China – A New Stage of Development
for an Emerging Superpower

T0336523

China

A New Stage
of Development
for an Emerging Superpower

Edited by

Joseph Y. S. Cheng

City University of Hong Kong Press

First published 2012
Printed in Hong Kong

ISBN: 978-962-937-197-5

Published by
City University of Hong Kong Press
Tat Chee Avenue, Kowloon, Hong Kong

Website: www.cityu.edu.hk/upress
E-mail: upress@cityu.edu.hk

Table of Contents

4.　Cadre Performance Appraisal and Fabrication of Economic Achievement in Chinese Officialdom

LI Jun and Joseph Y. S. CHENG...................................... **117**

5.　The Internet and Political Marketing in Globalizing China

Chin-fu HUNG **149**

6.　The Transitional Role of the Hu-Wen Leadership in China: A Case Study of Liu Xiaobo

Mobo GAO... **175**

Preface

China's achievements in economic development and improvement in international status have been impressive in the past decade. The adjustments in economic development strategy took place before the international financial tsunami in 2008–9, and the response to the crisis was decisive. The building of a social security net covering the entire population has been benefitting hundreds of millions people. Much credit goes to the Hu Jintao–Wen Jiabao administration in 2002–2012.

At the same time, there has been no significant political reforms in the past decade and more. Corruption has become more rampant; various vested interests have been more entrenched. Even official think-tank researchers admit that policy implementation often encounters strong resistance at the local level. Despite the raising of living standards, dissatisfaction and grievances continue to accumulate as reflected by the increases in frequency and scale of mass incidents. Unrest and riots in ethnic minority areas pose an obvious challenge.

The Chinese economy promptly recovered from the recent international financial crisis, but the economic downturn in the United States and Europe is expected to dampen China's exports. The external economic environment is less likely to offer strong support for sustainable high growth rates. Meanwhile, economic difficulties in the developed countries generate more pressure on China to adjust its high dependence on trade and assume greater responsibility for the reform of the international financial structure.

The high-profile "return to Asia" strategy of the Obama administration fully exploits the uneasiness of China's neighbours which have been concerned with the Chinese leadership's assertiveness in territorial disputes and its military modernization programme. Their hedging strategies in turn facilitate the United States' attempts to contain China's influence and secure a guiding role in the regional economic integration process. Beijing now experiences diplomatic setbacks and is aware that greater efforts are required to re-assure the countries in the Asia-Pacific region.

Assessment of the Hu-Wen administration's performance is a complicated task; it is important because the administration's apparent success tends to create a path-dependence orientation on the part of its successor. A team of experts has been recruited to offer a volume to evaluate the administration's achievements and difficulties in various policy areas, as well as the likely challenges and policy changes in the years ahead. Each author has been invited to focus on one important issue and offer his/her analysis, so that this book will provide a platform for further informed deliberations among academics, students, corporate executives and professionals who are interested in China's development.

I would like to take this opportunity to thank all the authors for their support and co-operation. Thanks are also due to the staff of the City University of Hong Kong Press for their professionalism and dedication throughout the publication process.

Joseph Y. S. Cheng
January 2012

China – A New Stage of Development
for an Emerging Superpower

1

Challenges for Hu-Wen and Their Successors: Consolidating the "Beijing Consensus" Model

Joseph Y. S. CHENG

Introduction

What will the Hu-Wen leadership be remembered for? Mao Zedong has certainly been recognized for his revolutionary model and the founding of the People's Republic of China (PRC), as well as his excesses such as the Great Leap Forward and the Cultural Revolution. Deng initiated the Four Modernizations, and he ultimately rejected political reforms, maintaining the Communist Party of China (CPC)'s monopoly of political power while exploiting economic growth as the source of the Party regime's legitimacy. Jiang Zemin and Zhu Rongji presided over a period of impressive economic growth and rising international status; Zhu skilfully managed the over-heated economy in the mid-1990s and the third-generation leadership promoted the full embrace of globalization. Yet they allowed serious problems, including rampant corruption, the widening of the gap between the rich and poor, environmental degradation, etc. to be exacerbated.

The Hu-Wen leadership has quietly achieved much. The Chinese economy is about to become the second largest in the world; China exports more than any other country and is the number-two trader in the global economy. Beijing held the Olympics in 2008 and Shanghai the Expo in 2010. Chinese people really feel that they have stood up, as claimed by Mao on 1 October 1949 when the PRC was founded. Though Chinese leaders avoid the use of the acronym G2 (the USA and China as the only two superpowers in the world); Chinese people are proud of the country's impact on international affairs. This national pride has become an important source of the Party regime's legitimacy too. The fourth-generation leadership has failed to tackle the problem of corruption, but it has a much soberer understanding of the challenges of rapid economic growth. Even before the global financial tsunami in 2008 and 2009, the Chinese authorities realized that for sustainable economic growth it would have to reduce its dependence on exports and investment in infrastructural projects. Instead, it would have to count more on domestic consumption. More resources have been allocated to environmental protection and the enhancement of energy intensity; as the structure of the economy improves and the service sector further develops, there is a better chance that pollution may be reduced very slowly. The Hu-Wen leadership in the past five or six years has begun building a basic social security net covering the entire population to contain the grievances generated by the widening of the gap between the rich and the poor. The emphasis on stability and prosperity is prominent, and the strategy and tactics adopted by the fourth-generation leadership are sophisticated.

The Party still has no intention of giving up its monopoly of political power; and in fact in the past decade there have been no significant political reforms. Parallel to this rejection of democratization, the Hu-Wen leadership has been very sensitive to potential unrest. There was a crackdown on dissidents, independent non-governmental organizations (NGOs), human rights groups, and freedom of information flow on the Internet in the two years or so before the Beijing Olympics. However, there has been no relaxation after the event, as 2009 was a year of significant anniversaries: the fiftieth anniversary of the Tibetan uprising, the ninetieth anniversary of the May Fourth Movement, the twentieth anniversary of the Tiananmen Incident, and the sixtieth anniversary of the establishment of the PRC. This acute sense of insecurity was best symbolized by the Chinese authorities' request that Beijing residents stayed home to watch television during the National Day parade in 2009.

The mainstream Chinese media often describes China today as *shengshi*, a traditional Confucian term for historical eras of peace, prosperity and achievements.[1] Hu Jintao has also been promoting his models of "harmonious society" and "harmonious world". These concepts are hardly Marxist-Leninist nor dialectical; and it is significant that the Chinese leadership and intelligentsia no longer care. Further, the "eight honours" and "eight shames" advanced by Hu as ethical standards for cadres are distinctly Confucian. These ideological trends initiated by the fourth-generation leadership are significant, though there is also a strengthening of traditional Marxist-Leninist ideological studies at the same time.

Chinese leaders do not use the term "Beijing consensus",[2] and they certainly do not discuss it in competition with the "Washington consensus".[3] But Chinese leaders reject the liberal democratic model advocated by the United States and the Western world as the only ideal model; and the Chinese experience of achieving impressive economic growth and social stability in the absence of democracy is perceived as an alternative to the "Washington consensus" by many Third World countries. Meanwhile, the Hu-Wen leadership has become very sophisticated in image-building and has acquired political skills comparable to those of Western politicians used to fighting elections. Their apologies for less than satisfactory performance and Premier Wen Jiabao's tears in public apparently have been well received by the people. The fourth-generation leaders have been innovative in political styles, though not in political reforms.

This introductory chapter attempts to examine the challenges facing the Hu-Wen leadership and its distinct policy programme orientations. It will analyse the important policy changes initiated, as well as their implementation and results. On this basis, an evaluation will be made and the implications for the fifth-generation leadership will be considered.

Leadership Succession, Cadre Cultivation and the Maintenance of Ideological Orthodoxy

Deng Xiaoping not only approved the replacement of Zhao Ziyang by Jiang Zemin and that of Li Peng by Zhu Rongji, he also anointed Hu Jintao as the core of the fourth-generation leadership. Despite the fact that Jiang had ambitious plans for arranging his successor, Hu ultimately managed to secure the Party leadership. However, it had been widely circulated that Jiang supported Xi Jinping; and Xi is expected to become the new Party general secretary at the coming Eighteenth Party Congress in 2012 rather than Li Keqiang, the protégé of Hu Jintao who now probably will succeed Wen Jiabao as premier or Wu Bangguo as chairman of the Standing Committee of the National People's Congress. Hu in turn will likely have a very significant say over the sixth-generation leadership line-up.

This may well become an accepted pattern for leadership succession arrangements. The succession of Jiang Zemin by Hu Jintao was the first orderly, peaceful and well-prepared leadership succession in the Party's history. In the absence of open, competitive election procedures, selection of future leaders through consultation and bargaining within the existing leadership seems to be the preferred norm and tends to be more institutionalized. The selected future leaders will go through about a decade of exposure, training and tests. Fifth-generation leaders like Xi Jinping and Li Keqiang are now going through this stage; and sixth-generation leaders are being identified, with former Communist Youth League (CYL) leaders including Hu Chunhua (Party secretary of Inner Mongolia), Zhou Qiang (governor of Hubei) etc. being shortlisted for the Eighteenth Party Congress in 2012.

This planned approach does not, and probably cannot, preclude political competition. In 2009–2010, Wang Yang (the youngest Political Bureau member and the provincial Party secretary of Guangdong) and Bo Xilai (Political Bureau member and the municipal Party secretary of Chongqing) offered two interesting examples. Wang Yang advocated seizing the opportunity provided by the global financial tsunami to "empty the cage and change the bird (teng long huan niao)", meaning to accelerate the phasing out of labour-intensive processing industries and the introduction of high-tech industries, using Japan during the oil crises of 1973–74 and 1979–80 as the model. Wang Yang attempted to use achievements in economic development to seek further promotion to the leadership core. Bo Xilai, a princeling, on the other hand, received the traditional Chinese Communist values and cracked down on gangster activities to enhance his popular appeal while pursuing advancement in his political career.

A planning process has gradually developed for the cultivation of future leaders. In February 2009, the Party Central Committee released the "2009–2020 National Party and State Leadership Reserve Cadre Corps Construction Plan". This was the first time that the Party leadership had prepared a cadre cultivation programme of this kind. On 3 April 2009, Li Yuanchao, head of the Party Organization Department, indicated at the opening ceremony of the First China-Singapore "Leadership Talents Selection and Cultivation" Forum that as the Chinese economy became increasingly internationalized, it would be important to develop the international understanding, international perspective and international horizon of leadership talents. Earlier, on 1 March, Xi Jinping stated in the Central Party School that leading cadres had to improve their competence in promoting scientific development. Xi further pointed out that leading cadres at all levels had to work hard to improve their competence in the following six areas: overall co-ordination, pioneering innovation, recognition and use of talents, risk management, maintenance of stability and the handling of the media.[4]

Since the Sixteenth Party Congress in 2002, the selection and cultivation of young cadres has revealed several orientations which are known as the "five insistences": (1) insistence on talents and high ethical standards with priority given to the latter including high political standards, strong conviction in the Communist ideals, firm adherence to the Party line and a good record in observing Party discipline; (2) insistence on outstanding service record in difficult and complicated localities as a test of young cadres' political qualities and problem-solving capabilities; (3) insistence on experiences in grassroots frontline work, in this connection, fresh university graduates have been encouraged to serve in administrative villages and rural communities; (4) insistence on cultivation and training of young cadres, especially those selected for further promotions; and (5) insistence on the strict management of cadres.

These orientations demonstrate a subtle yet significant difference between the Hu-Wen era and the previous Jiang Zemin-Zhu Rongji administration; now cadres believe that academic qualifications from leading universities and working experiences in the Western world are valuable assets in their career advancement. These new orientations actually reflect awareness on the part of the present Chinese leadership of the need to provide attractive incentives for talented young cadres to accept hardship posts; otherwise the most talented would concentrate on administrative positions in big cities and rich state-owned enterprises (SOEs). In this way, governance at the grassroots level and in the rural areas would suffer, and stability would be adversely affected. The decision in early 2010 to equalize the representation rights of rural and urban residents in people's congresses at various levels was aimed to produce the same effect too; the increase in the number of deputies from the rural sector in people's congresses at various levels would mean more opportunities to reward rural cadres who would then have better prospects for promotion.

The following statistical data on provincial/ministerial-level cadres born after 1960 may be interesting: 84% of them are party members, 13% belong to the democratic parties, and 3% have no party affiliations; 86% are Han people, while 14% belong to the ethnic minorities; 90% are male and only 10% are females; 93% hold the positions of deputy provincial governor or deputy minister, while 7% are provincial governors or ministers. Regarding their sources of recruitment: 35.2% were from the Party and State organs; 22.5% from universities; 18.3% from enterprises, 9.8% from the CYL and from research institutions respectively, and 4.2% from other sources.[5] Obviously the Chinese authorities have been broadening their net in cadre recruitment at the senior levels.

There is recognition of inadequacies in the cadre selection and promotion processes, especially at the local level, as reflected by commentaries in the mainstream media and academic studies. According to a sample survey of the China Association of City Mayors, from 2002 to 2006 over 80% of the 150 cities surveyed had one change of mayor. In big cities and cities in developed areas, the mayors basically completed their terms; but changes of mayor were more frequent in small cities and cities in less developed areas. The implication is that the mayors of the latter group were less satisfied with their positions, and they were relatively active in seeking transfers.

The usual criticisms against the processes include: lack of competitive mechanisms and reliance on an appointment system; decisions are made by the principal officials or very small groups of officials concerned; making promises and pledges of loyalty and engaging in factional activities; information leakages regarding discussions on candidates by the party committees concerned; active lobbying for promotions and transfers and even offering bribery for promotions and transfers.

In response to these criticisms, in October 2008 the Party Central Commission for Discipline Inspection and the Central Organization Department released a document suggesting measures to deter such undesirable practices. In May 2009, Li Yuanchao initiated an activity known as "Ten Thousand Organization Department Heads to the Grassroots", in which the heads of Party organization departments at lower levels would visit grassroots-level cadres to engage them in heart-to-heart conversations to discourage lobbying for promotions through strengthening routine cadre management and supervision. Since September 2008 when the campaign to deepen the study and practice of the scientific development perspective was launched, public opinion surveys on the satisfaction of the masses have gradually become a common practice. On 29 April 2009, the Central Organization Department released the results of its first public opinion survey on the satisfaction level concerning national organization work; and the score was 73.55%.

Within the Leninist framework, maintaining the Party's monopoly of power and political stability demands the accord of a high priority to Party-building work which in turn means the cultivation of a reliable cadre corps. In preparation for the Eighteenth Party Congress, in 2009 the Chinese leadership asked for lists of about 1,000 reserve cadres at the provincial/ministerial-level, over 6,000 reserve cadres at the prefectural/bureau-level, and about 40,000 reserve cadres at the county/departmental-level. These selection processes were designed to ensure the availability of talent to strengthen Party and state organizations on a long-term basis, including the appointment of younger cadres at all levels. The Central Organization Department also seriously warned against lobbying activities in these selection processes.

According to a report of the Chinese Association for Science and Technology in 2008, scientific and technical human resources in China surpass those of the United States in quantitative terms, but China still encounters a severe shortage in high-level scientific and technical personnel. In December 2008, the General Office of the CPC Central Committee released a document asking all ministries and local government to liberate thinking in attracting talent from overseas and a Central Talents Work Co-ordination Group was formed. At the same time, the Central Organization Department launched a "Thousand Persons Plan" to attract about 1,000 top-notch talents from overseas to come to work in China within five to ten years, and to build 40–50 innovation bases for them. The first list of 122 persons appeared in September 2009; 96 of them had been working in universities and research institutes, while 26 of them were hi-tech entrepreneurial talents. Following the example of the central government, Shanxi, Shaanxi, Sichuan, Yunnan, Anhui, Henan, etc. all initiated their own provincial plans to recruit talent from overseas, with Jiangsu appearing to be the most ambitious. The latter announced a plan in September 2008 to recruit more than 10,000 high-level overseas experts in the following five years.

The significance of introducing these overseas talents (*hoiguipai*) has attracted considerable attention. Following the model of Taiwan in the 1980s, by the turn of the century the Chinese authorities began to realize the importance of recruiting overseas talent in a systematic way. Chinese PhD students who have been going abroad to study since the early 1980s now constitute a pool of expertise not to be neglected. There are already obvious examples, like the former education minister Zhou Ji, and public health minister Chen Zhu. At the same time, the satisfaction of being responsible for major projects, being able to contribute to the motherland, improving living conditions in the major coastal cities and generous remuneration packages have made the offer quite attractive. There may well be problems of adjustment to the bureaucratic rules and operations, petty jealousies, etc. But the increasing role of overseas talent in China's modernization has definitely become an inevitable trend.

Ideological education remains an important part of cadre cultivation, however. The CPC Central Committee and State Council issued the "Opinions on further strengthening and improving ideological and political education of university students" in October 2004. The document reflected the Hu-Wen leadership's intention to give ideological and political direction to university students in conformity with the principles of Marxism-Leninism, Mao Zedong Thought, Deng Xiaoping Theory, and "the important thinking of the 'three represents'". This ideological and political education aimed to foster a "correct world outlook, life philosophy, and values" among university students, to educate them in civic virtues based on "essential moral standards", and to strengthen their patriotism. The document acknowledged that there were "many weak links" in university students' ideological and political attitudes; and highlighted the role of the CYL and student organizations in fulfilling the goals of the authorities.[6]

On 26 December 2005 (the birthday of Mao Zedong), the status of the Institute of Marxism-Leninism-Mao Zedong Thought in the Chinese Academy of Social Sciences was raised to that of a school with a much expanded establishment. In the year before, the Party centre endorsed a ten-year research programme on Marxist theory, including the writing of a series of textbooks for China's tertiary institutions.[7] In January 2005, the Party launched a mild rectification and education campaign for its seventy million members to be implemented in three stages; the basic objective was to study the theory of Deng Xiaoping, the "three represents" demand of Jiang Zemin and the scientific development perspective of Hu Jintao.[8]

These efforts achieved limited results. Cadres and university students are not interested in studying Marxism; in recent years many universities have dropped courses on the official ideology from their curricula. However, the Party as a power elite still has its attraction. To fill the ideological vacuum, Chinese leaders have adopted many pragmatic measures, ranging from the exploitation of nationalism and promotion of the rule of law to the restoration of traditional Confucian values symbolized by Hu Jintao's advocacy of the "Eight Honours and Eight Shames".

Nevertheless, the emphasis on ideological orthodoxy has continued. In commemorating the thirtieth anniversary of the watershed third plenum of the Eleventh CPC Central Committee held in December 1978, Hu Jintao reiterated the importance of adhering to basic Marxist tenets, while also promoting the "Sinicization" of Marxism. Hu declared: "Marxism is the fundamental guiding ideology for us in establishing the Party and state . . . At the same time, only if Marxism is integrated with China's national condition and the characteristics of the era and is continually enriched and developed in practice can it better play its role in guiding practice."[9]

This adherence to ideological orthodoxy has been accompanied by a lack of tolerance for political debates. In the first year or so of the Hu-Wen leadership, there were some expectations of genuine political reforms and in fact lively debates on constitutional changes and reform of political system emerged. The prompt dismissal of the mayor of Beijing, Meng Xuenong, and the minister of public health, Zhang Wenkang, who had covered up the spread of the severe acute respiratory syndrome (SARS) epidemic in April 2003, contributed to these expectations. But in the following year the political conservatism of the new leadership became apparent, signs of a crackdown appeared, and many topics and persons eventually became taboo in the mainstream media.

In June 2004, Dr Jiang Yanyong, who had earlier become a hero for exposing the SARS cover-up, was arrested for sending a letter of the Chinese leadership seeking a reversal of the verdict on the Tiananmen Incident in 1989. Chen Guidi and Chun Tao, authors of *Zhongguo Nongmin Diaocha* (*A Survey of Peasants in China*), a book critical of the problems in rural China which had attracted a lot of domestic and international attention, were sued for libel by a cadre of the Anhui provincial government. Jiao Guobiao, a journalism professor at Beijing University, came under a lot of pressure after severely criticizing the Central Propaganda Department of the CPC, and was eventually forced to leave the country. The outspoken *Nanfang Dushi Bao* (*Southern Metropolitan Daily*) had its editorial board overhauled and its leading editors prosecuted for embezzlement; a popular Beijing University electronic bulletin board service was terminated; and a reputable journal, *Zhanlüe yu Guanli* (*Strategy and Management*) supported by some retired Party elders, also ceased publication after leading with an article criticizing the North Korean leadership.[10]

This crackdown on dissidents, critics and the media continued as the Beijing Olympics approached, and was not relaxed subsequently because of the riots in Tibet in 2008, those in Xinjiang in 2009, and the sensitive anniversaries in the same year. In the previous years, local mainstream media in China had adopted a practice of being bolder in reporting on the scandals and darker sides of society in other provinces, as they had to show deference to the local authorities to which they were accountable. But the Central Propaganda Department stopped this practice, the sanctions on the deviant media became more serious, and they were sometimes closed instead of suffering from mere reshuffles in the respective editorial teams.

Lack of Political Reforms
and the Promotion of Intra-Party Democracy

Li Jingjie, the director of the former Soviet-Eastern Europe Institute at the Chinese Academy of Social Sciences, in an interview with David

Shambaugh in 2003, indicated that the break-up of the Soviet Union and the collapse of the Soviet Communist Party regime "had haunted the Chinese leadership ever since". Li said that Chinese leaders tried "to understand the implications and lessons, so that they don't make the same mistakes of Gorbachev . . .".[11]

It appears that the Hu-Wen leadership, despite the country's impressive economic growth, is still worried about the survival of the one-Party regime and would not entertain the introduction of democracy. The present leaders are ready to follow the hitherto adopted line of enhancing Party organization, propaganda and thought work among cadres, intra-Party supervision, the cultivation of cadres, etc. They repeat the same mantra of economic development before political reforms. They also caution against separatism among China's national minorities; and especially the Western world's "peaceful evolution" strategy, the "Westernization" strategy and the "division" strategy against China.[12]

China's official think tanks not only analyse the lessons to be drawn from the collapse of the Communist regimes in Eastern Europe and the Soviet Union, they also examine relevant issues of the existing Communist regimes. There are sometimes commentaries on North Korea, Vietnam and Cuba; apparently one cannot find many studies on Laos. In the elections of Party and state leaders, the Vietnamese Communist Party has introduced procedures more democratic than its Chinese counterparts in recent years, and these political reforms are quietly discussed among the reformers in China.[13] The lengthy, stable rule of the Cuban Communist Party has attracted considerable interest from the researchers in China's official think tanks. In recent years, exchanges between the two Communist parties have been frequent. In 2004, at the fourth plenum of the Sixteenth Central Committee of the CPC, Hu Jintao praised Cuba's mass media policy, which aroused many criticisms in overseas Chinese communities.[14]

Another focus regarding the Chinese leadership's concern for the survival of the Chinese Communist regime is the "colour revolutions" in the former constituent republics of the Soviet Union in the early years of this century, i.e., the "rose revolution" in Georgia in 2003, the "orange revolution" in Ukraine in 2004, and the "(yellow) tulip revolution" in Kyrgyzstan in 2005. David Shambaugh believes that the Chinese leadership is very worried about the causes and implications of the "colour revolutions" for the Chinese Communist regime. He identifies six major aspects of the Chinese analyses of the "colour revolutions" in his survey; the nature of the "revolutions", the role of the United States, the role of international non-governmental organizations (NGOs), the potential for more "colour revolutions" in Central Asia, the implications for Russia, and those for China.[15]

In response to the "colour revolutions", the Chinese authorities adopted certain measures to limit their potential impact. In general, the Chinese media did not report these events. The Chinese government also suspended a plan to allow foreign newspapers to be printed in China. When George Soros visited China in October 2005, the local media did not cover the event, and his scheduled lectures and meetings were all cancelled.[16] It was also said that President Vladimir Putin warned Hu Jintao at a 2005 Shanghai Co-operation Organization meeting about the subversive potential of the international NGOs; and partly as a result of this warning, the Chinese authorities began to scrutinize NGOs operating in China.[17]

In the absence of democratization, the Hu-Wen leadership offers its brand of populism. Soon after his assumption of the Party leadership position, in early 2003, Hu Jintao visited Xibaipo, a small town near Beijing where Mao planned the final attack on the Chinese capital in 1949. Hu tried to remind the nation of the fine traditions of the Party and appeal for the improvement of people's living standards. Then the Chinese leaders stayed in Beijing to work in the summer instead of holding their annual consultation in Beidaihe, the seaside resort near Beijing, breaking a half-century tradition. In the wake of the SARS epidemic, Wen Jiabao advocated the need to treat AIDS patients with "care and love", and he personally visited three AIDS patients in a Beijing hospital in an attempt to break a long-standing taboo in Chinese society. It has now become a convention for Hu and Wen to have the Lunar New Year's eve dinner with poor peasants, miners, etc. When Sun Zhigang, a Hubei migrant, was arrested and beaten to death in a detention centre in Guangdong in March 2003, the Chinese authorities abolished the existing national regulations which allowed urban governments to detain rural migrants without urban residential permits or employment and return them to their villages.[18]

To maintain the Party's monopoly of political power and the legitimacy of the Party regime, it has to deliver more than economic growth. To combat corruption and ensure a more responsive cadre corps, the Hu-Wen leadership intends to promote democracy within the Party. In December 2003, the "Regulations of the CPC on Internal Supervision (for final)" were enacted. At the fourth plenum of the Sixteenth Central Committee of the CPC in the following September, "Party construction" was the principal agenda item, and the plenum released a resolution on strengthening the Party's governance capability. "Party construction" again emerged as the main agenda item exactly five years later at the fourth plenum of the Seventeenth Central Committee of the CPC, at which several intra-Party democratization measures were planned to be promoted.

The Chinese leadership is keenly interested in enhancing the Party's governance capability and ensuring good performance as well as responsiveness to public opinion on the part of cadres at all levels; and intra-Party democratization measures are perceived as useful instruments. In the summer of 2009, China's mainstream media were highlighting several reform experiments. They included: (a) the direct election of the Party committee leadership by all Party members in Lingshan Township, Pingchang County in Sichuan; (b) the reform of the Party representatives congress into an active standing organ in Taizhou, Zhejiang; and (c) the reforms of the Party committee system in Minxing district, Shanghai, including the Standing Committee holding a question-and-answer session for all members of the Party committee and the election of the preliminary list of candidates for officials at the *chu* (county head) level with choices by the entire Party committee.

These reform measures were not new; they had been deliberated for at least three or four years. Apparently they had encountered some resistance; and at that stage Chinese leaders decided to promote them again. Because of the economic difficulties caused by the international financial tsunami, social stability had become an even more important concern. Rapid economic growth in the past decades has generated many contradictions; in the context of an economic slowdown, rising unemployment, etc. these contradictions have been exacerbated.

Chinese leaders are under considerable pressure to initiate policy programmes to reduce the people's hardships and grievances. To ensure that cadres at all levels pay more attention to these hardships and grievances, and are more responsive to local public opinion, rectification of the Party through intra-Party democratization measures appeals to the Chinese leadership. A more active crackdown on corruption in 2009 was probably aimed to reduce people's dissatisfaction and grievances too. After all, economic difficulties, unemployment, corruption, etc. constitute the recipe for social unrest in China.

The rise in the number of mass incidents and their expansion in scale, as well as the riots in Tibet and Xinjiang, are serious warning signals. The Han riots in Wulumuqi (Urumchi) in 2009 showed that the Party organizations at the grassroots level could not function well; that was why the city Party secretary was sacked promptly and publicly. Most of the Han people in Wulumuqi are descendants of the People's Liberation Army (PLA) and cadres, and today a considerable segment of them work in large state-owned enterprises. If they could not be persuaded to toe the Party line, i.e., to exercise self-restraint and restore calm immediately, the central leadership would naturally be angry. One of its responses was to dispatch cadres to strengthen the city's grassroots Party organizations.

Intra-Party democratization in political terms is similar to joining the World Trade Organization (WTO) in economic terms. Former Premier Zhu Rongji understood that economic reforms had reached a difficult stage; in order to overcome the resistance of vested interests, he had to rely on the commitments made to the WTO. Similarly, relying on mild campaigns and instructions from Beijing to rectify the Party would not be effective; intra-Party democratization measures can be useful instruments. These democratization measures demand strong consensus and political will on the part of the central leadership to make an impact before the eighteenth Party Congress to be held in 2012. Reform of the election system and turning the Party representatives congresses into standing organs would be relatively easy, as the competition in the elections and the effectiveness of the Party representatives congresses in monitoring the Party secretaries at the corresponding levels will depend on concrete circumstances.

On the other hand, declaration of assets on the part of leading Party cadres has encountered severe resistance despite the fact that the proposal has been discussed for more than a decade and there cannot be any good reason to argue against the proposal. Similarly, the earlier suggestion of making the commission for discipline inspection accountable to the Party committee one level above instead of to the Party committee at the same level has not been mentioned in the past year or so. The original intention of the proposal was to give the commission for discipline inspection at all local levels a freer hand to administer the Party leaders at the same level; and it is not difficult to understand why this was not supported.

In line with the emphasis on facilitating people to articulate their grievances to reduce their level of dissatisfaction, as well as to reduce their incentive to go to Beijing to lodge their complaints (*shang fang*), a series of channels has been opened up in recent years to receive complaints and reports on cases of consumption and abuses of power. They include: (a) a website for complaints run by the Supreme People's Procuratorate and a unified telephone service for complaints by the national procuratorate system both launched on 22 June 2009; (b) a website serving as a complaints centre against judges at all levels violating the law and their disciplinary code launched on 6 May 2009; (c) a website for complaints launched by the Party Central Commission for Discipline Inspection and the Ministry of Supervision on 15 July 2005; and a unified telephone service for complaints launched by the national party discipline inspection system and the state supervision system on 26 June 2008; (d) a website for complaints launched by the Party Central Organization Department on 26 February 2009; and a unified telephone service for complaints launched by the national Party organizational system on 29 March 2004; and (e) a website for suggestions on the prevention of corruption launched by the National Bureau of Corruption Prevention of China launched on 17 December 2007.

A bright spot has been administrative reforms at the city level which in general have improved transparency and services for the people. These reforms demonstrate keen competition among cities whose leaders are eager to establish models of reforms to enhance the respective images of their cities and advance their own career development. They certainly reflect a high level of tolerance for reforms at the centre and provincial enthusiasm among local governments to improve services. The following examples illustrate the broad orientations of administrative reforms at the city level.

In 2007, the commission for discipline inspection of the Yangzhan Party committee (in Jiangsu province) and the supervision bureau of the city government initiated a "Sunshine Project" to regulate the distribution of responsibilities and powers. In the following year, ten bureaux and their public-sector corporations of the city government which were closely associated with services deeply affecting people's livelihood were selected as experimental units. At the same time, the reforms were expected to proceed also in the counties, county-level cities and districts under the city government.

The reforms were aimed at achieving better services, higher efficiency and the avoidance of corruption opportunities. Initially, each bureau was asked to define a clear-cut allocation of tasks and powers without overlaps so as to generate effective checks and balances. Further they were to accelerate the work flow through implementation of procedures to delete over-concentration of powers. Strengthening risk management was also an objective, and the work units concerned were asked to locate their risk areas and rectify them. Finally, they had to establish monitoring and internal-control electronic mechanisms designed to combat corruption. Meanwhile, sharing of good practices was encouraged. In sum, the orientation was to modernize urban administration and quite a number of coastal cities have been engaging in similar reforms.

Hangzhou city (in Zhejiang province) approached its reforms with a different orientation and its emphases were "openness, transparency, participation and interaction". Starting from November 2007, the city government invited the deputies of the city people's congress and delegates to the city people's political consultative conference to attend its routine, scheduled meetings. In the following year, ordinary citizens were invited to attend and the meetings were directly broadcast on network television. On 21 January 2009, the city government's standing committee meeting was directly televised for the first time.

At the same meeting, the city government approved a set of regulations on its open decision-making procedures. Besides broadcasting its meeting, the city government and its organs would broadly consult the community who would not be satisfied with the agenda items. There would be many more hearings, and ordinary government documents would be available on the city government's website. The procedures of the hearings stipulate that the citizen participants may engage in debates with the personnel of the work units involved in the issues deliberated in the hearings. These work units, as far as possible, should present two or more options for cost-benefit analysis.

Finally, the labour and social security bureau of the Chengdu city government (in Sichuan province) concentrated on improvements in service delivery. In June 2008, the city government and the bureau signed contracts with the central government's Ministry of Human

Resources and Social Security and its China Scientific Research Institute on Labour and Social Security respectively to engage in reforms using Chengdu as a base of innovation. In the following month, the bureau listed fourteen types of services, ranging from registration to seeking employment, social security information enquiries to the calculation and release of pension fund payments, and pledged to deliver the services at the community and village level. Even if the service windows at this level could not handle the demands immediately, they would be responsible for the ultimate service delivery after consultations through the Internet information systems. The idea was that instead of people making efforts to seek services, the government would make the efforts to deliver services in the most convenient way for people.

As governments at all levels seek to secure legitimacy through better services, democratization has not made much progress. When village elections were first introduced in China in 1986–87, they attracted a lot of attention in the international media, the academic community and groups in Western countries interested in promoting democracy in China. At that time, Chinese leaders like Hu Yaobang and Zhao Ziyang were dedicated to pushing for political reforms in China. The democratic direct elections of village heads and village committees were in line with the promotion of "small government, big society" and Chinese leaders appreciated the advantage of transferring the unpopular tasks of tax collection and enforcing control to elected representatives of the people. But from an ideal point of view, supporters for political reforms certainly hoped that village elections would lead to town/township elections and even county elections.

Earlier, at the end of the 1990s, some interesting democratic innovations were introduced in the elections of town and township beads in Shenzhen, Sichuan and other places. Apparently these were local initiatives. The central leadership's response was quiet discouragement. The local officials concerned were not punished nor criticized; but the democratic experiments were not covered by the mass media.[19] These experiments were only studied by academics overseas.

The reform "bottleneck" was mainly related to the scope of cadres. Village heads and members of village committees are only members of grassroots autonomous bodies; however, they are not cadres of the state. On the other hand, heads of towns and townships are basic-level cadres. If they are directly elected, then the fundamental principle of Party appointing cadres at all levels may be compromised; and this is the most effective mechanism for the Party to maintain its monopoly of political power. This is exactly why, after more than two decades, village elections still cannot lead to town and township elections.

At the beginning of this century, direct elections were introduced in the urban sector at the level of community residents committees and owners' committees of housing estates. Regarding the latter, the rationale was that property owners naturally would like their community properly managed and the value of their properties enhanced. Hence they should be interested in participation in self-management.[20] These innovations attracted the attention of the media and academics within and outside China; but they have not led to significant breakthroughs. At this stage, Chinese leaders concentrate on administrative reforms and intra-Party democratic reforms.

The idea of elections, nevertheless, is gradually beginning to influence the values of the professionals and the intelligentsia in China. In August 2008, thirty-five lawyers who were members of the Beijing Lawyers Association asked for the direct election of the association's management council. The existing election method is that members of the incumbent management council will elect the members and chairman of the management council as well as members of the supervisory council. In this way, the judicial authorities would be able to exercise substantial influence in the elections, and make sure that dissidents would not be elected. The advocates for reforms subsequently received considerable pressure; some of them even lost their jobs.

According to some foreign experts who follow village elections in China, roughly one fifth to one quarter of them are competitive; the rest are mainly controlled by the Party organizations at the village and township levels. Competitive elections normally emerge in villages with valuable assets and/or profitable village enterprises. Hence the villagers consider that their concrete interests are involved, and the candidates believe they can achieve something. In poor villages without assets, often there may be no candidates at all because even the basic remuneration is in doubt. Under such circumstances, the Party organizations will have to work hard to find candidates. In the worst-case scenario, the township governments concerned will have to send their cadres to act as village heads to manage village affairs. There will be no elections then.

Harmonious Society through Social Security Net

At the beginning of this new century, many scholars in China realized that the country was approaching a complex and unstable stage of development. In 2003, per capita GDP in China reached US$1,090. Some official think tanks indicated that, on the basis of the historical experiences of foreign countries (mainly Latin American countries), in the stage when per capita GDP gradually climbs from US$1,000 to US$3,000 per annum, social stratification will be exacerbated, the middle class and its influence will grow, various cultural trends will emerge, the gap between the rich and poor will widen, and various social contradictions including ethnic contradictions will sharpen. These think tanks would like to see China follow the path of Japan and the "four little dragons of Asia" in making good use of this economic take-off to lay a firm foundation for subsequent economic development. On the other hand, they would like to see China avoid the precedents of Brazil, Argentina and Mexico, which were trapped in economic stagnation after the 1970s. In 1961, Argentina's per capita GDP already reached US$1,000; but in the following four decades and more, its per capita GDP only grew at an average annual rate of 1.9%.[21]

The sharpening of social contradictions in China has become conspicuous in the past decade. Inequality has been deteriorating, with the Gini Coefficient rising from 0.33 at the beginning of the reform era to 0.49 in 2005, indicating that China had drifted from being one of the most egalitarian countries in Asia to becoming one of the least. In June 2005, the National Statistics Bureau reported that the top 10% of the population owned 45% of the nation's wealth, while the poorest 10% received a share of 1.4% only. The president of the World Bank observed that there were still 150 million people living in acute poverty.[22] In the same year, the Ministry of Labour and Social Security admitted that the expanding income gap under current trends would likely lead to instability by 2010 if no effective solutions were implemented; and the State Council's Development Research Centre sponsored a research report claiming that health care reforms had not helped the poor in the rural sector, and criticized the Chinese authorities for avoiding their responsibilities in this area of social service.[23]

The Hu-Wen leadership has been very ambitious in building a

basic social security net covering the entire population to contain the grievances generated by the widening gap between the rich and poor, between the urban and rural sectors and among the regions. This ambition has been supported by China's impressive economic growth in the past decades and the accompanying increase in the central government's fiscal revenues.

In the mid-1990s, in view of the limited fiscal revenues at its disposal, the Chinese leadership emphasized the idea of "small government, big society". Li Tieying, then Politburo member and head of the State Commission for Restructuring the Economic System, emphatically stated in a conference in July 1995 that China could no longer afford "a high-level of social welfare (*gao fuli*)".[24] According to Li, the fundamental purpose of the new social security system was to promote productivity. It should stress the integration of rights and responsibilities as well as individual participation, so that most people would not have to rely on a redistribution of income. Li's statement reflected the Chinese leadership's policy orientation; but political stability required the provision of basic social security and the containment of the widening gap between the rich and the poor.

The introduction of bankruptcy for SOEs naturally produced millions of unemployed workers (initially known as *xiagang*, "stepping down from their posts"). At the end of the 1990s, the Chinese leadership originally designed a three-stage process to provide for their basic livelihood. In the first *xiagang* stage, the SOEs still had to offer the redundant workers their living expenses as well as continue contributing to their social security schemes. After two years or so, the unemployment insurance system would assume the burden. Finally, the social relief system known as the guarantee of minimum living standards would take over. But most of the bankrupt SOEs did not have the financial resources to support the redundant workers (there were many cases of fraud too in which the management pocketed the assets of the bankrupt SOEs). The unemployment insurance system basically did not even have a chance to accumulate funds in order to function. The guarantee of minimum living standards quickly became the last resort to the basic social security net for urban residents who could not support themselves.

The central government certainly did not adequately foresee the development and was not at all prepared. But it responded promptly, and within two to three years offered strong support to the provincial governments to set up social security nets with the guarantee of minimum living standards as the foundation. In September 1997, the State Council demanded that all cities and all towns where county governments were located had to establish a system for the guarantee of minimum living standards for their residents before the end of 1999. In September 1999, when the "Regulations on the Guarantee of Minimum Living Standards for Urban Residents" was promulgated, the system only covered 2.82 million people. In June 2002, the coverage expanded to 22.5 million, and then it stabilized at the 22 million level for some years.[25]

The central government was aware of its increasing financial burden, and began to seek to secure the necessary revenues. In 2002, the central government decided to take back a share of the personal income tax revenue (all of which used to go to local governments since the 1994 fiscal reforms) and of the corporate income tax revenue above the 2001 base figures. The Chinese leadership set the central government's share at 50% for 2002 and 60% for 2003, and the rates would be adjusted in the future depending on circumstances. The Chinese leaders' rationale was that the new revenues would go to the re-distribution of income among provinces through transfer payments from the central government.[26] The latter also accorded a higher priority to improving tax collection and the combat of tax evasion by individuals. The tax investigations in the year obviously targeted some high-profile private entrepreneurs.[27]

In his government work report to the National People's Congress (NPC) in early 2002, Premier Zhu Rongji strongly stressed the need to help disadvantaged groups (*ruoshi qunti*), the term he first used in 1998. At that stage, the principal target was the poor people in the urban sector. If they had no employment and no incomes, the probability of hunger was high. Even when their incomes could support their survival, they might still be deprived of the right to development, as they might not have access to education, health care and decent accommodation.

The system of the guarantee of minimum living standards in the urban sector celebrated its tenth anniversary in 2007. In view of high economic growth and substantial fiscal revenues, the Chinese leadership offered to increase the pensions of SOEs' retirees, raise the level of unemployment insurance benefit and that of the guarantee of minimum living standards (which had been extended to the rural sector already), and establish an urban medical relief system at the level of city districts and counties, so as to help those who did not have the cover of the existing urban employees basic medical insurance system.[28]

The Hu-Wen leadership then turned their attention to the other disadvantaged groups as well. In 2004, Wen Jiabao made wage arrears, especially those for migrant workers, a major issue after intervening personally in a single case. Rights protection for migrant workers then became a new priority in social security. In the third quarter of 2007, migrant workers participating in the pension system amounted to more than 17 million, more than 29 million in the medical insurance system, almost 11 million in the unemployment insurance system, and over 34 million in the work injuries insurance system.[29] Relative to the estimated flow of migrant workers, exceeding 120 million, the above figures were still rather low; but they certainly reflected the efforts of the Hu Jintao administration to help under-privileged groups. To demonstrate the priority accorded to the promotion of migrant workers' political rights, the Standing Committee of the NPC indicated that in future there would be a fixed number of seats in the NPC allocated to migrant workers.

The *san nong* issues (problems of the peasants, the rural sector and agriculture) obviously constitute a most significant focus of the policy programmes of the Hu-Wen leadership. In October 2003, the rural tax-for-fee reform was reported to have been "basically initiated" throughout China: the reforms were aimed at reducing the financial burden on the peasantry by terminating all types of fees imposed on them, mainly by the township and county governments. The central government allocated 35 billion *yuan* in transfer payments in support of the initiative. The tax on special farm products had been abolished in most areas to the benefit of many peasants too. At the same time, a rural co-operative medical care system and further improvements in education were being promoted throughout the countryside through increased allocations to educational, public health and cultural funds. Further, rural credit and then financial reforms were introduced; the central government selected eight provinces and municipalities to implement the pilot reform of rural credit co-operatives in order to serve agriculture, the rural sector and the peasants better.[30] There were the first series of measures to improve the living standards and the social security net of the peasants to narrow the gap between the urban and rural sectors. Enhancement of peasants' incomes also has important economic implications: the Hu-Wen leadership accepts that sustainable economic growth in China has to rely more on domestic consumption and less on exports and investment in the infrastructure.[31] As peasants have a high marginal propensity to consume, raising their incomes would help stimulate domestic consumption.

Despite the implementation of nine years of free education, some children in the rural areas still cannot afford to go to school. In response to their difficulties, in 2004 the central government introduced new initiatives including exemption of poor rural students from various fees, the provision of free or subsidized textbooks, as well as accommodation and living expenses for those who have to leave their homes.[32] Chinese leaders hope that education will serve as an important channel for upward social mobility for young people in rural areas.

In early 2007, Premier Wen Jiabao proposed in his government work report that a national system of the guarantee of minimum living standards would be established in the rural sector in the same year. It was estimated that, at the end of 2007, over 30 million people in difficulties had been included in the system.[33] At the Seventeenth Party Congress in 2007, Hu Jintao presented the public health policy goal of enabling the entire nation to enjoy basic medical and health services by 2020. This meant that China would be among the countries offering a national health service. Earlier in the 2003–2005 period, the Chinese authorities began to introduce the new rural co-operative medical care system. Initially all participants would have to pay 20 *yuan* per annum with half of this contribution coming from the government. By 2006, the minimum per capita contribution increased to 40 *yuan* per annum; and by 2008, it would rise to 80 *yuan* per annum.[34]

As financial resources in support of a medical insurance system, the sums involved were still far from adequate. But the rapid rise in the standards again reflected the Chinese leadership's determination to avoid the unacceptable scenario of poor peasants with serious illnesses waiting for their deaths because they could not afford medical care. The government's financial responsibility was to be assumed by various levels of government together. In central and western China as well as in the poor places along the coast, the central government would pay for half of the government's total contributions; and the remaining half would be absorbed by the provincial, prefectural city and county levels of government.[35]

In mid-2009, the central government released its "Opinions on Deepening Structural Reforms in the Medical, Pharmaceutical and Public Health Sectors". According to the policy document, in the following three years, various levels of government would spend 850 million *yuan* on the reforms, with 331.8 billion *yuan* from the central government. With a breakthrough in the medical insurance coverage of retired workers from closed and bankrupt enterprises, in the first half of 2009, urban workers and residents covered by medical insurance reached 336 million; and those who had participated in the new rural co-operative medical care scheme amounted to 830 million.

On 1 September 2009, the State Council formally announced its "Guiding Opinions on Development of the New Rural Social Retirement Insurance Scheme", asking for an initial coverage of 10% of the counties and county-level cities by the end of the year. This is based on individual contribution, and subsidies from the collectives and the governments; subsidies from the central government would go directly to the peasants' accounts. In the urban sector, the central government introduced temporary measures governing the transfers of accounts for employees at urban enterprises wherein the basic but important retirement insurance scheme can hitherto protect the benefits of workers, moving from one province to another, especially those of migrant workers. The central government has also been making efforts to raise the level of co-ordination for the urban retirement insurance schemes; at this stage, twenty-five provincial units have been practising co-ordination at the provincial level for the retirement insurance schemes. Finally, the State Council has introduced a set of rules governing participation in the basic retirement insurance scheme by migrant workers.

Meanwhile, the minimum living standard guarantee scheme in the urban and rural areas has been developing. In the urban sector nationally, about 11.205 million families (22.328 million people) received support from the scheme in July 2009; in the same month, 21.41 million families (45.34 million people) in the rural sector received support from the scheme.[36]

Chinese leaders understand well that an economic downturn, rising unemployment, the widening of the gap between the rich and poor and corruption together constitute the recipe for social unrest. In

February 2009, at the peak of the global financial tsunami, about 20 million migrant workers returned home early for the Lunar New Year because they had lost their jobs. About 80% of the 70 million migrant workers who had returned home for their traditional spring festival holidays came back to the urban centres to seek employment after their annual leave, and only 11 million of them succeeded. Fortunately, the Chinese economy recovered rapidly and by mid-2009 labour shortages began to emerge in the Tianjin area, and by the end of the year, most coastal cities again encountered difficulties in the recruitment of migrant workers. It is interesting to note that labour shortages first occurred in the Tianjin area where there is a relatively smaller concentration of labour-intensive processing industries, and they emerged later in the Pearl River Delta where the concentration of labour-intensive processing industries is relatively high.

Another group which had been badly hit by unemployment was the fresh graduates from tertiary institutions, who numbered 6.1 million in 2009. In the first half of the year, the unemployment rate for urban youth in the age group 16–24 years exceeded 11%; the unofficial estimates were much higher.[37] Various estimates placed the unemployment rate of fresh graduates at 30%; and at the edge of major cities like Beijing, there were tens of thousands of young graduates who lived in slums with monthly earnings of one or two thousand *yuan*. Among the newly employed workers, about 30%–40% of them belonged to the category of flexible employment; many of their jobs depended on government subsidies, and only half of them enjoy social security. These dissatisfied groups were potential sources of social unrest. It was reported that in 2009, there were about 217,900 cases of rallies, protests and mass meetings; and the public security and armed police were mobilized 243,600 times to suppress the riots.[38]

In response to the unemployment problem during the global financial tsunami, the Chinese authorities acted swiftly. Their measures demonstrated the efficiency and sophistication of the central government at the tactical level, and its understanding of the fundamental political challenges at the strategic level. Between September 2008 and February 2009, seven policy documents were released from the State Council and to ministries on the stabilization and expansion of employment including: a comprehensive policy measures document from the State Council; three from its general office on the employment of migrant workers, that of university graduates and the promotion of entrepreneurship to stimulate employment; and another three from the Ministry of Human Resources and Social Security and other ministries concerned on special training programmes, activities related to employment services, and measures to reduce enterprises' financial burden to stabilize employment. Regarding the latter, enterprises were allowed to delay their employees' social security payments; they were given reductions regarding the rates of these payments; and were given subsidies from the unemployment insurance fund to compensate for their social security payments and the maintenance of job positions so as to encourage enterprises in difficulties to avoid or reduce retrenchment.[39]

Economic Development Strategy

In the autumn of 2003, China's government economists observed that the national economy had entered a new era as reflected by six major changes: (1) easier market access, reduced government controls, improved investment and fund-raising conditions and a strengthened legal framework; (2) the industrial foundation of economic growth had shifted from labour-intensive sectors towards more capital- and technology-intensive industries (this explained why China's imports of new materials, minerals and energy resources expanded very rapidly in the past decade); (3) international as well as domestic markets had become a major force sustaining China's economic growth; (4) mixed forms of ownership at this stage characterized enterprise groups driving economic development; (5) a new regional structure of economic growth was emerging, exemplified by a shift from the primary role of the Pearl River Delta as a growth mode in the 1980s to the Yangtze River Delta in the 1990s, towards an even more diffused pattern of diverse economic development at the beginning at this century; and (6) simple pursuit of gross domestic product (GDP) growth was giving way to a more comprehensive pattern of co-ordinated and sustainable development.[40]

The tenor of the central economic work conference held in Beijing in late November 2003 attended by all the top leaders was that multipolarization and economic globalization remained the two main international trends. The emphasis in China was to maintain continuity and stability in macro-economic policy, by giving more emphasis to "regulation . . . control and structural optimization". Special efforts were needed to expand domestic demand, and to improve pro-active fiscal and stable monetary policies. State bonds and new treasury funds would go to the *san nong* issues, social development, the development of western China and the transformation of the old industrial bases in the north-west, ecological construction and environmental protection, employment expansion, improvements in the social security system, and raising the living standards of the poorest groups. It was also recognized that priority should be accorded to the strengthening of industry through the accelerated development of hi-tech (especially information technology) industries and the application of applied technology to upgrade traditional industrial activities.[41]

These priorities have been retained until now, but the Hu-Wen leadership was able to articulate a much more clearly-defined economic development strategy when the annual central economic conference was held in late 2005. By then, the "long-standing contradictions and problems in economic development" as well as some new circumstances and problems were identified, including the "extensive mode of economic growth, uneven development between urban and rural areas, imperfect systems and mechanisms, and problems affecting economic safety and the masses' vital interests". Hu's platform was strict adherence to the principles of sustainability and "people-centredness" in order to facilitate economic and social development "along the track of scientific development".

In practical terms, Chinese leaders agreed to "strive to expand domestic demand" and "re-adjust the relations between investment and consumption"; "achieve more co-ordinated development between the urban and rural areas and between regions including"; "building socialist new countryside"; intensify efforts to create "an independent innovation capability as the strategic base for scientific and technological development", and promote social harmony and facilitate a more equitable distribution of the benefits of reform and development.[42] At this time, government economists predicted that, between 2006 and 2010, economic growth would be 8.5% per annum, falling slightly to 8% per annum during 2010–2015. By 2010, per capita GDP would reach 19,000 *yuan*, and over 40,000 *yuan* by 2020. Consumption rates would by then exceed 60%.[43]

The high priority accorded to the *san nong* issues has been symbolized by the dedication of the first policy document issued by the Central Committee of the CPC to them every year since 2004. The communiqué of the third plenum of the Seventeenth Central Committee of the CPC, released in October 2008, noted that the issues of rural reform had been at the heart of the plenum.[44] The policy document on rural reform urged that a market be established to provide for the "transfer of the right to operate on contracted land"; and that "industry must feed agriculture in return, cities must support the countryside and cities must give the rural areas more and take from them less".[45] The plenum also set ambitious targets for 2020 including: (a) to put in place institutions and mechanisms to facilitate the integration of urban and rural development; (b) to achieve the "equalization" of basic public services for both urban and rural populations; and (c) to double peasants' per capita net income from the base of 2008. There was also a pledge to reform the land requisition system through the strengthening of measures to compensate and resettle those who had lost their land through requisition. The latter group certainly has been a conspicuous source of social grievances.

During the recent global financial tsunami, there were two interesting policy measures which illustrated the orientations of the Hu-Wen leadership regarding the *san nong* issues. The well publicized campaign of "household electrical appliances to the countryside" was aimed at changing the potential consumption demand of the peasantry into effective demand. One estimate considered that the implementation of this policy for four years would generate consumption of up to 920 billion *yuan*.[46] The other was encouragement and support for returned migrant workers to become entrepreneurs. Many provincial governments offered various policy packages to exploit their exposure and work experiences outside their villages and to reduce unemployment; many of these packages also tried to overcome the workers' difficulties in getting bank credit, which was a serious bottleneck in rural development.

The drafting of the Twelfth Five-Year Plan (FYP) (2011–2015) began at the end of 2009 with the impact of the global financial tsunami still in the background. The Chinese authorities' responses to the crisis were "protect economic growth, expand domestic demand, and adjust the economic structure"; the latter would likely remain a main theme in the coming FYP. As China's economic reforms adopt an experimental approach, the orientations and achievements of the seven comprehensive reform experimental regions (*zong gaishi yan qu* 综改试验区) would shed light on the key elements of the coming FYP too.

Pudong in Shanghai concentrated on its development as an international economic, financial, trade and marine transport centre. But there are criticisms that it has been losing momentum, and seems to promote reforms just for the sake of reforms, rather than in response to genuine needs. Binhai in Tianjin focused more on a management system oriented towards internationalization, as well as innovation in financial reforms and land management system. Shenzhen would like to engage in administrative management reforms including the amalgamation of administrative bureaux and the separation of decision-making, executive and supervision powers.

Wuhan and the Changsha-Zhuzhou-Xiangtan metropolitan complex are the two comprehensive reform experimental regions in central China. In 2007–2009, the latter completed its regional plan, and its experiments would be in the areas of resource conservation and environmental protection. The Hubei provincial government had also finished its Wuhan experimental region's framework programme with planned investment amounting to 1.3 trillion *yuan*.

The two experimental regions in the west, Chengdu and Chongqing, devoted their major efforts to building constructive and healthy relations between the urban and rural sectors. In 2008, they established a comprehensive property rights exchange and a land exchange respectively to promote the free circulation of land-use rights. Chongqing achieved considerable progress in the reforms of the land system and the changing status of peasants; while Chengdu tried to amalgamate its reform experiments with the reconstruction after the Wenchuan earthquake. It was reported that the Hu-Wen leadership articulated three major demands regarding the Twelfth FYP: (1) to accelerate the transformation of the economic development model proposing reform arrangement and action programmes to tackle the lack of co-ordination and sustainability as well as the imbalances in China's socio-economic development; (2) to emphasize social justice and the sharing of the fruits of development so as to achieve common prosperity, proposing reform plans and policy arrangements to reduce the gaps among regions, that between the urban and rural sectors and that between the rich and poor; and (3) to strive to promote developments in education, science and technology, and culture so as to raise the innovation capability of the state.[47]

There is an awareness on the part of the leadership of the inadequacies – including stagnation in raising the level of marketization, the strengthening of governmental intervention in and control of the market and the economy without improvement, imbalances in the economic structure, expansion in investment and decline in consumption, deterioration in the state of law and business integrity essential to the operation of the market economy, the choking pressures on the vitality of the market economy and social development exerted by the expansion of administrative monopoly, the degradation of the environment, and the widening gap between the rich and poor – but their improvements have encountered strong resistance by vested interests.

The above awareness and the recent global financial tsunami have reinforced the momentum for the transformation of the existing development model. In his keynote address to the annual World Economic Forum at Davos, Switzerland, in January 2010, Vice Premier Li Kaqiang said that "China will transform its current growth pattern and explore a new development model in the post-crisis era. As we stand at a new historical juncture, we must change the old way of inefficient growth and transform the current development model that is excessively reliant on investment and export."[48]

Hu-Wen's Foreign Policy Line:
A Harmonious World Perspective

At the time of the Seventeenth Party Congress in 2007, the Hu-Wen leadership appeared to have developed a comprehensive foreign policy framework with a harmonious world perspective as its central idea.[49] This perspective in turn is based on two important concepts: a new security concept and the democratization of international relations. The Hu-Wen leadership continues to work to maintain a peaceful international environment to allow it to concentrate on the nation's modernization. In view of China's impressive economic growth and rising international status, avoiding conflicts with the United States and other major powers has become more challenging. Beijing especially seeks to resolve the divergence in interests due to differences in political systems. It perceives that the Western world treats China unfairly because of its authoritarian regime. A harmonious world perspective emphasizes harmonious co-existence among countries with different cultures and systems, in contrast to the discourse of "the clash of civilizations" formulated by Samuel P. Huntington. [50]

A harmonious world perspective accepts that power politics continues to exist and the democratization of international relations has yet to be realized; but dialogue, exchanges and harmonious co-existence have become the mainstream in international relations, and mutual respect and equality among states have emerged as the consensus of the international community. These ideas are obviously influenced by constructivism. The Hu-Wen leadership, however, recognized that most Third World countries adopt systems different from those of the Western/United States' unilateralism and exert pressure on the Western countries to secure their respect for diversity and pluralism. These objectives naturally are in line with China's vital national interests, as Premier Wen Jiabao indicated in 2006: "China's insistence on its road of peace and development is determined by China's traditional culture, development needs and national interests".[51] The above foreign policy line has its difficulties too. In ideological terms, a harmonious world perspective has few elements of Marxism; this means that its claim as the critical inheritance of traditional Marxism is in doubt. Further, while the Hu-Wen leadership preaches the democratization of international relations, domestic political reform has hardly made any progress in the past decade. Concern over China's political and social stability is related to the human rights condition, political reforms, and corruption in China. Chinese leaders are obviously determined to combat corruption; there has been improvement in the human rights condition in the country, but the CPC has no intention of compromising its monopoly of political power. The fact that China is not a democracy and makes little efforts at democratization remains a handicap in China's foreign relations. After all, the international community tends to subscribe to the theory of democratic peace, i.e., democracies will not fight each other.[52]

Even in the most important international organization, the UN, Beijing has not been able to articulate a concrete plan to democratize its decision-making processes. Apparently it values its veto power in the Security Council; and it has not been working actively with Third World countries to come up with plans based on consensus to promote reforms.

The projection of China's image overseas is handicapped by the fact that the international media are mainly in the hands of the United States and other Western countries. In the 1990s, Chinese academics and thinktanks worked hard to rebuke Samuel P. Huntington's thesis of the clash of civilizations, but their efforts failed to make any impact in the international community. The Chinese authorities have been attempting to exploit the appeal of traditional Chinese culture; the Confucius Institutes project is a good example.

In the past decade, the Hu-Wen leadership probably has a well planned design to exploit international institutions and NGOs as global platforms to promote multilateral co-operation in various spheres to cultivate a peaceful international environment to facilitate China's development. According to a survey released in April 2007, China had joined 61.19% of all global inter-governmental organizations, ranking twenty-seventh among all countries; it had also joined 58.14% of all global NGOs, ranking thirty-first among all countries. [53] Although China's influence in defining international norms and setting agendas in the international community has remained limited, its level of participation has been improving, especially in recent years. In the wake of the global financial tsunami, China certainly has a more significant role in the definition of the new international financial structure, and its share in a number of specific cases in the Asian region, China's performance in setting agendas and defining norms has been impressive.

In these cases, the role of the United States is significant too. In the Six-Party Talks on the nuclear programme in North Korea, China has been enjoying the support of the United States. In the Sino-ASEAN relationship, there is considerable competition between China and the United States, perhaps best illustrated by the controversies over the membership of the East Asia Summit. This competition reveals the rise of China's influence and the relative decline of the United States; the latter was accused of a benign neglect of Southeast Asia after 1975. [54] Since 9/11, the region has been accorded considerable priority by the Bush administration in its efforts to combat terrorism; however, the USA's unilateral approach and its alienation of the Muslims in the region caused much resentment, which in turn contributed to China's rising influence.[55] Among the Shanghai Co-operation Organization countries, the alarm over the "colour revolutions" has facilitated renewed Sino-Russian co-operation and reduced the incentives of the Central Asian republics to use the USA to balance against their gigantic neighbours. In both cases, and especially in Southeast Asia, China has been avoiding open confrontation with the United States, and instead has chosen to concentrate on building the regional institutional frameworks.

Chinese leaders have not presented the Chinese development model as the "Beijing consensus" in competition with the "Washington consensus". But, as argued by Joshua Cooper Ramo, the Chinese model has begun to alter the global development parameters in the economic, social and political aspects. China thus has been able to reduce the influence of the United States, which is perceived to have been promoting its interests unilaterally. China's development model offers new ideas to guide developing countries to protect their respective lifestyles and political options, and to realize genuine independence while converging with the international order in their respective development courses. The recent global financial crisis has further discredited the "Washington consensus" because the Bush and the Obama administrations have pursued a course of action that was condemned by the United States during the previous regional financial crises, including the one in the Asia-Pacific region in 1997–98. Meanwhile, China has a good opportunity to seek a louder voice in the restructuring of the international financial architecture and better articulate the interests of the developing countries.

Both Jiang Zemin and Hu Jintao have also been building various international forums since the turn of the century to engage in Track-2 dialogue. In 2001, China established the Boao Forum for Asia. It was the first in Asia to consider major global economic issues from the perspective of Asians; it was modelled on the World Economic Forum in Davos and also aims at dialogue and exchanges with other regions to strengthen the economic ties within Asia and between Asia and the external world. In 2002, after the visit to Beijing University by a higher education delegation from South Korea, both parties reached agreement to hold the first annual meeting of the Beijing Forum on "The Harmony of Civilizations and Prosperity for All" in August 2004. Then in May 2005, Fudan University hosted the Shanghai

Forum on "Economic Globalization and the Choice of Asia" involving academics, experts, entrepreneurs and politicians from various countries to discuss the challenges of globalization.[56] The hosting of international forums at the civil society level has now become a trend in China's major cities.

The spread of Chinese culture and language now constitutes an important element in the cultivation of China's soft power. Following the examples of the British Council, the Alliance Française, the Goethe-Institut etc., China has also initiated its Confucius Institutes project. This is a step forward from the earlier "panda diplomacy"; it is a part of China's public diplomacy and its peaceful rise strategy.[57] In 1987, the Office of the Chinese Language Council International (Hanban) was formed with officials from twelve ministries and agencies including the State Council Office, education ministry, finance ministry and foreign affairs ministry.[58] Since the launch of the first Confucius Institute in Seoul on 21 November 2004, by mid-2007 there were already more than 170 Confucius Institutes in over fifty countries. According to the plan, there will be 500 Confucius Institutes by 2010.[59] The Institutes offer five types of service: promotion of Chinese-language teaching; training of Chinese-language teachers and provision of Chinese-language teaching resources; holding of Chinese-language examinations and certification of the qualifications of Chinese-language teachers; offer of information and consultation services on Chinese education and culture; and development of language and cultural exchanges between China and foreign countries. The use of the name Confucius Institute is interesting; it certainly shows a deliberate attempt to avoid the image of official propaganda and to exploit the appeal of traditional Chinese culture.

In response to the rising nationalism at home, however, Chinese leaders may have to adopt a hard-line position which does not conform to a harmonious world perspective. In November 2008, China postponed its summit meeting with the European Union because of the meeting between French President Nicolas Sarkozy and the Dalai Lama; at that time Sarkozy held the European Union presidency.

In December 2008 and in March 2009, Chinese monitoring and patrol vessels made high-profile appearances in the exclusive economic zones claimed by China near the Diaoyutai (Senkaku) Islands and the Paracel Islands in the South China Sea.[60] These gestures may adversely affect Chinese leaders' efforts to cultivate the image of a peaceful China; they also arouse the suspicion that Chinese leaders are more prone to hard-line gestures in times of domestic difficulties.

In sum, while trying to secure recognition as a major power satisfied with the status quo and keen to maintain a peaceful international environment to concentrate on development, the Hu-Wen leadership still has a long way to go to convince the world of the purpose and contribution of its pursuit.

Challenges and Constraints for Hu-Wen's Successors

Path dependence would likely be a strong characteristic of the policy programme of Hu-Wen's successors. It is widely suspected that Hu Jintao may follow the example of his predecessor Jiang Zemin and retain the chairmanship of the Party Central Military Commission for another two years or more at the Eighteenth Party Congress in 2012. In short, with the retired Party elders around, the new leaders will have to wait for at least two or three years before they can really make their mark in new policy programmes. They will need considerably more time before they can make enough key appointments so as to have their own teams to work effectively. Given the fact that the retired Party elders all have their protégés to reward and protect, the new leaders will encounter substantial resistance in their new appointments and promotions. They may actually prefer to be cautious and wait patiently.

Regarding the economic policy programmes, the broad directions analysed above enjoy strong support among the Party elite and the intelligentsia. The resistance mainly comes from vested interests. To take, for example, the issues of industrial upgrading and economic restructuring, they were policy goals set before the recent global financial tsunami and became even more pressing in the wake of the economic turmoil. It was also obvious that when China's economy recovered, labour shortages first appeared in Tianjin, then gradually spread to the Yangtze Delta and finally to the Pearl River Delta which has a higher concentration of labour-intensive processing industries. Wang Yang, the Party Secretary of Guangdong, had been pushing hard to implement the double transformation strategy of industries and the labour force to make Guangdong a high value-added world manufacturing centre through technological upgrading. But by early 2010, the progress of industrial and technological upgrading had been disappointing.

Local governments in Guangdong still accord a priority to maintain economic growth and secure jobs by preserving the low value-added, labour-intensive manufacturing factories, instead of engaging in ruthless industrial restructuring.[61] While in the eyes of the central government, Guangdong is notorious for "finding ways to bypass a red light", the Guangdong provincial authorities have the same problem with their own local governments. At the same time, the inadequacies of human capital in the Pearl River Delta are another bottleneck. While the unemployment of fresh university graduates remains a serious national problem, there is also an acute shortage of technicians and skilled workers in the country, and the shortage is more keenly felt in Guangdong than in the coastal cities to the north. Many entrepreneurs operating low-tech factories in the Pearl River Delta do not have the education and the management skills to meet the challenges of technological upgrading; and some of them choose to retire or engage in speculation in the real estate and stock markets.

As explained above, China's sustainable growth will have to depend more on domestic consumption, which means changing the pattern of "rich state but poor people (*guo fu min qiang*)" to "storing wealth among the people (*cang fu yu min*)", i.e., through the improvement of people's livelihood by raising their incomes and providing them with better social security and public services. This policy orientation, unfortunately, goes against the traditional values of the Party elite who consciously or unconsciously embrace "GDP-ism" which means that rapid economic growth should always be the state's highest priority because it will be the solution to almost all national problems and because it will raise China's international status. Moreover, there is also a strong inclination for governments at all levels to concentrate the resources at their hands for conspicuous projects, often infrastructural projects. Hence economic restructuring calls for adjustments concerning inputs, especially in terms of human resources, change in values and the overcoming of vested interests.

In his report on government work in early 2010, Premier Wen Jiabao indirectly indicated that income redistribution would become increasingly significant as the gap between the rich and poor widens.

Income redistribution takes place at two levels: between the state and society as a whole, and among the various socio-economic strata, and interest groups. The share of GDP going to people's income today is about 42%, compared with an average of 55% in developed countries; as the government has been ready to improve public services and social security, it may be reluctant to enhance the share going directly to people's income. It is therefore interesting to see whether new policies will be introduced in the coming decade towards this direction.

Real estate prices have been a key factor leading to a widening of the gap between the rich and poor. In early 2010, they became a severe test of good governance as the government's efforts to cool down real estate prices in the past eight years had proved to be ineffective.[62] They were a severe test because they caused a lot of dissatisfaction, and were a symbol of collusion between officials and enterprises at the expense of ordinary people. High real estate prices were related to the rapid urbanization supported by the Hu-Wen leadership, and to the fact that the urban authorities heavily depended on real estate development as a source of revenue. Yet the appropriation of land without adequate compensation by the urban authorities has been a significant source of grievances. Those who own property obviously would like to see further appreciation of property values; those who have yet to acquire their accommodation certainly desire a substantial decline in real estate prices. But the latter could possibly do much harm to the Chinese economy as consumption and purchasing power would be adversely affected.

The real estate prices issue therefore is a good illustration that income distribution and re-distribution have become very complicated and difficult as Chinese society has undergone profound division and stratification in the past three decades. Balancing various interests and considerations has become more challenging. Meanwhile, economically and politically powerful interest groups have emerged and, together with many local governments, they can effectively resist or combat government policy directives. Moreover, they can influence the mass media and public opinion too. Increasingly the successors to the Hu-Wen leadership will encounter challenges of this kind.

Environmental protection and energy efficiency present similar challenges. In his political report to the Seventeenth Party Congress in 2007, Party General Secretary Hu Jintao first introduced the concept of "ecological civilization" (*shengtai wenming*) as one of the key elements in "building a comprehensive well-off society". This is naturally a matter of balancing short-term and long-term objectives, as well as changing the values and behaviour patterns of cadres and ordinary people. In terms of policy implementation, the challenge for the leadership is to provide an effective package of economic and administrative incentives and disincentives as well as appropriate institutional changes.

In November 2007, the State Council included green indicators of per unit GDP energy consumption and reduction of major pollutants in the performance assessment of provincial-level officials. Under the new policy, the energy conservation and pollution reduction assessment results of all provincial authorities would be provided to the personnel system as an important basis for the assessment of their leading cadres. The application of the accountability system and the one-ballot veto system means that those leading cadres who fail to meet the targets would not be eligible to participate in the annual award competition or to receive any honorary titles.

The one-ballot veto system apparently is a crude but rather effective sanction. From 2006 to 2008, China's two major pollutants, sulphur dioxide (SO_2) and chemical oxygen demand (COD) dropped 8.95% and 6.61% respectively, and energy intensity decreased by 10.1%. The targets of the Eleventh FYP (2006–2010) were a 20% drop of energy consumption per unit GDP and a 10% reduction of major pollutants; hence the performance in the first three years of the FYP was satisfactory.[63] But in the first quarter of 2010, energy intensity rose 3.2% which made the fulfilment of the FYP target almost impossible.[64] An important reason was the accelerated growth of the electricity generation, steel, non-ferrous metals, construction materials, petrochemical and chemical industries in the same period; and these industries consume large energy resources. Up till now, 80% of the energy conservation in China has been achieved through the retirement of obsolete equipment; in the near future, it has to be achieved largely through industrial restructuring.

It is not expected that the fifth-generation leadership will demonstrate a keen interest in genuine political reforms, at least not in its initial years. But improvement of governance is recognized as an important objective in maintaining the legitimacy of the Chinese Communist regime. In the Sixteenth Party Congress held in 2002, the

Party leadership indicated that it would establish systems governing the tenure, resignation and accountability of leaders of the Party and the state. Two years later, the Party released the "Temporary Regulations on the Resignation of Leading Cadres of the Party and State", which demands resignations on the part of principal officials assuming responsibility for serious mistakes and negligence in their respective spheres of work. In 2005, the "Civil Service Law" was promulgated; and accountability enforced through resignation procedure has become a part of the management system for the civil service and was stipulated in legal form.[65]

In May 2007, the Party's Central Commission for Discipline Inspection released the "Certain Regulations on the Strict Prohibition of Abusing the Privileges of Official Positions to Secure Improper Interests". In the same month, the National Bureau of Corruption Prevention was established as an organ directly under the State Council, affiliated to the Ministry of Supervision.[66] In July 2009, the General Office of the Party Central Committee and that of the State Council released the "Communist Party of China Regulation on Inspection Work (Trial)", "Temporary Regulations on the Implementation of Accountability of Leading Cadres of the Party and State", and "Certain Regulations on Avoiding Consumption in the Work of the Leading Personnel of State-owned Enterprises".[67] There is obviously no lack of documents and institutions to combat corruption. The crux of the matter is that democracy and the rule of law violate the bottom line of the dictatorship of the Party, hence there are no effective checks and balances and the combatting of corruption has to rely on political campaigns.

Leaving democracy and the rule of law aside for the time being, even the supervision and monitoring of officials by the media and the people's congress system are still not acceptable to the Hu-Wen leadership; they are still perceived to erode the Party's monopoly of political power. The Chinese authorities today maintain a tight grip on the mass media. In the past few years, the suppression of media freedom, cyber society activities, NGOs, dissidents etc. had been strengthened. Many of the restrictions might have been related to the preparation for the Beijing Olympics, but there was no relaxation afterwards. The economic difficulties triggered off by the international financial tsunami and the politically sensitive anniversaries in 2009 were convenient excuses for rejecting any liberalization measures.

As the media and publications in China have to belong to or at least be affiliated in name to recognized official organs, there were attempts to report scandals in other provinces by a number of more adventurous newspapers and magazines, while avoiding embarrassing the local authorities with administrative control over them. For example, news magazines such as *Nanfang Zhoumo* (*Southern Weekly*) had established a reputation of investigatory reporting on scandals and the darker side of society outside Guangdong. In recent years, because of the deterrence measures of the Party's Central Propaganda Department, including the re-organization of the editorial board and even the termination of publication, these bold attempts to test the limits of media freedom have been in decline.

The Party also controls the people's congress system by ensuring the presence of a majority of Party members at all levels of the system. The Party groups in all people's congresses can therefore impose Party discipline to ensure their functioning in accordance with the Party line. To avoid challenges to the Party leadership and to protect the image of the Party and its leaders, the people's congresses at all levels have yet to exercise their supervision of government officials at the corresponding levels effectively. After the Tiananmen Incident, the "monopolistic leadership of the Party" has been emphasized, and the Party secretary usually also serves as the chairman of the standing committee of the people's congress at the same level. Under such circumstances, the people's congress system finds it even more difficult to serve as a checks and balances mechanism and to assume a supervisory role.

In the fifth-generation leadership, meaningful political reforms would probably begin in these two areas. Allowing more freedom of the mass media can be gradual and carefully monitored, some of the investigatory reporting prompting decisive action on the part of the leadership can be highly popular, enhancing its appeal and status. The same applies to strengthening the role of people's congresses at the county and prefectural-city levels. The experiments in Wenling City in Zhejiang in the past decade allowing the people's congresses at the town level to play an effective role in deliberations in the town budgets have presented a good model.[68] These political reforms will not immediately challenge the Party's monopoly of political power.

Many types of consultative mechanisms will continue to develop. Even a Leninist party has to establish its mass organizations; in the

Yan'an period the Party already promoted the Maoist "mass line". At this stage, consultative mechanisms will have their new packaging. The Hu-Wen leadership now demands cadres at all levels to win the support of public opinion; good governance aims to secure legitimacy and requires evidence of people's approval. Senior cadres today are already adept at Western politicians' political showmanship; no one will deny that Premier Wen Jiabao has set an outstanding example, and his successors will be even more sophisticated.

The redress of grievances would likely be another area in which the successors to the Hu-Wen leadership would be innovative. It was reported that in 2009 there were about 217,900 cases of rallies protests and mass meetings; and the public security and armed police were mobilized 243,600 times to suppress the riots.[69] In November 2008, over 2,000 Party secretaries of county-level Party committees were all called upon to attend a seven-day study course with a series of sessions to learn how to correctly handle contradictions among various interests and to cases of emergency. In 2009, the 3,000 county-level public security bureau chiefs, the 3,500 heads basic-level procuratorates, and the chief judges of the basic-level law courts all had to go through training sessions. The principal purpose of this national training for the responsible cadres of the basic-level law and order organs was to establish a harmonious society, and to learn how to avoid as well as handle mass incidents.[70]

Shenyang city in Liaoning offers an interesting model in the redress of grievances. Before 2008, complaint visits (*shangfang*) to the central government in Beijing from Shenyang ranked first among provincial capital cities. In response to this notoriety, the Shenyang city government spent 50 million *yuan* to build a conspicuous building along the main boulevard where the city government was located. The nineteen bureaux of the city government maintained reception desks in the building, and various types of complaints were handled at four levels depending on their complexity. The building had over four hundred stuff members who were more numerous than those at the complaints bureau of the Liaoning provincial government. The one-stop approach proved to be convenient for the people and attracted much publicity in the national media. It was a good example of how the initiative of the city leadership turned a bad name into fame, as complaint visits from Shenyang to the central authorities dropped markedly.[71]

It is difficult to anticipate significant top-down political reforms initiated by the governing political elite or a pro-democracy movement launched by the people at the grassroots level before the mid-2010s. In Japan, in response to the long-term predominance of the Liberal Democratic Party, Ozawa Ichiro proposed that its internal factions may split the governing party into two conservative parties engaging in competition.[72] This kind of scenario is unlikely to appear in China. The CPC is probably not strongly united by ideological commitment and discipline, but the strong common interest and consensus on the maintenance of its monopoly of political power are likely to prevent a split within the fifth-generation leadership.

In the foreign policy arena, the fifth-generation leadership may have a good foundation to be more assertive and perhaps more innovative. In the wake of the global financial tsunami, Chinese leaders perceived symptoms of a decline in United States hegemony. The annual report of the Institute of International Relations at the People's Liberation Army (PLA) College of International Relations stated in 2009 that "the United States has suffered a major blow", and it will "without doubt see its standing slide precipitously" in the future. The report also indicates that the global financial tsunami occurred at an extremely good time (for the emerging powers) to participate in the rebuilding of the international economic system and that they "will be able to exploit this opportunity to establish themselves as leading players, or as major supporting actors, in the global stage". The communiqué of the fourth plenum of the Seventeenth CPC Central Committee released in September 2009 more authoritatively claimed that "a new change has occurred in the framework of the global economy and a new global power balance can now be seen". Earlier, in July, President Hu Jintao told the Eleventh Meeting of Chinese Diplomatic Envoys that "the prospect of global multipolarization has become much clearer".

The successors to the Hu-Wen leadership are expected to continue to promote multipolarization and multilateralism, and to adopt a higher profile in championing Third World interests. At the second financial summit of G20 leaders in April 2009, President Hu Jintao spoke of the G20 as having a "broad representative nature" that includes the developing countries and described it as "an important and effective platform" for concerted international efforts to counter the economic and financial crisis. At the summit, Hu proposed that international financial institutions should give more assistance to developing countries and that the International Monetary Fund (IMF) and the World Bank should enhance the representation and voice of developing countries. The same messages were repeated by Hu at the following G20 financial summit in September.[73]

Today the Chinese leadership perceives "the collective rise of the emerging powers as an important characteristic of today's world", and it considers these powers to be a major force for promoting the democratization of international relations, the reform of international politics and economics, and the multipolarization of the world. Hence there is a growing recognition on the part of Beijing of the importance of the BRIC (i.e., Brazil, Russia, India and China), as a new arena for China's diplomacy. In an interview with the *Renmin Ribao*, Foreign Minister Yang Jiechi discussed strengthening relations among the BRIC within the framework of "major powers".[74] It appears that China considers its relations with the other three BRIC countries on a par with its relations with the United States, the European Union and Japan; and that China considers building close relations within the BRIC group an important element of its foreign policy. These trends would be significant agenda items in the fifth-generation leadership foreign policy programme.

In June 2009, the first BRIC Summit was officially held in Ekaterinburg, Russia. Earlier still, the Sino-Russian Joint Statement on Major International Issues concluded in May 2008 indicated that in addition to the dialogue between the G8 and the developing and emerging economics, both countries would strengthen and develop international cooperation mechanisms such as foreign ministers' meetings among the BRIC group and between China, Russia and India. Then in the China-Brazil summit held in July of the same year, President Hu called for an expansion of strategic co-operation with Brazil within a multinational mechanism including the BRIC.

Based on these agreements, the foreign ministers of the BRIC met in September 2008 during the regular session of the United Nations General Assembly. Two meetings of the BRIC finance ministers were then held in Sao Paulo in November 2008 and in Horsham, United Kingdom, in March 2009. In the following September, BRIC finance ministers and central bank governors also met. Each of these meetings took place before a meeting of the G20 finance ministers and central bank governors, thus allowing the BRIC governments to co-ordinate their positions regarding reform of the international financial architecture. For example, at their September 2009 meeting, the BRIC authorities announced their common proposal to allocate 7% of the quota contributions of the IMF and 6% of the member country contributions to the World Bank to developing countries, and to ensure that the latter would receive equal voting rights as the advanced countries.

China's expanding foreign exchange reserves and international economic reach bring their problems too. In the foreseeable future, China will continue to expand its trade and investment overseas, China's dependence on the international market, as reflected by the ratio of trade to GDP, is expected to rise further. China's increasing imports of oil, natural gas and other industrial raw materials plus its investment to secure their future supplies are similar to Japan's "resource diplomacy" in the years after the Yom Kippur War of 1973. China's approach to Africa, Latin America and the Middle East in recent years does have strong "resource diplomacy" considerations; it also reflects China's concerns for economic security.

China's investment in the Third World, however, has sometimes generated resentment. Whereas China was hailed for creating jobs and saving industries, more recently Chinese investors have been accused of discriminatory employment practices. Some of the more common complaints against Chinese firms in Africa include poor pay, lack of safety protection for workers in the textiles, copper and coal mining industries, and the use of short-term contracts. In 2004, the Zambian government asked the Chinese managers at Zambia-China Mulungushi Textiles in northern Kabwe to stop locking workers in the factory at night. In June 2006, the Zambian authorities shut down Collum Coal Mining industries in southern Zambia, indicating that miners had been forced to work underground without safety clothing and boots. Union officials in Chambishi Mining, a copper producer in Zambia, complained that miners there were the lowest paid in the country's entire mining sector, with the least paid earning US$100 a month, compared with US$424 in Konkola Copper Mines, the largest copper producer in Zambia. Chambishi Mining, sold to Chinese investors in 2003, was the scene of violent workers' protests in July 2006.[75]

Chinese enterprises have been active in infrastructural projects in Africa, such as the construction of roads, railways and housing. The major difference in operating styles between the Chinese companies and their Western counterparts is that the former often bring their own labourers. The arrival of tens of thousands of Chinese workers naturally creates ill feeling in African countries with very high unemployment rates. There are complaints against the contracts concerned, which normally require the successful bidders to contract only 30% of their work to local companies. Typical examples are the road and railway rehabilitation projects in Angola funded by Chinese credit backed by oil exports to China.[76]

There are many complaints regarding cheap Chinese products flooding the African continent too, as they sometimes force local industries to close, with severe job losses. In Lesotho, Chinese operators are licensed to operate only big retail shops or supermarkets, but locally owned grocery stores have largely disappeared. It was said that the local people had rented their shops to the Chinese because "they get a better profit from rent than from running the shops themselves".[77]

There are also complaints closer to China in the Greater Mekong Sub-region. The World Wide Fund for Nature, based in Switzerland, observed that the "New City Development Project" in the Lung Namtha province in Laos would damage the marsh land in the area and bring about more floods and other environmental damages. In Cambodia, environmentalists and local residents are condemning China's hydro-electric power projects there. Residents near the development sites perceived the projects as unnecessary; they told Western journalists that they did not want to see their ancestral lands "stolen" by the projects. The International Rivers Network (now International Rivers) in the United States criticized the dam projects as "poorly conceived . . . needlessly and irreparably damaging Cambodia's river system with serious consequences".[78]

China as a trade partner and a source of investment will enhance Third World countries' bargaining power vis-à-vis the developed countries, which tend to take a common stand regarding demands on democracy, human rights and the rule of law. China's demand for energy and raw materials has been a significant factor in driving up their prices in international markets, which has benefitted many Third World countries in recent years. Some Chinese experts consider that China can be an important source of intermediate technology, which is cost effective and appropriate for the stage of development of many Third World countries. However, China has yet to demonstrate that it can serve as a generous and effective source of technology transfer for the Third World in household electrical appliance industries, textiles and apparel industries, infrastructure construction, and so on.[79]

Establishing networks through education, both by sending teachers to Third World countries and providing scholarships to their students to study in Chinese universities, is an effective way to strengthen China's "soft power". From the mid-1950s to 2000, 5,582 African students had enrolled in tertiary institutions in China. These students typically took two years learning the Chinese language, and then pursued technical subjects, especially in the engineering disciplines. In 2003, about half of the African students in China were studying for postgraduate degrees. The Chinese government's hope is that these education exchanges will improve China's image in Africa, establish grassroots support in local communities, and cultivate networks and goodwill among the future elites. In the foreseeable future, these African talents are expected to contribute to the expansion of Sino-African economic ties in the high-tech fields.[80]

To succeed in the cultivation of goodwill, the Chinese authorities have to work hard to ensure that African students on university campuses in China do not suffer from discrimination and racist attitudes from Chinese students. The latter often value the friendship of their counterparts from the developed countries more than that of classmates from Africa. Discipline of African students is occasionally a problem. In the past, there were protests against discrimination among the African students, which were an embarrassment to the Chinese authorities.[81]

To deal with the emergence of the "ugly Chinese" syndrome, Beijing's generous aid programmes may not be enough. The Chinese authorities, while directing their SOEs to expand and invest in the Third World, have not directed them to operate as "model business partners". However, some of China's aid money can go to the SOEs so that they will be able to behave as "model employers" and contribute to community projects. It requires effective co-ordination at the central government level and new mechanisms have to be built to achieve the desirable outcomes. The Hu-Wen leadership is obviously aware of the emerging adverse publicity and will try to reverse the trend. This is one of the major challenges to the fifth-generation leadership's attempt to enhance China's soft power and its economic security.[82]

Conclusion

The Hu-Wen leadership naturally can claim that it has been successful not only in improving people's living standards, but it has also laid the foundation for a basic social security system although not for the entire population. While nationalism has been an increasingly significant element in Chinese politics, the improvement in China's international status has also become an important source of the regime's legitimacy. The Hu-Wen leadership has certainly been sophisticated in containing the growing discontent and grievances of the people, and it has developed a good grasp of the skills of Western politicians too. The adjustments in the economic development strategy are certainly reforms in the right direction. All these explain the appeal of the "Beijing consensus" especially after the recent global financial tsunami.

The achievements of the Hu-Wen leadership, however, had guaranteed a significant tendency towards path-dependence. As the Party elite become the most significant part of the vested interests, even though different factions may have various ideological orientations, the difficulty of arriving at an adequate consensus to promote major changes is substantial. And since the status quo plus the adjustments initiated by the Hu-Wen leadership at this stage represents the consensus of the mainstream, the reluctance to engage in major political reforms will be hard to overcome.

Concerns for political stability as well as the status of the incumbent and past leadership also mean that the Chinese authorities are unwilling to admit mistakes. In January 2010, the Fifth Tibet Work Conference of the Party was held in Beijing attended by all the top leaders. Yet in response to the riots in Tibet in March 2008, the observations of the conference were that "the major contradiction" in the autonomous region is between the increasing material demands of the people and the decreasing social productivity and a special contradiction is between "the people in Tibet" and the "Dalai Lama clique". Hence the focus of government efforts in the Tibetan region should be on economic development and political stability.

Finally, the Hu-Wen leadership already realizes that reforms of any kind would be bound to encounter serious resistance from vested interests, a good example is the non-ideological issue of real estate prices in major cities in China. The real danger for the fifth-generation leadership would be that while it may detect the need to initiate reforms, it would not have the political support to overcome the resistance. The Party regime will then deteriorate. It has been suggested that Chinese leaders look to Singapore as a model; but if the Party regime cannot overcome the vested interests, it might become like the Suharto regime in Indonesia.

Notes and References

1. Guoguang Wu, "China in 2009, muddling through crises", *Asian Survey*, Vol. 50, No. 1 (January / February 2010), pp. 29–30.

2. Joshua Cooper Ramo, *The Beijing Consensus* (London: The Foreign Policy Centre, 2004) pp. 11–13.

3. John Williamson, "What Washington means by policy reform", in John Williamson (ed.), *Latin American Adjustment: How Much Has Happened?*, Washington DC: Institute for International Economics, 1990, pp. 8–19.

4. Lian Yuming and Wu Jianzhong (eds.), *Zhong guo guo ce bao gao 2009–2010* (*Report on China's National Policies 2009–2010*) (Beijing: Zhongguo shidai jingji chubanshe, 2010), pp. 18 and 20.

5. *Ibid.*, pp. 19 and 21.

6. New China News Agency commentary, 14 October 2004.

7. *Oriental Daily News* and *Wen Wei Po*, 5 November, 2005; *Ta Kung Pao*, 25 November 2005 (all Hong Kong Chinese newspapers); and New China News Agency dispatch, 16 November 2005.

8. New China News Agency dispatches, 28, 29 and 30 November and 20 December 2005.

9. New China News Agency dispatch, 18 December 2008.

10. See Mary E. Gallagher, "China in 2004: stability above all", *Asian Survey*, Vol. 45, No. 1 (January-February 2005) pp. 27–28.

11. David Shambaugh, *China's Communist Party – Atrophy and Adaptation* (Washington DC: Woodrow Wilson Centre Press, and Berkeley CA: University of California Press, 2006) pp. 76–77.

12. Zhonglianbu Ketizu (International Liaison Department's Specialized Topic Research Group), "Sugong kuatai he sulian jieti gei zhizhong gongchandang ren de jingshi (The CPSU's fall from power and the Soviet Union's disintegration serve as a warming to ruling Communist Party members)", *Dangjian Yanjiu Neican (Party Building Research Internal Reference Materials)*, No. 4 (2001) pp. 13–15.

13. Chen Yanhua, "Yuenan de gaige kaifang de chengji he wenti (Successes and problems in Vietnam's reform and opening)," *Guoji Gongyunshi Yangjiu (Historical Research on the International Communist Movement)*, No. 1 (1993) pp. 11–13.

14. Willy Wo-Lap Lam, "Zhonggong yauxiang Guba xuexi? (The Communist Party of China has to learn from Cuba?)", *Apple Daily* (a Hong Kong Chinese newspaper), 24 October 2005, p. A22.

15. Shambaugh, *China's Communist Party*, p. 88.

16. *Ibid.*, p. 91

17. *Ibid.*

18. Richard Kraus, "China in 2003: from SARS to spaceships", *Asian Survey*, Vol.44, No.1 (January-February 2004), pp. 150 and 152.

19. See Joseph Y. S. Cheng, "Direct elections of town and township heads in China: the dapeng and buyun experiments", *China Information*, Vol. XV, No. 1 (2001), pp. 104–137.

20. See Yong Gui, Joseph Y. S. Cheng and Weihong Ma, "Cultivation of grass-root democracy: a study of direct elections of residents committees in Shanghai", *China Information*, Vol. XX, No. 1 (2006), pp. 7–31.

21. See Joseph Y. S. Cheng, "Introduction: economic growth and new challenges," in Joseph Y. S. Cheng (ed.), *Challenges and Policy Programmes of China's New Leadership* (Hong Kong: City University of Hong Kong Press, 2007), pp. 1–2.

22. Tony Saich, "China in 2005: Hu's in Charge," *Asian Survey*, Vol. 46, No. 1 (January–February 2006), p. 42.

23. Subject Group of the Development Research Centre of the State Council, "Evaluation and suggestions on reform of the Chinese medical health system (abstract and key points)," 29 July 2005, http://www.sina.com.cn.

24. *Hong Kong Economic Journal* (a Hong Kong Chinese newspaper), 29 July 1995.

25. Liu Xitang, "Chengshi benkun zhili zhong de jumi zuidi shenghuo baozhang zhidu (The minimum standards of living scheme and the urban poverty prediction in China)", in Bai Gang and Shi Weimin (eds.), *Zhongguo Gonggong Zhengce Fenxi, 2008 Nian Juan (Analysis of Public Policies of China, 2008)* (Beijing: China Social Sciences Press, 2008), pp. 159–160.

26. "PRC officials on income tax revenue sharing scheme aimed at common prosperity", New China News Agency dispatch, 12 March 2002; and "Finance Minister Xiang Hucheng says revenue sharing to benefit western China", New China News Agency dispatch, 11 March 2002.

27. Dali L. Yang, "China in 2002: leadership transition and the political economy of governance," *Asian Survey*, Vol. 43, No. 1 (January-February 2002), pp. 36–37.

28. Wang Fayan and Wang Xianming, "2007 nian Zhongguo shehui baozhang fazhan baogao" ("Development of social security in 2007"), in Ru Xin, Lu

Xueyi and Li Peilin (eds.), *Shehui lanpishu – 2008 nian Zhongguo shehui xingshi fenxi yu yuce (Blue Book of China's Society – Year 2008: Analysis and Forecast on China's Social Development)* (Beijing: Social Sciences Academic Press (China), 2008), pp. 50–51.

29. *Ibid.*, p. 51.

30. New China News Agency dispatch, 7 October 2003.

31. John Wong, "China's economy 2009 in review: rebound first and rebalance later," *East Asian Policy* (Singapore), Vol. 2, No. 1 (2010), pp. 13–22.

32. New China News Agency dispatch, 23 October 2005.

33. Zhang Shifei and Tang Jun, "Chengxiang zuidi shenghuo baozhang zhidu jiben xingcheng (The system of subsistence allowances for urban and rural residents in place)", in Ru Zin, Lu Xueyi and Li Peilin (eds.), *Blue Book of China's Society 2008*, pp. 57–58.

34. See Premier Wen Jiabao's report on the work of government delivered at the first conference of the Eleventh National People's Congress on 5 March 2008, section 6, http://big5.xinhuanet.com/gate/big5/news.xinhuanet.com /newscenter/2008–03/19/content_7819983.htm

35. Gu Xin, "Quanmin yiliao baoxian zoushang zhenggui (Towards universal coverage of health care insurance: China's new health care reform)", in Ru Xin, Lu Xueyi and Li Peilin (eds.), *Blue Book of China's Society 2008*, p. 95.

36. Li Peilin and Chen Guangjin, "Zhongguo Jinru Fazhan de Xin Chongzhang Jieduan – 2009–2010 nian Zhongguo shehui fazhan xingshi fenxi yu yuce (China steps into a new stage of growth – analysis and forecast, 2009–2010)", in Ruxin, Lu Xueyi and Li Peilin (eds.), *2010 nian: Zhongguo shehui xinshi fenxi yu yuce (2010 society of China: analysis and forecast)* (Beijing: Social Sciences Academic Press (China), 2009), pp. 4–5; and Wang Fayun and Li Yu, "2009 nian Zhongguo Shehui Baoxian Shiye" ("Social insurance in China, 2009"), in *ibid.*, pp. 49–60.

37. See Li Peilin and Chen Guangjin, "China steps into a new stage of growth", pp. 3–4; and Mo Rong, Zhao Liwei and Chen Lin, "2009 nian: gueji jinrong weiji xia de jiuye xingshi he zhengce (The employment situation and relevant policies under international financial crisis)", in Ru Zin, Lu Xueyi and Li Peilin, *2010 Society of China: Analysis and Forecast*, pp. 31–48.

38. Cen Chen, "Gongan wujing qunian chudong yi 24 wan ci (Public security and armed police were mobilized over 240,000 times last year)", *Cheng Ming* (a monthly in Chinese published in Hong Kong), No. 389 (March 2010), pp. 16–17.

39. Mo Rong, Zhao Liwei and Chen Lan, "The employment situation and relevant policies under international financial crisis," pp. 43–44.

40. *Renmin ribao* (Beijing), 12 November 2003.

41. New China News Agency dispatch, 29 November and 2 December 2003.

42. New China News Agency dispatch, 1 December 2005; and *Renmin ribao* editorial, 2 December 2005.

43. New China News Agency dispatch, 17 November 2005.

44. "Decision of the Central Committee of the Communist Party of China regarding a number of major issues in promoting rural reform and development" approved by the Third Plenum of the 17th Central Committee of the CPC on 12 October 2008; New China News Agency dispatch, 19 October 2008.

45. *Ibid.*

46. Lian Yuming and Wu Jianzhong (eds.), *Report on China's National Policies 2009–2010*, p. 121.

47. Wu Zhongtao, "'Shi er wu'gui hua Quanmian Gaige (The Twelfth Five-Year Plan aims at comprehensive reforms", *The Mirror* (a monthly in Chinese published in Hong Kong), No. 395 (June 2010), p. 19.

48. Zhao Hong, "China's Economic Restructuring Matters to the World Economy", *East Asian Institute Bulletin* (National University of Singapore), Vol. 12, No. 1, May 2010, p. 4.

49. See Joseph Y. S. Cheng "China's Foreign Policy after the Seventeenth Party Congress", in Dennis Hickey and Baogang Guo (eds.), *Dancing with the Dragon – China's Emergence in the Developing World*, Lanham MD: Lexington Books, 2010, pp. 23–52.

50. Samuel P. Huntington, "The clash of civilizations", *Foreign Affairs*, Vol. 72, No. 3 (Summer 1993) pp. 22–49.

51. "A record of Premier Wen Jiabao's replies to questions from Chinese and foreign journalists (Wen Jiabao zongli de zhongwai jizhe wen shilu)", *Xinhuanet*, 14 March 2006, http://news.xinhuanet.com/misc/2006–03/14/content_4301180.htm.

52. Spencer R. Weart, *Never at War: Why Democracies Will Not Fight One Another* (New Haven CT: Yale University Press, 1998), pp. 1–3.

53. "A comparison of various stated participation in international organizations" ("Geguo canyu gyoji zuzhi de bijiao"), China Internet Information Centre, 2 April 2007, http://big5.china.com.cn/node_7000058/2007-04/02/content_8047488.htm.

54. Diane K. Mauzy and Brian L. Job, "U.S. Policy in Southeast Asia: Limited Re-engagement after Years of Benign Neglect", *Asian Survey*, Vol. 47, No. 4 (July / August 2007), pp. 622–641.

55. Tsai Tung-chich and Hung Ming-te, "MeiZhong liangguo zai dongnanya diqu de ruanquanli gouzhu yu jingzheng (Constructing and competing for soft power in Southeast Asia between the U.S. and China)", *Prospect Quarterly* (Taipei), Vol. 10, No. 1 (January 2009), pp. 45–88.

56. *Ibid.*, p. 60.

57. Joshua Kurlantzick, *Charm Offensive: How China's Soft Power Is Transforming the World* (New Haven CT: Yale University Press, 2007), p. 61.

58. Tsai Tung-chich and Hung Ming-te, "Constructing and competing for soft power", p. 56; and Ding Sheng and Robert A. Saunders, "Talking up China: an analysis of China's rising cultural power and global promotion of the Chinese language," *East Asia: An International Quarterly*, Vol. 23, No. 2 (June 2006), pp. 3–33.

59. "Confucius institutes in the world", website of the Office of Chinese Language Council International (Hanban), http://english.hanban.org /kzxy_list .php?ithd=gzky.

60. Xiao Shi, "Zhongnanhai wenjian yu qiangying, shuangquan bingju (Chinese leaders demonstrate a stable and a hard line)", *The Mirror* (a monthly in Chinese published in Hong Kong), No. 379 (February 2009), pp. 22–23.

61. Yu Hong, "Guangdong's economic transformation and housing prices", *East Asian Institute Bulletin*, Vol. 12, No. 1 (May 2010), p. 6.

62. Yu Qiaofu, "Zhongyang zai liu meng yao bi lou shi 'tuishao' (The central leadership adopted tough measures again for 'cool down' the estate market)", *The Mirror*, No. 395 (June 2010), pp. 26–29.

63. Chen Gang, "China making progress in environmental protection and energy efficiency," *East Asian Institute Bulletin*, Vol. 12, No. 1 (May 2010), p. 7.

64. Xiao Shi, "Zhong yang 'tie wan' cu jing ji zhuan xing" ("The central leadership's 'iron fist' in promoting economic transformation)", *The Mirror*, No. 395 (June 2010), pp. 24–25.

65. Joseph Y. S. Cheng, "Introduction: economic growth and new challenges", p. 7; and New China News Agency dispatch, 2 December 2005.

66. Wen Shengtang and Li Yuanze, "2007 nian Zhongguo yufang he chengzhi fubai de xingshi" ("The trends in the prevention and punishment of corruption in 2007"), in Ru Xin, Lu Xueyi and Li Peilin (eds.), *Blue Book of China's Society 2008*, pp. 135–136 and 139.

67. Wen Shengtang and Wen Quan, "Dang qian fan fu chang lian xing shi fen xi yu qian zhan" ("Analysis on and Forecast of the Combat against Corruption and Advocating Integrity)", in Ru Xin, Lu Xueyi and Li Peilin (eds.), *Blue Book of China's Society 2010* , pp. 113–114.

68. Li Fan (ed.), Wen ling shi yan yu zhong guo di fang zheng fu gong gong yu suan gai ge (The Wenling Experiments and Public Budgetary Reforms in Local Governments in China), Beijing: zhi shi chan quan chu ban she, 2009.

69. Cen Chen, "Public security and armed police were mobilized over 240,000 times last year."

70. Lian Yuming and Wu Jianzhong (eds.), *Report on China's National Policies 2009–2010*, pp. 38–39.

71. *Renmin ribao* (Beijing), 7 August 2009.

72. Ichiro Ozawa, *Blueprint for a New Japan: The Rethinking of a Nation* (Tokyo and New York: Kodansha International, 1994).

73. The National Institute for Defense Studies, Japan, *East Asian Strategic Review 2010* (Tokyo: The Japan Times, 2010), pp. 119–121.

74. *Renmin ribao* (Beijing), 14 December 2009.

75. *Los Angeles Times*, 6 October 2006.

76. Ali Zafar, "The growing relationship between China and Sub-Saharan Africa: macroeconomic, trade, investment, and aid links," *World Bank Research Observer*, Vol. 22, No. 1 (Spring 2007), pp. 103–130.

77. *South China Morning Post* (Hong Kong), 14 August 2006.

78. Lim Tin Seng, "China's active role in the Greater Mekong Sub-region: challenge to construct a 'win-win' relationship," *East Asian Policy* (Singapore), Vol. 1, No. 1 (January-March 2009), p. 46.

79. For a more optimistic view, see Edward Friedman, "How economic superpower China could transform Africa," *Journal of Chinese Political Sense*, Vol. 14, No. 1 (March 2009), pp. 1–20.

80. Gao Qiufu, "Old friends, new partners", *Beijing Review*, Vol. 49, No. 22 (1 June 2006), pp. 12–13, http://www.bjreview.com.cn/expert/txt/2006-12/10/content_50411.htm; and Ni Yanshuo, "Confucius around the world", *Beijing Review*, Vol. 51, No. 10 (6 March 2008), pp. 26–27, http://www.bjreview.com.cn/ nation/txt/2008-03/04/content_102406.htm.

81. These observations are based on the author's frequent visits to universities in China.

82. See Deng Yong and Wang Fei-ling (eds.), *China Rising: Power and Motivation in Chinese Foreign Policy* (Lanham MD: Rowman and Littlefield, 2005).

2

Democratization within the CPC and the Future of Democracy in China

Feng LIN

Introduction

The Communist Party of China (CPC) is the ruling political party in China. Its policy and practice on democracy will have direct impact upon democratic progress in China. The official policy of the CPC is to develop and promote the people's democracy through realization of democracy within the CPC. Hence the future of democracy in China hinges upon the success of democratization within the CPC. This chapter focuses on the discussion of democracy within the CPC. It will start with an overview of the historical development of democracy within the CPC, showing that democracy within the CPC has only been taken seriously in the twenty-first century, and that there are deep historical and cultural reasons for this lack of democracy. Despite the lack of a democratic tradition, various policy statements of the CPC have mentioned the necessity of developing internal democracy and the Seventeenth Central Committee in 2007 made it clear that the CPC should develop internal democracy in order to achieve people's democracy in China. That has been regarded as essential to maintaining the governing position of the CPC in China. Part II of the chapter will discuss the justifications for the change of policy to embrace democracy within the CPC. There are various reasons for this, of which the democratic movement in the former Eastern European communist countries is an important external factor. In order to develop democracy within the CPC, the consensus is that a set of democratic mechanisms has to be established, which includes the means for competitive elections, the protection of the rights of CPC members, ensuring transparency, leadership within the CPC, the working of the CPC, supervision and so on. After an overview of the mechanisms to democratize the CPC, Part III of the chapter will focus on competitive election as a basis to discuss the actual development of democracy within the CPC. Discussion of different experiments in electoral reform within the CPC at different levels in the two recent rounds indicates that the element of competition has gradually been brought into elections within the CPC. It is also encouraging to see that the necessity for democratic election within the CPC has been appreciated by senior Party leaders. However, the development of competitive elections within the CPC is still at its preliminary stage and at the lower level of CPC organizations. There are also considerable obstacles in the lower-level CPC organizations for the expansion of competitive elections. Since the election reform within the CPC has broken through some existing rules within the Constitution of the CPC, it will be more desirable for the relevant provisions in the Constitution of the CPC to be amended before further electoral reforms are carried out. Part IV of the chapter will discuss the future of democracy within the CPC and the future of democracy in China. Given that the CPC has a clear policy on developing internal democracy, the establishment of various mechanisms and their reforms has proved to be moving in the right direction, and that those mechanisms seem to work in coordination with each other, the author remains cautiously optimistic about the future development of democracy within the CPC. However, the progress of the development of internal democracy has been very slow and it has even been argued that the development of internal democracy has encountered a bottleneck due to resistance to the reform from lower-level CPC organizations. Since the CPC is so powerful that it has no competitors at all at the moment, it is in the best interest of China and the Chinese people for the CPC to democratize itself first, which will lead naturally to popular democracy in the country. Without internal reform and external pressure coming from outside the CPC, the progress of internal democracy will lack momentum. Hence the chapter concludes by arguing that the increase of both internal and external pressure will force the CPC to take internal democratization seriously and assist the Central Committee of the CPC to remove resistance against internal democratization from local party organizations. That means China should develop democracy both within the CPC and nationally, so that the people's democracy will facilitate the development of democracy within the CPC. Once democracy is achieved within the CPC, there will be people's democracy in China.

Historical Development of Internal Democracy

A Change of Policy: From Centralism to Democracy

From the time the CPC was founded in 1921 to the time it came to power in 1949, the Party was at war, centralism was believed to be more important than democracy, and the conditions were not right for the CPC to develop internal democracy.[1] After the CPC came to power as a governing political party in 1949, it realized the necessity of developing democracy within the Party itself.[2] This interest in democracy within the CPC reached its first height in 1956 when the Eighth Central Committee of the CPC was held. The Eighth Central Committee decided that the CPC should insist on democratic centralism, collective leadership, the development of internal democracy and also people's democracy.[3] According to Professor Xu Yaotong,[4] the Eighth Central Committee made eight important decisions with regard to the development of internal democracy. First, the CPC must without exception implement the principle of collective leadership and expand internal democracy. Second, the principle of democratic centralism was defined as democracy under the guidance (rather than under the leadership) of centralism and the essence of the principle of democratic centralism is democracy rather than centralism.[5] Third, all the business of the Eighth Central Committee was made public. Fourth, there should be no idolatry. Fifth, the CPC should have regular deputies to Party congresses. Sixth, a strict and effective supervision mechanism should be established within the CPC. Seventh, the CPC should explore fixed terms of appointment (rather than life-long terms) for leadership positions. Eighth, the CPC should protect and expand the democratic rights of the CPC members – the Constitution of the CPC adopted by the Eighth Central Committee included seven specific rights.[6]

Unfortunately, the decisions made by the Eighth Central Committee were not fully implemented and their implementation was interrupted by a series of political movements starting from 1958, which culminated in the Cultural Revolution during which centralism became the norm within the CPC.[7] After the Cultural Revolution, especially from the Third Plenum of the Eleventh Central Committee, the CPC started to reflect on its painful experience. More critical reflection was made by Deng Xiaoping in 1980 in an article entitled "The Reform of the Leadership System of the CPC and the State", which is generally regarded as the very first serious discussion of its kind. Deng noted in his article that the CPC had in its history emphasized the necessity of unified leadership of the CPC which had seen the concentration of power in the hands of a few persons. One specific problem was the excessive concentration of power in the hands of party committees which was in turn concentrated in the hands of several party secretaries, especially the first secretaries. Most matters were decided by the first secretaries.[8] One year later, in 1981, "the Resolution on Several Historical Issues of the CPC after the Founding of the PRC", adopted by the Sixth Plenum of the Eleventh Central Committee, endorsed Deng's views as the official approach of the CPC.[9]

This approach was formally stated in the Report adopted by the Thirteenth Central Committee of the CPC in 1987. Furthermore, the Report announced that democracy should be developed within the CPC in order to promote people's democracy.[10] The development of democracy within the CPC was believed to be a feasible and effective means to develop a socialist democratic polity in China.[11] In 1994, the Fourth Plenum of the Fourteenth Central Committee of the CPC announced that an important route to developing a socialist democratic polity was by developing democracy within the CPC so as to promote people's democracy in China.[12] Ever since then, the issue of development of democracy within the CPC has frequently appeared in various documents of the CPC and its Central Committee. The Report adopted at the Sixteenth Central Committee has put democracy within the CPC into a more prominent position and stated that internal democracy is the life of the CPC and will be an important model and driving effect on people's democracy.[13] In September 2004, the Decision of the Central Committee of the CPC on the Enhancement of the Party's Governance Capability was adopted at the Fourth Plenum of the Sixteenth Central Committee. That document makes democratic rule one of the three basic pillars of the CPC[14] while democratic rule includes promotion of people's democracy by enhancing democracy within the CPC.[15] The White Paper entitled "Building Political Democracy in China" issued by the State Council in October 2005 confirms that the CPC will stick to the principle of promoting people's democracy by enhancing democracy within the CPC and states that the promotion of democracy within the CPC is an important component of the CPC's democratic rule.[16]

The policy of promoting people's democracy through the development of democracy within the CPC has become widely known among the general public in China since 2006, when the journal *Qiushi* (*Seeking Truth*) published an article written by Professor Zheng Xiaoying from the Central Party School, entitled "Promoting People's Democracy through Internal Democracy within the CPC".[17] That article attracted much attention and caused a great deal of discussion. Professor Zheng argues in the article that without having the people's democracy there will be no future for the CPC, and the development and implementation of democracy within the CPC is the proper route to develop people's democracy.[18] Shortly thereafter, Professor Li Junru, a Vice President of the Central Party School, echoed this view in an interview with Xinhua News Agency. Further, Professor Li argues that this is a new approach for the reform of China's political system.[19]

Professor Li is an expert on the development theory of the CPC. It is the common perception that the views expressed by scholars from the Central Party School represent the views of the Central Committee of the CPC. *Qiushi* is an official journal of the CPC and Xinhua News Agency is the official news agency of Chinese government. Furthermore, the Seventeenth Central Committee affirmed the policy made at the Sixteenth Central Committee.[20] It is now crystal clear that the CPC's roadmap for China to develop its democracy is to develop democracy within the CPC first. Once there is democracy within the CPC, it is expected that such internal democracy will promote and eventually lead to the development and realization of people's democracy in China.

Reasons for Lack of Internal Democracy

The above discussion shows that as early as 1956 the CPC decided to develop internal democracy and actually made some specific decisions to implement it, but there was no development of internal democracy in the two decades thereafter. Now the CPC has once again adopted a policy of developing internal democracy. In order to examine whether the current policy will lead to the same dead end, it is necessary to examine the reasons why there was so little democracy within the CPC for decades after it came to power.

Chinese scholars and politicians have identified several reasons which can be summarized as follows. First, the lack of democracy within the CPC is related to the social and historical circumstances in which the CPC was situated. China had traditionally been a country in which a patriarchal system played the dominant role. There were deep historical and cultural undemocratic elements in traditional China. These factors influenced the CPC from its formation.[21] Deng Xiaoping described it as the influence of the feudal autocratic system in ancient Chinese history.[22] Second, lack of democracy within the CPC may also be due to the influence of the tradition of various other communist countries, whose leaders often had an excessive concentration of power in the age of the League of Communism.[23] For example, in the early days of the former Soviet Union, there was not much democracy within the Soviet Communist Party. Third, the CPC historically never emphasized the necessity of avoiding an excessive concentration of power in the hands of a few persons.[24] Instead, it greatly emphasized centralism. Lack of internal democracy may also be due to other defects in the exercise of leadership power such as bureaucracy, and life-long tenure, and various phenomena of prerogatives.[25] Fourth, whether there was internal democracy was also related to whether the CPC had adopted a proper political policy at a particular time in its history. It has been observed that if the political policy is correct, implementation of the principle of democratic centralism is much better. This is because a proper political policy would have the support of the masses and all CPC members, could be implemented in practice, and officials would have more confidence and not be afraid of criticism from the masses and CPC members. But if the policies were not good, not in the interests of the general public and CPC members, then they would not get the support of the masses and CPC members. If certain officials still wanted to insist on the implementation of those policies, they would have no choice but to emphasize centralism improperly and to oppress democracy in order to control criticism from within the CPC.[26] Fifth, the working style of some senior officials in key positions also contributed to the lack of democracy within the CPC. The power of party organizations and officials comes from the CPC members, which is a point often not appreciated by some senior CPC officials. Hence, once they were in control of positions of power, they thought they were patriarchs and enjoyed prerogatives, and became very bureaucratic. Very often they would put themselves above CPC organizations and treat such organizations as instruments to implement their will.[27]

Out of the five reasons, the first is related to Chinese tradition which is something inherent in the system and may be more fundamental and difficult to remove. The second is a historical reason which no longer exists. The last three reasons are all related to the leadership style and decision-making mechanisms within the CPC. It is fair to say that those three reasons have not yet disappeared. On the one hand, that has made it more difficult to develop democracy within the CPC. On the other, it proves the necessity to develop democracy within the CPC because those are the issues that need to be resolved.

The Necessity to Democratize the CPC

Development of democracy within the CPC has become the official policy of the CPC and is also the common understanding among scholars.[28] But why does the CPC want to develop internal democracy at this moment of history? Scholars have identified several justifications. The first is the uniqueness of China's own historical development of democracy. One Chinese scholar has observed that in Western countries it has often been the case that there was a democratic state first before political parties were formed. Under the circumstances that people enjoyed widespread social democracy, it was difficult for political parties not to adopt a democratic system within their own organizations. In the case of China, when the CPC was founded it was a secret political party with the mission to overthrow the existing political power in China and eventually it came to power itself.[29] Due to the restriction of circumstances, there was often a lack of internal democracy. After it came into power, given the lack of a democratic tradition within the CPC and in society at large, a feasible choice was to develop democracy within the CPC first. In so doing, it could avoid certain risks and mistakes by having directly people's democracy in society. It could also avoid possible loss of control and a chaotic situation from occurring in China[30].

The second major reason is that both the CPC and scholars believe that democracy within the CPC is a proper means to develop and promote people's democracy in China. The CPC has carried out political reforms several times in its history without success. This time, the CPC has chosen the development of internal democracy to be the breakthrough point for political reform. Professor Wang Guixiu of the Central Party School has argued that development of democracy within the CPC is the best breakthrough point for political reform in China. The CPC has tried various means to reform China's political system, such as reform of administrative organs, separation of the CPC from the administration, transparency of politics, development of democracy at grassroots level, and reform of the personnel system. None of them has proven to be successful. In his view, the breakthrough point should focus on the fundamental issue a political reform needs to resolve and the fundamental aims the reform intends to achieve. The development of democracy within the CPC is the fundamental issue and therefore should be chosen as the breakthrough point.[31] Thus the development of democracy within the CPC has been regarded as a means to start political reform in China. One related advantage is that there is comparatively low risk of causing social disorder even if the reform fails.

The third reason is that development of internal democracy will contribute to maintaining the status of the CPC as a ruling political party in China. Jiang Zemin observed that since the 1990s some political parties in other countries which had been in power for decades have been removed from the ruling position, and some have already withered away. The fundamental reason is internal problems that occurred within those political parties.[32] That reveals the real purpose of carrying out internal reform of the CPC, i.e., to remove any internal problems so that the CPC can maintain its position as the ruling political party in China. This has been confirmed by various decisions and documents issued by the CPC. For example, the Report of the Sixteenth Central Committee has stated that internal democracy is the life of the CPC.[33] This shows, in my view, the determination of the CPC to carry out internal reform within the CPC.

The fourth reason is that development of internal democracy is necessary for the healthy development of the CPC under the current circumstances because China is opening itself to the outside world and developing a socialist market economy.[34] The fifth reason is that it is the internal requirement of the CPC's recently stated objective to establish a harmonious socialist society in China.[35]

Out of the five reasons mentioned above, the most important reason should be the third one. Changes in many former communist/socialist countries, especially the so-called "colour" revolutions, have made the CPC realize that it must change in order to maintain its ruling position in China. Democratization is the required change. The development of internal democracy will help to make the CPC more appealing to the public and therefore a stronger ruling political party in China.

Democratization of the CPC – from Policy to Practice

How to Democratize the CPC?

After adoption of the policy to democratize the CPC, the next issue is how to do it. As early as 1980, Deng Xiaoping mentioned that many problems occurred partly due to the mistakes of certain leaders but more importantly due to the lack of various mechanisms. The existence of some good mechanisms could, in his view, prevent leaders from exercising their powers arbitrarily.[36] According to Deng, Mao actually realized that problem and also the importance of establishing certain mechanisms, but he did not make a serious effort to establish them.[37]

Many scholars have also expressed the view that in order to develop democracy within the CPC it is necessary to establish various democratic mechanisms. One commentator has observed that lack of effective mechanisms in operation is one of the reasons for insufficient democracy within the CPC.[38] Another scholar has noted that in order to develop democracy within the CPC, the very first thing to do is to establish democratic mechanisms.[39] Professor Zheng Xiaoying has argued that the establishment of democratic mechanisms is one of the four means needed for development of democracy within the CPC.[40] The establishment of various democratic mechanisms is believed to be fundamental to the development of democracy within the CPC since mechanisms are stable and of long-term effect.[41]

Consensus therefore exists among scholars that the establishment of various democratic mechanisms is a necessity to develop democracy within the CPC. Different views, however, exist on what the democratic mechanisms should include. Professor Zheng Xiaoying, for example, mentions democratic mechanisms together with a democratic supervision mechanism, leadership mechanism and working mechanism within the CPC.[42] It seems that democratic mechanisms in her view do not include a supervision mechanism, leadership and working mechanism within the CPC. Some other scholars are of the view that a leadership mechanism, working mechanism and supervision mechanism are important democratic mechanisms.[43] This is a difference of classification rather than of substance because they all agree that the establishment of proper leadership, working and supervision mechanisms is essential for the development of democracy within the CPC.

Many Chinese scholars have mentioned the following mechanisms in their articles: competitive election mechanism, mechanism for the protection of rights of the CPC members, mechanism to ensure transparency, leadership mechanism within the CPC, working mechanism within the CPC, especially the relationship between different CPC organs and committees, supervision mechanism, and so on. Since it is impossible to discuss all the mechanisms mentioned above within the scope of this chapter, this part will focus on the competitive election mechanism as an example to discuss in detail.

Competitive Election and the Constitution of the CPC

According to the Constitution of the CPC as amended in 2007, all party organizations can be classified into three levels; national party organizations, local party organizations including those organs at provincial, municipal, district/county levels, and grassroots-level party organizations. The electoral system of the CPC can be summarized as follows. The highest organ of power within the CPC is the National Party Congress and the Central Committee elected by it. The CPC's organs of power at local levels are its local party congresses and party committees elected by such local party congresses. A party committee will be accountable to and report to the party congress at the corresponding level.[44] The CPC's organs of power at all levels should be formed through election.[45] Hence, the electoral system within the CPC includes the election of deputies to party congresses and the election of members to the Central Committee and various local party committees, as well as election of the first and deputy secretaries to party committees at all levels.

Since reform with regard to competitive election has been carried out only among grassroots and local party organizations, I will set out here just the two articles relevant to the election of delegates to party congresses and members of grassroots and local party committees, as well as the first and deputy secretaries thereof.

Paragraph 1 of Article 11 of the Constitution of the CPC provides:

> The election of delegates to Party congresses and of members of Party committees at all levels should reflect the will of the voters. Elections shall be held by secret ballot. The lists of candidates shall be submitted to the Party organizations and voters for full deliberation and discussion. The election procedure in which the number of candidates nominated is greater than the number of persons to be elected may be used directly in a formal election or this procedure may be used first in a preliminary election in order to draw up a list of candidates for the formal election. The voters have the right to inquire about the candidates, demand a change or reject one in favour of another. No organization or individual shall in any way compel voters to elect or not to elect any candidate.

Paragraph 1 of Article 27 of the Constitution provides:

> The local Party committees at all levels elect, at their plenary sessions, their standing committees, secretaries and deputy secretaries and report the results to the higher Party committees for approval. The standing committees of the local Party committees at all levels exercise the functions and powers of local Party committees when the latter are not in session. They continue to handle the day-to-day work when the next Party congresses at their levels are in session, until the new standing committees are elected.

From these two articles, we know that all elections must be carried out through secret ballot. The relevant CPC organs will have an important role to play in the election because the list of candidates will be formed through consultation between them and CPC members. Elections can either be direct or indirect in that preliminary elections can be organized to decide a formal list of candidates. Furthermore, the local Party committees will elect the first and deputy secretaries.[46] Discussion in later sections will focus on competitive election at grassroots and local levels and will show that the last requirement has not been achieved in the various experiments in electoral reform.

Election Experiments by Grassroots Party Organizations

Rules and Regulations

The Interim Regulations on Election Work of Grassroots Organizations of the CPC ("Interim Regulations") were adopted in 1990 with the intention of improving democracy within the Party.[47] The Interim Regulations apply to party committees, general branch committees, and sub-branch committees of grassroots organizations of the CPC, including factories, shops, educational institutes, institutions, residential groups in urban areas, cooperative societies, farms and townships, and also to the disciplinary committees established with the approval of grassroots party committees.[48] Article 4 of the Interim Regulations provides that committees of grassroots organizations of the CPC shall be elected by the general meeting of all CPC members. If the number of CPC members is more than 500 or the party organization is spread over a wide geographical jurisdiction, committee members can also be elected by deputies of CPC members after obtaining the approval of the party organization at the next level above. Article 5 provides that formal party members have the right to vote and to stand for election. Article 6 provides that the democratic rights of the CPC members should be respected and protected in elections, and that democracy should be fully enhanced in elections so that elections represent the will of the voters. No organization or individual should impose pressure on any voters to vote for or against a specific candidate. In summary, the committees of grassroots party organizations will be elected either by all CPC members or by their deputies.[49] All CPC members enjoy democratic rights in elections which should not be improperly interfered with.

As far as the election of deputies to grassroots party congresses is concerned, the relevant election unit, i.e., one specific grassroots party organization, shall organize all its CPC members to conduct consultations with regard to the nomination of candidates, and candidates will be determined according to the views of the majority of CPC members.[50] The number of candidates should be 20 per cent more than the number of deputies to be elected.[51] The exact number of deputies to a grassroots party congress shall be determined by that particular grassroots party organization, subject to the approval of the party organization at the next level above[52].

As for the election of members to a grassroots party committee, candidates will be determined by the incumbent party committee according to the opinion of the majority of party members.[53] The number of candidates should be 20 per cent more than the number of committee members to be elected.[54]

As for the election of the first and deputy secretaries of a committee of a grassroots party organization, its candidates shall be proposed by the incumbent party committee and submitted to the party organization at the next level above for approval before election by all members of the party committee.[55] For a general branch which does not establish a party committee, candidates for the first and deputy secretaries shall be proposed through adequate consultation among all CPC members and submitted to the party organization at the next level above for its examination and approval before election by all party members.[56] The number of candidates will be equal to the number of secretaries to be elected.

For a grassroots party organization which establishes a standing committee of its party committee, candidates shall be determined by the incumbent party committee according to the rule that the number of candidates should be one or two more than the number of standing committee members to be elected. An election will be held by all members of the party committee after the candidates are examined and approved by the party organization at the next level above.[57]

The elected members of a party committee shall be submitted to the party organization at the next level above for record. The elected members of the standing committee of a party committee and the first and deputy secretaries should be submitted to the party organization at the next level above for approval. Similarly, the first and deputy secretaries of the party disciplinary committee shall, once approved by the party committee, be submitted to the party organization at the next level above for approval.[58]

It is not difficult to see that the election of deputies to a party congress and members to a party committee is more democratic in that the number of candidates can be more than the number of persons to be elected. But for election of members to the standing committee of a party committee, and the first and deputy secretaries of a party committee, the party organization at the next level above has the right to veto not only the candidates but also the elected persons under the existing rules.

Electoral Reform Practices

According to one source, at the end of 2009, there were in total 3,792,000 grassroots party organizations, of which 183,000 were party committees, 235,000 general branches, and 3,374,000 sub-branches.[59] Various electoral reforms have been carried in the last decade for the purpose of enhancing democracy within the CPC. At village level, as early as 1997, one county in Shenyang City (Liaoning Province) had, with the approval of the Organization Department of the Central Committee of the CPC, experimented with direct election of the first secretary of a sub-branch of the CPC in a village by all CPC members in that village.[60] Since then, electoral reform of CPC organs in villages has been tested in different localities in China. In 2000, the Central Committee of the CPC actively promoted reform of the selection and appointment system of members of sub-branches in villages.[61] Reform has picked up pace since then and four different models have appeared. The first is called "two recommendations and one election", meaning recommendation by both the public and CPC members in a village and then election by all CPC members.[62] The second is called the "two votes system", meaning that it will be up to the public to cast a vote of confidence, and then all CPC members will formally cast their votes. The purpose of the "two votes system" is to win the support of villagers for the village CPC sub-branch.[63] The third is called "direct election after public recommendation", meaning that the CPC members and the masses will openly pre-elect candidates for the secretary of a village CPC sub-branch and then an election will be held.[64] The fourth is direct election by all CPC members in a village through one-person one-vote. It is a variation of the other three models and the candidates have been through four prior recommendations.[65] The essence of all the four models is that the election of a village CPC sub-branch is no longer regarded as an internal matter within the CPC. Instead, members of a village CPC sub-branch need to get the support of not only the CPC members of that village but also the majority of villagers (who are non-CPC members). Though the election will ultimately be held among CPC members, villagers who are not CPC members, and who constitute the majority of residents in the village, will almost determine the election results.[66]

The reform of elections in township party organizations also started in the last decade. Reform of township party committee elections has mainly been in the direct election of secretaries of a township party committee. In 2001, Pingchang County in Sichuan Province started an experiment in the direct election of members of township party committees on the basis of public nomination.[67] During the election in 2001-2, for all 175 townships under Ya An City in Sichuan Province, the first and deputy secretaries of party committees at township level were elected through public nomination and public voting. But that competitive election, according to one commentator, had its limitations. Firstly, only those within the system, i.e., cadres, could be qualified to stand for election. Secondly, election campaigning was prohibited although the candidates were allowed to make a speech before voters and answer voters' questions. Thirdly, there is often an age limit, which is set very low. The same commentator has observed that by 2002 some competitive elections occurred within CPC organizations[68] but they were very small in numbers. He has noted that quite a number of experiments have taken place in Sichuan Province, but even there, in big cities such as Chendu reform was not popular.

As to the reasons for the introduction of competitive elections within the CPC, the same commentator has identified several. Firstly, competitive election at township level was very often enthusiastically promoted by county and/or municipal party committees. Secondly, there was a crisis of confidence about the cadres of township party committees. Party organization at the next level, especially the first secretaries, wanted to resolve the problem by introducing a competitive election mechanism so that people could elect party cadres in whom they have confidence. Thirdly, party leaders at the next level above wanted to bring in persons who could contribute to local economic development. In Ya An City, for example, that was the fundamental reason. In the past, local leaders only listened to leaders above them, and lacked enthusiasm in their work. The participation of the public was limited and passive. The work carried out by township government did not have active support from ordinary people. Through competitive elections, the enthusiasm of cadres at lower level has been activated so that additional resources outside the system can be mobilized and used for local economic development. In Ya An, competitive election was not the result of a crisis of confidence, instead it is a means adopted by the municipal party committee to mobilize additional resources in order to achieve higher objectives.[69]

In 2006, Ya An City completed another round of election. From February to April 2006, Ya An City carried out a reform experiment with the election of CPC as well as governmental officials in four selected townships under its jurisdiction. As far as candidates for the first and deputy secretaries of party committees are concerned, there were two steps in the election process. First, all candidates must be publicly voted for by all voters in the specific jurisdiction (township). The party organization could only nominate candidates from those who ranked in the top ten in the public voting process. Secondly, the candidates will be put before all CPC members for election to determine the results. Again, as in the 2001–2 election, the conditions set for candidates were very high; only those within the system were qualified and they were required to have a certain number of years of experience as cadres. For example, in Renyi Township, only 26 persons were qualified to be candidates. After mobilization, 18 persons eventually participated in the election of CPC and governmental leaders. Voting was arranged for all qualified voters (including non-CPC members) to elect 10 out 18 preliminary candidates. After this public election, the county party committee decided the formal candidates through voting. For Renyi Township, the original first party secretary, Gao Geli, who ranked no. 1 in the public vote, and another candidate Zhang Min, who ranked no. 2 in public vote, were nominated by the county party committee as candidates for the first secretary. Gao was elected as first secretary. Then, Zhang Min together with two other candidates who ranked no.

3 and no. 4 respectively in the public vote were nominated as candidates for deputy party secretaries. Again, and surprisingly, Zhang Min lost the election.[70]

In addition to Ya An, experiments in competitive elections at lower levels of party organizations have also been carried out in some other places in recent years. For example, in Luotian County in Hubei Province, public nomination and public voting in township party committees, and direct election of deputies to county party congress by CPC members, have been implemented.[71] Mu Lan Town in Xin Du District of Chengdu City (Sichuan Province) had the secretary of its township party committee directly elected through "direct election after public recommendation" on 7 December 2003.[72] In 2004, 45 party secretaries of township party committees in Sichuan Province were produced through direct election on the basis of public nomination.[73] In Chendu City, as many as 46 township party committees have been elected through public nomination and public voting method. Similar reforms have also been carried in other provinces.[74] In Luxi County of the autonomous prefecture of Honghe hani ethnic minority and li ethnic minority, Yunan Province, all members of the party committees at township level have been elected through direct nomination and direct election by CPC members.[75] Up to October 2005, the method of direct election on the basis of public nomination has been experimented with in more than 210 townships in Sichuan Province. This has proved to be the trend in the election of members as well as the first secretary of a party committee at lower levels.[76]

A new round of elections is being held from 2011 to 2012 at four local levels.[77] The policy of the Organization Department of the Central Committee is to continue the experiment of "public recommendation in combination with direct election" in order to gain experience for further expansion of direct elections within the CPC.[78] Some new mechanisms have been experimented with under the guidance of the Organization Department. One is the election recently completed at township level in Fengxin County, which was the first of its kind, with the Organization Department in charge of the whole process. The Guidance Group sent by the Organization Department to Fengxin designed a set of rules to standardize the whole election process. The purpose was to change the phenomenon of the minority electing from among the minority by giving the majority the right to elect from among the majority of party members. The specific mechanism introduced by the Guidance Group is called "four publicity, three recommendations and two votes". The positions and their requirements, the selection process, nominations and recommendations, as well as relevant information about the candidates, will be made public. "Three recommendations" means that on the basis of self-nomination or nomination by relevant party organizations, the county organization department will first make its recommendation, then all leaders at county level will through secret ballot select candidates according to the ratio of two candidates for one position. Finally the senior leaders will select candidates according to the ratio of one and a half candidates for one position. Two votes means the final candidates will be decided through voting by both the county party committee and its standing committee.

In Chongqing, the initial target was to use the method in 60 per cent of township party committee elections. Surprisingly, due to strong popular demand, the method has been used in more than 80 per cent of township party committee elections.[79] One fundamental change which has been observed is that the attitude of elected members, especially first and deputy secretaries, of party committees at township level has changed. They feel that they are now accountable not only to the party organization at the next level above, but also to the voters who have elected them.[80]

These experiments have set good examples for other grassroots party organizations to follow. Xu Yaotong has noted that if all party organizations at grassroots level implemented internal democracy in elections, then the democratic progress of the CPC as a whole would become a completely new picture of healthy and orderly development.[81] He is of the view that democracy should be developed progressively by starting from grassroots party organizations and then gradually move upwards and eventually to the central party organization.[82]

At the moment, experiments with various means of direct election have been tried and achieved good effects. It has been suggested that on that basis direct election should be further expanded progressively to ensure that cadres of party organizations at grassroots level are more representative.[83] It is also encouraging to note that in the current round of election for the change of term, for the first time we are seeing that the method of "public recommendation and direct election" has been used to elect the secretaries of three municipalities directly under the provincial government of Jiangsu Province.[84] This means that direct election has been expanded upwards to municipal level.

Election Reform of Local Party Organizations

Rules and Regulations

The Regulations on Election Work of Local Organizations of the CPC were enacted in 1993 (the 1993 Regulations) for the purpose of improving democratic centralism within the CPC and the election system within the CPC, and strengthening local organizations of the CPC.[85] The 1993 Regulations apply to the election of members of party congresses, party committees and disciplinary committees of provinces, municipalities directly under the State Council, municipalities which are divided into districts, autonomous prefectures, counties, municipalities not divided into districts, and districts under municipalities.[86] Several general principles are laid down in the 1993 Regulations. The first is that the election of deputies to party congresses at all local levels, members of party committees, standing committees and disciplinary committees, must be held according to the principle that the number of candidates should be greater than the seats available.[87] The second is that election must be democratic and the democratic rights of voters must be respected and guaranteed.[88] The third is that voting must be by secret ballot.[89] There are also detailed rules on the election of deputies in the 1993 Regulations. Whether the election of deputies under these Regulations is democratic seems questionable, however. At local levels, all members of a party committee shall elect its first and deputy secretaries as well as members of the standing committee. The election results must be approved by the party committee at the next level above.[90]

Reform Practice

One fundamental reform at local level is to allow all CPC members to elect their deputies directly. The direct election of deputies to a CPC congress at county level in Ya An City in December 2002 is believed to have been the first of its kind in China.[91] In Ya An City, one county and one district were selected to experiment with public direct election of deputies to the party congress at county/district level by CPC members.[92] Related procedural reforms also included the procedure for a CPC member to nominate him/herself to compete in an election and the procedure for delivering campaign speeches. [93] Other experiments relating to the election of deputies include: (1) reduction of quota for deputies, which usually amounts to a decrease of more than 20 per cent in the number of deputies; (2) making election units smaller so that CPC members within an election unit will have a better understanding of and supervision over the candidates; (3) the number of candidates has been increased to 40 per cent more than the number of deputies to be elected.[94] Comments on these experiments have not been uniform. Some are of the view that the reform will make it possible for a CPC congress to play its role and contribute to democracy within the CPC. Others are of the view that the cost for such reform is too high and it may well affect the efficiency of decision-making within the CPC. [95] For instance, some cadres, including party secretaries of township party committees and governmental officials, lost their positions in the election.

Bai Gang, a professor with the Public Policy Research Centre of the China Academy of Social Sciences, observed that it had never happened in the past that democratic election was adopted for the election of deputies to a party congress. The experiment in Ya An City could be seen as a starting point of the development of internal democracy within the CPC. Such an experiment should have positive effect upon promoting change of governance style as well as democratization of decision-making processes within the CPC.[96]

From March to October 2003, direct election of deputies to county party congresses was also held in Yidu County and Luotian County (Hubei Province). As far as Luotian was concerned, all preliminary candidates were put before party members so that they could elect formal candidates in a preliminary election by secret ballot. Those formal candidates would then be voted on by CPC members to elect the deputies. Only those obtaining more than 50 per cent of the votes could become deputies. One election unit, for example, had a quota of ten deputies, but only eight candidates got more than 50 per cent of the votes. Therefore, only eight deputies were elected from that election unit.[97] Similarly, from November 2004 to March 2005, direct election of deputies to the party congress was also held in Luqiao District of Taizhou City (Zhejiang Province).

Several breakthroughs have been identified by a group of researchers from Beijing from the reforms carried out so far. Firstly, the nomination method has been changed and is different from that stated in the Constitution of the CPC. The new method allows nomination by a candidate him- or herself, the party organization or other party members jointly, while the primary method is voluntary nomination by party members themselves. Secondly, the difference between the number of formal candidates and number of deputies to be elected has been expanded from 20 per cent to more than 20 per cent, in some places up to 50 per cent. Thirdly, competition speeches were given by formal candidates. The formal candidates would be subject to direct election by party members and the votes would be counted on the spot. Fourthly, the whole process of election is public. It is also required that the names of the preliminary candidates and the formal candidates and the election results are publicly announced.

In the new round of elections held for the change of term of party organizations from the end of 2010 to 2011, direct election upon public recommendation has been experimented with at different levels. In Shenzhen, for example, four electoral units were chosen to try this method to elect 14 deputies to Shenzhen Municipal Party Congress in 2011. In these four units, out of 116 candidates, 78 were chosen as preliminary candidates and then 26 were chosen as final candidates.

Analysis

The above discussion shows that the relevant rules and regulations governing election within the CPC are not fully democratic and reveal the clear intention that the party organization at the higher level should have control of the election of senior officials of party organizations at the next lower level, including the first and deputy secretaries as well as members of the standing committees of party committees. That is the nomenclature system China learned from the former Soviet Union.

Electoral reform practices carried out in the last decade until 2011 indicates that electoral reform has been experimented with in elections within the CPC up to municipal level in different provinces. In some places it is upon the initiative of party organizations at the next higher level while in others the reform was carried out with the approval of the Organization Department of the Central Committee of the CPC. These reforms have shown a trend of expansion, which is important because elections were being carried out among four levels of CPC organizations from township party organizations to provincial party organizations from 2010 to 2011. From reports on the election results which were already known at the time of writing, such as for Shenzhen, it is encouraging to see that new and more democratic reform has been experimented with at higher levels.

In order to develop democracy within the CPC, it is necessary to have a competitive mechanism within the CPC, and elections in which the number of candidates is greater than the number of persons to be elected is one kind of competition. Such a view has been expressed by Professor Zheng Xiaoying in an interview with the *Journal of Finance* (*Caijin*). [98] Specifically speaking, competition is reflected through election. Hence, it has been suggested that there is a necessity to improve election mechanisms further within the CPC, and to expand democracy in the election of candidates and also the use of persons by the number one person either in the CPC or people's government. [99]

In internal elections, it has been proposed for the nomination of candidates that the party organization should decide the proportion and the structure of different kinds of candidates, and then specific candidates should be proposed from the bottom up by party members to ensure that recommendation is made on the basis of members' discussion and agreement. Party organizations should respect the will of their members, and not arbitrarily change the list of candidates. Before election, candidates should be allowed to meet with the CPC members or their deputies. Websites with information on candidates can be established and candidates be allowed to deliver campaign speeches. The introduction of candidates must be detailed and accurate so as to ensure that CPC members' right to information concerning the candidates and their rights as voters are properly protected. [100]

It is encouraging to see that the 2006 election in Ya An City met most of the criteria proposed above. In particular, the party committee at the next level above no longer dictates the candidates for secretaries of party committees at the next level down. Instead, it only selects formal candidates from those already approved by the CPC members. At grassroots level, the reform has been more dramatic in that decision-making power in the election of party secretaries and members of standing committees of party committees has more or less been given to voters, including CPC members and non-CPC members.

While it is undeniable that such reform has made election within the CPC at grassroots and local level (mainly county/district level) more democratic, it is a fact that such reforms are not consistent with the existing rules and regulations governing elections within the CPC. It is common phenomenon in China that reforms are conducted in violation of existing rules and regulations. But now China and the CPC as well has vowed to follow the rule of law principle and to do things according to law. It would be much more desirable for the rules and regulations to be amended before the relevant reforms are carried out.

However positive those electoral reforms are, one must remember that electoral reform within the CPC is still at its preliminary stage and is still limited to those levels at and/or below county level as in 2006. There are also different views with regard to whether competitive election is necessary, and the criteria to assess whether or not there is internal democracy within the CPC. [101] In the author's field study, concern has also been expressed by some party members. In one province, it was observed by a couple of CPC members that they work very hard and often need to travel to other parts in China for business. As a result they don't have much opportunity to socialize with their colleagues. That will affect negatively their competitiveness in elections and hence their opportunities for promotion within the party. Such concern needs to be addressed but it does not challenge the merits of democratic election within the CPC.

The Future of Democracy within the CPC and the Future of Democracy in China

The Future of Democracy within the CPC

The above discussion of competitive election experiments proves that various elections within the CPC, such as the election of deputies to party congresses, members of party committees, members of standing committees of party committees, and the first and deputy secretaries, have become more competitive in those places where reform has been implemented. The White Paper entitled "Building of Political Democracy in China", issued by the State Council in October 2005, has made positive comments on election reform within the CPC, and states that the difference between the number of candidates for election of deputies to CPC congresses and the number of deputies should be increased appropriately, and that the scope for direct election of officials of grassroots CPC organs should gradually be expanded.[102] Although CPC organization at the next level above still enjoys and exercises the power to determine certain formal candidates, such as candidates for the first and deputy secretaries of party committees at the next level below, the practice in Luotian shows that the exercise of that power has been based on the voting results of CPC members and proves that it is possible to converge the views of CPC members with the views of the CPC organ at the next level above. That is a good example of the implementation of the democratic centralism principle. What is also important to note is that electoral reform in Luotian and some other local party organizations has the endorsement of the Organization Department of the Central Committee of the CPC. It demonstrates that top-level officials within the CPC take the position that it is necessary to have electoral reform within the CPC.

CPC members and Chinese scholars have expressed mixed views about the future of democracy within the CPC. For example, in the author's interviews with some CPC officials and scholars during his field study trip to Guangzhou, Hunan and Zhejiang, several CPC officials who are in power expressed their confidence about the future development of democracy within the CPC. One official expressed the view that the CPC's primary objective is to maintain stability and develop the economy in China. Internal democracy will develop under those conditions and serve those purposes. In his view, the CPC is now more democratic than at any time before in its history, although in some aspects it is still not that democratic. He has even predicted that in 50 years China might be more democratic than the United States. Some ordinary CPC members are, however, less optimistic than those in power. Another official opined that there is no democracy at all and everything is decided by the first secretary within the CPC. One scholar specializing in research on the development of the CPC has expressed positive views about its future development, while some law professors are of the view that the policy on developing internal democracy within the CPC is only for window-dressing purposes, and the CPC has no real intention to develop democracy within the CPC and in China.

What the official in power has said about stability and economic development represents the common understanding in China, i.e., stability and economic development are top priorities of the CPC. Comparatively speaking, the development of internal democracy has a low priority. It is understandable that opinions differ between those in power and those not in power as they have different perspectives, but it is a bit surprising that the contrast is so great. Whether or not the policy on developing internal democracy is for window-dressing is a subjective judgment. It is, nevertheless, a fact that such policy has been promulgated and repeated in various normative documents issued by the highest organ of power within the CPC. There must be some factors which have prompted the CPC to adopt the policy. The "colour revolutions" in other former Communist countries must be one of them. The promulgation of such a policy is already a step forward. Once the policy is coupled with actual experimental practice, those who have benefited from such practice will add momentum to the implementation of the policy and promote internal democracy within the CPC, just as happened with various economic policies adopted by the CPC after 1978.

While the author remains optimistic about the future development of democratic election within the CPC, it should also be noted at the same time that the future is not yet that clear, and the goal of democracy may not be reachable in the new future. To take Luotian as an example, it was planned to complete in five years the experiment which started in March 2003 and hence was due to end in February 2008. [103] Thereafter, the Organization Department of the Central Committee would review the experience obtained in Luotian and decide whether or not to adopt the experimental practice as formal policy to be applied to elections in other local party organizations. During the current round of elections, Luotian has not yet completed its elections at the time of writing and hence we do not know whether Luotian will continue to move ahead.

It should also be noted that democracy within the CPC is not developing smoothly without any obstacles. Concerns have been raised as to: (1) whether democracy within the CPC will cause endless debate within the CPC and therefore harm the unity of the CPC, and with it social and political stability in China; (2) whether the development of democracy within the CPC would affect adversely the authority of party organizations and individual leaders. The answers by some scholars to the above two questions are negative. On the contrary, they are of the view that internal democracy will facilitate the decision-making and provide a means to resolve conflicts within the CPC. The exercise of democracy within the CPC by the members could provide a good basis/foundation for party organizations to practise centralization correctly. The existence of different opinions within the CPC is a common and healthy phenomenon. As to the second question, the authority and reputation of party organizations and individual leaders can only be truly established on the basis of genuine support from party members and the masses. Internal democracy could contribute to the establishment of genuine support. Oppression of democracy within the CPC would only lead to blind obedience. Authority established on such a basis would be superficial, weak and unsustainable. Furthermore, within party committees, the status of the party secretary and committee members is equal, rather than the relationship between a leader and those led by him. The Constitution of the CPC also clearly prohibits individual worship within the CPC and emphasizes that CPC officials must be under the supervision of the CPC and the people. In order to achieve this, it is important to develop democracy within the CPC.

In conclusion, despite the existence of many problems as discussed above in different aspects of the development of democracy within the CPC, the CPC has shown through a series of its official documents, including Decisions, Resolutions, and White Papers, clearly and consistently its policy to develop democracy within the CPC. Since it has established various mechanisms to facilitate the development of democracy within the CPC, the author remains cautiously optimistic about the future development of democracy within the CPC. One should never forget the fundamental objective for the CPC to develop democracy within the CPC, however. As noted by Deng in 1980, the objective is to strengthen the leadership of the CPC rather than to weaken it. [104] Hence, there exists a possibility that the Central Committee of the CPC would call off the development of internal democracy if it threatened the governing position of the CPC.

The Future of Democracy in China

Can democratization within the CPC eventually lead to people's democracy in China? While the majority of Chinese scholars are positive about the answer, there does exist a different view. One Japanese scholar has argued that the development of democracy within the CPC has encountered a paradox. On the one hand, the Central Committee of the CPC wants to push forward internal democracy. On the other hand, local party organizations are not enthusiastic about it, because it would mean members of party committees being elected by party members, and that the decisions within the party committee will be made by voting. That means the first and deputy secretaries will no longer be able to make whatever decisions they want. He argues that the only means to resolve this paradox is to resort to people's democracy. The proper method to develop democracy in China is to develop democracy in the society, i.e., people's democracy, then democracy within the CPC.[105]

What he has suggested is the development route and the practice in many Western countries where democracy developed before political parties were established. As a result any political parties will have no choice but to follow the rule of democracy within their parties. But as discussed above, in China the CPC came into being at a time when there was no democracy in China. China needs to determine how to develop democracy. What is needed to realize people's democracy in China is to empower the people. That means the CPC needs to let the Chinese people choose the ruling political party. That is clearly impossible at this stage because the Constitution states very clearly that the CPC is the ruling political party in China and the CPC has shown no intention to do so.

Recently people in some North African and Middle Eastern countries have taken to the streets to demand democracy. Such popular revolutions are successful in some countries but not in the others. Meanwhile, China has tightened its control of some dissidents who advocate democracy, human rights and rule of law in China.[106] One possible interpretation is that the CPC is concerned that its governing status might face similar challenge from the masses. Under such circumstances, it is even more difficult for the CPC to empower Chinese people by giving them the right to determine the future of China.

This means there are only two alternatives left for China. One is a radical change through mass movements, following the example of many countries in the former Socialist bloc. Informal interviews with Chinese people at different levels leads the author to the view that this is not a choice favoured by the majority of Chinese people. Furthermore, the CPC has now more than 8 million members, occupying all the important positions in all governmental organs at all levels. The total membership of all the other eight political parties together is 710,000, which is less than one per cent of the total number of the CPC members[107]. So if there were a radical change, no other political party could come out to replace the CPC. As a result, China might enter into a period of chaos.

The rational choice is for the CPC to democratize itself. That will lead to people's democracy. The issue is how to ensure that the progress of democratization within the CPC will move forward. On this point, I am of the view that both internal and external pressure for democracy will have an important role to play. The increase of both internal and external pressure will force the CPC to take internal democratization seriously and assist the Central Committee of the CPC to remove resistance against internal democratization from local party organizations.

In conclusion, China should develop both democracy within the CPC and people's democracy so that the people's democracy will facilitate the development of democracy within the CPC. Once democracy is achieved within the CPC, there will be people's democracy in China.

Note

This chapter is based on a research report funded by Civic Exchange. The author is solely responsible for any errors which may exist in this chapter.

Notes and References

1. See Lin Shangli, *Dangnei Minzhu – Zhongguo Gongchandang de Lilun yu Shijian* (*Internal Democracy – Theory and Practice of the* CPC) (Shanghai Academy of Social Science Press, Shanghai, 2002), pp.1–40; see also Xu Dongmei, *Zhongguo Gongchandang Dangnei Minzhu Yanjiu* (*Study of Internal Democracy within the* CPC) (Dangjian Duwu Press, Beijing, 2004), pp. 2–3.

2. See Lin Shangli, *Dangnei Minzhu – Zhongguo Gongchandang de Lilun yu Shijian (Internal Democracy – Theory and Practice of the CPC)*, pp. 40–50.

3. See Guanyu Jianguo, "Yilai dangde ruogan lishi wenti de jueyi (The resolution on several historical issues of the CPC after the founding of the PRC), para. 15, adopted by the 6th Plenary Session of the 11th Central Committee of the CPC on 27 June 1981, in *Resolution on CPC History (1949–1981)* (Pergamon Press, Oxford, 1981), pp. 23–24.

4. See Xu Yaotong, "Dang de ba da he dangne minzhu" (The 8th Central Committee and internal democracy within the CPC), http://guancha.gmw.cn/show.aspx?id=9901.

5. Before that, the principle of democratic centralism was defined as centralism on the basis of democracy and democracy under the leadership of centralism.

6. See Xu Yaotong, "Dang de ba da he dangne minzhu" (The 8th Central Committee and internal democracy within the CPC).

7. For detailed discussion after the 8th Central Committee, see Lin Shangli, *Dangnei Minzhu – Zhongguo Gongchandang de Lilun yu Shijian (Internal Democracy – Theory and Practice of the CPC)*, pp. 50–57.

8. See Deng Xiaoping, "Dang he guojia lingdao zhidu de gaige" ("The reform of the leadership system of the CPC and the state"), Part III: http://www.ccyl.org.cn/theory/dspws/page2/danghe.htm (accessed 26 November 2006).

9. See Guanyu Jianguo, "Yilai dangde ruogan lishi wenti de jueyi (The resolution on several historical issues of the CPC after the founding of the PRC) pp. 23–24.

10. See Zhao Ziyang, "Yanzhe you Zhongguo tese de shehui zhuyi daolu qianjin" ("March along the socialist road with Chinese characteristics"), Report delivered at the 13th Central Committee of the CPC on 25 October 1987, Part Six: http://www.china.org.cn/chinese/archive/131711.htm.

11. See Wang Yongbing, "Dangnei minzhu: zhidu kongjian yu fazhan lujin" ("Internal democracy within the CPC: room within existing system and route for development"), http://chinainnovations.org/read.asp?type01=1&type02=3&type03=5&articleid=3465.

12. See "Zhonggong zhongyang guanyu jiaqiang dangde jianshe jige zhongda wenti de jueding" ("Decision of the Central Committee of the CPC on several important issues concerning strengthening the establishment of the CPC"), adopted on 28 September 1994 by the 4th Plenum of the 14th Central Committee of the CPC, http://www.china.com.cn/chinese/archive/131752.htm.

13. See Jiang Zemin, "Zai dangde di shiliu ci quanguo daibiao dahui shang de baogao" ("The report delivered by Jiang Zemin at the 16th Central Committee of the CPC"), part 10, http://news.sina.com.cn/c/2002-11-17/2258809867.html; see also Wang Yongbing, "Dangnei minzhu: zhidu kongjian yu fazhan lujin" ("Internal democracy within the CPC: room within existing system and route for development").

14. See "Zhonggong zhongyang guanyu jiaqiang dang de zhizheng nengli jianshe

de jueding" ("The decision of the Central Committee of the Chinese Communist Party on strengthening the governing capacity of the Chinese Communist Party") ("the Decision"), http://www.china.org.cn/chinese/2004/Sep/668376.htm (accessed 26 November 2006).

15. See the White Paper entitled "Building of political democracy in China", Part Eight, Para. 2, http://www.china.org.cn/e-white/index.htm (accessed 26 November 2006).

16. *Ibid.*

17. Zheng Xiaoying, "Yi dangnei minzhu tuijing renmin minzhu" ("Promoting people's democracy through democracy within the CPC"), http://news.xinhuanet.com/newscenter/2003-06/18/content_925227.htm (accessed 26 November 2006).

18. *Ibid.*

19. See Liu Chang and Min Jie, "Wo dang yi dangnei minzhu daidong renmin minzhu zhanxian zhenggai zin silu" ("The CPC promotes people's democracy through internal democracy within the CPC: manifestation of new thoughts"), http://politics.people.com.cn/GB/1026/4539217.html (accessed 26 November 2005).

20. See Hu Jintao, "Report delivered at the 17th National Congress of the CPC", Part XII: http://news.xinhuanet.com/newscenter/2007-10/24/content_6938568.htm (accessed 10 April 2011).

21. See Xu Dongmei, *Zhongguo Gongchandang Dangnei Minzhu Yanjiu* (*Study of Internal Democracy within the CPC*), pp. 160–173.

22. See Deng Xiaoping, "Dang he guojia lingdao zhidu de gaige" ("The reform of the leadership system of the CPC and the state").

23. See Xu Dongmei, *Zhongguo Gongchandang Dangnei Minzhu Yanjiu* (*Study of Internal Democracy within the CPC*), pp. 147–160.

24. See Deng Xiaoping, "Dang he guojia lingdao zhidu de gaige" ("The reform of the leadership system of the CPC and the state").

25. *Ibid.*

26. See Lin Shangli, *Dangnei Minzhu – Zhongguo Gongchandang de Lilun yu Shijian* (*Internal Democracy – Theory and Practice of the CPC*), pp. 50–57.

27. *Ibid.*

28. The journal *Dang Jian Yanjiu* has published a series of articles, from volume 4 to volume 12 in 2005, discussing various aspects of the development of internal democracy of the CPC. For a summary, see "Fazhan dangnei minzhu zhuanti yantao guandian zongshu" ("Summary of views expressed around the theme of development of internal democracy within the CPC"): http://theory.people.com.cn/GB/49150/49151/4071358.html (accessed 26 November 2006).

29. See Xu Yaotong, "Yi dangnei minzhu daidong renmin minzhu" ("To Promote people's democracy through internal democracy within the CPC"), http://www.studytimes.com.cn/chinese/zhuanti/xxsb/1017450.htm (accessed 26 November 2006).

30. *Ibid.*

31. See Wang Guixiu, "Zhengzhi tizhi gaige de zuijia tuopokou: fazhan dangnei minzhu" ("The best breakthrough point for political system reform: development of internal democracy within the CPC"), in *Gaige Neichan (Internal Reference Material for Reform)*, vol. 21, 2003, http://www.zysy.org.cn/06/0605/Images/200559-111331-2003%E5%B9%B4%E7%AC%AC6%E6%9C%9F.doc#, 政治体制改革的最佳突破口：发展党内民主 (accessed 27 November 2006).

32. See Jiang Zemin, *Lun Dangde Jianshe (Study of the Development of the CPC)* (Zhongyang Wenxian Press, 2001), p. 442.

33. See Jiang Zemin, "Zai dangde di shiliu ci quanguo daibiao dahui shang de baogao" ("The report delivered by Jiang Zemin at the 16th Central Committee of the CPC").

34. *Ibid.*

35. *Ibid.*

36. See Deng Xiaoping, "Dang he guojia lingdao zhidu de gaige" ("The reform of the leadership system of the CPC and the state").

37. When Mao talked about the serious damage caused by Stalin to the former Soviet Union's socialist legal system, Mao said that it is impossible for such problems to occur in the UK and the USA.

38. See Ji Fang, available at http://www.bjpopss.gov.cn/bjpopss/xzit/xzit/20050427b.htm.zh.

39. See Wang Yongbing, "Dangnei minzhu: zhidu kongjian yu fazhan lujin" ("Internal democracy within the CPC: room within existing system and route for development").

40. See Zheng Xiaoying, "Yi dangnei minzhu tuijing renmin minzhu" ("Promoting people's democracy through democracy within the CPC")

41. See Xu Yaotong, "Yi dangnei minzhu daidong renmin minzhu" ("To Promote people's democracy through internal democracy within the CPC").

42. The four requirements mentioned by Professor Zheng Xiaoying are to implement the principle of ruling the country according to law and to insist on administration according to law. For details, see Zheng Xiaoying, "Yi dangnei minzhu tuijing renmin minzhu" ("Promoting people's democracy through democracy within the CPC").

43. See, for example, Ding Xiaoqiang, "Fazhan dangnei minzhu yao zhongshi zhidu jianshe" ("In order to develop internal democracy within the CPC attention needs to be paid to the establishment of mechanisms"), http://www.zgdjyj.com/default.aspx?tabid=99&ArticleId=143.

44. See para. 3 of Art. 10 of the Constitution of the CPC.

45. See para. 2 of Art. 10 of the Constitution of the CPC.

46. See para. 1 of Art. 11 of the Constitution of the CPC.

47. See Art. 1 of the Interim Regulations.

48. See Art. 2 of the Interim Regulations.

49. See para. 2 of Art. 29 of the Constitution of the CPC.

50. See Art. 9 of the Interim Regulations.

51. See Art. 8 of the Interim Regulations.

52. See Art. 7 of the Interim Regulations.

53. See Art. 13 of the Interim Regulations.

54. See Art. 12 of the Interim Regulations.

55. See Art. 16 of the Interim Regulations.

56. See Art. 16 of the Interim Regulations.

57. See Art. 17 of the Interim Regulations.

58. See Art. 18 of the Interim Regulations.

59. See the statistics issued by the Organization Department of the Central Committee of the CPC in 2010, http://cpc.people.com.cn/GB/64093/95111/11994237.html (accessed 10 April 2011).

60. See Yang Hai-feng etc, "Shencheng xiangzhen dangwei gaixuan huanjie, shixing dang daibiao zhijie xuanju fangshi" ("Election for the change of term of the CPC committees at township level in Shenyang City, the experiment of direct election by deputies to the CPC Congress at township level"), in *Huashang Chengbao* (*Huanshang Morning Post*): http://www.nen.com.cn/7797076757210726420050830/1749500.shtml.

61. *Ibid.*

62. See "Shangdong shixing cun dangzhibu zhijie xuanju qude shixiao" ("The trial of direct election of village CPC organ in Shangdong Province has achieved good results"), in *Dongfang Wang* (*Dongfang Net*), http://www.siica.org.cn/eastday/node4796/node12163/node12166/node12183/userobject1ai731890.html.

63. See Xu Yong, "Chongjian zhengzhi xinren de youye tansuo – du 'xiangcun xuanju zhong de liangpiao zhi'" ("Good experiment in re-establishing political confidence: reading 'two votes system' in village election"), http://www.weiquan.org.cn/data/detail.php?id=3463.

64. See "Jihuo dangnei gaige shidian, Sichuan cheng zhongguo zhengzhi gaige shiyantian" ("To activate reform within the CPC, Sichuan has become the experimental field for China's political reform"), 9 June 2005, 11:05, from *Fenghuangwang* (*Phoenix Net*), http://news.memail.net/050609/120,2,1525872,00.shtml; see also "Gongtui zhixuan de xianshi yiyi – Fenghua shi nongcun dangzuzhi xuanju zhidu gaige de sikao" ("The practical meaning of direct election after public recommendation – reflection on the reform of the election system of Village CPC organs in Fenghua City"), http://www.zjol.com.cn.

65. See "Zhixuan dangzhibu shuji, chuangxin xuanju moshi" ("Direct election of the secretaries of CPC branches and creation of new election model"): http://dj.sun0769.com/newsc.asp?id=2618; also "Dalingya Chun huanjie

shunli chanshen xinyijie zhibu shuji" ("The change of term election at Dalingya Village has smoothly produced the new team of branch committee"), at http://www.523170.com/article-446-1.html (accessed 10 April 2011).

66. See "Shangdong: wuqian duoge cun shixing zhixuan zhishu" ("Shangdong: direct election of the heads of village CPC organs in more than 5,000 villages"): http://news.xinhuanet.com/mrdx/2005-09/26/content_3544135.htm.

67. See Wang Yongbin, "Dangnei minzhu: zhidu kongjian yu fazhan lujin" ("Internal democracy within the CPC: room within existing system and route for development").

68. See Lai Hairong, "The development of competitive election at township level in Sichuan Province", p. 5, originally published in *Zhangnue Yu Guanli* (*Strategy and Management*), vol. 2, 2003. The author downloaded the article from: http://www.usc.cuhk.edu.hk/wk_wzdetails.asp?id=2242.

69. *Ibid.*, pp. 5–7.

70. See: http://cpc.people.com.cn/GB/64093/64387/4640945.html

71. See Xu Yaotong, "Yi dangnei minzhu daidong renmin minzhu" ("To Promote people's democracy through internal democracy within the CPC").

72. See "Chengdu kai quanguo xianhe, 639 ming dangyuan zhixuan chu zhen dangwei shuji" ("Chengdu leads the nation: 639 CPC members directly elected the head of the CPC Committee in a town"), http://www.chinaelections.org/readnews.asp?newsid={C8F5F99A-D7E1-4A18-B496-52920FBFBAE7}.

73. See Wang Yongbing, "Dangnei minzhu: zhidu kongjian yu fazhan lujin" ("Internal democracy within the CPC: room within existing system and route for development").

74. See "Jihuo dangnei gaige shidian, Sichuan cheng zhongguo zhengzhi gaige shiyantian" ("To activate reform within the CPC, Sichuan has become the experimental field for China's political reform"); see also "Sihong shiyan: 1.4 wan dangyuan zhixuan xiangzhen dangwei" ("Sihong experiment: 14,000 cpc members directly elect the CPC committees at township level"), http://www.chinaelections.org/readnews.asp?newsid={01BE8DED-934C-42AD-945E-9EA66B43E042}.

75. See Xu Yaotong, "Yi dangnei minzhu daidong renmin minzhu" ("To Promote people's democracy through internal democracy within the CPC").

76. See Wang Yongbing, "Dangnei minzhu: zhidu kongjian yu fazhan lujin" ("Internal democracy within the CPC: room within existing system and route for development").

77. They include township, county/district, municipal, and provincial levels.

78. See "Xiangzhen dangwei zhixuan guancha" ("Observation of direct election of the CPC committee at township level") in *Liaowang*: http://news.xinhuanet.com/politics/2011-04/17/c_121313565_8.htm (accessed 10 April 2011).

79. *Ibid.*

80. *Ibid.*

81. See Xu Yaotong, "Yi dangnei minzhu daidong renmin minzhu" ("To Promote people's democracy through internal democracy within the CPC").

82. *Ibid.*

83. See Ding Xiaoqiang, "Fazhan dangnei minzhu yao zhongshi zhidu jianshe" ("In order to develop internal democracy within the CPC attention needs to be paid to the establishment of mechanisms").

84. See "Neidi xuanju ji, xukuo gongtui zhixuan" ("The season of election in Mainland China, continuous promotion of 'public recommendation and direct election'") in *Ming Pao*, 21 April 2011: http://news.sina.com.

85. See Art. 1 of the Regulations.

86. See Art. 2 of the Regulations.

87. See Arts. 4 and 7 of the Regulations.

88. See Art. 5 of the Regulations.

89. See Art. 6 of the Regulations.

90. See Art. 27 of the Constitution of the CPC. According to the same Article, the standing committee of a CPC local committee will exercise the authority of that local committee while the latter is not in session; the standing committee will continue to be in charge of routine work when the next local CPC congress is in session until a new standing committee is elected.

91. See "Jihuo dangnei gaige shidian", "Jihuo dangnei gaige shidian, Sichuan cheng zhongguo zhengzhi gaige shiyantian" ("To activate reform within the CPC, Sichuan has become the experimental field for China's political reform").

92. See "Dangdaibiao dahui changrenzhi: Ya An shishui chengxiao lingren guanzhu" (Permanent deputies to party congress, experiment in Ya An and its effect catches attention), originally published in *Ban Yue Tan*. The author downloaded from http://news.xinhuanet.com/newscenter/2003-09/05/content_1064336.htm.

93. See "Jihuo dangnei gaige shidian", "Jihuo dangnei gaige shidian, Sichuan cheng zhongguo zhengzhi gaige shiyantian" ("To activate reform within the CPC, Sichuan has become the experimental field for China's political reform").

94. See Li Zhi-hong, "Guanyu dang daibiao dahui changrenzhi shidian gongzuo de diaocha" ("Investigation of the experiments with the standing system of deputies to the CPC Congresses"), in *Dangjian Yanjiu Neichan* (*Study of the CPC Development for Internal Reference*), vol. 2, 2003, http://www.djyj.com.cn/share/viewdjyjnc.asp?id=477.

95. *Ibid.*

96. See "Dangdaibiao dahui changrenzhi: Ya An shishui chengxiao lingren guanzhu" (Permanent deputies to party congress, experiment in Ya An and its effect catches attention).

97. See "Zhongzubu shidian dangnei minzhu gaige: Hubei Luotian xianwei sushe changwei" ("The Organization Department of the Central Committee of the CPC experiments with reform of internal democracy within the CPC: there will be no standing committee of county party committee in Luotian, Hubei Province"), http://politics.people.com.cn/GB/1027/3438031.html.

98. See engine.cqvip.com/content/l/81160x/2003/000/010/jy23_l4_9095942.pdf.

99. See note 28 above.

100. See Ji Fang, available at http://www.bjpopss.gov.cn/bjpopss/xzit/xzit/20050427b .htm.zh.

101. See Wang Yicheng, "Dui fazhan dangnei minzhu wenti de ruogan sikao" ("Several thoughts on the issue of developing internal democracy within the CPC"), originally published in *Zhengzhixue Yanjiu* (*Research of Politics*), vol. 2, 2005. The author downloaded from http://chinaps.cass.cn/readcontent .asp?id=4834

102. See the White Paper entitled "Building political democracy in China", Chapter 8, at http://www.china.org.cn/e-white/index.htm. It actually means that the CPC wants to develop democracy within the CPC first and hope that democracy within the CPC will naturally promote democracy in the society nationwide. That has been regarded as the policy for achieving democratic governance by the CPC.

103. See Wu Licai, "Luotian zhenggai: cong dangnei minzhu qidong de xianzheng gaige" ("Political reform in Luotian: a political reform starting from democracy within the CPC"), http://ganzhi.china.com.cn/xxsb/txt/2006-01/ 24/content_6104089.htm

104. See Deng Xiaoping, "Dang he guojia lingdao zhidu de gaige" ("The reform of the leadership system of the CPC and the state")

105. See Jiantian Xianzhi, "Zhongguo gongchandang dangnei minzhu jianshe de xianshi lilu ji lishi jingshi" ("The current practice of establishing democracy within the CPC and its historical lessons"), http://www.rmlt.com.cn/ News/201101/201101251435282365_3.html

106. For example, Ai Weiwei has recently been detained by the Public Security Authority.

107. Statistics from the United Front department of the Central Committee of the CPC, http://www.zytzb.org.cn/zytzbwz/ztlm/mzdphj/zhpl/80200712200209.html (accessed 10 April 2011).

3

Purchase of Office in China: A Shortcut for Career Advancement?

Jun LI

Joseph Y. S. CHENG

Introduction

Promotion is "a significant issue" to the cadre corps in China and its related mechanisms are important in Chinese politics. The system of cadre promotions and transfers to a considerable extent determines the performance of the Party regime in China. Cadre promotions, however, involve much corruption. This corruption ranges from senior officials taking bribes to help their subordinates win promotion to the outright sale of positions to the highest bidder. In the course of end-of-term reshuffles and promotions (*huan jie*), the phenomenon of "buying official posts and selling official posts" (*mai guan mai guan*) frequently occurs, and the temptation of money for officials is often stronger than Party ideology.

The purchase of official positions damages the legitimacy of the Chinese Communist Party regime, and the knowledge on the part of ordinary people of such corrupt practices compromises the image of the Party and its leadership. Selecting the best-qualified officials and promoting them according to commonly accepted criteria has been one of the most important expectations of the leadership since ancient times.[1] The purchase of official positions is perceived to work against the development of the country and serves to focus the blame for all evils perpetrated in the eyes of the people against the officials in power. The Chinese leadership is obviously aware of the seriousness of the problem; and it is most concerned with the maintenance of social and political stability. Stories of the purchase of official positions are issues that can easily generate mass incidents, because these stories also mean that decent officials supported by the people have been denied the positions or promotions they deserve. Owing to these considerations, the Seventeenth National Congress of the Communist Party of China (CPC) in 2007 declared the policy objective of "increasing public trust in cadre selection and appointment",[2] which was in fact an acknowledgement of a significant inadequacy.

This chapter aims at investigating the phenomena of buying and selling official positions in China in recent years through a case-study approach. It attempts to answer the question why it is so difficult to eradicate these corrupt practices. The latter obviously exposes the weaknesses of the CPC and its institutional mechanisms which have failed to overcome a well-known and serious problem. This study suggests that the supervision processes have not been effective, and that cadre promotion is largely at the personal discretion of higher-level cadres in the absence of objective criteria and transparent, democratic procedures.

The Spreading Practice of Purchasing Official Positions

On 23 January 2006, the Central Commission for Discipline Inspection of the CPC and the Organization Department of the CPC Central Committee held a joint press conference to inform the public of cases regarding the purchasing of Party and government official positions in local Party committee elections. The former sanctioned eight local officials for accepting or offering bribes in the promotion exercises. The press conference represented an important gesture on the part of the Chinese authorities to crack down on the corrupt practice of trading official positions in leadership reshuffles of local governments ahead of the Seventeenth Party Congress.[3]

The practice of trading official positions apparently had become rampant. In 2005, over 300 officials were reprimanded for taking or offering bribes in exchange for promotions. Some also abused their power to elevate relatives or friends to key government positions.[4] Bribery in exchange for promotion had become prevalent at all

Table 1:
Senior Officials (at Provincial Level) Involved in the Sale of Posts in Recent Years

Name	Rank	Bribe
Xu Guojian	Standing Member of Jiangsu Provincial Party Committee, Director of Organization Department	4.7 million *yuan* and US$8,000
Han Guizhi	Chairman of the Provincial People's Political Consultative Conference in Heilongjiang	9.5 million *yuan*
Liu Fangren	Secretary of Guizhou Provincial Chairman of Standing Committee of Guizhou People's Congress	6.6 million *yuan* and US$19,900
Li Jiating	Deputy Secretary of Yunnan Provincial Party Committee, Governor of Yunnan Province	18.1 million *yuan*
Pan Guangtian	Vice Chairman of the Provincial People's Political Consultative Conference in Shandong	1.53 million *yuan*
Tian Fengqi	President of Liaoning Higher People's Court	3.3 million *yuan*
Cong Fukui	Standing Member of Hebei Provincial Party Committee, Vice Governor of Hebei Province	9.36 million *yuan*
Wang Xuebing	President of China Construction Bank	1.15 million *yuan*
Wang Huaizhong	Vice Governor of Anhui Province	9.9 million *yuan*
Mai Chongkai	Deputy Secretary of Political and Legal Affairs Committee, Guangdong Provincial Party Committee	1.06 million *yuan*
Zhang Guoguang	Deputy Secretary of Hubei Provincial Party Committee, Governor of Hubei Province	0.57 million *yuan*

Source: Data Centre of the Beijing Research Institute of International Urban Development

government and Party levels nationwide, as was demonstrated by the increasing number of corruption cases revealed, the huge amounts of money involved, and the number of senior officials concerned, i.e., above prefectural level (see Table 1).

Trading in official positions apparently has been acknowledged as a "hidden norm in officialdom" (*guanchang qianguize*). A senior cadre interviewed by the authors in Beijing in 2009 described the situation as follows: "A senior cadre cannot expect any improvement in his position if he doesn't make courtesy calls and brings no gifts, he can only expect horizontal transfers. If he does both, then he can expect promotions."[5] Another senior Party cadre also admitted: "It has taken the CPC a long time to realize how serious this problem is."[6]

The cases reported in the media are likely to be just the tip of the iceberg. It is commonly believed that senior cadres have been easily able to secure personal gain and even bribes through their power to promote their subordinates. There is political gossip that even important political and administrative posts are up for sale at given prices. It appears that the widespread practice of purchasing official positions has gradually established a broad network of corruption, or even a trading system, that has become increasingly institutionalized. It extends upwards weaving a protective umbrella and goes downwards forging expectations and behavioural patterns. Despite the risks of exposure and heavy penalties for the convicted, corruption seems to persist.[7]

Trading of Official Positions: The Shangzhou Case[8]

This was not just a simple case of a corrupt official taking a bribe. What made the Shangzhou case notorious was that numerous posts were sold within the prefectural bureaucracy, which illustrated how widespread such trading of official positions was in China.

On 4 July 2006, Zhang Gaiping, a standing member of the Shaanxi Provincial Party Committee and secretary of the Shangzhou Prefectural Party Committee, was convicted of taking bribes from subordinates. Zhang received over 1.09 million *yuan* in bribes from officials who sought promotion during her tenure in Shangzhou from 2000 to 2005.[9] Zhang's misconduct was brought to light by media reports, and her trial by the Xian Intermediate Court revealed the value of power which could be traded for money. She was removed from office and expelled from the Party with a thirteen-year gaol sentence. The court heard in detail that she had accepted 380,000 *yuan* in one case to help a subordinate to advance in their career.

Zhang Gaiping was appointed a member of the Shangzhou

Prefectural Party Committee and its secretary in November 2000, and shortly afterwards she became the mayor of Shanglou, a prefecture-level city in south Shaanxi. Zhang's own career could be described as smooth; at the age of 40, she had reached the rank of deputy bureau head, which was not very common in Chinese officialdom, especially for a woman. Zhang was in fact the first female mayor in Shangluo's history. In Shangzhou, Zhang was initially widely regarded as a good leader: efficient, diligent, enthusiastic and caring. For instance, after she had become the mayor of Shangluo, the area was severely hit by an unexpected flood. Zhang, along with principal cadres from the relevant departments, immediately went to visit the affected area and console the local people. The effective disaster relief efforts gained her much respect from the local populace, who called her the "Shangzhou female Buddha (*shangzhou nu pusa*)".

Her lifestyle, however, gradually became corrupt after holding high office for many years. Her love of money led to her downfall. Zhang's business of selling offices started after her transfer from Xianyang to Shangzhou. As Party secretary of Shangzhou prefecture, Zhang was directly in charge of cadre promotion, especially for county-level officials. In the beginning, Zhang herself did not dare to accept bribes directly; the money transactions were all dealt with via a businessman named Yang Jiangxiong.

At the end of 2000, Yang attempted to bid for the contract of the building project of the "Red Mansion" hotel in Shangluo, and presented Zhang with 20,000 *yuan* as "commission" (*haochufei*). Yang won the bid and, with Zhang's blessing, became the constructor of the project. This deal led to their closer collusion. Yang then became Zhang's intermediary (*zhongjianshang*) through whom Zhang collected bribes for her subordinates' promotions. One day in November 2003, Chen Zhixin, deputy secretary of the Shangzhou Party disciplinary committee, asked Yang to help him secure his promotion to director of the Shangzhou Education Bureau, the position he had sought for many years. Yang visited Zhang to tell her Chen's expectation and gave her 100,000 *yuan*. In April 2004, Yang approached Zhang again and this time offered her 200,000 *yuan*. In addition to Yang's offers, Chen himself once talked to Zhang face to face about his promotion, and left 80,000 *yuan* for Zhang as a "gratitude fee" (*ganxiefei*). As the top leader in Shangzhou, Zhang had the final say in personnel decisions even under the guise of democratic procedure. In mid-2004, Chen's wish to become the director of the Education Bureau finally came true. At the candidate-nomination meeting attended by Standing Committee members of the Shangzhou Prefectural Party Committee, Zhang highly recommended Chen. Zhang's strong support was crucial to Chen's promotion.

Chen's promotion exercise gave Zhang the idea that she could take advantage of the power in her hands to create wealth through selling positions to the right persons. At first Zhang accepted bribes in secret and with caution; but she gradually became greedier and even attempted to sell positions with set prices. "Zhang took risks to solicit bribes, but her demands actually attracted bribery offers", a cadre responsible for disciplinary matters observed.[10]

In August 2002, Wang Junjie, manager of Shangzhou Tourism Company, came to Zhang's office to report on his work. Their talk deviated away from the set topic; during their conversations, Wang asked several times for a change of position at the year-end reshuffle. He offered Zhang 40,000 *yuan* with the hope that Zhang could exert her "key influence" in candidate selection for the director of the Shangzhou Tourism Bureau. This time Zhang did not make any promise because she certainly thought that the offer was too small for the important post requested. A month later, Wang presented Zhang with 10,000 *yuan* for his promotion. In early 2003, Wang was appointed the director of Shangzhou Tourism Bureau on Zhang's nomination and with her recommendation at a "democratic" selection meeting.

Similar transactions were a frequent occurrence during Zhang's tenure in Shangzhou. In the summer of 2000, Chen Xuzhong gave Zhang 50,000 *yuan* for his promotion to Zhuoshui County magistrate. In August 2001, Tang Kangxun offered Zhang 40,000 *yuan* for his elevation to director of the Shangluo Birth Control Bureau; and so on. The officials offering bribes to Zhang worked in departments and bureaux ranging from education and finance to transport, agriculture and welfare in the Shangzhou prefecture government.

When prosecutors investigated the cases, Zhang did not contest any of the charges against her and several times referred to the democratic procedure of cadre promotion set by the Central Organization Department of the Party. She said that she had not violated the rules and had only expressed her own opinions on who should be promoted within the framework of democratic consultations.[11] From Zhang's standpoint, within the formal and "democratic" procedural framework, she could naturally adopt a key role in cadre promotion.

When Zhang Gaiping was Party secretary of Shangzhou prefecture, she was the administrator of a region where the average monthly wage for a cadre was less than 600 *yuan*. But in one of the poorest parts of the impoverished Shaanxi Province in western China, Zhang was able to amass more than one million *yuan* in five years by peddling her influence in the government and Party bureaucracy. Shangzhou officials borrowed and embezzled public money in order to pay Zhang to further their careers.[12] To raise money for the bribes, some officials in Shangzhou either embezzled public funds and took bribes from their subordinates or borrowed money from banks and friends. Two family-planning officials took bank loans to cover their bribery expenses. The largest single sum Zhang received was from Chen Xinzhi, then director of the Shangzhou Education Bureau. Chen paid Zhang 380,000 *yuan*, including 40,000 *yuan* from the funding for a hygiene and anti-epidemic centre.

A total of 27 Party cadres and governmental officials in Shangzhou were found to have offered Zhang bribes between 2000 and 2005. Zhang Bin, former deputy director of the Transport Bureau in Shangzhou, in 2003 and 2004 embezzled 15,000 *yuan* from the public accounts to bribe Zhang so that she would endorse his promotion to head of the Shangzhou Administration Office. "It was well-known among Shangzhou officials that to get promoted, you had to pay Zhang Gaiping. If not, you had no chance", observed an unnamed official in Shangzhou.[13] When Zhang Gaiping was the Party secretary of Shangzhou prefecture, most leading officials of the Party and government agencies in that prefecture joined the "team" to buy offices.

The Shangzhou case attracted wide public attention in China because of the number of posts sold by Zhang, which was quite beyond the public's expectations. The press satirically labelled Zhang's crimes as a "wholesale" business.[14] The Shangzhou case unfortunately is not an exception. Li Jiating, former governor of Yunnan Province, was convicted in 2001 of taking over 18 million *yuan* in bribes to promote dozens of officials. In 2005, Ma De, former party secretary of Suihua, Heilongjiang Province, was sentenced to death for taking more than RMB 6 million *yuan* in bribes for promoting officials to important government posts during his ten-year tenure in various government positions.

The Chain of Trading Official Positions

Gaining public power and seeking more important positions is a common goal for most politicians. It has been said that "Perhaps the main driver for civil servants and politicians is career concerns. They are concerned by the effect of their current performance not so much on immediately monetary rewards, but rather on their reputation or image in view of future promotions, career prospects in private and public sectors, as well as re-elections."[15] This analysis conforms to the incentive consideration of officials in China, often described as "rank-seeking". There is naturally severe competition for promotions among cadres in officialdom.

In China today, not too many cadres at various levels follow the Party line that cadres should not think about their own interests but should serve the people wholeheartedly. Few cadres believe that promotion to higher posts is based on their capability and performance. As promotions lead to both improvement in economic welfare and the enhancement of social respect and reputation, cadres' top priority is often the remuneration and privileges that they receive corresponding to their rank in the hierarchy. The differences in privileges, including a variety of attractive perks, can be very substantial between cadres of lower ranks and their superiors. This explains why most cadres are so eager to secure promotions or strategic positions and why they are willing to do their utmost to realize their objectives.[16] In the eyes of ordinary cadres, rank determines not only salaries, and official status, it carries with it remuneration in terms of housing allocation, quality of medical care, travel arrangements, official cars and so on.[17] Despite the Party's official line against "careerism", with the decline of ideological and moral appeal, it is only natural that cadres want better living standards that go in tandem with promotions.

In the era of economic reforms and opening to the external world, the norms of a market economy become increasingly prevalent, and the influence of money in the political and administrative processes rises correspondingly. The trading of official positions emerged after 1979 and gradually spread, despite numerous anti-corruption campaigns in the subsequent decades. High-ranking and strategic public offices are perceived as a commodity for trading. The purpose of buying official positions is to secure public power, which is considered a precious resource in contemporary China.[18] Eagerness to seek promotion and the worry of stagnation in one's career in the context of rampant corruption encourages cadres to seek channels to offer bribes to their superiors. This is especially so when it is common knowledge that very few cadres would reject bribes, thus promotions through bribery gradually became commonplace. To seek fast-track promotions, some cadres concentrate on establishing networks and accumulating the resources to secure higher offices as the most effective way of career advancement.

Three types of cadres may be more enthusiastic in engaging in "buying posts": the first type involves mediocre cadres with no significant achievements during their term of office to support promotion; the second type is the average group who lack confidence that they will be promoted by merit. In general, any cadres who are qualified are potential "active buyers", as recognized by some academics.[19] The third type is those with a good record of achievements but who are afraid of being left-behind, out-competed by other competitors with stronger backgrounds and connections (*guanxi*); in their logic, "many cadres secure their high offices through offering money. I cannot afford not to join; otherwise, I will be left out".[20] Avoiding the corruption network is perceived as a severe handicap, they would therefore be squeezed out by the "active buyers". Hence they have to give in and accept the "hidden norm in officialdom". These types are "passive buyers";[21] but the obvious danger is that they slowly multiply when the perception is that trading of official positions has become a common practice.

As the Shangzhou case demonstrates, power can generate money either by selling public offices or by securing bribery through benefiting those who are ready to offer money. In the context of the hidden norm in officialdom, those who purchase posts can be confident that, after securing the promotion, they can easily get their bribe back through the collection of more bribes. In fact, in most cases, the bribes they offer to their respective superiors are money they collect from their respective subordinates. Chains of trading in official positions are thus established, and sometimes they expand beyond the Party and government hierarchies. For example, Li Gang sent 500,000 *yuan* to Ma De, the Party secretary of Shuihua, Heilongjing Province, for his promotion to Party chief of Shuiling, a county under the administration of Shuihua. When Li Gang got the position, he became a post seller, taking bribes from his subordinates amounting to over 2.1 million *yuan*. Li's profit rate was as high as over 300%. In another case, Ma De once spent 800,000 *yuan* for his promotion, and he subsequently managed to collect bribes amounting to nearly 6 million *yuan*, i.e., a profit rate as high as 600%. To recover the huge expense of buying offices, office buyers have to utilize the power in their hands to maximize their profits by squeezing money from their subordinates, which then further extends the chain downwards.[22]

The post seller is usually easily identified; the top leader (*yi ba shou*) in the hierarchy and the leader in charge of personnel and cadre affairs are most likely to be the suppliers in the official-positions trading chain. According to the regulations governing Party managing cadres (*dang guan ganbu yuanze*), promotions are to be decided collectively at Party Committee meetings and usually require further approval at the next higher level of the Party Committee. However, the procedures of promotion in practice can be manipulated by a few officials, principally the Party secretary and the top executive of the local government in charge of the personnel department. In practice, candidates for promotion are usually nominated by the Party secretary and the Organization Department. In committee meetings, the Party secretary would recommend a list of candidates to the members of the Party Committee according to the institutional arrangement of "initial nomination". If the Party secretary takes bribes for his subordinates' promotions, then those who offer bribes would be included in the candidate list nominated by the Party secretary. It is through the "initial nominations" controlled by the Party secretary that the bribe-offerers slip into the candidates lists for "democratic discussion". The Party secretary's opinions usually carry much more weight than those of other members, given his predominant status and influence in the Party committee. Consequently more time and attention are given to the top-of-the-list candidates. By manipulation of the candidate nomination process, the Party secretary can significantly alter a candidate's chance of promotion.[23] All this makes the Party secretary the most important target for office buyers.

Many senior leaders do not initially engage in the business of trading official positions. Many of them would refuse to take money for their subordinates' promotions. However, as more and more subordinates and junior cadres seek to be promoted as soon as possible, and approach senior officials offering bribes and luxurious gifts to facilitate their promotion, senior cadres may not be able to withstand the attack of "sugar-coated bullets" (*tangyi paodan*) and become corrupted.

A buyer of office will actively send gifts to his superior using various excuses. "Your promotion is under the control of your superiors. Every cadre has to show 'goodwill'."[24] It is said that an office buyer "is only afraid that a leader does not have difficulties or hobbies, which would prevent him into accepting the bribes".[25] Many subordinates now offer their superiors not only money, expensive home appliances or jewellery, but also shares, luxurious watches and overseas trips. Sometimes an office buyer needs to send money several times to satisfy his superior, as illustrated in the Shangzhou case.

Besides the temptation of corruption, serious cadres also want to establish their own clique in a given organization so that they can still control their subordinates and exert their own influence when they have to retire or leave the organization. They therefore would like to select the right cadres who are not only loyal to them but who can be controlled easily. Contracts between senior cadres as sellers of official positions, and their subordinates as buyers, in the absence of mutual trust being established, may involve high political risks. In the Shangzhou case, personal ties as a basis for reciprocity and mutual trust between buyers and sellers of official positions were secured through the promotion of personal alliances by leaders in bureaucracies. Senior officials worry about keeping their current posts and having subordinates follow their orders and show allegiance to them. Personal connections were therefore a crucial consideration in selecting the right persons to promote even though bribery would be accepted for the promotion.

China's leaders rely heavily on the cultivation of *guanxi* (personal connections).[26] These ties remain hidden and unknown to the public. A top cadre in a given bureaucracy acts like an authority towards those below him because he has substantial leverage over his subordinates[27] and can strongly influence their careers. A cadre showing loyalty and obedience to a superior may earn a cheaper promotion. A minority of cadres have pledged loyalty to their respective leaders and the network around their respective leaders, i.e., they have formed factions or cliques. Under such circumstances, personal connections are more important than performance and loyalty to the Party in determining the career advancement of such faction members. This is usually called nepotism or cronyism, referring to the willingness to break procedural rules in a system of corruptive practices in order to provide better opportunities or advantages to people belonging to the same faction. Senior cadres selling official positions often ensure, through networks of nepotism, that their faction members occupy strategic positions, which would allow them to maintain influence in a given organization. This is why it is often too subtle to judge from the outside to what extent a promotion indicates "caring" for a subordinate, promoting faction interests, or personal gain in terms of bribery.

Without the advantages of shared ties, such as coming from the same home town or graduating from the same university, many officials resort to monetary methods to build up good relationships with their superiors to boost their chances of promotion. Once a transaction is concluded, the two parties – buyer and seller – are in the same boat and share the risk of being caught. Both parties attempt to keep the secret and protect each other. Nepotism often constitutes a big umbrella for local cadres which protects them from being monitored. Under this umbrella, Party secretaries in cities and counties are often sellers and buyers of offices.

One consideration often dominates a senior cadre's mind. The selling of official positions frequently takes place under the table and only through face-to-face encounters between the buying and selling parties. The senior cadre is naturally concerned whether the buyer can keep his or her mouth shut so that the illegal transaction will not be disclosed. For example, Xu Guojian (see Table 1) would not accept bribes for a position from someone he could not trust.

Often bribery does not end even after one gets the position or promotion. Many cadres continue to send money to thank the leaders for their promotions to show their loyalty to their superiors, because they would like to maintain the relationship to seek further promotions or other benefits.

Party cadres and government officials have defined terms of service, and the trading of official positions becomes more active at the end of each cycle. The prices for offices vary with the rank of the position traded and with the personal relations between the superior and the subordinate. Generally speaking, the higher the rank of the position, the larger the amount of money demanded; ranging from about one million *yuan* charged for a provincial-level position down to several thousand *yuan* for a township-level position; and the amount of money changing hands normally represents a consensus already reached between the two parties concerned.

Table 2: Chain of Selling and Buying Official Positions in the Shangzhou Case

Office Seller	Office Buyer	Positions Bought	Bribe Offered
Zhang Gaiping	Wang Junjie	Director of Shangluo Tourism Bureau	30,000 *yuan*
	Chen Xuzhong	Magistrate of Zhuoshui County	50,000 yuan
	Tang Kangxun	Director of Shangluo Birth-Control Bureau	30,000 yuan
	Zhang Bin	Deputy Director of Shangluo Prefectural Government Administration Office	50,000 yuan
	Chen Zhixin	Director of Shangluo Prefectural Government Education Bureau	380,000 yuan
	Liu Zhishan	Director of Shangluo Prefectural Government Water Affairs Bureau	40,000 yuan

Source: Guojizaixian, http://www.crionline.cn/, 16 July 2006

The Weaknesses of the Current Institutional Mechanisms for Cadre Promotion

The Shangzhou case generated much discussion among the educated public in China. They were shocked not so much by the bribery involved, but by the problems of the entire cadre management system. The Party regime in China today largely retains its Leninist features;[28]

but the Chinese leadership understands that effective governance is essential to the maintenance of the regime's legitimacy.[29] As the Party line emphasizes the realization of a "relatively wealthy society (*xiaokang shehui*)" as the foundation of the regime's legitimacy, Party cadres must give people the confidence that they are capable of securing this objective.

The *Handbook* released by the CPC's Central Organization Department as a general reference for Party cadres states:

We promote cadres so that there can be successors to the Party's cause who will lead the people in realizing the Four Modernizations. The promotion is by no means intended to replace a certain leader occupying a certain office or to carry out some unfinished cause to which a leader is personally committed. Personal decisions on cadre appointments, utilization and promotions facilitate [the development of] a self-interested perspective, the abuse of position and power to place in office intimate friends and the development of personal influence. This not only violates regulations on Party life, but also makes it easy for unsuitable cadres and even opportunistic elements seeking personal gain to infiltrate our cadre ranks and leading groups. This is extremely dangerous . . . We must put an end to personal decisions on cadre appointments, utilization and promotions. Through the organizational system we must end appointments on the basis of favouritism.[30]

The Regulations on the Work of Selecting and Appointing Leading Party and Government Cadres (*Dangzheng Lingdao Ganbu Xuanba Renyong Gongzuo Tiaoli*) specifies that "cadres should ... be determined to carry out the reform and opening-up policy, be devoted to the cause of [national] modernization, and work hard for the building of socialism and the making of concrete achievements".[31] Following the traditional Leninist line, Chinese leaders consider that crucial to the success of all reforms is the major effort to establish and develop the Party's cadre management system. This consideration is reflected in the official repetition of Lenin's dictum "cadres decide everything", in line with the recognition that the current socio-economic transition requires first of all a transformation of the elite and that the deficiencies in the cadre system have been a serious obstacle to the transformation.[32] The Chinese leadership in fact has devised various incentive mechanisms and criteria to improve the work of cadre promotion at all levels.

To ensure effective Party management of cadres (*dang guan ganbu*), the organization department and Party secretary at all levels have been given almost monopolistic control over cadre management through the processes of candidate nomination, cadre evaluation and review, and the system of reporting for the record (*bei an zhidu*) to facilitate their monitoring of cadre performance.[33] It is this system that confers substantial authority on the Party organization department and the Party secretary at every level to make personnel decisions in cadre selection and promotion.

From 2000 onwards, the practice of trading official positions apparently infiltrated Party and government systems all over the country. To deter this corrupt practice, the central leadership has several times announced its stance against such misconduct. For example, Vice-president Xi Jinping called for "creating a clean and upright environment" for the election of new local leaders by firmly preventing and severely punishing misconduct such as selling and buying government posts.[34] In view of the Chinese leadership's concern, those who are found to have been involved in trading official positions will be punished severely and formally prosecuted. Even very senior officials who are found selling official posts or accepting bribes from their subordinates for promotion will be demoted and given legal and disciplinary sanctions. Top officials involved or implicated in such corrupt practices will be recorded as having made severe mistakes in decision-making, neglecting their duty, providing slack supervision and management of affairs under their jurisdiction, abuse of power, and improper nominations and promotions in cadre selection. In short, irregularities in official promotions will be dealt with case by case with zero tolerance and senior cadres involved are warned to expect "serious consequences".

On 7 July 2006, the Party's Central Organization Department promulgated a new cadre management system, based on the document "The Trial Method of Comprehensive Local Cadre Evaluation that Embodies the Requirements of the Scientific View of Development".[35] This system was supposed to serve as the basis of cadre selection and promotion for the new government of Hu-Wen's second term. It consists of six procedures: "democratic nomination", "democratic assessment", "public opinion poll", "analysis of actual achievements", "interview", and "comprehensive evaluation". According to the new design, "democratic nomination" entrusts the nomination of the candidates for promotion to their colleagues, i.e., cadres of the same locality; and "democratic assessment" emphasizes the opinions of the peers around the candidates, who must have the "majority support" of their peers in order to be considered for promotion. "Public opinion poll" is used to get an "outsiders' view" of the candidate. However, the "public" here refers not to the general public but to the grassroots level deputies of the People's Congress and delegates to the People's Political Consultative Conference. "Analysis of actual achievements" is mainly based on the data supplied by relevant agencies such as the statistics bureau, the bureau of audit etc., as well as the feedback from the general public. Typical indicators considered include local per capita GDP and its growth rates, per capita fiscal revenue and its growth rates, and certain items related to economic performance. The other specific items to be included are largely left to the discretion of the local authorities in adjustment to the local conditions. The "interview" is conducted by a team of cadres from the Party's Organization Department; it helps to clarify doubts and ambiguities from the earlier procedures and to assess the psychological quality of the candidate. The final stage is "comprehensive evaluation", which takes place in the meetings of the evaluation team, assessing and analysing the findings so far.[36] The goal is to reach an "objective and fair agreement" on the candidates. The ultimate decision, however, still rests in the hands of the next higher level Party authority, which is supposed to base its decision on the results of the comprehensive evaluation. Cadres must go through all six stages successfully to secure their promotions. This fulfils the requirement of the long-standing principle of the Party regime: "the Party controls cadres".

If implemented faithfully, which is by no means guaranteed, the new system would remove the nomination power from local Party secretaries, who had been nominating their own subordinates in the earlier practice of "initial nomination", and put it in the hands of larger circles of relevant cadres. It may then terminate the notorious "black-box operation" style in personnel decisions, which was perhaps the source of corruption. This may indeed generate a sense of popular accountability among cadres, the Party has not given up its control over cadres and the Leninist predisposition is still prevalent.[37] It essentially accepts elite rather than popular mass participation. It is limited within the Party-state system, with most representatives being drawn from among officialdom at different levels.[38] The public opinion survey is only used as a reference for the higher leaders to consider who should be promoted; it is very difficult to know the actual significance of public opinion in cadre promotion.

The recent institutional adjustments in the appointment, promotion, transfer and removal of local leaders is part of an overall post-Mao attempt at organizational rationalization in cadre management. It is hoped that the limited "democratization" will create a measure of responsiveness badly needed to deter misconduct in cadre management so as to build a "harmonious society", while maintaining the Party regime rule and political stability. Yet, the mild institutional adjustments do not guarantee effectiveness, as significant weaknesses still exist in the new system. By deliberate design the new system leaves abundant room for intervention by higher-level leaders when deemed necessary. These same loopholes, however, may also render the new cadre management system ineffective.

Party management of cadres is governed by an elaborate division of responsibility among various Party committees. In principle, no leading cadre's appointment, promotion, transfer or removal can be effected without the approval of the appropriate Party committees.[39] These Party committees are the legitimate decision-making organs for cadre promotion based on four aspects: (a) virtue (*de*), focusing on political standpoint and character; (b) ability (*neng*), focusing on professional ability and management skills; (c) work attendance and attitude towards work (*qin*); (d) achievements (*ji*), focusing on specific achievements in performance and general work efficiency.[40] However, the relevant Party committees are often unwieldy in size and may meet infrequently;[41] it seems likely that their standing committees or at the local level their secretariats play a crucial role in these decisions.

The common abuse of official power among senior leaders is influence peddling to obtain favours for their nominations of candidates for promotion. Within the existing bureaucratic framework, the power of promoting cadres still lies with a few key leaders. The standing Party committee, usually made up of seven to nine members, would convene to discuss the recommendation of candidates for promotion. For example, in the Shangzhou case, at the prefectural level, the Party secretary led the prefectural Party committee, which consisted of the mayor and vice mayors, as well as other officials heading important departments in the Party, including the organization and propaganda departments. The Party committee determined all the major issues in the personnel area. Inside the committee, the Party secretary, Zhang Gaiping, had the final say over almost everything, including policies and personnel appointments. The committee meetings did not offer many opportunities for bargaining and discussions. The decisions were then presented to the standing committee, which was unlikely to raise objections to the decisions made. The Party committee exercised authority over the appointment of senior personnel, as well as promotions, dismissals and transfers one level down the administrative hierarchy.[42] The final decisions were approved and released in the name of the standing committee, which was usually controlled by the Party secretary.[43]

Hence, it can be seen that if the leading officials want to give the green light to a candidate, they have ample latitude to do so without violating formal procedures. In addition, reciprocity is the prevailing norm among Chinese officials. Those who give support to the candidates picked by the Party secretary often receive future benefits in return. Once the Party secretary strongly supports a candidate, other committee members are often unable or reluctant to object.

In some cases, leading officials can freely make appointments. An investigation in August 2006 found a prefectural Party secretary in Shangqiu, Henan Province, convening four standing committee meetings to promote 94 cadres without going through any assessment procedures.[44]

It should be remembered that the Party actually controls the procedure of cadre promotion, which leaves much room for the Party secretary to manipulate the procedure. The Party secretary exerts personal influence in at least two ways. In the first place, he or she is the principal official responsible for cadre promotion and tends to monopolize the privilege of setting the criteria for application and the assessment of the applicants. The Party secretary can manipulate the criteria on age, education background and years of work experience to limit the field of applicants. Further, the initial nomination in the hands of leading members is very important in determining who is the most suitable candidate for a promotion. In fact, the nomination of candidates places substantial discretionary power in the hands of leading members, especially the Party secretary. Nomination by the Party secretary often means the assurance of a safe promotion. This places the official promotion process in a black box and distorts the incentives of most cadres waiting for promotion through their own hard work and integrity. It is common for potential candidates to spend most of their efforts working to please their superiors with little incentive to work for the people. This has been the root behind the increasingly common practice of "selling and buying official posts"[45] as illustrated by the Shangzhou case.

Under such circumstances, the concentration of power over personnel issues makes bribery more efficient, because it clarifies the potential targets subordinates need to bribe. Office selling is also made safer for senior cadres because they can easily hide their responsibility behind the collective decisions of the Party committees, since all final decisions have to be made unanimously, according to formal procedure.[46]

What is striking about the institutional mechanisms for cadre management is their adherence to an additional "majority support" principle, which could potentially conflict with the first principle in case public opinion concerning a candidate diverges widely from the opinion of his or her superiors. The Party's Central Organization Department makes it clear that cadres who do not have the "majority support of the masses" should not be considered for candidacy for promotion in the new system.[47] However, the term "masses" here refers not necessarily to ordinary citizens but to those people – usually cadres and support staff – who work for or together with the cadre under evaluation. Neither is the word "democratic" used in its conventional sense in this context. For example, the nominators in the "democratic nomination" procedure are, in the case of selecting members of the Party committee, limited to the incumbent members of the Party committee, i.e., the principal leaders of the government; the head of the Party's discipline inspection committee; leading Party members of the local people's congress and people's political consultative conference; and the leading cadres of the Party and government bureaucracies; the people's court; the people's procuratorate; and "mass organizations" including the Communist Youth League, the Women's Federation and trade unions.[48] Nomination may be done by formal ballot or informally by eligible cadres expressing their preferences personally to the Party organization department overseeing the process. The ultimate decisions, however, lie in the hands of the current Party standing committee which determines, on the basis of the "democratic nominations", the cadres to be promoted.

Further, the promotion criteria are difficult to define and assess. Although good economic performance and political credentials are believed to be significant for cadres to earn promotions, it is widely perceived by ordinary people, and verified by the authors' interviews with officials in China, that personal connections with one's superiors in charge of promotion are perhaps even more important.[49]

The fact that the institutional mechanisms for cadre promotion have not been able to fulfil the original functions is much related to the power abuse of the Party secretaries concerned. Obviously, the existing institutional arrangements have failed to eliminate personal influence in official promotions. In the first place, the role of the Party secretary concerned in candidate nomination remains ill-defined, and there is no clear consensus as to what the secretary should or should not do. Secondly, while the Party secretary has considerable leeway to adapt the centrally promulgated model to local conditions, it is unclear who has the final authority to determine which candidates should be included for consideration, thus opening the door to misconduct in the candidate nomination process. Responsible senior cadres do not appear to have violated regulations; but democratic selection often becomes a procedural facade, while the real successful candidates are determined by under-the-table deals.

Certainly, there exist serious obstacles to the monitoring of senior cadres. One important obstacle is the dependence of the monitoring work on local Party organizations. Since 1977, at every local government level, the relevant Party discipline inspection commission (*jilu jiancha weiyuanhui*) (DIC) has been given the responsibility to monitor the local leaders. The DICs are accountable to both the DIC one level up and the local Party committees, dominated by their Party secretaries. Before 1977, a local DIC was accountable totally to the local Party committee. This arrangement compromised the effectiveness of discipline inspection work, especially when "combating unhealthy tendencies" (*fan buzhengzhifeng*) is in conflict with the priorities of local Party leaders. The effectiveness of campaigns to combat unhealthy tendencies initiated by the central Party leadership is often largely determined by local support of the Party secretaries at different levels.[50] It is difficult to monitor the leading local cadres, especially the Party secretaries, because too much power is in their hands. The buying and selling of official positions does not leave much evidence for investigators. Investigation of such cases is difficult because it involves so many officials at various levels, from townships and counties even up to the central level. These officials usually reach agreements beforehand that once the investigation starts, they will cover up for each other.[51]

"A lack of supervision of top officials is still common in the government's internal structures."[52] In recent years, the Party has been trying to strengthen the supervision of local cadres and the enforcement of discipline; this is in line with the central leadership's constant concern to deter the development of local "independent kingdoms".

There are still suspicions among the general public, however, that the institutional mechanisms might not be as open and competitive as is suggested, and that very often a few key leaders have already secretly decided the candidates for promotion. The authors talked to cadres in Beijing and their views may be summarized as follows:

> Some leaders use the power of managing cadres for their private interests. Personal calculations take precedence over the Party line. They select candidates for promotion mostly based on their own interests. Unfortunately, few institutional mechanisms can stop this abuse of power. Without any supervision both from above and below, power in some leaders' hands is even used for private monetary gains, thus buying and selling official positions in some areas have become increasingly rampant.[53]

Conclusion: Consequences of Trading Official Positions

The CPC has mobilized considerable resources in recent years to enhance its political control over the process of cadre promotion. It seeks to improve personnel management by gradually reshaping the institutions that collect information, monitor the performance of local cadres, and sanction officials.[54] The network of Party organization departments, DICs and local Party committees is expected to remove cadres who do not follow central policies, who are guilty of "power-money transactions", and who are shown to be corrupt. "We must ensure the decision [to promote a cadre] should not be made by only one or two top leaders. It must be an open and democratic process. Otherwise, it will be very difficult to ensure it is fair and just," stated Wu Guangzheng, the secretary of the Central Commission for the Discipline Inspection.

The Party regime's maintenance and effective functioning to a considerable extent depend on its power to appoint cadres at all levels. However, as the above discussion demonstrates, this power is no longer highly centralized, as some academics have argued;[55] at the same time, the exercise of this power has not been institutionalized, as the official propaganda claims. The processes still leave considerable room for improper intervention by leading local cadres. Despite frequent demands and appeals for intra-Party democracy and collective leadership, the Party secretaries in the Party committees at the local level normally remain the dominant figures with decisive influence in personnel decisions.

In view of rampant corruption in China, there are naturally ample temptations on the part of cadres who seek promotion to bribe their superiors and for the latter to secure benefits through the exercise of their power and influence. As these practices spread, they gradually become a bureaucratic sub-culture, with consequent impact on the expectations of various parties concerned.[56] The cadre management system which is the foundation of the Party regime has been severely compromised; regular cadre promotion procedures have been contaminated by corruption and purchases of official positions, leading to the phenomenon of "bad cadres drive out good cadres".

The Leninist party doctrine is that cadres are the crucial determinant of party development. The Chinese leadership today accepts this principle and the people also regard it as the political reality. If corruption among cadres reaches such an extent that their promotions and career development are heavily influenced by bribery, it certainly affects people's trust and confidence in the regime as well as the regime's legitimacy. The situation has been exacerbated by the general perception that the Chinese leadership does not have the political will to combat corruption in general and the trade in official positions in particular effectively, despite the usual Party propaganda.[57]

Appendix
Interview Format

Time: April and May, 2009

Location: Beijing

Interviewer: The researcher

Interviewees: Eleven cadres from five government agencies in Beijing. Due to the sensitive nature of this research and potential risk for the interviewees, this research does not list the actual names of informants the researcher interviewed and surveyed.

Part one: Questions about the current system of cadre selection

1. What do you think about the current system of cadre selection in China? Please specify the reason?

2. What are the advantages and disadvantages of the current system of cadre selection and cadre management?

3. How does the current system of cadre selection operate in practice, for example, in the agency where you work?

4. What is, in your opinion, the effect of the current system of Chinese cadre selection?

Part Two: Questions about purchase of office in China

5. Why is the purchase of office so popular in Chinese officialdom?

6. What is the motivation of office buyers in China? Why? Please specify with an example from within your agency.

7. Why do some senior officials want to sell posts to their subordinates? Please use an example to explain.

8. What factors will affect the trade of posts in China? Why?

9. In what ways is nepotism conducive to the trade of posts? Why?

10. Any trade is interest-oriented. How do you think of it? Why?

11. Please comment on the phenomenon of office purchase, especially in the context of your agency.

12. Please list the chain of buying and selling office in China.

Part Three: Questions about measures to prevent the purchase of office in China

13. What is your opinion about how to eliminate the occurrence of office purchase in China? Why?

14. How to build the system to prevent office purchase in China? Why?

15. What is your suggestion about how to build a rightful system of cadre selection? Why?

Notes and References

1. "China punishes officials buying public posts", *BBC Monitoring Asia Pacific*, 23 January 2006, p. 1.

2. "China: senior party leader outlines criteria for official promotion", *BBC Monitoring Asia Pacific*, 15 January 2008, p. 1.

3. *Ibid.*

4. Chungyan Chow, "Cadres punished for buying and selling promotion. Corruption must make way for talent, says discipline chief," *South China Morning Post* (Hong Kong), 20 July 2006, p. 5.

5. Author's interview in Beijing, 21 April 2009.

6. Author's interview in Beijing, 10 May 2009. (interview format; if not applicable, state the reasons)

7. Huifeng He, "Shaanxi official's corruption case is the tip of iceberg", *South China Morning Post*. Hong Kong, 23 July 2006, p. 5.

8. Information from Guojizaixian: http://www.crionline.cn/ 16 July 2006 and authors' interview in Beijing, 20 April 2009.

9. "The list of 27 post trades in Shanxi Province" ("Shanxi nujutan ershiqici maiguan qingdan"), see http://www.crionline.cn. 16 July 2006.

10. *Ibid.*

11. *Ibid.*

12. *Ibid.*

13. *Ibid.*

14. Chungyan Chow, "Cadres punished."

15. Jean Tirole, "The internal organization of government," *Oxford Economic Papers*, new series, Vol. 46, No.1 (January 1994), p. 7.

16. Xiaobo Liu, "From rank-seeking to rent-seeking: changing administrative ethos and corruption in reform China," *Crime, Law and Social Change,* No. 32 (December 1999), p. 352.

17. *Ibid.*

18. Jiangnan Zhu, "Why are offices for sale in China? A case study of the office-selling chain in Heilongjiang Province," *Asian Survey*, Vol. 48, Issue 4 (July/August 2008), p. 559.

19. *Ibid.*, p. 565.

20. Author's interviews with officials in Beijing, 25 April 2009.

21. Jiangnan Zhu, "Why are offices for sale in China?" p. 565.

22. "Ma De: the trader of posts" ("Ma De: Wushamao pifashang"), http://news .sohu.com/s2005/rwmade.shtml.

23. *Ibid.*

24. Huifeng He, "Another top cadre snared as crackdown continues," *South China Morning Post*, 16 October 2009, p. 9.

25. Jiangnan Zhu, "Why are offices for sale in China?" p. 570.

26. Joseph Fewsmith, "Institutions, informal politics, and political transition in China." *Asian Survey*, Vol. 36, No.3 (1996), p. 235; Joseph Fewsmith, "The new shape of elite politics," *The China Journal* , Vol. 45 (2001), p. 87; Lowell Dittmer, "Chinese informal politics," *The China Journal* , Vol. 34 (1995), p. 21; Lowell Dittmer and Wu Yu-Shan, "The modernization of factionalism in Chinese politics," *World Politics*, 4784 (1995), p. 472; Xuezhi Guo, "Dimensions of guanxi in Chinese elite politics," *The China Journal* , Vol. 46 (2001), p. 82.

27. Jiangnan Zhu, "Why are offices for sale in China?" p. 567.

28. John P. Burns, "The People's Republic of China at 50: national political reform," *The China Quarterly*, No. 159 (1999), p. 580.

29. Wenfang Tang and William L. Parish, *Chinese Urban Life Under Reform: The Changing Social Contract (*New York: Cambridge, 2000), p. 36.

30. Central Organization Department, *Handbook (*1983), pp. 113–14.

31. Xin Zhong: *Regulations on the Work of Selecting and Appointing Leading Party and Government Cadres* (Beijing, Foreign Language Press, 2000).

32. Melanie Manion, "The cadre management system, post-Mao: the appointment, promotion, transfer and removal of party and state leaders," *The China Quarterly*, No. 102 (1985), p. 217.

33. Yasheng Huang, *Inflation and Investment Controls in China: The Political Economy of Central-Local Relations during the Reform Era* (New York: Cambridge University Press, 1996), p. 92.

34. "China: senior party leader outlines criteria for official promotion", *BBC Monitoring Asia Pacific*, London, 15 January 2008, p. 1

35. The system is the product of pilot programmes in three provinces but is still issued "on trial basis", meaning the localities are allowed to adapt it to local situations. It consists of 47 items in 9 chapters.

36. Liangping Guo, "China's new cadre evaluation system," *EAI Background Brief*, No. 324 (2007).

37. *Ibid.*

38. Tony Saich and Xuedong Yang, "Innovation in Chinese local governance: 'open recommendation and selection'," *Pacific Affairs*, Vol. 76 (2003), p. 197.

39. Manion, "The cadre management system, post-Mao," p. 211.

40. *Ibid.*, p. 207.

41. Local Party committees, for example, can meet as infrequently as once annually, see Constitution of the Communist Party of China, 1982, c. 4, art. 26.

42. John P. Burns, "China's nomenklatura system," *Problems of Communism*, Vol. 36, No. 5, 1987; *The Chinese Communist Party's Nomenklatura System: A Documentary Study of Party Control of Leadership Selection, 1979–1984* (Armonk, NY: M.E. Sharpe, 1989); and "Strengthening central CCP control of leadership selection: the 1990 nomenklatura," *The China Quarterly*, No. 138 (1994).

43. Saich and Xuedong Yang, "Innovation in Chinese local governance", p. 194.

44. Xianghan Wu, "Corruption behind cadre promotion," http://zqb.cyol.com/content/2009-09/16/content_2894591.htm.

45. Saich and Xuedong Yang, "Innovation in Chinese Local Governance," p. 192.

46. Jiangnan Zhu, "Why are offices for sale in China?" p. 578.

47. "Organization Department promulgates the trial methods of evaluating local leading teams and leading cadres", *People's Daily (Remin ribao)*, 7 July 2006, (section 10).

48. Liangping Guo, "China's new cadre evaluation system."

49. Pierre F. Landry, "Performance, markets, and the political fate of Chinese mayors," paper presented at the annual meeting of the American Political Science Association (APSA), Boston, MA, September 2002.

50. Jiangnan Zhu, "Why are offices for sale in China?" p. 573.

51. *Ibid.*

52. Huifeng He, "Shaanxi official's corruption case is the tip of iceberg", *South China Morning Post*, Hong Kong, 23 July 2006, p. 5

53. One party member in Beijing talked about buying and selling posts to the author.

54. Yasheng Huang, "Managing Chinese bureaucrats: an institutional economics perspective," *Political Studies*, Vol. 50 (2002), p. 69.

55. Harry Harding, *Organizing China: The Problem of Bureaucracy, 1949–1976* (Stanford CA: Stanford University Press, 1981), p. 76.

56. Li Yuanchao: "Buying and selling official positions will not be tolerated" ("Juebu guxi paoguan yaoguan maiguan maiguan"), See http://news.163.com/11/ 0320/06/6VIPS6D200014AED.html.

57. "Rectificating the phenomenon of 'buying and selling posts'" ("Zhongquan zhili maiguanmaiguan"), *Outlook Weekly (Liaowang Zhoukan)*, see http://news.xinhuanet.com/politics/2010-10/30/c_12719103.htm.

4

Cadre Performance Appraisal and Fabrication of Economic Achievement in Chinese Officialdom

Jun LI
Joseph Y. S. CHENG

The past three decades have witnessed the transformation of the Chinese economy from a centrally planned to a market-based economic system, a transformation that has been accompanied by significant political and social institutional changes.[1] The transition has brought about changes in the orientation and operation of governments at all levels, including cadre appraisal and promotion based on related evaluation.[2] The control of recruitment and career advancement has long been recognized as a central pillar of Chinese Communist rule, also serving as a system of social control (reward for political loyalty)[3] and a means of ensuring elite ideological conformity.[4]

In line with the impressive development of the Chinese economy, at an average annual growth rate of 9.5% over the past thirty years, the fabrication of economic achievements by local government has often been exposed by the Chinese media, gradually arousing the attention of academics and policy-makers alike. This chapter is an attempt to examine why and how Chinese local cadres fabricate their economic performance, based on a study of the theoretical literature on cadre promotion and empirical analyses of China's local governance experience. The article first reviews the literature on economic performance related to cadre promotion in China's local government authorities; then it discusses the dominant role of economic criteria in selecting candidates for promotion; thirdly, it explores the incentives for local cadres' economic achievements in terms of promotion standards; fourthly, it analyses the fabrication of economic performance among local cadres on the basis of information secured from the author's fieldwork in City H. Finally, it discusses the consequences of the predominance of economic standards in cadre promotion in China.

Economic Performance and Cadre Promotion in Local Governments

Within organizations, promotion is a powerful incentive as it determines members' career opportunities. It have thus been studied by researchers in many social science disciplines including economics,[5] politics,[6] sociology[7] and public administration.[8] For example, Andrew Walder examined the political logic underlying the construction of distinctive career paths in Chinese organizations.[9] Similarly, Zhou showed the impact of shifting state policies on varying opportunities and allocative mechanisms for managers and professionals over time.[10]

In the existing literature, most studies tend to focus on factors at the organizational level (organizational attributes) as well as at the individual level (individual characteristics).[11] In this research, two major questions have been asked. First, why do organizations use promotion to motivate employees when there appear to be other incentive schemes which are more appropriate? Second, what are the consequences of using promotion as an incentive?[12] These two questions have induced many interesting propositions in the fields of human resources management, organizational sociology, and the economics of incentives since "The Peter Principle" was put forward at the end of the 1960s.[13]

Some researchers[14] suggest that promotion-based incentive schemes are more common than monetary bonuses because there are plausible circumstances in which monetary bonuses and other incentive schemes have limited effect. In extreme cases, if employees can simply bribe managers to give them bonuses, the incentives the bonus schemes are intended to provide may be completely destroyed. Further, tournament schemes based on relative performance, which have often been assumed to be resistant to manipulation by employers, likewise lose their effectiveness if they rely on monetary bonuses or on promoting employees in rank while they continue to do the same job. On the other hand, promotion schemes that involve promoting highly performing employees to different jobs can still be effective.

Researchers observe that promotions in China are often path-dependent and regulated by organizational processes.[15] The "path" is related to the standards the organization uses to evaluate performance. In contemporary China, the criteria refer mainly to economic indicators, thus research has gradually narrowed to probe the relationship between local governments' economic performance and cadre promotion in Chinese officialdom.

Most prior studies find a significant positive relationship between government performance and political promotion in China, though the criteria of economic performance are diverse. Ho, for example, writes that rural cadres are judged primarily by their success in promoting economic development. He finds that economic targets take precedence over non-economic targets and almost 70% of composite work targets are concerned with industrial performance.[16] Fiscal revenue growth also increases the probability of cadres' promotion.[17] Lin's case study on township leaders in a city of Zhejiang Province in coastal China similarly highlights the significance of economic performance to cadres' political careers.[18] Qian and Xu have documented a significant positive correlation between the change of relative economic performance and the change of relative political position of a region, the latter measured by the ratio of the number of Party Central Committee members from the region to the region's population.[19] Likewise, using annual growth in provincial Gross Domestic Product (GDP) and average annual GDP growth rates during the periods of appointments as economic performance measures, Li and Zhou analysed the turnover rates of provincial leaders in China (1979–1995) and found that these economic performance indicators predicted their promotion and affected their tenure of office.[20] These empirical studies demonstrate that the likelihood of promotions (terminations of office) of Chinese local cadres increases (decreases) with their improved economic performance. The economic-performance–promotion nexus has thus been strengthening as the Chinese central government uses political career mobility as an incentive to motivate local officials to promote economic growth.

While a promotion scheme can certainly be used to provide incentives, there is also the risk that the incentives will distort the assignment of employees so that they may not be appointed to the jobs to which they are most suited,[21] and this may be viewed as the "negative effect of promotion". In China, government officials are preoccupied with the pursuit of higher positions by falsifying data to mark their achievements. This type of data fabrication appears to be routine in Chinese officialdom today and deserves academic attention. The difficulties involved in investigating this phenomenon have meant that there have been very limited studies so far. Are cadres in China totally motivated by economic criteria for career advancement as a result of the Chinese leadership's emphasis on economic development? This study reveals that despite some positive effects, problems have emerged due to the abuse of economic development indicators through performance fabrication for personal gain.

Economic Development Indicators and Cadre Performance Appraisal

The unique approach of Chinese cadre management has been carefully examined in the context of Chinese politics. In Western democratic countries, voters make decisions on who can be political leaders; in contrast, in China the upper levels of government, through the Organization Department and the Bureau of Personnel of the Communist Party of China (CPC), directly appoint all top officials at the subordinate level. Under the nomenclature system, all power over personnel is concentrated among the upper-level Party leadership in order to make certain that their subordinates implement Party policy. In the eyes of the Chinese leadership and some academics, "the Chinese political system seems to be able to select the 'right' people to the top level of governments".[22]

What determines the promotion of local cadres in China? Among the various approaches adopted by senior cadres, cadre appraisal and performance measurement is central, since the results of performance measurement may be used to determine the selections for promotion within the organizational human resource pools.[23] The measurement of performance of Chinese local cadres poses a challenge to the Party leadership. It becomes more severe in the context of China as a developing country in transition, where reliable data is rarely available.[24] In fact, the cadre management system in China, especially the regulations on cadre performance appraisal and selections for appointments and promotion, have changed substantially in the past decades.[25]

From the CPC's perspective, political stability and political campaigns rather than economic development were the dominant orientations of the society prior to the era of economic reform and opening to the outside world. The criterion for promotion before 1978 was mainly political loyalty, which was relied upon to maintain political legitimacy and social stability.[26]

From 1978 the task of economic development became dominant (*jingjiyadaoyiqie*), and it determined the logic of political promotions in China until the late 1990s.[27] How to motivate government officials and Party cadres to contribute to economic development became a key issue.[28] As a unitary state, the Chinese government system is hierarchical; higher-level units of the Party-state organization can conduct evaluations of the performance of lower-level units. Control of local cadres' careers linked with their economic performance could therefore be used as both a carrot and a stick to induce better local coordination and implementation of central policy.

Political loyalty and conformity to the Party line, which was the only important pre-reform criterion for appraisal and promotion of cadres, gave way to economic performance and other competence-related indicators,[29] although political loyalty to the Party's ideology was still the major factor in determining who should be promoted. In practice, measurement of cadres' loyalty to the Party was simplified to economic achievement based on the following reasoning: economic reform and development were the most important tasks for the maintenance of the Party's legitimacy and effective governance, all of the Party's work should therefore be oriented to these subjects. Top leaders usually screen candidates for promotion on the basis of political reliability and economic performance.

To alter the behavioural propensities of local government cadres in line with the Party's objectives, the authorities altered their incentive structure.[30] The "Regulations on the Work of Selecting and Appointing Leading Party and Government Cadres (*Dangzheng Lingdao Ganbu Xuanbarenyong Gongzuo Tiaoli*)" specifies that cadres should be determined "to carry out the reform and opening-up policy, be devoted to the cause of [national] modernization, and work hard for the building of socialism and the accomplishing of concrete achievements".[31] In 2006, the CPC Central Organization Department promulgated the "Trial Methods of Comprehensive Cadre Evaluation that Embodies the Requirements of the Scientific Outlook of Development (*Tixian Kexue Fazhanguan Yaoqiu de Defang Dangzheng Lingdaobanzi he Lingdao Ganbu Zonghe Kaohe Pingjia Shixing Banfa*)*" as the institutional framework for managing leading cadres and the basis of cadre selection and promotion during the second term of the Hu-Wen leadership. The "Trial Methods", in the Party's terminology, adopts the concept of "scientific development" as the important guiding ideology and standard for evaluating, assessing and appointing cadres. It upholds the principles of both moral integrity and ability, emphasizes actual performance and public recognition by the masses; and demands the application of such specific methods as democratic recommendation, democratic test and appraisal, public opinion polls, analyses of actual performance, individual discussions, and comprehensive assessment in evaluating and assessing cadres in an all-round way.[32] The document calls for measures to be adopted to ensure cadres are selected on their merits and that they are outstanding in political integrity and professional competence. Nevertheless, the superior Party committee still has the final say in personnel decisions; more specifically, it is the Organization Department at the appropriate level that submits information and report as it is in charge of the personnel dossiers (*dang'an*) and the evaluation materials on the cadres concerned.

Cadre evaluation consists of four main parts: political background (*shencha*); assessment made by the cadre's unit (*jianding*); screening, which has to include the opinion of the masses (*kaocha liaojie*); and the evaluation of competence as part of the cadre management responsibility system (*kaohe*). The meaning of competence here is multifaceted: the cadre's virtue (*de*), ability (*neng*), work attitude (*qin*), achievements (*ji*), and cleanliness, i.e., being free from corruption (*lian*), are all considered.[33]

The cadre responsibility system is a straightforward process in which cadres are rewarded for good performance – financially in the form of bonuses, and politically in the form of promotion. The "Trial Methods" demands analysis of the actual performance of the leading teams of local Party and government organizations as well as individual members of the leading teams. This is based mainly on information concerning the general conditions of economic and social development provided by the relevant parties as well as the opinions of the masses, and focuses on analysis of the cadres' ideas, inputs, and work results during their tenure. Specifically the analysis should include comprehensive statistical data and assessment opinions provided by the statistical departments at higher levels on local per capita GDP and its growth rates, per capita financial revenue and its growth rates, urban and rural residents' incomes and their growth rates, consumption of resources and production safety records, basic education, urban employment, social security, urban and rural cultural life, population and family planning, protection of farmland and other resources, environmental protection, scientific and technological inputs and innovations; as well as conclusions and assessment opinions provided by the audit departments at higher levels, including the masses' assessment.

Indicators have been developed and defined to govern the above areas. There are also specific items to be included, which are largely left to the discretion of local authorities to adjust to local conditions. Among all these areas, economic performance is generally considered to be of increasing weight when assessing cadres for promotion;[34] and the economic performance criteria are powerfully skewed towards GDP growth. The economic evaluation system of Chinese cadres has been formalized throughout the country since the release of the "Trial Methods".

Economic performance is easy to measure and manipulate. The Chinese system employs relative performance evaluation and thus strengthens the incentive effect.[35] Past economic performance of cadres serves as an important indicator of their potential competence, guiding promotion decisions at the upper levels; and this in turn is perceived as the underlying logic for incentive arrangement and personnel management.[36] The implication of the new "cadre evaluation and appointment system"[37] naturally has a significant political and economic impact, as it reflects a set of ideological orientations and values. As the performance evaluation system concerns the vital interests of all cadres, the re-designing of the evaluation system presents a window of opportunity for a redistribution of power. Bureaucratic in-fighting to some extent is inevitable and already underway, and the conceptual ambiguities and technical controversies concerning GDP are conveniently exploited for political purposes. With the clear emphasis on economic development, the tendency has been to appoint cadres to positions of authority and responsibility more on the basis of GDP growth than other indicators. For instance, in rural Jiangsu the slogan "Those unable to get rich won't be elected village cadres; those incapable of leading everybody towards wealth are not good cadres" soon became popular.[38] Economic achievement becomes the principal criterion to measure the competence or incompetence of local cadres.

The CPC's meritocratic standard still demands the enthusiastic implementation of the Party line. The emphasis on GDP growth is directly linked to the core issue of the Party line which considers economic growth as the principal task of the Party and the foundation of the Party regime's legitimacy. Successful implementation of the CPC line has led to the almost double-digit average economic growth rates of China during the past three decades, and it has also generated side effects in the social and environmental arenas. The enforcement of economic-based performance evaluation in China's officialdom has been facilitated by a number of institutional features. First, personnel control is centralized at the central government, and the economic performance of local leaders has become a crucial indicator in personnel evaluations. Second, local officials have substantial influence over the local economy through their control over key economic resources, including land, credit, and power over local economic policies such as taxation and government spending. Because of their direct powerful influence on the local economy, local officials are held responsible for local economic performance.

Economic performance indicators are the most important but not the only factors determining upward mobility for Chinese officials. One's ability and demonstrable career achievements (*zhengji*) matter. Economic-oriented promotion criteria for local cadres are dynamic; they must be presented in the context of political loyalty, and public service. Although they are not conflicting objectives, economic growth, social development and environment protection have variable priorities during different phases of reform, which imply that local cadres must not neglect the latter two; at least they must avoid major blunders in the latter two areas.

"What's measured is what matters."[39] The cadre performance evaluation system sends signals of policy orientations from the upper-level authorities and creates incentives for lower levels of government to follow orders. Local government officials realize that their promotions are largely determined by their economic performance.

Cadre performance is, however, always a qualitative concept and involves a comprehensive assessment of the achievements and contribution of the local government agency concerned. Performance evaluation based on a small number of quantitative indicators cannot be satisfactory; even if a comprehensive range of indicators can be developed, it is still difficult to achieve complete, accurate and reliable assessment. Emphasis on economic growth is still the tradition in the People's Republic of China, even in the era of "politics in command" (*zhengzhi guashuai*). Computerization and the promotion of e-government have certainly reinforced the tendency.

Guidance Target and Performance Contract

The emphasis on economic performance in cadre appraisal is a core principle; its operation requires some concrete strategies. The Target Responsibility System, which is the principal form of monitoring local cadres' performance, constitutes the main tool.[40]

The centralization of the appointment and monitoring of local cadres is probably the most important mechanism for the Party to stay in power. The central leadership has to accomplish the monitoring of local cadres by stipulating policy targets and evaluating cadre performance on the basis of how well or poorly these policy targets are achieved. As explained by Li Yuanchao, a member of the Politburo of the CPC Central Committee and Head of the Party Central Organization Department, "We should gain a thorough understanding of the importance and urgency of personnel reform regarding cadres; [and] act in accordance with the guiding ideology, guiding principles, as well as targets and tasks put forward in the 'Programme Outline'."[41]

Performance evaluation through target contracts in the Chinese government setting is "used chiefly to ensure that local officials comply with higher-level policy priorities" and "by binding local officials' target accomplishments to their future careers, the target-based responsibility system guarantees that local officials will follow the directives that come down from above".[42] With regard to tasks and targets, planning is still practised in China. Top-down policy targets are favoured because the Chinese government, both before and after the economic reforms of the late 1970s, has behaved essentially like a developmental state that is strongly motivated to realize economic progress to ensure its political legitimacy. Hence, various levels of government all have incentives to push their subordinates to demonstrate economic and social development through "objective" measurements. [43] Earlier accounts of this performance evaluation system have described it as a straightforward process in which local cadres worked towards fulfilling their performance targets and were rewarded financially as well as politically.[44]

In the reform era, guidance targets have gradually replaced mandatory targets from higher levels of government. In order to secure their own career success, senior government leaders often assign impractical targets to their subordinates. Local government cadres are frequently instructed to take up newly-designated "guiding targets" in addition to their routine administrative duties. These targets may be flagged as policy priorities, identified for immediate action or extra attention. Guiding targets are specified in the five-year and one-year plans that filter down level by level to subordinate cadres,[45] which are then written down in the individual responsibility documents (*gangwei zerenshu*) of all cadres. These individual documents may be regarded as performance contracts between the higher-level cadres and their subordinates, as part of the cadre management responsibility system.[46] Performance contracts are thus in place, with different contracts for different fields including industrial development, agricultural development, tax collection, family planning, and social order. These contracts are drawn up between the leading cadre and his or her immediate subordinates, and are signed either by the Party secretary or government unit head, depending on the contents of the contracts. In these performance contracts, leading cadres are assigned performance targets (*kaohe zhibiao*) which are internally ranked in importance: there are soft targets (*yiban zhibiao*), hard targets (*ying zhibiao*) and priority targets with veto power (*yipiao fojue*).[47]Soft targets are usually those that are difficult to measure and quantify, and policies that are not deemed important by the higher levels of government, such as cultural and social development. Hard targets are typically drawn from the economic and social development plan.[48]

Priority targets[49] with veto power (*yi piao fou jue*) is an institutional tool exclusively used for key policies of the central government and sometimes also for key policies of local government. The veto means failure to meet this important target and would bring no credit at all for the cadre's entire annual performance, irrespective of how well he or she had performed in other areas.[50] All targets play an equal role in the evaluation in terms of bonuses, but attainment of hard targets and priority targets are important for personnel decisions. From the ranking of targets, it can be deduced that under normal circumstances, the Party accords priority to the economic development of localities,[51] especially the annual GDP growth. Local cadres are given more autonomy in choosing the means to achieve the targets given them by their superiors, and economic incentives are provided to improve efficiency. While higher levels of government are not concerned with details like what products to produce, output quota, etc., performance targets are given for general economic indicators. Specific targets vary among areas, depending on local conditions and last year's performance, but the contents of targets remain much the same. For example, in the plan of a township the authors investigated in City H, comprehensive targets were given to the township government including: grain output, per capita income level, growth rate of industry, foreign exchange earnings, and level of foreign investment.[52] It is a well established fact that lower-level cadres and managers have stronger incentives to perform well economically; they are more economically oriented.

A local cadre is evaluated by his or her superior at the end of each year on the basis of how well the performance targets have been fulfilled. The two main incentives are bonuses and promotion prospects. There are two kinds of evaluation: one called work evaluation (*gongzuo kaohe*) which is related to bonuses, and the other is mainly an evaluation of ability and attitude which are related to promotion in position and rank. The two are separate evaluations but with some overlap.[53] The first kind of evaluation is carried out on a collective basic and is linked to the cadre's personal income. It is the overall performance that is evaluated and this determines whether the leaders in charge have fulfilled the work targets of the plan given to them. In a county in southern Jiangsu which the author visited, it was coordinated by the Party bureau of rural affairs and bonuses were calculated on the basis of a large number of targets.[54] The second kind of evaluation is related to appointment and promotion decisions, and therefore is carried out at the individual level. Promotion is probably the most important incentive for local cadres, and is linked to economic performance but also to other criteria. The Party committee still formally exercises the power to make appointment decisions at the next level down in the administrative hierarchy according to the nomenclature list.

Financial incentives are thus pegged to local cadres' work performance. There are so-called bottom lines that local cadres cannot fail to meet. Among the most important targets are: GDP growth, amount of profits, foreign investment and trade. If local cadres cannot fulfil these work targets secured by the state-oriented enterprises (SOE) under their jurisdiction, they will very likely not be able to keep their positions; at least that they cannot be promoted. The CPC spells out its economic targets, and the implementation of these targets weighs much more heavily than other policies in the evaluation of local leaders. There is a strong link between promoting economic development and work targets set by the superior concerned. In the first place, developing the local economy and promoting growth are work targets in themselves. Further, promoting economic development is essential to the fulfilment of other work targets such as providing welfare and so on. While it is recognized that local governments promote economic growth partly because they need the revenue, there is less consideration regarding what the revenue is needed for. The higher level government employs concrete performance criteria to determine each official's remuneration, tenure of office, and opportunity for advancement. [55] Above all, local economic performance is the most important criterion in the higher level officials' assessment of lower-level officials.

The management of economic performance behind career incentives is actually in the hands of upper levels of government, challenging the concept of downward accountability (*duixia fuze*) while creating much more room for upward accountability (*duishang fuze*). Local cadres understand that what matters most is the satisfaction of their superiors. In the words of a senior cadre, "performance can lead to promotion, but what matters is not so much to let ordinary people but the superior see the performance".[56] As Chinese government officials are all politically appointed rather than elected by the people, they are held accountable only to their superiors, and not to the general public. This upward accountability means that cadres would always be more sensitive to demands from the top, rather than requests from the bottom.[57] According to a recent poll conducted by Horizon Research, 54% of respondents believed that government officials cared more about currying favour with their superiors than serving ordinary people, and only 24.5% of them said otherwise.[58] Local officials are well aware that their "careers depend on their superiors within the CPC".[59] They do not have to rely on voters' support to maintain their positions as do their counterparts in Western countries, but a cadre has to "follow closely both his patron and his patron's faction, since they are the source of his authorities".

By setting the economic performance indicators, the central or upper-level authorities are able to play a very important role in intervening in and directing local development. The behaviour of local government is determined to a large extent by the evaluation indicators. Unfortunately, it is likely that the latter may not be consistent with local needs. According to an article in an official Chinese journal, some of the targets that come from the higher levels of government are impossible to reach; but since the leaders demand them, the lower levels of government simply apply more pressure. Plan indicators sent down by the superiors are ultimately reflected in statistical figures returned upwards.[60]

As the performance of local government officials at every level is evaluated according to a series of indicators imposed from above, in the process of political competition for promotion across all regions, local government officials understandably compete against each other to fulfil and over-fulfil the policy targets.[61] The economic-centred performance evaluation system, on which the cadre selection and appointment system depends, encourages the expansionary impulse to promote local economic growth.[62] It also encourages inter-regional competition and provides strong incentives for regional cadres to compete with each other in terms of regional economic performance, which is reinforced by the use of relative performance evaluation by the central government. While cadres prefer to avoid fabricating their performance, they are aware that if their competitors falsify data to boost their achievements, their own chances of being promoted will suffer. To avoid falling behind, each cadre is strongly motivated to fabricate his or her economic performance record, intentionally or unintentionally. For this reason, China suffers from an epidemic of false reporting of economic information, including official statistics on provincial economic growth.

Fabrication of Economic Achievement in Local Government

It is said that an official who does not know how to tell lies to his superior does not know how to secure promotion.[63] In China today, two kinds of fabrication of economic achievement in practice are frequently found in local government. The first is so-called "image projects"[64] (*xingxiang gongcheng*). In an interview conducted during fieldwork in the summer of 2009, a middle-aged township cadre in City H talked about how the city government initiated "image projects" to demonstrate its "performance":[65]

> I worked in a township government for eleven years and finally became the administrative chief of the town. The setting of the government's performance evaluation indicators at the township level deviates far from the actual practice in many areas, forcing the township cadres to engage in fraud to some degree. Take building biomass pools in our town for example. It is a beneficial thing to build biomass pools providing farmers with bio-fuel and saving energy costs. However there is a premise: farmers have to rear pigs. Many farmers in our township are unwilling to have pigs and [hence] there is simply no raw material for biomass pools. The city government, however, ordered our township to build at least 41 pools in a year. In addition to the funds allocated from the higher-level government, building a biomass pool requires 600 *yuan* [which had to be] paid from the township's finances which were already in a difficult situation. The biomass pools are of no use except as an "image project" for inspection from above.[66]

Among other political "image projects" in City H are an airport, a large power plant, and development of the cattle industry. Despite objections from the local people, the city government allocated several thousand *mu* of land to build an international airport costing 390 million *yuan*, which became a heavy burden on local finance because of its serious losses. The power plant, on which construction commenced in 1999 with a massive initial investment of several hundred million *yuan*, is known as the "most heartbreaking work" in City H. This power plant project was suspended until 2002 when the plan was revised because of the city's financial difficulties. Development of the cattle industry was a project very much boasted of by the government of City H, which convened a national conference on this topic. The route to the venue of this meeting went along a section of the provincial road (*shengdao*) stretching for ten miles. Just a few days before the meeting, city government officials ordered the rural people along the road to set up many cattle lots for the inspection of the higher authorities. Those who did not own cattle had no choice but to rent them at the cost of ten *yuan* per head per day. They had to spend almost two hundred *yuan* to build each lot, even though their per capita annual income was no more than several hundred *yuan*. City H, once the largest market for cattle trade in the region with an annual volume of more than two million head, actually had a stock of only a few hundred thousand in 2006.

The "image projects" in City H also featured the world's largest zoo, a project which would cover hundreds of acres of land to raise 1,000 tigers and crocodiles. To publicize this project, the city government mobilized tens of thousands of cadres, teachers and students to take part in the voluntary work of building the zoo, which occupied much fertile land. In the absence of well-planned design and financial support, the three-year project had to stop halfway with ten million *yuan* wasted.

> In our city, image projects are initiated usually after the replacement of the leading cadres. New officials who are eager to establish a performance record often "apply strict measures" (*xinguan shangren san ba huo*) to certain projects to attract media attention. The city government in policy implementation usually relies on massive campaigns or other mobilization approaches to complete the image projects. By highlighting the government's determination, mobilization campaigns help to overcome public resistance. Moreover, by placing political pressures on local officials to fulfil targets, mobilization is a convenient bureaucratic tool to overcome bureaucratic inertia.[67]

In practice, local officials in China, in order to demonstrate to their political superiors their competence and achievements and to secure rapid promotion, are often inclined to spend large sums of public funds on grand projects or programmes. While some of these image projects may benefit local economic development, many are ineffective or a waste of money. Worse still, they tend to aggravate local financial woes and impose a burden on local people with various fees and levies. These image projects usually also mean less money for improving social welfare.

The second type of economic achievement fabrication in China is fraud in economic statistics, especially GDP statistics. In City H, many township cadres confessed that they had to fabricate some statistical indicators about local economic development to meet the demands of higher authorities. A township government head in City H thus complained:[68]

> What is performance? Performance is infrastructure and investment. In our city, the government uses these two criteria to judge the performance of local cadres. Many infrastructure projects are going on, regardless of the actual local needs. Concerning absorbing foreign investment, the government assigns quotas to the heads of every town. As long as a town head attracts funds from the outside, no matter how poorly he performed in the past, he would be qualified for various awards and promotion. For example, in 2006 the city government established the item of absorbing investment project funding of more than 5 million *yuan*, including at least one foreign-funded project, as the indicator to assess township cadre performance.
>
> It was difficult for a township like ours in a remote rural area without any convenient transport facilities to attract foreign investment, but we reported that we successfully established three and four foreign investment projects in 2005 and 2006 respectively. The performance assessment programme stipulated very specific measures, including checking the enterprise business licences, tax certificates, and even inspections on the spot. To conceal the fact that we had cheated, our township had to invite a rich tycoon from City H to provide a variety of supporting

documents issued on behalf of our township government. Then we led the inspection team to a temporary construction site to check the projects that we had attracted. In order to conceal the true data, we even distributed documents to the local people enumerating methods to fool the inspection team sent by the city government. Even though the inspection team was well aware of our tricks, it was reluctant to expose our fraud because it knew the indicator demanded by the higher authorities was unrealistic.[69]

We are aware of the danger of fraud. But if we reported the true information to the superiors, we might be subject to criticisms, fines and even dismissals; On the other hand, those who have falsified data to the higher authorities may be praised, rewarded, and even promoted. There is a certain demonstration effect: if officials who lie may be promoted, how can others not imitate? The economy of our township several years ago ranked twelfth among a total of twenty-one townships in the county, and the township leaders were discredited by a few county leaders, which resulted in the economic indicators being overstated in our township in the following year's evaluation.[70]

Under the pressure to achieve the assigned targets, cadres in some regions have relied on deception to please their superiors:

Take peasants' annual income as an example, rural people in our township account for 95% of the total population of 19,000 people, with arable land per capita amounting to 0.87 *mou*, and the annual income mainly from agricultural products. Peasants living in our township by comparison enjoy a per capita income far behind that of other townships in the city. However, the reported per capita net income of peasants in our township surprisingly reached 4,300 *yuan* in 2005 and more than 4,600 *yuan* in 2006, which were at the leading position within City H. In fact, the peasants have little cash available, with an average of less than 600–700 *yuan* per capita per annum. Each year most peasants have no more money left after deducting the payments for pesticides, fertilizers and children's tuition fees. The reported high figures of peasants' per capita net income are mainly out of the consideration to achieve the "well-off" (*xiaokang*) evaluation criterion and to meet the higher-level authorities "political needs".[71]

The overstating of peasants' per capita net income results in pressures on the self-construction fund which exceeds the actual affordability of the population.

When the higher levels of government emphasize the GDP indicator, local officials have adopted a variety of ways to inflate the GDP figures, regardless of whether this growth has improved people's welfare or not. Wang Huaizhong, the former mayor of Fuyang in Anhui Province, who fabricated wildly inflated GDP figures, provides a good example. Wang asked his subordinates at the county level to report economic indicators and output values within their administration at the beginning of each year. Accurate reports encountered Wang's harsh criticism and personal insults, while reports that inflated the statistics would be praised and their writers often rewarded. In drafting Fuyang's Ninth Five-Year Plan (1996–2000), Wang did not take into account the real level of economic development in the region, but pursued sensational publicity marked by reports of high GDP growth. For example, the Planning Commission of Fuyang began by putting forward annual GDP increases of 13%, but Wang thought they were "too low" and rejected the proposal. In response, the Planning Commission changed the projected GDP growth to 15% per annum reluctantly, but Wang was still unsatisfied and finally the GDP growth was set at 22% per annum during the Ninth Five-Year Plan. However, the GDP growth rate in Fuyang only reached 4.7% even in 2002, which was far below the projected figure. As reported in 1997, the GDP in Fuyang had already reached 400 billion *yuan* and its fiscal revenue nearly 3 billion. But the fact, real GDP in Fuyang amounted to only 20.9 billion *yuan* and fiscal revenue was only 1.78 billion *yuan* even in 2002.[72]

Experience has shown that every cadre would like to be perceived as "serving the benefit of local people during his tenure" (*wei guan yiren zaofu yifang*). It is a common phenomenon in China that local government leaders go for a "quick economic fix" with the hope of faster and better development. Given the vastness of China, the central government does not have the resources and time to investigate the accuracy of local government reports. Central government officials certainly examine local government reports carefully to gain an understanding of what really happens in the localities and they naturally hold the following attitude: "All the statistics reported are discussed and passed in a meeting of the respective Party Standing Committee and government leaders, there is no reason not to believe their statistical reports."[73] What subordinates report is typically what the higher-level authorities demand. Obviously, the final statistics reported are designed to emphasize the excellent performance of the subordinate.

Local governments tend to believe that no figures are impossible in their economic reports; and playing with numbers becomes a "compulsory" skill for most local officials. In 2005, a Party secretary of a township in Ningbo City, Zhejiang Province, ordered his statisticians to make a false statement about gross industrial output value which was claimed to be 463 million *yuan*, in excess of the actual value by about 75%.[74] Earlier, at the end of 2001, the Jiangsu Provincial Bureau of Statistics, the Supervision Department and the Justice Department jointly carried out a law-enforcement inspection, and discovered that over a third of the local government units in Jiangsu had falsified statistics in order to seek political advancement.[75]

In the eyes of local government officials the political risk of falsifying statistics is very low.

> Compared with other types of fraud, digital fraud is least costly. Once the lie was passed, the benefits would be astonishingly impressive: making a fortune and securing promotion. An official who received a bribe of four million *yuan* would be sentenced to death, but an official who overstated the local GDP by four billion *yuan* would only be lightly punished.[76]

The upward accountability system exacerbates the information asymmetry problem inherent in a hierarchical structure. In any political system, local governments tend to distort the information that they pass on to their political superiors in order to place themselves in a good light. In China, as the general public can hardly oversee the activities of government organs, lower-level officials can deceive higher-level authorities more easily than their counterparts in liberal democracies.[77]

Consequences of Emphasizing Economic Criteria for Upward Career Mobility

The Cult of GDP

Gross Domestic Product (GDP) indicates the aggregate macro-economic output of the economy in a certain period of time. In the eyes of some local officials in China, however, GDP represents the achievement of the leadership, the most important demonstration of their work performance, and even their opportunities for promotion. Cadre promotion in China is becoming increasingly competitive in the bureaucratic cultural context; and securing promotion is the central incentive among local cadres to enhance regional economic growth and social development in the process of fiscal decentralization.[78] Local officials in China have therefore devoted tremendous attention and energy to promoting regional economic growth, an enthusiasm that is relatively rare in other transitioning or developing countries.[79]

Local government officials in China have a keen interest in keeping GDP levels high for two reasons. First, over the past decade and a half, GDP growth rates have been serving as the main criterion in the evaluation of the achievements of local officials, especially in terms of promotion or demotion. When "economic growth" becomes the key measure of local governments' "achievements", it is not difficult to understand why officials obsessed with promotion are enthusiastic about GDP growth. It is relatively easy for the local cadre to demonstrate his or her individual performance concerning the economy; this performance may be compared and it facilitates a sensible link between economic performance evaluations. One revealing indication of the importance of economic performance for local officials is their obsession with economic ranking among peers.[80] The expansionary impulse of local governments is a direct consequence of this "GDP cult" among local cadres as well as the central government's emphasis on economic growth in the past two decades. Second, local officials themselves make a great deal of money from infrastructure and property development projects. GDP has become the main pursuit of most local officials. Local officials trapped in the performance bind are in turn obsessed with promoting GDP growth by such projects regardless of the risk, efficiency and financial expenditure that these projects may entail. Government officials in regions short of resources and without comparative geographical advantages and other support may also be tempted to overstate their GDP figures.

The "GDP cult" may also be exacerbated by what is known as "yardstick competition" wherein jurisdictions are compared and evaluated by higher-level governments in accordance with a set of standardized performance criteria, which may or may not include some measurement of local citizen satisfaction.[81] In this way the upward accountability leads to problems of "selective policy implementation", i.e., cadres conscientiously enforce unpopular policies preferred by their superiors, while refusing to carry out other measures that local residents would welcome but which would be overlooked by their superiors.[82]

More importantly, quotas ultimately create a result-oriented bureaucracy in which only closely monitored targets are met and all other considerations are secondary to the attainment of assigned targets. Local cadres may have to resort to unusual, sometimes extreme, measures in order to produce the desired results. This only perpetuates the current spending-for-growth cycle.

The "cult of GDP" is a serious problem if China even wants to think of introducing policies to achieve sustainable development. The prevalence of fabrication of GDP figures among grassroots government officials leads to inefficient investment. The concern of the central government is that local government officials, in pursuit of their own interests, tend to ignore the demands of the local people. As the responsibilities of local governments are dictated from above, the cost of policy implementation is often not known to the upper-level of government. Various phenomena of soft-budget constraints among local governments prevail, and the focus on GDP often creates convenient excuses for local officials to pursue self interest, and seek bribes which cannot be monitored easily by the upper-level authorities. Local officials have often managed to find ways to overspend through illicit taxation, borrowing, and the requisitioning of farmland at low prices and then reselling it or letting it out for more lucrative development projects.[83]

This focus on GDP on the part of local governments is the consequence of the GDP-centred cadre performance evaluation system, on which the careers of local cadres depend. Shooting for the highest possible growth figures is the principal game of local rivalries. Leaders of local government authorities try hard to demonstrate results before their terms end, and the proven way to achieve this is more projects and more investment. The proliferation of the so-called "task economy", "term economy" and "landmark projects" where valuable resources are squandered has been the root cause of economic overheating. The problem is further aggravated by the fact that all levels of government in China are growth-driven. Since the reforms of the early 1990s, local governments across China have initiated new waves of urban expansion, establishing new development zones, building ambitious industrial parks and urban residential projects, and expropriating rural land at below-market prices. In this process of accelerated urbanization, millions of peasants have lost their land without adequate compensation, resulting in widespread complaints and social unrest.[84]

Digital government management demands many statistics for analysis. However, the blind pursuit of GDP growth at the expense of local ecology, environment, and humanitarian concerns tends to ignore people's interests and distort officials' behaviour. The emphases on scale expansion, quantity and speed often results in blind investment and loose approval procedures for projects. If governments at all levels evaluate their officials by indicators which lack adequate scientific basis, the results of the assessment exercise are distorted and generate adverse consequences.

Figures Are Paramount in Cadre Promotions (*shuzi chu guan*)

China has always been a "bureaucracy-oriented" society with priority accorded to an orderly hierarchy in which power is heavily concentrated in the official; the corresponding "official standard" (*guan ben wei*) means measuring the social status of a person in terms of the rank of his or her official position. This hierarchical and bureaucratic politics over thousands of years has generated a kind of quasi-religious devotion to and admiration of bureaucratic positions.

Power is the most cost-effective public good from the perspective of input-output ratio. Officials of the Party-machinery as state representatives of the people can easily manipulate the machinery to dispose of public resources and exercise bureaucratic authority to control the destiny of a large population. So it is natural for people to seek official positions and then promotions in the hierarchical bureaucracy, in pursuit of personal aspirations, honour, and even family fortunes.

For government officials, there is little opportunity for career advancement outside the bureaucracy. The "official standard" easily leads to careerism, i.e., their dedication is neither to the state and the people, nor to their responsibility and integrity, but only to gaining rank and titles. Hence, all the "economic achievement figures", true or spurious, are oriented to moving up the bureaucratic hierarchy, which in turn consumes officials' time, energy, experience and wisdom. In drafting development plans, the most important things that local governments consider are economic growth, their GDP rankings and their relative competitiveness against each other.

The "figures" originally come from officials, and naturally it is convenient and tempting for them to fake them. Over-reliance and over-emphasis on "economic achievement figures" in cadre performance evaluation and in promotion considerations therefore are responsible for the phenomenon that "figures are paramount in cadre promotions", and the latter in turn creates the temptation to falsify economic statistics. The authors encountered the case of a county magistrate in southeast China who was promoted to be the head of a prefecture mainly because of the impressive figures of local economic development. [85] In Chinese officialdom, there is thus a strong perception that fabrication of statistics is an easy means to secure political status, honours, promotions and economic returns. "It often happens that local governments interfere with the accounting work to make the figures look better than they are." According to a grass-roots official in a township in Zhumadian, a city in central China's Henan province, his colleagues have been almost numb to GDP indicators and have never carefully compiled GDP statistics; all the economic indicators they report to the higher levels of government are arbitrary.[86] Officials who are deft at playing with statistics can expect to have smooth careers.

Conclusion

There is a saying among people in China today: "Villages coax townships; townships coax counties; and counties coax provinces".[87] The National Bureau of Statistics has acknowledged that its investigation uncovered massive inaccuracies in China's economic data, much of it done by local officials who inflated economic growth statistics to advance their careers.[88] These spurious statistics present a serious challenge: higher-level authorities find it difficult to know what really happens below, the data upon which their decisions depend obviously are not reliable and may not lead to correct policy decisions. Attempts to evaluate officials' performance mainly by economic indicators are too idealistic. Officials are well aware that local economic achievements and the local GDP growth rates attract their impressive attention for promotion opportunities in the final analysis. Economic figures have gradually become the starting point and destination for all work. As long as the numbers look good, the cost of achieving these figures is irrelevant. Such a blind pursuit of major economic indicators is absolutely incompatible with long-term economic and sustainable development; the future costs to the nation may be huge.

To stop these malpractices, a more scientific promotion system should be created to evaluate the performance of officials. A more reasonable promotion system for government officials will help to control the fabrication of GDP indicators that is so prevalent in local government. A new or modified cadre evaluation system was released by the Political Bureau of the CPC Central Committee in 2009, in line with the launch of the "Scientific Outlook on Development" by the CPC Central Committee in 2004.[89] As explained by Li Yuanchao:

> We should standardize the system for the promotion, appointment, and nomination of cadres; and make sure that the mainstay of the system is clearly defined, relevant procedures are scientifically set, and responsibilities are stated in unambiguous terms. We should improve and perfect the mechanism for the assessment and evaluation of Party and government leading bodies as well as leading cadres, making sure that the mechanism contributes to promoting the country's scientific development; and should devote great efforts to making the assessment and evaluation work more scientific.[90]

The cadre performance appraisal system and its emphasis on economic indicators did not start with the Hu Jintao–Wen Jiabao administration, but the trends have been reinforced in the past decade. In recent years, there has certainly been an increasing awareness of the importance of sustainable development and the adverse effects of the over-emphasis on investment in infrastructural projects. In this connection, there are various proposals to adopt "green" indicators to better reflect the quality of economic growth and the achievements in environmental protection among local governments. In the Eleventh Five-Year Plan (2011–2015), the promotion of a low-carbon economy has emerged as a priority goal. Hence, while economic growth indicators remain significant in the evaluation of local cadre performance, considerably more attention has been paid to the transformation from the extensive mode to the intensive mode of development and to environmental protection. It is likely that priority targets with veto power concerning environmental protection and energy conservation may apply to local cadre performance appraisal in the near future.

There are obvious limitations too. Despite the promotion of sustainable development in the past of the top leadership, most money still goes to infrastructural projects, especially high-speed railways even after Premier Wen Jiabao introduced his four trillion *yuan* economic stimulus package in late 2008. Despite the talk of more spending on low-cost housing, education, medical care and health, the proportion of money from the package going to the improvement of social services remains small. Vested interests are very difficult to overcome, and changing the values and the mentality of the bureaucracy is time-consuming.

Returning to the incentive structure, local leaders realize that major projects are prominent showcases of their achievements; in comparison, improvements in local education and medical services will take much more time to accomplish and are more difficult to demonstrate to their superiors. However, infrastructural projects generate opportunities for corruption and rewards for supporters, family members and so on. There are signs that public opinion surveys will be used more frequently in cadre performance appraisal, and this is perhaps the most effective tool against fabrication of economic achievement.

Appendix
Interview Format

Date:

Interviewer:

Interviewee:

Part One: Questions about the current system of cadre performance appraisal

1. What do you think about the current system of cadre performance appraisal? Why?

2. What are the advantages and disadvantages of the current system of cadre performance appraisal?

3. How does the current system of cadre performance appraisal operate in practice, for example, in the agency where you work?

4. What is, in your opinion, the effect of the current system of Chinese cadre performance appraisal?

Part Two: Questions about GDP as the index of cadre performance appraisal

5. Do you think it is reasonable to use GDP as the index of performance appraisal? Why?

6. "The higher the GDP, the better the odds for cadre promotion". What do you think of that? Why?

7. In what ways is the GDP appraisal index conducive to the rising phenomenon of the "GDP cult" in China? Why?

8. Do you think that fabrication by cadres is relevant to GDP index? Why?

9. What do you consider to be the most significant elements in judging cadre performance in China?

Part Three: Questions about performance fabrication in practice

10. How do some cadres fabricate their performance, for example, in the government agency where you work?

11. Why are some cadres inclined to fabricate their performance in China? Please use examples to explain.

12. What is your suggestion for eliminating performance fabrication in Chinese officialdom? Why?

Notes and References

1. Wang Shaoguang. "Changing models of China's policy agenda setting," *Modern China*, 34(1) (2008), pp. 56–87.

2. Richard Walker and Wu Jiannan. "Performance evaluation in Chinese city governments: an examination of future prospects," 2009 IPMN/GSPA Conference, Seoul.

3. Andrew G. Walder. "Career mobility and communist political order," *American Sociological Review*, 60(3) (1995), pp. 309–328.

4. Walter Connor. "Workers, politics, and class consciousness," in A. Kahan and B. Ruble (eds.), *Industrial Labor in the USSR* (New York: Pergamon, 1979), pp. 313–332.

5. Sonja Opper and Stefan Brehm, "networks versus performance: political leadership promotion in China," 2007, http://www.isnie.org/assets/files/papers2007/opper.pdf.

6. Bo Zhiyue, *Chinese Provincial Leaders: Economic Performance and Political Mobility since 1949* (Armonk, NY: M.E. Sharpe, 2002).

7. Walder, "Career mobility and communist political order."

8. Oliver James and Peter John, "Public management at the ballot box: performance information and electoral support for incumbent english local governments," *Journal of Public Administration Research and Theory*, 17(4) (2007), pp. 567–580.

9. Walder, "Career mobility and the communist political order"; Andrew G. Walder, Bobai Li and Donald J. Treiman, "Politics and life chances in a state socialist regime," *American Sociological Review*, 65 (2000), pp. 191–209.

10. Zhou Xueguang, "Political dynamics and bureaucratic career patterns in the People's Republic of China, 1949–1994," *Comparative Political Studies*, 34 (2001), pp. 1036–1062.

11. Barbara S. Lawrence, "At the crossroads: a multiple-level explanation of individual attainment," *Organization Science*, 1 (1990), pp. 65–85.

12. James A. Fairburn and James M. Malcomson, "Performance, promotion, and the Peter Principle," *The Review of Economic Studies*, 68(1) (2001), pp. 45–66.

13. Laurence Peter and Raymond Hull, *The Peter Principle: Why Things Always Go Wrong* (New York: William Morrow and Company, 1969). The Peter Principle holds that "people are promoted to their levels of incompetence."

14. Fairburn and Malcomson, "Performance, promotion, and the Peter Principle".

15. Zhao Wei and Zhou Xueguang, "Chinese organizations in transition: changing promotion patterns in the reform era," *Organization Science*, 15(2) (2004), pp. 186–199.

16. Samuel P.S. Ho. Rural China in Transition, *Non-agricultural Development in Rural Jiangsu, 1978–1990* (Oxford: Clarendon Press, 1994), p. 213.

17. Guo Gang. "Retrospective economic accountability under authoritarianism: evidence from China," *Political Research Quarterly*, 60(3) (2007), pp. 378–390.

18. Lin Ting, *Economic Performance and Political Mobility: A Case Study of L City in Zhejiang Province* (Beijing: Peking University Press, 2003).

19. Qian Yingyi and Xu Chenggang, "Why China's economic reforms differ: the m-form hierarchy and entry/expansion of the non-state sector," *Economics of Transition*, 1(2) (1993), pp. 135–170.

20. Li Hongbin and Zhou Li-an, "Political turnover and economic performance: the incentive role of personnel control in China," *Journal of Public Economics*, 89(9–10) (2005), pp. 1743–1762.

21. Fairburn and Malcomson, "Performance, promotion, and the Peter Principle".

22. Huang Yasheng, "The industrial organization of Chinese government," MA Working Paper (Boston MA: Harvard Business School, 1998), p. 20.

23. Edward Lazear and Sherwin Rosen. "Rank-order tournaments as optimum labour contracts," *The Journal of Political Economy*, 89(5) (1981), pp. 841–864.

24. Wu Jiannan and Ma Liang, "Government performance and officials' promotion: a literature review," *Journal of Public Administration*, No. 2 (2009), pp. 172–196.

25. Walker and Wu Jiannan, "Performance Evaluation in Chinese City Governments."

26. Walder, "Career mobility and the communist political order."

27. Li Hongbin and Zhou Li-an, "Political turnover and economic performance: the incentive role of personnel control in China," *Journal of Public Economics*, 89 (2005), pp. 1743–1762.

28. Timothy Frye and Andrei Shleifer, "The invisible hand and the grabbing hand," *American Economic Review*, 87(2) (1997), pp. 354–358.

29. Li Hongbin and Zhou Li-an, "Political turnover and economic performance."

30. Guo Liang, "China's new cadre evaluation system," *EAI Background Briefs*, Singapore: East Asian Institute, National University of Singapore, 2007.

31. Zhong Xin, *Regulations on the Work of Selecting and Appointing Leading Party and Government Cadres* (Beijing: Foreign language Press, 2000), p. 78.

32. "Chinese Communist Party issues trial rules on local cadres' evaluation," *BBC Monitoring Asia Pacific*, 12 July 2006, p. 1.

33. Melanie Manion, "The Cadre management system, post-Mao: the appointment, promotion, transfer and removal of party and state leaders," *The China Quarterly*, 102 (1985), pp. 226–229.

34. Maria Edin, "Why do Chinese local cadres promote growth? Institutional incentives and constraints of local cadres," *Forum for Development Studies*, 1 (1998), pp. 97–127.

35. Chen Ye, Li Hongbin and Zhou Li-An, "Relative performance evaluation and the turnover of provincial leaders in China," *Economics Letters*, 88 (2005), pp. 421–425.

36. Peter and Hull, *The Peter Principle: Why Things Always Go Wrong.*

37. Guo Gang, "Retrospective economic accountability under authoritarianism: evidence from China," *Political Research Quarterly*, 60(3) (2007), pp. 378–390.

38. "Personal wealth promoted as criterion for selecting village elders," *China BBC Monitoring Asia Pacific*, London: 29 March 2006, p. 1.

39. Gwyn Bevan and Christopher Hood, "What's measured is what matters: targets and gaming in the English public health care system," *Public Administration*, 84(3) (2006), pp. 517–538.

40. Walker and Wu Jiannan, "Performance evaluation in Chinese city governments."

41. "China: Li Yuanchao Speaks of personnel reform in Beijing." *BBC Monitoring Asia Pacific*, London: 16 December 2009.

42. S. Chan Hon and Gao Jie, "Performance measurement in Chinese local governments: guest editors' introduction," *Chinese Law & Government*, 41(2–3) (2008), pp. 4–9.

43. Liu Mingxing, Song Binwen and Tao Ra, "Perspective on local governance reform in China," *China & World Economy*, 14(2), pp. 16–31.

44. Susan Whiting, *Power and Wealth in Rural China: The Political Economy of Institutional Change* (New York, Cambridge University Press, 2001), pp.110–118.

45. Edin, "Why do Chinese local cadres promote growth?"

46. *Ibid.*

47. Maria Edin, "Remaking the communist party-state: the cadre responsibility system at the local level in China," *China: An International Journal*, No. 1 (2003), pp. 1–15.

48. *Ibid.*

49. There are two priority targets which are enforced nationwide, mirroring the importance which the CPC places on these policies: family planning and social order (*shehui zhi'an*).

50. Rong Jingben et al, *Cong yalixing tizhi xiang minzhu hezuo tizhi de zuanbian: xianxiang liangji zhengzhi tizhi gaige* (*Transformation from the Pressurized System to a Democratic System of Cooperation: Reform of the Political System at the County and Township Levels*) (Beijing: Zhongyang bianyi chubanshe, 1998), p. 271.

51. Edin, "Remaking the communist party-state."

52. Interviews with local cadres during researcher's fieldwork in city H, 2009.

53. Edin, "Why do Chinese local cadres promote growth?"

54. Information source: http://review.jcrb.com/zywfiles/ca551759.htm.

55. Whiting, *Power and Wealth in Rural China*, pp. 110–118.

56. Cao Yong, "The 'performance' view of a vice governor," *Nanfang zhoumo*, 23 August 2003, http://www.people.com.cn/CB/8410/20020823/8D6416.html.

57. Huang Yanzhong. "The state of China state apparatus," *Asian Perspective*, 28(3)L, (2004), pp. 30–68.

58. Horizon Research, http://www.Horizonkey.com, 9 March 2004.

59. David S. G. Goodman, "The politics of regionalism: economic development, conflict and negotiation," in David S. G. Goodman and Gerald Segal (eds.), *China Deconstructs: Politics, Trade and Regionalism* (London: Routledge, 1994), p. 4.

60. Gan Xinmin and Li Tongyin. "To control falsification, we must control its foundations," *Zhongguo tongji* (November 1998), p. 21.

61. Liu Mingxing, Song Binwen and Tao Ra, "Perspective on local governance reform in China."

62. Guo Liang, "China's new cadre evaluation system."

63. http://www.360doc.com/content/07/0607/12/3549_543686.shtml.

64. A project designed to build up the image of local officials. An "image project" is viewed as an economic achievement fabrication in that it is not in use except to represent spurious economic prosperity for political gains.

65. Due to the sensitive nature of this study and the potential risk for interviewees, we have not used the actual name of the city and the informants interviewed.

66. Interviews with local cadres during researcher's fieldwork in city H, 2009.

67. Interviews with local cadres during researcher's fieldwork in city H, 2009.

68. Interviews with local cadres during researcher's fieldwork in city H, 2009.

69. Interviews with local cadres during researcher's fieldwork in city H, 2009.

70. Interviews with local cadres during researcher's fieldwork in city H, 2009.

71. Interviews with local cadres during researcher's fieldwork in city H, 2009.

72. Xu Zhibin, "The spurious achievements of Wang Huaizhong and their consequences," *Inner Review of Party Building*, 5 (2004), p. 23.

73. http://www.360doc.com/content/07/0607/12/3549_543686.shtml.

74. Information source: http://review.jcrb.com/zywfiles/ca551759.htm.

75. *Ibid.*

76. Interviews with local cadres during researcher's fieldwork in city H, 2009.

77. Susan L. Shirk, *The Political Logic of Economic Reform in China* (Berkeley CA: University of California Press, 1993), p. 57.

78. Li Hongbin and Zhou Li-an, "Political turnover and economic performance."

79. Olivier Blanchard and Andrei Shleifer, "Federalism with and without political centralization: China versus Russia," *IMF Staff Papers* (2001).

80. Li Hongbin and Zhou Li-an, "Political turnover and economic performance."

81. Liu Mingxing, Song Binwen and Tao Ra, "Perspective on local governance reform in China."

82. Kevin. J. O'Brien and Li Liangjiang, "Selective policy implementation in rural China," *Comparative Politics*, 31(2) (1999), pp. 167–186.

83. Liu Mingxing, Song Binwen and Tao Ra, "Perspective on local governance reform in China."

84. *Ibid.*

85. Information source: http://review.jcrb.com/zywfiles/ca551759.htm.

86. "New criteria for officials," *China Daily*, 17 May 2006, http://worldcup .china.com.cn/english/GS-e/168608.htm.

87. http://www.360doc.com/content/07/0607/12/3549_543686.shtml.

88. Michael Dorgan, "Official acknowledges massive misreporting of China's economic data," *Business News*, Washington DC, 1 March 2002, p. 1.

89. Guo Gang, "Retrospective economic accountability under authoritarianism."

90. "China: Li Yuanchao speaks of personnel reform in Beijing," *BBC Monitoring Asia Pacific*, London, 16 December 2009.

5

The Internet and Political Marketing in Globalizing China

Chin-fu HUNG

Introduction

Ever since the late Qing Dynasty in the second half of the nineteenth century, modernization has been the major national project for Chinese leaders, as they compete with their western counterparts, as well as their more recently developing neighbours in East Asia. The core of modernization at the time of the Qing Dynasty was to industrialize China in order to safeguard the country from western commercial and military aggression. In the early decades of the twentieth century, making China a strong (*qiang*) and wealthy (*fu*) state was the top priority of the newly established republican government. In Mao's China, the "Great Leap Forward" (*da yue jin*) of the late 1950s epitomized Mao's ambition to speed up the process of modernization, specifically industrialization. He conceived of this as a nationwide mobilization to construct a massive steel and iron sector, as the strategic industry in the national development of a communist society. Nevertheless, Mao did not succeed in hauling China out of its still desperate backwardness. Instead, following the disastrous Cultural Revolution, a series of government measures were implemented during Deng Xiaoping's reign, known as the "Second Revolution".[1]

Deng's successors, Jiang Zemin and the current President, Hu Jintao, have also addressed the theme of national development, with different national strategies that reflect the information age. In Jiang's words, "Digitalization will become a power house in the modernization process, and information technology (IT) is one of China's top priorities and a driving force behind the country's economic development".[2] In the present administration of Hu Jiantao, the "Eleventh Five-Year Plan for IT Application in National Economy and Social Development" as well as the "National Informatization Development Strategy, 2006–2020" have likewise stressed the importance of taking measures to accelerate the integration of IT application and industrialization. In addition, these strategies have focused on implementing a scientific outlook on development, with the aim of laying a good foundation for China to stride towards an information society.[3]

Additionally, when information and communications technologies (ICTs), principally symbolized by the Internet, converge on the political environment in most authoritarian and developing countries, they allow the public the possibility of gaining more latitude in expressing opinions and disseminating alternative information. Communist China is particularly significant in this respect. Here, the (mass) media were traditionally incorporated into the governing mechanism to serve tactically as tools of propaganda (*xuan chuan*) and thought work (*sixiang gongzou*), and for the purposes of agenda-setting (*yulun daoxiang*) in mostly major policies. Entering the Internet age, the state is seen as determined to assure its economic growth and competitiveness in such an increasingly globalized context, where information largely drives global, regional and domestic economies.

The central government in Beijing keenly advocates and supports the development of information and network technology. However, at the same time, it persistently attempts to minimize the undesirable socio-political effects that ICTs have brought about since they were introduced in the early 1990s. The social and political impacts of the Internet have caused the Beijing government unease, as they usually undermine its long-held monopoly over the flow of information. The party-state has accordingly adopted a variety of strategies to harness ICTs, limit the impact of this new information technology to an acceptable degree, and hopefully use it to the government's benefit, in areas like electronic commerce (e-commerce)[4] and electronic government (e-government).

For the development of e-government, the Chinese state has not only underscored the magnitude of authoritative and correct public opinion guidance and agenda-setting, but since 1998 it has also vigorously shaped it in the grand "Government Online Project" (*zhengfu shangwang gongcheng*). The year 1998 was dubbed China's "Government Online Year" (*zhengfu shangwang nian*) to demonstrate the milestone of China's e-government development. An official state source suggests that the People's Republic of China (PRC) had established more than 45,000 government portals by the end of 2009, in which 75 central and state organs, 32 provincial governments, and 333 prefectural governments, as well as over 80 per cent of county-level governments, had launched their official websites.[5] The e-government project can, in one sense, be interpreted as the authorities' proactive efforts to revive the propaganda machinery in the Internet age, as it has been continuously tarnished and weakened throughout the reformist period – especially with the gradual reduction in the state's monopoly over the provision of information and communications.[6]

Besides this, while the concepts of "public opinion" have been extensively addressed in Western democracies, there has been a relative dearth of scholarship on the part of China, before the advent of the Internet. This partly reflects the political reality in the PRC: that previously, publicly posting unauthorized bills – such as big posters (*da zi bao*) – on the street was prohibited and usually deemed a politically dangerous act. To some degree, those who have long been accustomed to perceiving communist China as an autocratic regime believe that the top communist leaders need not listen to what their people think, let alone heed the idea that public opinion might influence or even alter government-designated policies. Since the legitimacy of the regime is not based primarily on the majority support of the electorate, but rather more on economic performance (such as annual GDP growth), outsiders may form the impression of a total monopoly of control by the Chinese government over its mass media; not to mention its effective tools of political manipulation and mass persuasion. Simply put, under the cardinal guidelines of Chinese political correctness, the public were often perceived as unlikely to form any independent opinions concerning political expression, and consequently unlikely to make any significant impact upon policies or realize political change.

However, one has seen the rise of independent public opinion ever since the early 1990s, thanks to China's continuous economic reform and the introduction of modern information and mobile technologies. As many scholarly works have suggested, the power of the worldwide web has already presented the Chinese authorities with unforeseen and unprecedented challenges, which are contributing to undermining the information control of the Communist Party of China (CPC) and exposing party and government misconduct – instances of official corruption, social and economic problems, as well as injustice.[7] Against this backdrop, this article presents questions on how the CPC tackles and responds to the increasing challenges from cyberspace, in addition to its conventional methods of online filtering, surveillance, blocking, and criminal sanctions. What are the implications of electronic political marketing for China's propaganda regime and its politics in the Internet age?

Media and ICTs in China's Propaganda State

In Western literature, discussion of the mass media, ICTs, propaganda, and democracy have all become interwoven with one another. In general, there are two dominant approaches in the literature about the media's democratic potential; economism versus politicism. The latter includes radical Marxism (focusing more on critiques of the state) and liberal pluralism (focusing more on critiques of capital), while both of these approaches demonstrate rather different political images and normative expectations.[8] The liberal-pluralist approach usually suggests that free media/press can only exist in a free democracy and that true democracy is possible only with a free media/press. In this sense, a free media serves to promote and preserve democracy by safeguarding its watchdog role in holding the state to account for its governmental policies. Therefore, "media" are attributed the status of the fourth estate within the state.

Several scholars have also suggested that most Third World and former Communist countries fit into the liberal-pluralist perspective, as these late-developing states lead the country's modernization process.[9] In this perspective, because the media are capable of moulding the minds of people and influencing their decisions in both private and public life, there is a threat to full democracy if either the government or private individuals exercise monopoly control over the media.[10]

In Asia there is a greater variety of views, however. The function of the media serving as an independent check on government is somewhat dismissed and played down. A media scholar from Singapore, for example, held that, "In much of Asia, the justification for the media and for communications was instead to increase national unity and identity in nation-building".[11] In this view, unlike the Western normative notion of the media acting as a check on the government's actions, in Asia the media are instead supposed to "support" the incumbent government, by fostering the grand vision of the post-colonial process in nation-building or even consolidation of the political authority and regime. This viewpoint is shared by some who argue that there exists a unique historical and political experience, characterized as they are by their longstanding tradition of political philosophy, largely shaped by respective religions and social beliefs. This, to a larger extent, determines the process of political democratization. It creates unique features of democracy whereby value-laden words, like individual freedom, freedom of speech, freedom of expression, and human rights, including participation in political decision-making, are redefined.[12]

In this context, unlike the West, there are "official" media in many Asian countries. In China the media are either state-run or party-controlled mouthpieces, which largely act to monopolize news sources and serve the propaganda purposes of the state. This type of propaganda could therefore be viewed as disseminating what one (i.e., ruling party leaders) believes to be true and correct, with overtones of propagating orthodoxy. This leads to further questions about what propaganda is and its relations with public opinion.

The general view on propaganda is that it is the technique of influencing human action by the manipulation of presentations. Harold Lasswell, for instance, describes propaganda as the "control of opinion by significant symbols, or to speak more accurately by stories, rumors, reports, pictures, and other forms of social communication".[13] In a similar vein, Gareth S. Jowett and Victoria O'Donnell consider propaganda as a "deliberate and systematic attempt to shape perceptions, manipulate cognitions, and direct behavior to achieve a response that furthers the desired intent of the propagandist".[14] For his part, Peter Kenez has associated socio-political values with the purpose of propaganda. He defines propaganda as "…nothing more than the attempt to transmit social and political values in the hope of affecting people's thinking, emotions, and thereby behaviors".[15] As one observes, such pre-war techniques of mass propaganda still persist in many Asian countries, albeit they may have been reworked to conform to individual circumstances.[16] Admittedly, there has been a substantial tradition and political culture in Asian countries of managing information flows to ensure that the state is the primary, if not the sole, provider of information. From this perspective, holding the comparative advantage to release exclusive news in ways that serve their own interests, governments or political parties can seek to represent themselves in a more favourable light. This can be accomplished by using willing news reporters as conduits through which the authorities can publish news information as they wish.

In fact, Gary D. Rawnsley has cautioned us that factual-based propaganda raises further questions of selection: who is deciding which facts to report? Which facts are hidden, and why?[17] His reminders touch upon what is widely addressed in the present-day concept of "agenda-setting",[18] with particular reference to the "Internet commentators" (best known as *wumao dang* or *wangluo pinglunyuan*)[19] in the PRC. Obviously, where the state occupies and controls the press and mass media, it can utilize them either by denying access to information or by distributing it selectively, for propaganda purposes – as was commonly the case in Nazi Germany and the former Soviet Union.[20] It was in the totalitarian regimes of Soviet Russia and Nazi Germany that propaganda was most visible as a weapon of the state for the purposes of political indoctrination and social control.

The Chinese "propaganda system" (*xuanchuan xitong*) is institutionally headed by a member of the Politburo Standing Committee, who is in charge of news media with subordinate media institutions under the State Council. These institutions include the Ministry of Culture, Ministry of Industry and Information Technology, Ministry of Public Security, State Administration of Radio, Film and Television, General Administration of Press and Publication, State Information Office, and Xinhua News Agency. The Central Propaganda Department under the Central Party Committee has also supervised the propaganda institutions at different levels, guaranteeing that these news organizations adhere ideologically to the party line, propagate the party's messages, and obey the CPC's regulations.[21]

Prior to the launching of the opening and reform policies in the late 1970s, Chinese people were overwhelmed by official information and interpretations of reality in the media, in the workplace and even at home.[22] Mao Zedong made the role of the media unequivocally clear in 1942 when he demanded that, "a comrade thoroughly conversant with the party's correct line should read the gallery proof to amend its incorrect views before publishing".[23] Since the open-door policies came into effect, particularly after 1992, when Deng Xiaoping called for "more opening, deeper reform", China has been witnessing an unprecedented boom and liberalization of the media. At the same time, the country has been experiencing tension between rapid commercialization and continued ideological control.[24] The media sector needs to respond to increased market pressures and competition, while being under-subsidized or even deprived of any governmental financial support.

Under such circumstances, it has been suggested that the Chinese media has been transformed from being a mere tool of communist propaganda to a mixed agent of political stability, ideological control, economic growth and information provision.[25] Zhao Yuezhi, in particular, holds that the significant shift of the media's role in China has been from propaganda instrument to an industry, from leading the masses to serving consumers, and from tools to service providers.[26] In this sense, tight media controls may have given way somewhat to policies seeking to stimulate competition, reduce subsidies, and streamline organizational structures. Through media marketization and commercialization, or in Chinese parlance, "media industrialization" (*meiti chanyehua*), the range of media issues under political control has been reduced. These changes have, in turn, resulted in the reinforcement of decentralization, specialization, and the multiplication of production and distribution processes in the media sector, which may in turn further weaken ideological control and increase operational autonomy.[27] The Chinese mass media is thus said to be "one head, many mouths", with the single head of the Communist Party and the many mouths and tongues of media coverage.[28] In addition, this unique media culture has become further intertwined by ICTs, as China becomes more globalized and engages to a further extent with the world.

One aspect of this recent development is that China's authoritarian regime is under constantly increasing pressure from the public to hold the former more accountable, responsive and transparent about state policies. In responding to this surging public pressure, the Chinese government has decided both to shore up its governability and to promote political marketing in the Internet age. By means of renewing the conventional propaganda apparatus, top leaders think they could and should adapt to the new information environment. To them, the traditional measure of outright information control may only achieve partial success in strengthening the authority of the regime and the party in the Internet age. Promoting and enhancing positive public images of the party and government would instead outweigh the heavy-handed policies that entail heavy costs and consequences.

In other words, the authorities intelligently incorporate new information technology for the purpose of promoting and publicizing positive images of the party, which will in turn strengthen its governing techniques in the Information Age. Apart from its official presence in cyberspace, through the presence of e-government, the Central Propaganda Department has also actively established or encouraged the setting-up of government-sanctioned or -supported online discussion forums and blogs, and made use of popular social networking sites, such as Facebook and Twitter. Chinese leaders realize that these ICTs give Chinese citizens a conduit of expression that was not available before. Internet users are nowadays equipped with new communications tools to speak out and defend themselves, participate in public discourse, and more importantly, bring issues of social problems or injustices to national attention, despite all the "policing"[29] and surveillance in both the virtual and physical world.

Propaganda and Political Marketing in the Internet Age

Propaganda in China has traditionally been divided into two major categories; internal (*duinei*) and external (*duiwai*) propaganda. While the former is directed towards Chinese people, the latter is primarily targeted towards foreigners in China, overseas Chinese, and the general non-Chinese outside world.[30] For the past three decades,

China's economic reform has brought about transitions of the nation's social and political landscapes, causing the propaganda authorities and the associated thought work to undergo a evolutionary transformation, causing the state to reflect, respond to, and guide public opinion in a new social reality.

As Mike Wayne argues, "…the Internet as a communicative production force potentially outflanks, or at least acts as a counterweight to, the state's management of news in a crisis; …the media could make use of the increased possibilities for the production and dissemination of information by people 'on the ground', in the heart of crisis, as a means of diversifying their sources and becoming less reliant on the state".[31] Since Chinese people can now gain better access to other sources of news and information, audiences and readers are no longer willing to accept much of this propaganda from a single source.

Traditionally, the CPC usually resorted to uniform media norms and techniques of propaganda in managing the party's images. This is known as the guidance of public opinion (*yulun daoxiang*), which is directed by the Central Propaganda Department and implemented by the mass media. The goal of *yulun daoxiang* is not only to uphold the correct and unerring guidance of public opinion, but also to bring the public's opinions into line with the party and government, and to restrict or prevent print or broadcast content that is at odds with the Communist Party from being disseminated. To this end, "emphasizing positive news" (*zhengmian baodao*) is key, as former President Jiang Zemin remarked. He commented that, "Our Party highly values the news work and regards newspapers, broadcasting, and television as the mouthpieces of the party, government, and the People … As the media will directly impact people's thoughts, actions and political orientations, we should guide, motivate, inspire, mobilize, and organize the mass [of the] people through emphasizing positive news to support unity and stability".[32] This has also become the customary method for the Central Propaganda Department to "strengthen media to face competition by international media groups and face the global struggle for public opinion".[33]

However, the shift to promoting a positive image and political marketing is *per se* a proactive measure to boost the popularity of China's top leaders, mostly among the country's patriotic youth and citizens. They do this because it can strengthen positive and virtuous images of the party leaders. Moreover, this in turn restores the public's distrust in the government. In essence, it is a political marketing strategy, increasingly employed by the Central Propaganda Department, and one that shares techniques with commercial advertising and public relations. While China continues to remain interconnected with the outside world, the Beijing government realizes that any domestic problems may not only undermine (local) government's authority and capability, but also damage the public image and the popularity of the authorities if these issues, problems and crises are not appropriately addressed and dealt with.

Essentially, this is consistent with Anne-Marie Brady's observations, when she argues that "China's propaganda system has deliberately absorbed the methodology of political public relations, mass communications, political communications, and other modern methods of mass persuasion . . .".[34] In particular, Brady points out that current Chinese propaganda work has incorporated innovative new information technologies, such as the Internet and other multimedia communications, to strengthen the modern thought work of preserving the positive image of the Communist Party and government, achieving the goal of manipulating the public mind.[35]

On the one hand, the Internet and other mobile technologies are enhancing Chinese civil discourse by permitting public opinion and debates on national and foreign policies to be expressed and conducted in cyberspace. On the other hand, nevertheless, the authorities are also promoting "virtual" propaganda and thought work by launching electronic political marketing in the state's online battle against the seemingly unfettered democratic potential of ICTs. The following case study of Chinese Premier Wen Jiabao is of significance in this regard.

Case Study –
Wen Jiabao in the Cyberworld

Premier Wen Jiabao made his live debut with Netizens on 28 February 2009, in an online chat jointly hosted by the central government website (*gov.cn*) and the official Xinhua News Agency. Wen's chat occurred just days before the big political event of the annual "two sessions" (the National People's Congress and the Chinese People's

Political Consultative Conference) held in Beijing in March 2009. Wen's first ever online chat came a few months after President Hu Jintao's online address, when the latter had a brief Q&A with Netizens on the *People's Daily* website, in June 2009. Wen's two-hour online discussion attracted over 90,000 questions from nearly 300,000 Internet and mobile phone users in China and abroad. Diverse topics were raised, ranging from the shoe-throwing protest during his speech at Cambridge University in February 2009, corruption among officials, unemployment, the wealth gap, social justice and democracy. To reach out to Netizens, Wen shared his experiences of surfing the Internet almost every day and sometimes spending as long as one hour perusing the questions, comments and criticisms put forth by Netizens. A year later, on 27 February 2010, he had his second broad-ranging online chat, conducted in the same fashion.

In addition to joining the Internet craze, Wen has also earned the reputation of being one of China's most popular political figures due to his Facebook profile. Although the authorship of Wen's Facebook page is still unknown, he has gained tens of thousands of followers and supporters on this social networking site. His rising popularity was significantly boosted after he made a quick appearance, in May 2009, at the sites of the devastating earthquakes in Sichuan Province.[36] Apart from being referred to as the "People's Premier", Wen has also been called "bao-bao" (baby) or "Grandpa Wen" by many of his supporters. This was due to the fact that he had performed well during the earthquake relief efforts as the General Commander of the Earthquake Relief Efforts Committee.

In the aftermath of this natural disaster, Wen joined President Hu and other political leaders to quickly mobilize the country's resources, channelling vast funding into earthquake-hit regions, and – most significantly for this paper – broadcasting messages to the public on national media and in cyberspace. Given that the propaganda authorities had imposed restrictions on general news reporting in the first place, they later relaxed these regulations by allowing media and cyberspace users to cover and discuss the public efforts underway for aid to victims and earthquake-related issues. To a degree, the Chinese leadership kept its focus and leveraged the power of the authoritarian regime to good effect in order to be very responsive to the natural disaster.[37] During this time, leaders, including Premier Wen, forged positive reputations for themselves as "men of the people".

On Wen's Facebook page, he is reported to possess a down-to-earth character, something which has helped him both to get closer to grassroots organizations and to appeal to ordinary people; in particular, those who are marginalized and impoverished. He has done this through addressing concerns such as the increasing gap between rich and poor, the unbalanced development between the hinterland and coastal cities, and in part, through enacting policies like cutting farmers' taxes and heading campaigns against official corruption.

Creating and allowing more (positive) news stories and public discourses on Wen's Facebook can be best understood as China's updated propaganda tactics in the Internet age. As such, news and public opinion are critical for the ideological domain and thought work. Along with China's substantial economic growth, technological advances and innovations, and more importantly, the rise and awakening of *wei-quan* (rights defence) consciousness, the ways citizens communicate among themselves and the channels through which they acquire and transmit information have become numerous and varied. In recent years, citizen activists on the Internet have grown more vocal, and freewheeling social and political discussions have become more prevalent. In this sense, creating a new pattern of public opinion guidance has turned out to be an emerging prominent issue for the Chinese authorities. They will have to address this if they intend to enhance the effectiveness of media control and accommodate current changes to Chinese society both within and outside the country in the current Information Age.

Undoubtedly, the increasing globalization and commercialization of Chinese media outlets are expanding the space for public discussion. For China's propaganda leaders, however, increasing the ability to channel public opinion in this new era hinges on enhancing innovative power to revitalize news and propaganda work.[38] Creating a platform from which top leaders, such as Premier Wen, can interact face-to-face with people and Netizens at the grassroots level would be regarded as a renewed and innovative method to strengthen the effectiveness of public opinion guidance. This partly explains why Chinese leaders are increasingly participating in online chats and interviews. They are doing this in order to strengthen the interaction and intercommunication between the will of the state and the people. In so doing, they may increase the attractiveness of the party and the image of the government, in an open age in which the Internet is becoming ever more important for transmitting information and is acting as a new venue for public discourse.

The Politics of E-Political Marketing

The CPC has proactively shaped the use and development of the Internet medium from the very beginning of its introduction in the early 1990s. Adopting a series of measures to promote self-censorship among Internet users, the government is keen to attempt to control Internet use through a variety of means. These include constructing fundamental Internet network infrastructures and connection backbones, imposing online content filtering and censorship – such as the installation of the China-produced Net-screening device known as the "Green Dam" – and laying relentless criminal charges against offensive Internet users.[39] These measures effectively act as warnings and make an example of some, discouraging potential offenders of Internet laws and regulations. This reflects the increasing unease felt by Chinese leaders who are managing the propaganda and media systems; however, they cannot totally control the relatively free flow of information in cyberspace as they used to do with the harnessing of the traditional press and mass media.

This has, in turn, triggered the Chinese authorities to promote what they call "healthy online culture", a term Chinese President Hu Jintao put forth in January 2007, during a study session of the Political Bureau of the Central Committee of the CPC. He stressed, "Whether we can cope with the Internet is a matter that affects the development of socialist culture, the security of information, and the stability of the state".[40] As a result, the government will be looking to exploit advanced technologies to better guide public opinions voiced through the Internet.

On 20 June 2008, President Hu paid a high-profile visit to the party's mouthpiece, the *People's Daily*, where he made a speech and chatted briefly online with the Netizens on "Strong Country Forum", answering some of their queries. Hu's visit to the *People's Daily* was not accidental, but rather a deft move to incorporate electronic and web-based media to promote political marketing by raising his public profile and popularity among Chinese Netizens. The speech made during his official visit to the party-organ's newspaper office served a political purpose. It shored up the party-dominated Chinese media space in a context where market-oriented commercial and urban dailies are constantly challenging the party newspapers and broadcasting stations. These commercial and urban dailies include outspoken news outlets such as *Nanfang Dushi Bao* (*Southern Metropolis News*) and *Nanfang Zhoumo* (*Nanfang Weekend*), from the Nanfang Media Group in Guangzhou. What this demonstrates is that propaganda remains the defining framework for the Chinese mass media in the twenty-first century. In a broad sense, the waning or death of the propaganda state in China has not been realized, as some Western researchers have predicted.[41]

It is apparent that the public opinion mediated online has had a direct or indirect impact on China's domestic policies. In part, it is that the new media technology, in particular the Internet and related communications technologies, has substantially transformed the manner in which ordinary people and government officials communicate. The CPC has conventionally established vertical flows of top-down communications through the propaganda mechanism – such as the party or official media outlets – and thereby maintained a "healthy" media environment with political correctness; one in which the Party decides what is and is not correct. Some scholars have further suggested that "the news in China provides Chinese society with the basic knowledge needed for the building of a forced consensus, the basis of Communist rule and legitimacy".[42]

Nonetheless, the Internet and digital media like SMS messaging have been fostering a horizontal system of communications, and offering a more efficient conduit for the horizontal exchange and dissemination of information. The so-called "public opinion supervision" (*yulun jiandu*) is often seen as a refreshing and positive force to expose official corruption and social problems, as well as injustice. Cases like the Sun Zhigang investigation, the BMW case, and the Liu Yong trial have all highlighted public opinion supervision mediated and facilitated in cyberspace.[43]

This is also due to the enhancement of general awareness of the safeguarding of citizens' rights, better known as *wei-quan* consciousness.[44] Collective labour disputes in state-owned enterprises, collective-owned enterprises and private enterprises, protests over land requisition and subsequent relocation, as well as other social disturbances and riots, have in one way or another been triggered by specific economic grievances, rapid socio-economic transformation, and the poor quality of (local) governance.[45] Chinese citizens have become noticeably more adept at using the law and new communications tools to assert and defend their rights and interests against the government and others. As the country continues to deepen its economic reform and open-door policy, pluralized socio-economic interests are jointly taken up in the growing civic-oriented agendas, and may accordingly restrict the CPC's autonomy and governing capacity in solely determining policy orientation, content and delivery. Chinese citizens, instead of blindly accepting the government's agendas, are now being awakened and empowered to set their own policy agendas both in cyberspace and in physical life.

Moreover, just as the case study on Premier Wen illustrated, the new information technology has transformed the manner, speed and scope in which government officials communicate with citizens. Whereas ordinary citizens and Netizens are more empowered by new communications technologies to set their own policy agendas, defend their (statutory) rights, and organize to fight collectively against the state's attitudes and policies, the Chinese propaganda authorities have noticeably become politically alert towards this new social development. The combination of public pressure and widespread attention allows *wei-quan* activists to exert influence and bring pressure to bear on those who are in power but fail to live up to their obligations. Citizens of modern Chinese society may not simply insist that the regime addresses their social, economic and political demands through official mechanisms. If this were the case, they would certainly demand the creation of adequate institutions to allow them to have a voice in the first place. Engaging through the Internet and social media – through online discussion forums, blogs, instant messaging systems, Facebook, QQ, Twitter – and other Internet communications systems, allows more people to articulate their (policy) interests better and to set their own agenda proactively. Through these media, they can express grievances, discuss and debate public policies, and organize themselves into social movements to mobilize and coordinate collective action when needed.

Since the disruptive action of citizen resistance, in particular coordinated action of a political nature, is not tolerated by the government, more preventive or even preemptive measures seem necessary as well as pressing for effective governance, in the face of increasing cases of "mass incidents" (*quntixing shijian*) and "public order disturbances" (*raoluan gonggong zhixu fanzui*).[46] One method employed by the CPC to respond to reactionary forces and potential challenges is the remoulding of its traditional governing methods into those of cyber-political marketing techniques, mass communications, political public relations, and mass persuasion. These methods are commonly utilized in Western democracies and are re-adjusted and re-adapted to Chinese situations and needs by the authorities.

The initial attitude of Chinese officials towards the Internet was ambivalent. On the one hand, the Internet has become "a key battlefield in China's political and ideological struggles" and "a new realm for the struggle of international opinion".[47] On the other hand, the Internet has also extended the CPC's reach, rendering "political thought work more efficient".[48] Liu Yunshan, Director of the CPC Publicity Department, remarked on one occasion that "various non-Marxist thoughts and ideas have grown and affected social harmony and stability . . . how to utilize, develop and scientifically manage the Internet has become a major and pressing task".[49]

In ushering in the new brand of China's Fifth-Generation leaders, the propaganda regime seems more confident in tackling both the direct and indirect challenges posed by the new technologies. Instead of seeing the Internet as a threat to Communist rule, the authorities have come to view these new kinds of technology as a great opportunity for catalysing further economic prosperity, and more significantly in this context, an integral means through which the regime can utilize effective political tools in order to construct propaganda and thought work in the Information Age. If the work is successfully constructed, this may, in turn, strengthen the regime's governance and ensure its survival in the Internet age.

To this end, the CPC takes a positive and combative stance towards the management of information flows and Internet-facilitated expression of public opinion from the "emerging middle class"[50]in China. The State Council Information Office (*Guowuyuan Xinwenban*), for instance, has specifically learned from past experiences, when dealing with challenges deriving from mass incidents and emergencies facilitated or aggravated by the Internet. It has adopted the so-called "*Si Jiang*" (four "speaks") guidelines for Chinese publicity and security departments to follow: (1) *Speak* quickly to seize the commanding heights in disseminating information;

(2) *Speak* continuously to the public and inform them about the progress and latest developments of any ongoing incident; (3) *Speak* accurately in disclosing true and comprehensive information in order to seek public recognition; and lastly (4) *Speak* repeatedly to answer and clarify various public enquiries.[51]

The "*Si Jiang*" guidelines are closely associated with what the Chinese government is currently endeavouring to do: build and foster a good image of the CPC and people-oriented leadership in the government. In one sense, this serves to renew the CPC's withering official ideology of socialism by presenting to the public the "populist stance" of top Chinese leaders. The populist stance may be best conceptualized from what President Hu Jintao stated at the Central Party School in February 2003. He discussed the new "Three People's Principles" (*xin sanmin zhuyi*): power to be used by the people (*quan wei min suo yong*), concern to be showered on the people (*qing wei min suo xi*), and benefits to be enjoyed by the people (*li wei min suo mou*). Vice President, Xi Jinping, for his part, has added a new theory – power is bestowed by the people (*quan wei min suo fu*) – to these three principles. This "pro-people" theoretical shift functions effectively, on the one hand, to proclaim that the party mainly serves the demands and needs of the populace and to promote "human-centred" development. On the other hand, it also serves to enhance the CPC's legitimacy, providing better governance for the Chinese people during the tenure of this new generation of leaders.[52]

Under these three new principles, the directives from the party and government are to cater to the needs and concerns of the ordinary people. In this regard, the official role of the media is to cover more stories that truly reflect the daily lives of the public, effectively realizing what is being called the "three closes" (*san tiejin*): closer to the reality, closer to the public's lives, and closer to the masses (*tiejin shiji, tiejin shenghuo, tiejin qunzhong*).[53]

The Chinese state's means for using propaganda remain strong in the Information Age. This is the case not simply because propaganda is intended to shape public opinion, but also because it looks to guide and corral opinion, forming what the Beijing authorities call a "healthy and orderly"[54] environment of Chinese cyberspace. To this end, along with Internet regulations,[55] political marketing strategy has something to offer beyond the "black arts" of the Chinese propaganda system.

Chinese leaders have learned lessons from past experiences in handling various "mass or public incidents" (*qunzhong huo gongong shijian*), albeit these are all different types of cases, ranging from natural disasters and manufacturing/production incidents to public health incidents. They consider the lessons learned here important for the Chinese media (particularly the mainstream media, such as the party-run or controlled media outlets), so that they are able to keep a firm grip on the initiative in reporting. Essentially, this means that leaders in the propaganda regime believe the media ought to report incidents at the first available moment, so as to enhance the transparency of news reporting. They should also utilize the strengths of all sorts of media, especially the Internet and the mobile phone network, so as to strengthen authority effectiveness in covering news stories. This is a much more nuanced approach, employed by the propaganda authorities not simply to boast (moderate) media openness, but also to fortify its position on the commanding heights of discourse; discourse which is occurring in this current informational environment where new and alternative media outlets increasingly undercut the credibility and authority of the official agencies. This is what Chinese leaders have usually stressed as important to making the new propaganda work, so that it is "keeping pace with the times" (*yushi jujin*).[56]

Within this new informational setting, clamping down on public incidents with suppression and control may eventually incur serious consequences, such as social instability and a deepening mistrust of government. Nonetheless, in the aftermath of many of these incidents, such as the SARS epidemic, the Sichuan Wenchuan earthquake and the Sun Zhigang case, there has been an opening up of the media, particularly the Internet, after mounting pressure from the public and international media. Rather than simply suppressing news, the Chinese government is beginning to strike first to release authoritative information at the earliest moment and to grasp the initiative firmly in news propaganda work. Essentially, this means that the CPC wants to convince the general public with official accounts and coverage, rather than simply suppressing news and forcing citizens to look for information and news on "underground" channels and sites.

It can be argued that Chinese authorities have staked out a two-pronged strategy governing ICTs. This comes from a Chinese expression: "the soft get softer, the hard get harder" (*ruande gengruan, yingde gengying*). Whereas top Chinese leaders such as President Hu Jintao and Premier Wen Jiabao have constantly projected a kinder, gentler, more caring image, they have also tightened their grip over sensitive content and subjects in cyberspace. President Hu, for instance, made a live webcast on the "*Qiangguo Luntan*" (Strong Country Forum) during the 60th anniversary of the founding of the party's *People's Daily*, on 20 June 2008. During his twenty-minute chat, he answered three questions put forward by forum members, all of which were chosen by the party's webmaster. On this officially arranged occasion, Hu Jintao underlined that:

We pay great attention to suggestions and advice from our Netizens. We stress the idea of "putting people first" (*yiren weiben*) and "governing for the people" (*zhizheng weimin*). With this in mind, we need to listen to people's voices extensively and pool the people's wisdom when we take actions and make decisions. The Web is an important channel for us to understand the concerns of the public and assemble the wisdom of the public.[57]

Hu's debut appearance on the party-run chat room suggests that "the Party at least knows the importance of listening to the public".[58] Top leaders are aware that the Internet, serving as an effective horizontal communications channel among citizens, may augment grievances and dissatisfaction and act as a catalyst for socio-political change; especially, when institutional mechanisms cannot accommodate their needs and demands and alleviate their discontent.

Nowadays, the party-state persistently maintains socio-political control as one of the crucial pillars of the continuation of the authoritarian regime. The state has effectively exploited its "authoritarian power structures to crush any overt opposition and ride out any unrest".[59] At any rate, the state endeavours to sustain a relatively prolonged stability, despite increased challenges from subversive forces within political and socio-economic arenas. What is also noteworthy is the distinctive strategy that is currently being adopted by the Chinese authorities: the electronic political marketing scenario, which this section has explored. Within this scenario, the party-state, despite filtering and/or containing online activities, takes active measures to promote the public image of the party and of the government, maintains public relations/diplomacy at home and abroad, and looks to eventually reinvigorate and bring the propaganda machine back to China's increasingly globalized and digitalized society.

Conclusion

The Internet is facilitating political liberalization in Chinese society. The mushrooming online discussion forums and blogosphere have created and nourished a "virtual" space for Chinese civil society to emerge. Providing a platform for the public to express opinions and discuss (current) affairs, the cyber community has not only pushed for associative and communicative freedoms, but has also catalysed greater changes towards a new chapter for China's state-society relations in the Internet age.

Previously, the mass media in China was, in essence, an adjunct of the party apparatus and was controlled completely by the party-state. With the deepening of reform policies and China's opening up to the outside world, the nation has experienced an unprecedented boom and liberalization of the media. Yet the official media seems to be continuously attempting to play the role of guiding and shaping public opinion, and trying to realize the profound objective of enhanced ideological control.

The Chinese government has been under increasing public pressure to hold itself more accountable, responsive and transparent about its policies. To shore up China's governability in the Information Age, Beijing's technology-savvy propaganda machine has been subtly incorporating new technology to promote and strengthen public images of the party and government by intentionally launching their official presence in the virtual world.

These moves are employed not simply for opinion guidance, but also as proactive measures to seize on the top leaders' (rising) popularity, mostly among the country's patriotic youth and "angry youth" (*fen qing*).[60] This kind of political calculation is intended to boost the political marketing as well as governability of the party-state in the Internet age, at a time when China is deeply interconnected with the outside world. This is because any domestic issue that challenges the Chinese governing mechanism may also become a regional or global event that, in turn, could damage its image, both domestically and internationally. This article has demonstrated that China's propaganda regime has been resilient in updating its mechanisms and in keeping pace with the times in order to manage the new media aptly. And this may eventually reinvigorate China's propaganda machine in the globalized world.

Notes and References

1. In Deng's words, "The reform we are now carrying out is very daring. But if we do not carry it out, it will be hard for us to make progress. Reform is China's second revolution. It is something very important that we have to undertake even though it involves risks." Deng Xiaoping, "Reform is China's Second Revolution," *Selected Works of Deng Xiaoping*, 28 March 1985 (Beijing: Foreign Languages Press, 1998), http://english.peopledaily.com.cn/dengxp/vol3/text/c1360.html.

2. Hou Mingjuan, "Jiang says IT is a top priority," *China Daily*, 22 August 2000.

3. See "China's Eleventh Five-Year Plan and the Informatization Development Strategy", http://www.china.com.cn/policy/txt/2007-03/02/content_7891656.htm and http://news.xinhuanet.com/politics/2006-05/08/content_4523521.htm.

4. For more discussion about electronic commerce in China, see, for example, John Wong and Nah Seok Ling (eds.), *China's Emerging New Economy: The Internet and E-Commerce* (Singapore: Singapore University Press and World Scientific, 2001).

5. See Information Office of the State Council of the People's Republic of China, *Zhongguo Hulianwang Zhuangkuang* (*The Internet in China*), 8 June 2010, http://www.gov.cn/zwgk/2010-06/08/content_1622866.htm

6. Xiudian Dai, *The Digital Revolution and Governance* (Aldershot UK: Ashgate, 2000), pp. 151–152.

7. See, for example, Guobin Yang, *The Power of the Internet in China: Citizen Activism Online* (New York: Columbia University Press, 2009); Xiaoling Zhang and Yongnian Zheng (eds.), *China's Information and Communications Technology Revolution: Social Changes and State Responses* (London: Routledge, 2009); Tamara Renee Shie, "The Internet and single-party rule in China," in Suisheng Zhao (ed.), *Debating Political Reform in China: Rules of Law vs. Democratization* (New York and London: M.E. Sharpe, 2006), pp. 215–229; Jens Damm and Simona Thomas (eds.), *Chinese Cyberspaces: Technological Changes and Political Effects* (London and New York: Routledge, 2006); Zixue Tai, *The Internet in China: Cyberspace and Civil Society* (London: Routledge, 2006).

8. Chin-Chuan Lee, "Chinese communication: prisms, trajectories, and models of Understanding," in Chin-Chuan Lee (ed.), *Power, Money, and Media: Communication Patters and Bureaucratic Control in Cultural China*

(Evanston IL.: Northwestern University Press, 2000), pp. 26–36.

9. See, for example, Martin Staniland, *What is Political Economy?: A Study of Social Theory and Underdevelopment* (New Haven CT and London: Yale University Press, 1985).

10. Justice P. B. Sawant, "Media in democracy," *Media Asia*, Vol. 28, No. 1 (2001), p. 47.

11. Simon S. C. Tay, "Democracy and the media in ASEAN and Asia," *Media Asia*, Vol. 27, No. 4 (2000), p. 226.

12. See, for example, Vinod C. Agarwal, "Information and communication technology challenges to democracy in Asia," *Media Asia*, Vol. 28, No. 3 (2001), p. 132.

13. Harold D. Lasswell, *Propaganda Technique in the World War* (London: Kegan Paul & Co., 1927), p. 221. See also Harold D. Lasswell, "Propaganda," in Robert Jackall (ed.), *Propaganda* (London: Macmillan Press, 1995), p. 13. For more discussions about propaganda and public opinion, see, for example, Leonard William Doob, *Public Opinion and Propaganda*, second edition (Hamden CT: Archon Books, 1966).

14. Garth S. Jowett and Victoria O'Donnell, *Propaganda and Persuasion*, second edition (Newbury Park CA and London: Sage Publications, 1992), p. 4.

15. Peter Kenez, *The Birth of the Propaganda State: Soviet Methods of Mass Mobilization, 1917–1929* (Cambridge: Cambridge University Press, 1985), p. 4.

16. Pippa Norris et al. identify three main schools of thought have developed to account for the influence of political communications: pre-war theories of mass propaganda, post-war theories of partisan reinforcement, and recent theories of cognitive, agenda-setting and persuasion effects. See, Pippa Norris et al., *On Message: Communicating the Campaign* (London and Thousand Oaks CA.: Sage Publications, 1999), pp. 3–9.

17. Gary D. Rawnsley, "Selling Taiwan: diplomacy and propaganda," *Issues & Studies*, Vol. 36, No. 3 (June 2000), p. 4.

18. See Alex Chan, "Guiding public opinion through social agenda-setting: China's media policy since the 1990s," *Journal of Contemporary China*, Vol. 16, No. 53 (November 2007), pp. 547–559.

19. For more discussions about China's Internet commentators, see, for example, David Bandurski, "China's guerrilla war for the web," *Far Eastern Economic Review*, Vol. 171, No. 6 (July/August 2008), pp. 41–44.

20. John Street, *Mass Media, Politics and Democracy* (New York: Palgrave, 2001), 109. For more discussions about the relationship between communist states and propaganda, see, for example, Hannah Arendt, *The Origins of Totalitarianism* (New York: Harcourt Brace & Company, 1973); John C. Clews, *Communist Propaganda Techniques* (London: Cox and Wyman, 1964); and Richard Taylor, *Film Propaganda: Soviet Russia and Nazi Germany* (Kino: The Russian Cinema Series, 1998); David Welch, *The Third Reich: Politics and Propaganda* (London and New York: Routledge, 1993).

21. See, for example, Anne-Marie Brady, "Guiding hand: the role of the Central Propaganda Department in the current era," *Westminster Papers in Communication and Culture*, Vol. 3, No. 1 (March 2006), pp. 58–77.

22. Daniel C. Lynch, *After the Propaganda State: Media, Politics, and "Thought Work" in Reformed China* (Stanford CA: Stanford University Press, 1999), p. 3.

23. Mao Zedong, *Mao Zedong xinwen gongzuo wenxuan* (*Selected Writings on Journalism by Mao Zedong*) (Beijing: Xinhua Press, 1983), p. 155.

24. Joseph M. Chan, "Commercialization without independence: trends and tensions of media development in China," in Joseph Yu-Shek Cheng and Maurice Brosseau (eds.), *China Review 1993* (Hong Kong: The Chinese University Press, 1993), pp. 25.1–25.21; Yuezhi Zhao, "From commercialization to conglomeration: the transformation of the Chinese press within the orbit of the party state," *Journal of Communication*, Vol. 34, No. 1 (Spring 2000), pp. 3–26; and Chen Huailin and Joseph M. Chan, "Bird-caged press freedom in China," in Joseph Y. S. Cheng (ed.), *China in the Post-Deng Era* (Hong Kong: The Chinese University Press, 1998), p. 650.

25. Yu Guoming, *Jiexi chuanmei bianju* (*Interpreting the Transformation of the Media Industry*) (Guangzhou: The Southern Daily Press, 2002), pp. 6–7.

26. Zhao Yuezhi, *Media, Market, and Democracy in China: Between the Party Line and the Bottom Line* (Urbana IL.: The University of Illinois Press, 1998), pp. 47–51.

27. Eric Kit-wai Ma, "Rethinking media studies: the case of China," in James Curran and Myung-Jin Park (eds.), *De-Westernizating Media Studies* (London and New York: Routledge, 2000), pp. 21–34.

28. Wu Guoguang, "One head, many mouths: diversifying press structures in reform China," in Chin-Chuan Lee (ed.), *Power, Money, and Media: Communication Patters and Bureaucratic Control in Cultural China* (Northwestern University Press, 2000), p. 61.

29. The Internet police is said to be a division within the Ministry of Public Security that currently employs over 30,000 officers. They are tasked with monitoring online traffic, weeding out Net-based dissent, and censoring subversive material, in what is called the Golden Shield Project or the Great Firewall of China. See John Markoff, "Surveillance of Skype messages found in China," *The New York Times*, 2 October 2008, C1.

30. Anne-Marie Brady, *Marketing Dictatorship: Propaganda and Thought Work in Contemporary China* (Lanham MD and Plymouth: Rowman & Littlefield, 2008), p. 12.

31. Mike Wayne, *Marxism and Media Studies: Key Concepts and Contemporary Trends* (London: Pluto Press, 2003), p. 51.

32. Jiang Zemin, "Guanyu dang de xinwen gongzuo de jige wenti" (Regarding several problems with the Party's news work), *People's Daily Online*, 28 November 1989, http://news.xinhuanet.com/ziliao/2005-02/21/content_2600239 .htm. See also Zhang Shigang, "A timely progress for Marxist news studies –

study [of] Jiang Zemin's thoughts on the news," *Xinwen zhanxian* (*News Battle Front*), No. 5 (2002), http://www.people.com.cn/GB/paper79/6261/618513.html.

33. Hu Xiaohan, "Seizing the commanding heights – thoughts on the enhancing public opinion guidance under the new situation," *Zhongguo Jizhe* (*Chinese Journalists*), No. 9, 2009, http://media.people.com.cn/GB/ 10087872.html.

34. Brady, *Marketing Dictatorship: Propaganda and Thought Work in Contemporary China*, p. 3.

35. Anne-Marie Brady, "Regimenting the public mind: the modernization of propaganda in the PRC," *International Journal*, Vol. 57, No. 4 (Autumn 2002), pp. 563-578.

36. Edward Wong, "China leader makes debut in great wall of Facebook," *The New York Times*, 28 May 2008.

37. Dali L. Yang, "Forced harmony: China's Olympic rollercoaster," *Current History*, Vol. 107, No. 710 (September 2008), p. 246.

38. Ma Laishun, "Yi chuangxin tisheng dianshi xinwen de yulun yindao nengli" (Employing innovation to raise the level of public opinion channelling in television), *Zhongguo jizhe* (*Chinese Journalists*), No. 9 (2009), http://media.people.com.cn/GB/137684/8916813.html.

39. See, for example, Greg Walton, *China's Golden Shield: Corporations and the Development of Surveillance Technology in the People's Republic of China* (International Centre for Human Rights and Democratic Development, 2001); Reporters Without Borders China, *Journey to the Heart of Internet Censorship, Investigative Report*, 2007, http://www.rsf.org/IMG/pdf/Voyage_au_coeur_de_la_censure_GB.pdf; Michael Chase and James Mulvenon, *You've Got Dissent!: Chinese Dissident Use of the Internet and Beijing's Counter-Strategies* (Santa Monica CA: RAND, 2002); Robert Faris, Hal Roberts and Stephanie Wang, *China's Green Dam: The Implications of Government Control Encroaching on the Home PC* (The OpenNet Initiative, June 2009), http://opennet.net/sites/opennet.net/files/GreenDam_bulletin.pdf.

40. "Hu Jintao asks Chinese officials to better cope with Internet," *People's Daily*, 25 January 2007, http://english.peopledaily.com.cn/200701/24/eng20070124_344445.html.

41. See, for example, Lynch, *After the Propaganda State*.

42. Tsan-Kuo Chang, Jian Wang and Chih-Hsien Chen, "News as social knowledge in China: the changing worldview of Chinese national media," *Journal of Communication*, Vol. 44, No. 3 (September 1994), p. 66.

43. See, for example, Chin-fu Hung, "The politics of cyber participation in the PRC: the implications of contingency for the awareness of citizens' rights," *Issues & Studies*, Vol. 42, No. 4 (December 2006), pp. 137–173; Xiao Qiang, "The rising tide of Internet opinion in China," *Nieman Reports*, (Summer 2004), http://www.nieman.harvard.edu/reports/article/100852/The-Rising-Tide-of-Internet-Opinion-in-China.aspx; Sharon Hom, Amy Tai and Gabriel Nichols, "The rise of the Internet and advancing human rights,"

China Rights Forum, No. 3 (2004), http://www.ir2008.org/PDF/initiatives/Internet/ rise-of-internet.pdf.

44. Jonathan Benney, "Rights defence and the virtual China," *Asian Studies Review*, Vol. 31, No. 4 (December 2007), pp. 435–446.

45. See, for example, Kevin J. O'Brien and Lianjiang Li, *Rightful Resistance in Rural China* (Cambridge: Cambridge University Press, 2006); James C. Scott, *Weapons of the Weak: Everyday Forms of Peasant Resistance* (New Haven CT and London: Yale University Press, 1985); and David Zweig, "The externalities of development: can new political institutions manage rural conflict?", in Elizabeth J. Perry and Mark Selden (eds.) *Chinese Society: Change, Conflicts and Resistance* (London: Routledge, 2000), pp. 120–142.

46. A source from China's Ministry of Public Security puts the number of "mass incidents" (riots, protests, demonstrations, and mass petitions) as increasing from 8,700 in 1993 to 87,000 in 2005, and to over 90,000 in 2006. See Wang Weilan, "Making sense of 'mass incident'," *Global Times*, 30 May 2009, http://special.globaltimes.cn/2009-05/433271.html, accessed 25 October 2010.

47. "Internet brings unwelcome ideas," *South China Morning Post*, 10 August 2000; "War on Net hots up," *South China Morning Post*, 12 July 2000.

48. *Ibid.*

49. Liu Yunshan, "Huigu yu zhanwang" ("Review and prospect"), *Qui Shi* (*Seeking Truth*), No. 1, (22 June 2009), http://www.qstheory.cn/zxdk/2009/200901/200906/t20090609_1625.htm.

50. It has been suggested that China remains far from being a genuine "middle-class society" as the size and scope of the middle class is still small and it is establishing itself at a slow pace. See Yang Dali, "Economic Transformation and Its Political Discontents in China: Authoritarianism, Unequal Growth, and the Dilemmas of Political Development," *Annual Review of Political Science*, Vol. 9 (June 2006), pp. 143–164.

51. Yin Shuang, "'Caifang xu shenpi' daodi kazhu le shei?" ("Who has actually been stuck with 'Interview subject to approval'?"), *Guangming ribao*, 14 September 2010, http://view.gmw.cn/2010-09/14/content_1251752.htm (accessed 14 September 2010).

52. Joseph Fewsmith, "Hu Jintao's Approach to Governance," in John Wong and Lai Hongyi, eds., *China into the Hu-Wen Era: Policy Initiatives and Challenges* (Singapore: World Scientific Publishing, 2006), p. 93. See also Chih-jou Jay Chen, "Growing social unrest in China: rising social discontents and popular protest," in Guoguang Wu and Helen Lansdowne (eds.), *Socialist China, Capitalist China: Social Tension and Political Adaptation under Economic Globalization* (London and New York: Routledge, 2009), p. 25.

53. Chen Lidan, "Hu Jintao tongzhi guanyu xinwen xuanchuan gongzuo de lunshu han xin si wei" ("Comrade Hu Jintao's commentary on journalism, propaganda work, and the new thinking"), *People's Daily*, 27 July 2006, http://media.people.com.cn/GB/40606/4633009.html.

54. "Cai Mingzhao: insisting on developing online environment in a healthy and orderly manner," *China Radio International*, 5 December 2008, http://news.xinhuanet.com/zgjx/2008-12/05/content_10462100.htm.

55. Many regulations exist that actively guide people in surfing the Internet and managing websites. The most relevant regulations and laws include: "The Decision of the National People's Congress Standing Committee on Guarding Internet Security" ("Quanguo renmin daibiao dahui changwu weiyuanhui guanyu weihu hulianwang de jueding"), "Regulations on Telecommunications of the People's Republic of China" ("Zhonghua renmin gongheguo dianxin tiaoli"), "Measures on the Administration of Internet Information Services" ("Hulianwang xinxi fuwu guanli banfa"), "Administration of Internet News Information Services Provision" ("Hulianwang xinwen xinxi fuwu guanli guiding"), and the "Administration of Internet Electronic Messaging Services Provisions" ("Hulianwang dianzi gonggao fuwu guanli guiding").

56. See, for example, "Liu Yunshan: News propaganda need to keep pace with the times, greatly improve and innovate," *Xinhua News Agency*, 11 June 2004, http://news.xinhuanet.com/newscenter/2004-06/11/content _1521685.htm.

57. "Hu Jintao talks to netizens via People's Daily Online," *Renmin wang*, 20 June 2008, http://news.sina.com.cn/c/2008-06-20/103115784006.shtml.

58. Michael Bristow, "China's leader makes live webcast," *BBC News*, 20 June 2008, http://news.bbc.co.uk/2/hi/asia-pacific/7465224.stm.

59. Tony Saich, "Globalization, governance, and the authoritarian state: China," in Joseph S. Nye Jr and John D. Donahue (eds.), *Governance in a Globalizing World* (Washington DC: Brookings Institution Press, 2000), p. 224.

60. *Fen-Qing* mainly refers to Chinese youth who display a high level of Chinese nationalism. For more discussions about *Fen-Qing*, Chinese youth and the party-state, see, for example, Stanley Rosen, "Contemporary Chinese youth and the State," *The Journal of Asian Studies*, Vol. 68, No. 2 (May 2009), pp. 359–369.

6

The Transitional Role of the Hu-Wen Leadership in China: A Case Study of Liu Xiaobo

Mobo GAO

Introduction

This chapter argues that the Hu-Wen leadership basically has been playing a house-keeping role. It does not have any clear vision for the future of China, has no big ideas and has been unable to provide a narrative of how China should move forward or of how China should stand in the world of nations. In other words, the Hu-Wen leadership has been at best playing a transitional role and at worst has been hushing up problems and avoiding making difficult decisions as much as possible. It has to be said, however, the Jiang Zemin–Zhu Rongji leadership had also been mostly doing house-keeping work, although Zhu Rongji did take some tough decisions, some of which were disastrous, like the commercialization of health care and the entrepreneurization of education. Therefore, the transition in China has been going on for quite some time since the strong man Deng Xiaoping gave up power.

I would like to point out also at the beginning that what I mean by transition is not the same as how it is usually used by China watchers in the Western world. When Western China watchers talk about transition their basic assumption is Fukuyama's "End of History", though they may not be aware or admit this assumption. In other words, they either argue or assume that China is currently undergoing a transition from Communism and planned economy to capitalist democracy and private market economy. In this big picture of human society, all and any societies have to end up the same as they are now in the West,[1] and before that happens they are transitional.

What I mean by transitional is much narrower and it simply means that the Hu-Wen leadership has been house-keeping the Chinese political system and its economic structure, with a hammer and screwdriver to fix bits and pieces here and there, to ensure that the house is not going to fall apart. This leadership has not been thinking of doing any renovation of the house, let alone move house. The reasons why this is the case is not a major concern in this chapter, though it does no harm to have a little speculation. One possible reason might be that these people are intellectually very limited. They gained the leadership position not because they have any particular talent or intellectual vision but because they were in the right place at the right time. This leads to the second possible reason. Maybe it is just the sign of the times, a time when no one in China could intellectually envisage anything different from the End of History or clashes of civilization. Hu Jintao or Wen Jiabao, like so many politicians and thinkers in China, may not like communism and the planned economy any more, but they cannot convince themselves to embrace wholeheartedly the Western system of capitalist democracy and private market economy either. In this scenario the best you can do is hang around and maintain the current order. Therefore, the Hu-Wen leadership, like the majority of high- and middle-ranking party officials and bureaucrats in China, have no intellectual substance; nor do they have any political conviction. Their decisions and actions seem ad hoc and reactive. At best they stay there in their position in order to stay there. At worst they stay in their position to extract as much capital as possible for their families and children.

In this chapter I will make use of one case study to show how the lack of intellectual and political conviction makes the Chinese leadership insecure, reactionary and clumsy. This case is the treatment of Liu Xiaobo. This is a good case study not only because it is well known but also because it touches both the domestic and foreign policies of China.

Background Explanation of House Keeping

There is a Chinese television programme called *Getaway*, jointly produced by the Chinese and some foreign company. The idea is to showcase China's tourist spots in the way they are appreciated by foreigners. The assumption, a very right one I think, is that foreigners and Chinese tour China for different reasons and look for different things. One episode that I watched with great interest is about a small town, Wuzhen in Zhejiang Province. Unlike so many villages in China, this village has kept most of its traditional houses and layout. In some villages, though not in Gao Village where I grew up, there used to be a *geng fu* (night watchman) who would tell the *geng* (a two-hour period in the night), so there were supposed to be ten hours of night divided into two-hour periods, making five *geng*. The *san geng* (the third period) would be from 1 am to 2 am, which was considered midnight, thus the Chinese saying *san geng ban ye* (the midnight of the third period). The *geng fu* (the night watchman) would have to go around the village and bang on a gong three times to indicate that it was *san geng*, four times to tell the villagers of *si geng* (the fourth period of the night) and so on. The man has to wear a vest on which the character *geng* is written both on the front and the back. In this television documentary, the *geng fu* of Wuzhen was not just telling the time but also announcing that it was a very dry period in high summer and therefore all the villagers had to be careful not to cause a fire.

That is collective house-keeping; to prevent disasters, to put out a fire, and to maintain order. The Hu-Wen leadership, in many ways, has done an excellent job as a *geng fu* in keeping the Chinese house in order, and in preventing a fire breaking out. The best example is the Chinese leadership's handling of the Sichuan earthquake in 2008. Wen Jiabao personally was at the front of the rescue efforts and set a very good example. After learning the lesson of media handling from the Tibetan riots in 2008, the Hu-Wen leadership did a much better job in handling the media on the Xinjiang riots later. The Hu-Wen leadership has been a good *geng fu* in many ways.

Obviously the *geng fu* of China has to do more than the *geng fu* in Wuzhen, and this is not without cost. The cost of this night-watchman mentality is that order has to be kept at any cost, to the extent that it is rigid, suppressive, dictatorial and oppressive. All these are appropriate conditions for breeding misunderstanding, even contempt and resentment. This is one of the reasons why there are always dissidents emerging, every now and then and here and there. The 2008 Charter, which advocates constitutional democracy and universal values of human rights, and which was signed by hundreds of academics, journalists and freelance writers, is one of these examples.

Another example of dissent is the young blogger called Han Han, who has made very mild but very explicit criticisms of the Chinese government policies and behaviour. He has a huge following in the internet. [2] At various levels of governance all over China other examples of resistance against the oppressive regime can be found everywhere. People kill themselves as a way to protest against developers whose bulldozers level their houses; migrant workers jump from the top of their dormitories and kill themselves, like a dozen young workers from the Taiwan-run enterprise Foxconn. The management of Foxconn was so worried about this reccurring nightmare that safety nets were installed around the workers' dormitories. This is certainly unprecedented.

Indeed, any disturbance of any kind can be seen as failure of the government to maintain order, so much so that the bureaucrats at various levels watch their area closely and will try to stop any sign that may be the beginning of disorder. This paranoid fear of disorder is so intense that it is like the pressure inside a pressure cooker that is getting higher and higher because there is no outlet for the steam to get out. This is so dangerous that any small incident, like what happened in Tunisia in early 2011, can potentially lead to an eruption on a huge scale.

The lack of an overarching grand narrative makes house-keeping in China more difficult than in a country like Tunisia because conflicting narratives compete with each other, involving differences of approach to move China forward. For instance, the increasingly talked about "Chongqing model" initiated by Bo Xilai, a very charismatic leader and one of the most powerful figures in current Chinese politics, attempts to recall the values of the Mao era to claim the moral ground. In contrast, provincial leaders in regions like Guangdong attempt to move China further down the road of privatization and capitalist democracy. The latter is very much represented by the Southern Media Group (*nanfang baoye*), a group of media outlets, chiefly the *Southern Weekend* (*nanfang zhoumo*), officially run by the Guangdong Provincial Propaganda Department. Early in 2011, the propaganda boss in Beijing forced Guangdong to sack some of the journalists and editors of the Southern Media Group who appeared to be spreading the idea of political reform along the Western model of capitalist democracy. For instance, one of the Guangdong Media Group outlets, the *Southern Weekly* (*nanfang zhoukan*), set up in 2008, purposely claims to model itself on the American *Time* magazine. Towards the end of 2010, the *Southern Weekly* selected and published what it called the 100 most influential Chinese of that year. Almost all of those included in the list would be considered to be from the right-wing side of Chinese politics including several who had signed the very controversial 2008 Charter. Weeks later, an unnamed Deputy Minister of Propaganda in Beijing is reported to have told Guangdong that the Southern Media Group was meant to work for the Communist Party of China (CPC), and it could not and should not be the headquarters of anti-CPC propaganda.[3] The context of these remarks was a visit by Wen Jiabao to a centre in Beijing where *fangmin* congregated (*fangmin*, literally meaning those who travel to talk to officials of upper authority, these are people who go to Beijing to seek the official redress by the central government of injustices they have suffered from local government authorities). The Deputy Minister of Propaganda allegedly said that Wen "was making trouble" because what he did would encourage *fangmin* to travel from all over the country to Beijing and that would make things difficult, especially with the two big national conferences taking place in the city in 2011.[4] He accused Wen of making a token gesture of caring to enhance his reputation.[5] All the provincial media outlets followed the instruction from Beijing not to make a huge event of Wen's visit to the *fangmin*, except the Guangdong Media Group, which made a feast of it for two days. This clearly shows that there is a lack of consensus on where China is heading and there is no sign as which side the Hu-Wen leadership in Beijing wants to support. Wen Jiabao seems to be inclined to be on the side of the ideology that the Southern Media Group has been trying to direct, while Hu Jintao is considered to be more inclined towards the traditional revolutionary ideology. The division is not very clear, however.

Liu Xiaobo and the Nobel Prize for Peace

The case of Liu Xiaobo is very illuminative as a study of the Hu-Wen house-keeping behaviour. It shows that the Hu-Wen leadership feels insecure, and therefore has been obsessed with maintaining the house in order, that China's domestic concern influences its foreign policy and that the perceived foreign interference influences its domestic decisions. The case of Liu Xiaobo also illustrates the conflicting political and value forces currently competing in China. One political and value force is the narrative that China should move quickly into a Western style of capitalist democracy. To put it in nutshell, this narrative represents the aspiration of what is called "the colour revolution" in China. But this narrative is being strongly resisted in China, possibly from Hu Jintao, and certainly from influential leaders like Bo Xilai and possibly Xi Jinping, the likely successor of Hu Jintao. Some of those in power are the princelings of the old revolutionary vanguards, that still have the revolutionary ideology that was instilled in them. On the other hand, there are many of these princelings who are actually bosses of capitalism enterprises. There are signs that these two forces, i.e., the princelings of power and the princelings of money, have already joined together to run the country.

But there are also many ordinary people who actually look back to the era of Mao with fond memories and who think the current leadership has betrayed the cause of Mao and his colleagues. According to this version of what is happening in China now, these are the capitalist roaders and Deng Xiaoping did exactly what Mao had accused him of: restoring capitalism in China. This ideological position can clearly be found in the internet website of *wuyouzhixiang* (The Utopia). The problem, however, is that those who resist the "colour revolution" model cannot really provide an alternative narrative. What is instructive is that in spite of its power and capacity to suppress dissent the Hu-Wen leadership actually allows the existence at the same time of both *wuyouzhixiang* and the Southern Media Group. The apparent tolerance of diversity indicates that there is a lack of conviction and a lack of agreed narrative. Thus the difficulty of house-keeping in China, as demonstrated by the Liu Xiaobo case.

Liu Xiaobo

Liu Xiaobo is a maverick literary writer, very much a product of the 1980s post-Mao "thought liberation" movement (*sixiang jiefang*), when the backlash against the Cultural Revolution and the rigid ideological and political control of the Mao era was at its loudest. There emerged the intellectual daring of the farewell to revolution,[6] not only the Cultural Revolution, but also the 1949 Revolution, the Russian Revolution and even the French Revolution, and the cry for Enlightenment, i.e., humanism, individualism and Western style of democracy. This Enlightenment narrative is especially critical of Chinese tradition which has been condemned in terms of "feudalism".[7] Chinese traditional ideas and practicum are narrated as feudalistic, backward and dark, whereas Western ideas of individualism and humanism are praised as progressive, modern and bright. This is basically a re-visiting of the landmark May the Fourth Movement usually referred to as having started in 1919.[8] The May the Fourth Movement focused on modernizing China with two interrelated strategies: to import Western ideas and to sweep away the ugly Chinese traditional values.[9] During this movement of soul-searching and ideological turmoil there emerged thinkers like Lu Xun, who launched scathing but nonetheless sympathetic attacks on the so-called Chinese national character (in *The Story of Ah Q* and *The Madman's Diaries*, for instance), and Hu Shi, who advocated wholesale Westernization. Two of the most outstanding and lasting impacts of this movement were the creation of the CPC in 1921 and the abolition of classical Chinese writing and the literary development known as plain speech.

How extraordinary it is that after more than half a century of transformation, the result of which has rendered China unrecognizable, compared with what China was like at the beginning of the twentieth century, the forward thinking Chinese in the 1980s were actually looking backwards,[10] to the beginning of the century, the very century through which the Chinese strove hard and made enormous sacrifice. And they called this looking backwards "thought liberation"! Of course, the Chinese intelligentsia elite used modern technology and new rhetoric, new metaphors and new images to re-play the veteran anti-tradition themes. For instance, the then very popular television series *He shang* (*The River Elegy*), controversial but supported by the then General Party Secretary of the CPC, Zhao Ziyang,[11] proclaims that the Chinese mentality is enclosed by the Great Wall and that the Yellow River symbolizes the misery and backwardness of Chinese civilization. It is the May the Fourth Movement revisited, but with more vivid images.

Liu Xiaobo is one of those 1980s Chinese intelligentsia who took the cultural essentialism seriously. For some there could be nuances in this ideology. However, in the case of Liu Xiaobo there has been none. Unlike Wei Jingsheng, an electrician who had the originality and courage to put up a wall poster that advocated the explosive theme that what China needed was the "fifth modernization", i.e., the modernization of democracy[12], and Li Zehou[13], who developed the idea that there was a narrative tension between Chinese nationalism and Enlightenment and that the tragedy for China was that Enlightenment had to give way to nationalism amidst foreign invasions[14], Liu Xiaobo did not have any new ideas. What makes Liu Xiaobo stand out as the "black horse", a status Liu clearly enjoys, is his knife-cutting, sharp way of saying something that has the effect of shocking his audience.[15] For instance, he declares that the reason why Hong Kong is so civilized and modern is that it was a British colony for 200 years. Therefore, for China, a country so big and backward, to reach the status of Hong Kong 300 years of Western colonization would still not be enough.[16] Liu Xiaobo both espouses a self-hatred of China and the Chinese,[17] and would go all the way to praise the West, especially the United States of America. Liu Xiaobo not only supported the U.S. invasion of Iraq in 2001[18] but also declared that what was good for the USA was good for humanity and that none of the wars waged by the USA, with the possible exception of Vietnam, was a war of aggression.[19]

While there is a lack of ideas there is no shortage of courage in Liu Xiaobo. When the 1989 Tiananmen events were taking place, Liu Xiaobo was actually in the USA as a visiting scholar. He immediately flew back to Beijing to be part of the events. He was one of the mature intelligentsia, as opposed to the young students, who had staged a hunger strike to support the protests against the Chinese authorities. To be fair to Liu he was also one of the few who, in the last phase of the events, helped to get the students out of the square in time to avoid further casualties. Liu Xiaobo is not a thinker, but a brave political activist. The initiation, the work to get people to sign and then to publicize the *ling ba xuan zhang* (the 2008 Charter) typical of his political activism. The Charter does not have anything really new to say and it basically apes the Eastern Europe precedent of the 1977 Charter, but it had the desired political and publicity impact. One aspect of the impact is that the Chinese regime under the leadership of Hu-Wen arrested Liu Xiaobo and put him in gaol. This is an act of cowardice on the part of the Hu-Wen leadership that shows its sense of insecurity and lack of intellectual conviction. It was a very bad house-keeping decision that was counter-productive to its own good.

The Nobel Prize for Peace

More than the Nobel Prize for Literature, the Nobel Prize for Peace is blatantly political.[20] It really has nothing to do with peace. Some would argue that the prize has often been awarded to war criminals, like Henry Kissinger.[21] Among the controversial awards there was also the Israeli Prime Minister Menachem Begin, who had been head of the militant Zionist group Irgun, which is often regarded as a terrorist organization and responsible for the King David Hotel bombing in 1946. In a less damaging but nevertheless farcical case, the year 2009 prize was awarded to the sitting U.S. President Obama who had just came into power. Even Obama himself seemed to find the award embarrassing. One sometimes wonders what these elderly Norwegians of the Nobel committee think they are doing. Since the prize has been politically motivated,[22] it is beside the point whether Liu Xiaobo deserves the award of the 2010 Nobel Prize for Peace. However, it is not beside the point to discuss how the Hu-Wen leadership handled Liu Xiaobo and its behaviour towards the award of the Nobel Peace prize to him. Of course we are not sure whether the arrest of Liu Xiaobo and the diplomatic endeavour to boycott the award ceremony was directly taken by the Hu-Wen leadership high up in Beijing. However, it can be surmised that neither Hu Jintao nor Wen Jaobao could be isolated from the events surrounding Liu Xiaobo or that the actions could be taken without their approval.

What Is at Stake and Why

Because the award of the 2010 Nobel Prize for Peace aroused such fierce debate,[23] especially on the internet media, somehow the Nobel Prize for Peace committee felt the need to respond. One of the committee members, Geir Lundestad, said that "Beijing's decision 'solved the problem' of how to recognise Chinese activists". He said the judges had gradually come to believe they had to "address the China question". He further added during a talk at Oxford University,

"If we had given a prize to a dissident from Cuba or Vietnam, fine, there are difficult situations in those countries, but the question would then be: why don't you address China?"[24]

What is interesting is his automatic admission of two important points. The first is that the prize has to be awarded to a dissident activist. The second point is that it has to be awarded to a dissident in what is considered to be a communist country. Why does not the committee think of awarding the prize to someone who really has worked for peace, for instance, the President of Taiwan who has genuinely promoted peace between the two sides of the Taiwan Straits? Secondly, why does not the committee think of giving the prize to a dissident in a country other than the so-called communist states, for instance, the United States of America, like Noam Chomsky? Or some dissident in Saudi Arabia, or Tunisia or Egypt, or Israel?[25]

One can easily name tens of countries where human rights abuses can be described as worse than those in China. The answer of course is that the award has to be made in accordance with the geopolitical interests of the Western powers, whatever that interest is perceived to be in any particular year.[26] That is of course also why the American National Endowment for Democracy (NED) funds Liu Xiaobo for his dissident activities.[27]

The award of the Nobel Prize for Peace to Liu Xiaobo seems to show that it has nothing to do with peace,[28] but it has everything to do with the "colour revolutions". Therefore in this respect the Chinese authorities are right and the Hu-Wen leadership has legitimate worries. What is at stake for the Hu-Wen leadership is what Liu Xiaobo does represent and that it does indeed threaten the rule of the CPC.

The Hu-Wen Leadership's Management of the Liu Xiaobo Case

Liu Xiaobo is just a freelance writer, not a drug dealer, a political party organizer, not an activist who holds a gun and organizes an underground army or who wages a guerrilla war. Therefore, it is totally idiotic and infantile for the Hu-Wen regime to be paranoid about Liu Xiaobo and the likes of him. It is understandable that for the regime to hang on to power it would not like what is advocated in the 2008 Charter. But people inside and outside of China have been saying these things for years. So what if hundreds of the intelligentsia elite signed the 2008 Charter?[29] It is very likely that most of the middle-class young people, let alone the vast majority of the working people, in China could not care less. It is understandable that the regime does not like the idea that a foreign organization, NGO or otherwise, pays for people like Liu Xiaobo to write anti-Chinese government propaganda. But have they not been doing that for years, like the Laogai Foundation headed by Harry Wu, or the Fanlungong and its media outlets, and so on? If they could do these things outside of China, what difference does it make if people like Liu Xiaobo do it inside China, since the internet makes national boundaries more or less meaningless anyway?

The Hu-Wen leadership, like the leadership of Jiang Zemin before them, reacted to this kind of criticism and this kind of activity badly, clumsily and idiotically, because they do not have a proactive policy of dealing with criticism. They do not have a proactive policy because they do not have a narrative of what they themselves are and what they should move China forward to. In other words, they do not have the intellectual guts or, in a Chinese phrase that expresses the phenomenon better, they have no *diqi* (底气, "the air on which they can stand"). They do not have the intellectual guts because they do not know what to do with China. They do not even know what to do with themselves except to hang on to power.

Lack of Substance in Ideas and Policies

This lack of substance in terms of ideas is very different from even Deng Xiaoping, let alone Mao Zedong. Mao could afford to launch so many political campaigns, and even to launch the Cultural Revolution which attacked all officials and bureaucrats of an entire state machine, from civil to military and from top to bottom, because Mao had a narrative of creating a new system and new society by keeping the revolution alive. Mostly Mao did not have to react to policy problems domestically and internationally because he dictated what would happen and what would not happen. The grand narrative of *xin zhongguo* (new China) was an endless source of ideas and policies.

Deng Xiaoping did not have many original ideas;[30] but he knew that what China needed to do soon after the downfall of the Gang of Four was to reverse many of the Maoist policies in the name of correcting the wrong ones and upholding the right ones. He knew that China had to develop a market economy and to make use of technological and management innovations developed in developed countries, especially in the USA, Japan and Europe. This was the substance of ideas that formed the bedrock of the Deng period. True, Deng Xiaoping handled the Tiananmen protests idiotically and terribly badly, but he managed to move China forward and he handled the foreign powers that had imposed diplomatic, technological and military embargoes with confidence. However one might appraise Deng Xiaoping, one cannot deny that he had *diqi*.

However, when we come to the Hu-Wen generation, the state machine is completely filled with careerists who have been promoted and could be promoted only if and when they follow those above them. Hu Jintao and Wen Jiabao do not have ideas of their own of how to move China forward. Hu's predecessor Jiang Zemin did not have much of an idea either. But he pretended to be a statesman of vision and ideas by floating the slogan of the "three representatives" which, justly, became a joke for many Chinese people. And now Hu Jintao talks about "scientific development" and "harmonious society". The former aims to address the excesses of the "development at all cost" strategy implemented since Deng Xiaoping came to power after the Cultural Revolution, and the latter to address the issue of tension and even local unrest as a result of increasing disparity and inequality.

But there is no such thing as "scientific development". You can have balanced or unbalanced development, depending what you mean. You can have development that favours the rich and the powerful only or development that brings along the poor and the advantaged. You can have development that harms the environment and exhausts the resources or you can have sustainable development that protects the environment and leave resources for future generations. But neither of these is either "scientific" or "non-scientific". Science may aim to pursue the truth; but what is perceived or agreed to be "scientific" does not mean it is good for human society. Furthermore, there is no such thing as the holy grail of the "scientific".

Nor is there such thing as "harmonious society". People can be taught to behave towards each other civilly and politely; but there are always tensions and conflicts among different sectors and different stratum of any society. A successful leadership is one that has the power and the imagination to allocate resources in such a way that innovation and creativity is encouraged and at the same time even the most disadvantaged feel that there is something worth living for, or at least feel that they are cared for.

Clearly the Hu-Wen leadership does not have ideas of substance to stand on. They therefore feel insecure, uncertain, unconfident and therefore very defensive. That explains their clumsiness in handling the Liu Xiaobo affair. They should not have put Liu Xiaobo in gaol in the first place. They should not have done that not because they should be expected to believe in individual human rights, but rather for their own good. The Norwegian Nobel prize committee might not have even awarded the Prize to Liu Xiaobo if he had not been gaoled. Furthermore, the Chinese leaders should not have attempted to coerce people to stay away from the prize ceremony. This kind of foreign relations behaviour dictated by ill-conceived domestic politics can only lead to the effect opposite to what the Chinese authorities wish.

If the Hu-Wen leadership had any idea of substance they would have been more confident of themselves. As a result of that confidence they would not have censured the news about the 2008 Charter or the Peace Prize. They could have published the whole case and let people debate about it. It is quite likely that, after debate and after full exposure of what Liu Xiaobo does and thinks, the majority of the Chinese would have agreed that Liu Xiaobo was no more and no less than an egocentric, harmless and empty chatterbox.

The Hu-Wen leadership does not seem to have conviction of any kind – they want to hang on to what they think is or what they call socialism. At the same time they think capitalism works better for the economy. So they call this capitalism with Chinese characteristics "socialism with Chinese characteristics". For the harmonious society idea they have to resort to Chinese tradition, especially the sage Confucius. Recently the Chinese authorities put up a huge statue of Confucius on the Tiananmen Square, an act that has caused a huge controversy and debates on the internet. The CPC was one of the children of the May the Fourth Movement that made a huge issue of "down with Confucius shop". In fact the first leader of the CPC when it was established in 1921 was Chen Duxiu, one of the foremost May the Fourth Movement leaders. For many the ideologies of the CPC are the very antithesis of Confucianism[31], but now Confucius stands there on the Square, looking over the dead body of Mao Zedong, whose one last political campaign was to criticize Lin Biao and Confucius.[32]

Conclusion

Because there is a lack of substance in the Hu-Wen leadership all they can do is maintain order by playing a leadership role (*zuo xiu*), as if they were leading and as if they cared. The most recent example, recalled above, is when Wen Jiabao visited a centre frequented by *fangmin* (people of other regions who travel to Beijing to seek official rectification of injustice), early in 2011. The Southern Media Group outlets hailed this event as historical in that it was the first visit to meet a group of *fangmin* by a premier in the 61-year history of the PRC. But in fact it was all a show without any substance. If Wen really cared or could do something about their problems, why has he not done anything about them in all these years, until he is about to step down, in 2011? During this staged visit, Wen actually said that he could not solve the problems of individuals, their cases had to be dealt with by the relevant departments and could best be resolved at the locality where the problem arose. As one *fangmin* said, if their problems could have been resolved locally, why would anyone choose to travel all the way to Beijing to seek justice?[33] Instead of making any improvement to any one of the *fangmin* at the centre, Wen's visit led to a police round-up which resulted in the detention of many *fangmin* before his visit, to ensure security!

To conclude this chapter, a few words have to be said about where the transition will lead. I have argued in this chapter that the Hu-Wen leadership does not have a narrative of what they are doing or of where China is heading, and that consequently all they can do is house-keeping. I have also argued, by using the case study of Liu Xiaobo, that the house-keeping job by the Hu-Wen leadership has mostly been done very clumsily and badly. In other words, as suggested by the title of this chapter, the Hu-Wen leadership has only played a transitional role. Then there is the question of transition; from what to what? I have pointed out at the beginning of this chapter that what I mean by transition is not what is usually referred to in the field of China studies, in which the Chinese regime is always assumed to be, or talked about as if it were, transitional from communist authoritarian state to liberal democracy and from planned economy to capitalist market economy. There are many democracies in the world that are not liberal and many authoritarian or even dictatorial one-party states that are not communist. China seems to have a mixture of a robust market economy and a planned economy. The state machine has been changed from dictatorial to authoritarian. What is somewhat unique in China is that it is being run by one party that still calls itself communist, though there is hardly anything communist about what it does.

What to do with this party? What is the relevance of the CPC to the people of China? What is the future of the CPC? To where does the CPC want to lead China? What is the CPC's ideology? What does the CPC aim to achieve by hanging onto power? Any leadership unable to find answers to these questions is transitional.

Notes and References

1. The so-called global financial crisis that started in 2009 has poured some cold water on this self-congratulating confidence in the Western world, but it looks like the water was not cold enough.

2. "Han Han, China's most popular blogger," *China Digital Times*, http://chinadigitaltimes.net/china/han-han/ (accessed on 19 February 2011).

3. Boxun, "中宣部副部长失控，斥温家宝是麻烦制造者" http://news.creaders.net/china/newsViewer.php?nid=459751&id=1038932, 28 January 2011.

4. The National Conference of the Representatives of the People's Congress and the National Conference of the Representatives of the Political Consultancy.

5. Boxun, "中宣部副部长失控，斥温家宝是麻烦制造者"

6. 刘再复、李泽厚，《告别革命》(香港：天地图书有限公司，1997).

7. 李慎之，《风雨苍黄五十年》(香港：明报出版社，2000).

8. 杜光，"送别包.遵.信 推进新启蒙 — 曾经沧海，" 2007, http://www.360doc.com/content/071130/08/16239_859121.html (accessed on 15 June 2009).

9. 柏杨，《丑陋的中国人》(台湾：林白出版社，1985).

10. 李泽厚、刘再复，"五四 90 周年仍缺民主与科学"，《亚洲周刊》二〇〇九年第十八期, http://www.gongfa.org/bbs/viewthread.php?tid=2362 (accessed on 15 June 2009).

11. 赵紫阳，《赵紫阳软禁中的谈话(宗凤鸣 记述)》(香港：开放出版社，2007).

12. The idea of "fifth modernization" was to follow the "four modernization" theme that was being floated around during the early 1970s when, in the terms of Zhou Enlai, the four modernizations were; agriculture, industry, science and technology, and national defence.

13. 李泽厚《中国现代思想史论》，北京，东方出版社，1987.

14. According to Wang Luoshui, 王若, in He Qinglian, 《20世纪后半叶历史解密》 (Hong Kong, 博大出版社, 2009), pp. 6–21), it was Vera Schwarcz (*The Chinese Enlightenment: Intellectuals and the Legacy of the May Fourth Movement of 1919*, University of California Press, 1986) who first proposed the idea that the priority of saving the nation (by revolution) overwhelmed the project of the Enlightenment.

15. 黎阳，"孔子像给庆祝建党出了个难题"，华岳论坛，6 February 2011, http://washeng.net/HuaShan/BBS/shishi/gbcurrent/173459.shtml (accessed on 7 February 2011).

16. Barry Sautman and Hairong Yan, "Liu Xiaobo Stands for War Not Peace," *The Guardian*, 25 October 2010, http://www.mg.co.za/article/2010-10-25 -liu-xiaobo-stands-for-war-not-peace (accessed on 4 February 2011).

17. Channa Li, "A Nobel peace prize for cultural self-hatred," *New American Media*, 12 October 2010, http://newamericamedia.org/2010/10/a-nobel-peace-prize-for-cultural-self-hatred.php (accessed on 4 February 2010).

18. 刘晓波，"伊战与美国大选" in 观察网 China Observer, 31 October 2004 (accessed on 9 February 2010).

19. Mobo Gao, *The Battle for China's Past: Mao and the Cultural Revolution* (London: Pluto, 2008).

20. Fredrick S. Heffermehl, "Norwegian jurist calls Nobel peace prize wrong, Illegal", Hidden Harmonies China Blog, 13 October 2010. http://www.asianews.it/index.php?l=en&art=13971 (accessed on 8 February 2011).

21. BBC Documentaries, "The trials of Henry Kissinger," 3 April 2006 http://www.bbc.co.uk/bbcfour/documentaries/features/feature_kissinger.shtml (accessed 8 February 2010).

22. William F. Engdahl, "The geopolitical agenda behind the 2010 peace prize" in *Liu Xiaobo Deserves an Ig Nobel Peace Prize – The latest reaction to Buzz the West*, Hidden Harmonies China Blog, 2 December 2010, http://blog.hiddenharmonies.org/2010/10/liu-xiaobo-deserves-an-ig-nobel-peace -prize-the-latest-reaction-to-buzz-the-west/ (accessed on 8 February 2011).

23. James Fallows, "Liu Xiaobo and the '300 years' problem," *The Atlantic*, 21 October 2011; David Kelly, "Liu Xiaobo and universal values," *East Asian Forum*, 11 October 2010, http://www.eastasiaforum.org/2010/10/11/liu -xiaobo-and-universal-values/ (accessed 4 February 2011); Julia Lovell, "China's quest for a suitable Nobel," *East Asian Forum*, 21 October 2010, http://www.eastasiaforum.org/2010/10/21/chinas-quest-for-a-suitable-nobel/ (accessed 4 February 2011).

24. Geir Lundestad, "China made peace prize decision for us, says Nobel judge,"

The Guardian, 28 October 2010, p. 26, http://guardian.co.uk, 27 October 2010.

25. Here is "Ruthie", one of the respondents to Tariq Ali's article, "The Nobel War Prize" (see note 28 below) at *The London Review of Books* website, 11 December 2010 (accessed on 4 February 2011):

> "Here in Tel Aviv some of the peace activists like myself often wonder why no Israeli dissidents have ever been honoured. Uri Avineri, Amira Hass, Gideon Levi are obvious names. And the person whose courage has become legendary: Mordechai Vanunu, who revealed that Israel was a nuclear state and is still under house arrest, not allowed to leave the country. Each year from 1988 to 2004, Joseph Rotblat wrote to the Nobel Prize Committee suggesting his name. Finally Vanunu wrote himself and withdrew his name. He stated: "I am asking the committee to remove my name from the list for this year's list of nominations. I cannot be part of a list of laureates that includes Shimon Peres, the President of Israel. He is the man who was behind all the Israeli atomic policy. Peres established and developed the atomic weapon program in Dimona in Israel. Peres was the man who ordered the kidnapping of me in Italy Rome, Sept. 30, 1986, and for the secret trial and sentencing of me as a spy and traitor for 18 years in isolation in prison in Israel. Until now he continues to oppose my freedom and release, in spite of my serving full sentence [of] 18 years. From all these reasons I don't want be nominated and will not accept this nomination. I say No to any nomination as long as I am not free, that is, as long as I am still forced to be in Israel. WHAT I WANT IS FREEDOM AND ONLY FREEDOM."

> It seems that our fighters for peace are invisible to the Norwegian politicians. I always wondered why. This blog debate has been enlightening. I now know why.

26. William F. Engdahl, "The geopolitical agenda behind the 2010 Peace prize," in *Liu Xiaobo deserves an Ig Nobel Peace Prize – The latest reaction to buzz the West*, Hidden Harmonies China Blog, 2 December 2010, and http://blog .hiddenharmonies.org/2010/10/liu-xiaobo-deserves-an-ig-nobel-peace-prize-the -latest-reaction-to-buzz-the-west/ (accessed 8 February 2011).

27. Fallows, "Liu Xiaobo and the '300 years' problem". For the details of Liu's NED support see: http://www.zoominfo.com/people/Xiaobo_Liu_378792980 .aspx. ICPC received $135,000 (USD) from the NED in 2007 (http://www .ned.org/grants/07programs/grants-asia07.html); $135,000 from the NED in 2006 (http://www.ned.org/grants/06programs/grants-asia06.html) and $85,000 from the NED in 2004 (http://www.ned.org/grants/04programs/grants -asia04.html). ICPC is not the only avenue by which my tax dollar benefits Liu Xiaobo. He also receives financial support from the U.S. to publish the magazine *Minzhu Zhongguo* (*Democratic China*): $145,000 in 2007 (http://www.ned.org/grants/07programs/grants-asia07.html); $136,000 in 2005 (http://www.ned.org/grants/05programs/grants-asia05.html) and $135,000 in 2004 (http://www.ned.org/grants/04programs/grants-asia04.html).

28. Tariq Ali, "The Nobel War Prize," *London Review of Books*, 11 December 2010.   http://www.lrb.co.uk/blog/2010/12/11/tariq-ali/the-nobel-war-prize/ (accessed 4 February 2011).

29. "Over 300 Sign 'Charter 08' a Manifesto for Human Rights in China, But Some Are Already Arrested," http://*Asiannews.it*, 12 October 2008 (accessed 8 February 2010).

30. The black cat and white cat theory has been popular for thousands of years in rural China and is hardly original.

31. 黎阳，"孔子像给庆祝建党出了个难题。"

32. After the author wrote this chapter the statue of Confucius was removed quietly from the Tiananmen Square. This is a further example of how insecure and unsure the Chinese authorities are.

33. 尚好，"把皮球踢给地方 温家宝访民秀演砸了"，万维读者网，7 February 2011, http://news.creaders.net/headline/newsViewer.php?nid=460917&id=1041282 &dcid=16 (accessed 8 February 2011).

7

China Wages Quasi-Superpower Diplomacy

Willy Wo-Lap LAM

Introduction

By most measurements of national strength, including economic and military prowess, the People's Republic of China is closing the gap with the world's lone superpower, the United States. In mid-2010, China replaced Japan as the second-largest economic entity in the world. Having made a spectacular recovery from the global financial crisis, China is widely regarded as the prime locomotive for economic recovery worldwide. The People's Liberation Army (PLA) is building nuclear submarines and aircraft carriers, and the country's first astronaut is expected to set foot on the moon before 2020. Taking advantage of the damage that the financial crisis has dealt the American laissez-faire system, the Communist Party of China (CPC) is gunning for a novel international financial architecture, or one that is not dominated by the United States. Most significantly, Beijing is pulling out all the stops to project hard and soft power to augment its global influence.

Even though Beijing has made friends and enhanced its influence in regions as far as Africa and Latin America, it is also coming up against unprecedented challenges. While the USA and China are poised to enhance cooperation on the financial and trade fronts, these two "strategic competitors" are expected to cross swords on a number of security and foreign-affairs issues. China's relations with important neighbours such as Japan and India will also be affected by the growing popularity of the "China threat" theory. Friction between China, on the one hand, and Southeast Asian nations including

Vietnam, Malaysia and the Philippines, on the other, has intensified owing to sovereignty disputes over a score or so of islets in the South China Sea. There are also indications that countries including Australia, India, Japan and South Korea may consider it advantageous to join hands with the USA to check China's ascendancy. This is why despite the Middle Kingdom's formidable economic and military heft, the CPC leadership has become more nervous than ever about the exacerbation of a Washington-led "anti-China containment policy".

This chapter traces the efforts that China is making to attain quasi-superpower status in the foreign and security arenas – and the implications of this high-powered diplomacy for the global balance of power, including China's relations with key countries such as the USA. Given the prevalence of the "China threat" theory, this chapter will also examine whether the CPC leadership is nimble and creative enough to convince status-quo powers that its precipitous rise will not upset the world order or spell disaster for individual nations. For example, Beijing has done much to boost its soft power by playing up the benign – and universally acceptable – values of the China model. And while it has continued to maintain close ties with rogue regimes such as Burma and Zimbabwe, the CPC leadership has tried hard to become a "responsible stakeholder" in the international community by, for example, chairing the Six Party Talks on the North Korean nuclear issue and enthusiastically taking part in United Nations-mandated peace-keeping missions in Africa. Beijing has also played the "economic card" by pouring investments into neighbouring countries – particularly members of the Association of Southeast Asian Nations (ASEAN).

The Hu Jintao administration, however, has adamantly refused to reform China's outdated ideology and political institutions. Since China's socio-political systems and norms do not mesh well with the forces of globalization, the Chinese leadership's refusal to undertake genuine reforms could undermine its international reach. President Hu has reiterated that the CPC will "never go down the deviant path" of Western political ideals. In this age of globalization and IT-dominated economies, Beijing still subscribes to the theory of indivisible sovereignty, meaning that no country should interfere in the internal affairs of others. And even as the CPC is committing unprecedented resources to muffling dissent, it is trying to bolster its legitimacy by appealing to nationalist sentiments especially among the young. While the leadership has set aside tens of billions of dollars to project Chinese "soft power," its commitment to quasi-Leninist norms will militate against its aspirations to become a superpower in the coming decade or two.

Much then depends on whether the fourth generation of CPC leadership headed by President Hu is willing and able to make the necessary changes in both internal politics and diplomacy to persuade major international players that an enhanced role for the fast-emerging quasi-superpower will spell benefits for them. How China will make adjustments to meet the world's expectations – and how global stakeholders will accommodate the aspirations of the quasi-superpower – will constitute the major story of the first half of this century.

Genesis of China's Quasi-Superpower Diplomacy

China's rapid recovery from the global financial crisis has given the CPC leadership more confidence in its global power projections. This has been made possible not only by China's fast-growing economic and military might but also the decline of America's international influence in the wake of its interventions in Iraq and Afghanistan and the meltdown of its financial institutions. President Hu Jintao, who heads the CPC's Leading Group on Foreign Affairs (LGFA), is pushing "quasi-superpower diplomacy" to consolidate China's preeminence in the new world order. China's new-found prominence and much-elevated status was evident during the G20 meeting in London in April 2009, when Hu was seated right next to Queen Elizabeth II and host Prime Minister, Gordon Brown, for the opening photograph. U.S. President Barak Obama, who was trying hard to shed his predecessor George W. Bush's much-criticized unilateralist foreign policy, had to settle for a much humbler place in the back row.[1]

The official Chinese media has made much of comments by Western observers that the G20 has morphed into the G2, namely the world's lone superpower and the rising quasi-superpower. There is also talk of a Pax Americhina, or Chinamerica, dominating 21st century geopolitics.[2] This was pretty much confirmed by President Obama in the "Strategic and Economic Dialogue" (SED) between both countries that first took place in Washington in July 2009. "The relationship between the United States and China will shape the 21st century, which makes it as important as any bilateral relationship in the world," Obama said while opening the SED conclave. "That really must underpin our partnership. That is the responsibility that together we bear."[3]

So confident is Beijing about its global stature that it seems oblivious of the fact that the image of a China that is throwing its weight around may conjure up latter-day versions of the Yellow Peril. The Middle Kingdom as fire-spitting dragon was etched onto television screens around the world as the Chinese navy celebrated its sixtieth birthday in the port city of Qingdao in April 2009. Military representatives from twenty-nine countries were on hand to witness the Chinese navy showing off its first indigenously manufactured nuclear submarines and assorted state-of-the-art hardware.[4] One month earlier, Defence Minister Liang Guanglie told his visiting Japanese counterpart Yasukazu Hamada that the PLA was going ahead with its programme of building aircraft carriers.[5] Western experts think the PLA has plans to construct up to four flat-tops in the coming decade. Beijing is also pulling out all the stops to land a Chinese astronaut on the Moon by 2015. All these add up to a no-holds-barred projection of power that is rare in China's 5,000-year history.

For reasons including reluctance to fan the flames of the "China threat" theory, Chinese officials and scholars have not yet used the term "quasi-superpower diplomacy" or its equivalent. Yet the facts speak for themselves. Hu, who is also Chairman of the Central Military Commission, the equivalent of commander-in-chief, has made major revisions to the foreign and security policies of his predecessors. Deng Xiaoping, the late patriarch, laid down this series of dictums in the late 1980s and early 1990s: in foreign policy, "take a low profile and never take the lead"; and regarding the USA, "avoid confrontation and seek opportunities for cooperation".[6] Former president Jiang Zemin, from the mid-1990s onward, pioneered a so-called "great power diplomacy under the global climate of one superpower, several great powers". This meant that China should work together with other great powers such as Russia, Japan and the European Union to transform a "unipolar world order" – one that is dominated by the USA – into a "multipolar world order". However, China avoided direct conflicts with the lone superpower, and the relationship between the Jiang leadership and the Bill Clinton administration was by and large stable.[7] At the same time, Jiang tried to persuade China's neighbours that Beijing was sticking to a "peaceful rise" strategy, that is, the Middle Kingdom's emergence would not pose a threat to them. The term "peaceful rise", however, has seldom been used by Chinese diplomas and senior cadres since the early 2000s.[8]

China's economic, military and diplomatic clout had expanded dramatically by the time Hu took over the helm at the Sixteenth CPC Congress in November 2002. Seeing itself as a quasi-superpower, Beijing is no longer shying away from frontal contests with the USA, China's strategic competitor. For the Hu-led Politburo, "quasi-superpower diplomacy" means China will expand its influence in regions ranging from the ASEAN bloc to Africa and Latin America – and in global bodies such as the United Nations, the World Bank and the International Monetary Fund.[9] Blaming Washington for failing to regulate its multinational financial firms, Beijing is lobbying hard for a "new global financial architecture" shorn of U.S. domination. Equally significantly, Beijing is trying to prevent American naval and air power from dominating the Asia-Pacific Region. And the PLA is developing enough firepower to thwart an "anti-China containment policy" supposedly spearheaded by Washington and abetted by such U.S. allies as Japan, South Korea, the Philippines and Australia.[10]

A trademark of Beijing's new-found "quasi-superpower diplomacy" is that Chinese diplomats and generals are gunning for a paradigm shift in geopolitics, namely, new rules of the game whereby the fast-rising quasi-superpower will be playing a more forceful role. In particular, Beijing has served notice that it won't be shy about playing hardball to safeguard what it claims to be "core national interests" (see following section). The pugilistic turn in China's Great Leap Outward was evidenced by a number of incidents in 2001: the Hu leadership's unexpectedly vehement reaction to Washington's arms sale to Taiwan in January 2001, and to Obama's meeting the Dalai Lama; and Beijing's high-decibel objection to the summer war games conducted by the USA and South Korea in the Yellow Sea.

According to Li Wei, the president of the high-profile China Institute of Contemporary International Relations (CICIR), there is a reawakened resolve on the part of Beijing to do whatever it takes to defend "core interests" such as Taiwan and Tibet. Referring to the country's new-look foreign policy since late last year, Li said: "We have become a more pro-active and much more mature [global player]".[11] Professor Yuan Peng, an America expert at CICIR, which is affiliated with the Ministry of State Security, is even more forthright about his country's global strategy. He said Beijing's unusually harsh reactions to Washington's arms sales to Taiwan and President Obama's meeting with the Dalai Lama amounted to a game changer. "China wants to change the rules of the game," said Professor Yuan. "The U.S. leadership had sold arms to Taiwan and met with the Dalai Lama, and we had scolded the U.S. before. But this time, it's real rebuke and real *fanzhi* (counter-control)."[12]

More significantly, Beijing is determined to boost its global clout by taking advantage of the decline in American power. According to Professor Liu Jianhua of Zhongnan University of Economics and Law, "China should seize upon the opportunity provided by the shrinkage of America's strategic [resources]" by expanding its international exposure. He pointed out that in the coming decade or so, "America's needs for China will grow and its ability to contain China will decline". Beijing should not miss this golden opportunity to pursue a more proactive foreign and security policies.[13] As we shall see below, the quasi-superpower diplomacy of a newly ascendant China will clash with the USA, the status-quo superpower, which is not about to yield its predominance without a fight.

No-holds-barred Projection of Hard Power

The most obvious manifestation of the new quasi-superpower diplomacy is the projection of hard-power by China's increasingly well-equipped military. Not only is the PLA given big budget boosts every year, but the generals also seem to be having a bigger say in foreign and security policies. This is evidenced by the fact that a relatively large number of senior PLA officers, in addition to military media commentators, have dominated the media with their hawkish views on diplomacy. When asked about the preeminence of military voices in foreign policy, Major-General Xu Guangyu indicated in 2010 that "it's natural for the PLA to speak out first on these issues". Xu, a researcher at the China Arms Control and Disarmament Association, added, "It's the PLA's sacred duty to defend China's territory and interests".[14] It is probable that Hu is giving the generals more authority over security matters in return for their backing for his Communist Youth League Faction (CYLF). The Eighteenth CPC Congress – which will witness the transition of power from the fourth- to the fifth-generation leadership – is scheduled for late 2012, and support of the generals is key to the elevation of a large number of CYLF affiliates to key slots.[15]

According to Air Force Senior Colonel Dai Xu, China's military capacity is simply not equal to the task of maintaining national security – or protecting the country's vast global interests. Dai, a popular commentator on military affairs for Beijing websites, compares the U.S. defence force to an eagle – "which stands tall and has unimpaired vision" – and that of Russia to an ostrich, "which can't fly too high but can run very fast", The PLA, on the other hand, "can neither fly nor run fast".[16] Yet Dai is confident that the Chinese military machine will catch up soon. For the strategist, military power consists of two elements; *shili* ("power and capacity") and whether a country is determined and daring enough to use *shili*. There seems little question that a new generation of assertive generals and strategists will not shy away from projecting military power to sustain the country's quasi-superpower status.[17]

Expanded Role for the People's Liberation Army and a New Stance on Settling Territorial Disputes

In an apparent revision of the "peaceful rise theory", China's military officers and analysts are saying that to attain a global status commensurate with China's comprehensive strength, the PLA should not only seek sophisticated weapons but also be constantly primed for warfare to defend China's core interests. Indeed, while the main objectives of China's defence forces up to the early 2000s were defending its borders and ensuring national reunification – mainly thwarting Taiwan independence – the goal under the "new historical circumstances" is to protect China's global interests. According to General Zhang Zhaoyin, the PLA must abandon the outdated doctrine of "building a peace-oriented army at a time of peace". Writing in the official *Liberation Army Daily*, General Zhang argued that "preparing for battle, fighting wars, and winning wars have always been the fundamental tasks of the army". "The PLA must never deviate from the doctrine of 'being assiduous in preparing for warfare, and seeking to win wars," added Zhang, who is the deputy commander of a Group Army in the Chengdu Military Region.[18]

Strategist Jin Yinan has posited the theory that "China can not emerge in the midst of nightingale songs and swallow dances", a reference to the placid pleasures of peacetime. Jin, who teaches at the National Defence University (NDU), indicated that China had to "hack out a path through thorns and thistles" in its search for greatness. "When a country and a people have reached a critical moment, the armed forces often play the role of pivot and mainstay" in ensuring that national goals are met, Jin noted.[19] That these theorists were evincing mainstream opinion within the leadership was made clear when Jin was invited in July 2009 to give a special lecture to the Politburo on military strategies.[20]

What is alarming, particularly to China's neighbours, is that a sizeable number of hawkish PLA officers want to fine-tune yet another Deng doctrine on handling sovereignty disputes with nearby states, namely, *gezhi zhuquan, gongtong kaifa* (搁置主权 共同开发) "shelving sovereignty disputes and focusing on joint development". This concept was first raised by then Vice-Premier Deng when he visited Japan in 1978. Deng told his hosts that disputes regarding the Diaoyu (known as Senkakus in Japan) islets should be "left to later generations" while both countries should concentrate on joint economic development.[21] The *gezhi zhuquan* idea is also the principle underpinning China's early 2000s agreements with ASEAN regarding sovereignty rows over the Spratly and the Paracel Islands. In 2002, Beijing and ASEAN signed the Treaty of Amity and Cooperation, which was followed closely by the Declaration on the Conduct of Parties in the South China Sea (DOC).[22] This *modus operandi* was also used during the theoretical accord reached between President Hu Jintao and then-Japanese Prime Minister Yasuo Fukuda in 2008 for settling sovereignty disputes over the East China Sea. Yet, Beijing and Tokyo have since failed to go one step further by formalizing the Hu-Fukuda agreement into a full-fledged treaty. One possible reason is opposition to the "joint development" formula expressed by Chinese nationalists as well as PLA generals.[23]

Various opinion leaders, particularly those from the PLA, however, have lobbied for a revision of the *gezhi zhuquan, gongtong kaifa* doctrine. According to Rear Admiral Yang Yi, an NDU professor, Deng's recommendation about joint development "must be based on the premise that sovereignty belongs to China". He warned unnamed countries that it is "dangerous" to assume that Beijing would not resort to force simply due to its anxiety to foster peaceful development and to polish its international image. "Strong military force is a bulwark for upholding national interests," Yang pointed out. "The Chinese navy is a strong deterrent force that will prevent other countries from wantonly infringing upon China's maritime interests."[24]

According to Li Jinming, an expert on maritime rights at Xiamen University, the *gezhi zhuquan, gongtong kaifa* formula was responsible for China's "massive loss of oceanic sovereignty rights". "What has happened is that while China has suspended sovereignty disputes, other countries have made a go of developing the disputed areas [without China's consent]," he said.[25] Lieutenant-General Luo Yuan noted that the *gezhi zhuquan* principle had become a "one way street" that resulted in the marginalization of Chinese interests. "China must make known its sovereign rights so that neighbouring countries will take note and beat a retreat," he said. While Luo did not explain why these neighbours would want to beat a retreat, it is presumably due to the aggrandizement of China's navy and its readiness to project power.[26] According to Chinese statistics, some 1.2 million sq km of China's oceanic territory are under dispute with foreign countries – and a large number of strategic islands are occupied by neighbouring states.[27] Beijing's apparent desire to firm up these claims has, however, alarmed neighbours such as the Philippines, Malaysia and Indonesia (see following section).

Ever-expanding Concept of China's "Core National Interests"

The "China threat" theory gained considerable mileage in March 2010, when the Chinese leadership told the Americans that the entire South China Sea belonged in China's "core national interest". This assertion raised eyebrows because traditionally, Chinese "core interests" had meant mostly maintaining territorial integrity, especially preventing Taiwan, Tibet and Xinjiang from breaking away from the motherland.[28] The South China Sea, however, is a different matter.

Not only are islets within the South China Sea contested by various countries, but it contains vital sea lanes through which one-third of world trade passes. Fears have been raised particularly among China's neighbours that as the PRC becomes stronger – and requires more resources to sustain its march toward superpower status – its list of *hexin liyi* or core interests will grow accordingly. This was indirectly confirmed in July 2010 by Chinese Foreign Ministry spokesman Qin Gang, when he was asked by foreign reporters to define the concept of core interests. "Areas relating to national sovereignty, security, territorial integrity and developmental interests all belong to China's core interests," he said.[29]

Qin was speaking as civilian and military authorities were raising a hue and cry over the series of naval exercises that were conducted by American and South Korean forces in the Yellow Sea. Popular PLA commentator Lieutenant General Luo Yuan referred to the Yellow Sea as a virtual Chinese sphere of interest when he explained Beijing's objections to the war games: "How can we let strangers fall sound asleep right outside our bedroom?" The Chinese Foreign Ministry lodged no fewer than nine protests with Washington, which maintained that since the exercises were in international waters, the USA was abiding by international law.[30] However, questions, have been raised as to whether Beijing also considers this patch of water wedged between China and the Koreas as China's *hexin liyi*. It is little wonder that the South Korean media has recently been blasting Beijing for putting the entire Korean Peninsula into its sphere of influence.[31]

The concept of ever-expanding *hexin liyi* was first propounded by military commentator Huang Kunlun. In an article in *Liberation Army Daily* in April 2009, Huang raised the notion of "the boundaries of national interests". The nationalistic theorist argued that China's national interests had gone beyond its land, sea and air territories to include areas such as the vast oceans traversed by Chinese oil freighters – as well as outer space. "Wherever our national interests have extended, so will the mission of our armed forces," Huang wrote. "Given our new historical mission, the forces have to not only safeguard the country's 'territorial boundaries' but also its 'boundaries of national interests'". "We need to safeguard not only national-security interests but also interests relating to [future] national development," he added.[32]

Han Xudong, a national security expert at the NDU, seemed to argue against the "expansionist" definition of *hexi liyi* when he indicated in July 2010 that China should adopt a cautious attitude when staking out the country's "core interests". Han pointed out that "our [China's] comprehensive national strength, especially military power, is not yet sufficient to safeguard all our core national interests". Yet what he was opposed to was merely the premature proclamation of these core interests. Professor Han recommended that Beijing release China's list of *hexin liyi* in a phased, step-by-step fashion. "As China becomes stronger, we can publicize by installments those core interests that our country can effectively safeguard," Han added.[33] In other words, the NDU professor has confirmed Beijing's adoption of a continually aggrandizing definition of national core interests.

Experts who caution against the no-holds-barred conception of *hexi liyi* are in the minority. For example, Da Wei, a senior researcher at CICIR, has warned against the "arbitrary expansion" of China's core interests. Da advocated a "minimalist definition" of *hexin liyi*, adding that "we must prevent the arbitrary extension of the parameters of *hexin liyi* in the wake of the rise of [China's] national power". The respected expert on U.S. affairs indicated that a country should adopt a "broad and rough" rather than "narrow" interpretation of its core interests. He cited the issue of territorial integrity, which is considered of core interest for most countries. "When handling territorial disputes, many countries often adopt compromises such as exchanging [disputed] territories or recognizing the status quo," he pointed out. "Often, big powers may 'let go of' some disputed areas. This doesn't mean that such countries have forsaken their core interests."[34]

"Red-Line Diplomacy"

So-called red-line diplomacy is a natural extension of China's re-definition of its *hexin liyi*. In internal papers, the CPC leadership has made reference to "drawing red lines" around areas and issues deemed vital to China's "core interests" – and which foreign powers will not be allowed to cross.[35] Red-line diplomacy is based on the largely successful experience that the party-state apparatus has accumulated in isolating Taiwan – including the two pro-independence bugbears, former presidents Lee Teng-hui and Chen Shui-bian – from the international community. Beijing successfully obliged even Western countries to openly profess their opposition to Taiwan independence – and not to receive senior cabinet officials from the "breakaway province".[36] Given the remarkable thaw in relations between mainland China and Taiwan in the wake of the election of the Kuomintang's Ma Ying-jeou as president in March 2008, Chinese diplomats have used the same tactic to circumscribe the international wiggle room of the Dalai Lama and Rebiya Kadeer, leaders respectively of the Tibetan and Xinjiang exiled movements.

Red-line diplomacy has been deployed with a certain degree of success to isolate the Dalai Lama, the Nobel Peace Prize winner who is the spiritual leader of Tibetans worldwide. In March 2009, the South African government barred the spiritual leader from participating in an international peace conference in Johannesburg. After the surprise decision of Pretoria, several Nobel Prize winners who were originally invited to the conference boycotted the session, which was then cancelled.[37] Earlier, Beijing suspended normal ties with France after President Nicolas Sarkozy met with the Dalai Lama in November 2008. Relations were restored – and Messrs Hu and Sarkozy held a bilateral "mini-summit" on the sidelines of the G20 enclave in London – only after Paris had issued a statement saying it did not support Tibetan independence. However, the revered lama showed up in Paris in June 2009 at the invitation of the municipal government – and the Chinese Foreign Ministry could do little more than blast the city authorities. More significantly, neither Poland nor Germany heeded Beijing's warnings: in July, the Dalai Lama was made an "honorary citizen" Prague before visiting Germany for the thirty-fifth time.[38]

After the international profile of the Uighur International Congress and its leader Rebiya Kadeer was raised in the wake of the Urumqi riots of 5 July 2009, Beijing has bent over backwards to dissuade various countries from granting visas to the renowned dissident. In mid-July, New Delhi obliged Beijing by refusing to allow her to visit India, and Chinese authorities were spared the embarrassment – and colossal loss of face – that would ensue from a get-together of the two prominent "splittists". However, both Australia and Japan issued visas to the exiled Uighur leader. Beijing was particularly incensed with Tokyo, which allowed the former Xinjiang businesswoman to hold press conferences freely and to blast the CPC on Japanese soil.[39]

It is emblematic of the Middle Kingdom's heft that Beijing has also sought to intervene in the activities of foreign NGOs and quasi-official organizations. In August 2009, the Chinese government raised eyebrows when it successfully put pressure on the organizers of the Frankfurt Book Fair to disinvite two Chinese dissident writers – Dai Qing and Bei Ling – who had been scheduled to speak at the world-famous forum.[40] Beijing has the past few years also been leaning heavily on the Norwegian authorities not to award the Nobel Peace Prize to Chinese dissidents such as Hu Jia, the Tiananmen mothers, and Liu Xiaobo. This is despite the fact that the Peace Prize is awarded by the Nobel Peace Prize Committee, which is an NGO and not a government agency.[41]

It is expected that Beijing will encounter more resistance when it ups the ante of its red -line diplomacy by applying it to the South China Sea – and the Yellow Sea. Despite repeated objections raised by both the Foreign Ministry and the PLA, the USA and South Korea have conducted several war games in the Yellow Sea. The nuclear-propelled aircraft carrier *George Washington*, which is a symbol of twenty-first-century U.S. military technology, took part in the October exercises despite earlier indications that Washington might think otherwise out of respect for Chinese sensitivities.[42]

A New Relationship with the U.S.: Cooperation and Contention on an Equal Footing

There seems little doubt that the hawkishness displayed by PLA officers and other power blocs in China is in large measure aimed at the USA, which is seen as the most serious constraining factor against China's rise. After all, one purpose of China's developing Blue Fleet Navy, is equipped with nuclear submarines and aircraft carriers, is to break out of the "anti-China containment policy" supposedly spearheaded by Washington. The theory goes that by forming alliances with a host of countries including Japan, South Korea, the Philippines, and so forth – and by stationing naval resources in islands from Hawaii all the way down to Okinawa, Guam and beyond – the USA wants to contain and encircle China through an "island chain".

As the Chairman of the Joint Chiefs of Staff, Admiral Mike Mullen put it in May 2009, the PLA is developing capacities that are "maritime and air focused... They seem very focused on the United States Navy and our bases that are in that part of the world."[43]

The relative depletion of American power due to the Afghan and the Iraqi quagmires – and the superpower's growing budget deficits in the wake of the financial crisis – has emboldened the Hu administration in its policies vis-à-vis its once-and-future antagonist. Hu's strategy is precisely to step into the vacuum in global influence that resulted from the truncation of American might. That U.S. troops are bogged down in Iraq and Afghanistan has to some extent hampered Washington's ability to play the role of global policeman. Worse, the USA has lost much of the moral high ground – as well as soft power – that it used to have. The wholesale collapse of American banks, insurance companies and manufacturing giants has shown up weaknesses in the "American model of laissez-faire capitalism". By contrast, the "China model" – a Chinese-style socialist market economy coupled with tight government control over many aspects of life – seems to have gained respect in disparate parts of the world.[44] More specifically, at a time when the Pentagon was forced to limit its budgets in developing state-of-the-art weapons, the PLA sees an opportunity to close the military gap with the USA.[45] And as we shall see in a later section, Beijing also wants to use its huge foreign-exchange war-chest to acquire strategic assets in the U.S..

Indeed, the mutating power equation between China and the U.S. is a key factor behind the Hu leadership's geopolitical calculus. In the early 1990s, then-president Jiang began asking his foreign-affairs aides this question: Does China need the USA more than the USA needs China, and by how much? If, in quantitative terms, an equal degree of interdependence is characterized as 50:50, the "ratio of interdependence" between China and the USA in the early to mid-1990s was reckoned by Chinese experts as around 70:30. This figure had changed to 65:35 by the turn of the century. In the wake of the Iraq conflict and, particularly, the financial tsunami, a number of Beijing strategists think the ratio has changed to between 60:40 and 55:45.[46] Recent developments have testified to the fact that in economic and other realms, a kind of rough parity has obtained between the two countries. The changing relations between the two countries were evident during Obama's first trip to Beijing in

November 2009. The international media made much of the fact that Obama and Hu were talking as equals when both pledged to "deepen bilateral strategic trust", "take concrete actions to steadily build a partnership" and enhance "positive, cooperative and comprehensive".[47]

While the USA is China's largest export market, China is the biggest buyer of American government bonds and other securities. Some 35% of the PRC's $2.4 trillion worth of foreign-exchange reserves are held in U.S. Treasury bills.[48] Given that officials including Premier Wen Jiabao have openly queried the "safety" of Chinese-held U.S. assets, American officials have been at pains to reassure the Chinese. During the first SED between the two countries in July 2009, Vice-Premier Wang Qishen went so far as to demand that the U.S. government cut its budget deficits so as not to exacerbate the depreciation of the greenback. That Washington was forced to entertain what can be construed as "interference in the domestic affairs of the U.S." was evident from the fact that the Obama administration trotted out several senior officials – including Federal Reserve Chairman Ben Bernanke – to give the country's largest creditor detailed explanations and elaborate promises.[49]

It is partly due to these new realities that the Obama administration has toned down its criticism of China's exchange rate policy and other controversial trading practices. After appreciating by about 20% from mid-2005 to September 2008, the *renminbi* was virtually pegged to the greenback at 6.83 *yuan* to one dollar. Washington – and particularly the U.S. Congress – was disappointed when the *yuan*'s value did not change much after Beijing decided in June 2010 to lift the peg and allow the currency to be more responsive to market fluctuations. Yet unlike a number of Congressmen, Obama's officials refrained from harsh rhetoric on the issue. Lawrence Summers, Obama's chief economic adviser, kept to a low-key approach when he visited Beijing in September 2010 to discuss the renminbi issue with the Chinese leadership. Treasury Secretary Timothy Geithner has consistently opposed naming China a "currency manipulator" or imposing retaliatory tariffs on Chinese imports.[50]

More significantly, the U.S. has curtailed negative comments on Beijing's human rights record as well as its policy toward Tibet and Xinjiang. It is notable that during her maiden visit to China as Secretary of State in early 2009, Hillary Clinton told American reporters that disputes about human rights "should not get in the way" of bilateral cooperation on fronts such as finance and climate change. Moreover, Washington's reactions to the Tibet protests in March, and particularly the incident in Urumqi, Xinjiang, on 5 July 2009 – in which close to 200 people were killed – were muted. Regarding the Xinjiang issue, Clinton merely said that Washington had "expressed our concerns" to the Chinese and that "it was certainly a matter of great interest and focus". She also "called on all sides to exercise restraint", which is diplomatic speak for the USA not getting involved at all. No wonder that Chinese Vice-Foreign Minister Wang Guangya expressed appreciation for the "moderate attitude" taken by Washington on the Uighur issue.[51]

Sino- U.S. contention, is expected to intensify over geopolitical issues, however, particularly in the crucial Asia-Pacific theatre. The Obama administration shifted to a more assertive stance beginning in 2010, especially after Beijing refused to criticize Pyongyang for its role in the sinking of the South Korean vessel *Cheonan* in March of the year. The U.S. navy organized a series of manoeuvres with its South Korean counterpart in areas close to China including the Yellow Sea. More importantly, in her appearance at the ASEAN Regional Forum held in Hanoi in July, Hillary Clinton indicated that the peaceful resolution of the South China Sea sovereignty dispute was a matter of America's "national interest". Subsequently, American naval vessels made a symbolic port call on Vietnam (see following section). All these signalled not only that the USA was "back in Asia" but that it was ready to help small countries stand up to "big bully China".[52]

Beijing was of course worried that Washington was resuscitating its time-honoured "anti-China containment policy" by co-opting Asian nations that have territorial disputes with China. Chinese scholars expressed the fears that particularly after U.S. troops began pulling out of Iraq at the end of August 2010, the U.S. would be earmarking more resources in "encircling" China. The Chinese media also raised the bogey of an "Asian NATO" that is aimed at the PRC.[53] However, it is a mark of Beijing's new-found confidence – and its determination to wage quasi-superpower diplomacy – that the Hu leadership has refused to give ground. It is unlikely that the renminbi will appreciate significantly in the coming year or so. Despite verbal promises, Beijing does not seem to be cooperating with Washington on the North Korea or the Iran front. Sino-DPRK relations were consolidated during the two visits of Dear Leader Kim Jong-il to

China in 2010.[54] And government-controlled Chinese companies, especially those in the oil and resources sector, have boosted investments in Iran even as Western countries observe the UN boycott on the pariah state. As of mid-2010, the three major Chinese oil monopolies had invested an estimated $40 billion in oil-and-gas assets in Iran.[55]

Regarding Sino-United States relations in the near to medium term, it is hard not to agree with the assessment of a leading China specialist on the USA, Yan Xuetong of Tsinghua University. Yan characterizes bilateral ties as where "enmity outweighs friendship". While noting that both countries share common interests mainly in the economic and trade areas, Yan pointed out in early 2010 that such commonalities were overshadowed by rapidly growing rivalry in a number of geopolitical spots. "China and the U.S. are active competitors and passive cooperative partners," he said. The America expert indicated that "both sides do not want to openly admit that their conflict outweighs common interests". While Yan noted that the two countries "want to maintain [the façade of] fake friendship," he implied that this won't last long.[56]

Projection of Financial Power

Challenging the Predominance of the Greenback and Other Bold Initiatives

According to Chen Xiangyang, a senior strategy scholar at the CICIR, Beijing wants to "occupy the vantage point" and "seize the initiative" in global geopolitical contention. "We want to articulate China's voice, safeguard China's image and expand China's national interests," he pointed out.[57] Apart from the military arena, Beijing is exploiting its economic heft to push for a "new global financial architecture". This essentially means that, not unlike China's long-standing search for a "multi-polar world order", Beijing is gunning for an international economic order that is unencumbered by American predominance.[58]

Economics-driven diplomacy has always been one of the trump cards of Chinese diplomats. Until relatively recently, however, this was limited to these areas: providing economic and technological aid to developing nations; "forgiving" the debts of poor countries, especially those in Africa; and allowing developing countries to pile up sizeable trade surpluses with the PRC. China has also been active in cementing free trade agreements with a number of regions and countries. The China-ASEAN Free Trade Area (CAFTA), which became operational in January 2010, has vastly expanded the country's clout in Southeast Asia. Encompassing a population of some 1.8 billion, the CAFTA is billed as the third largest global trading bloc behind the EU and the North American Free Trade Area.[59]

At the G20 Meeting in London in early 2009, however, it became evident that Beijing's projection of financial power had reached a new level. On the eve of the London conclave, Beijing caught world attention by challenging the supremacy of the greenback as the world currency. Senior finance officials in Beijing suggested that "special drawing rights" of the IMF should replace the U.S. dollar as the "new global currency" in which countries hold their reserves.[60] While China's proposal about the new world currency was not seriously discussed in London, such of its recommendations as setting up an international agency to monitor the activities of financial multinationals and raising developing countries' representation at the IMF were adopted. Moreover, in a historic move in April 2010, the IMF and the World Bank boosted the "voting rights" of developing and transition countries by 4.59%. Thus China's voting power increased from 2.77% to 4.42% while that of India was augmented from 2.77% to 2.91%.[61] The Middle Kingdom's profile as the originator of global initiatives was raised tremendously.

In the meantime, the PRC has pulled out all the stops to raise the global status of the renminbi. This has been helped by the unlikelihood that the depreciation of the U.S. dollar will end any time soon. Since 2008, Beijing has begun to settle trade and other transactions with other countries in currencies other than the dollar. In 2009, the PBOC signed a total of 650 billion *yuan* in bilateral currency swap agreements with the central banks in South Korea, Hong Kong, Malaysia, Indonesia, Belarus and Argentina. And in June 2010, the PBOC vastly expanded a pilot programme to allow for imports and exports with all its trading partners to be settled in *yuan*. Experts say that some $2 trillion in China's trade flows – or about 50% of the total – could be settled in renminbi by the year 2012, compared with just 10% today.[62]

"Going-out Policy" in Acquisition of Foreign Assets

Not unlike the overseas acquisition spree undertaken by cash-rich Japanese companies through the 1980s, Chinese government-held corporations are revving up their *zou chuqu* or "going out" game plan of snatching up foreign firms with strategic assets. According to the Chinese government, the country's cumulative outbound direct investment (ODI) was $240 billion as of the end of 2009, making it the world's fifth largest investor in foreign countries. In 2008, its ranking was twelfth in the world.[63] By 2010, Beijing seemed to have emerged out of the shadow of state-run Aluminum Corp of China's (Chinalco) failed attempt in 2009 to snap up 18% of the British-Australian mining giant Rio Tinto, the third largest mining company in the world. Given the relentless augmentation of China's foreign-exchange reserves, China may surpass the U.S. as the world's largest global investor by the end of the decade.[64]

In light of Beijing's obsession with energy supplies to feed its industrialization, it is not surprising that oil and gas figure prominently in China's ODI agenda. Most of such acquisitions have to do with oil and other resources – and competition between Chinese oil firms on the one hand, and counterparts from the U.S., Japan and India on the other, has become red-hot. In 2009, China's three oil monopolies – China National Petroleum Corp (Petrochina), China Petrochemical Corp (Sinopec) and China National Offshore Oil Corp (CNOOC) – spent more than $18.2 billion in acquisitions of oilfields and related businesses. These outlays, which included Petrochina's $7.22 billion purchase in June 2009 of the Canadian oil firm Addax – represented 13% of global ODI in this competitive sector.[65] In the first four months of 2010, these three monopolies spent $29 billion in worldwide acquisitions of oil and gas assets. Unlike Western multinationals – which need to worry about factors such as shareholders' views or public opinion – Chinese conglomerates can more effectively push the agenda of the CPC leadership.[66]

Apart from targeting particular sectors, Beijing's hungry and aggressive buyers also have strategies for entire nations. Brazil is a case in point. In the first half of 2010, Chinese investment in the Latin American giant topped $20 billion, more than ten times the PRC's cumulative investment in the fast-developing country. That put China on track to be Brazil's No. 1 investor for 2010, compared with No. 29

in 2009. So far, Chinese firms, mostly state-controlled conglomerates, have bought farms, car plants and steel mills in addition to stakes in oilfields. Chinese companies are also bidding to expand and modernize Brazil's telecommunications, electricity and rail networks.[67]

Compared with state-run conglomerates such as the three oil majors, the central government's sovereign-fund vehicle, Chinese Investment Corporation (CIC) – which was set up in 2007 with a war-chest of $200 billion – has displayed a more cautious attitude. CIC, headed by former Deputy Minister of Finance Lou Jiwei, has indicated that its main interest is to maintain the value of China's reserves rather than make money. As of early late 2009, CIC had only acquired small stakes in two American financial firms, Blackstone and Morgan Stanley.[68] Given their huge volumes, however, even seemingly unadventurous purchases such as government bonds by CIC and Chinese banks can be of major geopolitical significance. Apart from American Treasury Bills, Beijing has become a major owner of Japanese and South Korean bonds. In the first eight months of 2010, Beijing snapped up $27 billion worth of Japanese government bonds, or six times as much as it had accumulated in the last five years. Vowing to find out Beijing's "true intention" behind the buying spree, then Japanese Finance Minister Yoshihiko Noda indirectly accused China of pushing up the value of the yen.[69]

China's Great Leap Outward: The Relentless Projection of Soft Power

The cash-rich Chinese government has since 2009 earmarked some $6.62 billion to boost "overseas propaganda", that is, to spread Chinese soft power globally. As the nationalistic paper *Global Times* put it, "we must let the world see the thousand faces of China". There is, however, little question that the CPC leadership is gunning for a leap forward in its spin-doctoring prowess. The image that Beijing is selling is a country that is embracing globalization and earnestly seeking a win-win solution to world issues. As veteran commentator Ding Gang indicated, "an important test in the course of China's globalization is how to use its power to shape the world's perception of China".[70]

Prominent state media including CCTV and Xinhua News Agency will vastly enhance their programmes and news-feeds in different languages for Western, Asian and even Middle East and African audiences. Also on the drawing board is an English news channel modelled upon Al Jazeera that will let the world get the Chinese take on issues ranging from politics and finance to culture and religion.[71] Beijing has also set up about 350 Confucius Institutes around the world. Patterned after quasi-official language-and-cultural organizations such as the Goethe Institute of Germany, Confucius Institutes serve to spread Chinese culture in addition to acquainting foreigners with the latest policies of the PRC. This "soft" approach is geared toward promoting people-level diplomacy in addition to enhancing the overall attractiveness of the "China model".[72]

A key thrust of Beijing's self-laudatory hard-sell is to exploit the precipitous drop in the esteem of American-style, laissez-faire capitalism in the wake of the financial tsunami. The Hu leadership wants to convince the world that the sorry state of the American model has thrown into sharp relief the superiority of the Chinese way of doing things. According to a recent commentary by the Xinhua News Agency, the results of thirty years of Chinese reform have amounted to "the realization of innovation and creativity on a gargantuan scale . . . nothing less than an epic poem about expeditious development". "Not only ordinary people but the media and academia in China and abroad have paid close attention to 'the China miracle' or 'the China model'", proclaimed the party mouthpiece.[73]

Further, Peking University political scientist Yu Keping claimed that the China model has "enriched our knowledge about the laws and paths toward social development and promoted the multi-pronged development of human civilization in the age of globalization". And, according to Central Party School Professor Zhao Yao, the China model is worth maximum exposure because "it has saved the world socialist movement". "Through the reform and open door policy of China, new vistas have been opened up for socialism", Zhao noted.[74] Dong Manyuan, a researcher at the China Institute of International Studies, which is a Chinese Foreign Ministry think-tank, argued that Chinese soft power is different from – and potentially more appealing than – Western brands because the former exudes a wholesome sense of "peace and harmony . . . Characteristics of Chinese soft power include respect for heterogeneity of world [cultures], openness and tolerance, friendliness and inclusiveness . . . respect for politeness and benevolence."[75]

It seems obvious, however, that there are severe limits to the attractiveness of Chinese culture and mores – as long as CPC authorities refuse to tolerate generally accepted practices regarding human rights and freedom of expression. In an article on the difficulties facing the mass marketing of Chinese values, Tsinghua University media scholar Li Xiguang noted that "the soft power of a country manifests itself in whether it has the power to define and interpret 'universal values' such as democracy, freedom and human rights". Li pointed out that in order to enhance the attractiveness of "socialism with Chinese characteristics", "we must let the whole world hear the stories that Chinese citizens have to tell about their democracy, liberty, human rights and rule of law".[76] The problem is that intellectuals bold enough to air their views on democracy and political reform have been harassed if not incarcerated by the authorities.[77] This is true of the dozens of well-known writers and professors who in early 2009 signed a manifesto called Charter '08, which asked the CPC leadership to do nothing more than allow the Chinese to enjoy civil rights enshrined in United Nations covenants. The incarceration of renowned writer Liu Xiaobo, a leader of the Charter '08 movement, has elicited protests from politicians and scholars around the world.[78]

Obstacles to Beijing's Quasi-Superpower Diplomacy and Power Projection

The quasi-superpower is meeting daunting challenges as it goes on the prowl. The hurdles come from not only status-quo powers such as the USA and Western European countries, but also developing nations who fear being seared by the fire-spitting dragon. This reality is succinctly explained by CICIR President Cui Liru, an adviser to the CPC leadership. "In the past ten years, China developed from a relatively weak posture to a relatively strong posture, and conflicts between China and the world were not particularly vehement," Cui said. "However, in the coming ten years, China will be progressing from a relatively strong posture toward an even stronger posture.

China's impact on the world will be bigger – and the world's worries about China will increase."[79]

China's global putsch is meeting obstacles galore on the military front. This is perhaps not surprising in light of the PRC's dazzling hard-power projection in the past two years. Manifestations of the PLA's new-found aggressiveness have included increasingly frequent cat-and-mouse games in the Pacific between Chinese submarines and naval vessels on the one hand, and those of the USA and Japan on the other. And China has apparently overtaken Japan and India in the three-nation race to put an astronaut on the moon. A ferocious arms race between China, India and Japan is also in the offing. Even China's neighbours which lack the resources to spend big on state-of-the-art weapons are taking different strategies to handle the "China threat".[80] An examination of China's increasingly testy relations with a host of Asian countries will throw this issue into sharper perspective.

Sovereignty Disputes in the South and East China Seas – China's Growing Tension with ASEAN, Japan and India

The PLA juggernaut has become so fearsome that most of China's neighbours – particularly countries that have territorial disputes with the PRC – have taken drastic measures to protect themselves. The best example is the intensifying conflict between China on the one hand, and the Philippines, Malaysia and Vietnam on the other, regarding sovereignty over a few dozen islets in the South China Sea.

In the spring of 2009, Manila passed a law legitimizing its sovereignty claims over the Scarborough Shoal (known as Huang Yan Island in China) and other islets of the Spratly archipelago; it also registered such claims with the United Nations. Hanoi and Kuala Lumpur have ignited acrimonious debates with Beijing over other islets. In the meantime, all three countries have announced plans to upgrade their navies and air forces. For example, Hanoi has reportedly ordered six kilo-class submarines as well as twenty-four SU-30 MK2 jetfighters from Russia. The trio have also been wielding the "America card" against China. Malaysia conducted wide-ranging war games with U.S. forces in June 2009, and the Philippines and Vietnam have professed willingness to let the U.S. navy use their deep-sea ports and other bases.[81] Most alarmingly for Beijing, the U.S. nuclear aircraft carrier *George Washington* made a port call on Danang, Vietnam, in August 2010, thus signalling the emergence of a possible "anti-China U.S.-Vietnam axis". Little wonder that Chinese opinion-makers have called for counter-measures against this latest U.S. "plot". Shanghai Academy of Social Sciences expert Cai Hongpeng indicated that Beijing should strive to boost ties with Hanoi so as to "prevent foreign enemy forces from driving a wedge in Sino-Vietnamese relations". "Don't push Vietnam toward the U.S.", Professor Cai warned.[82]

Indeed, for Beijing, Washington seems to be taking advantage of the increasing popularity of the "China threat" theory to consolidate its "anti-China encirclement policy" by cementing ties with allies and friends ranging from Japan, South Korea, Australia and India to the Philippines and Malaysia. Of particular importance is Washington's bid to boost ties with ASEAN, which the George W. Bush administration all but neglected. During her participation in the ASEAN Regional Forum (ARF) held in Phuket, Thailand, in July 2009, Secretary of State Clinton signed the Treaty of Amity and Cooperation with the regional bloc, thus becoming the sixteenth country to do so.[83] According to the *Global Times*, "the U.S. has acceded to the Treaty of Amity and Cooperation in order to counterbalance China". One of Clinton's main messages at the ARF was that the USA had "come back" to the ASEAN region, and that it was ready "to lay the groundwork for even stronger partnerships as we move forward".[84]

One year later, Clinton further challenged Beijing's perceived "hegemonic" claims over the South China Sea by pointing out at the ARF conclave in Hanoi that the resolution of sovereignty rows was a key American "national interest". More significantly, she pointed out that Washington would spearhead a diplomatic and legal initiative toward "resolving the various territorial disputes without coercion". Without naming China, the Secretary said: "We oppose the use or threat of force by any claimant". U.S. officials further disclosed that Vietnam, Malaysia and the Philippines had asked for American help in their tussle with China. Apparently taken aback by the fusillade, Chinese Foreign Minister Yang Jiechie said Clinton's initiative amounted to "an attack on China".[85] At the same time, Washington indicated its readiness to intervene in Beijing's disputes with countries including Vietnam, Laos, Cambodia and Thailand regarding water rights over the Mekong Delta. The four lower riparian states have complained that Chinese authorities, which have jurisdiction over the upper reaches of the Mekong, had siphoned off too much water for their own use.[86]

Relations with Japan and India – with both of which China was engaged in armed conflicts last century – have become more crisis-prone. This is despite the fact that after the retirement in 2006 of former prime minister Junichiro Koizumi – who infuriated Beijing by his repeated visits to the Yasukuni Shrine – genuine efforts have been made by Beijing and Tokyo to emphasize positive aspects such as trade while downplaying bilateral differences. While visiting Tokyo in May 2008, Hu reached a historic agreement with counterpart Yasuo Fukuda on joint development of undersea gas fields in the East China Sea with the understanding that sovereignty-related arguments would be set aside.[87] However, both governments have been unable to do follow-up work to produce a formal treaty on the East China Sea.

Moreover disputes over the sovereignty of the Diaoyu, or Senkaku archipelago, which is close to Taiwan, erupted with new ferocity in September 2010 following Japan's detention of the captain of a Chinese fishing vessel just off the Diaoyu. Beijing reacted by freezing high-level meetings with Tokyo. More significantly, the Chinese government began discouraging Chinese tourists from visiting Japan; it also cut down on the export of rare-earth metals to high-tech Japanese companies. The CPC leadership's apparent aggressiveness on the Diaoyu/Senkaku issue has reinforced the voices of politicians within both the ruling Democratic Party of Japan and opposition parties that Tokyo has no choice but to bolster defence ties with Washington.[88] Over the longer term, Tokyo remains nervous about the relentless aggrandizement of the PLA as well as Chinese military projection in the Pacific Region.[89] From Beijing's viewpoint, however, the enhanced Japan- U.S. military alliance simply confirms the fact that Tokyo is again playing the role of "lead hit man" in Washington's "containment policy" against the PRC.

Relations, particularly economic ties, with India had by and large improved until the flare-up in 2009 and 2010 over the age-old issue of the delineation of their boundaries in the Himalayan region. Additional troops from both countries have been massed along the disputed border. While confidence-building measures between two neighbours' armed forces have been put in place, an arms race between the two Asian giants is in the offing. Beijing is particularly unhappy with New Delhi's apparent "tilt" toward the USA, which first began overtures to India during the latter half of the Clinton administration. While India is still reliant upon Russia for state-of-the-art weapons, it wants to boost ties with Washington both to undercut Pakistan and to hedge against possible aggression from the quasi-superpower to its east. New Delhi was amply rewarded during the agreements reached with the Obama administration, which made it possible for India to buy billions of dollars' worth of weapons as well as nuclear technology from American firms.[90]

China's Rise and the "Clash of Civilizations"

In the second half of the Bush administration, politicians and opinion leaders in the USA, Japan, India and Australia talked much about a possible "Coalition of Values". The idea was that since the four major Asia-Pacific nations share common Western democratic values, they should deepen their security cooperation. For many, including Chinese strategists, however, this concept smacked of the "Cold War" goal of "containing China". While the term "coalition of values" seems to have dropped out of popularity recently, ties, particularly between the U.S. and India, as well as Japan and India, have increased markedly.[91]

One stumbling block to China's rise is that the socialist country has radically different ideological values and political institutions from those of the established powers, with the partial exception of Russia. Particularly given the spectacular performance of the Chinese economy, even the USA has been eager to involve China in international forums. However, the fact that China is still an authoritarian, one-party-ruled state that does not honour global norms such as human rights and elections has become a formidable impediment to its rise. Using the well-known formulation of the late political science guru Professor Samuel Huntington, the "clash of civilizations" between China and the West has hardly abated with the latter's rise and the partial integration of the Chinese economy into the international marketplace.[92] This is despite public-relations efforts undertaken by Beijing to sell the "China model" or the "Beijing consensus" to the world. Little wonder that in the wake of the Western world's criticism of Beijing's harsh treatment of Xinjiang's Uighur minority, a commentary by the official *Global Times* complained that China bashers had indiscriminately invoked "the dictatorial Chinese system" when laying into negative developments in the PRC. Whenever problems or disturbances happen in China, the commentator noted, "targeting the sins and mistakes of the Chinese system" had become the "first reaction" of the Western media.[93]

Yet the fact remains that internal problems that have arisen due to China's institutional drawbacks – including riots by Uighurs and dispossessed peasants – have dented the efficacy of Beijing's quasi-superpower diplomacy. Nothing illustrates this better than President Hu's embarrassing absence from the "G8 plus Five" Summit held in L'Aquila, Italy, in July 2009. After spending a day meeting Italian leaders, the Chinese commander-in-chief had to scurry back to Beijing to handle the aftermath of the 5 July Urumqi disturbances.[94] While it was a coincidence that one of the worst instances of ethnic violence since 1949 flared up at this juncture, there is no denying that problems of the "China model" – particularly stern one-party rule and the ruthless repression of dissent – have become a legitimate concern for the global community. After all, CPC authorities' suppression of the religious, linguistic and cultural rights of Uighurs as well as Tibetans is well documented.[95]

One rhetorical weapon frequently used by CPC authorities is that, given Beijing's subscription to the nineteenth-century version of indivisible sovereignty, it is no business of foreign countries to interfere in the country's internal affairs. This is inherent in the PRC's long-standing diplomatic principle of "non-interference in the internal affairs of other countries" – a cornerstone of the Five Principles of Peaceful Co-existence first propounded by the late premier Zhou Enlai in 1954.[96] The Chinese authorities have also invoked this precept to defend their connivance in human-rights violations by allies ranging from North Korea to Myanmar. Times have changed since the 1950s, however. The well-publicized trials of dictators charged with crimes against humanity – including former Serbian president Slobodan Milosevic and former Liberian president Charles Taylor – at the International Court of Justice in the Hague has buttressed the argument that international humanitarianism overrides national sovereignty.[97] Beijing's stubborn rejection of well recognized global norms and trends would render it difficult for the country to play a leading role in world affairs outside narrowly defined financial or technological realms.

China's Domestic Politics as a Constraint on its Great Leap Outward

As Prussian philosopher Carl von Clausewitz put it, "war is an extension of domestic politics". The same can be said of the intimate correlation between a country's diplomacy and global power projection on the one hand, and its domestic politics on the other. Given that the predominant portion of the Chinese economy is still controlled by the party-state apparatus – including about 130 state-held, monopolistic conglomerates in sectors ranging from petroleum and steel to banking and telecommunications – can Beijing convince the world that China is a "full market economy"?[98] And in light of China's problematic political institutions, particularly the ruthless suppression of most forms of freedoms and rights recognized by relevant United Nations covenants, can Beijing persuasively argue that the "Beijing consensus" is superior to the "Western model"?[99] Moreover, top leaders including President Hu and National People's Congress Chairman Wu Bangguo, both senior Politburo members, have reiterated that China will "never go down the deviant path" of adopting Western institutions such as universal suffrage and multi-party politics. All that the CPC has promised the nation in the way of political reform is that it will assiduously go about "perfecting the socialist system".[100]

Apart from the Beijing leadership's systematic violation of the civil liberties of its citizens, there are salient areas where China's domestic politics would undercut its international appeal. Just consider two areas: the country's neglect of the environment, and the CPC's pandering to growing nationalism especially among the young. Given the accelerated pace of globalization, no country can claim that its environmental policy falls solely within its "internal affairs". Since the turn of the century, China has been subject to increasing criticism for spreading acid rain and dust to areas including Japan, South Korea and even the West Coast of the USA. These and other countries have also complained that China-originated mercury and other metallic and chemical substances have polluted neighbouring fishing grounds. Since a number of international waters, including the Brahmaputra and the Mekong, originate from mountains in Western China, China has been blasted by countries including Vietnam, Laos and India for selfishly over-exploiting water and hydraulic resources in the upper reaches of these waterways.[101] Even more disturbing to the international community has been the inexorable rise of Chinese nationalism, particularly among the younger generation. Major manifestations have included the series of anti-Japanese demonstrations in April 2005 and anti-French protests in April 2008.[102] Foreign observers have noted that given the irrelevance of socialism and Communism, the CPC has sought to bolster its legitimacy – and consolidate its so-called "perennial ruling-class status" – by pandering to citizens' feel-good and even jingoistic feelings about the greatness of the Chinese nation. Chat-rooms in mainstream websites are choc-a-bloc with xenophobic attacks on countries and politicians who are seen as belittling China's achievements or finding fault with shortcomings in the Chinese model. How emotional the Chinese public can get was illustrated in the summer of 2009 by its vitriolic reaction against Australia for reasons including providing a platform for Rebiya Kadeer. A survey by the popular *Global Times* paper showed that 87% of Netizens supported a boycott of tourism visits to Australia or studying in Australian universities. At the same time, the leadership has cited popular support for military modernization to justify its decision to spend billions of *yuan* on expensive weapons such as nuclear submarines or aircraft carriers.[103]

Conclusion: China and the World Must Learn to Adjust to Each Other

Will the Hu leadership succeed in its global power putsch? Much of the Middle Kingdom's claim to quasi-superpower status rests on its economic might: a 9% growth rate for the past two decades and foreign-exchange reserves totalling more than $2.4 trillion. That Beijing has become the largest buyer of American bonds has obliged Washington to tone down its critique of China's human rights record as well as its alleged manipulation of the value of the *yuan*. The success of Beijing's quasi-superpower diplomacy could hinge on the extent to which the Chinese economy can contribute to global recovery. Responsible actions by PRC policymakers such as extending loans to the IMF and the Asian Development Bank, setting the renminbi's value in accordance with market forces, and putting emphasis on domestic consumption – instead of just exports – as the major engine of growth will boost China's image as a dependable bulwark of healthy economic development worldwide.[104]

Yet sheer economic might alone is far from sufficient in propelling China toward superpower status. On the global scene, it is important to take stock of the number of true allies and friends that China has made in the past two decades versus those of key competitors such as the U.S.. The deterioration in China's relations with Japan, South Korea, India and several ASEAN states speaks more about Beijing's ability to project power than whatever state-of-the-art weapons the PRC is acquiring. Much hinges on whether Beijing is willing and able to function as a law-abiding member – what former U.S. deputy Secretary of State Robert Zoellick once called a "responsible stakeholder" – of the international community. Firstly, the CPC administration must make more substantial efforts to counter the "China threat" theory. These include reaching at least temporary agreements with neighbours including Japan, Malaysia, Vietnam and the Philippines over the joint developments concerning the East and South China Sea islets. Equally importantly, the Hu-led Politburo must put a damper on remarks by hawkish generals and strategists about the untrammelled assertion of Chinese military might in the Asia-Pacific and other regions.[105]

Rather than sabre rattling, Beijing may well encourage relatively moderate – and innovative – ideas such as that proposed by Renmin University professor Pang Zhongying regarding the diffusion of tension in the South China Sea. Pang suggested in the summer of 2010 that Chinese authorities should actively consider a *duobian*, or multilateralist strategy. In an article in *Global Times*, Pang argued that "there will be considerable difficulty for Beijing to maintain its 'bilateral' approach" to ironing out territorial rows with countries and regions including Vietnam, the Philippines, Malaysia, Brunei and Taiwan. Beijing has insisted for decades that sovereignty-related negotiations be conducted on a one-on-one basis between China on the one hand, and individual claimants on the other. The CPC leadership has refused to consider options including China-ASEAN negotiations or "internationalized" talks involving third parties such as the United States. "In the past two decades, China has accumulated a lot of experience in multilateral [diplomatic] operations," Pang wrote, adding that the South China Sea issue could be resolved on a multilateral platform that involves parties including ASEAN, the U.S.,

Japan and even the United Nations. "Ruling out multilateralism will be tantamount to giving [China's] opponents pretexts to attack China," he indicated.[106] Given its economic, military and diplomatic heft, Beijing is better placed than ever to make solid contributions to defusing regional and global flashpoints. The denuclearization of the Korean Peninsula is a case in point. The PRC has reaped a bonanza of good will by playing host to the Six Party Talks on denuclearization since 2003. However, it has yet to demonstrate strong leadership in reining in redoubled attempts by the D.P.R.K. regime to develop a full-fledged nuclear arsenal.[107] The same goes for Beijing's dubious ties with a host of pariah states such as Myanmar, Sudan, Angola and Zimbabwe. It is partly due to China's support that these rogue regimes have managed to remain in power – and to trample upon the human rights of their citizens in addition to threatening world peace. For example, after Myanmese democracy heroine Aung San Suu Kyi was sentenced to an 18-month house detention in August 2009, Beijing said "the world should respect Myanmar's judicial sovereignty".[108]

Yet another major factor hampering China's "great leap outward" is stagnation in political reform. President Hu has since late 2008 reinstated with gusto Maoist institutions such as "democratic centralism", a euphemism for boosting the powers of the Politburo Standing Committee. Political liberalization has been frozen.[109] The PLA's clout, meanwhile, has been augmented because of its role in not only bolstering China's global reach but also suppressing the estimated 100,000 cases of protests, riots and disturbances that break out annually. Unlike military forces in most countries, the PLA is a "party army" not a state army.[110] This means that it is answerable to only a handful of top CPC cadres such as Hu, who also requires the backing of the top brass in order to maintain the preeminence of his own faction. That the Chinese armed forces are not subject to meaningful checks and balances has raised fears among China's neighbours that the generals might, for their own benefits, be pushing the country toward an expansionist and adventurous foreign policy. The CPC leadership's refusal to give up Maoist norms such as the "party's absolute leadership over the armed forces" and "the synthesis of [the requirements of] peace and war" has dented the global appeal of the China model – and detracted from the viability of Beijing's quasi-superpower diplomacy.[111]

In late 2008, as China's clout appeared to grow in direct

proportion to the severity of America's financial haemorrhage, Beijing temporarily suspended exchanges with France in protest at a meeting between President Nicolas Sarkozy and the Dalai Lama. At the G8 conclave in L'Aquila, Italy, in July 2009, however, a host of leaders including Sarkozy and German Chancellor Angela Merkel were openly critical of Beijing's Xinjiang policy. And in the wake of Turkish Prime Minister Tayyip Erdogan's accusation that Beijing was committing "genocide" in Xinjiang, the Hu leadership is nervous about hostile reactions in the Muslim world. [112] Beijing's concept of total or indivisible sovereignty – as well as "non-interference in the internal affairs of other countries" – has become an obstacle to its game plan of enhancing the country's global influence.

Given that China has for centuries been relegated to the margins of history – if not bullied by "imperialistic powers" – President Hu and his comrades can perhaps be forgiven for getting somewhat impatient in claiming what they perceive as China's rightful place in the sun. The CPC leadership, however, will be naïve and myopic if it underestimates international misgivings about the precipitous rise of China, which is still perceived as a country that follows an outmoded if not also immoral system of governance. While there is little doubt that the world, especially status-quo powers led by the USA, must learn to engage more creatively with the quasi-superpower, the onus is on the Beijing leadership to demonstrate to all its ability to assume the responsibility – to both the global community and its own citizens – that comes with its world-sized clout.

Notes and References

1. "G20 leaders open summit in London to tackle financial, economic crisis," Xinhua News Agency, 2 April 2009, http://news.xinhuanet.com/english/2009-04/02/content_11120490.htm.

2. For a discussion of the G2 and related concepts, see, for example, Irwin Stelzer, "The real action will be at the G2: China and the US," *Sunday Times* (London), 29 March 2009, http://business.timesonline.co.uk/tol/business/columnists/article5993143.ece?openComment=true; "China-US co-operation a must for world economy to recover," Xinhua News Agency, 7 March 2009, http://www.chinadaily.com.cn/bizchina/2009-03/07/content_7549936.htm.

3. "China-U.S. dialogue avoids confrontation," UPI, 4 August 2009, http://www.upi.com/Emerging_Threats/2009/08/04/China-US-dialogue-avoids-confrontation/UPI-45421249399200/; "Breaking   through   the   G-2

framework: Seeking a real balance," *People's Daily* (English), 3 August 2009, http://english.people.com.cn/90002/96417/6717152.html.

4. Cited in "China kicks off celebration to mark 60th anniversary of navy," Gov.cn, 20 April 2009, http://english.gov.cn/2009-04/20/content_1290703.htm.

5. Cited in "High echelons of the Chinese military say the country cannot do without aircraft carriers," China News Service, 23 March 2009, http://www.chinanews.com.cn/gn/news/2009/03-23/1613085.shtml; "China tells Japan it wants aircraft carrier," AFP, 22 March 2009, http://www.google.com/hostednews/afp/article/ALeqM5iLX9Q4jSaza-kDFWyJmogPBGX4dg.

6. For a discussion of Deng's foreign-policy precepts, see, for example, Wang Yusheng, "Looking into some issues concerning the idea 'keeping a low profile'," Chinese People's Institute of Foreign Affairs website, 5 December 2005http://www.cpifa.org/en/Html/2005125111547-1.html.

7. Cited in Willy Lam, "China learns to be a superpower," *Far Eastern Economic Review*, May 2009, http://www.feer.com/essays/2009/may/beijing-learns-to-be-a-superpower.

8. For a discussion of "peaceful rise" concept, see Li Kexian, "An explication of China's diplomacy of 'peaceful development'," *Leaders* (Hong Kong journal), April 2009; Esther Pan, "The promise and pitfalls of China's 'Peaceful Rise'," Council on Foreign Relations, New York, 14 April 2006, http://www.cfr.org/publication/10446/; Ma Zhengang, "China's strategic choices regarding peaceful development," China.com.cn, 25 March 2008, http://www.china.com.cn/book/zhuanti/qkjc/txt/2008-03/25/content_13541060.htm

9. For a discussion of Beijing's efforts to reach out to different continents, see "Top leaders begin intensive overseas visits to beef up diplomacy," *Outlook Weekly* (Beijing), 9 February 2009, http://www.ce.cn/ztpd/xwzt/guonei/2009/hjtcf/fxpl/200902/09/t20090209_18153589.shtml.

10. For a discussion of Beijing's perception of the "containment policy," see, for example, "Is the US 'encircling' China?" Therealnews.com, 9 July 2008, http://therealnews.com/t/index.php?option=com_content&task=view&id=31&Itemid=74&jumival=1838; Bill Emmott, "China's accidental empire is a growing danger," *The Times of London*, 22 May 2009, http://www.timesonline.co.uk/tol/comment/columnists/guest_contributors/article6337443.ece.

11. Cited in Willy Lam, "China seeks paradigm shift in geopolitics," *China Brief*, Jamestown Foundation, Washington DC, 5 March 2010, http://www.jamestown.org/single/?no_cache=1&tx_ttnews%5Btt_news%5D=36120.

12. "Yuan Peng: China will take counter measures to inflict real pain on the US", Phoenix TV News, 4 February 2010. http://itv.ifeng.com/play.aspx?id=f772b9a5-02b9-427f-b726-8744ca4755af.

13. Cited in "China should seize the opportunities provided by America's strategic retreat," *Global Times*, 10 September 2010, http://opinion.huanqiu.com/roll/2010-09/1089844.html.

14. Cited in Chris Buckley, "Chinese admiral says U.S. drill courts confrontation," Reuters, 13 August 2010, http://uk.reuters.com/article/idUKTRE67C0NV20100813.

15. For a discussion of reasons behind the rise of hawkish voices in China's foreign and security policy, see, for example, Willy Lam, "Hawks vs. doves: Beijing debates 'core interests' and Sino-U.S. relations," *China Brief*, 19 August 2010, http://www.jamestown.org/programs/chinabrief/single/?tx_ttnews %5Btt_news%5D=36769&tx_ttnews%5BbackPid%5D=25&cHash=4462bfb6da.

16. "PLA Air Force Senior Colonel: The US army is an eagle, our army is a penguin," *Global Times*, 28 June 2009, http://mil.huanqiu.com/Exclusive/ 2009-06/499442.html.

17. Cited in Dai Xu, "China's army must have a game plan for breaking out of encirclement," *Global Times*, 24 July 2009, http://opinion.huanqiu.com/ roll/2009-07/525254.html.

18. "Resolutely beef up the construction of core military capability," *Liberation Army Daily* (Beijing), 2 December 2008, http://www.chinamil.com.cn/ site1/xwpdxw/2008-12/02/content_1568916_3.htm.

19. Jin Yinan, "China's rise cannot be accomplished in the midst of nightingale songs and swallow dances," *Liberation Army Daily*, 31 December 2008, http://news.xinhuanet.com/mil/2008-12/31/content_10585102_1.htm.

20. "Hu Jintao stresses the importance of the fusion of military and civilian development at a Politburo collective study session," Xinhua News Agency, 24 July 2009, http://www.chinesetoday.com/news/show/id/266967.

21. For a discussion of Deng's dictum on the Diaoyu and related developments in the tussle with Tokyo, see, for example, Zhongqi Pan, "Sino-Japanese dispute over the Diaoyu/Senkaku Islands: the pending controversy from the Chinese perspective," *Journal of Chinese Political Science, Volume 12, Number 1*, 71–92, http://www.springerlink.com/content/b2306611125nw526/.

22. For a discussion of the formula of "setting aside sovereignty" in relation to the South China Sea, see, for example, Vaudine England, "Why are South China Sea tensions rising?" BBC news, 3 September 2010, http://www.bbc .co.uk/news/world-asia-pacific-11152948; Ian Story, "Conflict in the South China Sea: China's relations with Vietnam and the Philippines," *Japan Focus*, 30 April 2008, http://www.japanfocus.org/-ian-storey/2734.

23. For a discussion of the Hu-Fukuda agreement on the East China Sea, see, for example, James Manicom, "Hu-Fukuda summit: The East China Sea dispute," *China Brief*, 6 June 2008, http://www.jamestown.org/programs/ chinabrief/single/?tx_ttnews%5Btt_news%5D=4968&tx_ttnews%5BbackPid %5D=168&no_cache=1.

24. "New ideas required for China's oceanic strategy," *International Herald Leader* (Beijing journal), 3 March 2009, http://news.xinhuanet.com/world/ 2009-03/03/content_10932738.htm.

25. Cited in "Half of oceanic territory where we have sovereignty has been taken," *International Herald Leader*, 3 March 2010, http://www.laizhouba.net/ thread-21467-1-1.html; Li Wei, "The internationalization of the South China Sea," *Hong Kong Economic Daily*, August 23, 2010.

26. Cited in "PLA Major-General: the US has formed a 'crescent moon' circle to

contain China," *Guangzhou Daily*, 18 July 2010, http://club.bandao.cn/ showthreadm.asp?boardid=101&id=1604283.

27. "China has 1.2 million sq km of oceanic territory that is in dispute with other countries," *Global Times*, 14 March 2009, http://news.hunantv.com/ x/j/20090313/168883_2.html.

28. For a discussion of China's "core interests," see, for example, Cary Huang, "A bolder China asserts 'core' interests – but will it act?" *South China Morning Post*, 12 August 2010, http://www.viet-studies.info/kinhte/china _asserts_core_interest.htm; Claude Arpi, "China's core interests," *Indian Defence Review*, 30 August 2010, http://www.indiandefencereview.com/ 2010/08/china%E2%80%99s-core-interests.html.

29. "Foreign Ministry clarifies parameters of China's core interests," *Global Times*, 13 July 2010, http://news.qq.com/a/20100714/001265.htm

30. For a discussion of military reactions to U.S. manoeuvres in the Yellow Sea, see, for example, "Chinese major-general blasts the U.S., 'If people offend us, we'll certainly punish them," *Ming Pao* (Hong Kong), 13 August 2010; Chris Buckley, "Chinese admiral says U.S. drill courts confrontation," Reuters, 13 August 2010, http://www.reuters.com/article/idUSTRE67B11W20100813 ?type=politicsNews.

31. For a discussion of South Korean views on China's stance over the Yellow Sea, see , for example, "South Korean think tank criticizes China for being 'immoral', saying that China wants to take profit from the division of the Korean Peninsula," *Global Times*, 13 August 2010, http://world.huanqiu .com/roll/2010-08/1010297.html; "Korea makes use of military maneuvers to vent its anger," *Global Times*, 30 July 2010, http://world.huanqiu.com/ roll/2010-07/971337.html.

32. Huang Kunlun, "Our army must transcend concepts of [the protection of] territorial integrity so as to safeguard national security," *Liberation Army Daily*, 1 April 2009, http://www.hlkmil.com/news/milcn/200901/20090104 093409_5.html.

33. Han Xudong, "We should be careful with the concept 'national core interests'," *Outlook Weekly*, 25 July 2010, http://news.xinhuanet.com/ world/2010-07/25/c_12369991.htm.

34. Da Wei, "Why should China manifest its core interests?" *People's Daily*, 27 July 2010, http://world.people.com.cn/GB/12261419.html.

35. Cited in Zhang Wenmu, "China should draw the red line in its diplomacy with Europe," *International Herald Leader*, 8 December 2008, http://news.sina.com.cn/pl/2008-12-08/100816804452.shtml.

36. For a discussion of Taiwan's limited diplomatic wiggle room, see, for example, Vincent Wang, "Bush snubs democracy in Taiwan," *Taipei Times*, 17 December 2003, http://taiwantt.org.tw/taipeitimes/DOC/2003/12/ 20031217.doc; "Taipei's costly search for friends," The Associated Press, 27 April 2006, http://www.asiafinest.com/forum/index.php?showtopic=72985&pid =1792334&mode=threaded&start=.

37. "Dalai Lama's South Africa conference ban causes uproar," *The Guardian* (London), 23 March 2009   http://www.guardian.co.uk/world/2009/mar/ 23/ dalai-lama-south-africa-world-cup-ban.

38. "Dalai Lama kicks off four days of religious talks in Germany," *Deutsche Welle* (Berlin), 30 July 2009, http://www.dw-world.de/dw/article/ 0,,4528699,00.html.

39. Deng Yajun, "Japan has caught the 'syndrome to split China'," Xinhua News Agency, 3 August 2009, http://news.china.com/zh_cn/international/1000/ 20090803/15584543.html; "Australia's permission for Rebiya's visit chills bilateral ties," *People's Daily* (English), 11 August 2009, http://english.people.com.cn/90001/90780/91343/6724986.html.

40. "Furor over Chinese dissidents at Frankfurt Book Fair symposium," *Deutsche Welle* News, 12 September 2009, http://www.dw-world.de/dw/ article/0,,4675700,00.html.

41. For a discussion of Liu Xiaobo's Nobel possibilities and Beijing's pressure on Norwegian authorities, see, for example, "Nobel arms-twisting," *Wall Street Journal*, 1 October 2010, http://online.wsj.com/article/SB10001424052748 703882404575520912261103800.html; Pavol Stracansky "Chinese dissident wins more backing for Nobel," IPS News, 10 February 2010, http://ipsnews.net/news.asp?idnews=50278.

42. For a discussion of the new China-US tussle in the Yellow Sea, see Sunny Lee, "A 'new Cold War' in the Yellow Sea," *The National* (Dubai), 5 September 2010,   http://www.thenational.ae/apps/pbcs.dll/article?AID=/20100906/FOREIGN/ 709059911/1140.

43. Cited in "China's peripheries face a new military 'ring of encirclement'," China News Service, 12 June 2009, http://www.chinanews.com.cn/hb/ news/2009/06-12/1731654.shtml; "China military buildup seems US-focused, says Mullen," Reuters, 5 May 2009, uk.reuters.com/article/idUKTRE54363 X20090504.

44. Geoffrey York, "Self-confident China sees its own star rising," *The Globe and Mail* 5 December 2006; "China to the rescue: growing out of the financial crisis," Yaleglobal.yale.edu, 28 July 2009, http://yaleglobal.yale.edu/ display.article?id=12601.

45. "Defense secretary scores big wins on weapons cuts," The Associated Press, 25 July 2009, http://www.google.com/hostednews/ap/article/ALeqM5hfww NXQTZv9N3QvIdEAzFRGzXIfwD99LSJEO1.

46. Cited in Lin Heli, "Characteristics of China's quasi-Superpower diplomacy," *Leaders*, April 2009.

47. For a discussion of the US and China as equals, see Willy Lam, "Equals at least, for better or for worse," *New York Times*, 18 November 2009, http://www.nytimes.com/2009/11/19/opinion/19iht-edlam.html?_r=1.

48. "China and the dollar," *The Economist*, 9 July 2009, http://www.economist.com/businessfinance/displayStory.cfm?story_id=13988512 ; "China continued to purchase US government bonds in April; total holdings to reach US$900 billion," China News Service, 16 June 2010.

49. Tom Barkley and Deborah Solomon, "Chinese convey concern on growing US debt," *Wall Street Journal*, 29 July 2009, http://online.wsj.com/article/SB124878817147386753.html.

50. For a discussion of Summers' September 2010 visit to Beijing, see, for example, Andrew Batson, "U.S., China avoid touchy issues in talks," *Wall Street Journal*, 9 September 2010. http://online.wsj.com/article/SB10001424052748704362404575479354122402446.html?mod=googlenews_wsj.

51. "China welcomes 'moderate' US response to riots," The Associated Press, 28 July 2009, http://www.google.com/hostednews/ap/article/ALeqM5hqLramON8toBQBppkuM6zEzExUZgD99NOON80.

52. See Gordon Chang, "Hillary Clinton changes America's China policy," *Forbes* magazine, 28 July 2010; http://www.forbes.com/2010/07/28/china-beijing-asia-hillary-clinton-opinions-columnists-gordon-g-chang_print.html.

53. For a discussion of Chinese perceptions of Washington's "containment policy", see, for example, "The U.S. is forming a 'C-shaped encirclement ring' round China," *Guangzhou Daily* (Guangzhou), 14 August 2010, http://www.chinanews.com.cn/gj/2010/08-14/2467638.shtml; "Editorial: Beware of the emergence of a psychological 'Asian NATO'," *Global Times*, 11 August 2010, http://opinion.huanqiu.com/roll/2010-08/1003401.html.

54. For a discussion of President Hu's meetings with Kim Jong-Il in 2010, see, for example, Lin Heli, "Beijing pays heavy price for supporting the Kim dynasty," *Ming Pao* (Hong Kong), 11 September 2010.

55. See "China to invest $40 billion in Iranian oil and gas," AFP, 31 July 2010, http://www.rawstory.com/rs/2010/07/china-invest-40-billion-iranian-oil-gas/.

56. Cited in "Yan Xuetong: the China-U.S. relationship is one in which 'enmity outweighs friendship'," *International Herald Leader*, 22 March 2010, http://www.wyzxsx.com/Article/Class20/201003/139241.html.

57. Cited in Willy Lam, "Beijing launches diplomatic blitz to steal Obama's thunder," *China Brief*, 20 February 2009, http://www.jamestown.org/programs/chinabrief/single/?tx_ttnews%5Btt_news%5D=34387&cHash=64c53060b0.

58. "Wang Qishan: Developing countries should have a bigger say," *Ming Pao*, 28 March 2009; "The world asks the G20 to provide leadership for financial reform, and to raise the representation and say of developing countries," *People's Daily*, 27 March 2009, http://world.people.com.cn/GB/1030/9035650.html; "China displays image of a responsible power in maintaining the financial stability of the global economy," *People's Daily*, 30 March 2009, http://www.chinanews.com.cn/cj/plgd/news/2009/03-30/1623190.shtml.

59. For a discussion of China-ASEAN ties, see, for example, "China-ASEAN free trade ahead," *China Daily*, 23 June 2008, http://www.chinadaily.com.cn/bizchina/2008-06/23/content_6787069.htm; "China-ASEAN free trade area to be completed on schedule," Xinhua News Agency, 6 August 2009, http://www.china.org.cn/international/2009-08/06/content_18291636.htm.

60. David Pilling, "China is just sabre-rattling over the dollar," *Financial Times*, 2 April 2009, http://www.ft.com/cms/s/0/3f34d71c-1ee5-11de-a748-00144feabdc0.html?ftcamp=rss.

61. For a discussion of developing countries' enhanced status in the IMF and World Bank, see Si Tingting, "China urges voice for developing nations," *China Daily*, 24 July 2009, http://www.chinadaily.com.cn/china/2009-07/24/content_8466358.htm; "China, U.S. agree on reforming international financial bodies," Xinhua News Agency, 5 August 2009, http://news.xinhuanet.com/english/2009-08/05/content_11831594.htm; William Ide, "World Bank increases voting rights for China,", Voice of America, News, 26 April 2010, http://www.voanews.com/english/news/World-Bank-Increases-Voting-Rights-for-China-92075809.html.

62. For a discussion of the global role of the *yuan*, see, for example, Peter Garnham, "China plans global role for renminbi," *Financial Times*, 14 July 2009, http://www.ft.com/cms/s/0/e161ea5c-70a2-11de-9717-00144feabdc0.html; "The yuan goes global: A Mao in every pocket," *The Economist*, 23 September 2010,http://www.economist.com/node/17093527.

63. For a discussion of China's overseas investments, see "China surges to 5th largest global investor," *People's Daily*, 6 September 2010, http://english.peopledaily.com.cn/90001/90776/90883/7129663.html.

64. "Rio Tinto scuttles its deal with Chinalco," *Wall Street Journal*, 5 June 2009, http://online.wsj.com/article/SB124411140142684779.html.

65. "The right moment for Chinese enterprises to make overseas acquisitions," *Guangzhou Daily* (Guangzhou), 27 April 2009, http://news.xinhuanet.com/comments/2009-04/27/content_11264358.htm; "China's oil enterprises involved in overseas mergers and acquisitions worth more than RMB 80 billion," China News Service, 11 July 2009, http://www.chinanews.com.cn/cj/cj-cyzh/news/2009/07-11/1770799.shtml; "Chinese oil majors mull bids for Iraq oil," www.chinaview.cn, 7 July 2009; "Petrochina snaps up Canadian oil firm," *Ming Pao*, 25 June 2009.

66. Cited in "China overseas oil and gas investment gathering pace – IEA," www.energia.gr, 10 June 2010, http://www.energia.gr/article_en.asp?art_id=22402.

67. See John Pomfret, "China invests heavily in Brazil, elsewhere in pursuit of political heft," *Washington Post*, 26 July 2010, http://www.washingtonpost.com/wp-dyn/content/article/2010/07/25/AR2010072502979_pf.html.

68. Cited in "China's wealth fund, heavy in cash, lost 2.1% in '08," *Wall Street Journal*, 8 August 2009, http://online.wsj.com/article/SB124963635852013973.html.

69. For a discussion of Tokyo's attitude to Beijing's purchase of Japanese government bonds, see, for example, Alex Frangos, "China's yen buying spree adds to strained Sino-Japanese relations," *The Wall Street Journal*, 10 September 2010, http://www.theaustralian.com.au/business/news/chinas-yen-buying-spree-adds-to-strained-sino-japanse-relations/story-e6frg90x-1225917053721.

70. For a discussion of China's spin-doctoring efforts, see, for example, "Open the thousand-faced China for the world to see," *Global Times*, 3 September 2010, http://www.huanqiu.com of China," *Oriental Morning News* (Shanghai), 2 September 2010, http://opinion.huanqiu.com/roll/2010-09/1068819.html

71. "Beijing plans global media expansion," AFP, 14 January 2009, http://www.google.com/hostednews/afp/article/ALeqM5juSqW75T9CV55CR1AN52DTTfMdeg.

72. "Booming Confucius institutes enhance China's soft power," Xinhua News Agency, 2 November 2008, http://news.xinhuanet.com/english/2008-11/02/content_10294081.htm.

73. Willy Lam, "Chinese State Media Goes Global: A Great Leap Outward for Chinese Soft Power?" *China Brief*, Jamestown Foundation, 22 January 2009, http://www.jamestown.org/programs/chinabrief/single/?tx_ttnews%5Btt_news%5D=34387&cHash=64c53060b0.

74. Yu Keping, "The 'China Model' and thought liberation," *Beijing Daily*, 18 November 2008, http://news.xinhuanet.com/theory/2008-11/18/content_10373496.htm.

75. Dong Manyuan, "How to extend soft power with Chinese characteristics," *Outlook Weekly* (Beijing), 8 December 2008, http://news.xinhuanet.com/politics/2008-12/08/content_10473539.htm.

76. Li Xiguang, "Major difficulties facing the construction of Chinese soft power," *People's Daily* net, 5 January 2009, http://unn.people.com.cn/GB/22220/142506/8625983.html.

77. See Xu Youyu, "From 1979 to 2009: 20 years of evolution in Chinese thought," Chinadigitaltimes.com, 15 May 2009, http://chinadigitaltimes.net/2009/05/xu-youyu-%e5%be%90%e5%8f%8b%e6%b8%94-from-1989-to-2009-20-years-of-evolution-in-chinese-thought-22/.

78. Keith Bradsher, "China accuses dissident of subversion," *New York Times*, 24 June 2009, http://www.nytimes.com/2009/06/24/world/asia/24liu.html; Phelim Kine, "Free Liu Xiaobo," *Far Eastern Economic Review*, July 2009, http://www.feer.com/politics/2009/july58/Free-Liu-Xiaobo.

79. Cui Liru "The possibility of China developing conflicts with the world in greater than in the past," *Global Times*, 22 July 2009, http://opinion.huanqiu.com/roll/2009-07/523024.html.

80. "The new space race," BBC World Service, 10 August 2009, http://www.bbc.co.uk/worldservice/specials/1744_spacerace/page2.shtml;Madhur Singh, "India gains on China in Asia's space race," *Time* Asia Edition, 21 October 2008, http://www.time.com/time/world/article/0,8599,1852608,00.html.

81. Lin Heli, "China's battle to protect interests in the South China Sea," *Apple Daily* (Hong Kong), 4 July 2009.

82. For a discussion of a possible "anti-China U.S.-Vietnam axis", see, for example, "Could Vietnam be America's new counterweight to China?" http://www.newamericamedia.org, 8 September 2010, http://newamericamedia.org/2010/09/could-viet-nam-be-americas-new-counterweight-to-china.php; also see Cai Hongpeng, "Don't push Vietnam toward the US," *Global Times*, 25 August 2010, http://opinion.huanqiu.com/roll/2010-08/1043380.html.

83. "Clinton signs landmark U.S.-ASEAN friendship pact," AFP, 22 July 2009, http://www.google.com/hostednews/afp/article/ALeqM5gZaMHq5XgxGQZVkqEAj

_DRB4SKlg; "U.S. signs TAC with ASEAN," Xinhua News Agency, 22 July, 2009, http://news.xinhuanet.com/english/2009-07/22/content_11755447.htm.

84. "Remarks of Secretary Clinton at the ASEAN Regional Forum," State Department website, 23 July 2009, http://www.state.gov/secretary/rm/2009a/july/126373.htm; Wang Si, "The U.S. accedes to the 'ASEAN Treaty of Amity and Cooperation' in order to counterbalance China," *Global Times*, 22 July 2009; http://www.qthdaily.com/news/content/2009-07/23/content _115508.htm; Lachlan Carmichael, "US deepens ties with Asia," *Canberra Times* (Australia), 23 July 2009.

85. Cited in "Washington warned over South China Sea," *Global Times*, 26 July 2010. http://china.globaltimes.cn/diplomacy/2010-07/555737.html.

86. For a discussion of the Mekong's lower-riparian countries' fight for water resources with Beijing, see, for example, Jonathan Manthorpe, "China succumbs to Mekong nations," *Vancouver Sun*, 30 August 2010; http://www.vancouversun.com/business/China+succumbs+Mekong+nations/ 3461842/story.html; Simon Roughneen, "The US dips into Mekong politics," *Asia Times*, 14 August 2010, http://www.atimes.com/atimes/Southeast_Asia/ LH14Ae01.html.

87. James Manicom, "Hu-Fukuda Summit: The East China Sea Dispute," *China Brief*, Jamestown Foundation, 6 June 2008, http://www.jamestown.org/ programs/chinabrief/single/?tx_ttnews%5Btt_news%5D=4968&tx_ttnews %5BbackPid%5D=168&no_cache=1.

88. For a discussion of the aftermath of the China-Japan clash over the Diaoyu/Senkaku islets, see for example, "Japan-China tensions enter new phase," *Wall Street Journal*, 26 September 2010; Masami Ito, "Senkaku spat hurts Beijing as well," *Japan Times*, 30 September 2010, http://search.japantimes.co.jp/cgi-bin/nn20100930f1.html

89. "Japan is worried about the increase in the strength of the Chinese Air Force," *Global Times*, 11 August 2009, http://world.people.com.cn/GB/ 9835414.html; Christopher W. Hughes, "Japan's military modernization: a quiet Japan-China arms race and global power projection," *Asia-Pacific Review*, Vol.16 (No.1). pp. 84–99. http://dx.doi.org/10.1080/13439000 902957582.

90. For a discussion of Indian imports of US arms, see Anjana Pasricha, "New Delhi new deal paves way for US companies to sell sophisticated arms to India," Voice of America, 24 July 2009, http://www.voanews.com/ english/2009-07-24-voa13.cfm.

91. "Emerging trends in the security architecture in Asia: Bilateral and multilateral ties among the United States, Japan, Australia and India," Congressional Research Service Report for Congress, 7 January 2008; http://www.au.af.mil/au/awc/awcgate/crs/rl34312.pdf.

92. "US-China partnership needs new mindset," *Global Times* (English), 21 July 2009, http://opinion.globaltimes.cn/editor-picks/2009-07/449561.html; Ding Gang, "Anxieties about clashes between China and the West," Chinaelections.net, 16 January 2009, http://en.chinaelections.org/newsinfo .asp?newsid=19809.

93. See "Do not always link disturbances in China with 'the Chinese system'," *Global Times*, 30 July 2009, http://world.people.com.cn/GB/9749859.html.

94. "China's Hu skips G8 to deal with Xinjiang riots," Reuters, 7 July 2009, http://www.reuters.com/article/latestCrisis/idUSPEK60499.

95. For a discussion of China's policy toward ethnic minorities, see, for example, "Behind the violence in Xinjiang," Human Rights Watch, 9 July 2009 http://www.hrw.org/en/news/2009/07/09/behind-violence-xinjiang; "China and Tibet: another year of the iron fist," *The Economist*, 26 February 2009, http://www.economist.com/opinion/displaystory.cfm?story_id=13184714.

96. "'Five Principles' still shaping global peace," *China Daily*, 29 June 2004 http://www2.chinadaily.com.cn/english/doc/2004-06/29/content_343578.htm.

97. "In depth: Milosevic on trial," BBC news, 24 July 2008, http://news.bbc.co .uk/2/hi/in_depth/europe/2001/yugoslavia_after_milosevic/default.stm; Lauren Comiteau, "Charles Taylor Trial Starts," *Time*, 7 January 2008, http://www.time.com/time/world/article/0,8599,1700945,00.html.

98. Austin Ramzy, "Why China's state-owned companies are making a comeback," *Time*, 29 April 2009, http://www.time.com/time/world/article/ 0,8599,1894565,00.html; "State-owned companies still biggest taxpayers in China," Xinhua News Agency (English), 11 October 2008, http://www.chinadaily.com.cn/china/2008-10/11/content_7097249.htm.

99. For a discussion of Beijing's human rights record, see "UN misses opportunity o push China on human rights," Amnesty International, 9 February 2009, http://www.amnesty.org/en/for-media/press-releases/un-misses-opportunity-push-china-human-rights-20090209; Willy Lam, "Hu's recent crackdown on political dissent," *China Brief*, 7 June 2005, http://www.jamestown.org/single/?no_cache=1&tx_ttnews%5Btt_news%5D= 30495.

100. Cited in "Hu Jintao's speech at conference to mark the 30th anniversary of the Third Plenum of the CPC 11th Central Committee," *People's Daily*, 19 December 2008, http://cpc.people.com.cn/GB/64093/64094/8544901.html; "Wu Bangguo's work report to the Second Plenary Session of the 11th National People's Congress," *People's Daily*, 10 March 2009, http://cpc.people.com.cn/GB/64093/64094/8934228.html.

101. For a discussion of the global implications of China's environmental problems as well as China-Indian arguments over river rights see, for example, "China dust storm hits East Asia," BBC news, 3 March 2008 http://news.bbc.co.uk/2/hi/asia-pacific/7274718.htm; Hari Sud, "China's future water war with India," UPI, 13 May 2008, http://www.upiasia.com/ Security/2008/05/13/chinas_future_water_war_with_india/3300/; "India expert claims China wants to use water resources to control India," *Global Times*, 11 August 2009, http://world.people.com.cn/GB/9834712.html.

102. For a discussion of nationalist forces behind Chinese diplomacy, see Jane McCartney, "French supermarket Carrefour faces wrath of Chinese protesters," *Times of London*, 21 April 2008, http://www.timesonline.co.uk/ tol/news/world/asia/china/article3784932.ece; Paul Mooney, "Internet fans

flames of Chinese nationalism," *YaleGlobal*, 4 April 2005, http://yaleglobal.yale.edu/display.article?id=5516.

103. For a discussion of the impact of the rise of nationalism, see, for example, "China's rulers look to space to maintain Olympic pride," AFP, 10 September 2008, http://afp.google.com/article/ALeqM5it_tnj1X28nnzGHN wh4WgORD1v-w; "China's risky support of Internet activism," Stratfor.com, 15 April 2008, http://www.stratfor.com/memberships/114779/ analysis/chinas_risky_support_internet_activism; "87% of Chinese Netizens support a boycott of visiting or going to college in Australia," *Global Times*, 10 August 2009, http://world.huanqiu.com/roll/2009-08/541338.html.

104. For a discussion of China's contribution to global economic recovery, see, for example, Bill Powell, "Can China save the world?" *Time* Asia edition, 10 August 2009, http://www.time.com/time/magazine/article/0,9171,1913638 ,00.html.

105. Cited in Willy Lam, "China learns to be a superpower," *Far Eastern Economic Review*, May 2009.

106. Cited in "Renmin University Professor: China should accept America's 'multilateral suggestion'," *Global Times*, 5 August 2010, http://mil.huanqiu .com/ Exclusive/2010-08/986900.html.

107. For a discussion of Beijing's "accommodation" of the DPRK, see, for example, Willy Lam, "Beijing's calculated response to NK missile launch," *China Brief*, 16 April 2009, http://www.jamestown.org/programs/chinabrief/ single/?tx_ttnews%5Btt_news%5D=34867&cHash=61ca5a28bd; "Diplomacy urged in North Korea nuke row," *New York Times*, 12 August 2009, http://www.nytimes.com/reuters/2009/08/12/world/international-uk-china-arms.html; Lin Heli, "Beijing has to pay stiff price for being a patron of North Korea," *Ming Pao*, 11 September 2010.

108. "Respect Myanmar sovereignty, China says after trial," Reuters, 12 August 2009, http://www.reuters.com/article/topNews/idUSTRE57B0O020090812.

109. For a discussion of the revival of "democratic centralism" and other Leninist values, see Jeffrey N Wasserstrom, "China's political colors: from monochrome to palette," Opendemocracy.net, 14 May 2008, http://www.opendemocracy.net/article/institutions/china-s-political-colours -from-monochrome-to-palette.

110. See Party Military History Research Centre of the National Defence University, "Why we must resolutely counter [efforts to] delink the army from the party," *Liberation Army Daily*, 4 May 2009, http://www.chinamil .com.cn/site1/xwpdxw/2009-05/04/content_1749539.htm.

111. For a discussion of the implications of the PLA being a "party army," see, for example, Willy Lam, "China to roll out the big guns," *Asia Times* Online, 14 August 2009, http://www.atimes.com/atimes/China/KH14Ad01.html.

112. For a discussion of Turkey's reactions to the Xinjiang events of the summer of 2009, see, for example, "Turkish PM told to take back Xinjiang genocide remark," Reuters, 14 July 2009, http://www.reuters.com/article/latestCrisis/ idUSPEK53133.

8

New History Inside
Hu Jintao's Foreign Policy:
"Harmony" versus "Hegemony"

Ronald C. KEITH

It is said that "only when the coffin lid is down can a man's reputation be fixed (*gai guan lun ding*)". As Hu Jintao's term of leadership is nearing completion and as China officially achieved new status as the world's second largest economy in the third quarter of 2010 now would seem to be an appropriate time to begin to consider the implications of Hu's foreign policy accomplishment.

Under Hu's leadership the underlying rationale of Chinese foreign policy has matured at a time when China's status in the world has undergone qualitative change. After a fitful start and debates over how to describe China's new place in the world, Hu dropped references to "peaceful rise" 和平崛起. "Rising" was problematic in that it failed to capture China's "developing status" and it failed to disassociate China from the "rise and fall of great powers"[1] Perhaps foreign policy under Hu Jintao is a bit "more activist",[2] but it is largely built on past perspective, style and principle.

By 2003 a clear policy emerged whereby Hu used the Confucian concept of "harmony" further to consolidate an established set of CPC principles and strategies concerning China's foreign policy and diplomacy. This elaboration updated the continuous synthesis of foreign policy with domestic policy; it defended the contemporary relevance of Zhou Enlai's "five principles of peaceful coexistence" 和平共处五项原则 and the companion strategy of "seeking common ground while reserving differences"求同存异; it reiterated the importance of Deng Xiaoping's "independent foreign policy" and his policies for "peace and development" 和平与发展; and it elaborated on Jiang Zemin's formulations regarding China's New Security Concept 新安全观, the "democratization of international relations" 国际关系的民主化 and "the diversity of civilizations" 各国文明的多样性.

The Hu Jintao years have been characterized by a surprisingly substantive trend to learn from Chinese history, hence the idea of 温故而知新 or "revisit the past and know new things". Mao had instructed "make the past serve the present" (*yi gu wei jin* 以古为今), but he was mainly interested in peasant rebellion as a harbinger of the modern Chinese revolution. Mao was hardly inclined to look for Confucian principles to serve as a conceptual basis for foreign policy and diplomacy. Hu's elaboration is a faithful extension of the thinking of the three previous "generations" of leadership, but it is also distinctive in the way that it draws on Chinese history. The celebration of Chinese civilization informs the current official interpretation of China's changing status in the world. The Party's Chinese civilization is enduring and ancient, but not unique and superior, thus Chinese civilization has refused to serve as justification for modern day imperialism, preferring instead to become an integral part of the "diversity of civilizations". The upshot of this is that China now subscribes to "harmony" 和谐 and still refuses to play the role of superpower in global contention for "hegemony" 霸权主义.

Ancient Chinese history has become a surprisingly important source of justification and legitimacy for contemporary foreign policy in a globalizing world. The 2005 white paper on peaceful development, for example, brought the past together with present and future in the following manner: "Looking back upon history, basing itself on the present reality and looking forward to the future, China will unswervingly follow the road of peaceful development, making great efforts to achieve a peaceful, open, cooperative and harmonious development".[3] The implications of Hu Jintao's notion of harmony needs a full analysis particularly with reference to "realist" assumptions as to China's emergence as a "superpower" that will challenge American "hegemony".

Hu continues to maintain the five principles of peaceful coexistence at the core of foreign policy, but he has further reconciled this core with his interpretation of both the near-term and long-term trends of Chinese history. His current notion of the "peaceful coexistence of civilizations", for example, extends the 1950s logic of the five principles of peaceful coexistence as against the contemporary "clash of civilizations". His notion of "harmony with differences" 和而不同 draws on the history of ancient Chinese civilization to consolidate Zhou Enlai's operative strategy of "seeking common ground, while reserving differences", in the contemporary arenas of state and civilizational interaction.

The Relevance of the Original Conceptual Core[4]

At Bandung in 1955, Zhou Enlai acknowledged that indeed there were serious ideological differences between states struggling with the dynamics of the Cold War, but that states could honestly acknowledge such differences as they promoted their common national and developmental aspirations. Moreover inclusive diplomacy and ever widening recognition that challenged the containment of China would contribute to China's peaceful development by allowing for the "learning of the strong points of *all* countries" regardless of whether such countries were "capitalist" or "socialist".

Zhou faulted Cold War bourgeois ideology for failing to achieve this kind of intelligent approach. Such ideology confused "right from wrong" whereas China had tried to "seek the truth from the facts".[5] Zhou's response to containment was deliberately inclusive and self-defensive rather than combative. The five principles of peaceful coexistence, namely; equality and mutual benefit, mutual respect for state sovereignty and territorial integrity, non-aggression, non-interference in each other's affairs and peaceful coexistence, offered an alternative guarantee for peace and development in Asia as opposed to war and the inequalities, interference and humiliating second-class status associated with the balance of power.

Zhou criticized the Cold War thrust of U.S. diplomacy: "Though there are many different views among us that should not affect the aspirations we all have in common".[6] The Asian and African states, regardless of their constitutional and ideological preferences, did have a serious interest in national economic development and Cold War politics had fanned the flames of "mutual suspicion and mutual exclusion". Each country's ideology deserved respect, but it was not to be exported. "Common aspirations" then co-exist with the "different viewpoints" that together constitute "an objective reality".[7]

Hu Jintao and the Four Generations
of Foreign Policy Leadership

Hu Jintao might well be faulted by some critics either for his lack of imagination or his apparently realist intention to deceive the world with disingenuous reference to peace. It is hard to believe that the entire edifice of policy is motivated by the desire to deceive.[8] Hence, my alternative argument here is that Hu's elaboration on an existing foreign policy ethos at a time when China's status in the world is undergoing great change is a stabilizing international development, as this established content rejects extreme nationalism and competition for hegemony while it continues to provide a consolidated positive basis for China's further integration with the world political economy.

Rather than altering Deng's low-posture foreign policy requiring disavowal of leadership, never seeking hegemony, and espousing a principle of modesty consistent with the national goal of creating a "moderately prosperous society" (*xiaokang shehui* 小康社会) in accordance with China's actual level of development, Hu has chosen to extend Deng's policy logic on the basis of a historical reading of the natural Chinese penchant for harmony.

Hu's foreign policy thinking is constructive in that it is based upon what might be called Chinese pragmatic idealism which prefers cooperation to conflict. Hu puts the relation between war and peace in historical context and has attempted to consolidate the policy preference for cooperation with a deeper reference to Chinese civilization and history. This particular reference to history has not fed an ambitious nationalist ego. The Chinese approach to China's changing status is neither bombastic nor celebratory; it is measured, constructive and consistently coherent.

The continued subscription to "diversity of civilizations" (*geguo wenmingde duo yangxing* 各国文明的多样性) confidently acknowledges the importance of Chinese civilization without stoking the fires of an extreme nationalism that builds on the putative superiority of Chinese civilization. In the context of 9/11, the "clash of civilizations" and the War on Terror, it was Jiang Zemin who came up with the diversity of civilizations, including China's civilization within human civilization.[9] Hu's foreign policy has elaborated on world harmony as the positive interaction between various civilizations, insisting that no one civilization is superior to the other and that they all contribute to human civilization.

Daniel Bell has studied the contemporary relevance of the Confucian notion of "*tian xia wei gong*", but his analysis overlooks the inclusiveness of Hu's putative Confucian approach that integrates the diversity of civilizations within the totality of human civilization. Bell advises the Chinese on policy:

> Rather than arguing for cosmopolitan political institutions inspired by Confucian principles – with the not so implicit agenda that the Chinese state will take the leading role in promoting China's soft power might be better off pointing to the Confucian emphasis on modesty, tolerance and willingness to learn that Confucians have often shown when engaging with other cultural and moral systems . . .[10]

Arguably willingness to learn has been a hallmark of the Chinese approach to development and globalization. The open-ended nature of learning was stressed by Hu when he commented on Bertrand Russell in London on 9 November 2005:

> The famous British philosopher Russell said, "In the past, contact between different civilizations often proved to be milestones in mankind's progress." Mr. Russell's words stressed the importance of dialogue and interaction and strengthened understanding and borrowing between different countries, different peoples, and different civilizations. In our age, with the advance of multipolarity in the world, and economic globalization, if people hope to promote the development of their own country, and work together to build a harmonious world with lasting peace and prosperity in common, then they must strengthen mutual understanding and enhance mutual trust.[11]

One might at this point consider Bertrand Russell's views on Chinese civilization and the "problem of China". Hoping that China would not follow in the footsteps of "the great military nations of the modern world", Russell had argued in 1926:

> But if Chinese reformers can have the moderation to stop when they have made China capable of self-defence, and to abstain from the further step of foreign conquest; if, when they have become safe at home, they can turn aside from the materialistic activities imposed by the Powers, and devote their freedom to science and art and the inauguration of a better economic system – then China will have played the part in the world for which she is fitted . . . .[12]

The present day Chinese discussion on harmony would probably have suited Bertrand Russell very well.

Hu has followed in the footsteps of the second and third generations of leaders in his independent search for security that is based on a basic principle of non-interference and an inclusive approach to national self-determination. He rejects the "realist" approach to anarchy in the state system through bilateral and collective defence alliance arrangements in favour of a collective security approach highlighting multilateral fora that seek common security and development. Middle Kingdomism, predicated in the superiority of China's unique civilization, explicitly conflicts with the assumptions underlying Hu's contemporary interpretation of "harmony".

Hu's Confucian policy of harmony is anti-hegemonic and conflicts with the exclusive and hierarchical dimensions of empire. Hu Jintao is no "Son of Heaven" such as Qian Long. The analysis herein thus disagrees with popular Western analysis that equates contemporary China with imperialism. Ross Terrill, for example, calls for a "liberalized China" that "will shed its imperial role". He castigates the CPC's imperial pretension: "Like the age-old dynastic court, the CPC views itself as the enlightened ruler of fringe peoples and the guardian of an unassailable doctrine". Terrill characterized the PRC as a twenty-first century "misfit" as it is "the last remaining major multicultural empire" and as its "imperial idea" is "dysfunctional in the world of nation-states".[13]

Especially in light of the provocative dimensions of containment, Chinese foreign policy has effectively dealt well with the evolution of modern nationalism in the state system and China's own entry into world politics was accompanied by a sensitive reading of the importance of the nationalism of other states. Chinese policy has tended to value the importance of stability on its borders and this has required a studied measure of respect for the national self-determination of border states that for the most part were also struggling for development. Jiang Zemin summed up this point by quoting the sages, "close neighbours with benevolence are a national treasure" (*qinren shanling, guozhi bao ye* 亲人善邻，国之宝也).[14] Hu has offered an interpretation of the Chinese philosophical tradition concerning harmony to strengthen this reading of the importance of nationalism in a state system that is presently contending with the advantages and disadvantages of globalization.

While American "realist" analysis has expressed considerable angst over China challenging the USA for hegemony, Chinese foreign policy has rationally focused on China's comparatively low level of development requiring a modest posture in international affairs that corresponds to China's low per capita income. American terms of reference have not predetermined the Chinese terms of reference. In 1982, Deng pointed out that there is no triangle, as the China angle is hardly an angle. China is, under Deng's "Goldilocks" analysis, neither a "minor" nor a "major" country:

> Some people are talking about the international situation in terms of a big triangle. Frankly, the China angle is not strong enough. China is both a major country and a minor one. When we say it is a major country, we mean it has a large population and a vast territory . . . But, at the same time, China is a minor country, an underdeveloped or developing country.[15]

This modest reading of China's place in the world connects with the domestic focus on development as the basis for foreign policy; and this modesty avoids imperial over-reach, dysfunctional arms races and the unacceptable cost of world leadership for a developing economy.

Even now Hu's foreign policy continues to advocate China's "developing" rather than "developed" status. In his remarks to the Seventeenth National Party congress on 15 October 2007, Hu described China as "a large developing socialist country with an ancient civilization" and, taking his cue from Deng Xiaoping, he reiterated China's "goal of building a moderately prosperous society in all respects [by 2020]".[16]

Chinese thinking values continuity as the basis for political consensus and legitimacy. Party policy and related diplomatic thought prefers to view change from within continuity Four generations of Party leaders have self-consciously treated foreign and domestic policy as part of the rolling synthesis of developmental priorities. In 2008, the ancient ideas of "feeding the people" and "letting them have their say" were symbolized in the character for "harmony" as it was bolded on the floor of the Bird's Nest stadium during the opening ceremony of the Olympic Games. "Harmony' called for "inter-civilization coexistence" and the harmony of peoples in their common aspirations for development and happiness.

The following *Renmin ribao* (*People's Daily*) gloss on "harmony" as "*hexie*" locates the source of Zhou Enlai's core principles in the Confucian notion of "harmony":

> The idea of "*hexie*" or "harmony" is deeply ingrained in Chinese history; it is a part of the Chinese nation's fine culture. The character "*he*" in "*hexie*" is written with the character "*he* 楪" meaning "grain" next to the character "*kou*" meaning mouth, and together they convey the sense that when the people are warm and well-fed, all is harmonious in heaven and earth. The character "*xie*   " is written with the character "*yan*" on the left side and "*jie*" on the right side, conveying the meaning that everybody has the right to speak up. Since China's first philosophers advanced the well-known concept of "harmony is precious," the concept has been handed down from generation to generation. From the Chinese government's *advancement of the five principles of peaceful coexistence* and the idea that all nations big or small are all equal to the advancement of the guiding principle of "be kind to the neighbours and be partners with the neighbours" ... and to its vigorously advocation (*sic*) of building a new international political and economic order that is fair and reasonable and its advocation of dialogues between different cultures as equals, they all give expression to the idea of harmony. [17]

China's former Foreign Minister Li Zhaoxing saw a constructive rationality in China's "culture of harmony" in its emphasis on "coordination, combination, integration and peace among different elements" and Li claimed: It is a reflection of the Chinese people's ethical quality and a basic thought of China's modern diplomacy."[18] The Mencean philosophical explanation of harmony celebrated differences, hence, *fuwuzhi buqi, wuzhi qingye* 夫物之不齐，物之情也. The original Cold War five principles of peaceful coexistence now serve as the basis of post-Cold War foreign policy thinking, which is said to originate in China's ancient "culture of harmony". The irony of this is perhaps readily appreciated by historians of the Cultural Revolution when Zhou was attacked as a big "Confucian" who would "restore the rites".

Deng Xiaoping once said that no matter how much international conditions change, Chinese foreign policy will still use Zhou Enlai's five principles of peaceful coexistence as its Post-Cold War base.[19] In his Harvard address of December 2003, Premier Wen Jiabao celebrated China's 5000-year civilization with reference to an abiding dialectical intelligence and the importance of contemporary inter-civilization dialogue that specifically builds on Zhou Enlai's five principles of peaceful coexistence and "seeking common ground while reserving differences":

> The Chinese nation has an extremely deep cultural foundation. The Chinese people love peace dearly. "Harmony with differences" was a great thinking put forward by the Chinese ancient philosophers. [This] kind of harmony is not the run of the mill one. The kind of differences is not the ones that contradict with each other. Harmony is for the sake of living and growing together. Differences are aimed at achieving complementarity. Adopting the *"harmony with differences"* attitude to view and handle problems is not only conducive to our warm treatment of our friendly neighbours, but also to helping defuse *contradictions* in the international community.[20]

The five principles may have been created to deal with Cold War differences, but they have nonetheless been conscripted to deal with today's differences in a globalizing world.

In his commentary of 19 April 2005, Xiong Guangkai, Director of the China Institute for International Strategic Studies, noted the long-term Chinese subscription to the idea of "harmony" and claimed that

". . . the Bandung Conference provided a great historic example of harmonious accommodation of various civilizations and cultures and a convincing denial of the 'clash of civilization' theory. It lends immediate significance to the current efforts to promote respect for the world's diversity."[21]

Premier Wen Jiabao eulogized Zhou Enlai's Bandung thinking of 1955. Although the five principles and the idea of "reserving differences" originated in the post-World War II context of new states emerging from colonial dependence, Wen argued that they are now applicable throughout today's international system: ". . . They are still needed to transcend differences of social system and the unevenness of North-South development and to foster common development."[22] Wen confirmed that China remains "an active proponent" and also "a faithful practitioner of the Five Principles of Peaceful Coexistence" as the latter are "enshrined in China's Constitution" and serve as "the cornerstone of China's independent foreign policy". Wen claimed: "That the Five Principles of Peaceful Coexistence still have vitality and remain relevant with the passage of time is due, basically speaking, to its conformity with the purposes and principles of the UN Charter, with the basic requirements of the development of international relations, and with the fundamental interests of the people in the world."[23]

The current notion of "harmony with differences", or "harmony without uniformity", self-consciously parallels Zhou Enlai's "seeking common ground, while reserving differences". Underlying Zhou's strategy was a diplomatic directness or style of modesty and honesty. This was the style that had initially appealed to Nehru, who originally joined with Zhou in crafting the five principles. Nehru disagreed with the US depiction of China. He expected that the rough edges of China's revolution would be smoothed out in the inevitable resurgence of China's ancient civilization.[24]

Western biographers commented on Zhou Enlai's personal grace as if he were the modern reincarnation of the Confucian scholarly gentleman. Zhou's style assumed the direct expression of viewpoint as well as respect for the views of others. The contemporary Chinese discussion of "harmony without uniformity" recalls the ageless wisdom of Confucius. Confucius said: "A gentleman gets along with others, but does not necessarily agree with them; a base man agrees with others, but does not coexist with them harmoniously".[25] Hence the rational man does not fear to disagree with others, but does respect different viewpoints. The "mean man" is more likely to agree only to promote an illusion of harmony so as to further his own interest. Such a lesson in moral character may well have informed Zhou Enlai's interaction with Kissinger in the drafting of the first Shanghai communiqué where the two sides resorted to an honest statement of "differences" so as to kick-start Sino-U.S. normalization.

The *Renmin ribao* (*People's Daily*) glossed Hu's "harmony" highlighting the moral connections between individuals and then moving to the international level of analysis featuring the cooperation between states. The positive nature of "harmony" is actually embedded in "the rational composition of different things" whereas the negativity of "uniformity" is sterile in "the simple duplication and coincidence of things of different natures". Thus the *Renmin ribao* prescribed three principles to facilitate "harmony without uniformity". First, the individual person ought "to take his or her own initiative". Secondly, persons should allow others to take the initiative. Thirdly "one must be good at engaging in friendly cooperation with others".[26] Substituting states for persons on the basis of this "harmony without uniformity" presumes respect for national self-determination and non-interference, as well as acceptance of differences as the critical precondition to the creation of a "harmonious world".

Chinese commentators eulogize the traditional wisdom, or "political intelligence", that lies behind Zhou Enlai's five principles of peaceful coexistence and Deng Xiaoping's "independent foreign policy". Wu Genyou, for example, sees this "political intelligence" as a valuable contribution to the countries of the world:

> As a country with a longstanding cultural and historical tradition, China will follow the philosophy of "harmony with differences" . . . The political intelligence gradually accumulated through political practice over the longstanding historical period and used to administer a country with such a huge territory must be a valuable characteristic, hard to obtain and valuable to people both in China and the countries of the world.[27]

Wu repeats the common Chinese argument that security starts at home with attention paid to the livelihood and moral contentedness of the people. The moral power that derives from "benevolence" in politics is more powerful than the force that comes from "hegemony". Wu specifically cited Xun Zi on this point:

> Benevolence is above everything; justice is above everything; and prestige is above everything. When benevolence is above everything, everybody without exception will be close to the ruler. When justice is above everything, everyone will respect him. When prestige is above everything, no one will dare to make him an enemy. Relying on the invincible strength and political principle to conquer the hearts of people, he will be able to defeat anybody without waging wars and will possess lands without attacking others. [28]

Ancient "political intelligence" has been conscripted into the thinking of the four generations of Chinese leadership, and such ancient "political intelligence" as it focuses on the moral dimension of cultural power, anticipates the modern day notion of "soft power."

Hu Jintao has rooted Chinese foreign policy in a domestic politics that it is self-consciously based on a rolling synthesis of ideas linking the various generations of Chinese political leaders in their attempts to maintain Party focus on national economic development. General Xiong Guangkai, a senior interlocutor of Chinese policy, explained this in "generational" terms:

> . . . since the founding of New China, the first-generation leadership-collective of the Party with Mao Zedong as the core put forward and jointly initiated together with the leaders of India and Burma as early as in 1954 the five principles of peaceful coexistence. The second-generation . . . with Comrade Deng Xiaoping as the core put forward the important thesis, "peace and development are two major issues of the contemporary world" and actively called for the establishment of a new international political and economic order. The third generation . . . with Jiang Zemin as the core further put forward the establishment of a new security concept of "mutual trust, mutual benefits, equality and cooperation," [that] called for maintaining the world's

diversification and promoting the world's multi-polarization and advocated democratization of international relations. [29]

Hu then threw *"he"* into the dialectical mix of generational wisdom. According to General Xiong, Hu Jintao, in his programmatic speech to the UN on 1 September 2005, accordingly "held aloft the banner of peace, development and cooperation" and called for ever greater international cooperation on the basis of the Five Principles of Peaceful Coexistence". Hu's speech dismissed the "clash of civilizations" in favour of achieving harmony between different civilizations on the basis of "seeking common ground while reserving differences." Highlighting "inclusiveness" in building a "harmonious world", Hu reasoned:

> Diversity of civilizations is a basic feature of humanity and an important driving force behind human progress . . . various civilizations have made positive contributions to human progress . . . . Various civilizations can learn from one another and improve together because there are differences. Seeking uniformity with force only leads to the decline and ossification of human civilizations because of a loss of a driving force. There is a difference in the length of history of civilizations, but civilizations cannot be distinguished as superior or inferior . . . We should strengthen dialogues and exchanges among different civilizations, learn from each other's strong points to offset one's weaknesses in the course of competition and comparison, *develop together in the course of seeking common ground while reserving differences.*[30]

"Harmony" is now synthesized with "peaceful coexistence" and the "diversity of civilizations" aspires to "coexistence" between civilizations within the common development of mankind

In his speech to the Seventeenth National Party Congress in October 2007, Hu Jintao emphasized the importance of applying "seeking common ground, while reserving differences" in dealing with the "diversity" of the world in order to make common cause in advancing "human civilization".

We maintain that the people of all countries should join hands and strive to build a harmonious world of lasting peace and common prosperity. To this end, all countries should uphold the purposes and principles of the UN charter, observe international law and universally recognized norms of international relations, and promote democracy, harmony, collaboration and win-win solutions in international relations. Politically, all countries should respect each other . . . and endeavour to promote democracy in international relations. Economically, they should cooperate with each other, draw on each other's strengths and work together to advance economic globalization in the direction of balanced development, shared benefits and win-win progress. Culturally, they should learn from each other in the spirit of seeking common ground while shelving differences, respect the diversity of the world and make joint efforts to advance human civilization.[31]

The internal argument for "harmony" based on "coexistence" may have been very easy to make within the Party. On the basis of "coexistence", Chinese foreign policy negotiated the collapse of containment, the entry of the PRC into the UN, sequential normalizations with the U.S., Japan, the USSR and Russia, the re-establishment of international trade and open-door policies after Tiananmen Square. It has contributed positively to regional stability in Central Asia even in the wake of the spectacular collapse of the Soviet Union and the creation of new states in ethnically inflamed Central Asia.

Conclusion

Under Hu Jintao there has been important foreign policy continuity that is reinforced in an interpretation of Chinese history that negates any likely form of Middle Kingdomism based on extreme nationalism. Arguably such interpretation offers a very powerful rebuttal against the "China Threat" and provides amply for the effective development of China's "soft power".

Chinese analysis has become so comfortable with nationalism that it argues that Chinese civilization will engage with other civilizations on a positive basis of positive diversity and coexistence. There is no room for aggressive irredentism in this policy. Chinese nationalism requires respect, but it does not require a unique national destiny. Nationalism and internationalism can work together in a harmonization of differences.

This is an interesting difference in and of itself from the earlier thinking of Sun Yatsen. Worried that China was a loose grain of sand, Sun proclaimed nationalism as "the most precious possession by which humanity maintains its existence". Sun's exclusive interest in nationalism resulted in his rejection of cosmopolitanism, 世界主义, as it distracted Chinese nationalists from the singular task of nation-building. He was worried not only about Western cosmopolitanism that claimed nationalism was a passing phase in the progress of new material civilization, but he also eschewed Chinese imperial cosmopolitanism for having regarded China's moral culture as more important than the Chinese nation-state.[32]

Mao later claimed that Confucianism had spawned "a sense of superiority in the relation to the outside world which was inappropriate to the practical study and investigation of modernity".[33] The contemporary discourse on Chinese history and foreign policy, while similarly emphasizing the importance of modesty, has claimed that Confucian principle in its acceptance of differences was open to learning from the outside world. Ignoring the unique moral supremacy of the "Son of Heaven", the contemporary policy on harmony demurs from placing the Middle Kingdom at the centre of the world, but it conscripts the Confucian "harmony with differences" to support the "coexistence" of diverse civilizations in a positive reconciliation of Chinese nationalism and internationalism.

In his 2008 speech to the faculty and students of Waseda University, Hu spoke of a long relationship which began the studies of Liao Zhongkai, Li Dazhan, Chen Duxiu and Peng Pai at the university. Hu applauded the University's goal to build "an international university that trains people for the whole world". Hu then offered his own related interpretation of ancient philosophy:

"If one day there may be a renovation, then every day there may be, indeed, daily there must be." "As Heaven keeps vigour through movement, a gentleman should unremittingly practice self-improvement." The ancient Chinese philosophers put forward these important thoughts from their observation of the universe. These maxims reveal the perseverance and resilience of the Chinese nation . . . China is firmly committed to peaceful development. This is a strategic choice the Chinese Government and people have made in light of China's national conditions and the trend of the times. It reflects the unity of China's domestic and foreign policies and the unity of the fundamental interests of the Chinese people and the common interests of the people of the world.[34]

Hu's diplomatic thought has synthesized four generations of policy thinking with an extended interpretation of the history of Chinese civilization, and this ultimate synthesis has been featured in China's growing "soft power" which supports economic cooperation rather than military competition and rejects hegemonism in favour of the inclusive practice of the five principles asserting common prosperity and China's expansive opportunities for national economic development as against the great game practised by great powers seeking to build alliances and the balance of power.

What then is Hu Jintao's foreign policy legacy? Arguably, it lies in his consolidation of a rational continuity that deliberately synthesizes the wisdom of four generations of leadership on how to develop China. This synthesis has always located foreign policy within national economic policy. The same synthesis has often sought regional and international stability so as to support domestic economic growth. Hu Jintao's "harmony" builds on a critique of "hegemony" as repressive empire. Even while Chinese policy seeks technology and investment through globalization, it denies American assumptions of "hegemonic stability" that promise the delivery of "public goods" under the leadership of the single superpower.

Undoubtedly, the above analysis is controversial; and Western analysis will likely have trouble interpreting Hu Jintao's legacy. After all, China is not liberal democratic; it is led by a Communist Party that is not above misappropriating China's past to serve its Leninist present. Presumably Communist leaders are by their very nature predisposed to repression at home and hegemony abroad.[35] Such an assumption derives from an ideological oversimplification of China as a regime type, but Hu's profession of "harmony" and his rejection of "hegemony" as China' "rises" then becomes a convenient hyperbole, or monumental disinformation that risks an unnecessary loss of international and regional diplomatic opportunity for greater cooperation in an anxious time of geo-political and geo-economic flux.

Joseph Nye once wrote that how China behaves once it becomes powerful is an "open question". Claiming that "official ideological holds little appeal", he warned against self-fulfilling prophecy in unthinking American opposition to China: "Nonetheless, the rise of China recalls Thucydides's warning that belief in the inevitability of conflict can become one of its main causes."[36]

What then would be the consequences of Western failure to accept "harmony" and the Western inclination to expect "hegemony"? How would China's leaders respond to Western suspicion and ill will? History may provide the clue as Chinese foreign policy has enduring thematic coherence. In the early 1950s Party leaders persevered against the hostile and aggravating assumptions of containment and in so doing came up with "peaceful coexistence" which is now converging with the logic of "harmony" as suitable to China's status as a large developing state with increasing international influence.

Without too much effort and cost China can easily extend its "soft power" on the basis of "harmony". On the other hand, resort to "hegemony" would confirm the China threat at the expense of China's economic development and deny China's modern history of liberation from colonialism, thus inviting the political and economic costs of blatant hypocrisy in the Third World and elsewhere. Politically the Party has been remarkably steady in its handling of the transition to the market, the collapse of the Soviet Union, globalization and China's changing status in the world. This steady response to the world has been rooted in a persisting generational consensus that prefers change within continuity, and what is more deeply embedded in the Chinese mind than "harmony"?

Hu Jintao may pass from the scene, but the foreign policy that he helped consolidate is anchored deep in a considered sense of China's place in the world that is based on the "diversity of civilizations" and in an enduring political consensus on the priorities of China's development. Indeed, this is more important than occasional changes in the tone of foreign policy statements. Assuming the regime can survive the mounting social contradictions of fast economic growth it is not likely to abandon the current basis of proven foreign policy success to adopt a more aggressive policy of hegemony overseas that would undermine the key importance of domestic national economic development.

Notes and References

1. For related comment on "rising" see Chu Shulong and Jin Wei, *Zhongguo waijiao zhanlue he zhengce* (*China's Foreign Strategy and Policy*) (Beijing: Shishi chubanshe, 2008), p. 112.

2. Rosemary Foot, "Chinese strategies in a US-hegemonic global order: accommodating and hedging," *International Affairs*, Vol. 82, No. 1, pp. 85–87.

3. "China's peaceful development road," People's Daily Online, 22 December 2005, http://english.peopledaily.com.cn/200512/22/eng20051222_230059.html (accessed 8 September 2010).

4. This relevance is explored more fully in Ronald C. Keith, "Zhou Enlai heping gongchujiaode dangdai yiyi: xianshizhuyi yu lixiangzhuyide wanmei jiehe" ("The contemporary relevance of Zhou Enlai's five principles of peaceful coexistence diplomacy: a consummate synthesis of realism and idealism"), in Xu Xing (ed.), *Ershiyi shiji Zhou Enlai yanjiude xin shiye* (*New 21st century perspectives on the study of Zhou Enlai*), Vol. 2 (Beijing: Zhongyang wenxian chubanshe, 2009), pp. 991–1004.

5. Zhou Enlai, "Strengthen party unity and oppose bourgeois individualism," 10 February 1954, *Selected Works of Zhou Enlai*, Vol. II (Beijing: Foreign Languages Press, 1989) p. 136.

6. *Ibid.*, p. 163.

7. *Ibid.*, p. 163.

8. This is what is implied in realist focus on the term "hide our capacities" in Deng Xiaoping's famous twenty-four character instruction, "Observe developments soberly, maintain our position, meet challenges calmly, hide our capacities and bide our time, remain free of ambition and never claim leadership". Realists have focused on "hide our capacities" as indicative a grand strategy of deception. See Guan Li, *Deng Xiaoping yu Meiguo* (Beijing: Zhonggongdangshi chubanshe, 2004), p. 606. Also see Foot, "Chinese strategies in a US-hegemonic gobal order," p. 84.

9. See, for example, "Dangjin shijiede sange da wenti" (Three big problems in todays' world) 14 October 2002, in Jiang Zemin, *Jiang Zemin wenxuan*, Vol. III (Beijing: Renmin chubanshe, 2006), p. 520. Also see Jiang Zemin, "Speech at the CPC 80th anniversary celebration," in *Jiang Zemin on the "Three Represents"* (Beijing: Foreign Languages Press, Beijing, 2001), p. 216.

10. Daniel Bell, *China's New Confucianism* (Princeton NJ: Princeton University Press, 2008), p. 25.

11. "Speech by Hu Jintao at welcome banquet hosted by the Lord Mayor of London," *Xinhua*, 10 November 2005, NewsEdge Document No: 20-0511101477.1_68f604451bf3b436 (accessed 19 May 2008).

12. Bertrand Russell, *The Problem of China* (London: George Allen & Unwin, 1926), p. 252.

13. Ross Terrill's assumptions essentially differ from those of Bertrand Russell, both of whom explicitly addressed the "problem of China". See *The New Chinese Empire* (New York: Basic Books, 2003).

14. Jiang Zemin, "Gongtong chuangzao yige hoping fanrongde xin shiji" ("Together creating a prosperous new century of peace"), *Jiang Zemin wenxuan* (*Selected works of Jiang Zemin*), Vol. 3 (Beijing: Renmin chubanshe, 2006), p. 475.

15. Deng Xiaoping, "Peace and development are the two outstanding issues in the world today," 4 March 1982, *Selected Works of Deng Xiaoping*, Vol. III, p. 111.

16. Hu Jintao, "Hold high the great banner of socialism with Chinese characteristics and strive for new victories . . . ," Report to the 17th National Congress of the Chinese Communist Party, http://en.chinaelections.org /newsinfo.asp?newsid=12146, p. 17 (accessed 29 September 2008).

17. Lu Hong, "Work together to build a harmonious world (International Forum)", *Renmin ribao*, 13 May 2005, NewsEdge Document No.: 200505131477.1_9c5600c51359538c, author's italics.

18. "PRC FM Li Zhaoxing: ancient philosophy guides China's modern diplomacy of harmony", Xinhua, 5 September 2003, NewsEdge Document No: 200509051477.1_eced600830ef80892.

19. Ye Zicheng, *Xin Zhongguo waijiao sixiang cong Mao Zedong dao Deng Xiaoping* (*New Chinese diplomatic thought from Mao Zedong to Deng Xiaoping*) (Beijing: Beijing daxue chubanshe, 2000), p. 423.

20. "Wen Jiabao delivers speech marking Five Principles of Peaceful Coexistence anniversary," Xinhua, 28 June 2004, p. 3, author's italics.

21. Xiong Guangkai, "an epoch-making conference, a powerful trans-century voice," in *Guoji xingshi yu anquan zhanlue* (*International Situation and Security Strategy*), (Beijing: Tsinghua daxue chubanshe, 2006), p. 273. Xiong elaborates on the "*he*" character in a second speech in the same volume, "For common security in a harmonious Asia-Pacific", p. 308.

22. "Wen Jiabao delivers speech marking Five Principles of Peaceful Coexistence anniversary," p. 3.

23. *Ibid.*, p. 2.

24. Keith, *Diplomacy of Zhou Enlai*, p. 2. For a comment on "Nehruvian" diplomacy's representation of India as a civilization, see Amitra Narlikar, "Peculiar chauvinism or strategic calculation? Explaining the negotiating strategy of a rising India", *International Affairs*, 82:1 (2006), p. 72.

25. "RMRB article views global popularity of Confucius, China's peaceful rise", *Renmin ribao*, 29 September 2005, NewsEdge Document No.: 200509291477.1_81f600bc65024ac0.

26. "RMRB article views global popularity of Confucius, China's peaceful rise", *Renmin ribao*. Perhaps the reference to the Confucian adage, "cultivate the self, regulate the family, rule the state and then there will be peace under heaven" (*tianxia yijia, xiushen chijia, zhiguo, tianxiaping*) is the origin of such reasoning.

27. Wu Genyou, *Peace: The Roots of the Cultural Tradition and Values of the Chinese People* (Beijing: Foreign Languages Press, 2007), p. 195.

28. As cited by Wu, *Peace: The Roots of the Cultural Tradition*, p. 73.

29. "Xiong Guangkai's article says PRC's development, peaceful, open and cooperative . . .", Xinhua, 28 December 2005, NewsEdge Document Number: 200512281477.1_10ce00b009feb426.

30. Hu Jintao, "Strive to build a harmonious world where there are permanent peace and prosperity", Speech at the 60th anniversary of the UN, 1 September 2005, Xinhua, 16 September 2005, NewsEdge Doc. No.: 200509161477.1_4eb805b96f4909f9c, p. 4, author's italics.

31. Hu Jintao, "Hold high the great banner of socialism with Chinese characteristics and strive for new victories . . ..", Report to the 17th National Congress of the Chinese Communist Party, http://en.china elections.org/newsinfo.asp?newsid=12146., p. 37 (accessed 29 September 2008).

32. See Sun Yatsen (Frank Price trans.), "Lecture three", in *San Min Chu I*, (Shanghai, 1927), pp. 14–16.

33. This is to repeat the analysis in R. Keith, "Mao Zedong and his political thought," in Anthony Parel and R. Keith (eds.), *Comparative Political Philosophy* (Lanham MD: Lexington Books, 2003), p. 96, author's own italics.

34. Speech by Chinese President Hu Jintao at Waseda University, 20 July 2008, http://www.china-embassy.org/eng/zt/768675/t476528.htm (accessed 12 July 2010).

35. Hugh White has started a controversy in Australia on these points. He argues that China is more likely interested in some form of collective leadership in Asia rather than in imposing "on Asia a harsh hegemony backed by armed force and political repression." Hugh White, "Power shift: Australia's future between Washington and Beijing," *Quarterly Essay*, No. 39 (2010), p. 21.

36. Joseph Nye, Jr, *The Paradox of American Power: Why the World's Only Superpower Can't Go it Alone* (Oxford: Oxford University Press, 2002), p. 19.

9

Battle Ready?
Developing a Blue-water Navy.
China's Strategic Dilemma

Joseph Y. S. CHENG
Stefania PALADINI

The development of China's navy can be interpreted from different perspectives. From a hawkish perspective, it is getting ready for an inevitable clash with the United States or, in terms of realpolitik, China is upgrading its naval military capabilities to the rank of the great economic power it has become while pursuing a peaceful rise. It is without doubt that China's recent maritime developments have been regarded with suspicion, and recent clashes in regional waters have done nothing to improve this perception. However, on a deeper examination of the internal Chinese debate, things are far more complex, and there are different currents of opinion on China's maritime future. China's grand strategy will be determined not only by internal power plays but also by how the regional powers and the United States behave in this regard.

Introduction: Building a First-class Naval Power

Nobody will deny that China's military is entering a period of intense transformation. While China has the biggest army in the world, its backwardness and limited global reach have long been acknowledged. However, this started to change after the first Gulf War, when China commenced a resource-intensive, RMA-driven transformation of the People's Liberation Army (PLA) with the objective of becoming a first-class military power. This is meant to occur in two phases,[1] with the government first modernizing the existing structure;[2] then, supposedly in the next decade, the PLA would achieve a leapfrog, information-led advance putting China on the same ground as the United States in "comprehensive science and technology strength" (*zonghe keji jingzhengli*). The military budget has been growing exponentially, although there is disagreement about the real figures, with the United States Department of Defense (DoD) normally approximately doubling the amount of supplied by PLA sources (US$27.9 billion in 2008 according to the DoD, 2009; US$13.7 billion for the same year according the PLA).[3] In any case, both calculations reflect the impressive growth of the defence budget during the period 1996–2008, an average rate of 12.9% in real terms over the period, while GDP grew at 9.6%. China's military expenses are estimated at 4.3% of GDP, a rate that does not even place it among the first twenty in the world, and far less than the United States, even if the war budget is not taken into account. One area which has been expanding substantially in its capabilities is the PLA Navy (PLAN) traditionally the weakest of China's armed forces but now thriving on the flourishing Chinese shipbuilding industry.[4]

Since 2005, Chinese scholars and central government policy-makers have been debating the necessity of building a blue-water navy, with the objective of constructing multiple aircraft carriers and associated ships by 2020.[5] President Hu Jintao called China a "sea power" and advocated a "powerful people's navy" to "uphold our maritime rights and interests" during a speech at a Navy CCP Congress in 2006. This is also apparent by looking at the composition of the top brass, which has seen the balance recently shifting toward the navy and air force away from the traditional pre-eminence of the ground forces.[6] According to a recent military appraisal, the Chinese navy is now the largest in Asia and, through the new submarine facilities located on Hainan Island, it enjoys direct access to international sea lanes and a considerable strategic position. There are currently two doctrines confronting each other. The first, known as "offshore active defence", which fosters coastal defence operations (*jinyang fangyu*) within the so-called "first islands chain", has defined China's strategy since the 1950s. The focus here is clearly Taiwan and the defence of national territories. While this looks far more conservative than the second, there are problems related to what

China considers as part of the nation, which is in some cases quite controversial. The second, more hawkish approach, advocates a "far-sea defence" (*yuanyang fangyu*). This has been developed very recently following Hu's new doctrine of multi-dimensional precision attacks beyond the first island chain, combined with operations outside of China's claimed 200-nautical mile Exclusive Economic Zone (EEZ) to defend China's national strategic interests. This approach could affect not only Asia but also other continents and pose a strategic challenge to the United States on the domain of the seas. As recently declared by Rear Admiral Zhang Huachen, deputy commander of the East Sea Fleet, "With our naval strategy changing now, we are going from coastal defense to far sea defense".[7] However, the problem with this strategy is clearly that China's global range is much more limited than that of the United States. As of June 2009, the United States had 285,773 active-duty personnel deployed around the world in more than 700 bases (even if nobody seems to know exactly how many bases the U.S. has abroad, and different sources have given different estimations).[8] On the contrary, China still operates no overseas bases and has few PLA personnel stationed abroad – in embassies or as members of United Nations peacekeeping operations. Also, a cursory analysis of PLAN's order of battle clearly shows it is "sized and shaped primarily for defending claims on China's disputed maritime periphery as opposed to conducting extra-regional blue water sea control operations".[9] More controversy surrounds the aircraft carrier project;[10] it is well-known that, while Jiang Zemin promoted the development of a strong navy, he did not fully endorse the desire of the late Admiral Liu Huaqing to build an aircraft carrier, feeling it was not necessary for containing Taiwan's independence.[11] It was only when Hu Jintao became commander-in-chief of the China Military Commission (CMC) that the emphasis was shifted to the role of the PLAN in securing strategic sea lines for energy security and talks about far-sea operations, which made the development of a carrier more relevant.[12]

The plan was publicly endorsed for the first time by the central government in 2007 in a declaration to the press after the annual National People's Congress, and since then a few statements have been issued by military personnel. Therefore while it is at present no longer in doubt that China will actually build an aircraft carrier, and maybe more than one, the motivations and purposes are open to discussion even within the Chinese military. Nobody disputes that China should have an aircraft carrier, because such a vessel, as the pinnacle of any fleet, is a mark of Great Power status, and a financial and technical achievement. Past hesitations due to lack of funding for the PLAN, in view of the huge costs required for the development and maintenance of a carrier, appear now to have been largely overcome. [13] Furthermore, it is a way to preserve sea routes, especially the Malacca Straits which are so important for China's oil supply, and in general to protect its expanding maritime interests. This second aspect, while not officially covered in China's latest White Paper on defence, is nevertheless gaining importance in Chinese strategic thinking.[14] Again, in the words of Zhang Huachen, in line with the expansion of China's economic interests "the navy wants to protect the country's transportation routes and the safety of our major sea lanes".[15] It is worth observing that China is the only permanent member of the UN Security Council that does not have an operational carrier, while some non-permanent members deploy one (India, Thailand), or even two (Italy). This was officially acknowledged by the Chinese Minister of Defence, General Liang Guanglie, in 2009, when he declared that China cannot go on being the only great power without an aircraft carrier.[16] Still, a Chinese carrier will alter the current dynamics of air power in the Asian region, and this may well represent a major problem, no matter Chinese's intentions, without even mentioning that it would be a tool to project force beyond Asia. The Malvinas war of 1982 remains a good example of the importance of a naval intervention force. A likely issue will be the type of carrier China chooses to put into service.[17] The complexity of the development of a large, CATOBAR carrier suggests that China will probably start with a medium-size vessel in order to gain expertise and then switch to something more appropriate for far-sea operations. Confirming this scenario, recently China stepped up efforts to build its own carrier, while working on upgrading the Russian-built, medium-size STOBAR Ukrainian Varyag aircraft carrier it bought in 2006 and which is now undergoing renovation and complete refurbishment at the Dalian shipyards. Nevertheless, China is not likely to have an operational carrier and associated ships before 2015, even, according to more recent estimates, 2011.

China openly acknowledged for the first time its plans for domestically built carriers in December 2010, while the Varyag will be put into service as a training ship as early as 2012.[18] Training for navy pilots is actually well on the way, even if negotiations for acquiring SU-33 Russian fighters stalled after the Chinese angered the Russians by reverse-engineering the planes. China is also working in other development areas together with its carrier project, and this seems to worry the neighbours significantly more, if possible. A watershed was represented by the impressive display at the November 2010 Zhuhai Air Show, which for the first time showed to the world an integrated "Coastal Defence System" made by China Aerospace Science & Industry Corporation (CASIC), one of the biggest Chinese defence manufacturers. The diagrams showcased how Chinese forces, an integrated mix of ground, naval, air and space assets, would track down foreign vessels approaching a small group of islands not far from mainland territorial waters. Here the enemy was represented by an unflagged aircraft carrier group and the attack was initiated by an UAV (unmanned aerial vehicle) which collected location details and passing them to the anti-ship missiles. Other units would finish the operation after the strike.[19] The ballistic anti-ship missiles, DF-21D, represent currently one of the most feared features of this emerging naval power, as they can effectively sink a carrier in the event of a conflict, should they work as expected. While the DF-21D was notably absent from the Zhuhai show, other anti-ship cruise missiles were on display, especially the C-802A (YJ-82), a subsonic device endowed with terminal guidance radar seeking for better performance.[20] Also worth mentioning are the amphibious units, deployed in the "Blue Strike 2010" Sino-Thai Marine Corps joint exercises in October 2010, and that, according the Taiwanese, China has substantially upgraded its "transport capacity up to a full division".[21]

Another valuable addition has been the two maritime Haiyang satellites, which have entered into service over the last decade to join the dual-use Yaogan earth surveillance satellites, which gave China an enhanced capability "to monitor and conduct operations along its disputed maritime periphery".[22] The PLAN was again in the news with its manned deep-water Jiaolong submersible; the vehicle performed a test operation, diving to the depth of 3,759 metres below the sea surface in the South China Sea in 2010.[23] While the vehicle is still experimental, few personnel have been trained on it, and a big share of the technology deployed was foreign-manufactured,[24] its importance cannot be underestimated. With a maximum depth of 7,000 metres, and therefore capable of reaching 99.8% of the earth's seabed, it illustrates an area of rapid Chinese achievements.

Naval exercises are routinely carried out by all navies and they normally do not attract too much attention. This was not the case, however, with PLAN's East Sea Fleet exercises of April 2010, which gathered worried commentaries especially from Japanese sources. In these exercises, not only did China venture for the first time beyond the first islands chain with a fully integrated naval force of frigates, destroyers and submarines, but it also passed along Japanese's Miyako Strait territorial waters without informing the Japanese government.[25] The interest of a powerful navy for China also lies in the possibility of retaliation should the United States venture too much into China's backyard. In the words of Colonel Dai Xu, "If the U.S. can start a fire in our backyard, we also can do the same in theirs". He also talked about "a crescent-shaped strategic encirclement" of China by the United States.[26]The colonel is not alone; General Yang Yi, a well-known scholar at the National Defence University in Beijing, has long warned of the danger of the emergence of an "anti-China coalition" in the West.

Given the attention paid by Chinese to the Monroe doctrine, it is clear that the objective in that case would be Latin America. Ship calls in China by South American navies are becoming far more frequent since 2000. Peruvian, Mexican, Chilean and Colombian vessels have all visited mainland ports in the past few years. China reciprocated, and two Chinese naval missions have been sent to the Western hemisphere so far. The first was in 2002, where the PLAN conducted its first circumnavigation of the globe, and a missile destroyer and a supply ship visited Ecuador, Peru, and Brazil. The latest one was in December 2009,[27] in which the Chinese North Sea Fleet visited the Southern Cone, visiting Chile, Peru and Ecuador, with its destroyer *Shijiazhuang* and the support vessel *Hongzehu*.

Still, without a clear projection force, this kind of initiative will not constitute a threat to the United States, which nevertheless in July 2008 reconstituted its Fourth Fleet to look after Latin America seas. Allegedly, there has been a change of perception in the U.S. military regarding China, shifting, in the words of Admiral Mike Mullen, chairman of the U.S. joint chiefs of staff, from "being curious about where China is headed to being concerned about it".[28]

The final contentious point has been on the so-called "string of pearls", a series of ports across Asia in which China has been investing in developing infrastructure and upgrading naval facilities. Defined as a "nexus of Chinese geopolitical influence or military presence",[29] the pearls include Sittwe, Coco, Mergui, Sihanoukville, Chittagong, Hambantota, Jeddah, Gadwar and Singapore among others (the list varies according different reports). In some cases, like Hambantota in Sri Lanka and Gadwar in Pakistan, the cooperation involves the joint development of deep-water port facilities. The definition and the underlying theory, stemming from a 2004 study commissioned by the U.S. DoD,[30] has found wide acceptance but India has been expressing concerns about China's rising influence in South Asia and fearing encirclement by a series of Chinese naval bases in the Indian Ocean.

However, with a more detached view, the establishment of fully-fledged U.S.-style bases seems quite unlikely, especially where, as in Bangladesh and Sri Lanka, the countries clearly enjoy a privileged relationship with India that would be harmed by such a move. The same would happen with Singapore, which has long enjoyed civil and military ties with both the United States and China. This also seems to be contrary to Chinese interests themselves, especially since this move could trigger reactions of containment of the very kind China seems to frown upon more than anything else. It is possible then that the "string of pearls" would remain what it currently is, a series of friendly "places" (as opposed to "bases") where Chinese ships can call on their way to overseas missions, in which China has recently starting to participate.

Even though all these recent advances may help in forming a balanced understanding of the situation, an overall evaluation of the actual Chinese naval power can prove elusive, and different estimations have been proposed over time by scholars, defence ministries and various think tanks. The one elaborated by the London-based International Institute of Strategic Studies puts China ahead of the United States in terms of available warships and combatants.[31] Still, as the U.S. Defence Secretary Robert Gates has commented on more than one occasion, statistics do not tell the whole story, and even pure military prowess may prove insufficient; as rightly observed, states as well as scholars should "strive for a nuanced, multidimensional, geographically informed understanding of naval power, lest they base their strategies on faulty assumptions".[32]

The Dilemma of Sea Power: Literature and the Present Political Debate in China

Any discussion about the Chinese internal debate about military and naval upgrades, and foreign policy in general, is quite complex, due to the plurality of views and actors involved in policymaking at different levels. While it is sometimes difficult to interpret when a position is actually endorsed, or even shared, by the central government, it is safe to say that there is quite a range of opinion in China regarding the course of action that the state should take regarding its sea power development, spanning from hawkish views to more pragmatic stances. A Chinese scholar described China's sea power as an issue which "cannot be forgotten, is difficult to discuss and come to a consensus, and will expose China's weakness when it comes to a final showdown".[33] Sea power obviously has become a significant issue in China's academic discussions in the last decade in line with China's impressive economic growth, its rising international status, its consideration of a grand strategy, and the expansion of its navy. In these discussions, scholars in China all refer to Alfred T. Mahan[34] whose work has been translated into Chinese.[35] There are ample references, too, to the strength of the U.S. Navy, which is considered to have played an important role in securing victory in World War II and defeating Japan, ensuring the safety of its trade, deterring the Soviet Union in the Cold War era, and making a significant contribution in recent wars in Iraq and Afghanistan.

The implicit and explicit conclusions in these discussions are: a country will become strong if it has adequate sea power; and if a state wants to emerge as a major power, it has to build up its sea power. China's trade and its security naturally have become an important consideration. In 1978, China's trade dependence or openness, i.e., trade as a percentage of GDP, was less than 10%, but in the first decade of this century, it has been consistently over 60%. In recent years, over 45% of China's oil has had to be imported. This is expected to climb upwards steadily. Ninety per cent of China's oil imports are carried by foreign oil tankers. Though China has a lot of coal, it still imports more than 10 million tons of it per annum from Australia, Vietnam, Indonesia, Russia and North Korea.[36] When energy security becomes a serious concern in China, the security of supply routes naturally becomes a significant issue. Today, China still has territorial disputes with a number of its neighbours, including the Paracels dispute with Vietnam, the Spratlys dispute with Taiwan, Vietnam, the Philippines, Malaysia, Brunei, and indirectly Indonesia, and the Diaoyutai (Senkaku) Islands dispute with Japan. These disputed territories are all very important in terms of international navigation and fisheries resources, as well as oil and natural gas. In view of rising nationalism in China, the Chinese leadership is under pressure to be seen effectively protecting China's sovereign rights.

At the same time, the Chinese media and international relations scholars have been paying considerable attention to the naval developments in the United States, Japan, India and neighbouring Asian countries. The natural implication of these reports and studies is that China has to strengthen its navy as well. Chinese people are especially concerned with the naval expansion of Japan, particularly the deployment of major naval escort vessels equipped with helicopters, which are perceived as pseudo-aircraft carriers.[37] There is considerable interest in the construction and deployment of aircraft carriers on the part of the Indian navy too; the Chinese perception is that if India can afford aircraft carriers, then China should have no difficulty in developing them.[38]

Chinese scholars are aware of the possible contradiction between its "harmonious would" perspective and the development of a blue-water navy including the deployment of aircraft carriers. Wang Yizhou, a leading international relations expert of the Chinese Academy of Social Sciences, offers the following explanation:

If China possesses strong armed forces, and at the same time acts fairly, being reasonable and respecting people's feelings, while firmly preserving the principles of peace, independence and self-reliance, following international law and commonly-recognized principles, carefully and continually managing its maritime boundary disputes with the countries concerned, China can then safeguard its legitimate maritime rights, generate an effective deterrence and restraint effect in potential troubles, and display to the world a kind of positive image of loving peace as well as [being] good at promoting good-neighbourliness and common developments.[39]

Other scholars argue that sea power construction offers an important momentum for China's rapid economic development. According to the State Oceanic Bureau, in 2008, China's oceanic products amounted to 2.9662 trillion *yuan*, an increase of 11% over the previous year, and equivalent to 9.87 of annual GDP. In the same year, the maritime sector employed 32.18 million persons, an increase of 0.67 million over that of 2007.[40] The ocean is most valuable economically in terms of natural resources and maritime transport. Further, the deterrent effect of sea power is also emphasized; it helps to avoid conflicts and allows China to concentrate on its economic development. Finally, sea power has an important role in non-traditional security in terms of deterrence of maritime terrorism, protection of marine ecology, prevention of the spread of diseases, and the combatting of transnational crimes, smuggling, drug trafficking, illegal immigration, and piracy. China believes that, as a rising major power, it would like to make a greater contribution to the international maritime public good.[41]

At the Sixteenth Party Congress in 2002 and the Seventeenth Party Congress in 2007, the Chinese leadership proposed "the implementation of the development of the ocean" and "the development of oceanic industries" respectively. Subsequently the State Council released two documents; "Outline of National Oceanic Economic Development Planning" and "Outline of National Oceanic Enterprise Development Planning". Chinese scholars have been at pains to explain that China's economic development involves its emergence as a maritime major power whose basic objective is to be able to defend against external encroachment and safeguard national interests.[42]

In geostrategic terms, China and South Korea have disputes over jurisdiction concerning the Yellow Sea involving some 180,000 square km. Due to China's position on the natural extension of the continental shelf and that of Japan on the middle line over the jurisdiction of the East China Sea, the Chinese authorities consider that Japan has unreasonably over-claimed 160,000 square km of the East China Sea. Further, China believes that the two island claims at the edge of its continental shelf control its entry into the Pacific and the Indian Oceans. These two island claims are currently the territories of the United States, Russia, Japan, the Philippines, Brunei, Indonesia, Malaysia and Singapore, plus Taiwan which is claimed by China but not under its actual control.

These claims constitute a strategic squeeze against China's coastline, and are perceived as a threat to China's maritime security.

This threat was highlighted by a series of naval exercises in the summer of 2010 with the United States assuming a leading role. In late July, the United States and South Korea held a joint naval and air military exercise in the Sea of Japan. The initial plan involved the aircraft carrier, USS *George Washington* operating in the Yellow Sea; the plan was abandoned only after strong protest from the Chinese government.[43] The PLAN then held a large-scale naval exercise on the second day of the previous exercise in the South China Sea involving its North Sea, East Sea and South Sea fleets. The exercise took place after mutual criticisms by the delegates of the United States and China at the Shangri-la Dialogue in Singapore in June 2010, and another verbal clash between the two countries in the following month at the ASEAN Regional Forum foreign ministers' meeting in Hanoi, in which the U.S. Secretary of State Hillary Clinton declared that the South China Sea involves U.S. interests.[44]

On the other hand, there is also a more cautious view regarding China's rapid expansion of its navy. Some scholars argue that in its sea power contribution, China has to avoid confrontation with the United States. The historical precedent of Germany before World War I has been cited as a negative example. They support the maintenance of the existing oceanic order based on the United Nations Law of the Sea Convention, affirming the principles of sovereign equality, joint development and peaceful use. Challenging the existing international order is perceived to be too costly, and there is a danger that it may terminate China's path of peace and development.[45] These scholars therefore see the development of China's sea power within the existing international order, maintaining the peaceful and friendly external environment for China's growth, continuing to exploit the public goods provided by the existing order for China's development, thus upholding China's status as a responsible major power. Some academics have articulated an even stronger opposing view. They think that over-emphasizing the importance of sea power may actually have a negative impact on China's security. In the first place, the historical function of sea power had a definite context in terms of technology and productivity; but in view of the present and future technological evolution, the role of sea power may decline. In other words, history determines the role of sea power, not the other way round. Further, there is the "security dilemma" argument; war as a means to win a competition between major powers has become considerably less important. Thirdly, given China's geographical location, its security threats come from many directions, and it cannot afford to concentrate on the construction of sea power alone. Finally, China at this stage should not act as the principal challenger against the sole superpower as it is very costly and China is not yet ready.[46]

In the discussions on China's sea power, mention is frequently made regarding Chinese *non-military maritime enforcement capabilities*, and the necessity for China to establish a strong maritime police force along the lines of the U.S. Coast Guard, Japanese Coast Guard or the Taiwan Executive Yuan Coast Guard Administration. It is considered that such a maritime police force would be more appropriate for the tasks of "showing the flag" and law enforcement within the Territorial Sea and EEZ under Chinese jurisdiction during peace time. Its operations would be better able to avoid escalation of tensions with China's neighbours in disputed waters, especially in view of rising nationalism in the countries concerned.[47] In 1998, the State Oceanic Bureau established the China Maritime Surveillance under the State Oceanic Administration, which has been expanding in personnel and equipment in recent years.[48] This acts much like a Coast Guard, even if it is considerably weaker that its neighbours' counterparts. Moreover, critics observe that it has been handicapped by the fact that several, namely five, similar forces co-exist, the so-called "five dragons stirring up the sea".[49] The State Oceanic Bureau has no control over the local maritime police force, their duties and jurisdictions tend to overlap and have not been clearly defined. This can seriously weaken the extent of the cooperation in non-traditional security issues in the East China Sea, resulting in a threat in itself for the mistrust it provokes among its neighbours. Finally, another problem is represented by the plurality of actors in charge of the overall military strategy, which also affects the naval activities and has already led to some international incidents. The one with the U.S. aircraft carrier *Kitty Hawk* in 2007, when a Chinese submarine surfaced in the middle of a U.S. Navy exercise (*Daily Mail*, 10 November 2007) or the other with the surveillance ship USS *Impeccable* in 2009 (*Die Welt*, 10 March 2009) are only two of the most famous. But it is important to notice that both events occurred at moments in which China's civil leadership, with President Hu Jintao, was willing to maintain a sound and stable relationship with the United States, suggesting a possible lack of coordination and dialogue among military and civil powers in China (Li, 2010). Whether correct or not, this adds up to the opaqueness and lack of transparency generally considered one of the major problems of China's foreign policy, and further complicates China's relations.

Toward a Grand Strategy: Implications for Foreign Policy and External Reactions

Parallel to the substantial research work and the discussion on the Chinese foreign policy and naval power debate in official think-tanks, the academic community and the media, there is a smaller yet significant volume of research on China's grand strategy. On 24 November 2003, the Political Bureau of the Communist Party of China (CPC) organized a collective study session on "the history of the development of the world major powers since the fifteenth century". As a result, Central Television produced a series of twelve documentaries on "The Rise of Major Powers", covering the emergence of Portugal, Spain, the Netherlands, Britain, France, Germany, Japan, Russia, and the United States from the fifteenth century onwards. A series of eight volumes were then published on the basis of the television documentaries.[50] The leaders as well as the intelligentsia have been eager to learn the lessons and avoid the pitfalls in the rise and decline of previous major powers.

The Chinese academic community in the international relations field tends to accept the following narrative of the evolution of China's world view. From ancient times until the Opium War (1839–1840), the Chinese believed that "China is the world" (*tianxia*). From the Opium War until the end of the last century, China first suffered under Western imperialism and struggled to survive after the founding of the People's Republic of China. It was eager to establish its place in the international community; and in the era of economic reforms and opening to the external world since then it has been trying hard to fuse with the international community and especially the international capitalist economy. In recent years, China has been attempting to co-exist with the world harmoniously.[51]

In defence of the official line, Chinese academics articulate that the harmonious world perspective represents China's pursuit of a new international political and economic order. It integrates China's domestic harmony with that in the international community; it also places China's national interests in harmony with those of the human race. In other words, China exploits the opportunity of world peace and development to concentrate on its own development, while it utilizes its own development to facilitate the maintenance of world peace and promotion of global prosperity. Harmonious co-existence would be the natural ultimate objective of China's peaceful rise; it surpasses the narrowness of democratic peace, i.e., that democratic countries would not go to war against each other[52] and the bias of "the clash of civilizations".[53] The harmonious world perspective is a response to the "China threat" perception;[54] and represents an advance of the earlier advocacy of peaceful co-existence.[55]

There is also a more ambitious aspect to China's grand strategy, however. In the last decade, Chinese academics have considered that in the intermediate and long-term future, China's fundamental objectives are to emerge as a world power, to achieve this objective without going through large-scale wars among major powers, and to sustain its status as a top-level world power avoiding a quick decline. There is recognition that the emergence of top-level world powers has been based on innovations with global and historical significance; and in most cases, these innovations are related to values. Reliance on economic and military power alone is usually inadequate to achieve global dominance.[56]

The Chinese leadership has been articulating that China has entered "a significant period of strategic opportunity" for its peaceful rise. Chinese academics have also been engaged in a discourse on the theoretical and historical standards regarding a major world power in the contemporary world. There is a fairly broad consensus on the following criteria: it has broad global political, economic and strategic interests; it has adequate comprehensive national power including sufficient long-distance projection capabilities so that it can effectively protect its interests during peacetime, and present credible deterrence and defence capabilities in war against other major world powers; it should be widely perceived as having the legitimate right to participate in the management of important international issues, and, to a certain extent, it shares fundamental common interests with other major powers based on common values and common international consultative mechanisms, with expectations of its assumption of a coordinating role. A powerful blue-water navy therefore is essential in this context.

There are different assessments concerning the extent to which China has achieved or is about to achieve the prerequisites to qualify as a major world power. In general there is ample sobriety on the part of the leadership and in the mainstream academic community.

Paul Kennedy's book *The Rise and Fall of the Great Powers* (1987) has attracted a lot of attention in China. Kennedy discussed the emergence of China as a major power; he indicated that China was the poorest among the world's major powers and at the same time probably located in the worst strategic position. He argued that two conditions would be essential to China's rise as a major power, namely, a visionary strategy formulated by the Chinese leadership and sustainable economic growth.[57]

Scholars in China engaged in the study of its grand strategy certainly consider that a national strategy is essential to a state's survival and development. Zhang Wenmu, for example, considers that a state's strategic capability may be divided into three linked elements; strategic culture, strategic thinking and strategic management. Strategic culture means the political consciousness of the citizenry, i.e., its consciousness of grasping the principal contradictions in its national life. Strategic thinking is limited to the elites and the intelligentsia; and it reflects the reserve of a state's strategic knowledge and experiences. Competence in strategic management is a quality of the leadership, which in turn depends on the support of the strategic thinking of its think tanks. Academics in China in general acknowledge that its grand strategy is at best in its developmental stage; it remains under-developed, although some progress has been made since the Sixteenth Party Congress in 2002.[58]

China's grand strategy has been formulated in the context of its embrace of globalization, especially economic globalization. China's opening to the external world allows it to exploit its comparative advantage and narrow the gap between China and the advanced countries. While China has succeeded in transforming itself from an outsider into a full participant in the international institutional framework, it has been emphasizing its right of participation. At the present stage, China strives to play an active role in the construction of international institutions, share their benefits, and secure its right to improve and reform the existing international norms.[59]

China realizes that its participation in globalization at all levels will not be cost free; there are opportunities as well as challenges. China therefore must ensure the protection of its core interests, especially its sovereignty and strategic interests.[60] As nationalism in China rises while its international status improves, the protection of state sovereignty to the maximum extent becomes an increasingly important consideration. Hence the development of a blue-water navy has moved up the agenda of the Chinese leadership.

Meanwhile regional strategies have been accorded a considerable priority since the mid 1990s. They were much neglected in the Maoist era because China's foreign policy was defined within the framework of the leadership's world view. Men Honghua of the Institute of International Strategic Studies at the Central Party School, for example, stresses the value of the significant supporting role of regional strategies in China's grand strategy. China's regional strategies, with an emphasis on its neighbours, are expected to contribute to the realization of its grand strategy. In the first place, efforts should be made to improve China's relations with East Asian countries and especially the members of ASEAN to remove the perception of a "China threat" and establish a new perception of China as an opportunity whose rise will be a contribution to the global community. This involves building a regional foundation for China's grand strategy as well as establishing international public opinion support for China's peaceful rise. Further, China has to construct a balance-of-power framework in East Asia to facilitate cooperation between major powers to avoid opposition from the United States and Japan. Regarding Taiwan, China has to work to strengthen cross-straits economic integration and to contain its influence in Southeast Asia. Approaching Central Asia is also perceived to have a positive impact on the development of western China, leading to the expansion of China's domestic market. Finally, China should strive to play an active role in regional institutional building in preparation for the improvement in its international status and influence.[61]

Men Honghua and many of his colleagues in the international relations field believe that China at this stage is in a better position to lead regional integration in East Asia. But the regional strategic situation demands coordination in an open regionalism, and it will be difficult for China alone to assume leadership. Hence China has to actively participate in existing regional organizations, as well as engage in promoting new ones like the Shanghai Cooperation Organization (SCO). These scholars consider that China's experiences in establishing the SCO and the China-ASEAN Free Trade Area are valuable for its future work in international institution building.

A Security Dilemma in the Making?
Reactions to China's Growing Power

China's rise has attracted much attention for some years, especially in the United States, and literature abounds on the topic. However, especially in recent times, the on-going modernization of the PLAN coupled with a new assertiveness from the Chinese in foreign policy has produced a mixed reaction and fierce criticism, especially from South Korea and Japan. The main problems have been caused by the tense situation in the Korean peninsula, which China failed to address by sanctioning the belligerent North, and continuous incidents in the East China Sea, which culminated in October 2010 when Japan seized a Chinese vessel, provoking a diplomatic crisis. Even more unwelcome has been the offer of mediation by the United States and the enraged Chinese reaction to Hillary Clinton's acknowledgement of U.S. strategic interests in the South Asian Sea, which speaks volumes about likely future fault lines in the area. Nevertheless, the U.S. appraisal of the Chinese threat has so far generally been quite moderate, even though there have been diverging views. Scholars have been long divided between the supporters of the thesis of "China's rise", a scenario in which China will become the hegemon of Asia and replace the United States in the regional architecture as dominant power, and others who instead believe that the United States will go on being a key player in the area and balancing the growing power of China. Mearsheimer sees conflict between China and the United States as unavoidable, as China is the new emerging power, interested in redefining the existing order. China's rise cannot be peaceful, and it will result in "an intense security competition between China and the United States, with considerable potential for war".[62] With some nuances, many scholars share this view, considering it is in the long-standing interest of the United States not to allow any single power to rule East Asia, whether at strategic and military level – the USSR during the Cold War or Japan in the 1940s, or economically – Japan in the 1980s and China now. Bergsten is less categorical,[63] but still warns of the systemic issue of a clash between a China-led Asia and a U.S.-led West for global economic dominance. Some have pointed out, as has Agnew,[64] how China now enjoys a degree of "structural" power. Others[65] have blamed the United States for the sort of vacuum of power left in the region since 9/11, which facilitated China's rising influence.

Some analysts caution about misreading the figures. Shambaugh noted that China is at least twenty years behind the United States in terms of military and technology, and this is one of the reasons for China to focus more on a less traditional, and more attractive, definition of power.[66] Beeson remarked that a form of hegemonic transition from the United States to China in Asia is unlikely to occur,[67] as China, notwithstanding its soft power, lacks a distinctive vision or ideology around which neighbours can coalesce. This is true even in front of the diminishing attraction of U.S. power. Realists such as Brzezinski have also observed that "conflict is not inevitable or even likely" between China and the United States, as China has nothing to gain in confronting the United States militarily.[68] And there are others[69] who regard integrating China and making it a stakeholder in the present liberal order as the best way to engage its rising power.

Finally, the recent assertiveness of China will eventually benefit U.S. interests and clout in East Asia, as Asian countries will quite naturally look to the Americans to maintain the balance of power in the area. The Philippines have for the first time in years filed a complaint against the harassing behaviour of two Chinese vessels in the Spratly Islands flashpoint, bringing the country even more back into the U.S. embrace for its defence. Even Vietnam is drawing closer to its former enemy, worried by a renewed Chinese presence near the Paracel Islands and in August 2010, Vietnam and the United States held their first defence talks since decades.[70] Pax Americana seems, again, to represent the best option.

On the more sensitive issue of China's growing naval power, the view of the United States seems cautious. While watching and analysing with attention China's increasing power, the Obama administration refuses to acknowledge the inevitability of a confrontation and appreciates the increased transparency of the Chinese government about military matters, through the publication of Defence White Papers and institutional websites. It is generally acknowledged that the Chinese naval build-up will impact U.S. maritime strategy in the Asia-Pacific region, and it may even challenge American primacy of the seas.[71] Even Chinese ventures outside coastal waters, as in the April 2010 incident with the Japanese Maritime Self Defence Force, or the September 2010 diplomatic spat after the Japanese arrest of the captain of a Chinese vessel, have not provoked a general outcry. Scholars have been nuanced in their views, with some warning about a more assertive and confrontational China and others inviting a more relaxed approach. Military analysts' attention has concentrated on the evolution of the Chinese military from Mao's times until today and its increasing role in politics and on the evaluation of new vessels and armaments.[72]

Japanese critics, of course, have been considerably more vocal, and this is not surprising given the geographic position and the maritime disputes between the two countries. However, it is important to remember Japan's role in facilitating China's reinsertion into East Asian regional politics and the importance given to its relation with China as one of the cornerstones of its long-term politics.[73] In the words of a former Japanese Prime Minister, Shigeru Yoshida, "Red or white, China remains our next-door neighbour",[74] and this alone would have been enough to motivate decades of Japanese engagement policy. However, China's rise and its new dominant position in East Asia has started to worry the Japanese,[75] especially since China began confronting them on maritime issues and taking over Japan's place as the world's second biggest economy and the reference for the rest of ASEAN.[76] Some scholars have suggested that Japan has shifted from a friendly attitude to a more nuanced one that mixes positive engagement with hedging against a Chinese potential future threat.[77] More recently others have observed that, while still regarding North Korea as a short-term major threat, China is now considered the most serious long-term national security threat.[78] The disruption of the supply of rare earth elements (REEs), absolutely vital for Japanese industry, has been another ominous signal. In this case, following the East China Sea incident when a Chinese fishing boat captain and his crew were held for trial in Japan, China, the world monopolist of the REEs with up to 97% of the global supply, suspended shipments. This episode was trumpeted by the Japanese press,[79] and around the world, as an example of China not living up its new responsibility as a new world great power, and contributing even more to international distrust. As well, it is widely believed that the way China manages its relationship with Japan is a sort of test, giving indications about China's future foreign policy towards its neighbours,[80] and there is some evidence that ASEAN countries generally share this view.

One of the relationships which promises to become the most problematic is that between China and India. The two countries, divided by ancient territorial claims and one conflict that still has not been fully settled,[81] appear to be competing fiercely for securing leadership in South–South dialogue and the acquisition of natural resources around the world. Both Chinese and Indian scholars acknowledge the complexity of this bilateral relationship[82] even if only a few[83] dared to produce a frank appraisal of the difficulties of cooperation. Also, China and India have long accused each other of aiming at regional "hegemony", while trying to secure allies with offers of cooperation and grants. The two countries, therefore, irrespective of the newly-developed dialogue, appear to be still locked in a military security dilemma.[84] However, it has been rightly observed that there always has been a sort of asymmetrical threat perception between the two Asian giants,[85] with India over-worrying and China generally dismissing India's worries as exaggerated. This is not going to change, or if it does change, it will not be for the best. As a fact, India has recently been visibly upset by the new Chinese assertiveness in defending its "core interests", both in the East and South China Seas, and even more about its growing presence in the Indian Ocean. The "string of pearls" theory is discussed in Indian think tanks, while issues like the recent Chinese presence in Kashmir are regarded as threatening the good relations among the two neighbours. Even more chilling for India are the Chinese territorial claims on Arunachal Pradesh, labelled since 2005 "South Tibet" or *Tawang* and now considered part of the Chinese expansionist agenda.[86] China, on the other hand, seems to assume that the real motivation of the new military cooperation between the United States and India is represented by "the Chinese factor", i.e., a China-containment strategy.[87] As a consequence, and as is explained well by the comments of one Chinese analyst, Dai Bing, "While a hot war is out of the question, a cold war between the two countries is increasingly likely".[88] Eventually, an enhanced Chinese presence in the Indian Ocean, in whatever form, may well push India to reciprocate by sending its navy closer to China's territorial waters. In the end, as noted by more than one Indian scholar, India has a maritime tradition in its history that enables it to compete with Zheng He's legacy in naval soft-power.[89] It is therefore to be expected that India will follow China outside its territorial waters in order to protect its national interests and the security of its sea lanes, as already stated in the Indian Maritime Doctrine published in 2004. "Since trade is the lifeblood of India, keeping our SLOCs (Sea Lane of Communication) open in times of peace, tension or hostilities is a primary national maritime interest".[90] A central and still debated point is whether East and South-East Asian waters may become the centre of an arms race, in the well-known logic of security dilemmas, and therefore threaten the emerging regional convergence and the economic rise of the region. It is clear that an antagonistic attitude toward Chinese naval operations and an upgrade of other countries' navies could trigger in the Chinese an encirclement syndrome and accelerate the military build-up by all sides even more. The new friendliness shown by Vietnam toward India and the United States in terms of military cooperation is something to be closely watched.

In the end, the peacefulness of China's rise will depend not only on China's willingness to exercise its power in a UN-based, internationally accepted fashion, but also on the way the rest of the world, primarily the United States, will allow space for the new big power. In the words of Australian scholar Hugh White, "The fact that China's government is repressive at home makes us uneasy, but it does not automatically mean it will behave unacceptably abroad".[91] While it is correct that historically it has been easier to leave space to a power sharing the same roots, values and political beliefs (the United Kingdom with the United States) than menacing authoritarian countries (Germany in the first part of the twentieth century), this does not mean that history necessarily has to repeat itself.

Conclusions

It has been recently observed that, after having long downplayed its military capabilities and strengths, now China is "publicizing its capacity to inflict damage while cultivating uncertainty about its precise intentions to induce caution in adversaries".[92] While the reasons for this changed attitude can be discussed at length, the consequences are starting to become evident. In the foreseeable future, China still needs a peaceful international environment to concentrate on economic development, but at this stage, it is becoming increasingly interested in raising its international status and enhancing its international influence. It is certainly true that, so far, as "China's power has grown, Beijing's relations with major powers around the world have improved rather than deteriorated";[93] but this may no longer be the case. In time, China's interests have become more diverse, and their defence in the eyes of its leaders requires improvements in its military power, especially naval projection capabilities including aircraft carriers. These developments have exacerbated the "China threat" perceptions of its neighbours which are more inclined to strengthen their hedging strategies, i.e., establishing closer security ties with the United States and increasing defence expenditure. As a result, a deteriorating "security dilemma" emerges in East and Southeast Asia.

At the meeting held on 30 December 2010, the director of SASTIND, Chen Qiufa, presented the new Twelfth Five-Year Plan (2011–2015), which will be China's blueprint for the next five years. On that occasion, he pointed out among China's main objectives the upgrade of the core military industry capabilities through innovation and a sustained growth of the military-defence complex.[94] This will accomplish the plan enabling China to leapfrog technologically to compete with the most advanced military powers by 2020, and it is not going to reassure anybody.

A question that seems linger is one that asks what kind of sea power China is becoming – an essentially defensive one, confined to protecting its national interests and territories, however broadly defined, or an aggressive one, venturing in far oceans to challenge other dominant powers, primarily the United States. As rightly observed by Holmes and Toshiyara, it will more likely be neither. In a way, the question itself is misleading, and not correspond to the internal debate currently held in China. There are choices to be made, but they are of a different type, and are more related to the role that China wants to play, first in Asia and then in the world, and what kind of power it is willing to become. China's main concerns seem to be social stability at home and avoiding encirclement abroad. The development of a powerful military may well appease the nationalists at home and help with the target of social stability. Still, a naval build up and a more assertive foreign policy may well reverse China's gains in its charm strategy toward South-East Asia and make neighbours gather closer to the United States in search of reassurance. There are already signals that this is happening, and this will be contrary to Chinese interests. A major problem is represented here by a certain lack of coordination (real or only apparent) between civil and military powers, with erratic consequences in recent Chinese foreign policy.

China's internal debate about the country's grand strategy and its naval development is a clear sign that scholars and policy-makers alike are not blind to these formidable challenges. A possible alternative, proposed by Goldstein,[95] is to give more emphasis to the development of a coastguard force instead of a fully-fledged blue-water navy, as considered more politically acceptable and justifiable.

It is not likely that Chinese leaders will cut back their naval expansion programme. In fact, the programme may be accelerated because of the escalation in tensions in 2010 along China's coast and the substantial fiscal reserves at the central government's disposal. China believes that its economic growth will benefit its neighbours, and it is willing to make concessions, especially to the small developing countries at its periphery. But this may no longer be adequate to reduce the "China threat" perception which in fact has become an obstacle to further regional economic integration and may undermine the very long-term results in terms of grand strategy that China would like to achieve.

Notes and References

1. Zhang Zhaoyin, "Firmly seize the period of important strategic opportunities to promote leap-type development," *Jiefangjun Bao*, 25 February 2003.

2. Robert Bitzinger, "Towards a Brave New Arms Industry", *Adelphi Paper* 356 (London: OUP, 2003).

3. SIPRI gives instead an intermediate estimate, at about 1.4 times the official PLA figure. However, in 2010 the Report to Congress of the U.S.-China Economic and Security Review Commission proposed a much higher estimation, a defence budget of 532.115 billion *yuan* (US$81.3 billion) and even more for 2011 (601 billion *yuan*).

4. G. Collins and M. Grubb, "A Comprehensive Survey of China's Dynamic Shipbuilding Industry. Commercial Development and Strategic Implications",

China Maritime Study, vol.1, 2010, available at www.usnwc.edu/Research---Gaming/China-Maritime-Studies-Institute.aspx.

5. F. Liang, "Status and role of the oceans in national security and policy response," *Junshi xueshu (Military Art Journal)*, No. 1 (2005); W. Zhang and H. Zheng, "On strategic necessities and opportunities for developing our navy," *Junshi xueshu (Military Art Journal)*, No. 10 (2005).

6. Y. Lin, "The changing face of Chinese military generals: evolving promotion practices between 1981 and 2009," *The Korean Journal of Defence Analysis* (March 2010).

7. *China Brief*, 29 April 2010.

8. C. Johnson, *The Sorrows of Empire: Militarism, Secrecy, and the End of the Republic* (New York: Metropolitan, 2004).

9. A.S. Erickson, "Chinese defense expenditures: implications for naval modernization," *China Brief*, Volume 10:8 (16 April 2010), available at http://www.jamestown.org, accessed on 10 December 2010.

10. N. Li and C. Weuve, "China's aircraft carrier ambitions. an update," *Naval War College Review*, Vol. 63, No. 1 (Winter 2010).

11. Liu Huaqing, *Liu Huaqing huiyilu (Liu Huaqing's Memoirs)* (Beijing: Liberation Army Press, 2004). Admiral Liu Huaqing, who died in January 2011, is generally considered "the father of the modern Chinese Navy" (*China Daily*, 15 January 2011); he served as PLAN's supreme commander from 1982 to 1988 and was second-in-charge of the CMC, the highest military body, from 1989 to 1997. He lobbied for the construction of an aircraft carrier from the 1970s, while advocating the necessity to provide air cover for naval operations over the first island chain; the Spratly and Paracel Islands in the South China Sea. Jiang Zemin was always against the development of a carrier, which would have negatively affected his policy of cooperation with South-East Asia in line with the "New Security Concept" and China signing the Declaration of a Code of Conduct with ASEAN with regard to the South China Sea. It is also worth noticing that, while advocating the development of an aircraft carrier, Liu was putting emphasis on near-seas defence and territorial claims over the Spratlys, while leaving to far-sea action just a supporting and definitively secondary role in Chinese naval strategy.

12. Tang Fuquan and Wu Yi, "A study of China's sea defense strategy," *Zhongguo junshi kexue (China Military Science)*, No. 5 (2007).

13. Lu Ting, "China's finance is sufficient to fulfill the 'aircraft carrier dream'," *Junshi wenzai (Military Digest)*, No. 5 (2008), pp. 12–13.

14. *Ta Kung Pao*, 26 February 2010.

15. *New York Times*, 23 April 2010.

16. *Taipei Times*, 24 March 2009.

17. Aircraft carriers can be divided into four main typologies; CATOBAR (catapult-assisted takeoff but arrested recovery), the largest and most capable, but also the most expensive and complex to operate, like the USS *Nimitz*

class or the French *Charles de Gaulle*; the STOBAR (short takeoff but arrested recovery), medium-size, like the Russian *Kuznetsov* class; the STVOL (short takeoff vertical landing), like the British vessels, considered the minimum for operating fixed-wing aircraft; the VTOL (vertical takeoff and landing) normally used only for helicopters. A good analysis of the different types is provided by Li and Weuve, "China's aircraft carrier ambitions. an update."

18. *The Hindu*, 17 December 2010. According to some unconfirmed reports from Taiwanese newspapers (*Asia Times*, 12 April 2011), the career could be at sea as early as July 2011, with the quite frightening name (to Taiwanese ears) of *Shi Land*, the naval warfare genius of the Ming Dynasty, who invaded and conquered Taiwan.

19. *China Brief*, 19 November 2010; *Defence News*, 16 November 2010.

20. *Wen Wei Po*, 17 November 2010.

21. *Taipei Times*, 19 July 2010.

22. Erickson, "Chinese defense expenditures", p. 2.

23. Xinhuanet, 27 August 2010.

24. *New York Times*, 11 September 2010.

25. *Yomiuri Shimbun*, 27 April 2010.

26. Xinhua News Agency, 27 May 2010.

27. Xinhuanet, 9 December 2009.

28. *Financial Times*, 19 December 2010.

29. C. Pehrson, "String of pearls: meeting the challenge of China's rising power across the Asian littoral," Strategic Studies Institute, United States Army War College, July 2006, available online at http://www.strategicstudiesinstitute .army.mil/pdffiles/pub721.pdf.

30. J. MacDonald, A. Donahue, and B. Danyluk, *Energy Futures in Asia, Booz-Allen Hamilton Report* (November 2004), commissioned by the U.S. Department of Defence.

31. *The Economist*, 9 August 2010.

32. J. Holmes and T. Yoshihara, "Understanding Asia-Pacific sea power," *The Diplomat* (2010), available at http://the-diplomat.com, p. 3.

33. Chen Lim, "Lun Zhongguo bianjiang haiquan wenti de zhili" ("The settlement of disputes in China's frontier sea power"), *Academic Exploration*, No.1 (February 2010), p. 17.

34. Alfred Thayer Mahan, "The influence of sea power upon history, 1660–1783," in *Encyclopaedia Britannica* (2010), retrieved 9 August 2010, from Encyclopaedia Britannica Online: http://www.britannica.com/EBchecked/ topic/ 287784/The-Influence-of-Sea-Power-upon-History-1660-1783

35. A Chinese translation of Alfred T. Mahan's important book, by Xiao Weizhong and Meiran, was published by the Zhongguo Yanshi Chubanshe in Beijing in 1997.

36. Zhang Si Ping, *China's Sea Power* (Beijing: Renmin ribao chubanshe, 2009), p. 35.

37. Zhang Qian, "Aimei de Riben de rixiang – haikou ziweidui hangmuxing 'huweijian' jiedu" ("The ambiguous 'Hyunga' of Japan – an interpretation of the name of the aircraft carrier-type naval escort vessel of the maritime self-defence force"), *World Outlook*, No. 571, No. 17 (September 2007), pp. 40–41.

38. Zhang Ming, "Cong Yinduyang chufa – Yindu haijun de weilai hangmu zhanlue" ("Launching from the Indian Ocean – the future aircraft-carrier strategy of the Indian navy"), *World Outlook*, No. 568, No. 14 (July 2007), pp. 74–79.

39. Wang Yizhou, *Quanqiu zhengzhi yu zhongguo waijiao tanxun xin de shijiao yu jiesi* (*Global Politics and Chinese Foreign Policy's Search for New Perspectives and Explanations*) (Beijing: Shnijie zhishi chubanshe 2003), p. 240.

40. *Renmin ribao*, 14 February,2009.

41. An Xiuwei, "Zhongguo heping fazhan zhanlue shiye xia de hanquan jianshe" ("Sea power construction under China's peaceful development strategy"), *Shandong Shifan daxue xuebao (Renwen shehui kexueban) Journal of Shandong Normal University* (Humanities and Social Sciences Edition), Vol. 55, No. 2 (General No. 229) (2010), pp. 150–151.

42. *Wang Shuguang Haiyang kaifa zhanlue yanjiu (A Study of the Oceanic Development Strategy)*, Beijing: Haiyang chubanshe, 2004; and Sun Zhihui, "ouanmian shishi kejixinghai guihua gangyao,cujin haiyang jingji youhaoyoukuai fazhan (Implement Comprehensively the Outline Plan to Develop the Ocean with Science and Technology, Promote the Good and Rapid Development of the Oceanic Economy)", *Haiyang kaifa yu guanli (Oceanic Development and Management)*, No. 10, 2008.

43. Luo Yuan, "Big brother flexes muscles," *China Daily*, 31 July 2010, p. 5. the author is a major- general of the PLA at the Academy of Military Science. See also *Ming Pao* (a Chinese newspaper in Hong Kong), 26 July 2010.

44. *Ming Pao*, 28 and 30 July, 2010; see also *China Daily*, 31 July 2010 and *South China Morning Post* (an English newspaper in Hong Kong), 31 July 2010.

45. Fu Mengmei, "Zhongguo jueqi yu guoji zhixu de hepingbiange" ("China's rise and the peaceful reform of the international order)", *Xiandai guoji guanxi (Contemporary International Relations)*, No. 10 (2005).

46. Xu Qiyu, "Haiquan de wuqu yu fansi" ("The wrong thinking on sea power and reflections)", *Zhanlue yu guanli (Strategy and Management)*, No.5 (2003), pp. 15-21.

47. Song Zenghua, "Haiquan de fazhan qushi ji zhongguo haiquan fazhan zhanlue gouxiang – jianlun haishang xingzheng zhifa liliang xingqi dui zhongguo haiquan fazhande yingxiang" ("The development trend of sea power and the vision on china sea power development strategy – the

influence on China sea power development by the rising maritime force in administration law enforcement"), *Ruankexue yanjiu chengguo yu dongtai (Research Results and Activities Concerning Soft Sciences)*, No. 7 (2009), pp. 191192.

48. Wu Liang and Wu Dan, "'Landun' haiyang weiquan" ('Blue Shield' protecting oceanic rights)", *Liaowang xinwen zhoukan* (*Outlook Weekly*), No. 21 (May 21 2007), pp. 34-35.

49. He Zhonglong, Ren Xingping, Feng Shuili, Luo Xianfen, and Liu Jinghong, *Research on the Building of the Chinese Coast Guard, (Zhongguo Hai an jingweidui zujian yanjiu)* (Beijing: Ocean Press 2007).

50. Editorial and Publishing Committee of the Book Series "The Rise of Major Powers" in "Daguo Jueqi" Xilie Congshu Bianjichuban Weiyuanhui (Yuan Zhengming, Yang Ruixue, Guo Linmao et al.), *The Rise of Major Powers (Daguo Jueqi Congshu)* 8 Vols. (Beijing: Zhongguo minzhu fazhi chubanshe, 2006).

51. Wang Xiwei, "Hexie shijie guan de sanchong neihan" ("The Three Layers of Contents Regarding the 'Harmonious World' Perspective"), *Jiaoxue yu yanjiu (Teaching and Research)*, No. 2, 2007, pp. 67–68, from http://www.cnki.net.

52. Spencer R. Weart, *Never at War: Why Democracies Will Not Fight One Another* (New Haven CT: Yale University Press, 1998), pp. 1–3.

53. Samuel P. Huntington, "The Clash of Civilizations?", *Foreign Affairs*, Vol. 72, No. 3 (Summer 1993), pp. 22–49.

54. Herbert Yee and Ian Storey (eds.), *The China Threat: Perceptions, Myths, and Reality (*New York: Routledge Curzon, 2002), pp. 1–19.

55. The Five Principles of Peaceful Co-existence were jointly initiated by China, India and Burma in 1953-54; they are to apply to relations among countries with different social systems. They are: respect for territorial integrity and sovereignty, non-interference in domestic affairs, equality and mutual benefit, non-aggression and peaceful co-existence.

56. Qin Yaqing, Zhou Jianming, Wen Tiejun, Shi Yinghong, Zhang Wenmu et al., "Zhongguo da zhanlue wenti yu silu (China's Grand Strategy: Issues and Trends of Thinking"), *Xueshujie (Academics in China)*, No. 117, No. 2 (March 2006), pp. 15–16, http://www.cnki.net; see especially Shi Xinhong's contribution.

57. Paul Kennedy, *The Rise and Fall of the Great Powers* (New York: Random House, 1987), pp. 447–457.

58. Qin Yaqing et al., China's Grand Strategy: Issues and Trends of Thinking, p. 25.

59. Hu Angang (ed.), *Quanqiuhua tiaozhan zhongguo (Globalization Challenges China)* (Beijing: Peking University Press, 2002), pp. 12–13; Men Honghua, "Zhongguo heping jueqi de guoji zhanlue kuangjia" ("The international strategic framework of China's peaceful rise)", *Shijie jingji yu zhengzhi (World Economics and Politics)*, No. 6 (2004), pp. 14–19; and Men Honghua, "Zhongguo jueqi yu guoji zhixu" ("China's rise and the

international order)", *Taipingyang xuebao (Journal of Pacific Studies)*, No. 2 (2004), pp. 4–13.

60. Wang Yizhou, "Mianxiang ershiyi shiji de zhongguo waijiao: sanchongxuqiu de xunqiu jiqi pingheng" ("China's foreign policy facing the 21st century: the pursuit and balancing of three types of needs"), *Zhanlue yu guanli (Strategy and Management)*, No. 6 (1999), pp. 18–27.

61. Meng Honghua, "Canyu chuangshe yu zhudao, yi guoji zhidu jianshe wei zhongxin tuijin dongya yitihua" ("Participation, innovation and guidance – promoting East Asian integration through the central task of international institutional building"), *Guoji wenti luntan(International Issues Forum)*, No. 37 (Winter 2004), pp. 1–16.

62. J. J. Mearsheimer, *The Tragedy of Great Power Politics* (New York: W.W. Norton, 2001).

63. C. Fred Bergsten, Gill Bates, Nicholas R. Lardy and Derek Mitchell, *China: The Balance Sheet: What the World Needs to Know Now About the Emerging Superpower* (New York: Public Affairs, 2006).

64. J. Agnew, *Hegemony: The New Shape of Global Power* (Philadelphia: Temple University Press, 2005).

65. R. Sutter, *China's Rise in Asia: Promises and Perils* (New York: Rowman and Littlefield, 2005).

66. D. Shambaugh, "China engages Asia: reshaping the regional order", *International Security*, 29:3 (2005).

67. M. Beeson, "Hegemonic Transition in East Asia? The Dynamics of Chinese and American Power," *Review of International Studies*, 35 (2009), pp. 95–112

68. Z. Brzezinski, "Make money, not war," *Foreign Policy* 146 (Jan–Feb), 46 (2005).

69. J. Ikenberry, "The rise of China and the future of the West," *Foreign Affairs*, 87, 1 (2008); Nicholas R. Lardy, *Integrating China into the Global Economy* (Washington: Brookings Institute, 2002).

70. *Navy Times*, 17 August 2010.

71. J. Holmes and T. Yoshihara, *Red Star over the Pacific: China's Rise and the Challenge to U.S. Maritime Strategy* (Naval Institute Press, 2010).

72. Li Ni, "Chinese civil-military relations in the post-Deng era," *China Maritime Study*, Vol. 4 (2010), available athttp://www.usnwc.edu/Research---Gaming/China-Maritime-Studies-Institute.aspx

73. C. Hughes, "Japan's response to China's rise: regional engagement, global containment, dangers of collision," *International Affairs*, 85: 4 (2009), pp. 837–856.

74. S.Yoshida, "Japan and the crisis in Asia," *Foreign Affairs* 29: 2 (January 1951), 179.

75. Y. Cooper Ramo, *The Beijing Consensus* (London: Foreign Policy Centre, 2004).

76. A. Macintyre and B. Naughton, "The decline of a Japan-led model of the East Asian economy," in T. J. Pempel (ed.), *Remapping East Asia: The Construction of a Region* (Ithaca, NY: Cornell University Press, 2005), pp. 77–110.

77. M. Mochizukia, "Japan's shifting strategy toward the rise of China," *Journal of Strategic Studies*, 30:4-5 (2007), pp. 739–776.

78. C. Hughes, "'Super-sizing' the DPRK threat: Japan's evolving military posture and North Korea," *Asian Survey*, 49: 2 (2009).

79. *The Japan Times*, 18 November 2010.

80. B. Emmott, *Rivals: How the Power Struggle between China, India and Japan Will Shape Our Next Decade* (London: Allen Lane, 2008); D. Roy, "The sources and limits of Sino-Japanese tensions", *Survival* 42: 2 (Summer, 2005), pp. 191–214.

81. Y. Dompierre, "China and India: rivals always, partners sometimes", *China Analysis: European Council of Foreign Relation* (November 2009), available at http://eufr.eu.

82. Yin Bin, "Structure, themes and changes: a systemic analysis of the progress of China-India relations," *Nanya yanjiu*, No. 1 (2009), pp. 7–17; Zhao Gancheng, "India: look east policy and role in Asian security architecture," *India Ocean Digest* (2006); Zhao Gancheng, "Analysis of China's strategy with regard to India," *Nanya yanjiu jikan*, No. 1 (2008), pp. 3–9.

83. Sun Shihai, "Perspectives on China-India relations in the 21st century", in *Zhongguo yu zhoubian ji 9-11 hou de guoji jushi* (*China, Its External Environment and the International System after September 11*) (Beijing: Zhongguo shehui kexue chubanshe, 2002).

84. J. Holslag, "The persistent military security dilemma between China and India," *Journal of Strategic Studies*, 32: 6 (2009), pp. 811–840.

85. J. Garver, "Asymmetrical Indian and Chinese threat perceptions," in Sumit Ganguly (ed.), *India as an Emerging Power* (London and Portland OR: Frank Cass 2003).

86. M. Malik, "China Unveils the Kashmir Card" *China Brief*, 10 (19), 24 September 2010. Available on line at: http://www.jamestown.org/, accessed on 22 January 2011.

87. Zhang Li, "The Chinese Factor in Strategic Relations between the United States and India", *Nanya yanjiu jikan*, no. 136, 2009.

88. http://china.org.cn, 8 February 2010.

89. K. M. Panikkar, *India and the Indian Ocean: An Essay on the Influence of Sea Power on Indian History* (New York: Macmillan, 1945).

90. Government of India, *INBR-8, Indian Maritime Doctrine* (New Delhi: Integrated HQ, Ministry of Defence (Navy), 25 April 2004).

91. H. White, "Power shift: Australia's future between Washington and Beijing," *Quarterly Essays*, 39 (2010), pp. 34–99.

92. J. Newmyer, "The revolution in military affairs with Chinese characteristics," *Journal of Strategic Studies*, 33:4 (2010), pp. 483–504.

93. Q. Zhao and G. Li, "The challenges of a rising China," *Journal of Strategic Studies*, 30-4 (2007), pp. 585608.

94. Xinhua News Agency, 30 December 2010.

95. L. Goldstein, "Five dragons stirring up the sea. Challenge and opportunity in China's improving maritime enforcement capabilities," *China Maritime Study*, Vol. 5 (2010), available at http://www.usnwc.edu/Research---Gaming/China-Maritime-Studies-Institute.aspx.

10

The Twelfth Five-Year Plan: Strategic Adjustments, the Impact of the Global Financial Tsunami, and the Socio-Political Challenges

Joseph Y. S. CHENG

Introduction

The basic strategy of the Chinese leadership to maintain the Party's monopoly of political power includes promoting economic growth, building a social security net for the underprivileged groups, and absorbing the elites of various sectors into the vested-interest strata. Chinese leaders are eager to pursue good governance if the measures concerned do not adversely affect the leadership of the Party. Today they have an accurate assessment of the situation, and the Twelfth Five-Year National Economic and Social Development Programme, 2011–2015 (henceforward referred to as the 12th FYP), is a good example of this sober assessment.[1]

The Hu Jintao–Wen Jiabao leadership has quietly achieved a great deal economically. The Chinese economy is now the second largest in the world; China exports more than any other country and is the number two trader in the global economy. Beijing held the Olympics in 2008 and Shanghai the Expo in 2010. Chinese people really feel that they have stood up, as claimed by Mao on 1 October 1949 when the People's Republic of China (PRC) was founded. Though Chinese leaders avoid the use of the acronym "G-2" (the U.S. and China as the only two superpowers in the world), Chinese people are proud of the country's impact on international affairs. This national pride has become an important source of the Party regime's legitimacy too. The fourth-generation leadership has failed to tackle the problem of corruption, but it has a much more realistic understanding of the challenges of rapid economic growth. Even before the global financial tsunami in 2008 and 2009, the Chinese authorities realized that sustainable economic growth would have to reduce its dependence on exports and investment in infrastructural projects. Instead, it would have to rely more on domestic consumption. More resources have been allocated to environmental protection and the enhancement of energy intensity; as the structure of the economy improves and the service sector develops further, there is a better chance that pollution may be reduced very slowly. The Hu-Wen leadership in the past six or seven years has begun to build a basic social security net covering the entire population to contain the grievances generated by the widening of the gap between the rich and the poor. The emphasis on stability and prosperity is prominent, and the strategy and tactics adopted by the fourth-generation leadership are sophisticated.

The achievements of the Hu-Wen leadership have generated a significant path-dependence tendency. As the Party elite becomes the most significant part of the vested interests, even though different factions may have various ideological orientations, the difficulty of arriving at an adequate consensus to promote major changes is substantial. Since the status quo plus the adjustments initiated by the Hu-Wen leadership at this stage represent the mainstream consensus and appear to work, continuity tends to prevail, as reflected by the 12th FYP.

China's economic performance during and after the global financial tsunami has been impressive. While 2009 was labelled "the most difficult year", the following year was described as "the most crucial year". In 2010, the Chinese economy began to recover, the employment situation improved, and the income levels of the urban and rural populations increased. By the end of the year, China's GDP surpassed that of Japan, and it became the second-largest economy in the world. In 2011, the Chinese authorities considered an economic growth rate of 8% per annum as healthy and desirable, and their major worry was inflation, especially in the overheated real estate market.

The global financial tsunami demonstrated that China's economy had become well integrated with the international economy, the business cycles of which unavoidably affected China. The risks of an export-oriented economy were exposed. The international crisis, however, reinforced the policies that had already been implemented before the crisis; in the middle of the previous decade, Chinese leaders had already fully recognized that China's economic growth had to depend more on domestic consumption and less on exports and infrastructural development. Further, China had to improve its industrial structure and gradually abandon its labour-intensive processing industries, at least in the coastal provinces.

Recognition of China's economic vulnerabilities has made its leadership more committed to the building of a social security net covering the entire population in order to maintain social stability. The rapid economic recovery has strengthened the legitimacy of the Party regime domestically and enhanced the country's international influence, increasing the appeal of the "Beijing consensus" over that of the "Washington consensus" in many developing countries.[2]

China's Exposures, Challenges, and Lessons Learnt in the Global Financial Tsunami

The overdependence of China's economic growth on exports and investment was well demonstrated during the global financial tsunami. From 1980 to 2008, China's ratio of foreign trade to GDP increased from 12.5% to 59.2%. After its entry into the World Trade Organization (WTO), this ratio rose by 20.7% in the period 2001–2008.[3] When the impact of the crisis spread from the financial sector to the real economic sector, the traditional extensive economic growth model suffered severe constraints. Although the size of the Chinese economy was impressive, the economic structure and economic efficiency were still at a low level. There were difficulties in stimulating long-term domestic demand, and the over-reliance on exports exacerbated the contradictions and frictions in China's trade relations with other countries.

China's economy appears to be highly trade-dependent. However, since "processing trade" constitutes slightly more than half of China's annual exports, its gross exports only generate a small share of the domestic value-added in its GDP. Hence, the external demand normally contributes less than 20% of China's total GDP growth. In 2009, China's exports fell by 34% because of the slump in the global demand for China's goods; the external demand therefore made a negative contribution to its economic growth. In fact, the latter was mainly supported by the fiscal stimulus package and liberal bank credit. Of the 9.2% GDP growth in 2009, investment contributed 8.7% and consumption 4.1%, while net exports (exports minus imports) caused a decline of 3.7%. In 2010, of the projected 10% economic growth (the actual growth subsequently reached 10.3%), the domestic demand (investment and consumption) was expected to contribute 7.8% and the external demand 2.2% as China's export growth turned around.[4]

In 2010, China's foreign trade, exports, and imports amounted to US$2,972.8 billion, US$1,577.9 billion, and US$1,394.8 billion, respectively, achieving increases of 34.7%, 31.3%, and 38.7%, respectively. As imports grew faster than exports, China's trade surplus shrank by 6.4% to US$183.1 billion compared with that of the previous year.[5] There was an obvious consensus among Chinese leaders and economists even before the global financial tsunami that China's economic growth should rely less on exports and investment in infrastructure and should depend more on domestic consumption. Hence, the decline in China's trade surplus is not necessarily a bad sign; at least it will help to reduce the international pressure on the Chinese authorities to appreciate the *renminbi*.

In the autumn of 2010, when the Chinese economists were analyzing the prospects for China's economy in the coming year, warnings were already being issued regarding the severe challenges facing China's foreign trade. They include: a) the rapid expansion of exports of products of high energy intensity, which in turn created pressure on achieving the targets regarding energy conservation and the reduction of pollutant emissions; b) the rise in the global prices of basic commodities increasing the costs of exports; c) rising protectionism in foreign markets and the targeting of China in their protectionist measures; d) increasing international pressures on the *renminbi* to appreciate; and e) rising labour costs adversely affecting the international competitiveness of China's exports.[6] At the same time, there was a concern that the economic recovery in the developed countries might not be very strong, thus dampening the demand for China's exports.

It is not surprising that in the first quarter of 2011 China reported a trade deficit of US$1.02 billion. Other economic statistics for the quarter, however, continued to paint a bright picture. The GDP grew at a rate of 9.7%, compared with 9.8% in the previous quarter; exports and imports increased by 26.5% and 32.6%, respectively, amounting to US$399.64 billion and US$400.66 billion. The trade deficit did not help to reduce the pressure for the revaluation of the *renminbi* though, as China's foreign exchange reserves broke the US$3 trillion mark (US$3.0447 trillion).[7]

China's economic development experience shows that the expansion of investment is the most direct and effective way to stimulate economic growth. As China is in a stage of industrialization and accelerating urbanization, the expansion of investment has been easy to implement, and the enthusiasm of the local governments concerned is obvious. The fiscal stimulus package initiated in 2008 exacerbated the dependence of economic growth on investment. In 2009, the ratio of investment to GDP amounted to 50.4%, the highest level since 1978. It was forecast in the autumn of 2009 that the ratio would reach 52.2%, and the ratio of fixed-asset investment to GDP would rise to 71.7% in 2010.[8]

In this period of rising investment, a new change in the investment structure emerged. In the first place, domestic investment became predominant, and investment in the private sector became more active. Since the global financial tsunami in 2008, the share of domestic investment has consistently increased in view of the 4 trillion *yuan* fiscal stimulus package. At the end of 2009, regarding fixed-asset investment in the urban sector, the share of domestic investment climbed to 92.2%, 2.3% higher than that in 2008. In 2009, some private-sector capital adopted a wait-and-see attitude, and private-sector investment amounted to 63.09% of domestic investment, dropping 2.05% compared with that in 2008. In the first half of 2010, the share of private-sector investment rose to 66.42%. This is significant because in the earlier period, there was criticism of "the advance of the state sector and the retreat of the private sector". The phenomenon emerged because the fiscal stimulus package favoured the state sector, which was also in a strong position to secure credit from the state-owned banks. At the same time, there were waves of mergers and acquisitions in times of economic hardship; major state-owned enterprises (SOEs) were able to make use of the opportunity to absorb smaller private enterprises in difficulties. On May 13, 2010, the State Council issued a document on the encouragement and guidance of private-sector investment, demonstrating an awareness that private-sector capital had to be mobilized and given a level playing field.

In response to the global financial tsunami, the Chinese leadership actively used investment to promote economic growth, especially exploiting investment projects funded by the central government to mobilize local investment. For several years before the crisis, the share of local investment projects had actually been expanding. This trend was reversed in 2009, when the share of centrally funded projects increased by 1.1% compared with the previous year. Apparently there was a time lag in this mobilization process. In the first half of 2010, local project investment rose by 26.7%, almost 14% higher than the growth rate of central project investment.

In recent years, the respective growth rates of fixed-asset investment in central and western China were considerably higher than that in eastern (coastal) China. This trend was maintained in 2009, when the respective rates for western, central, and eastern China were 36%, 35%, and 23.9%, reflecting the priority of the Chinese leadership aimed at redressing the regional disparities. In 2010, the growth rates in central and western China slowed down slightly, while that of eastern China showed a rebound. In the autumn of the year, it was estimated that the latter's fixed-asset investment share rose back to 54.1%, 6.6% higher than that in 2009. It appears that the coastal provinces remain the most attractive region for investors in a stable economic climate.

This reliance on investment to stimulate growth has two undesirable consequences, and both were exacerbated during the global financial crisis. The first is the increasing debts of the local governments, and the second is low consumption. According to a study by Golden Sachs, at the end of 2009, the total debts of various levels of government in China amounted to 15.7 trillion *yuan*, about 48% of China's GDP in the year. The debts of the central government amounted to 20% of the annual GDP, those of the local governments 23%, and the rest were non-performing loans absorbed by the state-owned asset-management companies from the restructuring of the state-owned commercial banks in 2000–2001. [9] The central government, with its healthy revenues and impressive foreign exchange reserves, would not consider the debts an unbearable burden, unlike many local governments.

A study by the office of the Ministry of Finance in 2005 already indicated that many provincial governments had accumulated debts exceeding their respective annual fiscal revenues, and that their debt-service ratios surpassed 10%. The situation in the wake of the global financial tsunami was certainly worse because local governments had to come up with matching funds to attract investment from the central government's fiscal stimulus package. More seriously still, the debt problems of many local governments were well hidden, and a significant proportion of their debts were not direct debts, i.e., they did not have to repay them immediately. However, when their corporations bankrupted, they would have to assume the responsibility for loan repayment. Chinese leaders were aware of the problem, and in June 2010, the State Council issued a notice demanding local governments to tighten the management of their corporations regarding the finance of local projects.[10]

The problem obviously cannot be resolved by a government directive. The root cause was the sharing system of tax revenues between the central and the local governments introduced in 1994; the latter suffered from the fact that while fiscal revenues were concentrated at the central government level, various services had been decentralized. The urbanization process, the improvement of social services, and the strengthening of the social security net all added to the financial burden of local governments. The latter had been eager to assume responsibility for various infrastructural projects too, instead of mobilizing the private sector. Meanwhile, various measures to reduce taxes and restrict local real estate development projects resulted in a decline in local revenues. All these factors mean that a major reform is called for to enhance the revenue sources of local governments so that they will be able to meet the new demands for their services. They should also be allowed to tap into a local government bond market yet to be better developed.

There has been a general consensus on stimulating domestic demand to support long-term sustainable economic growth. China's domestic consumption has been low because its savings ratio has been very high, averaging 48% of GDP in the 2001–2008 period. It rose further to 52% in 2009, higher than the average of all the high-savings East Asian economies and twice that of the OECD countries. China's high savings ratio has been attributed to many factors, including a low dependency ratio, a relatively low level of urbanization, strong economic growth, a weak social security network, and high income inequality.[11] The other side of the same coin of high savings is low consumption, 36% of GDP in 2009 compared with the U.S. level of 70%. For many years to come, domestic consumption will continue to trail behind domestic investment as a major source of China's economic growth. While China's consumption level has been relatively low, the consumption growth rates in the past decade (2000–2009) amounted to an average of 8.6% per annum, which was actually quite high.

Adjustments to China's Economic Development Strategy to be Reflected in the 12th FYP

At the beginning of this century, many scholars in China realized that it was approaching a complex and unstable stage of development. In 2003, the per capita GDP in China reached US$1,090. Some official think tanks indicated that, on the basis of the historical experiences of foreign countries (mainly Latin American countries), during the stage when the per capita GDP gradually climbs from US$1,000 to US$3,000 per annum, social stratification will be exacerbated, the middle class and its influence will grow, various cultural trends will emerge, the gap between the rich and the poor will widen, and various social contradictions including ethnic contradictions will sharpen. These think tanks would like to see China following the path of Japan and the "four little dragons of Asia", making good use of this economic take-off to lay a firm foundation for subsequent economic development. On the other hand, they would like to see China avoiding the precedents of Brazil, Argentina, and Mexico, which were trapped in economic stagnation after the 1970s. In 1961, Argentina's per capita GDP had already reached US$1,000, but in the following four decades and more, its per capita GDP only grew at an average annual rate of 1.9%.[12]

Chinese leaders understand well that an economic downturn, rising unemployment, the widening of the gap between the rich and the poor, and corruption together constitute a recipe for social unrest. In February 2009, at the peak of the global financial tsunami, about 20 million migrant workers returned home early for the Lunar New

Year because they had lost their jobs. About 80% of the 70 million migrant workers who had returned home for their traditional spring festival holidays came back to urban centres to seek employment after their annual leave, and only 11 million of them succeeded. Fortunately, the Chinese economy recovered rapidly; by mid-2009, labour shortages began to emerge in the Tianjin area, and by the end of the year, most coastal cities encountered difficulties in the recruitment of migrant workers. It is interesting to note that labour shortages first occurred in the Tianjin area, where there is a relatively smaller concentration of labour-intensive processing industries, and they emerged later in the Pearl River Delta, where the concentration of labour-intensive processing industries is relatively high.

Another group that was badly hit by unemployment was the fresh graduates from the tertiary institutions, who numbered 6.1 million in 2009. In the first half of the year, the unemployment rate for urban youths in the age group of 16–24 years exceeded 11%; the unofficial estimates were much higher.[13] Various estimates then placed the unemployment rate of fresh graduates at 30%, and at the edge of major cities like Beijing, there are tens of thousands of young graduates who live in slums with monthly earnings of one or two thousand *yuan*. Among the newly employed workers, about 30%–40% belong to the category of flexible employment; many of their jobs depend on government subsidies, and only half of them enjoy social security. These dissatisfied groups are potential sources of social unrest. It was reported that in 2009, there were about 217,900 cases of rallies, protests, and mass meetings, and the public security and armed police were mobilized 243,600 times to suppress the riots.[14]

In response to the unemployment problem during the global financial tsunami, the Chinese authorities acted swiftly. Their measures demonstrated the efficiency and sophistication of the central government at the tactical level and its understanding of the fundamental political challenges at the strategic level. Between September 2008 and February 2009, seven policy documents were released from the State Council and various ministries on the stabilization and expansion of employment, including: a comprehensive policy measures document from the State Council; three from its general office on the employment of migrant workers and university graduates and the promotion of entrepreneurship to stimulate employment; and another three from the Ministry of Human

Resources and Social Security and other ministries concerned with special training programmes, activities related to employment services, and measures to reduce enterprises' financial burden to stabilize employment. Regarding the latter, enterprises were allowed to delay their employees' social security payments; they were given reductions regarding the rates of these payments; and they were given subsidies from the unemployment insurance fund to compensate for their social security payments and the maintenance of job positions in order to encourage enterprises in difficulties to avoid or reduce retrenchment.[15]

The efficient response on the part of the Chinese authorities and the rapid economic recovery in 2009 were reflected by labour shortages in most coastal cities at the end of the year. The labour shortages in turn encouraged migrant workers to demand improvements in their wages and working conditions; these demands led to a wave of strikes in the early summer of 2010. In this year, labour disputes involving 11 to 49 workers numbered more than 4,000, participated in by 118,000 workers, and those involving more than 50 workers amounted to 216, participated in by 29,000 workers. Major labour disputes were usually handled by government mediation. Of the collective labour disputes, 64.4% were related to labour remuneration and overtime wages, and they were concentrated in the textiles, electronics, and construction industries. These disputes mainly involved migrant workers and female workers, with a high concentration in Guangdong (49.1% of the cases and 60% of the workers). It became obvious that workers considered collective struggles more feasible and more effective in fighting for their rights, leading to an increase in cases of collective disputes. Apparently, the workers participating in these disputes were better organized and the disputes lasted longer.[16]

In the era of economic reforms and opening to the external world, China's economic growth had been exploiting the comparative advantage of the low wages of migrant workers from rural areas. China's labour-intensive, export-oriented processing industries participated in economic globalization and generated a distinct pattern of international division of labour. This economic development strategy had been at the expense of workers' interests, whose improvement in wages lagged behind China's impressive economic growth rates for a long time. Corruption and the anomalies in the rule of law also led to frequent abuses of labour rights by enterprises.

The wave of labour strikes in the early summer of 2010 reflected the rejection of the minimum wage standards by the younger generation of migrant workers. In 2004, the export processing zones in southern China had already encountered labour shortages; migrant workers then "voted with their feet" to articulate their dissatisfaction with low wages under the conditions of an abundant labour supply. In the wake of the global financial tsunami, they began to use collective action to articulate their interests and demands, and their mode of action spread. The Chinese authorities are aware that they have to adjust their low-cost economic growth mode and industrialization strategy, which have been at the expense of cheap labour. Chinese leaders now advocate a scientific development perspective and promote "inclusive economic growth", i.e., to build harmonious labour relations and to ensure a "respectable and dignified" living for workers. In the aftermath of the global financial tsunami, the concern regarding the weak economic recovery in the developed countries is putting pressure on the Chinese leadership to reduce the country's reliance on export-oriented industrialization and to promote domestic consumption. Raising workers' wages is an important element of stimulating domestic consumption. It is significant that the Chinese leadership adopted a tolerant attitude towards the wave of labour strikes in 2010.

The message is clear. The Chinese authorities are encouraging labour wages to rise; industrial enterprises have to plan seriously for improvements in productivity and cost cuts in order to absorb the wage rises and enhance their international competitiveness. They therefore have to upgrade their products, increase the value-added components, or move to places in interior China or outside China where the labour costs are cheaper. The Ministry of Human Resources and Social Security planned to complete the drafting of the "Enterprise Wage Regulation (draft)" by the end of 2010, to be released by the State Council in 2011.

The reality is less optimistic. The share of labour remuneration in GDP was in decline from 56% in 1995 to 41% in 2005, and the share in 2010 remained at slightly more than 42%.[17] As the Chinese authorities emphasized increases in GDP and the launch of major infrastructural projects, the resources in the public sector were concentrated on monopolistic or oligopolistic state-owned enterprises, which would then reap huge profits from the people. Small and medium-sized enterprises secured fewer and fewer resources, adversely affecting the benefits of their owners and employees. These phenomena caused polarization in income distribution and exacerbated the imbalances in the economic structure; worse still, they might lead to social conflicts and instability. Hence, Chinese leaders were aware that from the points of view of both promoting sustainable economic growth and protecting labour rights, they had to abandon the economic growth mode, which was dependent on low labour costs.

The emergence of labour shortages means that the unemployment of migrant workers is no longer a pressing problem today; however, that of fresh graduates remains so. In 1999, the Chinese Government introduced a policy of vastly expanding the intake of tertiary students, so much so that China produced 6.3 million graduates from tertiary institutions in 2010 (6.6 million in 2011), 7.6 times the number in 1998. In 1982, the unemployment rate of university graduates under 30 years of age was only 0.1%; according to a national sample survey conducted by the Sociology Institute of the Chinese Academy of Social Sciences, this unemployment rate rose to 11.2% in 2008.[18] It is generally believed that even in the wake of the economic recovery, the unemployment rate of fresh graduates remains at the 30% level at the end of the year of their graduation. The official targets set in a document released by 6 ministries including the Ministry of Human Resources and Social Security and the Ministry of Education on April 7, 2010 indicated that the authorities intended to tackle the problem of 7 million unemployed graduates in the year (6.3 million fresh graduates plus 0.7 million past graduates still unemployed); they hoped to achieve an employment rate of 70% when the fresh graduates left the tertiary institutions, and an employment rate of over 80% at the end of 2010. Various programmes were introduced to help create job opportunities, promote entrepreneurship among them, offer assistance and services in seeking employment, and organize recruitment activities as well as internship projects.

Chinese leaders realize that the unemployment of young graduates can be a serious cause for political instability, as demonstrated by the "jasmine revolution" in Tunisia, Egypt, etc. In fact, their general dissatisfaction may become a source of trouble. There are hundreds of thousands of young graduates living in the poor suburbs of Beijing and Shanghai and earning a monthly salary of about one thousand *yuan* (US$154) or slightly above, which can hardly support a satisfactory living standard. In view of the keen competition to be admitted to universities, the costly inputs of the students and their parents, and the elitist expectations on their part, the psychological imbalance is natural and inevitable. Parents with wealth, social status, and connections are often in a position to help their children attain good jobs, and this further exacerbates the sense of injustice among the educated youth who are unemployed or who have unsatisfactory jobs.

Quality Economic Growth

Economic Growth Rates

Economic development remains the principal source of legitimacy for the Chinese Communist regime, as the 12th FYP claims that "development is still the key to solving all the problems in our country" (chapter 2, second paragraph). However, as the leadership and the leading economists have been advocating for more than a decade, economic growth in China will have to move from an extensive mode to an intensive mode, i.e., instead of relying on increases in inputs of capital, labour, and natural resources, it has to depend on improvements in efficiency, technology, the quality of labour, etc.

The 12th FYP sets an average annual economic growth rate of 7% for the five-year period, compared with 11% in the 11th FYP period. Following the central policy line, Beijing and Shanghai lowered their respective target growth rates for 2011 to 8%, and Shenzhen is only aiming at an average annual growth rate of 10% for the 12th FYP period, compared with 13.5% for the preceding FYP period.[19] Though the 12th FYP considers that "our country's development is still in an important period of strategic opportunities during which it can achieve much" and that "the international environment in sum still favours our country's peaceful development" (Chapter 1, second and third paragraphs), it is explicitly concerned with the significant impact of the international financial crisis and the consequent slowing down of the global economic growth, which are expected to lead to obvious changes in the global demand structure and more intense competition for markets, resources, talents, technology, and standard-setting.

On the other hand, the 12th FYP reveals stronger optimism regarding the domestic scene. China is said to have been experiencing an in-depth development of industrialization, informationization, urbanization, marketization, and internationalization; stable growth in the per capita national income; an accelerated transformation of the economic structure; immense potential in market demand; an abundant capital supply; a comprehensive raising of the level of science, technology, and education; an improvement in labour quality; progressing satisfactory development of the infrastructure; a prominent strengthening of the dynamics of the institution; and an obvious raising of the government's capabilities in macro-control and the handling of complex situations, as well as the maintenance of the stability of the broad social situation.

The 12th FYP also identifies the weaknesses of the domestic economy, i.e., the outstanding issues of imbalances and the lack of co-ordination and unsustainability, as follows: the exacerbation of the constraints imposed on economic growth by the resource environment; the imbalance between investment and consumption; the relatively large gap in income distribution; the low capabilities in innovation in science and technology; the irrational industrial structure; the still weak foundation in agriculture; the lack of co-ordination in urban/rural and regional development; the pressures of unemployment and the structural contradictions in employment; the increasing pressures of inflation; the obvious deterioration in social contradictions; and the many obstacles in the institutions and mechanisms concerned restraining scientific development.

Technological Development, Infrastructure, and the Private Sector

According to a study group of the Institute of Economics, the Chinese Academy of Social Sciences, in the era of economic reforms and opening to the external world, the appropriate range of economic growth rates should be from 8% to 12%, with the mid-range of the potential economic growth rate being 10%.[20] In the 12th FYP period, economic growth will be affected by three factors: a) in the wake of the global financial tsunami, external demand will decline and stay at a low level for a period of time; the competition for markets and resources will be more intense, and trade protectionism will rise; b) the restraints imposed by resources, energy, the environment, etc., will become more severe; c) the emphases will increasingly be the quality, efficiency, and cost-effectiveness of economic growth, the transformation of the mode of growth, and adjustments to the economic structure. Hence, the study group considers that the upper limit of the appropriate range of economic growth rates should be adjusted downwards by 2% for the 12th FYP period, i.e., between 8% and 10%, and the mid-range of the potential economic growth rate should then be 9%.[21]

A member of the study group further indicates that certain policy dilemmas will emerge during the programme period, because it has some of the characteristics of the previous cycle of economic decline as well as the characteristics of the new cycle of economic expansion. At the same time, there are pressing current problems and long-term structural problems; their co-existence makes tackling them complicated. Six major dilemmas are identified.

In the first place, after the series of economic stimulating policies introduced in the wake of the global financial tsunami has achieved considerable results, its withdrawal involves a timing problem. If it is terminated too soon, the rate of economic growth may decline, and if it is stopped too late, the inflationary pressures may become too high. Similarly, adjustments in the real estate market are controversial. High housing prices left uncontrolled can easily become a serious social problem. However, a sharp decline in the housing market would adversely affect economic growth, and many migrant workers in the construction industry may lose their jobs.

The reform of income distribution poses a third dilemma. Increases in the incomes of the low-income and middle-income groups are the key to raising the contribution of consumption to economic growth and reducing the income gap. These increases, however, will raise the costs of enterprises and generate challenges to their operation. Distributional adjustments among the state, enterprises, and individuals may involve serious reforms of the taxation system, which are likely to be controversial. Price adjustments constitute another dilemma. Transforming the mode of economic growth and promoting energy conservation and the reduction of emissions of pollutants require the existing relatively low prices of natural resources to be raised. However, as the revival of the economy has already generated great inflationary pressure, price adjustments will be bound to exacerbate such pressure.

The exchange rate of the *yuan* is a well-recognized international issue. If the *yuan* is allowed to appreciate too rapidly, exports may decline and the employment of migrant workers may be adversely affected. Future financial crises, on the other hand, may bring about substantial devaluation pressure. Sharp fluctuations in the exchange rate are undesirable. However, international pressures for the appreciation of the *yuan* at this stage are hard to defend; a series of minor upward adjustments will easily attract massive inflows of "hot money". Finally, exports are a dilemma too. The revival of the global economy in the wake of the international financial crisis offers an opportunity to expand China's exports. However, the revival appears unstable and the sovereign debt crisis in Europe may seriously deteriorate; China's expansion of its exports and trade surpluses may attract a lot of international criticism too.[22]

The 12th FYP still emphasizes economic growth, but the basic orientation is the intensive mode of growth, with priorities accorded to quality, balances, co-ordination, and efficiency. The difficulties perceived in the external environment and the lessons learnt during the recent global financial tsunami have reinforced the reliance on domestic consumption. The latter as well as investment and exports constitute the three pillars supporting economic growth, which in turn depends on the co-ordinated development of the primary, secondary, and tertiary sectors. The value-added in the latter is expected to rise by 4% in terms of its share in the GDP.

As Chinese leaders plan to reduce the weight of labour-intensive processing industries and develop strategic emerging industries, they have identified the key sectors for the leapfrog type of development. They include energy-saving, environment conservation technology, new-generation information technology, bio-tech, high-end equipment manufacturing, new energy, new materials, new-energy automobiles, etc. It is expected that the value-added of these new strategic industries will reach 8% of GDP at the end of 2015. To this end, the government has pledged that research and development expenditure will amount to 2.2% of GDP by the end of the programme period.

In fact, a more detailed blueprint has been provided regarding the development of the strategic industries to be given priority support. Energy-saving environment conservation technology will focus on the key technology, products, and services for high-efficiency energy saving, environment conservation, and resource recycling. The new-generation information technology industries will concentrate on the development of new-generation mobile communication, new-generation Internet, three-network convergence, Internet of things, cloud computing, integrated circuits, new displays, high-end servers, and information services. In the biological industrial sector, the highlights will be bio-pharmaceuticals, bio-medical engineering products, bio-agriculture, and bio-manufacturing. In the high-end equipment manufacturing industry, the priorities will be the development of aviation equipment, satellites and their application, rail traffic equipment, and intelligent manufacturing equipment. In the new industry, the development foci will be new-generation nuclear energy, solutions to energy utilization, photovoltaic and photo-thermal power generation, wind power technological equipment, intelligent power guides, and biomass energy. In the new materials sector, the areas identified for priority support are new functional materials, advanced structural materials, high-performance fibres and related compound materials, and common basic materials. Finally, in the new-energy automobile industry, the strategic foci will be the development of plug-in hybrid electric vehicles, pure electric vehicles, and fuel-cell automobile technology.

Despite the concern about raising domestic consumption, investment is still perceived as a very important element supporting economic growth and long-term economic development. While more resources will be assigned to research and development, the cultivation of innovation capabilities, and education, the bulk of the investment fund will still be devoted to infrastructure. In the 12th FYP, the construction of a comprehensive transportation system has been given top priority; while improving inter-regional traffic networks and the construction of inter-city express networks are the key tasks ahead, the authorities also pledge to pay serious attention to public transport and improving transport services. Improving inter-regional traffic networks is considered to contribute to the acceleration of the development of central and western China, and high-speed railways assume a key role in this as well as in the development of inter-city express networks.[23]

The development of the oceanic economy is given a chapter in the 12th FYP, with emphasis on the development and implementation of an oceanic development strategy and improving China's oceanic development, control, and comprehensive management capabilities (Chapter 14). Shandong, Zhejiang, and Guangdong have been identified as experimental sites for the development of China's oceanic economy. This is related to technological and infrastructural development, and also has significant foreign and defence policy implications.

It has been mentioned that the 4 trillion *yuan* economic stimulus package in response to the global financial tsunami has strengthened the state sector, sometimes at the expense of the private sector, which was more severely affected by the crisis. The substantial increases in research and development funding as well as the impressive investment in infrastructure in the 12th FYP similarly will chiefly benefit the large state-owned enterprises (SOEs). In Chapter 9, on the renovation and improvement of the manufacturing industry, there is a section on the guidance of the mergers and re-organization of enterprises and one on the promotion of the development of small and medium-sized enterprises (SMEs). The former are actually feared by SMEs in China, while the latter only repeats the well-known principles.

After the release of *Several Opinions on the Encouragement, Support and Guidance of the Development of the Non-Public Sector Economy Including Individual and Private Enterprises* in 2005, the State Council on May 13, 2010 further released *Several Opinions on the Encouragement and Guidance of the Healthy Development of Private Investment*. Apparently the Chinese authorities wanted to boost the confidence of the private sector after its setbacks in the previous years, reaffirming their recognition of its significant role in economic development, adjustments to the industrial structure, and especially generating employment.[24]

In 2010, among the over 80 trades and sectors, foreign investment enjoyed access to 62 while private investment only secured access to 41. In the traditional monopolistic sectors and trades, the respective weights of private investment were relatively low: 13.6% in the generation and supply of electricity and heat; 12.3% in education; 11.8% in health, social security, and social welfare; 9.6% in finance; 7.8% in information transmission, computer services, and software; 7.5% in transport and communication, storage, and postal services; 6.6% in irrigation and water supply, environment, and public facilities management; and 5.9% in public management and social organization.[25] Private investors have been complaining that they have been blocked by three types of doors in their access to monopolistic sectors, social enterprises, infrastructural facilities, and public services: steel doors, meaning that they have been completely blocked off; glass doors, implying that apparently they have been granted entry but in fact there are serious obstacles in terms of administrative approvals; and spring doors, meaning that after entry, non-market factors finally result in expulsion.

The May 2010 document pledges to establish and regulate the access threshold of private investment, define clearly the government's investment scope, treat civilian social enterprises as a significant supplement to public social enterprises, and encourage and guide private investment into trades and sectors not explicitly prohibited by law. Further, the document seeks to identify trades and sectors in which to encourage participation by the private sector in order to adjust the structure of the state sector. These trades and sectors include: the infrastructural facilities in transport, telecommunications, and energy; urban and public utilities; scientific and technological industries in the defence sector; social security housing; as well as participation in the establishment of financial institutions; commercial, trade, and logistics enterprises; and cultural, educational, sports, medical, and social welfare enterprises. The authorities in the document also define the channels for private sector participation, including: tendering, contractual responsibility system, leasing, transfer of property or operational rights, participation in reorganization and restructuring of SOEs, etc. Finally, the government will offer incentives that include compensation mechanisms in addition to charging fees, government subsidies, and purchases; credit supply and credit guarantee; land supply, etc. In sum, the government promises to offer the private sector fair treatment on a level playing field, better supporting services, and an improved investment environment.[26]

Environmental Protection and Urbanization

The 12th FYP demonstrates the Chinese authorities' commitment to sustainable development and their realization of the limits of the extensive mode of economic growth. The FYP stresses the importance of building a resource-saving and environment-friendly society to push for the transformation of the economic development mode; the Chinese authorities pledge to save energy, reduce greenhouse emissions, tackle global climate change, and develop a circular economy and low-carbon technologies.

The determination has been well reflected by the concrete targets set. They include: maintain farmland reserves at 1.818 billion *mu* (about 121.26 million hectares); cut water consumption per unit of value-added industrial output by 30%; raise the water efficiency coefficient in agricultural irrigation to 0.53; increase non-fossil fuel resources in primary energy consumption to 11.4%; reduce energy consumption per unit of GDP by 16% and carbon dioxide emissions per unit of GDP by 17%; cut chemical oxygen demand and the emissions of sulphur dioxide by 8%, and those of ammonia and nitrogen oxides by 10%; and increase the forest coverage rate to 21.66% and national forest stocks by 600 million cubic metres (Chapter 3).

In the first four years of the 11th FYP period, the targets for energy conservation and the reduction of emissions of pollutants were not met. One of the major causes for the setback was the lack of technological innovations on the part of most SMFs. Hence, energy saving and the reduction of pollution have to be integrated into the promotion of new technologies, exerting pressure on enterprises to renovate their technologies and upgrade the industrial structure, thus achieving the transformation of the mode of economic growth as well.[27] In the final year of the 11th FYP, some local governments actually restricted industrial and construction activities to reduce pollution to meet the targets. This sacrifice reflected the seriousness of the central government and the local leaders' concern to avoid its sanctions.

Urbanization is also an important part of the economic development strategy at this stage (Chapter 20). The Chinese authorities hope to achieve the co-ordinated development of large, medium-sized, and small cities as well as small towns, and the development of a transportation network is the key to the realization of this objective. Urbanization means changing the rural population into an urban population. The plan is for super-large cities to exercise rational control of their populations, and for large and medium-sized cities to strengthen their population management while assuming the role of absorbing the migrant population. Medium-sized and small cities as well as small towns are expected to relax their terms for the settlement of migrants according to their respective conditions. To protect the peasants, Chinese leaders promise to respect their choice and guarantee their legal rights, especially the rights to their existing contracted land under the rural responsibility system and those for their accommodation. Migrant workers with stable employment who have been working in the urban sector for a number of years are expected to secure urban residents' status.

For migrant workers who do not yet qualify, the Chinese authorities promise to offer them better public services and protection of their rights. The 12th FYP states that the children of migrant workers should enjoy equal rights to compulsory education, and the primary and middle schools of the cities or towns that have received the migrant workers should ensure the continuity of their children's middle-school and high-school education. Migrant workers with stable employment in enterprises should be included in the latter's basic retirement insurance and medical insurance schemes for urban workers. Provincial-level governments should co-ordinate funding for subsidies for the basic training of migrant workers. Finally, attempts should be made to involve qualified migrant workers in the urban social-security housing schemes and to adopt various channels to improve their housing conditions.

These measures are in line with the understanding that urbanization at this stage is significant in the promotion of sustainable economic development, as the 12th FYP stipulates that during the programme period, employment will have to be created for 45 million people (maintaining the urban registered unemployment rate at under 5%) and the urbanization rate raised by 4%. Urbanization will help to narrow the urban-rural gap and, hopefully, reduce the related social inequalities; it will also contribute to the general improvement of living standards as well as the expansion of domestic consumption.

The 12th FYP calls for better and co-ordinated planning of above-ground and underground urban public utilities to satisfy the demand generated by the rapid urbanization process. However, this in turn greatly exacerbates the financial burden of urban governments at all levels; many of them are now in debt and this has become a considerable financial risk.

Public Services in Support of Social Stability

Perhaps the most important contribution of the Hu Jintao–Wen Jiabao administration is the commitment to establishing a basic security net coving the entire population. Initially, this was perceived as a strategy to contain the grievances generated by the widening gap between the rich and the poor, between the urban and the rural sectors, and between the coastal and the interior provinces. The worsening social unrest has certainly reinforced this commitment; at the same time, the social security net not only enhances the legitimacy of the Party regime, but also contributes to economic development through the expansion of the tertiary sector, which is expected to increase its share of GDP by 4% within the 12th FYP period.

Lessons from the Global Financial Tsunami

Chinese leaders still offer their policy programmes within a socialist framework, as this remains the justification of the rule of the Communist Party of China. It is interesting to examine how the official think tanks interpret the responses to the global financial tsunami on the part of other Communist parties and the left-wing academics in the Western countries. In late November 2008, the Tenth International Meeting of Communist and Workers Parties released the Sao Paulo Proclamation, "Socialism is the Alternative!".[28] It concluded that this large-scale economic crisis cannot be separated from the irreconcilable internal contradictions and the nature and characteristics of capitalism.

The Communist Party of Greece further identified the fundamental contradiction of capitalism leading to the global financial tsunami as that between "surplus production and inadequate consumption demand". It explained that the keen competition among corporations and the pursuit of excessive profits by various trades and industries had exacerbated the imbalances and contradictions in capitalist economic development; the disorderly, unbalanced development in various sectors had worsened the contradiction between production and consumption by the masses.[29] Similarly, the Portuguese Communist Party argued that the international financial crisis first emerged in the capitalist hegemonic state, and it originated from surplus production, excessive accumulation, the shrinking market, and insufficient consumption demand. The latter in turn was due to the lowering of wages, socio-economic polarization, the reduction in public-sector expenditure, etc. The Party therefore considered that attempts on the part of the governments facing the crisis to increase the credit supply would only benefit the holders of financial capital; these measures were inadequate, temporary, and in fact would exacerbate the crisis. The increasing debts of the government and those of small enterprises would worsen the situation. The Party believed that it would be important to raise workers' wages and the incomes of ordinary people (including their pensions).[30]

From an ideological point of view, researchers in China's mainstream think tanks recognize that the analyses of the Communist Parties and the left-wing scholars in the Western world are important for their understanding of the international financial crisis. They consider that these analyses are valuable for China to strengthen and improve its macro-economic adjustments and control, accelerate the transformation of its mode of economic development, insist consciously on its strategy of expanding its domestic consumption, and accord even higher priority to the protection and improvement of people's livelihood. It is difficult to trace the impact of these analyses on China's 12th FYP, but it is reasonable to suggest that the global financial tsunami has provided added impetus to China's expansion of domestic consumption, and to that end, raising the incomes of the lower socio-economic strata.

These official think-tank researchers differ from the left-wing views in the Western countries in that while they recognize that the trend towards multipolarization and neo-liberal capitalism's need to encounter severe future challenges and adjustments are new historical trends, these changes are only in quantitative terms, and the present international political configuration remains that of one superpower and several major powers. These researchers consider that the United States was badly hurt in the crisis, but it has not lost its capability and political will to maintain its hegemony.

In parallel to this sober assessment, these think-tank researchers are not very optimistic regarding the opportunities for the left-wing political forces in the Western world and in development countries. These researchers are critical of the former that while they are now free from the neo-liberal ideological influences, they are still trapped in the ideological net of democratic socialism. While most European Union member countries were in serious economic difficulties, their continued advocacy for an enhancement of social welfare might be unrealistic. Regarding the newly established left-wing governments in Latin America, the Chinese researchers believe they will have to face severe challenges ahead. The latter had slightly expanded social services expenditure in their combat of poverty, but they had not been able to alter fundamentally the neo-liberal economic structure they had inherited. The economic recovery in recent years is highly dependent on the exports of primary commodities and the inflow of "hot money"; the capitalists are still in a predominant position relative to labour. The brittleness of these governments has in fact been exposed by the global economic difficulties.[31]

Major Public Service Commitments

The 12th FYP states that the ultimate goal of the acceleration of the transformation of the mode of economic development is the protection and improvement of people's livelihood. It promises to accord priority to the promotion of employment, accelerate the development of various social enterprises, implement the equalization of basic public services, and strengthen the adjustment of income distribution. These are the relatively new objectives of the 12th FYP, reflecting an increasing emphasis on social equality and justice in this stage of economic development and downplaying the earlier slogan of Deng Xiaoping, "let a segment of the population become rich first".

In terms of concrete targets, the FYP aims to control population growth to below 1.39 billion at the end of the programme period; raise the average life expectancy by 1 year to 74.5 years by 2015; and increase the per capita disposable income of the urban population and the per capita net income of the rural population by more than 7% per annum, respectively, i.e., higher than the economic growth rate. Regarding social security, the new rural social retirement insurance scheme is expected to attain full coverage, while the participants in the urban basic retirement insurance scheme will reach 357 million people; the three types of basic medical insurance schemes for the urban and rural sectors are expected to raise their respective participation rates by 3% too. The FYP pledges to build 36 million social security housing units in the urban sector during the programme period, and the central government then set the target for 2011 at 10 million units (p. 15).

These priorities and targets are in line with the broad strategy of providing a basic social security net covering the entire population to maintain social stability, contain grievances, and enhance the legitimacy of the Party regime. In view of the emerging and deteriorating socio-economic problems, the Hu-Wen leadership has actually been reversing the "small government, big society" policy trends of the Jiang Zemin–Zhu Rongj administration, which worked hard to reduce the social security burden of the government. In the middle of the last decade, the new Chinese leadership offered subsidies to rural children to ensure that they would have access to education; almost at the same time, it helped migrant workers to recover their pay arrears, provided them with opportunities to settle down in the urban sectors, and improved their access to social services and social security; then it worked to expand vastly the coverage of the minimum-income guarantee system in both the urban and the rural sector. In recent years, its focus of attention turned to the reform of medical insurance schemes and the improvement of medical services. At this stage, the priorities will be housing and employment; inflation has again become a matter of serious concern.

The sixth plenum of the Sixteenth Central Committee of the Party in 2006 released the "Resolution on Several Important Questions Concerning the Construction of the Socialist Harmonious Society". It offers an analysis of the issues brought about by economic structural reforms, changes in social stratification, competition among interest groups, and the emergence of new ideas and values as perceived by the Hu-Wen leadership. "*Maodun duofa* (breakouts of several contradictions)" is a term often used by social scientists in recent years in their comments on the current social scene in China.[32] Chinese leaders today are aware of the challenge and at the same time they are concerned about spreading civil consciousness among the people. In 2009, civil organizations registered by the Ministry of Civil Affairs and its counterparts in local governments numbered over 431,000, showing an increase of 34.8% from 2005.[33] The number of mass incidents and labour disputes/strikes has been increasing even faster. With more than US$3 trillion of foreign exchange reserves, the Hu-Wen leadership is naturally willing to spend more on public services, symbolized by the fact that for the 2011 budget, the planned expenditure on the "maintenance of stability" exceeded that for national defence.[34]

At the same time, the State Council in 2010 and 2011 behaved like a city government working hard to moderate real estate prices and tame inflation. Premier Wen Jiabao was acutely aware that these two issues were closely related to people's general level of satisfaction and social grievances. The evaluation of the performance of the central government by the people to a considerable extent depended on its handling of these two issues. The housing prices issue also tested the central government's control of the local governments. The definition and scope of public service in China have been evolving and broadening.

Education, Labour Issues, and Income Distribution

In China, education is assuming an increasingly important role in economic development; and it is also a very significant factor in providing upward social mobility opportunities and therefore a key element concerning social equality and justice. The Hu-Wen leadership first tackled the education of rural children exactly because of these considerations. The specific targets as stipulated in the 12th FYP are: significantly raising the quality of the nine-year free education and increasing its coverage rate to 93%; raising the admission rate to senior-high schools to 87%; accelerating the establishment of first-rate universities and high-level universities; and exerting huge efforts to develop vocational education and that serving the rural sector. Pre-school education has been made a priority area too, and the FYP pledges to raise the admission rate to 85% for children one year before their entry to primary schools.

Equality and social justice issues are to be addressed in the programme period. The FYP pledges that public education resources will favour rural, distant, poor, and ethnic minority districts, through the standardization of schools in the free-education sector, the equalization of remuneration for teachers in the urban and rural sectors within the same county and city, and the abolition of elite schools and elite classes in the free-education sector. Newly established tertiary institutions will favour the central and western provinces in their admission plans, and coastal universities will increase their student intakes from the interior provinces (Chapter 28, section 2). The FYP also promises to give private schools and public schools equal legal status and to raise the fiscal expenditure on education to 4% of GDP by 2012.

The global financial tsunami highlighted the problem of unemployment, and the 12th FYP discusses detailed measures to generate job opportunities (chapter 31, sector 1). They include: the development of labour-intensive manufacturing industries, service industries, and small and micro enterprises; the improvement of policies on tax reduction to create jobs; subsidies for job positions, training, social insurance, and job skill certification; and policies to promote the employment of graduates from tertiary institutions, workers moving out of the rural sector, and labourers in the urban sector with employment difficulties. There will also be policy measures to encourage entrepreneurship through small-loan guarantees, fiscal subsidies for interest payments, site arrangements, etc. Major projects funded by the government will also pay attention to job creation.

As mentioned in Section III, the recent labour shortages facilitated workers to bargain for better wages and working conditions. These were accepted by the Hu-Wen leadership as the 12th FYP promises that both the initial income distribution and the income redistribution have to handle the relationship between efficiency and justice well, and the income redistribution has to place greater emphasis on justice. The programme further pledges that the proportion of residents' incomes in the national income distribution will have to be raised and the same will apply to the proportion of labour remuneration in the initial income distribution (Chapter 32). To this end, the 12th FYP agrees to expand the scope for collective bargaining to determine wages and gradually raise the level of minimum wages. At the same time, the programme also promises to reduce the wage gaps among different trades, i.e., to reduce the exorbitant wage level of some monopolistic trades.

In February 2010, Jiangsu was the first provincial unit to raise the minimum wage. By the beginning of 2011, 29 of them had already done so, with an average increase rate of 24.1%. The "Regulation on Minimum Wage" was implemented in 2004, and in the following two years, all the provincial units raised their respective minimum wage levels. In 2007, 29 provincial units did so again, but the global financial tsunami delayed adjustments for two years. Following the economic recovery, the exercise was resumed in 2010. At this stage, raising wages is perceived to encourage enterprises to improve management and operations, engage in technological innovations, and increase their efficiency in the use of energy and resources. Differentiation in provincial wage levels also facilitates the upgrading of the industrial structure and the relocation of industries, leading to better regional economic co-ordination. Finally, wage improvement will promote consumption and increase domestic demand.

At the beginning of the 12th FYP period, some provinces had experimented with the implementation of wage collective bargaining at the trade on district level. The All-China Federation of Trade Unions in early 2011 planned to implement wage collective bargaining in all the enterprises with a trade union in three years, and propose legal sanctions against enterprises rejecting such collective bargaining. Regarding migrant workers, the authorities concerned would strengthen the systems of establishing wage guidelines, wage guidance indicators in human resources markets, and information on labour costs by trade as references for enterprises.[35]

The National Development Reform and Commission is expected to release an income distribution reform plan in 2011, with proposals to raise the incomes of middle- and low-level wage earners, adjust and control the wage volumes and wage levels of monopolistic trades, and strengthen the use of the taxation system to adjust income distribution, etc. The All-China Federation of Trade Unions is concerned with the minimum-wage system. It advocates the promulgation of a Minimum Wage Law; the establishment of a mechanism to adjust minimum wages regularly, ideally once a year, with upward adjustments at rates not lower than those increases in GDP and average wage; and finally, the raising of the ratio of minimum wage to average wage to a level of about 40–60%.[36]

The improvement of equity in income redistribution may rely on the taxation system too, instead of being mainly dependent on social services. The 12th FYP promises to achieve a fair tax burden and to use the tax system to regulate distribution relations (Chapter 4, section 3), but it is brief regarding the details. According to experts, the priority areas in tax reform in the 12th FYP period will be: the transformation of the value-added tax to include investment in housing and property; the introduction of a comprehensive personal income tax while allowing limited separate categories like incomes from interest payments on individual deposits; and the introduction of a property tax. These tax reforms are aimed at narrowing the gap between the rich and the poor.

Conclusion: The Leadership Succession Process and the Way Forward

Economic recession often brings political and social instability. There is awareness on the part of the Chinese leadership that economic recession, unemployment, and corruption together constitute a recipe for social unrest. Its formula for political stability and the maintenance of the legitimacy of the Party regime is economic growth, a basic social security net covering the entire population, and good governance in the absence of democracy. The rapid economic recovery after the global financial tsunami has strengthened the argument that China needs a strong government to concentrate on economic and social development, and the advantages of a strong government were well demonstrated by the prompt response to the global crisis, including the four trillion *yuan* economic stimulus package, the launch of major infrastructure projects, and various measures to reduce unemployment. The rise in China's international status has contributed to the legitimacy of the regime too, as the Chinese people desire an improvement in China's international influence, and national pride has been fully exploited by the Chinese leadership. Nevertheless, the latter has been cautious not to accept the notion of "G2".

In the absence of democratic elections, in the past twenty years, a leadership succession process has emerged and been refined to ensure stability and predictability. The choice of Jiang Zemin was a surprise in the wake of the Tiananmen Incident, but the successions of Hu Jintao and Xi Jinping were predictable. The heir apparent was selected ten years ago, joined the Party's Political Bureau as one of its youngest members, entered the Standing Committee of the Political Bureau in the next Party Congress, and emerged as the top leader in the following Party Congress. In the case of Xi Jinping, he became vice-chairman of the Party Central Military Commission two years before the crucial Party Congress, and was given the glamorous assignment of organizing the Beijing Olympics.

The maintenance of impressive economic growth and social stability means that the leadership succession process would not be challenged, and that the broad policy programmes of the Hu Jintao era would be closely followed by Xi Jinping. He would be likely to introduce adjustments, but not to initiate significant reversals. Hu Jintao would have a decisive say in selecting the new members of the Political Bureau in the Eighteenth Party Congress in 2012, and the youngest members are expected to become the top leaders in 2022. The upgrading of the industrial structure and the development of the western provinces were policies established in the Jiang Zemin era. Jiang and Premier Zhu Rongji decided to make the concessions demanded by the U.S. in joining the World Trade Organization; Premier Zhu also played a crucial role in developing China's banking and financial sector. In short, continuity can be anticipated in the broad policy programme in the leadership succession processes.

Hu Jintao and Wen Jiabao recognized the threat of the widening gap between the rich and the poor, that between the coastal and the interior provinces, and that between the urban and the rural sector. Their solution has been the building of a basic social security net covering the entire population. The increasing integration of the Chinese economy with the world implies that China will be more affected by the global business cycles, and the global financial tsunami had a significant impact on the unemployment of migrant workers at the end of 2008 and in the first half of 2009. The successors of Hu-Wen will definitely continue to complete the establishment of the basic social security net in the hope of maintaining social stability, which certainly has become even more challenging in the context of rapid economic growth. This continuation has to a considerable extent been pledged by the 12th FYP.

The global financial tsunami has reinforced the importance of upgrading China's industrial structure, spending more on research and development, stimulating domestic consumption, to which the building of the social security net will make a contribution, reducing China's dependence on exports, stepping up the urbanization process, etc. Improvements in the quality of life, urbanization, and the better supply of social services in turn will contribute to the expansion of the tertiary sector, and this is in line with the Chinese leadership's plan to secure a more balanced economic structure.

The imperative to stimulate domestic consumption and the concern for the maintenance of social stability have facilitated the Chinese leadership's promise to promote social justice and improve income distribution. Hence, the protection of labour rights and the raising of wages have become legitimate demands; the Chinese authorities adopted a tolerant attitude towards the labour strikes in the early summer of 2010. In the 12th FYP, the Chinese authorities promise that the growth in residents' income should be in line with economic development, and the improvement in labour remuneration should be in line with that in labour productivity; further, efforts will be made gradually to raise the share of residents' income in the national income distribution and the share of labour remuneration in the initial income distribution; finally, it is planned that the per capita disposable income of urban residents and the per capita net income of rural residents will grow more than 7% per annum in real terms during the programme period.

Sustainable growth has become a more significant goal after more than three decades of rapid growth, while environmental protection, climate change, energy intensity, etc. have become serious concerns. International pressures have also grown because of China's increasing weight in the international economy, but the Chinese leaders and Chinese people are aware that these policy objectives are in China's own interest. This awareness, however, still appears weak when challenged by greed, corruption, and vested interests.

In late 2010 and early 2011, Premier Wen Jiabao made a number of open appeals for political reforms, but his seemed to be a lone voice among the Chinese leaders. Socialist democracy takes up one chapter (chapter 54) of the 12th FYP, but there are no indicators of serious political reforms being scheduled; in fact, there have been no important breakthroughs in political reforms in the past decade. In view of the impending leadership succession and the concern regarding the "jasmine revolution", stability remains the top priority of the Chinese leadership, and the success of its economic development strategy has provided strong support for stability and maintenance of the status quo.

Notes and References

1. For the complete Chinese text of the 12th FTP, see http://www.sina.com.cn, March 17, 2011; for an English translation by the Delegation of the European Union in China, see http://cbi.typepad.com/china_direct/page/5/.

2. Joshua Cooper Ramo, *Beijing Consensus* (London: Foreign Policy Centre, 2004), pp. 11–13; and John Williamson, "What Washington means by policy reform," in John Williamson (ed.), *Latin American Adjustment: How Much Has Happened?* (Washington, D.C.: Institute of International Economics, 1990), pp. 8–19.

3. Research Group on the "Analysis and Forecast of Social Development," Chinese Academy of Social Sciences, "China's social construction in a new stage of growth – analysis and forecast on social situation in China, 2010 – 2011 (in Chinese)," in Ru Xin, Lu Xueyi, and Li Peilin (eds.), *Blue Book of China's Society – Society of China Analysis and Forecast (2011)* (Beijing: Social Sciences Academic Press (China), 2011), 9.

4. John Wong, "China's economy 2010: continuing strong growth, with possible soft landing for 2011," *East Asian Policy* (Singapore), 3(1) (Jan/Mar 2011), pp. 20.

5. For the statistics on China's economy in 2010, see http://www.china.com.cn/economic/txt/2011-01/20/content_21779966.htm.

6. Pei Changhong, "Characteristics of China's foreign trade in 2010: recovered growth but lack of power (in Chinese)," in Chen Jiagui and Li Yang *(eds.)*, *Blue Book of China's Economy – Economy of China Analysis and Forecast (2011)* (Beijing: Social Sciences Academic Press (China), December 2010), pp. 210–212.

7. For the statistics on China's economy in the first quarter of 2011, see http://www.etnet.com.hk/www/tc/news/categorized_news_detail.p.

8. Project Group on the "Analysis and Forecast of China's Economic Situation," "analysis and forecast of china's economic situation – report of Fall 2010 (in Chinese)," in Chen Jiagui and Li Yang (eds.), *Blue Book of China's Economy – Economy of China Analysis and Forecast (2011)*, pp. 5–6.

9. Qiao Hong and Song Yu, "Risk assessment of potential real estate adjustments and excessive debts of governments (in Chinese)," Research Report of the Goldman Sachs Group, 10 May 10 2010.

10. Huang Yanfen and Wu La, "The debt risks of China's local government: status, causes and impact on society (in Chinese)," in Ru Xin, Lu Xueyi, and Li Peilin (eds.), *Blue Book of China's Society – Society of China Analysis and Forecast (2011)* pp. 229–243.

11. See Li Cui, "China's consumption myth," paper presented by the Hong Kong Monetary Authority at the PBoC/IMF Workshop of "Catalysing Domestics Demand", Beijing, 21 January 2010; and Hung Juann and Qian Rong, "Why is China's saving rate so high? a comparative study of cross-country panel data," Working Paper 2010–07, East Asian Institute, National University of Singapore, November 2010).

12. See Joseph Y. S. Cheng, "Introduction: economic growth and new challenges", in Joseph Y. S. Cheng (ed.), *Challenges and Policy Programmes of China's New Leadership* (Hong Kong: City University of Hong Kong Press, 2007), 1–2.

13. Li Peilin and Chen Guangjin, "China steps into a new stage of growth (in Chinese)," in Ru Xin, Lu Xueyi, and Li Peilin (eds.), *Blue Book of China's Society – Society of China Analysis and Forecast (2010)* (Beijing: Social Sciences Academic Press (China), December 2009), pp. 3–4; and Mo Rong, Zhao Liwei, and Chen Lan, "The employment situation and relevant policies under international financial crisis (in Chinese)," *ibid.*, pp. 31–48.

14. Cen Chen, "Public security and armed police were mobilized over 240,000 times last year," *Cheng Ming* (a monthly in Chinese published in Hong Kong) 389 (March 2010), pp. 16–17.

15. Mo Rong, Zhao Liwei, and Chen Lan, "The employment situation and relevant policies under international financial crisis (in Chinese), *pp.* 43–44.

16. Qiao Jian, "The situation of China's working class in 2010 – calling for the sharing of economic gains and collective labour rights (in Chinese)," in Ru Xin, Lu Xueyi, and Li Peilin (eds.), *Blue Book of China's Society – Society of China Analysis and Forecast (2010)*, pp. 253–254.

17. Li Jing Rui, "All-China Federation of Trade Unions official indicated that the share of labour remuneration in GDP had been falling continuously for 22 years (in Chinese)," *Xin Jing Bao* (Beijing), May 12, 2010.

18. Li Chunling and Lut Peng, "Employment situations of graduates among the '80s generation' – a report of graduates from six '985' Chinese universities (in Chinese)," in Ru Xin, Lu Xueyi, and Li Peilin (eds.), *Blue Book of China's Society – Society of China Analysis and Forecast (2011)*, pp. 138 and 143.

19. See http://www.worldjournal.com/view/aChinanews/11667216/artical, 26 February 2011.

20. Macro Adjustments and Control Study Group, Institute of Economics, the Chinese Academy of Social Sciences, "An analysis of the 11th FYP and planning for the 12th FYP in terms of Macro Adjustments and Control Targets (in Chinese)," *Economic Research Journal* 2 (2010): 4–17.

21. *Ibid.*; see also Liu Shucheng, "The characteristics of China's economic situation in 2010 and an analysis of economic growth rate during the 12th Five-Year Plan Period (in Chinese)," in Chen Jiagui and Li Yang (eds.), *Blue Book of China's Economy – Economy of China Analysis and Forecast (2011)*, p. 32.

22. *Ibid.*, pp. 27–28.

23. The fatal high-speed train crash on July 23, 2011 near Wenzhou, Zhejiang may well result in a delay to these high-speed railway projects; see media reports in the week after the accident.

24. Li Bing, "Economic democratic protection intensified (in Chinese)," in Liu Jie (ed.), *The Process of China's Political Development 2011* (Beijing: Shi shi Chu banshe, 2011), p. 292.

25. "The National Reform and Development Commission Discusses the '36 Articles' on Private Sector Investment: The Long-Term Policy of Perfecting the Economic System (in Chinese)," *Renmin ribao* (Beijing), 15 May 2010.

26. Li Bing, "Economic democratic protection intensified (in Chinese)," pp. 293–296.

27. Research Group on the "Analysis and Forecast of Social Development," Chinese Academy of Social Sciences, "China's social construction in a new stage of growth – analysis and forecast on social situation in China, 2010 – 2011 (in Chinese)," p. 13.

28. For the text of the Sao Paulo Proclamation released on 23 November 2008, see http://www.kommunisten.ch/index.php?article_id=543.

29. For the text of the contribution of D. Koutsoumpas, member of the Political Bureau of the Control Committee of the Communist Party of Greece (KKE), at the Tenth International Meeting of Communist and Workers Parties in Sao Paulo in November 2008, see http://inter.kke.gr/News/2008news/2008-kkecontribution/view?sear.

30. For a Chinese translation of an article by the Secretary-General of the Portuguese Communist Party, Jeronimo de Sousa, "An Analysis by the Portuguese Communist Party on the current international crisis of capitalism and its response measures" released on October 6, 2008, see http://www.cctb.net/lldt/zdyj/20090305_3803.htm.

31. Liu Zhiming, "Reflections on the financial crisis by western left-wing scholars and communists (in Chinese)," in Li Shenming and Zhang Yuyan (eds.), *Yellow Book of International Politics – Annual Report on International Politics and Security (2011)* (Beijing: Social Sciences Academic Press (China), 2011), 302–306; see also He Bingmeng, "New development in contemporary capitalism: the transition from state monopoly to international financial capital monopoly (in Chinese)," *Hongqi Wengao* 3 (2010): 9–13.

32. See, for example, "Foreword (in Chinese)" by the editors, in Ru Xin, Lu Xueyi, and Li Peilin (eds.), *Blue Book of China's Society – Society of China Analysis and Forecast (2011)*, p. 1.

33. Research Group on the "Analysis and Forecast of Social Development," Chinese Academy of Social Sciences, "China's social construction in a new stage of growth – analysis and forecast on social situation in China, 2010–2011 (in Chinese)," p. 4.

34. In the 2011 budget, expenditure on public security amounted to 624.4 billion *yuan*, while defence expenditure amounted to 601.1 billion *yuan*. See Chris Buckley, "China's Internal Security Spending Jumps Past Army Budget", *Reuters* (Beijing), March 5, 2011, http://uk.reuters.com/article/2011/03.05/uk-china-unrest-iduktre7240b72011030.

35. Shi Dongxu, "Quick development of social democracy (in Chinese)," in Liu Jie (ed.), *The Process of China's Political Development 2011*, pp. 253–255.

36. Wang Hongru, "Breakthrough development will take place in the reform of income distribution (in Chinese)," *Zhongguo Jingji Zhoukan* 1 (2011): p. 21.

11

China's Financial Development under Hu-Wen's Leadership: The Unfinished Revolution

Baozhi QU
Yang LI

Introduction

The on-going financial crisis that began in 2008 has resulted in a tremendous downturn in the financial industry and the world economy. China's financial industry, in stark contrast, has achieved remarkable progress since the 1990s and appears to have been virtually unharmed by the crisis. Further, its global influence has even increased. For instance, the People's Bank of China (PBC), the main regulator of the country's financial system, has been appointed to membership of the committee engaged in revision of the well-known Basel framework for banking regulation. Chinese financial institutions have undergone significant expansion since the financial crisis began, with the country's major commercial banks now among the largest in the world in terms of market capitalization. For instance, the China Construction Bank (CCB) completed its acquisition of AIG Finance (Hong Kong) Limited (AIGF) in November 2009, acquiring a 100% stake in the company for US$70 million (approximately RMB 478 million). The Industrial and Commercial Bank of China (ICBC) has proposed the acquisition of Thailand's ACL Bank. On 15 July 2010, the Agricultural Bank of China (ABC) made its stock market debut (Shanghai first, and Hong Kong on the following day). Raising US$19.3 billion with an option to issue an additional US$2.7 billion in the near future, ABC set the world record for the largest initial public offering (IPO).

China's financial system has undergone significant changes since the 1990s, particularly in the complex period of Hu Jintao's leadership over the past eight years. However, this revolution has not been completed and the successors of Hu-Wen will still face significant challenges in this area. This article analyses China's financial development during this crucial period and considers the prospects for the future. We first provide a brief review of China's financial development in the 1980s and 1990s. We then examine the contemporary development of the country's financial markets under the leadership of Hu Jintao in the first decade of the 2000s, with a focus on the banking sector, equity market, and bond market. The final section of the article discusses the future prospects for China's financial development and the likely agenda items under the next generation of leadership.

A Brief History
of China's Financial Reform

Prior to the initiation of economic reform in 1978, China had a centrally planned economy, with the financial sector fully controlled by the central government. The system featured the state monopoly of the banking sector (a mono-banking system), absolute state control of interest and exchange rates, and the direct allocation of financial resources by the central planning authority. When the country began its transition from a planned to a market economy in 1978, the development of an effective, modern, and market-oriented financial system became an urgent need. The financial reform that followed can be divided into three stages, each of which had different goals. Figure 1 outlines the three stages and summarizes the main changes that took place in each.

The first stage (1978–1992) of financial reform was aimed at establishing a market-oriented financial system by abolishing the mono-banking system and establishing a variety of new financial institutions. The PBC, which had once assumed the functions of both central bank and commercial bank, was transformed into a purely central bank. The CCB, ABC, and Bank of China (BOC) were separated from the PBC and the Ministry of Finance in 1979 and assumed commercial banking functions. The ICBC was established in

1984 to take over the PBC's deposit-taking and lending functions. Other types of financial institutions soon emerged, and the security market was established in 1990.

Figure 1: Three Stages of China's Financial Reform

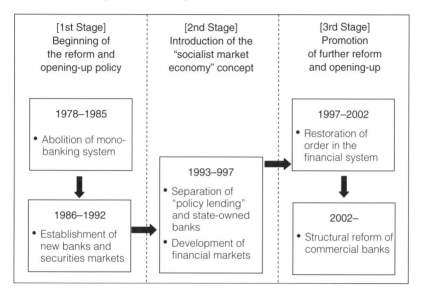

In the second stage (1993–1997) of reform, China focused on the commercialization and liberalization of the financial sector. The emphasis of banking sector reform in this period was on relieving the four aforementioned major state-owned commercial banks (the Big Four) of their policy-lending business (mainly to loss-making state-owned enterprises (SOEs)) and transferring it to three newly established policy banks. In addition, modern corporate governance and a risk management system were introduced into the Big Four, and the interest rate system and exchange rate policy were partially liberalized.

In the third stage (1998 to present), China focused on enhancing the risk management and capital adequacy of its financial institutions following the experiences learned from the 1997/98 Asian financial crisis. The so-called "One Central Bank, Three Supervisory Commissions" regulatory framework was formally established in 2003, and China subsequently diversified its financial markets and opened them up to foreign institutions.

Financial Development under the Hu-Wen Administration: An Overview

Financial Reform in the Context of the Broad Economic Development Strategy

The economic development strategy under the Hu-Wen leadership has a change- and risk-averse nature. Unlike the Jiang Zemin administration, which favoured the development of the eastern area and promoted an export-oriented economic structure, the Hu-Wen administration emphasized reducing the surging economic disparities between different regions and sectors and optimizing policies closely related to people's lives (such as easing the burdens on the farmers). While significant economic reforms took place in almost all sectors of the economy, the government followed a gradualism approach that had been implemented by previous leaderships. Drastic reforms that may cause significant structural changes and social disturbances were avoided. For instance, little was done in the field of political reform under the Hu-Wen leadership.

The same change-and-risk-averse strategy was also applied to financial reform under the Hu-Wen administration. Needless to say, significant progress had been made at this stage. The greatest achievement of the Hu-Wen leadership is probably the overhaul of China's banking sector. Burdened by the huge amount of non-performing loans and poor capital base, the Chinese banking system was in a near-crisis situation in the 1990s. A great reversal has taken place since then. By now the major Chinese banks are much more financially healthy and they are among the largest and most profitable banks in the world since the global financial crisis. In addition, China's stock market and bond market have also experienced significant advancement under the Hu-Wen leadership. Finally, the regulatory framework of the financial sector has been greatly strengthened. These reforms took place gradually under the Hu-Wen leadership and they will have a far-reaching impact on the future perspective of China's financial development.

However, the gradual approach also means that some of the most difficult and challenging reforms are left incomplete. The influence of various levels of government remains very strong in the operation of the banking sector as well as in the financial markets, which makes it difficult for the financial institutions to operate purely on business principles. Furthermore, the most important price signals in a financial system, the exchange rate and interest rates, are still not determined by market forces, which distorts the resource allocation in the entire financial system. Successors of the Hu-Wen administration need to face these serious challenges in the years to come.

China's Entry into the WTO and Financial Opening

China's financial development under Hu-Wen's leadership has been heavily influenced by international pressures. This can be seen best from the significant impact of China's accession to the World Trade Organization (WTO) in 2001 on its financial reform. China's financial system (especially the banking sector) had been fragile since the 1990s. Therefore the financial sectors, including banking, insurance, and securities, were the most disputed fields in the negotiation of China's accession to the WTO. China committed to open its financial markets significantly upon entry into the WTO: (1) Regarding foreign exchange business, foreign financial institutions would be permitted to provide services in China without any geographic or client restrictions; (2) Regarding RMB business, foreign banks would be allowed to do RMB business in twenty cities stage by stage over four years after accession. Five years after accession, all geographic restrictions would be removed; (3) Regarding business licences, the financial regulatory authorities would grant business licences solely on the basis of the prudential principle. In general, China's financial sector would be open to foreign competition to a great extent and foreign financial institutions would be allowed to deal with a wide range of business instantly upon accession.

China's entry into the WTO and the resulting higher degree of financial opening to the world introduced great pressure on the reformers under the Hu-Wen leadership. How to reduce financial risks and enhance the competitiveness of Chinese banks in both domestic and foreign markets became an immediate matter of urgency. This led to a series of fundamental reforms in China's financial sector in the following several years after its WTO entry, including the drastic reform of the state-owned commercial banks, aggressive development of non-state financial institutions, transformation of the domestic stock and bond markets and strengthening of the regulatory system.

Landscape of the Financial Sector: The Status Quo

Entering the twenty-first century, China now has a diversified financial system consisting of the banking sector, equity market, bond market, insurance industry, and other financial institutions, as shown in Table 1.

Table 1: Two Snapshots of China's Financial System

1978	2008
PBC	Financial authorities
(BOC, PICC)	• 1 CB (including the SAFE)
	• 3 Regulators
	Financial institutions
	• 8,734 Banking institutions
	• 148 Non-bank financial institutions
	• 264 Insurance institutions
	• 133 Securities firms
	• 184 Futures brokerage firms
	Organized marketplaces
	• 2 stock exchanges
	• 3 futures exchanges

PICC – The People's Insurance Company (Group) of China; CB – central bank; SAFE – the State Administration of Foreign Exchange.
Source: Yibin Mu, *China's Financial Reform and Opening-up over the Past Three Decades*, World Bank working paper series (2008).

Commercial financial institutions are playing an increasingly important role in the process of China's financial deepening. Since Hu Jintao assumed leadership in 2002, the country has witnessed remarkable progress in the reform of its banking sector, and the regulatory framework has also undergone significant changes to accommodate the development of financial markets and institutions. Generally speaking, the key feature of China's financial system is that it is highly bank-dominated. Figure 2 illustrates the structure of China's financial assets in 2008 in comparison with that of a number of other countries. It can be seen that bank deposits accounted for 58% of overall financial assets in China, which is well above the average level for emerging markets and the highest among all countries on the list. For instance, the corresponding figures for the U.S. and India are 23% and 44%, respectively.

Figure 2: Structure of Financial Assets by Region ($ trillion, %, 2008)

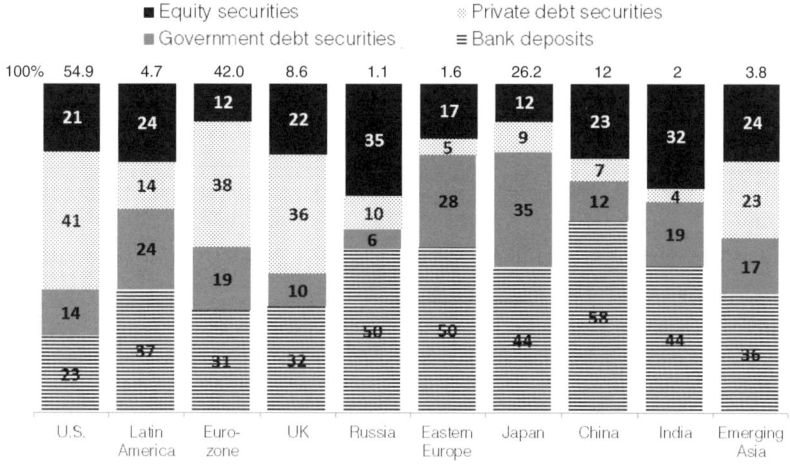

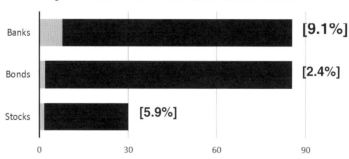

Source: McKinsey Global Institute, "Global Capital Markets: Entering a New Era." September 2009.

Figure 3: China's Share of the Global Financial Market

Notes: Bank assets (2007), debt securities outstanding (2008), stock market capitalization (2008), China and global total, US$ trillion and China % of total.
Source: Deutsche Bank Research, "China's Financial Markets – A Future Global Force?" 16 March 2009.

Relative to the banking sector, China's share of the global bond and stock markets remains quite low, accounting for 2.4% and 5.9%, respectively, in 2008, as shown in Figure 3. If we use the world market as a benchmark, then China's equity and bond markets should assume a more important role in allocating financial resources in the economy. Finding a way to promote the development of these markets is an important task to be faced by the next generation of leadership in China.

The Regulatory Framework

A country's financial regulatory framework is the foundation of its financial system. The PBC was the main regulator of China's financial sector before 1998. Following the 1997/98 Asian financial crisis, the country realized that financial liberalization should proceed gradually and that effective regulation and supervision were crucial. Hence, a new supervision framework that would segregate regulatory responsibilities was proposed. The aim was to ensure the soundness of the financial system so as to avoid a similar financial crisis in China. Accordingly, in 1999, the China Securities Regulatory Commission (CSRC) and the China Insurance Regulatory Commission (CIRC) were established to supervise the capital market and insurance industry, respectively. The PBC's role shifted to monetary policymaking and supervision of the banking sector. The China Banking Regulatory Commission (CBRC) was set up in April 2003 to supervise the banking industry, thus heralding the formal establishment of the supervisory system known as "One Central Bank, Three Supervisory Commissions".

Within this regulatory framework, the PBC, CBRC, CSRC, and CIRC are at the same administrative level, but specialize in different areas. The PBC, for example, primarily specializes in monetary policymaking, such as setting the interest rate and required reserve ratio, managing the foreign exchange and gold reserves, and regulating the inter-bank foreign exchange market and the gold market. The CBRC specializes in formulating the supervisory and regulatory rules governing the country's banking institutions; authorizing the establishment, termination, and business scope of these institutions, as well as approving any changes therein; conducting tests on the institutions; and publishing statistics on and solutions for them. The CSRC's area of specialization is the formulation of rules and regulations concerning the supervision of the securities market, supervising the offering, listing, custody, clearing, and settling of securities, investigating violations of relevant laws and regulations, and disclosing industry information. Finally, the CIRC's role is to formulate guidelines and policies for developing the insurance business, examine and approve the establishment of insurance companies, investigate and penalize unfair competition and illegal conduct among these institutions, and collect information and statistics on the insurance industry.

Supervised by this highly segregated regulatory system, China's financial institutions were strictly guided by the principle of the segregation of financial operations until 2008. The country's banks could not engage in trust, insurance, or securities business, and nor could they invest in trust or investment companies. Similarly, securities and insurance institutions could not be involved in banking or the trust business.[1] Since 2008, however, financial institutions in China have been consolidated across different lines of financial operation. For instance, mergers and acquisitions between insurance companies and banks are now allowed. The current segregated financial regulatory system thus requires reformation to accommodate these new developments.

The Banking Sector

The banking sector is the backbone of China's financial industry. The country now has a large number of banking institutions that provide diversified banking services in both urban and rural areas. These institutions are owned by the state or private investors, including foreign investors. Figure 4 depicts the structure of China's banking industry.

As of the end of 2008, the total assets of the Chinese banking sector amounted to RMB 62.4 trillion. Of these assets, 71.8% were held by the Big Four, shareholding banks, and city commercial banks (CCBs), whereas the shares held by rural cooperative financial institutions (including rural commercial banks, rural cooperative banks, and rural credit cooperatives), policy banks, the postal savings bank, foreign financial institutions, municipal credit unions, and other types of financial institutions were just 11.5%, 9.1%, 3.6%, 2.16%, 0.13%, and 1.9%, respectively.

Figure 4: China's Banking Sector

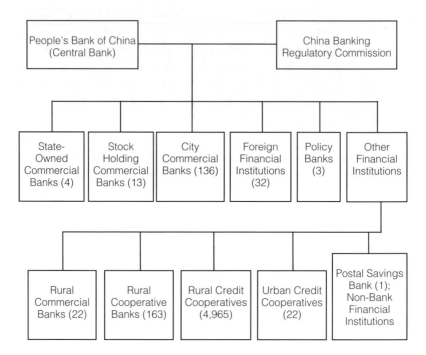

Source: People's Bank of China.

State-owned Commercial Banks

The Big Four (ABC, BOC, CCB and ICBC) were initially specialized banks, but were transformed into commercial banks between 1994 and 1997. Although they accounted for the majority of lending in the market, their financial performance was quite poor in the 1990s. As illustrated by Table 2, the Big Four were much less profitable than their counterparts in the developed market economies. For example, Citibank had a return on assets (ROA) ratio of 2.18% in 1996, compared with 0.3% of the Big Four in the same year. These banks were also heavily burdened by a large number of non-performing loans (NPLs) as a result of policy loans made to loss-making SOEs in previous years. Overall bank capital in China was only 3.1% of assets in 1996, which is much less than the capital adequacy requirement of 8% specified by the Basel Agreement at the time.

Table 2: Performance of China's Big Four in the 1990s

Year	RMB millions	Return on assets (%)
1985	13,103	1.4
1987	20,416	1.4
1989	25,950	1.1
1991	30,699	0.9
1993	23,354	0.4
1995	25,558	0.3
1996	26,900	0.3

Source: Nicholas Lardy, *China's Unfinished Economic Revolution*, Brookings Institution Press (1998), Table 3–8, p. 100.

Removal of NPLs

With the aim of cleaning up the balance sheets of the Big Four, most of the NPLs that fell into the "loss" and "doubtful" categories were transferred into state-owned Asset Management Companies (AMCs) including Changcheng (corresponding to the ABC), Huarong (corresponding to the ICBC), Dongfang (corresponding to the BOC), and Xinda (corresponding to the CCB). These AMCs were financed by the PBC and the Ministry of Finance, which means that the NPLs were actually purchased by the central government. At the end of 2002, there were RMB 814 billion worth of "doubtful" NPLs, with RMB 778 billion transferred to the AMCs. It is estimated that the BOC, CCB, and Bank of Communications (BOCOM) and the ICBC had RMB 633 billion worth of "loss" NPLs at the end of 2002 and 2004, respectively, with RMB 456 billion worth transferred to the AMCs. The initial objective of setting up the four AMCs was to remove RMB 1400 billion in NPLs from the Big Four.[2] By 2004, however, they had actually absorbed about RMB 2000 billion worth. In addition, only a relatively small number of NPLs were sold on the open market by the Big Four, with some of the buyers being foreign institutional investors. For example, CCB sold about 500 million in NPLs to Morgan Stanley and Deutsche Bank in 2004.

Capital Injection

In 2003, the Chinese government implemented a special scheme to inject capital into the state-owned banking sector. The Central Huijin

Investment Company (Huijin) was established as the government's capital injection vehicle, funded by the country's foreign exchange reserves managed by the State Administration of Foreign Exchange (SAFE). Huijin injected a total of RMB 499.6 billion (approximately US$60.4 billion) into the Big Four, with RMB 372.2 billion injected into the BOC and CCB in December 2003, RMB 3 billion into the BOCOM in June 2004, and RMB 124.05 billion into the ICBC in April 2005. Combined with the capital injection before 2003, this amounted to a total injection of RMB 785 billion (or US$95 billion), which is equivalent to 10% of the central government's revenue from 1998 to 2005. The capital injection into the last major state-owned bank in the Big Four, the ABC, is still in progress, and the amount is expected to be huge.

Foreign Strategic Investors

To improve the efficiency level of China's banking sector, the CBRC issued a document in December 2003 allowing foreign equity investment in Chinese financial institutions, one of the most drastic policy changes implemented since the country opened up its financial sector. According to this regulation, the combined shares held by foreign investors in any Chinese bank must be less than 25%, with an individual foreign entity permitted to own only less than 20%. The objective of this policy change was to allow foreign strategic investors to bring additional long-term capital into Chinese banks, transfer new management systems and techniques, and improve these banks' corporate governance and risk management systems. The policy has been welcomed by the capital market, and most of the major state-owned banks now have foreign strategic investors among their large shareholders.

Public Listing

After the removal of the NPLs and massive capital injection into the major state-owned commercial banks, these banks were transformed into public companies that are listed on the domestic stock exchanges or the Hong Kong Stock Exchange (HKSE). In addition to obtaining new capital, going public also helped to solve various other problems resulting from China's banking reform. After listing on the equity market, for example, banks have to become more transparent, and their operations are disciplined by the capital market to a greater extent. In addition, their ownership structure becomes more diversified, meaning that their management is more closely monitored, even though the controlling stake is still in the hands of the state. Last but not least, becoming listed companies means that banks have to follow the rules of the capital market and maximize profits for all of their shareholders, which may help to reduce government intervention.

From June 2005 to May 2007, the BOCOM, CCB, BOC, and ICBC all underwent successful initial public offerings (IPOs) and were listed on different stock exchanges (Hong Kong and Shanghai). The first two IPOs (BOCOM and CCB) were carried out on the HKSE, and the second two (BOC and ICBC) on both the HKSE and the Shanghai Stock Exchange (SHSE). In May 2007, the BOCOM was also listed on the SHSE.

Although the world banking industry was significantly weakened by the global financial crisis that began in 2008, the major Chinese banks have continued to perform relatively well. In terms of market capitalization, three of the Big Four, namely, the ICBC, CCB, and BOC, are now ranked among the top five banks in the world, as shown in Table 3.

Table 3: Top 10 Banks in the World (market cap., US$ billion, Feb. 2008)

Rank	Bank Name	Market Capital- ization	Rank	Bank Name	Market Capital- ization
1	ICBC (China)	277.51	6	JPMorgan Chase (U.S.)	159.62
2	Bank of America (U.S.)	195.93	7	Citigroup (U.S.)	140.70
3	HSBC Holdings (U.K.)	176.79	8	Wells Fargo (U.S.)	112.37
4	CCB (China)	165.23	9	Banco Santander (Euro zone)	109.86
5	Bank of China (China)	165.09	10	Mitsubishi UFJ Financial (Japan)	105.41

Source: *The Banker Magazine*, 2009.

Current Situation

The reform of China's large commercial banks, especially during the period of Hu Jintao's leadership, has proved to be a great success. The major commercial banks have been significantly strengthened, and have experienced rapid expansion over the past several years, even in the midst of the global financial crisis. As can be seen from Table 4, China's banking sector has grown steadily since 2003, in terms of both assets and deposits. For example, the total assets of banking institutions increased from RMB 27,658.38 billion in 2003 to RMB 62,387.63 billion in 2008, a compounded annual growth rate of 17.67%.

Table 4: Total Deposits and Loans of China's Banking Institutions (2003–2008)
(Unit: RMB 100 Million)

Item/Year	2003	2004	2005	2006	2007	2008
Total Deposits	220,363.5	253,188.1	300,208.6	348,015.6	401,051.4	478,444.2
Company deposits	76,784.9	89,438.1	101,750.6	118,851.7	144,814.1	164,385.8
Savings deposits	110,695.3	126,196.2	147,053.7	166,616.2	176,213.3	221,503.5
Trust deposits	2,572.3	2,082.5	3,524.7	3,134.5	3,215.5	3,955.4
Other deposits	30,311.1	35,471.3	47,879.5	59,413.3	76,808.4	88,599.5
Total Loans	169,771.0	188,565.6	206,838.5	238,279.8	277,746.5	320,128.5
Short-term loans	87,397.9	90,808.3	91,157.5	101,698.2	118,898.0	128,609.0
Medium-long-term loans	67,251.7	81,010.1	92,940.5	113,009.8	138,581.0	164,195.0
Trust loans	2,473.0	1,926.1	3,208.1	2,581.1	2,397.0	3,035.0
Bill financing	9,233.6	11,618.4	16,319.2	17,333.4	12,884.4	19,314.2
Other loans	3,414.8	3,202.8	3,213.3	3,657.3	4,986.1	4,975.4

Source: CBRC, *2009 Annual Report.*

In addition, the capital position of the Chinese banking industry has grown stronger since 2003, as witnessed by the increased number of banks meeting the capital adequacy requirement (see Table 5). China employs the common capital adequacy ratio (CAR), a measure of a bank's capital expressed as a percentage of its risk-weighted credit exposure, as its major risk-management tool for banks. The CAR of most Chinese commercial banks meets or exceeds the safety line recommended by the Basel Committee. It is expected that China will further increase the CAR requirement for commercial banks to between 11% and 12% by the end of 2010.

Table 5: CAR Requirement for Commercial Banks in China (2003–2008)

(Unit: Number of Banks, per cent)

Item/Year	2003	2004	2005	2006	2007	2008
Number of banks meeting CAR requirements	8	30	53	100	161	204
Share of total banking assets	0.6	47.5	75.1	77.4	79.0	99.0

Source: CBRC, 2009 Annual Report.

Because of the restrictions imposed by the country's banking regulations, China's major commercial banks engage in substantially fewer high-risk activities than do their counterparts in other countries. The banking sector's performance has also improved remarkably since Hu Jintao took the helm. For instance, the NPLs appearing on the banks' balance sheets have been significantly reduced over time (Table 6), with their share as a percentage of total loans decreasing from 17.9% in 2003 to 2.4% in 2008.

Table 6: NPLs of Major Commercial Banks in China (2003–2008)

(Unit: RMB 100 million, percentage)

Item/Year	2003	2004	2005	2006	2007	2008
Outstanding balance of NPLs	21,044.6	17,175.6	12,196.9	11,703.0	12,009.9	4,865.3
Substandard	3,201.1	3,074.7	2,949.6	2,270.7	1,844.3	2,248.9
Doubtful	11,130.7	8,899.3	4,609.0	4,850.3	4,357.5	2,121.5
Loss	6,712.8	5,201.6	4,638.4	4,581.9	5,801.1	494.9
NPL share of total loans	17.9	13.2	8.9	7.5	6.7	2.4
Substandard	2.7	2.4	2.2	1.5	1.0	1.1
Doubtful	9.4	6.8	3.4	3.1	2.4	1.1
Loss	5.7	4.0	3.4	2.9	3.3	0.2

Source: CBRC, 2009 Annual Report.

Development of City Commercial Banks in China

One of the most important changes in the Chinese banking sector over the past decade or so has been the emergence and rapid development of a new breed of dynamic regional banks – the city commercial banks (CCBs) – which were created only in 1995, following the State Council's issue of "Guidelines on the Establishment of City Cooperative Banks" on 7 September of that year. City cooperative banks (the precursors of CCBs) were established in 35 medium-sized and large cities. The first-generation CCBs were formed through the mergers of 2,194 urban credit cooperatives, rural credit cooperatives, and local financial service institutions. Hence, CCBs were also regarded as joint-stock banks at the time. Similar banks were later established in other cities. By the end of 2008, the number of CCBs had increased to 136, with at least one in almost every major city. The CCBs are unevenly distributed, however, with more branches in the economically developed eastern provinces (such as Guangdong) than in the less-developed western provinces (such as Qinghai). According to banking regulations, a CCB can provide financial services only in its own administrative region. Therefore, the typical CCB is much smaller than a Big Four bank. For instance, the amount of total loans per CCB was RMB 6.22 billion in 2008 (2000 price level), compared with RMB 1,841.05 billion for a Big Four bank and RMB 173.87 billion for a stockholding bank.

CCBs also differ from the Big Four in other ways. For example, they have more diversified shareholders from different classes of society, including individuals, private enterprises, institutional investors, SOEs, and the treasuries of local governments. On average, only about one-quarter of CCB shares are held directly by SOEs. Hence, these banks are less subject to state intervention and may enjoy better corporate governance relative to the Big Four.[3] According to the research carried out by Qu et al., the efficiency of CCBs is generally greater than that of the Big Four, and it improved significantly over the 1999–2008 period (see Table 7).[4] Analysis of the factors that influence that efficiency reveals a high degree of market development and a good institutional environment in a region to be significantly related to greater banking efficiency. More specifically, CCBs operate more efficiently in regions with less government intervention in the market, a high share of non-state business, and better market intermediaries and legal institutions.

Table 7: Profit Efficiency of Different Types of Banks

Year	Profit efficiency model		
	Big Four	Stockholding banks	CCBs
1999	0.3900	0.7981	0.6500
2000	0.6258	0.8988	0.7067
2001	0.7581	0.8997	0.7593
2002	0.7895	0.9002	0.8101
2003	0.8542	0.9085	0.8202
2004	0.8601	0.9180	0.8412
2005	0.8346	0.9149	0.8716
2006	0.8286	0.8976	0.8743
2007	0.8997	0.9156	0.8890
2008	0.9029	0.9010	0.8767
Average	0.7743	0.8952	0.8099

Source: Baozhi Qu, Zhong Xu, Peng Wang and Jianhua Zhang, "Bank Efficiency, Market Development and Institutional Environment: Evidence from City Commercial Banks in China," City University of Hong Kong, working paper (2010).

Foreign Banks

As one of the largest emerging economies in the world, China has attracted a large amount of foreign direct investment (FDI) from other countries and regions, especially from the developed economies. Table 8 shows that total foreign investments in the Chinese banking system have increased sharply since 2003, with the total amount reaching US$78.29 billion by 2008.

In addition to holding a non-controlling stake in Chinese banks, foreign financial institutions have also established local offices or branches in China. In 1979, Japan's Tokyo Bank became the first foreign bank to operate in China. However, because of the tight regulations, the number of foreign institutions in China was quite

Table 8: Entry of Overseas Investors (2003–2008)

(Unit: Number of banks, USD 100 million)

Item/Year	2003 Cumulative amount	2004 Current amount	2005 Current amount	2006 Current amount	2007 Current amount	2008 Current amount	2008 Cumulative amount
Number of commercial banks with foreign capital	5	6	7	6	5	6	31
Total amount of investment	2.6	23.5	116.9	52.2	17.6	115.2	327.8
Total amount of capital raised in listed overseas markets	–	–	113.9	299.0	42.2	0.0	455.1
Total amount	2.6	23.5	230.8	351.2	59.8	115.2	782.9

Source: CBRC, 2009 Annual Report.

limited until 2001 when the country joined the WTO and, accordingly, promised to open its financial market within three years. By 2004, 64 foreign banks from 19 nations and regions had established 192 operations, 88 of which were approved for RMB business. On 11 December 2006, new regulatory rules for foreign-funded banks were announced, thus symbolizing China's fulfilment of its WTO commitments. In April 2007, HSBC, Standard Chartered, the Bank of East Asia and Citibank became the first foreign banks to be chartered with full banking licences. By the end of 2008, there were 32 foreign financial institutions (including two finance companies) in China. The current rules require that foreign banks must wait three years after establishing a branch in China, and demonstrate profitability for no less than two years, to become eligible for an RMB licence. The requirements for a full banking licence are even more stringent, which means that China's domestic banking market still enjoys significant protection from foreign competition.

According to a recent report from PricewaterhouseCoopers (PWC), foreign banks still have a limited presence in the country's retail banking business, with only six such banks receiving 10% or more of their funds from retail deposits.[5] Foreign banks have a comparative advantage in terms of asset management and other high value-added financial activities, and thus it is more profitable for them to specialize in more lucrative financial services, such as project financing and investment banking. Foreign banks also tend to be located in major cities and to provide banking services to high-value customers.

Major Problems Remaining in China's Banking Sector

The reform of China's banking system in the first decade of the twenty-first century has proved to be successful. The major Chinese commercial banks have expanded rapidly and have significantly improved their performance, thus becoming more competitive in the global financial market. China has also become increasingly influential in international organizations such as the World Bank and the IMF, and is active in establishing international banking standards such as the Basel II Agreement. However, a number of problems remain in the country's banking industry, which may affect its future development. Two of these problems are discussed in the following paragraphs.

Lack of Small and Medium-sized Banking Institutions

One of the Chinese economy's comparative advantages is its large number of small and medium enterprises (SMEs), most of which are privately owned. Since 1978, these firms have been very active and become an integral part of the Chinese economy. They have contributed significantly to the country's GDP and have helped to create a large number of jobs for its vast labour force. During the recent credit crunch, however, most of these firms suffered considerably from the resulting market turbulence. Although the central government has employed various methods to increase the supply of bank loans in the market, total lending remains dominated by state-owned commercial banks that favour the large SOEs over private firms. It has been difficult for SMEs to obtain loans from these banks because of their lack of collateral and private ownership status.

In a developed financial market, small and medium financial institutions are most effective at financing SMEs, as large financial institutions incur higher transaction costs and may not have the information advantage their smaller counterparts enjoy. The establishment of small and medium-sized banking institutions would also make China's banking industry more competitive, and thus more efficient. At present, such institutions are lacking in China, and the influence of those that exist remains insignificant.

Policy Burden and Government Intervention

Although an important goal of China's banking reform was to force the commercial banks to operate on business principles, the lending decisions of these banks are quite often influenced by government policies and subject to state intervention. Since the eruption of the global financial crisis in 2008, the Chinese government has taken aggressive measures to stimulate the economy. To help the government achieve its policy goals, the major commercial banks have implemented a very loose credit policy and flooded the credit market with more than RMB 10 trillion in new loans. Figure 5 illustrates the large number of loans granted by Chinese financial institutions in 2009. To date, there have been no formal reports on the credit risk associated with these loans. When the market is turbulent and risk is high, a commercial bank operating on market principles would usually be more, rather than less, cautious in granting new loans. It is thus clear that China's commercial banks still carry a heavy policy burden and, despite their greater market orientation, have been unable to operate solely on business principles. It is likely that many of these loans are risky, and thus that the NPL ratio of the major banks will rise again in the next several years.

Figure 5: Monthly Loans Granted in China in 2009

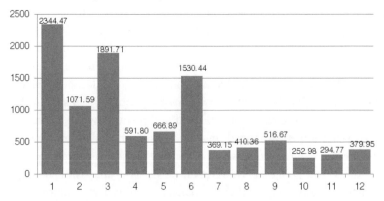

Source: Calculated from a summary of "Sources and Uses of Credit Funds of Financial Institutions (RMB) in 2008 and 2009" from the PBC website.

China's Stock Market

The inception and development of an equity stock market has been one of the most important changes in China's capital market since the 1990s. The two domestic stock exchanges, the SHSE and the Shenzhen Stock Exchange (SZSE), were established in 1990, and have experienced remarkable growth since then (see Figure 6). As of December 2009, the market capitalization of the SHSE and SZSE had reached RMB 16.94 trillion and RMB 8.97 trillion, respectively, and the overall capitalization of the two markets in that year was equivalent to 77.27% of China's GDP. China's stock market is now the second largest in the world by value and the largest among emerging economies.

Figure 6: China's Stock Indices

Source: CEIC database.

Types of Stocks

A basic feature of China's stock market is that it is still, to a large degree, isolated from the world capital market. This feature also partially explains why China was less affected by the 1997/98 Asian and 2008 global financial crises. The country's stock market has two types of stocks, called A and B shares. The A share market is open only to domestic investors, with shares traded in the domestic currency (the RMB), whereas the B share market is open to both domestic and foreign investors, and shares are traded in US dollars.

The market capitalization of the A and B share markets was RMB 27.74 trillion and RMB 632.18 billion, respectively, by April 2010. The B share fraction is thus only 2.23% of overall market capitalization, providing clear indication of the relatively small influence of foreign investment in China. By separating foreign and domestic investors, the Chinese government has, to a large extent, retained control over the market turbulence created by foreign speculators. By the end of 2009, there were 1,718 companies listed on the SHSE and SZSE (Figure 7), of which only 108 issued B shares. In addition to the A and B shares traded on the mainland Chinese exchanges, H shares are traded on the Hong Kong Stock Exchange. These shares are issued by Chinese registered companies that have been approved by the CSRC and the Hong Kong Securities and Futures Commission (SFC) for listing on the HKSE. As of 2009, there were 159 H share companies listed on the HKSE. Although the HKSE is a free market and is open to investors all over the world, it remains difficult for individual investors from the mainland to trade H shares directly due to the country's tight capital account control.

Figure 7: Number of Listed Companies in the SHSE and SZSE (2009)

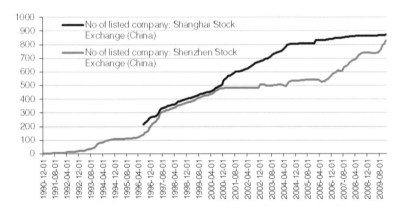

Source: CEIC database.

The majority of the 1,718 listed companies in China's stock market are the result of the corporatization of the SOEs. Such corporatization typically involves the carving out of an operational unit of a large SOE whose net assets are then converted to non-tradable shares at a certain rate. The remaining shares are issued to the public and can be traded. Figure 8 illustrates the typical procedure involved in restructuring a SOE into a shareholding company.

Figure 8: Restructuring of a Typical SOE into a Shareholding Company

Local government as ultimate shareholder			A-shares (Chinese citizens + QFIIs)
State asset management bureau	Parent firm, an SOE or incorporated firm (Former SOE part I)	Individual shareholders	B-shares (foreign individuals and investors)
Shareholding firm with productive assets (Former SOE part II)			H-shares (mainland incorporated & listed abroad)

Notes: QFII – qualified foreign institutional investors.
Source: Waltraut Urban, *The Chinese Stock Market Waking up – Will It Shake the World?* The Vienna Institute for International Economic Studies, 2000.

Development of the Multi-layer System

When the stock market was first created in China, the Main Board was the only market in which qualified Chinese companies could become listed. The Main Board has very stringent listing requirements in terms of company size and performance, however, and only the largest and most mature companies are successful in becoming listed on it. Hence, most SMEs are excluded. It became clear that a multi-layer stock market was needed to ensure that SMEs could obtain financing from the equity market. Accordingly, the SZSE began preparing a market for high-growth enterprises in 2001 and successfully launched the SME Board in 2005.

To further diversify the financing channels available to Chinese firms, especially newly qualified start-ups and high-growth enterprises, the Chinese authorities experimented with a Development Board, which was formally launched on 23 October 2009. According to official guidelines, the Development Board will give priority to firms with "two high" and "six new", namely, those with "high technology, high development" and "new technology, new economy, new energy, new service, new material, and new business model". As of April 2010, there were 70 listed companies on the Development Board, with total market capitalization of RMB 291.47 billion. These firms are mainly new technology and energy companies in a variety of industries.

Regulation and Openness

The CSRC is the main regulator in China responsible for supervising the equity market. The Securities Law published in 1999 was the first national law to regulate the issuance and trading of securities. In the same year, China also published the Company Law, which regulates the companies listed on the stock exchanges. The Law was amended by the National People's Congress (NPC) in 2003 in response to the extensive reforms in the financial sector and the development of the capital markets. These revisions were announced in 2005 and enacted in 2006.[6]

Under current regulations, capital accounts in China are not generally convertible. In other words, investors cannot freely convert foreign currencies to RMB (or vice versa) unless the transaction is trade-related or categorized as FDI. International investors are thus restricted from investing in Chinese A shares and domestic investors from access to international capital markets. As the Chinese economy becomes increasingly integrated into the world economy, there is a pressing need for a greater flow of international capital. To promote the opening up of the domestic capital market, the Qualified Foreign Institutional Investor (QFII) scheme was introduced in December 2002 to allow licensed foreign institutional investors to trade A shares on the secondary market. As of March 2010, 88 foreign financial institutions had obtained QFII certification, and the approved quota reached USD 17.07 billion (see Figure 9).

Similarly, to provide domestic investors with opportunities to invest in foreign equity markets, the Qualified Domestic Institutional Investor (QDII) scheme was launched in 2004, thus allowing qualified domestic investors to invest directly in foreign stock markets, subject to a maximum quantity set by the regulator. As of March 2010, 76 domestic institutional investors had got licences and the approved investment quota reached USD 64.26 billion (see Figure 9). The Hong Kong market dominated the allocation of the QDII investment portfolio, accounting for a 71.77% share, followed by the U.S., Australia, and other foreign markets.[7]

Figure 9:
Approved Quota under QFII & QDII Programmes (USD Billion, 2003–2009)

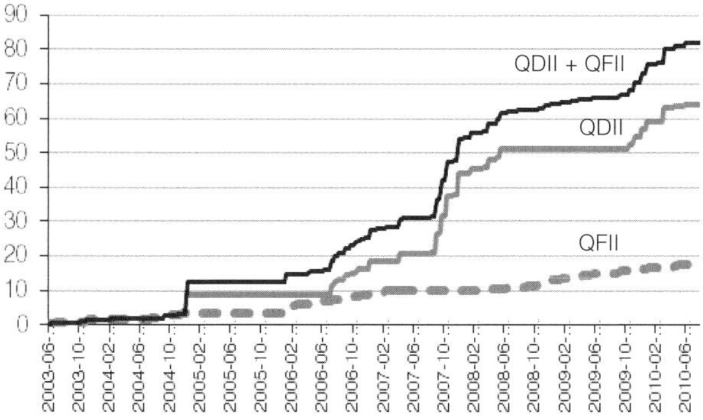

Source: Windnet, 2010.

Problems Remaining in China's Equity Market

Market Structure

The SME Board in the SZSE is still in the early stages of development, and its market capitalization is much smaller than that of the Main Board. In fact, by April 2010, only 390 companies with a market capitalization of RMB 2.15 trillion, were listed on the SME Board, about 7.77% of overall A share market capitalization. In other words, only a small fraction of the country's large number of SMEs are able to actually utilize the market for their funding needs, and the overall amount of capital available remains limited. Further, most of the firms listed on the Development Board have very high price-to-earnings (P/E) ratios due to the limited listing opportunities and optimistic expectations of their future growth. As of April 2010, the overall P/E ratio in the Development Board was 78.06, according to the Wind databases. The market features heavy speculative trading, and its volatility (a measure of market risk) is quite high compared to mature financial markets.

The inadequate development of the SME and Development Boards not only limits the direct equity financing available to SMEs and high-growth enterprises, but it also constrains the development of the venture capital and private equity industry in China due to the lack of a viable exit strategy for investors. In addition, China lacks a well-regulated over-the-counter (OTC) market, on which unlisted stocks can be traded directly between two parties. Such a market is crucial to the equity financing of the large number of non-listed corporations in mature financial markets, but still requires development in China.

Diversification of Financial Instruments

Futures and other derivative instruments are useful tools for the management of financial risks by investors and financial institutions, but they remain lacking in Chinese financial markets, although the CSRC launched its first stock index futures contract in April 2010. The regulator has been very cautious in developing a derivative market, especially a market for financial derivatives. The key concern is that these derivative instruments, if not properly used and managed, could add to, rather than reduce, the financial risks, as illustrated by the near collapse of the credit derivatives market and its negative impact on the overall financial market during the global financial crisis that began in 2008. It is expected, however, that the diversification of financial instruments in China will increase gradually as the equity market matures and becomes more sophisticated.

Non-tradable Shares

As noted previously, the shares of listed companies on China's stock exchanges can be categorized into "tradable" and "non-tradable". Non-tradable shares entitle their holder (usually the state) to the same rights that tradable shares confer upon their owners except that they cannot be traded publicly on the stock exchange. These shares quite often represent the controlling stake in listed companies, which effectively ensures state control over these firms and makes any mergers or acquisitions in the secondary market extremely difficult. As a result, there have been very few examples of such activity in the Chinese stock market, which may be an indicator of the low degree of efficiency in the capital market. The limited supply of tradable shares also increases the price of shares, reduces market liquidity, and adds to price volatility in the market.

China introduced a reform on non-tradable shares in May 2005 when the CSRC issued a "Notice on the Pilot Reform of Non-tradable Shares of Listed Corporations" (the Notice). This Notice states that "the non-tradable [share] reform is [designed] to optimize the governance structure of the company, solidify the mutual interest ground of all shareholders, [encourage] . . . listed companies to use various innovative financial tools to improve . . . capital operation efficiency, optimize [their] capital structure, and bring in better investment returns". This reform is recognized as one of the most important experiments in structural reform in the Chinese stock market, and it is widely considered to have been a success. However, to date, non-tradable shares still account for a large percentage of overall market capitalization. As of April 2010, the overall market capitalization of A shares in the two domestic stock exchanges was RMB 27.69 trillion, whereas that of non-tradable shares amounted to about 12.711 trillion, accounting for 45.88% of the market.[8] The non-tradable share reform is on-going, and whether its goals can be fully achieved remains to be seen.

Role of the Government

As previously noted, the majority of listed firms in China are the result of SOE corporatization. As in other countries in which the government retains a controlling stake in listed (and partially privatized) SOEs, the Chinese central and local governments remain, either directly or indirectly, the controlling shareholders of these firms.[9] According to Chen et al. (2006), in a typical listed SOE, 30% of the shares are owned by the government or government-related agencies, and another 30% are held by legal entities, which are usually controlled by the state. The remaining 40% are owned by individuals (including management and employees), private institutions, and foreign investors. Such an ownership structure implies that the minority shareholders have little influence over the management and governance of listed companies. For example, the board of directors is usually chosen by the government, and therefore these directors are responsible to the government rather than to the shareholders overall. Consequently, the government may play a dual role in China – both the supervisor of the market and the controlling shareholder in listed companies – which may result in serious governance issues such as conflicts of interest.

Bond Market

Overview of the Bond Market

The bond market in China experienced a slow rate of growth in the 1990s and remained an insignificant component of the country's financial system until 2005. In the early 1990s, SOEs issued a large number of corporate bonds that later ended up in default and resulted in large losses to the state-owned banks that were their major holders. The State Economic Planning Commission subsequently decided to close down the corporate bond market, which thus came to a standstill until 2004 when securities companies were approved to issue public bonds and short-term financing bills. Government bond and outright repo transactions were introduced at the same time.

Figure 10: China's Bond Market (RMB 100 million; face value)

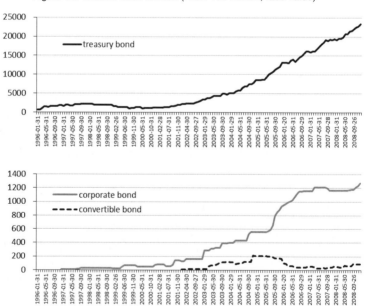

Source: CEIC database.

In terms of market capitalization, China's bond market is about the same size as its stock market. It is dominated by treasury bonds, although commercial bonds have shown significant growth in recent years (see Figure 10).

Market Structure of the Bond Market

In the primary market, the majority of bonds are first offered to investors through syndicated bond issues. Government bonds are mostly underwritten by the Big Four, whereas other financial institutions, such as the CCBs and the securities companies, form syndicates to underwrite corporate and commercial bonds. The secondary market, in contrast, consists of three segments: the inter-bank market, the exchange market, and the OTC market, as shown in Figure 11.

The inter-bank market is where counterparties negotiate with each other to arrive at a final agreement under PBC regulation. The three instruments that are by far the most actively traded products in the Chinese bond market, namely, central bank bills, corporate commercial paper (CP), and mid-term notes (MTNs), are solely traded in the interbank market. This market thus dominates the bond market. According to a Standard & Poor's report (2009), the total amount of the bonds outstanding in this market was RMB 13,900 billion at the end of 2008, which was about 97% of total bond market capitalization in that year.[10] The exchange market is a standardized market, and is relatively small, whereas the commercial OTC market is a good supplement to the other two, as it allows the participation of individual investors. Table 9 presents the trading volume of the different bond markets as of 2008.

The inter-bank market is where counterparties negotiate with each other to arrive at a final agreement under PBC regulation. The three instruments that are by far the most actively traded products in the Chinese bond market, namely, central bank bills, corporate commercial paper (CP), and mid-term notes (MTNs), are solely traded in the interbank market. This market thus dominates the bond market. According to a Standard & Poor's report (2009), the total amount of the bonds outstanding in this market was RMB 13,900 billion at the end of 2008, which was about 97% of total bond market capitalization in that year.[11] The exchange market is a standardized market, and is relatively small, whereas the commercial OTC market is a good supplement to the other two, as it allows the participation of individual investors. Table 9 presents the trading volume of the different bond markets as of 2008.

Figure 11: Structure of China's Bond Market

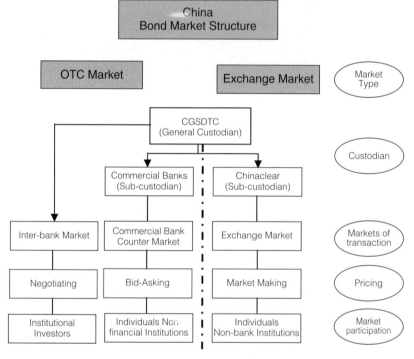

Notes: CGSDTC – Government Securities Depository Trust Clearing Ltd. Source: www.chinabond.com.cn.

Table 9: Trading Volume in China's Bond Market (2008)

Market	Spot Trading	Repo Trading	Total
Shanghai Stock Exchange	205.87	2,430.68	2,636.55
Shenzhen Stock Exchange	21.88	0.00	21.88
Interbank Market	37,090.52	57,526.25	94,616.78
Total	37,318.28	59,956.93	97,275.21

Notes: A repo (repurchase agreement) allows a borrower to use a financial security as collateral for a cash loan at a fixed rate of interest. Source: Wind database.

Table 10: China's Bond Issuance Volume in 2008 and 2009

	2009		2008	
	No.	Volume	No.	Volume
Sum	935	86,474.71	643	10,734.11
Government Bonds	117	16,213.58	29	7,246.39
Treasury Bonds	59	12,718.10	26	6,665.00
Savings Bonds (Evidence)	0	0.00	0	0.00
Savings Bonds (Electronic)	8	1,495.48	3	581.39
Local Government Bonds	50	2,000.00	0	0.00
Central Bank Bonds	81	39,740.00	122	42,960.00
Financial Bonds	105	14,759.10	85	11,783.30
Policy Bank Bonds	54	11,678.10	58	10,809.30
China Development Bank	25	6,700.00	24	6,200.00
Export-Import Bank of China	12	1,963.70	14	1,793.70
Agricultural Development Bank of China	17	3,013.80	20	2,815.60
Commercial Bank Bonds	43	2,846.00	27	974.00
Special Finance Bonds	0	0.00	0	0.00
Non-bank Financial Institution Bonds	8	225.00	0	0.00
Securities Co. Bonds	0	0.00	0	0.00
Securities Co. Cps	0	0.00	0	0.00
Corporate Bonds	192	4,252.33	71	2,366.90
State-owned Corporate Bonds	39	2,029.00	27	1,683.00
Local Corporate Bonds	153	2,223.33	44	683.00
Commercial Papers	263	4,612.05	269	4,338.50
Asset-backed Securities/ Mortgage-backed Securities	0	0.00	26	302.01
Middle Term Notes	172	6,885.00	41	1,737.00
SME Collective Notes	4	12.65	0	0.00
Foreign Bonds	1	10.00	0	0.00
International Institution Bonds	1	10.00	0	0.00
Others	0	0.00	0	0.00

Source: www.chinabond.com.cn (December 2009 Monthly Data).

Instruments

Of the different types of bonds traded in China's bond market, government bonds, central bank bonds, and policy bank bonds comprise the majority of bonds outstanding. As of 2009, these three types of bonds accounted for 18.75%, 45.96%, and 13.50%, respectively, of the gross volume of bonds outstanding, and 78.21% in total (see Table 10). CPs and MTNs are also important instruments. It can be seen from Table 10 that the issuance volume of corporate bonds grew to RMB 4,252 billion in 2009 from RMB 2,366 billion the previous year, an annual growth rate of 79.66%, although their share of the overall bond market remained small (4.92%).

Problems Remaining in the Bond Market

Market Participants and Liquidity

Although the bond market has grown rapidly in size over the past several years, it has had a limited group of participants, and trading in the bond market is far less active than that in the stock market. On the supply side, the government (including the central bank) and certain financial institutions such as the policy banks are the main bond issuers. As for corporate issuers, only the largest companies in China, most of which are owned by the state, have access to the bond market to raise funds. On the demand side, the state-owned financial institutions are the primary buyers. Although bond mutual funds are emerging in China, their number remains much smaller than that of equity mutual funds. Such a structure of bond market participants may lead to a lack of counterparties, and thus result in a low degree of liquidity in the market.

Lack of Market Infrastructure and Institutions

To develop a modern bond market in China, it is important to ensure that credit risk can be properly assessed and that relevant information is sufficiently disclosed to the market. China's accounting standards also need to be brought into line with international best practice to provide accurate and comparable financial information on borrowers.

A mature bond market requires credit rating agencies, which are lacking in China. The country has attempted to foster domestic rating agencies and to allow international rating agencies to set up joint ventures, but such measures have been slow to get off the ground due to the strong protectionist mentality of the past. In 2006, China issued the Three Gorges Bond, which was the first corporate credit bond without a bank guarantee. However, much remains to be done to improve the market infrastructure and institutions before the bond market can become a fully functioning marketplace.

Lack of Risk Management Instruments

An integral part of mature bond markets are derivative instruments that can be used to manage the credit, market, and interest rate risks of a bond portfolio, instruments that are still very limited in the Chinese bond market. When treasury futures were first traded in 1995, massive speculative trading in the market led to a government ban on such instruments, and moves to develop other fixed income derivatives has been slow to take off since then. At present, the only fixed income derivative contracts allowed in China are bond forwards, which are traded solely in the inter-bank market. Swap contracts are still being experimented with at the central bank level. The further development of fixed-income derivatives should be encouraged, although proper regulatory measures need to be developed at the same time.

Lack of Interest Rate Flexibility

Another major constraint on the development of the bond market in China is the heavy control of interest rates by the government. The authorities have been very conservative in dealing with the liberalization of interest rates, which may limit the price-discovery function of the financial market (the uninformative bond yield curve) and cause inefficiency in the bond market.

The regulator currently allows only the safest borrowers to tap the bond market, and defaults are extremely rare. However, when the credit risk of borrowers in the bond market is not sufficiently differentiated and the borrowing cost is heavily regulated, investors have only limited choices and their degree of interest in investing in this market is low, thus possibility leading to a low degree of market liquidity and slow market growth.

Prospects for China's Financial Development in the Next Decade

China has achieved tremendous progress in its financial development since 1978, especially since Hu Jintao assumed leadership. The banking system has been completed transformed, and the performance of its financial institutions has improved significantly since the 1990s. Aided by the country's rapid economic growth, the Chinese capital market surpassed Japan to become the world's second-largest stock market by value in 2009. A sizable bond market has also emerged in China and has grown rapidly in recent years.

Despite these great successes, however, China's financial system is still in the early stages of development compared with the developed economies. The prospects for its financial development depend on whether the country can deal successfully with the problems that remain in various financial sectors. The next generation of leadership needs to initiate further market-oriented reforms in the following key areas.

Institutional and Legal System Reform

The development of a modern financial system is crucially dependent on a well-functioning legal system and a market-based institutional infrastructure. For instance, the legal rights of creditors and shareholders need to be clearly defined and well protected by law, with that law properly enforced. Such protection is still weak in China, due to the lack of relevant laws or ineffective law enforcement, which represents a major constraint on the country's further financial development.[12]

Reform of the Regulation and Supervision System

China's current regulatory framework, which consists of "one central bank, three regulatory commissions", is segregated with each organization responsible for the supervision and regulation of one type of financial institution or market. The different regulators are at the same administrative level, which inhibits coordination among them. Such a segregated system may result in either regulatory gaps (e.g., financial transactions and institutions being under-regulated) or excessive regulation, consequently reducing the overall effectiveness of the regulatory framework. At a time when the consolidation of different types of financial institutions is becoming increasingly popular, and increasing numbers of full-service financial institutions are emerging in China, better cooperation among regulators is clearly needed.

It seems that the government has already recognized these problems and begun to deal with them by periodically holding joint conferences attended by the central bank and three regulatory commissions. However, a more fundamental restructuring of the regulatory framework is called for to ensure the better coordination of the regulatory efforts of the separate regulators.

Restructuring of the Financial Markets

China's financial system is currently heavily bank dominated. Previous research has shown that Chinese banks are not very efficient in allocating financial resources, [13] although their efficiency and performance have improved significantly in recent years.[14] In most mature market economies, the stock and bond markets play a more important role in such allocation than they do in China, where they are much smaller and less important than the banking sector.

China may need to take more decisive steps if it wishes to encourage the further development of its capital market. The government should be mainly responsible for maintaining a transparent and fair market environment, with its direct intervention in the market reduced. For a capital market to function well, it is important that there be a large body of financial institutions and investors with a diversified ownership structure that operates on commercial principles and acts as the dominant market force. The structure of the country's available financial instruments also requires diversification if they are to meet the needs of investors with different risk preferences and allow financial risks to be properly managed.

Openness and Internationalization

Integrating China's financial system with the world financial system would not only give China more access to the global capital markets, but it would also help to enhance the efficiency of domestic financial markets. The country's financial development has benefited significantly from greater openness and internationalization over time. For instance, the introduction of foreign strategic investors has proved to be a crucial factor in the success of its banking reform. The partial opening of China's capital market to foreign investors (e.g., through the QFII scheme) and the emergence of foreign financial institutions have helped to introduce international best practice to and increase the competitiveness of China's financial industry. Although a completely open financial market remains unfeasible in China due to the non-convertibility of its capital accounts, the further openness and internationalization of its financial system should be encouraged.

As the Hu-Wen administration prepares to hand power over to fifth-generation leaders like Xi Jinping and Li Keqiang in 2012, what are the likely agenda items for the new leadership in the field of financial development? Will the new leadership be able to meet these challenges successfully? While it is difficult to predict the exact policies of China's next generation of leadership, it seems that more drastic political and structural changes necessary for further reforms may be in the playbook in the Xi-Li administration. Recently at a meeting meant to solicit proposals for the twelfth Five-Year Plan (FYP) of the Chinese Communist Party (CCP), which is supposed to lay the framework for the implementation of economic and social policies for the decade to come, Vice Premier Le Keqiang declared that, "The transformation of the economic growth pattern is a comprehensive and profound change, and it involves new ideas and innovative approaches. We must accelerate reform and opening-up in order to achieve it."[15] If this is the case, it will be a significant departure from the change- and risk-averse nature of the Hu-Wen leadership. In the field of financial development, fundamental reforms in the key areas such as the exchange rate determination mechanism, the marketization of interest rates, and further relaxation of China's capital account control, are likely to be the top agenda items under the Xi-Li leadership.

The future reform in China's financial sector has profound global implications and the period covered by the twelfth FYP (2011–2015) will be especially important for both China and the world because of the relative weakness of the Western financial industries and economies. China is attempting to play a more active role in the re-definition of the international financial architecture. To do this, China must further transform its financial system so that it is more compatible with the world standard. Chinese financial institutions are likely to expand their international operations and become stronger competitors in the world financial markets. China will also be more open to the world and have much more interaction with the world financial markets. Obviously, this may reshape the current international financial architecture in the years to come.

Acknowledgments

We thank Professor Kenneth Chan and Professor Joseph Cheng for their helpful comments on this article. All remaining errors are our own responsibility.

Notes and References

1. E-sheng Cai, "Financial supervision in China: framework, methods and current issues," Bank of International Settlement, policy paper No. 7 (1999).

2. Yifu Lin, Fang Cai, and Yong Cao, *The Chinese Economy. Reform and Development* (McGraw Hill Education (Asia), 2009).

3. Giovanni Ferri, "Are new tigers supplanting old mammoths in China's banking system? Evidence from a sample of city commercial banks," *Journal of Banking and Finance* 33 (2009), pp. 131–140.

4. Baozhi Qu, Zhong Xu, Peng Wang and Jianhua Zhang, "Bank efficiency, market development and institutional environment: evidence from city commercial banks in China," City University of Hong Kong, working paper (2010).

5. PWC report, "Banking and capital market, foreign banks in China," June 2009.

6. China Securities Regulatory Commission, "China capital markets development report" (2008).

7. Shusong Ba, "Estimation and prospect of QDII and QFII in China," Development Research Centre of the State Council (China), working paper (2010).

8. All of the data are taken from the Wind Financial Database and are current as of 21 April 2010.

9. Gongmeng Chen, Michael Firth, Deniel Gao, and Oliver Rui, "Ownership structure, corporate governance, and fraud: evidence from China," *Journal of Corporate Finance* 12 (2006), pp. 424–448.

10. Standard & Poor's, "Chinese bond markets – an introduction," March 2009.

11. *Ibid.*

12. Frank Allen, Jun Qian, and Meijun Qian, "Law, finance, and economic growth in China," *Journal of Financial Economics* 77 (2005), pp. 57–116.

13. Allen, Qian, and Qian, "Law, finance, and economic growth in China."

14. Qu, Xu, Wang, and Zhang, "Bank efficiency, market development and institutional environment: evidence from city commercial banks in China."

15. Xinhua News Agency, 23 June 2011.

12

Labour Policies under Hu-Wen's Regime: Transformation and Challenges

Chris King-chi CHAN

Introduction

This chapter reviews the development of labour policies in China from 2003 to 2011 under the leadership of President Hu Jintao and Premier Wen Jiabao. In 2002, Hu Jintao put forward the concept of "harmonious society" (*hexie shehui*), which was officially defined in 2004 as "democracy and rule of law, justice and equality, trust and truthfulness, amity and vitality, order and stability, and a harmonious relation with nature". [1] This chapter argues that the idea of "harmonious society" has not been successfully achieved in the field of labour politics. On the contrary, the new socio-economic policies initiated by the party-state during the Hu-wen regime have created conditions and opportunities for the rise of the new labour activism. Among others [2], the radicalization of migrant workers' activism has exerted challenges to the governance of the local state. The governments have responded to the emerging patterns of migrant workers' protests by strengthening labour legislation and enhancing the minimum wage rate significantly. However, the share of wage over Gross Domestic Product (GDP) remains at a low level, and there is no sign that the labour discontent has been alleviated, especially after the economy started to recover from the second half of 2009. Trying to pacify the increasingly intense labour unrest, the central government and many provincial authorities are in the process of making collective bargaining laws. However, the barrier of building up effective workplace trade unions and collective bargaining system rests on the rising influence of the global and national corporations on China's labour policies, and the lack of institutional support towards workplace labour activism due to the ACFTU's integration with the party-state and the local government's client-patron relationship with global capital. This situation will be worsened when the local governments compete with each other to provide favourable policies to the global investors by lowering their labour standards. This dilemma can only be ultimately sorted out by a democratic reform which Hu Jintao and Wen Jiabao have failed to deliver during their regime.

The first part of this chapter highlights the significance of the socio-economic development since 2003 and explains its impact on the changing labour policies in China. It is followed by a historical review of the state, labour and capital relations in three periods: from shortage of labour to global recession (2003 to 2007); during global recession (2008 to 2009); and after the Chinese economic recovery (2010 onwards). Data were collected through the authors' fieldwork in China, systematic media reviews and documentary research. In the conclusion, a number of prospects for labour politics, as well as a general evaluation of the effectiveness of the labour policy in the decade of Hu-Wen's rule will be suggested.

2003 – A New Socio-economic Context?

Chinese labour politics experienced a milestone year in 2003 for many reasons. First, politically, President Hu Jintao and Premier Wen Jiabao took power in this year and began a period of socio-economic reform, especially on the protection of peasants and peasants-workers. At the beginning of 2004 Central Committee and the State Council of the Communist Party of China (CPC) issued a "No. 1 Document", entitled "Opinions on Policies for Facilitating the Increase of Farmers' Income". From then onward, the problems of "*san nong*" (peasant, rural village, and agriculture) were addressed in the party's "No. 1 Documents" for consecutive seven years (from 2003 to 2010).[3] While the stabilization of food production, the increase of farmers' income and the infrastructure in rural villages are three major foci of the policies, the rights and interests of "peasant-workers" were also highlighted as a part of the problems facing peasants. For example, in 2004, the "No. 1 Document" stated that "peasant-workers are an important component of production workers and hence deserved state protection and basic civic rights". It signified that the peasant migrant workers, who are mostly working in the foreign-invested enterprises (FIEs) and the private sector, had replaced the state workers as the key concern of the state's employment and welfare policies.[4] As a matter of fact, the number of rural–urban migrant workers has escalated dramatically while the number of state workers has significantly declined (See Figure 1). From 1990 to 2003, the number of industrial workers employed in state-owned enterprises (SOE) declined from 43.64 million (68.4% of the total industrial workers) to 13.34 million (36.3%). In terms of industrial output, the state-owned or state-controlled sectors dropped from 75% in 1981 to only 28% in 1999 and 38% in 2003.[5]

Figure 1: The Decline in Total Number of SOE Workers as a Percentage of Urban Employment from 1978 to 2005[6]

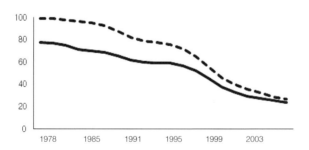

On the other hand, the national census in 2000 showed that the number of rural–urban migrant workers was as many as 120 million and the peasant migrant workers represented 57.5% of the manufacturing workforce.[7] However, the number of rural–urban migrant workers has jumped to approximately 230 million, according to a state council report to the People's Congress in 2010.[8] Most of the boom in manufacturing has taken place in the labour-intensive and export-oriented light industries in the coastal regions, especially the Pearl River Delta (PRD) in southern China and the Yangtze River Delta (YRD) in the east. Therefore, labour exploitation in these sectors had been intensified.[9] In 2004, a study by the Ministry of Labour and Social Security (MOLSS) showed that the salary of migrant workers in the PRD has grown by just 68 *yuan* (US$8.2) over the past twelve years, an increase which is less than that of living expenses; as a result the real wage was in fact declining. The report has pointed out that because of the detrimental working conditions, wildcat strikes and other forms of resistance have erupted rapidly.[10]

Table 1: Foreign Direct Investment in China, 1990–2005[11]

Year	Utilized FDI (US$ billion)	Change on Previous Year (%)
1990	3.5	+3
1991	4.4	+26
1992	11.0	+150
1993	27.5	+150
1994	33.8	+23
1995	37.5	+11
1996	41.4	+9
1997	45.2	+8
1998	45.5	+1
1999	40.4	-11.2
2000	40.8	+0.94
2001	46.9	+14.9
2002	52.7	+12.4
2003	53.5	+1.5
2004	60.6	+13.3
2005	72.41	+19.42

In short, the rising number of migrant workers, their significant contribution to the Chinese economy, and their poor working and living conditions, had forced the Hu-Wen regime to reprioritize the focus of social development from the cities to the rural villages, and the labour policy from urban workers to migrant workers. Under the direction of the "No. 1 Document", some provincial governments started to abolish agricultural taxes or even provided agricultural subsidies to peasants. This policy was extended to the whole country under the central government's campaign of "building new socialist rural villages" in 2006. This new policy initiative attracted some older migrant workers to return to their villages,[12] and thus contributed to a phenomenon of "labour shortage" that will be elaborated later.

Second, economically, after China was admitted into the World Trade Organization (WTO) in November 2001, the growth rate of Foreign Direct Investment (FDI) inflow returned to double digits: 14.9% in 2001, 12.4% in 2002 and 13.3% in 2004, after a slow-down since 1994 (see Table 1). Since 2003 China has surpassed the US to become the country with most FDI inflow in the world.

Export-oriented light manufacturing industries, such as garments and textiles, toys and electronics benefited from a tariff reduction after China joined the WTO and rapid growth of production in the country; thus there have been more job opportunities in these industries. In fact, since its transition to the market economy in 1978, China's economy has always been heavily dependent on its export industry. But the years after 2003 until the outbreak of the global economic recession were a period of particularly rapid growth in the export industry. According to the World Bank, Chinese exports of goods and services as a percentage of GDP jumped from 23% in 2003 to 42% in 2007.[13]

In short, the economic and social landscapes changed significantly after Hu-Wen came to power in 2003. In the following sections, the historical development of the relations of state, labour and capital in three periods (2004 to 2007; 2008 to 2009; 2010 onward) after Hu-Wen took power will be examined.

Labour Shortage and Growing Labour Conflict: 2004–2007

The dramatic changes in China, both urban (rapid economic growth driven by the export-oriented manufacture) and rural (improvement in social economic conditions under the state's new policy direction), gave rise to the phenomenon of "shortage of labour" (*mingong huang*) reported in the media from late 2003, which was in contrast to the "tidal wave of peasant workers" (*mingong chao*) in the early 1990s. The labour shortage spread from Fujian province to the PRD, and then to the YRD and to the country as a whole. The surveys conducted by the Guangdong Provincial MOLSS revealed that enterprises in the province employed 13% more migrant workers in 2004 than 2003,[14] but still the province lacked two million "skilled workers". Another survey suggested that the number of workers who had left the rural villages for jobs increased by 3.8% in 2004.[15] The official source also revealed that there was a shortage of 2.8 million workers in the whole country, with one million in the region of PRD and 300,000 in Shenzhen.[16]

The sudden emergence of labour shortage, as previously elaborated, had political and economic causes; and it helped breed labour activism in China. Labour historians suggest that economic boom can strengthen workers' confidence and lead to proactive strikes.[17] Similarly, labour shortage and increasing job opportunities in China have conferred on workers who have gained greater bargaining power in the labour market the courage to rebel in the form of semi-organized strikes. These have occurred since 2004, especially in the export-oriented industrial areas such as Shenzhen and its surrounding cities.

While statistics on the labour market are well presented by the official reports, the numbers of strikes are not officially documented by the state as striking is not recognized as a legal action.[18] Ethnographic study, however, revealed that there was a significant rise of number of strikes in the PRD since 2004.[19] When I started my fieldwork in 2005, a veteran labour organizer in Guangzhou told us that around 50% of migrant workers she encountered had experiences of strikes.

The sudden intensification of labour conflict since 2004 could also be reflected by other relevant statistics. One of the frequently cited indications in labour studies of China is the number of labour disputes handled by the labour dispute arbitration committee. Table 2 shows that as soon as the arbitration mechanism was established in 1993, it was promptly used by workers; and the number of arbitrated disputes and workers involved in these cases, as well as the number of arbitrated collective labour disputes, has escalated over the years. In Figure 2, we put the number of arbitrated labour disputes from 1999 to 2008 into a curve and found that the increase rate suddenly rose from 2004. The total number of arbitrated disputes has increased by 15% from 226,391 in 2003 to 260,471 in 2004 while the collective disputes in the same period skyrocketed by 77% from 10,823 to 19,242 (Table 2).

Table 2: Arbitrated Labour Disputes in China: 1993–2008[20]

Year	Arbitrated Labour Disputes	Workers Involved in Arbitrated Labour Disputes	Arbitrated Collective Labour Disputes
1993	12,368	35,683	684
1994	19,098	77,794	1,482
1995	33,030	122,512	2,588
1996	48,121	189,120	3,150
1997	71,524	221,115	4,109
1998	93,649	358,531	6,767
1999	120,191	473,957	9,043
2000	135,206	422,617	8,247
2001	154,621	467,150	9,847
2002	184,116	608,396	11,024
2003	226,391	801,042	10,823
2004	260,471	764,981	19,241
2005	313,773	744195	16,217
2006	317,162	679,312	13,977
2007	350,182	653,472	12,784
2008	693,465	1214,328	21,880

Figure 2: The Number of Labour Dispute Cases
Handled by the Labour Dispute Arbitration Committees
at All Levels in China from 1999 To 2008

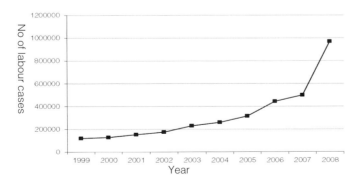

As further evidence, Table 3 shows the number of workers' collective actions in the PRD as collected by a NGO activist-cum-student, which indicates a trend of mounting labour protests.

While there were only three cases of strike reported in 2002, the number had risen to 10 in 2003, 22 in 2004 and 35 in 2005. It is worth noting that workers' strikes as reported by the media in China only show the tip of the iceberg and it is difficult, if not totally unachievable, to formulate a comprehensive picture. Yet, it is still possible to give us some hints about the historical trend.

Table 3: Workers' Collective Action in the PRD from 2002 to 2005[21]

	2002	2003	2004	2005
Incidents reported	3	10	22	35
Incidents involving in excess of 1,000 workers	0	2	9	13
Incidents resulting in physical conflicts with police	0	2	7	12

All these illustrate that workers' grievances are increasingly articulated in a radical and collective form. Many strike cases during this period in the PRD shared some general characteristics. First, workers demanded better implementation of legal labour rights, especially the minimum wage rate and social insurance. Starting from 2007, as the minimum wage had been basically enforced by enterprises, there was a trend for workers attempting to ask for a "reasonable wage" higher than the minimum wage. Their actions have forced city governments to increase the minimum wage promptly. Second, many strikes were led by hidden leaders who were usually skilled workers or lower level supervisors. Workers learned from experiences in which their representatives were dismissed by the management during the strike and that was why they started to declare that there was no representative in their actions. To establish a trade union or include grass-roots representatives into the existing trade union is sometimes a formal demand of workers during the strike. But there were not many successful stories, except in the case of the crane operators' strike in the Shekou port.[22] Third, in many cases, with their demands unmet, workers ended up walking away from their factory and blocking the main road in the city to attract public attention and invite the government's positive interventions.[23]

It is against the backdrop of the above mentioned labour shortage and waves of labour activism that the state's regulation of the workplace relations was strengthened from the period of 2004 to 2007, which has led to higher labour rights standards in the country.[24] Its interventions are mainly manifested in three ways. First, many local governments has raised the minimum wage level significantly. Take the Shenzhen Special Economic Zone (SEZ) as an example – its minimum wage rate has been raised by 40% from 2004 (610 *yuan*) to 2008 (850 *yuan*), compared with the minor adjustment of 6% from 2001 (574 *yuan*), a period before the labour shortage and the waves of workers' strikes, to 2004 (610 *yuan*) (see Table 4).

Table 4: The Level of the Legal Minimum Wage Rate in Shenzhen SEZ[25]

Year	Minimum wage (yuan)	Increase rate
2001–2002	574	
2002–2003	594	3.5%
2003–2004	600	1.0%
2004–2005	610	1.7%
2005–2006	690	13.1%
2006–2007	810	17.4%
2007–2008	850	4.9%
2008–2009	1000	17.6%
2009–2010	1000	0%
2010–2011	1100	10%

A minimum wage rate has been implemented in the SEZ since 1993 and became a national policy in 1994, enshrined in the Labour Law.[26] As can been seen, although the minimum wage rate has been adjusted almost annually, it was only after 2005 that the rate has been considerably increased. This reflects two sources of pressure for the local government when analysed within the new socio-economic context; one is the "shortage of labour" and the other is the wave of strikes.[27]

Since 2005, the minimum wage in the SEZ has been generally higher than the inflation rate, signifying a possible escalation in the real wage level (see Table 5 for the national inflation rates), while before 2004, as commented by Anita Chan, the real wage standard in the PRD was declining.[28]

Table 5: The National Inflation Rate[29]

Year	Inflation rate
2005	1.8%
2006	1.5%
2007	4.8%
2008	5.9%
2009	-0.7%

However, against the rising trend of minimum wage rates and probably the real wage of migrant workers, the share of employee's (*zhi yuan*)[30] income of the GDP in China has declined dramatically since 1978 and has not increased much in recent years (see Table 3). In 1980, it reached a peak of 16.99% and decreased to 15.81% in 1990 and 10.74% in 2000. In 2008, it increased slightly to 11.21%.

Table 6: The Share of Employees' (*zhi gong*) Wages on GDP[31]

Year	GDP (100 million *yuan*)	*Zhi Gong*'s Total Wages (100 million *yuan*)	Percentage of Wage on GDP
1978	3,645.2	568.9	15.61%
1980	4,545.6	772.4	16.99%
1990	18,667.8	2,951.1	15.81%
2000	99,214.6	10,656.2	10.74%
2005	183,217.5	19,789.9	10.80%
2008	300,670.0	337,131.8	11.21%

Apart from adjusting the minimum wage, the second manifestation of stronger regulation of workplace relations by the state is the strengthening of the legal regulatory framework in response to the sprouting of labour protests. A legal framework was basically established in China by the mid-1990s in order to replace the "socialist" administrative regulation.[32] One of the most important pillars of such a framework was the Labour Law, passed in 1994, which enshrines workers' legal and contractual rights, basically at the individual level, e.g., working hours and rest days, minimum wage, social insurance, labour dispute mechanism, occupational health and safety and special protection for children and women. Other crucial pillars include the Trade Union Law in 1992, the Arbitration Law (*Zhongcai Fa*) in 1995, the amended Trade Union Law and the revised Labour Law in 2001. Unfortunately, the proliferation of labour strikes has proved that this legal framework is ineffective in regulating labour relations. On the one hand, many labour laws are laxly enforced at the local level, as it is not uncommon for local authorities to be more inclined to protect the interests of capital due to their patron-client relations with business;[33] hence workers are often paid below the legal minimum wage and are deprived of their legal rights. On the other, under the present labour regulatory framework, the official arbitration and adjudication system is supposedly the last legal channel to which workers could appeal in order to resolve individual or collective disputes with their employers. However, the procedure is extremely complicated and highly time-consuming.[34] As a consequence, despite the increasing number of labour dispute cases handled by the government, as shown in Table 2, the past decade has seen the proliferation of workers' collective actions, such as strikes and work stoppages.

All in all, the failure of the labour regulatory framework to handle workers' grievances properly has provoked waves of labour activism that in effect bypass the trade unions and laws.[35] The migrant workers' unrest since 2004 is a testimony to the limitation of the current labour regulatory regime and has induced the legislation of three new laws – the Employment Promotion Law, the Labour Dispute Mediation and Arbitration Law, and the Labour Contract Law. The Employment Promotion Law aims to provide a guideline to the local government at the county level on how to monitor the employment agencies and facilitate the occupational and skills training of workers. The Labour Dispute Mediation and Arbitration Law simplifies the legal procedure of mediation and arbitration and reduces workers' economic and time costs. The Labour Contract Law is regarded as the most important among the three new laws. In view of the widespread practice of employers evading their legal responsibilities by not concluding a written contract with workers, the Law seeks to stabilize and regulate the employment relations by making it a legal obligation of employers to sign up labour contracts with workers. Moreover, the Labour Contract Law clearly states under what conditions and with what procedures employers can legally terminate or dissolve a labour contract and what their legal responsibilities are if they fail to do so.

It should be noted that, like their predecessors, these three new laws are also made under an individual right based framework. For instance, the Labour Dispute Mediation and Arbitration Law tries to channel workers' grievances into the legal channel, thus pre-empting their collective protests. The Labour Contract Law seeks to strengthen workers' individual contract rights, instead of alleviating collective discontent with a collective means.

Up to this point, my major argument is that the increasing job opportunities and labour shortage from 2004 to 2007, which were largely caused by the expansion of global production in the country since China joined the WTO and the state's new social development policies in the rural area, have fuelled the workers' struggles. This in turn has pressured the Hu-Wen government actively to reformulate its policies and strategies in stabilizing workplace relations, and thus has contributed to the improvement of workers' individual rights pertaining to minimum wage rate, employment contract and other legal protections.

Global Economic Crisis and Recession: 2008–2009

The year 2008 witnessed a severe downturn of the global economy and China could not stay immune to the global economic crisis. As mentioned, the Chinese export of goods and services in percentage of GDP had jumped to 42% in 2007. However, the recent economic crisis has had detrimental impacts on China's export trade, which plummeted 17.5% year-on-year to US$90.45 billion in January 2009. External trade with the EU dropped by 18.7% to US$27.93 billion while trade with the US decreased by 15.2% to US$22.25 billion.[36] As a result, the GDP growth of China in the last quarter of 2008 had slumped to 6.8%.[37] The slumping export trade had tremendous negative impacts on both capital and labour. On the one hand, it has been reckoned that 20 million migrant workers were laid off in the wake of the economic crisis.[38] On the other, the global capital in China has deployed various strategies in rising to the financial challenge, very often at the expense of workers. This means the labour rights standards in China have been seriously threatened by the economic crisis.

The first tactic used by investors to cope with the economic crisis was to lower labour costs by slimming down the workforce. It is reported that 900 workers were made jobless when a firm owned by a Hong Kong businessman shut down a factory in Shenzhen in October 2008.[39] And in the town of Zhangmutou (Dongguan) the number of Hong Kong enterprises has dropped from over 600 to less than 200 after the economic crisis, while that of Taiwanese enterprises fell from 103 to 60.[40] Apart from massive layoffs, many enterprises made workers quit by encouraging resignation, scheduling no paid leave and no overtime work. According to the observation of a labour service centre staff member,[41] for example, factories in the Baoan district in Shenzhen employed about one-third to one-half less workers at the end of 2008; some small-scale factories were said to have kept only 20% of their original workforce.

The second strategy deployed by the owners of capital was to evade their legal responsibility. It was found that many factories had shut down without paying due compensation to workers. For instance, the owner of a Taiwanese factory in the town of Changan (Dongguan), a major export-oriented city next to Shenzhen, fled the country in November 2008 without paying his 2000 workers the two months of wages they were owed. Third, the factory owners also sought to pressure the local and central government for assistance and allowances. For example, the Taiwanese business association had strongly requested the governments in the PRD via the Taiwanese politicians to cut down their operational costs by, for instance, waiving employers' contribution for workers' social security, reducing taxes and land charges, as well as postponing the implementation of the Labour Contract Law.[42]

The Chinese government responded promptly to this pressure from the owners of capital and it temporarily and selectively retreated from the legal regulatory regime. The central state advised the provincial and local governments in February 2009 to take temporary measures, such as the suspension of social insurance premiums, reduction of social insurance rates and freezing the minimum wage rate, to lower firms' labour costs.[43] As a result, the Guangdong Province froze the minimum wage rate, put off the wage consultations in enterprises and reduced enterprises' contributions to social insurance. It is reported that the Dongguan city government announced the deferred implementation of the Labour Contract Law, though this decision was later rejected by the central government.[44] Furthermore, the Shenzhen government revised the Regulations of the Shenzhen Municipality on the Wage Payment to Employees (*Yuangong gong zi zhifu tiao li*) in October 2009, which removed the clauses imposing punitive sanctions on wage arrears. Also the definition of wages and overtime work was altered; some allowances that used to be counted as a basis for overtime premiums were excluded from the calculation. The minimum wage rate in the city used to be adjusted annually but now was changed to a bi-annual basis.

Also in January 2009 Guangdong Province put forward the "The Guangdong Province government's various policies in supporting the Hong Kong, Macau and Taiwanese enterprises in coping with the global economic crisis and speeding up enterprise upgrade" (*Guangdongzhen zhichi gangaotaizi qeye yingdui guoji jingrong weiji he jiakuai zhuan ying shengji ruogan zhangce cuoshi de yijian*). These policies include spending 100 million yuan to facilitate the upgrading of enterprises in the value-added trade industries, tax reduction for Hong Kong, Macau and Taiwanese enterprises, and so forth.[45] Moreover, when the Labour Contract Law was first introduced in 2007, the central government showed great determination and a strong will in redressing the imbalance in capital-labour relations and restraining the owners of capital by means of the new law. However, its position has been softened in the wake of the economic crisis. In July 2009, the Supreme People's Court issued a guideline to all courts on how to handle labour dispute cases better, which emphasizes the protection of workers' legal rights and the survival and development of enterprises at the same time, so that "harmonious labour relations" could be preserved and a "win-win situation" could be reached. The guideline also reiterates that the courts' duties of settling labour disputes and preserving "social stability" serve one larger goal, which is to facilitate the economic development of the country.[46]

In the face of pressure from capital and the state's inclination to protect the former, workers' rights in China have been seriously threatened. By January 2009, the official urban unemployment rate, which did not count the internal migrant workers, had reached 4.3%; but the real level as estimated by the Chinese Academy of Social Sciences was 9.4%. Many laid-off workers were unable to get their wages, severance payments and other compensation due to them legally because their employers had simply disappeared.[47] Disgruntled workers appealed to two channels to pursue their rights after the economic crisis broke out. First, many of them sought help from the legal system. The Supreme People's Court reports that the total number of labour disputes in the country increased drastically, by 30% in the first half of 2009. Increases of 41.63%, 50.32% and 159.61% were recorded in the Guangdong, Jiangsu and Zhejing provinces respectively.[48]

Second, collective protests seem to be a more effective means to defend workers' rights as the legal process is tedious and complicated for workers. The state-run *Liaowang* magazine reported labour protests in the first ten months of 2008 increased 93.52% when compared with the same period of the previous year. Even more dramatically, a 300% increase in workers' protests was recorded in Beijing.[49] Apart from labour protests, the total number of "mass incidents", an official term referring to both work-related and non-work-related protests, is also on the increase. It jumped from 90,000 in 2006 to 120,000 in 2008; and there were 58,000 mass incidents alone in the first three months of 2009. An example of workers' collective action is workers from a Dongguan factory who launched a protest in November 2008 because they were owed severance payments.[50]

Waves of workers' protests after the explosion of the financial crisis created huge pressure on the state and in some cases were met with swift response from the government. In the event of workers' collective action in Shenzhen and Dongguan during the crisis, the government would intervene quickly and thus workers did not have to go through the tedious legal process. With the intervention of the government, laid-off workers usually received compensation quickly within a week and the government would pay workers their legal compensation in case their factories shut down. For example, the Shenzhen government gave 500 yuan to the employees of a factory whose owner suddenly disappeared in December 2008; the local government of Guangzhou offered 300 yuan to 900 workers of a Taiwanese factory that was shut down.[51]

During the economic crisis, workers' protests were defensive in nature, with wage arrears and dismissal compensation as their main demands. Still, they created huge pressure on the state and forced it to pay compensation to workers on behalf of business. This policy agenda, in fact, had been highlighted in China's slogan to battle the global recession: "maintain economic growth, people's livelihood and social stability" (*bao zengzhang, bao minsheng, bao wending*), and is in tune with what Louis Rocca has observed in China: "in many cities social stability is 'bought' by localities through money given to protesters".[52]

On the Road to Economic Recovery: 2009–2010

On the surface, China has been managing the economic crisis effectively and was able to prevent its economy from derailing. It set the target of maintaining 8% growth in the year 2009, which was safely secured; its GDP has reached 8.7% in 2009 and it is anticipated that it will increase to 9.1% in 2010.[53] China's housing market and automobile industries have experienced the greatest expansion, with increasesin sales of 32.3% and 42.1%.[54]

This economic recovery has been reflected by the revival of the labour market since early 2009. In the PRD, instead of downsizing, many factories had recruited more workers in mid-2009 as overseas demand started to rekindle.[55] However, increasing overseas orders do not necessarily mean a concomitant improvement of workers' welfare and wages; on the contrary, their work intensity and pressures escalated. Due to the unstable and fluctuating overseas demand, factories now received orders of smaller scale but of greater frequency.[56] This compelled many factories to adopt a flexible production model so as to save costs, which means the time for production has been shortened from a few months to one to two months. Hence workers are forced to work overtime and sometimes even do not enjoy any rest days.

Since the third quarter of 2009, the phenomenon of labour shortage has re-emerged. Newspapers report that a total number of two million workers are needed in the PRD and some production lines have been suspended due to the labour shortage.[57] According to observations and interviews with workers and labour organizers, the shortage is not of workers in general, but skilled or semi-skilled workers. The causes of this specific labour shortage are three-fold. First, when the economic crisis first broke out in 2008, the central state directed the surplus labour, mainly the migrant workers, back to the rural areas with the help of the ACFTU.[58] It contacted the transportation department and the railway system to make all the necessary arrangements[59] and paid the train fares for the migrant workers.[60] Moreover, to absorb the surplus migrant labour being relocated to the rural areas temporarily, the central government took four measures to achieve the goal of stabilizing employment for migrant workers. These include promoting and implementing active employment policies, providing employment services to migrant workers, offering specific vocational training to migrant workers in order to upgrade their skills, and encouraging migrant workers to start their own businesses by rendering them relevant training and financial assistance.[61]

The second cause of the labour shortage was the greater emphasis given to the development of the interior cities, which has attracted more investment, factories and capital to move to cities in the north and west of China and has thus created increasing job opportunities there. One of the effects of this trend is that workers now prefer to stay in cities near to their home town and are more reluctant to work in the southern industrial cities because prices there are high but wage levels are not satisfactory. My fieldwork in rural villages in the province of Henan in February 2009 after the Chinese New Year, and in Hebei in May 2009, found that under the central government's policy "every village connected to the road" (*chunchun tong gonglu*) many returned migrant workers had found work in the local infrastructure projects. Others took up casual jobs in the construction sites or the light industry factories in the nearby towns.

Third, the labour shortage to a large extent is a manifestation of workers' discontent towards the aggravating alienation and exploitation, especially during the global economic recession from 2008 to 2009, when labour was under serious assault. Many workers

I interviewed indicated that the deteriorating working conditions in their original factories left them frustrated and thus they wanted to move to other factories.[62]

All these explain the high turnover rate and labour shortage during the period of Chinese economic recovery. Endeavouring to cope with the re-emergence of the labour shortage, both the owners of capital and the state have taken the initiative in improving workers' wages and working conditions so as to stabilize the labour supply. On the one hand, many factories have lowered their job requirements starting from 2010; for instance, the age limit in general has been extended from 25 to 40; more male workers are recruited; a lower education level is required, and so forth.[63] On the other hand, many local governments have started to adjust the minimum wage rate. In April 2010, the Guangdong Province government announced an upward adjustment, with a maximum of 21% increase in some cities. After the government's announcement of the increase of the minimum wage rate, enterprises started to raise workers' wages accordingly.

However, the significant increase of the minimum wage could not easily pacify the aggrieved workers any longer. A new wave of strikes in China was sparked in mid-2010. Table 8 shows eighteen strike cases from late April to early June 2010 reported by *Asian Weekly* (*Yazhou Zhoukan*), a Hong Kong based magazine. The state media has always been sensitive and restrictive about reporting strike cases. It definitely does not provide a full picture of strikes, but through analysing the coverage of local and overseas media and conducting fieldwork in some of the industrial cities, we can still identify some quantitative and qualitative changes in the strikes in the country.

One of the strikes listed in the above table that attracted nationwide as well as international attention was staged by workers at the Honda automobile factory in Foshan in May 2010. The coordination, persistence and nature of the workers' demands in this strike were as never before. It was well organized, involved over 1,800 workers and lasted for seventeen days. It caused disruption of the production not only in that particular factory, but also in three other Honda factories in other parts of China and led to a loss of 240 million yuan per day for the enterprise.[64] The strikers had clear and specific demands which included a wage increase of 800 yuan, that is beyond the minimum wage rate adjustment and a democratic reform of trade unions as the existing trade unions could barely represent

Table 8: Strikes in China in mid-2010 reported by a Hong Kong journal [65]

Date	Detail of the strikes
29 April to early May	Poisoned workers from a Nikon factory in Wushi staged a few days' strike
4 May	Workers from factory producing thermo energy in Nanjing launched a strike
	Workers from a cotton factory in Shangdong struck
5 May to 11May	Workers from a metal and plastic factory in Shenzhen struck for the second time
12 May	Workers from a factory in Jiangsu were on strike
14 May to 1 June	Workers from a factory in Henan blocked the entrance of the factory
17 May to 1 June	Workers from the Honda factory in Foshan were on strike
18 May to 21 May	Workers from a factory in Datong blocked the road to traffic for three days
19 May to 21 May	A few hundred workers from a state enterprise in Kunshan struck for over three days
19 May	Workers from Vision Tec in Suzhou were on strike
23 May	Workers from a factory in Chongqing were on strike after some workers died of fatigue
25 May	Over 200 taxi drivers were on strike in Dongguan
27 May	Bus drivers from 13 cities in Yunan launched a strike
27 May	Workers from the Gloria Plaza Hotel in Beijing were on strike
28 May	Workers from a factory provider to Hyundai and from Xingyu automobile factory in Beijing were on strike
28 May	Frontline workers in a factory in Lanshou staged a strike
30 May	Over 100 taxi drivers in Dongguan struck against illegally operated taxis
1 June	Truck drivers in Shenzhen's Shekou harbour staged a strike over the entrance fee charges

their interests. The enterprise was at first reluctant to enter into any negotiation with workers, but later it had to bow to pressure and facilitate the democratic election of thirty workers' representatives, who later entered negotiations with the company in the presence of government officials and the illegitimate trade union representatives. At the end, both parties reached an agreement to raise workers' wages to 2044 yuan with a 32.4% increase and intern students' wages to around 1500 yuan with an increase of 70%.

The Honda workers' strike was generally seen as launching a new stage of labour resistance in China[66] and not only because of its success. It is also due to its duration (17 days) and level of organization when compared with other strikes in the past decades. Equally important, the strikers went beyond the individual interest of pay rises to call for democratic trade union reform. Apart from these, what merits special academic attention is the knock-on effect of the strike on the car industry, as well as other industries. Workers from many car companies and suppliers have followed the example of their counterparts and struck to demand higher wages. Almost at the same time as the Honda workers strike, it was reported that workers from a supplier to Hyundai in Beijing also launched a strike to demand higher wages. And shortly after the Honda strike in Foshan, workers from another Honda factory in Zhongshan, a city next to Foshan, staged a strike demanding higher wages and a reform of the enterprise trade union. Added to this, workers from two Toyota factories in Tianjin, Atsumitec Co. (a supplier to Honda) and Ormon (a supplier to Honda, Ford and BMW), followed the example of their counterparts and were on strike in June and July. The linkage of these strike cases is at least confirmed by that fact that a leader of the Zhongshan Honda strike contacted workers' representatives in the Foshan factory and tried to seek their advice.[67]

My review of the current wave of strikes in 2010 through media reports and interviews with worker activists of the Honda factory found that workers' protests departed from earlier strikes in at least three respects. First, while previous tides of strikes were concentrated in a specific geographic area,[68] the strike waves since May 2010 took place all over the country, including Beijing, Tianjin, Jiangsu, Henan, Yunnan and Chongqing.[69] Second, the demand for a "real" workplace trade union has become more clearly and consistently articulated by workers; it has also gained wider support from the ACFTU, the central government and the civil society.

Subsequent to the Honda workers' strike, the central and local governments have sought to push forward the collective interest based labour regulations by reforming the trade unions and establishing a better collective consultation system in the workplace. Commenting on the Honda workers' strike, the Xinhua agency, the official press, highlighted that it is of great urgency to push forward collective wage consultation in enterprises, so as to further safeguard workers' legal rights and promote harmonious labour relations.[70] On 5 June 2010, the ACFTU issued the policy document, "Further strengthen the building of workplace trade unions and give them full play",[71] which advocates the election of workplace trade unions in accordance with legal regulations and the role of workplace trade unions in ensuring the effective implementation of the Labour Law, Trade Union Law and the Labour Contract Law in enterprises. It also emphasizes workers' right to information, participation, expression and monitoring in workplace trade unions.

Besides, the vice-president of the Guangdong Provincial Federation of Trade Unions (GDFTU), Kong Xiang Hong, confirmed that the GDFTU would speed up the democratization of trade unions so that members could elect their own president. He also announced a pilot scheme of democratic election of workplace trade unions and training in ten factories, including the Honda factory.[72] Also, Wang Yang, the CPC secretary of Guangdong province, emphasised that when handling workers' collective grievances, workplace trade unions should position themselves as representatives of workers and help safeguard workers' rights according to legal regulations.[73]

Moreover, the Guangdong provincial government was debating the second draft of the Regulations on the Democratic Management of Enterprises in August 2010, while the Shenzhen Collective Consultation Ordinance (amended draft) was also under public consultation.[74] At the central level, the government requested local governments to initiate local regulations to promote collective wage consultation. It was reported that thirteen provinces had issued documents in the name of the CPC committee or government to push forward collective wage consultation, according to a media report on 9 June 2010.[75]

All these new legal initiatives seem to suggest that the Chinese government has realized the inadequacy of the individual right based legal approach in handling collective unrest. However, in reality it is undetermined and the attempt to move towards a collective interest based legal framework has been halted by pressure from the owners of capital. It is reported that the overseas business chambers were strongly against the legislation on collective negotiation. In Hong Kong, over forty business associations published their petition in newspapers, while some of their representatives paid official visits to the Guangdong government to reflect their concern.[76] As a consequence, the Regulations on the Democratic Management of Enterprises and the Shenzhen Collective Consultation Ordinance have been put off.[77] A new Enterprise Wage Ordinance (*qiye gongzi tiaoli*) has been drafted by the State Council since 2008 to regulate the payment, determination and adjustment of wages. The draft was sent to the State Council's Office on Legislation (*fa zhi ban*) in 2010. Similar to the cases of the Guangdong and Shenzhen legislation, opposition from enterprises has delayed its announcement. The newspaper report quoted an anonymous person who participated in drafting the law that many central government owned enterprises (*yang qi*) did not support the law.[78]

Apart from opposition from capitalists, there is also scepticism over the possible success of the collective bargaining system in China which rests on the nature of trade unions in China. This point can also be well demonstrated in the Honda strike. A trade union existed in the factory before the strike but workers were angered by its chairperson, a department vice-manager, as he was not helpful in their campaign for better working conditions. On 31 May, about 200 people who claimed themselves to be district and town level trade union officers entered the factory complex and persuaded the workers go back to work. After workers turned down the request, a physical confrontation took place between the strikers and the trade union officers. A few of the strikers were hurt and taken to hospital. This incident attracted vast attention from both the local and international media, with a Hong Kong newspaper using the headline, "Trade union beat workers up" (*gonghui da ren*).[79] Official sources did not declare where the 200 "trade unionists" had come from, but a reliable source of information said that they were actually mobilized by the local government. They wore yellow caps and held a "trade union membership card" (*gonghui huiyuan zheng*), according to workers. This incident served as a turning point, after which the company and trade unions came under even greater pressure and sought to resolve the dispute with a stronger initiative, including facilitating a department based workers' representative election and collective bargaining between the elected representatives and the management on 4 June 2010. The Nanhai District Federation of Trade Unions (NDFTU) and Shishan Town Federation of Trade Unions (STFTU) later issued a letter of apology to all strikers, but hinting at the faults of workers who insisted on striking.

As we see in the Honda case, the existing enterprise trade union had little positive role in promoting workers' interests and therefore it is hard for them to negotiate with the management on behalf of the workers. The local trade union centre, which is supposed to support workplace trade unions, is fully integrated into the local party-state which maintains a patron-client relationship with global and local capital. Under such circumstances, if the party-state wants to pre-empt radical workers' protests which may challenge the "social stability", to what extent can it support the enterprise trade union to articulate workers' interests with its ACFTU arm? The answer to this question remained uncertain in the Hu-Wen period.

Conclusion: The Challenge to "Harmonious" Labour Regulations

The idea of "harmonious society" which was highlighted in the political and policy agenda of the Hu-Wen regime has not materialized in the country's labour politics. While Jiang Zemin and Zhu Rongji laid down the foundation for the export-orientated economic model for China by restructuring the SOEs in the 1990s and entering the WTO in 2001, they also left their heirs, Hu Jintao and Wen Jiabao, some new social and political challenges. While the coastal industrial areas, especially the PRD and YRD, have been well developed, a large part of the country, especially the rural villages, is underdeveloped. While the problems of SOE workers were basically settled, the new challenges of migrant workers have emerged. While more and more migrant workers are employed in the FIEs, their working conditions are extremely detrimental and workplace conflicts are prevalent. As reflected in the party-state's No. 1 Documents in 2004, Hu-Wen's strategy to tackle these challenges is to promote social and economic development in the rural areas as so to achieve a more balanced or "harmonious" society.

However, the economic model laid down by Jiang and Zhu and the social development strategies deployed by Hu and Wen have worked together to create conditions and opportunities for a pattern of increased workers' activism. This workers' activism in turn has exerted pressure continually on the party-state to strengthen workers' rights by new labour regulations.

Soon after China's entry to the WTO in 2001, the higher demand for labour boosted workers' confidence and provoked waves of strikes against violations of workers' legal rights from the period 2004–2007. Responding to this socio-economic change, the Chinese state reformulated its policies to stabilize the labour relations by raising the minimum wage level and implementing three new labour laws; the Employment Promotion Law, the Labour Dispute Mediation and Arbitration Law, and the Labour Contract Law. However, the share of wage over GDP remained at a very low level, and there is no sign that labour discontent has been alleviated.

The advent of the global economic crisis in 2008 tilted the balance in favour of the owners of capital who, with the support of the state, sought to shift the financial burden to workers by downsizing, flexibilization of work, increasing work intensity and evading their legal obligations. This has compelled many workers to take to the street, which in turn has pressured the state to intervene in the capital-labour relations by partially meeting workers' economic demands.

The global economic crisis sowed the seeds of workers' discontent and indignation towards the worsening of labour rights. Once China's economy showed signs of recovery and the labour shortage re-emerged, labour protests turned from the defensive to the proactive. A new wave of strikes is booming in many parts of the country with workers demanding higher wages, better working conditions and in some cases democratic election of trade unions. Like in previous periods, workers' activism has once again shaped the response of the state, which includes an upward adjustment of the minimum wage rate and new labour legislation. But unlike 2004 to 2007, the state has tried to introduce a collective interest based labour regulatory framework, departing from the individual right oriented framework underlying earlier legislation, by initiating the national and provincial legislation of collective bargaining and promulgating the reform of workplace trade unions.

However, the barrier to effective workplace unions and collective bargaining rests on two fronts: first, the rising influence of global capital on China's labour policies; second, the lack of institutional support for workplace trade unions due to the ACFTU's integration into the party-state and local government's client-patron relationship with global capital. Without sorting out this dilemma, a "harmonious" labour relations and so a "harmonious society" cannot be achieved. The incapacity of the Hu-Wen regime to maintain social harmony is because of its failure to reform the party-state bureaucratic arms by democratic means. In this paper, I have highlighted the subordination of the AFCTU local branches to the local party-state, and the local party-state to the interests of global capital using the case of Honda strike.

The collusion of interest between the local party-state and global capital can also be better evidenced in the relocation of Foxconn from Shenzhen to Henan province. Foxconn is a Taiwanese electronic factory which employs over 0.4 million migrant workers solely in the city of Shenzhen. Thirteen workers had committed suicide since early 2010 in the factory and it attracted tremendous media attention in the same period as the Honda workers' strike. Although workers in Foxconn did not take any action, pressure from the civil society forced Foxconn to announce wage adjustments twice in one week; workers' basic monthly salary was increased from 900 to 2000 *yuan*. However, the company was reported to foster a relocation strategy from Shenzhen to the interior province of Henan, where the minimum wage rate ranged from 600 to 800 *yuan* in 2010, while that in Shenzhen was 1100 *yuan*.[80] The report also said that the city government in Henan would grant workers who work for Foxconn for more than six months a subsidy of 600 *yuan*; this indicates the active role of the local government in facilitating the relocation. The company plans to employ 0.3 million workers in Henan. To help the electronics giant to recruit sufficient workforce and tackle the challenge of "labour shortage", the Education Department of Henan provincial government issued an "urgent notice on organizing middle-level vocational school students to do placement in Foxconn" in September 2010. According to its official, 25,000 student workers from over 100 schools in the province had been mobilized to work in Foxconn by October.[81] While it is not the intention of the central government, the competition between different provinces and cities for the economic development in terms of GDP growth has made many local governments come to terms with the interests of global capital by lax implementation of the labour regulations.

Now the term of the Hu-Wen regime has almost come to an end, its labour regulatory regime is also at a crossroads. On the one hand, the individual right based legal framework has been proven ineffective in coping with the escalating labour discontent which has taken the expression of collective action and strikes. On the other, the attempt to transform the existing legal framework into a collective interest based one has been facing huge challenges. This year, 2011, is the first year of China's twelfth five-year plan. "Adjusting a reasonable income redistribution relation" (*heli diaozheng shouru fenbei guanxi*) was highlighted as one of the policy priorities.[82] It is a continual policy and political challenge for the central government to achieve the goal of "reasonable income redistribution". The key is how to introduce the institutional reforms so that local government has more incentives to protect workers' rights, and trade unions can conduct collective bargaining on wages. As long as the local and enterprise level trade unions do not represent the genuine interests of workers, and there is no effective mechanism to institutionalize and resolve labour conflicts, workers' eruption into massive unrest to a certain extent is inevitable as conflict of interest is embedded in the capitalist mode of production.[83] Hence, it is of prime importance to initiate effective workplace trade unionism in China to protect workers' rights so that the capital-labour relations can be stabilized and the goal of building a "harmonious society" will not remain so far-fetched.

Acknowledgments

This paper is partially supported by a City University start-up grant. A significant part of this paper is based upon the assistance of and collaboration with Ms Elaine Hui. Miss Mei Leung also provided assistance in the data collection. The author is grateful for their help and bears all responsibility for errors and faults.

Notes and References

1. Heike Holbig, *Ideological Reform and Political Legitimacy in China: Challenges in the Post-Jiang Era*, Working Paper (German Institute of Global and Area Studies, 2006).

2. Other forms of significant activism include the peasants' protests against land expropriation and the liberal intellectuals' Charter Movement in 2008.

3. Xinhua Net, 1 February 2010.

4. In the mid-1990s, in order to pacify the laid-off SOE workers' grievances, the state and the ACFTU introduced a series of retraining and welfare programmes to help the urban workers. See, e.g., W. Hurst and K.J. O'Brien, "China's Contentious Pensioners", *The China Quarterly*, 170 (2002), pp. 345–360; Yongshun Cai, *State and Laid-Off Workers in Reform China: The Silence and Collective Action of the Retrenched* (London: Routledge, 2006).

5. National Bureau of Statistics of China, 2000; 2005; cited by C. K. Lee, *Against the Law: Labor Protests in China's Rustbelt and Sunbelt* (Berkeley CA: University of California Press. 2007), pp. 39–40.

6. Source quoted from *China Statistical Yearbook 2006*, see J. Andreas, "Changing Colours in China," *New Left Review*, 54 November-December (2008).

7. See Lee, *Against the Law*, p. 6.

8. See http://www.npc.gov.cn/npc/xinwen/2010-04/28/content_1570903.htm

9. See A. Chan, *China Workers under Assault: Exploitation and Abuse in a Globalizing Economy* (New York: ME Sharpe, 2001).

10. See MOLSS report (2004) Online, http://www.molss.gov.cn/new2004/0908a.htm ; Beijing: Ministry of Labour and Social Security, cited by A. Chan, "Realities and possibilities of Chinese trade unionism" in C. Phelan (ed.), *The Future of Organised Labour: Global Perspectives* (Oxford: Peter Lang, 2006), p. 285.

11. Data from the Ministry of Commerce (various years) "Foreign direct investment in China," http://english.mofcom.gov.cn/ (Accessed 27 October 2007).

12. During the author's fieldwork in the cities of Guangzhou, Shenzhen, Dongguan and Huizhou in May and June 2005, many workers told me that the migrant workers aged over 40 years chose to return to villages as the economic conditions there had improved, while the policy of tax cancellation and agricultural tax did not have a big attraction for the younger generation of migrant workers who preferred to stay in the cities.

13. See World Bank, *Key Development Data and Statistics*, 2009, http://web.worldbank.org/WBSITE/EXTERNAL/DATASTATISTICS/0,,contentMDK:20535285~menuPK:1390200~pagePK:64133150~piPK:64133175~theSitePK:239419,00.html (Accessed on 15 August 2009).

14. *Nanfang Ribao*, 10 February 2004; *Nanfang zhoumo*, 15 July 2007.

15. *Min ying jingjibao*, 8 May 2004.

16. *Nanfang zhoumo*, 9 September 2004; *USA Today*, 12 April 2005.

17. See R. Franzosi, *The Puzzle of Strikes: Class and State Strategies in Postwar Italy* (Cambridge: Cambridge University Press, 1995).

18. The right to strike has not yet been recognized by the law since it was removed from the Constitution of the PRC in 1982, but any action to disrupt social order is illegal under Section 158 of the Penal Code. See B. Taylor et al., *Industrial Relations in China* (Cheltenham (UK): Edward Elgar, 2003).

19. For details of the strike cases, see C. K. C. Chan, *Challenge of Labour in China. Strikes and the Changing Labour Regime in Global Factories* (New York and London: Routledge, 2010).

20. National Bureau of Statistics of China, *Zhongguo Laodong Tongji Nianjian.* (*China Labour Statistical Yearbook*), (Beijing: China Statistical Publishing House [in Chinese], 2009.

21. The data, with detailed sources and short descriptions, was produced by Parry Leung who has worked in independent labour NGOs in Hong Kong and researched labour conditions in the PRD since 2000. In an interview he informed me that the data was produced from his wide scanning of NGO publications and media research with the search engine of the internet database, Wisenews. I am indebted to Leung for sharing his research data.

22. The report on the port workers' strike can be read at: *Guangzhou Ribao*, 8 April 2008.

23. See Chan, *The Challenge of Labour in China*, for a general analysis and detailed case studies of workers' strike in Shenzhen.

24. *Ibid.*

25. Shenzhen Municipal Statistics Bureau (various years) "Standard of minimum wage", http://www.cn12333.com/writ_view.asp?id=2272. (Accessed 2 July 2008) [in Chinese].)

26. The power to set the minimum wage is delegated to local authorities according to the cost of living and economic development conditions.

27. See Chan, *The Challenge of Labour in China*, chapters 4 and 5, for a detailed elaboration of this point.

28. Chan, *China Workers under Assault.*

29. Sources: website of China Statistics Bureau.

30. *Zhiyuan* does not cover all the migrant workers in the country. There is a complicated definition in the government statistics, referring to wage labourers in state owned enterprises, collective owned enterprises, joint-ventures, shareholders' companies, foreign-owned enterprises and other institutions. But here it gives us a hint of the historical change of workers' wage share.

31. *China Statistics Yearbook* (various years).

32. S. H. Ng, and M. Warner, *China's Trade Unions and Management* (London and New York: Macmillan/St Martin's Press, 1998); Taylor et al. *Industrial Relations in China.*

33. Chan, *China Workers under Assault.*

34. See Lee, *Against the Law*, for a detailed elaboration of the labour administrative complaint and arbitration procedure.

35. Chan, *The Challenge of Labour in China.*

36. "China's export down 17.5% in January," *The China Daily*, 11 February 2009, http://www.chinadaily.com.cn/china/2009-02/11/content_7467126.htm (Accessed on 15 August 2009).

37. CLB, *Twenty Million Returning Unemployed Migrant Workers to Put Strain on Local Government* (Hong Kong: CLB, 2009); http://www.china-labour.org.hk/en/node/100380, Hong Kong: China Labour Bulletin. (Accessed on 12 August 2009).

38. *Ibid.*

39. IHLO, "ACFTU in a time of crisis: back to the old ways?" Hong Kong Liaison Office of the International Trade Union Movement, 2009, http://www.ihlo.org/LRC/ACFTU/070509A.html (Accessed on 14 July).

40. *Industry and Commerce Times*, 20 January 2009.

41. I conducted an interview with a veteran staff member of a labour NGO in March 2009 and clarified some information with her in May 2010.

42. Information from Guangdong province government website, "Window of Guangdong and Taiwan" (*yuetaizhichuang*), http://www.huaxia.com/gdtb /sthd/2009/01/1285133.html.

43. IHLO, "ACFTU in a Time of Crisis".

44. *Nanfangwan*, 25 November 2008.

45. *Dongguan Daily*, 18 January 2009.

46. Supreme People's Court Guidelines to better handle labour dispute cases in the current situations (*guany dangqian xingshixia zuohao laodong zhengyu jiufenanjian shenpang de zhidao yijian*), 2009, http://www.chinacourt.org /flwk/show.php?file_id=136928 (Accessed on 14 August 2009) [In Chinese].

47. IHLO, "The Observer: China fears riots will spread as boom goes sour," Hong Kong Liaison Office of the International Trade Union Movement, 2009, http://www.china-labour.org.hk/en/node/100376 (Accessed on 10 August 2009).

48. IHLO, "As labour disputes rise 30 percent in the first half of 2009, courts emphasize stability," Hong Kong Liaison Office of the International Trade Union Movement, http://www.china-labour.org.hk/en/node/100518 (Accessed on 15 August 2009).

49. *Ibid.*

50. *Ibid.*

51. *Ibid.*

52. Quoted in C. K. Lee, "Is labour a political force in China?" in Elizabeth J. Perry, and Merle Goldman (eds.), *Grassroots Political Reform in Contemporary China* (London: Harvard University Press, 2008), pp. 228–252, at p. 244.

53. Xinhua Net, 21 January 2010.

54. *Ibid.*

55. Interviews with migrant workers and staff in a labour NGO in Shenzhen from September 2009 to January 2010, when the author paid regular visits to the organization for a project evaluation.

56. *Shenzhen Special Zone Daily*, 22 April 2010.

57. *Chendu Commercial Daily*, 22 February 2010.

58. IHLO, "ACFTU in a Time of Crisis," and CLB, "ACFTU plans for 2009 and union vigilance against 'hostile forces'," Hong Kong: CLB, 2009, http://www.china-labour.org.hk/en/node/100387 (Accessed 15 August 2009).

59. The Central People's Government of PRC, "The ACFTU pushed forward the mutual agreement campaign with mutiple means" (*"quanzong duocuo bingju tuijing "gongtongyueding xingdong" shenruyouxiao kaizhan"*) 2009, http://big5.gov.cn/gate/big5/www.gov.cn/jrzg/2009-03/04/content_1250498.htm [In Chinese] (Accessed on 12 August 2009).

60. IHLO, "ACFTU in a time of crisis."

61. Ministry of Human Resources and Social Security and ACFTU, "Notice on supporting the trade unions' 'millions peasant workers assistance campaign' to maintain stability and facilate employment" (*"guanyu zhichi gonghui kaizhan qianwang nongningong yuanzhu xingdong gongtong zuohao wending he cujin jiuye gongzuo de tongzhi"*) 2009, http://www.lm.gov.cn/gb/employment/2009-06/11/content_308292.htm [In Chinese] (Accessed 12 August 2009).

62. Chan, *The Challenge of Labour in China*.

63. *Chengdu Commercial Daily*, 22 February 2010.

64. *Jingji guanca bao*, 28 May 2010.

65. The source of this table is *Yazhou zhoukan*, issue 23, 2010.

66. E.g. *The Economist*, 31 July–6 August 2010; *The Observer*, 4 July 2010.

67. Information from the Honda workers.

68. Apart from my own study (Chan, 2010) on the PRD, Feng Chen also studied the role of trade unions in a wave of strikes in eighteen Japanese and Korean electronics factories in the city of Dalian, see F. Chen, "Trade unions and the quadripartite interactions in strike settlement in China," *The China Quarterly* 201 (2010), pp. 104–124.

69. See media reports, e.g., *Asian Weekly*, Vol. 23, 2010; *The Economist*, 31 July–6 August 2010.

70. *Ta Kung Pao*, 2 June 2010.

71. ACFTU. "Further strengthen the building of workplace trade unions and give them full play" (*jinyibu jiaqiang qiye gonghui jianshe congfen fahui qiye gonghuii zouyong*), 2010.

72. *Ta Kung Pao*, 14 June 2010.

73. *Yangchengwanbao*, 13 June 2010.

74. *Hong Kong Commercial Daily*, 30 September 2010; *Guangdong China News* 5 August 2010.

75. China News Net, 9 June 2010.

76. *Sing Tao News*, 27 September 2010.

77. *Wen Wei Pao*, 18 September 2010.

78. *Zhongguo chuang*, 27 May 2010.

79. See, e.g., *Ming Pao*, 1 June 2010

80. *United Morning Post*, 29 June 2010.

81. *Beijing Youth Daily*, 12 October 2010.

82. *People's Daily*, 28 December 2010.

83. This view is from the Marxist perspective on industrial relations, on which the analysis of this paper is based. See Richard Hyman's seminal work, *Strikes* (Basingstoke UK: Macmillan, 1989).

13

New Labour Law and Its Implication for the Human Rights Regime in China

Alvin Y. SO

Introduction

Liu Xiaobo won the Nobel Peace Prize in recognition of "his long and non-violent struggle for fundamental human rights in China".[1] Since Liu is still serving an eleven-year term on subversion charges in a Chinese prison, the Nobel Prize award has again led to growing criticisms of the worsening of human rights in China. As China becomes an economic powerhouse and has lifted millions of its people from poverty, Western nations complain that China's political change has not kept up with its economic reforms. The rise of China would lead the world to expect that China would start acting like a responsible global leader which will embrace universal values like freedom, democracy and human rights.[2]

Human rights agencies often see China's post-socialist state as the bad guy and Western nations and transnational corporations as the good guy in promoting human rights in China. For example, the US Department of State pointed out in 2009 that the Chinese government's human rights record "remained poor and worsened in some areas. . . . The government continued to monitor, harass, detain, arrest, and imprison journalists, writers, activists, and defence lawyers and their families, many of whom were seeking to exercise their rights under the law. . .".[3]

Similarly, Amnesty International's 2008 report on human rights in China provided the following account:

> Growing numbers of human rights activists were imprisoned, put under house arrest or surveillance, or harassed. . . . Millions of people had no access to justice and were forced to seek redress through an ineffective extra-legal petition system. . . . Preparations for the 2008 Olympic Games in Beijing were marked by repression of human rights activists. Censorship of the internet and other media intensified.[4]

Although the post-socialist party-state is regarded as the violator of human rights, globalization and its corporate sponsors are often looked upon as the agencies to promote human rights in China. Santoro, in his book on global capitalism and human rights in China, for example, describes "how multinational corporations are making a positive contribution to democratization and human rights in China".[5] U.S.-based corporations have repeatedly argued that they are raising human and labour rights standards abroad. The American Chamber of Commerce of Hong Kong, for example, asserts that American business plays an important role as a catalyst for positive social change by promoting human welfare and guaranteeing to uphold the dignity of the worker and set positive examples for their remuneration, treatment, health and safety".[6]

However, in this chapter I will argue that, in the battle for a new labour contract law in China at the turn of the twenty-first century, the bad-guy image of the post-socialist state and the good-guy image of the transnational corporations are reversed. In this struggle, the Chinese post-socialist state is seen as actively promoting the expansion of labour rights in good faith, whereas the transnationals are seen as blocking or cutting back labour rights in China. This chapter has several sections. First, it will briefly review the transformation of human rights and social rights in China before and after 1978. It will then examine the origins of the new labour law. After that, it will report how the transnationals have tries to modify the new labour law to suit their interests. At the end, this chapter will discuss how labour and business react to the new labour law as well as the implications of this labour law for the making of the human rights regime in post-socialist China.

Human Rights and Social Rights
in Socialist China before 1978

T. H. Marshall's (1950) classic work on citizenship spells out that the modern state has granted the following rights to its citizens:

- *Civil rights*: rights necessary for individual freedom, including personal liberties, property rights, and the right to due process of law etc.
- *Political rights*: the right to participate in the exercise of political power, such as the rights to vote and be elected to public office.
- *Social rights*: a whole range of rights from economic welfare to employment.

However, drawing upon the experience of Great Britain, Marshall stresses the importance of *individual* civil, political, and social rights; his rights formulation further assumes a linear progression from civil rights to political rights, and then to social rights. In other words, Marshall assumes that social rights are a product of free individuals when they are freed to form political organizations and engage in political activities to secure their interests.

Marshall's citizenship theory does not fit the rights situation in socialist China during the 1950s and the 1960s. In socialist China, this emphasis on *individual* rights was taken as a bourgeois device to mystify class inequalities, domination and exploitation in capitalist society. As a result, the Chinese socialist party-state seldom used the term "citizens" during the Maoist era. The discourse of citizens and human rights gave way to the discourse of class, and an *individualistic* perspective on citizens and rights was replaced by a state-centric view of the collective and the people.

In addition, there was an asymmetry between social/political rights and social rights in socialist China. Although the Chinese socialist party-state was very restrictive in granting individual civic and political rights, it was very generous in promoting social rights for urban workers. In the cities, workers in the state sector had gained all sorts of social rights that far exceeded those in Western welfare states. For instance, the Chinese working class as a whole made great strides in wages, welfare, employment security, and social status. Chinese workers could enjoy stable, secure income; socially provided housing, medical care and children's education; guaranteed lifetime employment; a work environment that often involved considerable workers' power, and social and political prestige. Starting in the 1950s, Chinese workers benefited from a way of life and a standard of living to be envied by their fellow workers in other countries.

Post-Socialist China
and Global Production after 1978

However, by the mid-1970s, the revolutionary fervour gradually subsided. Instead of class struggle and mobilization politics in the Maoist era, the reform era since 1978 emphasized economic development, Four Modernizations, and marketization. Subsequently, there was profound transformation of the rights regime in post-socialist China after 1978.

The main concern in the post-socialist era is to promote economic development and to catch up with the West as fast as possible. To do so, the socialist mode of governance had to be discarded, the selfless collective ethic needed to be dropped, and mass mobilization campaigns had to be discontinued. Subsequently, a whole new neoliberal economic discourse found its way into the mainstream popular culture: such as "smashing the iron rice bowl" (job security and lifelong employment), the law of value, supply-demand economics, material incentives, efficiency, productivity, maximization of profit etc.

Therefore, the post-socialist party-state began to take back the social rights that it previously granted to urban workers in the pre-1978 socialist era. State enterprises were condemned as highly inefficient, losing money, and corrupted. Social rights were condemned as making workers lazy and making the state enterprises lose money. Thus, workers would face layoff or market discipline if state enterprises went bankrupt. Workers were told that they should no longer depend on the state for jobs, welfare, and other benefits. In the late 1980s, a new labour market was introduced, creating a flexible labour force that was responsive to the ups and downs of the market. After the labour market was set up, the state enterprises were no longer required to provide life-long employment and job security to their workers; they were given the autonomy to hire and fire workers in the name of enhancing productivity and efficiency as called upon by neoliberalism.

In addition, the post-socialist party-state adopted the strategy of export-led industrialization. The Chinese economy was characterized by an "extrovert" economy, i.e. the economy was driven by foreign direct investment (FDI) and export-led industrialization, and its economic growth relied upon integration with the global commodity chains. For example, with regard to the commodity chain of athletic shoes, the 1990s observed the trend that transnationals (such as Nike and Reebok) moved their factories from their subcontractors in Taiwan to Guangdong and Fujian. Most of the raw materials were shipped from Taiwan, and the shoe factories in Guangdong were ran by Taiwanese resident managers.

China's export oriented developmental model has attracted a flood of transnational corporations seeking to take advantage of China's docile and low-wage workers and business friendly policies; three decades of rapid economic growth from the 1980s to the 2000s have transformed China from an economic backwater into the workshop of the world. How important are these transnationals to China's development? Roughly two-thirds of the increase in Chinese exports in the past twelve years can be attributed to non-Chinese owned global companies and their joint ventures. Foreign owned global corporations account for 60% of Chinese exports to the US. In 2004, retail giant Wal-Mart was China's eighth largest trading partner, ahead of Russia, Australia, and Canada.[7]

Violation of Labour Rights
in Post-Socialist China after 1978

What did the transition from a socialist economy to the workshop of the world mean to the Chinese working class? First of all, the dismantling of the state sector has led to severe problems of unemployment. From 1995 to 1999, the number of state-owned industrial enterprises fell from approximately 100,000 to 60,000. This decline translated into massive layoffs of state-sector workers. From 1996 to 2001, some 36 million state-enterprise workers were laid off; over the same period, collective firms laid off 17 million workers.[8]

Moreover, economic reforms led to the worsening of income inequalities. The Gini coefficient for household income in China rose from 0.33 in 1980 to 0.40 in 1994 and to 0.46 in 2000. The last figure surpasses the degree of inequality in Thailand, India and Indonesia. Most observers suspect that China's Gini coefficient now exceeds 0.50, placing its income inequality near the levels of Brazil and South Africa.[9]

In addition, the demise of the state sector has also meant that most workers have now lost their social safety net, including pensions, housing, health care, and increasingly even primarily and secondary education for their children. For example, state-owned enterprises (SOE) no longer provide pension benefits. Individual workers are now supposed to be served by a nationally organized system funded by worker, state, and employer contributions.

If workers in the state sector suffered from the above neo-liberal reform policies, workers employed by the small and medium firms (which are the subcontractors of the transnationals) in the private or foreign sectors suffered even more. The literature uses the label "sweat shop" to highlight a despotic labour regime in the foreign sector. For example, Tim Pringle[10] reported that abuses of Chinese workers' rights have been widely documented both inside and outside China over the past five years. Forced overtime, illegal working hours, unpaid wages, and dreadful health and safety conditions are commonplace. The general pace of work has increased dramatically as competition forces the prioritizing of order deadlines and production targets over safe and dignified working environments. "There is no such thing as an eight-hour day in China anymore," explained a private employment agency in Shulan, northeast China.

Furthermore, Anita Chan[11] points to the troubling fact that many of the tens of millions of workers who work in the so-called township and village enterprises as well as in the foreign-funded enterprises are victims of labour rights violations, including:

- *Migrant workers' lack of rights.* Chinese peasants working in urban areas are subjected to tight "immigration" controls under China's household registration system. They are not entitled to any of the benefits enjoyed by local residents, such as social welfare, schooling, and employment for their children. Periodically the police carry out raids to round up those peasants who do not possess a temporary resident permit to stay in the city. Those workers are harassed, humiliated, thrown into detention centres, and then deported from the cities.

- *Forced and bonded labour.* Under China's "neo-apartheid" system, workers are required to pay for a temporary work permit in one lump sum. In a seller's labour market, factories dictate the terms of employment and also charge a "deposit" of about half a month to a month's wages, further bonding the workers. Workers have to forfeit the "deposit" if they quit without management permission before the contract expires, or if they are fired. In some cases, the factory simply keeps a portion of the workers' wages each month, promising to return the money at the end of the year.

- *Subsistence or below subsistence wages.* In recent years the Chinese government has introduced a common standard for its urban workers, and has made these minimum wages mandatory in the Labour Law. In 1997, for forty-four hour work week, the minimum standard per month for Shenzhen Special Economic Zone was set at 420 *yuan* (US$54). However, despite the already low minimum wage, managers engage in a wide repertoire of manipulations to get away with paying *less* than the minimum wage. A monthly pay packet that looks on paper to be above the minimum wage is usually earned by a large amount of forced overtime. It is not uncommon for workers to work two or three hours of overtime each day with only one or two days off every month. The wage system is constructed on a rigid system of penalties, deductions and fines. Factories devise their own sets of arbitrary rules and regulations in open breach of China's labour laws. Workers caught in violation of such rules will be fined.

- *Intimidation, physical violence, corporal punishment and control of bodily functions.* The use of private security guards in factory and dormitory compounds is very common in China. In fact, factories sometimes hire policemen in their off-duty hours to serve as their security guards. This type of internal security system set up behind factory walls is extremely effective in intimidating and controlling workers. Under this atmosphere of intimidation, some factories impose strict rules that control workers' bodily functions by drastically restricting the frequency and length of time allowed for going to the toilet. Physical mistreatment and control of bodily functions are more prevalent in Korean and Taiwanese-invested firms.

• *Lack of occupational health and safety.* The factories are also known to lack workers' compensation insurance. There is a high level of accidents at the shop floor, numerous factory fires, explosions, severed and maimed limbs, and the use of poisons without safeguards, with little or no medical treatment or compensation for injuries. In footwear factories, there is the widespread use of toxic glues in poorly ventilated workplaces, where workers are provided with neither gloves nor masks.

Origins of the New Labour Law in 2008

How do the Chinese working class and the state respond to the violations of labour rights in the post-socialist era?

Labour Response: Rightful Resistance

Chinese working people have responded to the labour rights violations by a new wave of protests. *China Labour Bulletin*[12] reports that "almost every week in Hong Kong and mainland China, newspapers bring reports of some kind of labour action: a demonstration demanding pensions; a railway line being blocked by angry, unpaid workers; or collective legal action against illegal employer behavior such as body searches or forced overtime."

Although comprehensive figures on the number of strikes and worker protests are not made public, official figures on so-called collective action (usually strikes or go-slows with a minimum of three people taking part) can give an indication of the extent of labour unrest. According to *China Labour Bulletin*, in 1998 there were 6,767 collective actions involving 251,268 people in 1998, and the figure jumped to 8,247 collective actions involving 259,445 workers in 2000.[13] Figures on the number of officially-arbitrated labour disputes also tell a similar story: there are 135,000 labour dispute cases in 2000, and the number jumped to 314,000 labour dispute cases in 2005.[14]

Most of the working class' collective actions can be classified as "rightful resistance[15]" because workers frame their claims with reference to protections implied in the ideologies or policies of the Chinese party-state, like demanding the factories to pay their wages on time and pay their back wages, to pay the statutory minimum wage, to reimburse medical expenses for on-the-job injury, or to compensate their forced and excessive overtime work. It is rightful resistance because the workers' protests stay within the bounds of the existing regulations imposed by the state, and they usually appeal to the leaders in the Central Government to look into their grievances. In other words, Chinese labour protests in the post-socialist era can be called "rightful resistance" because they are merely defensive struggles, aiming to get back their "rightful" share promised by the state and factory management (like wages paid on time, minimum wages, medical compensations for on-the-job injury, and compensations for overtime work, etc.); they are not aimed at challenging the authority of the post-socialist party-state or the existing capitalist system.

State Response: Legal Absorption of Labour Conflict

Since the labour protests are not directed at the post-socialist party-state, and they are only directed at individual enterprise on a case-by-case basis, the Chinese party-state articulates a response that can be called "legal absorption of labour conflict" by setting up new labour legislation more congruent with the interests of labour. The aim is to divert the surging labour conflict into a formal legal channel, and to improve the individual rights of the working class without improving its collective rights. In other words, the aim is to improve the wages and other compensation for *individual* workers without at the same time leading to the rise of working class at a *collective* level to form a class-wise organization or to engage in a collective social movement.

The post-socialist party-state has always tried very hard to suppress the formation of the working class and it accomplishes this goal through setting up a nation-wide official trade union. Workers are deprived of the right of organization to form independent trade unions in China. Instead, they are only allowed to join the All China Federation of Trade Unions (ACFTU), the only trade union officially sanctioned by the party-state. It is always clear that the ACFTU is an organization of the party-state rather than a working-class organization. The ACFTU is obliged to obey the leadership of the Communist Party of China, as stated in the trade union regulations: "[A] Trade Union shall observe and safeguard the Constitution . . . uphold the socialist road, the people's democratic dictatorship, leadership of the Communist Party of China and Marxism-Leninism, Mao Zedong Thought and Deng Xiaoping Theory".[16]

It is under this historical context of post-socialist development which aims to safeguard individual rights while suppressing the collective rights of the Chinese worker class that the new labour law was formulated at the turn of the twenty-first century. The labour law was first presented to the Chinese public for comment in December 2005; it was formally approved by the National People's Congress in June 2007, and took effect in January 2008.

What Issues Are at Stake in the New Labour Law?

The new labour law is often labelled the new "labour contract law" by analysts because it stipulates clearly that every Chinese worker needs to be protected by a written contract. Millions of the migrant workers working in small and medium-sized enterprises (SMEs) in the foreign sector do not have contracts, leaving them in legal limbo, unable to access existing rights and benefits however limited. In particular, the new labour contract law has the following distinctive features:

- A *valid written labour contract* must be offered by the employer before a worker is asked to start working. If an employer has not given a worker a contract after 30 days, a contract is automatically assumed providing wages and working standards prevalent in the industry in which the worker is employed.

- *Open-ended contracts* for employment are required for those workers who have completed two fixed term contracts or with more than ten years of service in a firm. That means a permanent contract of legally valid labour relationship is automatically formed from the date a worker begins to provide substantial labour service to the employer, and workers are protected from dismissal without a valid cause.

- *Severance payment.* Employers are now obliged to give a severance payment which is about one month's pay for every year the worker has worked in the firm. Previously, employers could offer fixed term contracts that automatically end without the need for termination or severance pay.

- *Contribution to social security and set labour standard.* The new labour law also requires employers to contribute to their employees' social security accounts and set wage standards for workers on probation and overtime.

- *Consequences for violations.* The new law states that if employers fail to sign contracts or pay wages on time, workers can not only ask for compensation from the employer, but they can also ask the court to recover their wages. The law also states that government officials will face administrative penalties or criminal prosecution for abusing their authority if it results in serious harm to the interests of workers.

- *Expands the scope of bargaining over company policies and work rules.* The new law requires companies to negotiate company rules and regulations on a broad array of issues from compensation to health and safety issues, to vacations and days off.

- *Expands the role of (official) unions.* The new law expands the role of official unions by allowing a broader scope for collective bargaining at the enterprise level.

China Daily reported that when the draft labour law was completed in December 2005, the Chinese leaders decided to seek public comments on the draft, an action which *China Daily* describes as "rare, if not unprecedented".[17] This action indicates that the party-state wants to involve interest groups and the public at large in the formation of the new labour law; it is a step on the long march of making the post-socialist party-state more transparent and more responsive to social forces in society.

The public comment period of one month generated a huge reaction. *China Daily* reported that the party-state received a total of 191,849 responses through the internet, media, and mail. Most of the comments came from individual workers and Chinese trade groups, but there were comments from transnational corporations and their Chambers of Commerce.

Transnational Corporations' Battle against the New Labour Law

In 2006 US-based global corporations like Wal-Mart, Microsoft, Nike and AT&T, commenced a concerted effort to lobby actively against the new labour law, acting through the following three US business organizations:

- *The American Chamber of Commerce in Shanghai* which represents over 1,300 corporations, including 150 "Fortune 500" companies
- *The US-China Business Council*, representing 250 U.S. companies doing business across all sectors in China
- *The European Union Chamber of Commerce in China*, representing more than 860 companies

They also threatened that foreign corporations would withdraw from China if the labour law was passed.[18]

What explains the keen interests of the transnational corporations on a new labour law in China? The business lobby was worried that strict contract requirement of the new labour law could raise costs and give the transnationals less flexibility to hire and fire in China. The transnationals were also concerned about the major role that China's officially sanctioned trade union would play in collective bargaining.[19]

For transnationals, the new labour law is a battle they have to fight because efforts to improve the wages and the conditions of Chinese workers have profound implications for workers everywhere. In the 2000s, one in four workers in the global economy is Chinese. Business lobbies worry that improving the wages and labour standards in China will drive up wages and labour standards not only in China but also in other parts of the world. Improving labour conditions in China can help workers in the rest of the world to resist the so-called "the race to the bottom" in the globalization era.[20]

Global Labor Strategies reported in 2008 that the transnationals' battle over the new labour law in China is not a one-sided victory; instead the battle has gone through twists and turns. In the beginning, in April 2006, the transnationals started the battle by launching an all-round attack. The American Chamber of Commerce in Shanghai (AmCham), for instance, issued a 42-page submission on behalf of its 1,300 corporate members to the Chinese government. AmCham demanded a list of revisions and outright reversals of "rigid" regulations, including provisions making it harder to fire workers, new protections for temporary workers, and restrictions on non-competitive agreements. Similar submissions were sent to the Chinese government by the EU Chamber of Commerce and other lobby organizations. AmCham warned that the new labour law may negatively impact the PRC's competitiveness and appeal as a destination for foreign investment. AmCham made threats to withdraw its members' investments from China if the current version of the legislation passed, arguing that the Chinese government was turning the clock back twenty years.

According to a lawyer at a firm representing AmCham members in China, comments from the business community appear to have had an impact. Whereas the March 2006 draft offered a substantial increase in the protection for employees and greater role for unions than the existing law, the [new draft] scaled back protections for employees and sharply curtailed the role of unions.[21]

Corporate lobbies largely concentrated their efforts on eliminating new contractual rights for workers, including mandatory collective bargaining requirements over health and safety, wages, and layoffs; limitations on probation periods; mandated severance payments; and new protections for temporary workers. While some protections for workers remain in the second draft of the legislation, Global Labor Strategies' analysis shows that many important provisions have been seriously weakened or eliminated wholesale in response to global corporate threats and demands.[22] For example, the new law has watered down the role of trade unions in collective bargaining. The revised law now states that employer need *only listen to the advice (but need not seek the approval)* of the union before the company makes any layoff of over 20 employees or 10% of total employees.

Labour and Human Rights Groups Worldwide Fight for Rights of Chinese Workers

However, the transnational's offensive against the new labour law was not without resistance from labour and human rights groups. After the global media had exposed the role of foreign corporations in lobbying against reform of Chinese labour law, a series of fissures emerged between the corporations in China and the business lobbies that represent them. Obviously, we do not know what happened behind the closed doors of the corporate chambers, but Global Labor Strategies has pieced together the information from the mass media to infer what may be going on.[23]

For example, Nike suddenly distanced itself so far from AmCham's position that it prompted a headline: "Nike Repudiates AmCham Position on Chinese Law Reform" in the new release of the International Textile, Garment, and Leather Workers' Federation (ITGLWF).[24]

An even more remarkable shift occurred in the attitude of the EU Chamber of Commerce in China. Initially, it had criticized the draft labour law and issued a veiled threat that European corporations that it represented would abandon China if the new labour law were passed. On 8 December 2006, however, the EU Chamber suddenly reversed its position in a public statement stating that the Chamber believes that there is a serious need to improve working conditions in China and the Chamber stands firmly behind the Chinese government's efforts to improve working.[25]

A number of corporations too have tried to put distance between themselves and the original positions of the foreign business lobbies. Ericcson, for example, dissociated itself from the threats of withdrawing from China initially made by the EU Chamber of Commerce:

> Ericcson supports the Chinese government's legislative efforts to improve the labour law and regulations for working standards . . . Ericsson is in no way actively lobbying against the proposed legislation by the Chinese government. Nor has Ericsson threatened to pull out of China if the new labour laws were to be passed . . . Just because we are a member of the European Chamber of Commerce does not necessarily mean we endorse every lobbying initiative.[26]

What then explains the reversed position of some transnationals and their business lobbies? Global Labor Strategies[27] suggests two explanations. First, there is the explanation of a divided corporate world. The emerging division may reflect differences of interest among different foreign sectors. Nike's image is a crucial part of what it sells, and it has been intent to project itself as a leader in human rights ever since its image was damaged by labour rights campaigns. Some companies hope to sell products in China, and regard both a positive image and rising wages in China to be to their benefit. Some foreign corporations, conversely, view China primarily as a source of cheap labour for exports and oppose anything that might raise their labour costs. The breakup of a common front among foreign corporations offers the promise of reducing one of the main barriers to effective labour legislation for the benefit of Chinese workers.

The other explanation is social struggles. The emerging division in the corporate world is the product of the social struggles waged by labour and human rights groups worldwide on behalf of Chinese workers. A leading role in this social struggle has been taken by the ITGLWF. It issued a statement entitled "Multinationals Accused of Hypocrisy over China Labour Law Reform", demanding that EU and US corporations halt their lobbying campaigns against the modest improvements embodied in the new law.[28] Neil Kearney, General Secretary of the ITGLWF, approached numerous apparel and footwear employers to request that they "distance themselves from the position of their industry associations. Many industrial corporations like Nike have reversed their previous position as a result of this pressure from unions".[29]

Similarly, the European Trade Union Confederation (ETUC) has played a primary role in forcing the EU Chamber of Commerce to "clarify" its position after its aggressive lobbying campaign against the new labour law was exposed. After the Chamber's initial actions, John Monks[30], the General Secretary of the ETUC, demanded that "European companies should behave outside Europe as they are supposed to do inside. They should certainly not act to drive standards down." Later, ETUC further condemns the "disgraceful occurrences" of threats by the European Chambers of Commerce in Beijing to reconsider new investment in response to the proposal to improve labour laws. Subsequently, the EU Chamber revised its position, saying that it now stands firmly behind the Chinese government's efforts to improve working conditions.

Observing the changing tide of the EU Chamber of Commerce, other trade unions and their officials, including the AFL-CIO, European Metal Workers, and the Dutch Federation of Trade Unions, soon issued press releases, exposed U.S. and EU Chambers' efforts on their blogs, and used a host of other campaigning techniques to draw public attention to the issue.

Many human rights groups and other NGOs have also been involved in the fight to protect the workers' rights included in the new law, including the German Toy Campaign, PC-Global, India Committee of the Netherlands, Centre for Research on Multinational Corporations, and the CSR Platform, a coalition of forty unions and NGOs working on corporate social responsibility issues. The Business and Human Rights Resource Centre, chaired by former UN Human Rights Commissioner Mary Robins and affiliated with Amnesty International, asked leading companies about their role in opposing the law, then posted their responses on its website. As Chris Avery, Director, and Gregory Regaingnon, Senior Researcher for the Centre, explained:

> Respect for labour rights is a core aspect of companies' human rights obligations. Companies' position on labour rights issues, including on labour law reform in countries such as China, are a major part of their human rights

impacts, as are the lobbying activities of companies' associations.[31]

Observing the split in the business community and getting the support of the global labour and human groups, the Chinese government held its position in promoting the labour law despite receiving earlier threats from the transnationals and their business lobbies to withdraw their investment in China. In January 2008, the new labour law was finally put into effect. The final version has the following three major features:

- The final version said companies only need to *"consult"* the state-backed union if they plan workforce reduction, suggesting a softening from earlier drafts that gave the union the right to *"approve or reject"* layoffs before they could take place.
- The final version, however, retained language that limits "probationary contracts", which many employers use to deny employees full-time status. It also states that severance pay will be required for many workers and tightens the conditions under which an employee can be fired.
- In addition, the new labour law empowers company-based branches of the state-run unions or employee representative committees to bargain with employees over salaries, bonuses, training, and other work-related matters.

What then is the reaction of workers and businesses to the new labour law? What is the implication of the labour law for the making of a human rights regime in China?

Reaction to the New Labour Law

Labour Reactions

Parry Leung reported in 2008 that the legislation of the labour law, even before it took effect in 2008, had triggered a new round of labour protest beyond the established legal channel.[32] In the industrialized zone in the Pearl River Delta, a dozen large-scale worker protests and collective actions were reported in the Hong Kong and Guangzhou media in November and December 2006 (see Table 1).

Table 1: Reported Labour Conflicts Triggered
by the New Labour Contract Law Legislation

Date	Location	Employer	Details
Dec 22	Shenzhen	Massage service	Over 200 blind massagers took strike action for 4 days against employers' termination of existing employment contract.
Dec 20	Shenzhen	IT company	Over 1,000 workers took strike action and blocked Shennan Avenue against employers' termination of existing employment contracts and reduction of benefits.
Dec 14	Guangzhou	Taiwan invested electronics factory	Over 700 workers took strike action and blocked a nearby road for 3 hours, asking for minimum wage protection and protesting against termination of existing employment contracts.
Dec 13	Dongguan	Hong Kong invested paper factory	Over 600 workers took strike action and blocked a nearby road against employers' termination of existing employment contracts.
Dec 10	Shenzhen	Hong Kong invested factory	Over 2,000 workers took strike action for 3 days against employers' termination of existing employment contracts and reduction of benefits in new contracts.
Dec 5	Hainan	Foreign invested brassiere factory	Over 1,000 workers took strike action against employer's arbitrary dismissal of 3 senior workers.
Nov 27	Dongguan	Hong Kong invested electronics factory	Over 8,000 workers took strike action and blocked a nearby road for 6 hours, asking for higher wages and protesting against the increase of food prices.
Nov 23	Dongguan	Electronic factory	Over 800 workers took strike action against dismissal due to factory relocation.
Nov 20	Shenzhen	Not applicable.	A labour activist working for an NGO was assaulted for promoting labour contract law.

Source: Leung (2008, Table 1)

For example, over 700 workers started to strike in a Taiwan-invested electronic factory on 14 December 2007 and blocked a nearby road for three hours. These workers asked for minimum wage protection and protested against the termination of existing employment contract.

The labour law also provided an opportunity to raise workers' consciousness of their rights when they discussed the details the law in 2005–2007. When the legislation was open for public discussion and input, over 190,000 comments were received from civil society in China. Many NGOs, like the Shenzhen Dagogzhe Migrant Worker Centre, actively spread the knowledge of the new labour law and aroused workers' enthusiasm to discuss it.

When the labour law took effect in January 2008, the *Wall Street Journal* reported there was a big jump of labour disputes, showing the rising rights- consciousness of the workers.[33] Just in the city of Guangzhou, the local arbitration office received more than 60,000 cases from January to November, about as many cases as it handled over the previous two years combined. Huang Huping, deputy director of the labour bureau in Dongguan, said, "Before we would try to mediate more disputes before going to arbitration, but now that workers have the right to go to arbitration, they choose to do that right away". The Chinese media in 2009 also reported numerous recent incidents of labour unrest, from taxi strikes to protests by factory workers over unpaid wages.

The labour law also makes the official trade union more active. The ACFTU, the official labour union, opened 866 legal aid centres in preparation for a national-wide campaign for enforcement of the new labour law.[34] Hon DongFang, a well-known labour activist, also pointed out that during the drafting of the labour law, official unions had to respond to the workers' demands once their consciousness of their rights was aroused.[35]

Business Reactions

Taking advantage of the global recession, businesses protested by closing down or relocating. Canaves reported that in the first months of 2008, 15,661 enterprises in Guangdong, the southern province with a great deal of manufacturing industry, shut their doors.[36] Workers say companies avoid paying claims by liquidating or by just disappearing without properly settling their obligations.

There was also a scramble by companies to circumvent the labour contract requirement before the law came into effect. The most publicized case was Huawei Technologies – China's largest telecommunication equipment manufacturer and a former state-owned firm. Huawei asked 7,000 employees with more than eight years of service to resign and accept re-employment as "new staff". Divjak also reported "creative" employers in China had already worked out ways to get around the minimal restrictions contained in the new legislation.[37] Donald Straszheim, vice chairman of Los Angeles-based Roth Capital Partners, said: "We are seeing new labour contracts, two half-time shifts, the use of outside staffing companies, the creation of new companies to do the same work, so-called voluntary resignations before year-end only to be rehired on 1 January 2009".[38]

State Reactions

When a series of wildcat strikes broke out against Honda and Toyota in several cities in southern China in summer 2010, the post-socialist party-state allowed the Chinese mass media to cover the strikes in detail. The government's tacit approval of coverage of the strikes seems to reflect a genuine desire of the party-state to see higher wages for the workers so as to increase domestic consumption during the global economic crisis. The above speculation is confirmed by the fact that soon after the strike wave in summer 2010, various local governments in Shenzhen, Nanhai and Beijing quickly announced that they would raise the minimum wage by 10–20% in the following months.[39]

In August 2010, Chinese Premier Wen Jiabao further bluntly warned Japan "that its companies operating in China should raise pay for the workers" during a high-level Japan-China meeting. Wen told the Japanese officials that the background of labour troubles was the relatively low level of pay at some foreign companies.[40]

Conclusion: Implications for the Making of a Human Rights Regime in China

This chapter studies the battle for the new labour contract law between the post-socialist party-state and the transnational corporations at the turn of the twenty-first century. The new labour contract law is important because it may indicate the turning point of China's development.

Before the turn of the twenty-first century, China's "workshop of the world" model of development was built upon its linkages to the tail end of the global production, that is, it provided the subcontractors of the transnational corporations and engaged in low value-added, labour intensive industries whose profitability is dependent upon the "super-exploitation" of docile migrant workers in a sweat-shop factory. However, increasing labour unrest over the past decade showed this sweat-shop mode of production is no longer sustainable as the first wave of migrant labour matured and became organized. Therefore, in the early 2000s, the post-socialist party-state decided to phase out the low value-added, labour intensive, polluting industries and moved China's economy up the value chain. Since China's development is no longer dependent on the sweat-shop model, the new labour code is aimed to move toward a more humane industrial relationship like that in Western Europe.

The new labour code also has significant implications for the making of a human rights regime in China. First, using the "rule of law" and developing a European labour code instead of intensifying the repressive apparatus (like police and prison) to deal with labour unrest is a very good sign that the post-socialist party-state is committed to transforming itself into a modern state commensurate with the rise of China in the inter-state system.

Second, the way that the state promotes the new labour law is also very promising. Instead of imposing the new labour law from above, as the state did many times before, the labour legislation was first open for public discussion and input before the state enacted the final draft. This fact shows that the party-state is more transparent and more open to the inputs of civil society than before.

Third, Chinese workers responded to the new labour law not only by giving their opinions (190,000 comments) to the party-state, but they also now rise up in protest and engage in labour disputes to defend their rights. NGOs and trade unions are also more active than before in spreading consciousness of rights to the working class. Together with other indicators, such as the "rightful resistance" move-ment of the peasantry in the countryside and the "rights resistance" protests of the new middle class in the urban areas, the rising number of labour disputes during and after the passing of the labour law may indicate rights consciousness is rising in post-socialist China.

Finally, the new labour law serves to draw the attention of the human rights community onto China's workers. Before, the human rights literature seldom mentioned the issues of labour rights. In the US government's criticism of China's human rights violations, for example, China's violations of labour rights were barely brought up as a problem.[41] In the latter part of the labour law battle, it was the efforts of the global human right groups and labour unions that pressured the transnational corporations and their business lobbies to change their position against the labour law. The fusion of human rights and labour rights issues would greatly expand the concerns of the human rights organizations. If global human rights groups would continue pay attention to China's labour condition (like ensuring the basic human rights of Chinese workers to organize, bargain collectively, and strike), it would certainly help to pressure the Chinese government and the Chinese civil society to move in the direction of a modern human rights regime.

In short, the battle of new labour law at the turn of the twenty-first century is a very promising step in the long march for the creation of a modern human rights regime in China as Chinese citizens are becoming more rights conscious in asserting their rights in the workplace, as the Chinese post-socialist party-state wants to use "the rule of law" in resolving the growing conflict in society, and as the global human rights groups lend their support to the Chinese workers.

Note

An earlier version of the paper was presented to an international human rights conference entitled "Human Rights and the Social: Making a New Knowledge" at Seoul National University, 5–6 November 2009.

Notes and References

1. Andrew Jacobs and Jonathan Ansfield "Nobel Peace Prize given to jailed Chinese dissident," *The New York Times*, 8 October 2010.

2. Susi Dennison, "Where does Liu Xiaobu's Nobel leave Europe?" *European Council on Foreign Relations*, 8 October 2010, http://ecfr.eu/content/entry /commentary_liu_xiaobo_and_the_nobel/ (accessed 17 October 2010). See also Nicholas Kristof, "Liu Xiaobo and Chinese democracy," *The New York Times*, 8 October, 2010.

3. U.S. Department of State, *2008 Human Rights Report: China (includes Tibet, Hong Kong, and Macau),* http://www.state.gov/g/drl/rls/hrrpt/2008 /eap/119037.htm. (Accessed 17 October 2010).

4. Susanne Ure, *Amnesty International Report 2008: The State of Human Rights in China,* http://www.amnesty.ca/blog_post2.php?id=183 (accessed 27 October 2009).

5. Michael A. Santoro, 2000. *Profits and Principles: Global Capitalism and Human Rights in China* (Ithaca NY: Cornell University Press, 2000).

6. Global Labor Strategies, "Why China matters: labor rights in the era of globalization," 2008, p. 2, http://labourstrategies.blogs.com/global_labour _strategies/files/why_china_matters_gls_report.pdf (accessed 27 October 2009).

7. Stephen Roach, "Doha doesn't matter anymore", *The Business Times* (Singapore), 8 August 2006.

8. Marc J. Blecher, "Hegemony and worker's politics in China", *The China Quarterly,* 170 (2002), pp. 282–303.

9. Martin Hart-Landsberg and Paul Burkett, "China and socialism: market reforms and class struggle", *Monthly Review*, 56(3) (2004), pp. 8–123.

10. Tim Pringle, "The path of globalization: implications for Chinese workers." *Asian Labor Update,* No. 41 (2001).

11. Anita Chan, "Labor standards and human rights: the case of Chinese workers under market socialism." *Human Rights Quarterly*, 20 (1998), pp. 886–904.

12. "Industrial unrest in China – A labour movement in the making?" *China Labour Bulletin,* (31 January 2002), p. 1, http://www.hartford-hwp.com /archives/55/294.html (accessed 13 April 2003).

13. *Ibid.*

14. *Labour Statistical Yearbook* (*Laodong tongji nianjian*) (Beijing: Beijing State Statistical Publishing House, 2006).

15. Kevin J.O'Brien, "Rightful resistance", *World Politics* 49 (1996), pp. 31–55.

16. Parry Leung, "Legality and labor politics in China: the labor contract law legislation" (Unpublished manuscript, 2008).

17. Andrew Batson and Mei Fong, "China toils over new labor law", *China Daily,* 7 May 2007, http://www.chinadaily.com.cn/world/2007-05/07 /content_867071.htm (accessed 29 October 2009).

18. Jonathan Tasini, 2006. "U.S. corps blocking China labor law", *Front Page Posts,* 13 October 2006, http://www.workinglife.org/blogs/view_post.php ?content_id=4665 (accessed 29 October 2009).

19. Batson and Fong, "China Toils over new labor law."

20. Philip McMichael, *Development and Social Change: A Global Perspective* (London: Pine Forge Press, 1996).

21. Andreas Lauffs, "Employers face tougher rules: upcoming changes to employment contract law are likely to further constrain the policies of foreign companies in China," *Financial Times,* 31 January 2007.

22. Global Labor Strategies, "Undue influence: corporations gain ground in battle over China's new labor law," 2007, http://laborstrategies.blogs.com /global_labor_strategies/files/undue_influence_global_labor_strategies.pdf (accessed 29 October 2009).

23. *Ibid.*

24. International Textile, Garment, and Leather Workers' Federation, press release, "Nike repudiates AmCham on Chinese labor law reform," 2006, http://www.itglwf.org/DisplayDocument.aspx?idarticle=15269&langue=2 (accessed 29 October 2009).

25. EU Chamber of Commerce, "Statement on draft labour contract law," 2006, http://www.europeanchamber.com.cn/events/news.php?id=286 (accessed 30 October 2009).

26. Ericsson, "Ericsson's response to the Business Human Rights Resource Center," 5 January 2007, http://www.business-humanrights.org/Documents /Ericsson-response-China-labour-law-16-Jan-07.pdf (accessed 29 October 2009).

27. Global Labor Strategies, "Undue influence: corporations gain ground in battle over China's new labor law."

28. International Textile, Garment, and Leather Workers' Federation, press release, "Nike repudiates AmCham on Chinese labor law reform."

29. Global Labor Strategies, "Undue influence: corporations gain ground in battle over China's new labor law," p. 33.

30. John Monks, 2006. "Europe's trade and investment with China: challenges and choices," 2006, http://www.etuc.org/a/2612 (accessed 29 October 2009).

31. Global Labor Strategies 2007, pp. 35–6.

32. Leung, "Legality and labor politics in China: the labor contract law legislation."

33. Sky Canaves, "Factory closures strain China's labor law," *Wall Street Journal,* 17 January 2008.

34. Global Labor Strategies, "Undue influence: corporations gain ground in battle over China's new labor law," p. 38.

35. Hon DongFang, "Chinese Labour Struggles," *New Left Review* 34 (July–August 2005).

36. Canaves, "Factory closures strain China's labor law."

37. Carol Divjak, "China enacts new labour law amid rising discontent," 2008, *World Socialist Web Site,* http://www.wsws.org/articles/2008/feb2008 /clab-f06.shtml (Accessed 30 October 2009).

38. *Ibid.*

39. Insurgent Notes. 2010. "Wildcat Strikes in China," *Insurgent Notes,* 17 June 2010, http://insurgentnotes.com/2010/06/wildcat-strikes-in-china/ (accessed 10 October 2010).

40. Andrew Browne and Norihiko Shirouzu, "Beijing pressures Japanese on wages," *The Wall Street Journal,* 29 August 2010.

41. Chan, "Labor standards and human rights: the case of Chinese workers under market socialism."

14

China's Green Challenges in the Rise to Global Power under the Leadership of Hu Jintao

Carlos Wing-Hung LO
Yok-shiu F. LEE
Xueyong ZHAN

Introduction

China's ecological footprint has become increasingly visible and enlarged in the course of its rapid economic development since the 1970s. With an annual GDP growth of over 10% on average for three consecutive decades, China has rapidly evolved from being an emerging economy to replacing Japan as the second largest economy in the world at the close of 2010, with considerable potential to surpass the USA in GDP terms in the foreseeable future. The price for this rise to becoming a global economic giant is the heavy environmental cost of China's development strategy of high energy and high resource consumption which has sustained a prolonged period of successive industrial leaps founded upon backward and polluting technologies. According to the latest report from the Global Footprint Network, China has quadrupled its ecological footprint in the last forty years and is currently one of the top two countries, the other being the USA, that demand the most from the planet.[1] Indeed, China tops the world's rankings in pollution statistics, most notably in the emissions of CO_2, SO_2 and other major green house gases (GHGs). As the China Ecological Report 2010 warns, "China's per capita footprint was two times greater than its available biocapacity by

2007", and there is no sign of a reversal of this aggravating trend as its ecological footprint "is still increasing more quickly than its biocapacity".[2] Concerned by this growing threat to the planet's sustainability, international pressure has quickly mounted in the last decade to demand that China become environmentally responsible by pursuing a greener path of economic development,[3] first in the process of concluding the Kyoto Protocol and later at the Copenhagen climate summit. At the same time, as the country moves away from abject poverty toward relative affluence, domestic demand for expending greater efforts on ecological protection to improve the quality of the living environment has become increasingly pronounced. Thus China is now presented with the formidable task of transforming itself from an ecologically black dragon to an environmentally-friendly green giant.

On the road from being a Third World nation to becoming a global power, China is well aware of the implications of becoming a major polluter in the world community.[4] The resolution for the adoption of sustainable development as the national strategy for long-term development in the wake of the 1992 Rio Earth Summit signalled an environmental awakening of the Chinese Communist leadership, distancing itself from the polluting path of development characterized by the "pollution-first, remedy-second" approach. The immediate impact of this first green paradigm shift on stopping ecological degradation was symbolic rather than substantive, and the preoccupation with quantitative economic growth to lift the nation out of poverty has constrained political leaders at all levels from according a high priority to environmental protection. Nevertheless, the promulgation of China's Agenda 21 by the State Council in 1994 formally inaugurated the nation's green path to development and provided an important platform for green capacity building.[5] The Ninth Five-Year Plan (1996–2000), which is regarded as China's first green national development plan, was a manifestation of this green strategic thinking, reflecting a serious attempt to bring "aggravating pollution and ecological damage under initial control".[6] The institutional foundation for the nation's green commitment was eventually laid down at the close of Jiang Zemin's era when Zhu Rongji, then Premier, engineered China's farewell to "GDP driven" development by advancing the progressive concept of "qualitative economic growth" to reduce the ecological burden of economic prosperity. This pro-environment tone was set in his 2000 Government Report, which paved the way for the eventual President Hu Jintao to steer China toward a greener future:

> We must positively implement the strategy of sustainable development, foster the adjustment of economic structures, raise the overall quality of the economy, and promote coordinated economic and social development.[7]

This green thinking of socialist modernization essentially focused on industry's environmental performance while maintaining the industrial sector as the country's key growth engine in the era of sustainable development.

To what extent have President Hu Jintao and Premier Wen Jiaobao been able to act on Zhu's green platform to green China? In this chapter, we will examine three major green challenges that China has to deal with in its rise to becoming a global power as it enters the twenty-first century under the leadership of Hu Jintao. We begin with a review of China's changing environmental perspectives in the past few decades, followed by an examination of the progress made in reversing the aggravation of environmental conditions. On this basis, we will consider the nature of the challenges posed by the urgency to strengthen regulatory control of polluting industries, the imperative to take up environmental leadership internationally and domestically, and the necessity to cultivate an environmental civil society to leverage green NGOs' resources and capacity to enhance environmental governance. We will conclude by summing up the achievements made in these three domains and assessing the potential for China to becoming a fully-fledged green citizen in the world community in the near future.

China's Changing Environmental Perspectives under Hu Jintao: From Passive Control to Active Environmental Stewardship

China's environmental perspectives have been heavily shaped by the development orientation of its political leaders at different stages of economic progress in the reform era. In the first decade of economic reform, China was desperate for rapid industrial growth to recover from years of political turmoil and economic stagnation caused by the Cultural Revolution. The pro-growth orientation of Deng Xiaoping and his reform team was so single-mindedly focused that it effectively led them to the decision to subordinate environmental well-being to economic interests without much hesitation. They were ready to accept the adverse consequences of ecological destruction and heavy pollution in return for an accelerated pace of economic development. The development path of "pollution first, remedy second" clearly reflected this mind-set of sacrificing the natural environment almost unconditionally in order to achieve economic success within a short period of time.[8]

In the second decade of the economic reform era, the influence of the pro-growth legacy remained strong among Jiang Zemin's team as Jiang readily accepted that his primary task was to build on the first decade's spectacular economic success to attain an economic take-off and lift the nation out of poverty. As the sense of urgency in the need for economic growth gradually subsided and the country's material conditions greatly improved, a sentiment that the environmental costs of economic growth needed to be appropriately addressed in the pursuit of quantitative leaps emerged in response to the alarming statistics on environmental conditions and the pollution situation. Reflected in China's subscription to the idea of sustainable development proposed in the 1992 Earth Summit was a growing pro-environment orientation among China's leadership stratum to move the nation away from a polluting path of development. The prevailing view in this post-summit period was that a certain balance should be sought between economic growth and environmental protection, one which favoured a proactive over a remedial approach to pollution control. Accompanying the emergence of this greener development ideology was the growing recognition of the unsustainability of a pollution-dominating path in the long run and its inability to take China's economy to a higher and better quality level of growth.[9] An environmentally friendly approach based on technological innovation was eventually deemed the most viable alternative to transform the nation's development trajectory from quantity-focused to quality-oriented. As a result, the idea of passive control of pollution finally came to an end under the Jiang-Zhu leadership, giving way to a more progressive view of active prevention enshrined in the conceptual scheme of sustainable development. At the same time, the predominance of the utilitarian thrust of the prevailing development paradigm also declined at the end of the second decade of economic reform.[10]

The third decade of the economic reform era was dominated by a green paradigm of active environmental stewardship. Building upon Jiang-Zhu's development strategy of greening socialist modernization, the leadership of Hu-Wen at first struggled to formulate a coherent conceptual construct to develop the green idea of quality economic growth in their early years. In the search for an original perspective on environmental stewardship, their first major endeavour was the introduction of the concept of "resource-saving and environmentally-friendly society" (advanced in 2004).[11] This concept was in fact an attempt to consolidate the fragmented action plans of "cleaner production", "circular economy" and "saving energy, reducing emissions". It was encapsulated initially in the Eleventh Five-Year Plan (2006–2010) and then propagated in the 2008 Government Report.[12] However, this green society concept was too loosely defined and fragmented to provide a coherent sense of green vision and mission to underpin the long-term development of the socialist market economy.

The inspiration for the leading architects of China's reform to strive for a conceptual breakthrough came from the renewed international effort to tackle the increasing threat of climate change in the post-Kyoto period. The attainment of a global economic power status has apparently strengthened the confidence of China's political leaders to take an active and leading role in addressing global environmental problems. In response to growing expectations from the international community that it reduce the ecological footprint of its economic growth, China has advanced the strategic idea of building a "low carbon economy" to exercise active environmental stewardship.[13] This notion of a "low-carbon economy", made public by Premier Wen Jiabao at the Asia-Pacific Economic Cooperation Economic Leaders Meeting in 2009, has indeed helped facilitate China's global reach. It provides a global perspective for China to integrate its national economic development and environmental protection agendas with those of the world community. The promulgation of the Twelfth Five-Year Plan earlier in 2011 marked the completion of China's green ideological transformation, as the Hu-Wen leadership has effectively translated Jiang-Zhu's abstract idea of pursuing quality economic growth into a pragmatic agenda of building a low-carbon economy by committing to active environmental stewardship.[14] As such, this second green Five-Year Plan in Chinese history has also set forth a major challenge for the forthcoming leadership in the fourth decade of economic reform: to consolidate the ideological basis for enhancing China's capacity for environmental stewardship to help build a low-carbon economy.

China's Recent Environmental Conditions: Reversing the Aggravation of Environmental Conditions?

Due to a set of entrenched institutional constraints, the mounting allocation of resources to tackle environmental ills in the past three decades has not been effective in averting and reversing the continuing deterioration of environmental conditions in China. Air and water pollutions remain intractable problems, even though they have topped the nation's environmental policy agenda since the Ninth Five-Year Plan. Based on an assessment of the latest efforts in curtailing externalities nationwide, we believe that the chance of controlling and reversing environmental and ecological degradations in the near future remains slim.

First of all, surging air pollution has become a highly noticeable problem in many major metropolitan regions in the past two decades. In 2008, about one-quarter (23%) of the 519 cities regularly monitored for their air quality rated theirs as poor (grade III or worse than grade III). Only 4% of these cities reported grade I air quality. Three major air pollutants – PM10, sulphur dioxide and nitrogen dioxide – have become the major causes of poor urban air quality. In general, cities in the north emitted more pollutants than their southern counterparts. Although the concentration levels of some key pollutants have started to decline in recent years, albeit only modestly, acid rain has become increasingly frequent and is detected all over the country. In 2008, out of a total of 477 cities monitored for acid rain occurrence, 252 were found to be affected by acidic precipitations to varying degrees; 34% of cities suffering from acid rain reported an occurrence rate of 25% per annum, and about 24% suffered from severe acid rain with pH values below 5.0. Most of the acid rainfall was concentrated in areas situated to the south of the Changjiang River in Sichuan

Province, and to the east of Yunnan Province, including Zhejiang, Fujian, Jiangxi, Hunan and Chongqing.[15]

Secondly, water pollution has remained a prevalent issue and shows no sign of abating. The two major sources of water pollutants are untreated or partially treated industrial effluence and domestic sewage. The central government report on China's environment for 2008 stated that the water quality of the country's seven major river systems and their tributaries was moderately contaminated.[16] The quality of the water found along 45% of the length of these rivers was classified as poor or worse (i.e., grades IV, V, and worse than grade V). Water in Haihe was the most polluted, while that in Huanghe, Huaihe, and Liaohe was found to be moderately polluted. Only the water quality in the Pearl and the Changjiang Rivers was deemed to be clean. In addition, largely as a consequence of excessive discharge of nitrogen and phosphorus, the water quality in major lakes and reservoirs has continued to decline. The water quality in Taihu, Dianchi, Baiyang Lake and Dalai Lake was found to be very poor (i.e., worse than grade V) because these water bodies were subject to a high degree of eutrophication. Ten key large reservoirs nationwide have also suffered from increasing levels of nitrogen pollution and widespread eutrophication.[17]

Thirdly, one worrying trend in the nation's deteriorating environmental landscape is a surging level of pollution detected in rural areas which have become increasingly populated with industrial enterprises in the past two decades. Industry-induced degradation in rural areas was recorded at its worst in 1995 and pollution control efforts have been stepped up since then to reverse the situation. The outcome of such control measures has been somewhat mixed, however. Data gathered for the Eleventh Five-Year Plan period of 2001–2005 showed that the amount of major industrial pollutants declined markedly: particulates, COD and solid waste dropped by 8.0%, 8.7%, and 42.8% respectively. However, in the same period, the amount of industrial SO_2 and smoke/dust emission jumped by a hefty 38.4% and 11.4% respectively. Industrial emissions have thus remained a major source of air pollution in both urban centres and the countryside.[18]

Fourthly, in addition to pollution, the degradation of land resources in the western provinces has also become an increasingly challenging ecological issue. Despite the implementation of the cropland-to-grassland conversion programme in 2003, the scale of cattle-ranching activities still exceeds the carrying capacity of pasture areas. For instance, in recent years, as a consequence of overgrazing, the carrying capacity of the pasture areas in Inner Mongolia, Qinghai, Gansu, Xinjiang Autonomous Region, Sichuan, and Tibet was exceeded by between 20 to 40%.[19] Overgrazing has posed a major threat to the country's land resources, leading to an increased rate of occurrence, and an escalating scale of severe dust storms. Dust storms were the most severe in the spring of 2006, with eighteen episodes recorded in northern China.[20]

Against an overall deteriorating trend in environmental conditions, only two topical areas have reported some modest improvements: the quality of seawater in offshore water bodies and forest coverage. As a consequence of the prevalence of inorganic nitrogen and phosphate pollution originating from land-based sources, the quality of offshore water along the country's major population centres has been found to be only modestly satisfactory. In the 1990s, the occurrence of algae blooms in offshore areas became very frequent and their scale increasingly large. Data collected in the 2000s showed a reversing trend, however: in 2008, for instance, the number of reported algae bloom incidents was 68, which was 14 cases fewer than in 2007.[21] The total area affected by algae blooms has also reported a modest decline: dropping from 15,000 square kilometres in 2000 to 13,738 square kilometres in 2008.[22] Forest coverage has also made modest gains in recent years, as a consequence of intensified central government interventions. Noting that the nationwide forest coverage figure, at 18.2% in the early 2000s, was unsatisfactory when measured against historic trends, the central government tackled this deficiency by increasing the number of nature reserves from 2,395 in 2006 to 2,538 in 2008.[23] In addition, afforestation programmes were implemented to counter the impact of tree felling. In 2006, for instance, the net annual tree growth was recorded at 497 million cubic metres, while the annual logging figure was 365 million cubic metres.[24]

The evidence gathered from an overall assessment of China's environmental conditions suggests that nationwide clean-up efforts expended in the past three decades have not been able to arrest and reverse the downward trends of environmental pollution and ecological degradation. Enormous challenges remain in the fight against air and water pollution not only in major metropolitan regions but also in an increasingly industrialized rural sector gradually extending from the eastern part of the country to the interior provinces in the west. The western provinces, the destination of a sizeable industrial relocation programme instituted by the coastal cities, are therefore suffering increasingly from the double-whammy effects of pollution and ecological degeneration.

Green Challenge One:
Regulatory Control of Polluting Industries:
Adopting Cleaner Production
and Building a Circular Economy

Weak Regulatory Control of Pollution in the 1980s and 1990s

In the protection of the environment, China has adopted the approach of "environmental management by law" to control[25] industrial pollution since 1978. Through a series of active efforts in environmental legislation, China has basically built quite a comprehensive environmental legal regime.[26] All major types of environmental pollution have virtually been put under the regulatory control of the emerging system of law. In particular, most of the legal regulations are quite advanced and complete in terms of their structure, format and content, because the related laws and regulations in the American and European environmental legal systems were widely consulted in the drafting stage. However, despite the steady progress in environmental law-making, environmental pollution was not brought under control.[27] This was mainly because local environmental protection bureaus (EPBs) were not able to perform strict enforcement, aggravated by the incompleteness of most pollution control measures and supporting systems. As a result, the effectiveness of regulatory enforcement was doubtful and environmental pollution was persistently out of control.[28] Most notably, under the prescriptions of environmental laws and pollution control regulations, a large number of highly polluting enterprises and factories should have been ordered to shut down their production facilities, suspend production, convert their production line to manufacture other cleaner products, or relocate their plants to other industrial areas. Major reasons for this failure were the higher priorities accorded by governments at all levels to economic interests and workers' employment, together with the tremendous pressure from government authorities which owned or sponsored these polluting enterprises and factories.[29] In the absence of active support from local governments and cooperation from other bureaucratic agencies, it was difficult for local EPBs to take a tough stand in regulatory enforcement against the old-fashioned polluting plants (the so-called "15-small").

This regulatory stalemate persisted until 1996 when the central government began to show greater determination to curb the rampant industrial pollution, as the green strategy and agenda had gradually taken hold in China's Five-Year Plans starting from the Ninth. At that time, an instruction was issued by the State Council to governments at all levels to take a hard line in the enforcement of pollution control regulations and to set deadlines for enterprises and factories with serious pollution to close down or stop their production activities.[30] However, the outcomes of these clean-up efforts depended very much on whether local EPBs could strictly enforce environmental rules and regulations consistently in the long run, whether they could secure active support from local governments, whether they could obtain adequate enforcement power and resources, and whether they could sternly penalize enterprises and factories for their unlawful polluting acts. Here, the control of water pollution in the Huai River provides a notorious example of regulatory enforcement in China, which ended in complete failure after years of organized effort to control and reduce industrial pollution.[31] Thus it was a nationwide phenomenon that the bulk of pollution control regulations were not being uniformly implemented across China, and that many of the country's pollution problems appeared to be getting worse. In short, the enforcement gap in the regulatory control of pollution remained pronounced at the close of the Jiang-Zhu leadership.[32]

Tightening up Regulatory Enforcement under the Hu-Wen Leadership

The changing landscape in the regulatory control of pollution in China came in the Hu-Wen era under the new green thinking of active environmental stewardship, which pushed for adopting cleaner production and building a circular economy first, and developing a low-carbon economy later. In reality, the rise in people's living standards as a result of rapid economic development has provided governments in major cities such as Beijing, Shanghai and Guangzhou with improved material conditions and stronger public support for taking environmental protection more seriously. The most outstanding examples were Beijing, in fulfilling its promise to stage a green Olympics, and Guangzhou, in achieving its aspiration to be a green model city. In addition, the introduction of a new leadership responsibility system for local environmental quality and the withering away of state-owned enterprises have both brought support to stricter regulatory enforcement.[33] For example, with the blessing of the municipal government and after years of futile effort, the Guangzhou EPB finally closed down more than 60 garment factories causing serious pollution in a nearby county.[34]

Nationally, the effect of the growth of enforcement was visible in data from China's annual statistical reports on the environment (see Table 1). These data show a 30% increase in the number of administrative enforcement cases during the period from 2001 to 2006. Meanwhile the same data show that the average fine per case increased substantially from RMB 3,377 in 2001 to RMB 10,427 in 2006, an increase of 208%. This indicates not only that there are more frequent enforcement actions, but that each individual action is more stringent. Moreover, this happened at a time when the number of written environmental complaints (*xinfang*) increased by 67%. Thus, increasing external pressure on EPBs for greater enforcement effectiveness is clearly evident.[35]

Our study has shown that Guangzhou has followed a similar pattern, as shown by data obtained from the Guangzhou EPB. The number of administrative enforcement cases grew from 256 in 1998 to 1,547 in 2006, while the average fine was RMB 5,207 in 1998 and RMB 45,639 in 2006, with the number of written complaints about pollution increasing from 5,300 in 1999 to 20,192 in 2006. Assuming that pressure for enforcement is matched with support, our surveys also confirm this shift as they included a series of questions asking enforcement officials about their perceptions regarding support for enforcement from various societal sectors (i.e., the public, mass media, business, and social environmental organizations). Except for business, all showed a substantial and statistically significant shift in the level of support for enforcement.[36]

Table 1: China: National Statistics on Enforcement
of Environmental Regulations, 1998–2006

Year	Administrative enforcement cases	Average fine per case (RMB)	Citizens' written complaints about pollution
1998	39,754	n/a	n/a
1999	53,101	n/a	n/a
2000	55,209	n/a	n/a
2001	71,089	3,377	369,712
2002	100,103	3,017	435,420
2003	92,818	3,546	525,988
2004	80,079	5,747	595,852
2005	93,265	6,868	608,245
2006	92,404	10,427	616,122

Indeed, in the period between 2000 and 2006 in Guangzhou, there was even a measure of urgency about prioritizing regulatory enforcement, with the municipal government embracing the designation of "green model city" as a priority in its Tenth Five-Year Plan (Pearl River Environment News, 2006). This led to the establishment of the "Achieving Model City Target Responsibility System" at all levels of the municipal government. Of particular interest to this study was that enforcement officials were advised to modify their enforcement styles in three ways: (1) to be more assertive in collecting pollution discharge fees; (2) to become more strict with polluting enterprises (i.e., regardless of their "connections"); and (3) to enforce the legal requirements of two specific policies – the "three synchronizations" and the "imposition of deadlines on enterprises to control and reduce their pollution levels" (Pearl River Environment News, 2006). Taken together, this would appear to be a rallying cry for the styles of formalism and coercion. This call to action also seems to have been picked up by the media and the public, which has led to more frequent complaints, sometimes even when there was no violation of the law. Such public pressure had become a major source of influence on EPB agents by 2006, according to most agents interviewed in depth in the eleven Guangzhou district EPBs.

Overall, this system has led to somewhat tougher punishment for violations of pollution regulations and an increased allocation of financial resources (to an average of 2% of GDP per year during this period). In addition, at about this time, the Guangzhou EPB also began periodically to publicize habitual violators.[37] The stress on a more legal approach was further underscored when the Chief of the EPB symbolically appointed an environmental official who was a law graduate to head the enforcement team. With this legalistic mandate and external support in the task environment, enforcement officials were encouraged to shift their enforcement style elements away from prioritization and accommodation and toward formalism and coercion.

However, the general view is that the government's determination and its long-term commitment are always open to doubt as it has been widely reported that efforts in pollution control have been relaxed following a prolonged period of tight control.[38] In 2007 a survey jointly conducted by the Centre for Environmental Publicity and Education of the State Environmental Protection Administration and the China Academy of Social Science found that the general public is disappointed with regulatory enforcement, with 72.4% of respondents considering that the enforcement of environmental regulations was not strictly performed.[39] Greater national and local efforts for ensuring stringent enforcement are badly needed.

Strengthening Regulatory Enforcement in Sub-Urban and Rural China

While there has been steady improvement in tightening up the enforcement of environmental regulations in urban China, what has been the situation in sub-urban and rural areas? The problems and difficulties of regulatory control in rural areas were alarming, as reported by some studies,[40] under the large-scale and rapid development of township and village enterprises (TVEs) in the pursuit of rural economic transformation since the early 1980s.[41] Contributing factors were multiple, including the lack of properly organized and structured environmental agencies in rural jurisdictions; shortage of enforcement officials with technical competence; inadequate resource support and poor technical equipment; a wider territorial coverage;

the backward production technologies of the majority of factories; and local citizens with lower environmental awareness. After all, the core of the problem at that time of feverish growth was that most governments in rural towns and villages had almost completely ignored the importance of environmental protection and pollution control in favour of the overriding concern of local economic development.

As the polluting consequences of rural industrialization posed a growing threat and the scale of pollution was gradually extending beyond regulatory control, both provincial and local governments began to make a concerted effort to reorganize regulatory enforcement in rural jurisdictions. After years of efforts, how far have the preconditions for effective enforcement of environmental regulation been created in rural China? How effectively have the enforcement officials of rural EPBs been able to enforce environmental regulations? Our earlier study of regulatory enforcement in four local jurisdictions in the Pearl River Delta Region provides answers to these questions.[42]

There are several factors facilitating more effective environmental enforcement. First of all, the EPB officials in the rural areas of the Pearl River Delta Region in general have pro-environmental values. This is an encouraging sign, as their positive environmental orientation will help to legitimize the regulatory policy, motivate their enforcement action, and increase the demand for positive enforcement outcomes. In addition, EPB officials have received at least a modicum of governmental support in performing their enforcement duties.[43] This indicates that governments in rural areas may be less obsessed with economic growth than previously reported and, on average, more balanced in giving some weight to environmental protection. The implementation of a system of accountability for the administrative leadership on environmental quality may account for this positive development. Thus there has been growing pressure on governments at lower levels from their superiors to increase their commitment to combating industrial pollution. For example, the main reason the Zengcheng EPB obtained stronger government support was that the city mayor was severely criticized by both provincial and municipal governments for the city's poor performance in pollution control. Finally, the EPB officials reported that they have obtained significant levels of support from society in the performance of their enforcement duties. The general public and the mass media are the two major sources of social support. According to the Zengcheng EPB, a rise in complaints about pollution from local citizens has created palpable popular pressure on them to step up their enforcement measures. The local media have also been critical of the slow progress in reducing industrial pollution and are aggressive in reporting cases of pollution.[44] However, the influence of social forces on supporting enforcement, as independent, active, and established green non-governmental organizations (NGOs), is basically non-existent in suburban and rural Guangdong.

What are the obstacles to enforcement in these suburban and rural regulatory settings? The organizational capacity of the local EPBs in regulatory enforcement appears to be constrained by lack of resources, inadequate administrative authority, and environmental officials' lack of technical training and knowledge. In addition, the strong economic orientation of local governments, which is generally presumed to be especially pronounced in the PRD region, has consistently put environmental agencies in a weak position in the bureaucratic setting. Because of their inferior bureaucratic rank, it should not be surprising that respondents indicated that it is far more difficult to get active support and cooperation from other bureaucratic authorities for conducting stringent enforcement. Finally, the problem of human resource management in local EPBs is expressed in the difficulty of building a competent enforcement team. Greater budget constraints, inferior living conditions, and meagre career prospects have all put local governments in rural jurisdictions in a disadvantageous position compared with their urban counterparts in the recruitment of highly qualified candidates to take up positions within their local EPBs. One recent practice has been to recruit from urban EPBs. For example, the current deputy chief of the Kaiping EPB was formerly a leading official in a district EPB in Guangzhou. Upgrading the knowledge and technological competence of existing environmental officials, either through offering training programmes or financing continuing education, may be difficult given the tight manpower situation after several rounds of bureaucratic streamlining, heavy enforcement duties, and lack of proper staff development policies. With increasing external support and a growing ability to conduct uniform enforcement, environmental officials assessed the effectiveness of their enforcement actions quite positively. The higher rating on effective enforcement may indicate that major obstacles to more rigorous regulatory enforcement are gradually being removed.[45]

On the whole, our studies provide solid evidence to demonstrate that the contextual setting for regulatory control of environmental pollution in both urban and rural China has begun to change from one marked by hostility and resistance to one featuring more receptivity and greater support. It is expected that the institutional environment will lend additional support for stricter and more stringent regulatory control of industrial pollution under the Twelfth Five-Year Plan.

Green Challenge Two: Taking up Environmental Leadership in Addressing Climate Change (International) and Creating a Low-Carbon Economy (Domestic)

After China became the world's largest emitter of greenhouse gases in 2006, it faced increasing pressure from the West to commit itself to an absolute carbon reduction target. Confronted by such a demand, China, in the second half of the 2000s, replaced its earlier position of passive compliance with international agreements with an assertive activist stance in the global arena. This assertive posture is the most prominent in regard to its position on how the burden for climate protection should be shared between developed and developing countries. Specifically, China insists that no cap should be imposed on its carbon dioxide emissions because, under the 1997 Kyoto Protocol, it was considered a developing country and was therefore exempted from any emission reduction. Instead, China subscribes to the principle of "common but differentiated responsibilities" in mitigating climate change.[46]

China's Rebuttal of Western Criticisms

China's assertive stance in regard to the international carbon agenda is driven by its perception of unfairness in how it has been criticized for its rapidly increasing emissions of greenhouse gases. The Chinese government's rebuttal runs along the following lines of argument. First, the increased levels of carbon emissions recorded on China's territory come mostly from industrial production transplanted from the West to China. This relocation of manufacturing industry constitutes, in effect, the export of a large portion of the West's carbon footprint to the People's Republic.[47] Western countries are therefore hypocritical in criticizing China for increased emissions when they are investing in industrial production with heavy pollution in China and, at the same time, reaping the benefits of such industrial investment in the form of low-cost manufactured imports.

Secondly, while total emissions in China have increased, they are still less than one-quarter of those of the United States on a per capita basis. For instance, China, with a population of 1.3 billion people, released 4,760 kg of carbon dioxide per capita in 2007. China's per capita emission was considerably lower than the United States' emission figure of 19,280 kg per capita.[48] An objective assessment of China's contribution to overall GHG emissions should hence take into consideration the broader parameters, such as historical contribution to current carbon concentration. International comparisons of total cumulative carbon emissions have in fact shown that, measured on a historical per capita basis, China ranks seventy-eighth in the world, not first.[49]

China's Opposition to Absolute Emission Reduction Targets

Resisting the call to introduce mandatory emission caps on its greenhouse gases, China's position on the global carbon debate has therefore shown a new-found sense of confidence in negotiations over international environmental governance matters. In preparation for intensive international negotiations over climate change at the 2009 Copenhagen Conference, China announced its decision to reduce carbon dioxide emissions per unit of GDP in 2020 by 40–45% in comparison with the 2005 levels. It has, however, continued to oppose the imposition of any legally binding emission reduction targets on developing countries. Insisting that the international community should respect the developing countries' "right to develop", China has repeatedly argued that the burden of protecting the global climate should largely rest with the rich industrialized countries.[50] Specifically, China wants developed nations to commit to more ambitious reduction targets, to share their low-carbon technologies with developing countries, and to set up a United Nations fund that would help finance the cost of purchasing low-carbon technology for use across the globe.[51]

Given China's insistence on the allocation of reasonable carbon emission quotas to allow its economy to continue to grow, in pace with the twin processes of rapid industrialization and urbanization, and given that the "high-carbon" character inherent in China's energy structure could not be fundamentally altered in the short term, the carbon question will in all likelihood remain a highly contentious international environmental governance issue between China and the West in the years to come.

China's Domestic Climate Change Policy Is Energy-Focused

Within China, the central government unveiled its first national programme to combat climate change in 2007.[52] Devoid of any specific GHG emissions reduction targets, its principal thrust was energy-oriented: high priority was given to developing low-carbon energy sources and to raising energy efficiency levels in the industrial and agricultural sectors.[53] China's climate-related legislation is likewise energy-focused. The objective of the Energy Conservation Law, enacted in 1997 and revised in 2007, was directly related to the overall goal of the country's climate protection strategy. It declared energy conservation as an important strategic objective of long-term national economic development and mandated economy-wide reduction goals in energy consumption through efficiency gains in energy use in the manufacturing, construction, and transport sectors. The Renewable Energy Law, enacted in 2005 and revised in 2009, is another piece of climate-related national legislation. For the first time, it introduced a set of legally-binding targets in making renewable energy an important element of the nation's energy supply mix. As depicted in the 2007 *Medium- and Long-Term Development Plan for Renewable Energy*, Chinese planners aim to generate, by 2020, 15% of the country's overall energy supply from renewable sources (including hydropower, wind, biomass and solar energy), leading to a reduced emission of 1.2 billion tons of carbon dioxide.[54] Given that China's annual carbon dioxide emission was recorded at around 6 billion tons in 2007,[55] the planned reduction of GHG emissions through the development of renewable energy sources is quite significant.

Translating the National Climate Agenda into Local Actions

Most of the localization efforts of the national climate protection agenda have been steered by the central government. Only a small number of provincial and city governments have taken initiatives on the climate issue and voluntarily drawn up their own climate agendas.[56] In 2008, fourteen provinces, autonomous regions and direct-controlled municipalities were selected by Beijing in a pilot scheme and asked to formulate their own provincial- and city-level climate agendas.[57] In July 2010, five provinces[58] and eight cities[59] were tasked by the National Development and Reform Commission to turn themselves into "low-carbon provinces" and "low-carbon cities" respectively in a trial to implement the national low-carbon policy at the provincial and municipal levels.[60] The selected local authorities were merely asked to complete the following tasks: (i) prepare a low-carbon development plan; (ii) formulate a comprehensive policy framework in support of low-carbon development; (iii) expedite the establishment of a low-carbon economic structure; (iv) establish a greenhouse gas emission statistical and management system; and (v) promote a low-carbon lifestyle and consumption model.

However, in regard to the specific task of turning their cities into "low-carbon cities", mayors have not been given much guidance by central government agencies. As a consequence, cities that have formulated localized climate agendas have produced a diverse set of measures and actions that do not conform to any nationwide, standardized criteria. For instance, while both Shanghai and Hangzhou have introduced similar measures that focus on energy efficiency and clean energy production, the planning priorities and standards of their respective low-carbon projects are markedly different.[61] Although the absence of a national prescription allows cities to come up with their own innovations, the lack of a standardized policy matrix – comprising broad goals, specific objectives and fine-tuned targets – makes it difficult to measure and evaluate the comparative progress made by the local authorities.

In addition, the initial climate-related actions introduced by many local governments have been narrowly confined to the energy sector and mostly piecemeal in nature. For instance, while Baoding has striven to become a low-carbon city, its mayor has merely emphasized the importance of manufacturing solar power panels and wind power turbines for export.[62] In a similar vein, Xiamen's notion of a low-carbon city consists primarily of the development of the LED lighting industry and the building of an energy museum. Wuxi's attempt at this stage is even more rudimentary than Xiamen's – it plans merely to set up a low-carbon city development research centre.[63] The building of a truly low-carbon settlement or, better yet, the conversion of an existing city into a low carbon version, would involve transitions from high-carbon emissions to low-carbon emissions in multiple dimensions – ranging from infrastructure, urban planning, transport network and lifestyle to economic structure. Thus, the pilot schemes reportedly being run in some of China's cities at the moment are woefully inadequate in terms of capturing the essence of the low-carbon city concept.

Furthermore, in localizing the national climate protection agenda, city-level authorities have shown that they do not automatically and fully embrace all the key concerns of the central government and, instead, are highly selective in regard to the incorporation of national-level concerns into local measures. While Beijing has given equal weight to the three broad policy issues of climate change, energy conservation and pollution reduction, local governments are mostly only interested in implementing measures to conserve energy, because they accept the argument that intensive energy use would increase the cost, and thus affect the sustainability, of local economic growth.[64] Policy actions designed to reduce pollution and control greenhouse gas emissions, on the other hand, are still generally considered by local authorities to be impediments to local economic growth and are therefore given much lower priority when compared with the adoption of energy conservation measures. In addition, even though a number of emission-reduction projects have purportedly been introduced by provincial and city governments in order to combat climate change, they have turned out to be mere pollution control measures repackaged or dressed up as climate change measures.[65]

Only recently have the initial steps been taken in China's transition from a high-carbon economy to a low-carbon structure. The central government has assigned a high priority to this task, but not entirely out of a concern for global climate change. Instead, the push for local authorities to build low-carbon economies and low-carbon cities stems mostly from domestic considerations such as the imperative to ensure the country's energy security position and the need to develop a new, globally competitive economic sector based on clean and renewable energy. Overall, without any practical guidelines issued by the central government or a coherent policy framework structured at the local level, genuine climate protection policy actions at the urban and regional scale are still far and few in between.

Green Challenge Three: Cultivating Environmental NGOs as an Institutional Support for Improving the Capacity of Environmental Protection – From Weak Civil Society to Active

The emergence and development of environmental NGOs in the last two decades have been stimulated by rising public concerns regarding environmental degradation and pollution resulting from China's rapid industrialization and urbanization.[66] In the 1990s, Chinese environmental NGOs focused primarily on environmental education and other apolitical conservation projects, and they played a very limited role in China's environmental policy arena, since most of them were constrained by their limited access to the policy process and weak organizational capacity.[67] This passive and accommodative approach has led to criticism of the actual autonomy and the proper roles of environmental NGOs in China. Most notably, Ho remarked that Chinese environmental NGOs profess a "female mildness" – a tendency to avoid any conflict with the state.[68] However, since the inauguration of President Hu Jintao's leadership in 2003, environmental NGOs have been increasingly active in both domestic policy debates and international environmental collaborations. In the past few years, China's environmental civil society has been developing fast, with greater involvement of NGOs in policy advocacy; in many situations a few environmental NGOs have successfully negotiated with local governments to achieve their environmental goals.[69] For example, in 2004, environmental NGOs collectively persuaded Premier Wen Jiabao to defer the development of numerous hydropower stations on the Nu River in Yunnan Province. A few environmental NGOs, such as the Beijing-based Friends of Nature and the Institute of Public and Environmental Affairs, have become national leaders of environmental policy advocacy. Despite the fact that environmental NGOs have yet to become key players in China's environmental governance, recent development has shown the path of an incremental institutional transition to integrate them in the environmental policy process as supporting institutions for green development.

Weak Civil Society and Environmental Governance in the 1990s

The development of China's environmental civil society has received strong encouragement from a few dedicated members of social elites. For example, the four founders of Friends of Nature – Liang Congjie, Liang Xiaoyan, Wang Lixiong and Yang Dongping – were either famous public intellectuals or political activists in the 1980s. [70] However, the restrictive political ecology in the wake of the 1989 Tiananmen Democratic Movement was not conducive to the rapid development of environmental NGOs for many years under the Jiang-Zhu leadership. Most notably, restrictive measures that controlled the registration and activities of grass-roots organizations or civic NGOs had been introduced to ensure political stability. [71] In addition, there was a lack of legal channels and administrative avenues enabling environmental NGOs to interact with the state and local governments or to participate in the policy-making process. Besides these constraining factors, the institutional basis for grooming a green civil society was still weak as environmental awareness among the general public was found to be low, [72] making it difficult to nurture a stronger popular desire for public participation in environmental protection.

While the lack of political space for the growth of environmental NGOs prevented them from playing an active role in China's environmental politics, they did not find it necessary to take on the government in environmental issues. [73] Instead, they basically adopted a non-confrontational approach to work with governments at all levels in the 1990s. Seeing the cultivation of a more environmentally aware society as the most urgent task in supporting environmental protection in China, environmental NGOs committed most of their efforts to environmental education in urban areas in order to lift people's environmental awareness and urge them to adopt environmentally-friendly behaviours.[74] Their plans and actions in environmental education were indeed geared to the policy objectives of both the central and local governments to publicize the message of environmental protection and to mobilize the public to take part in it. This common chord of environmental education with the official line made governments reconsider the supporting role of environmental NGOs and their possible contributions. Indeed, these two parties were brought together under the support of international green foundations and organizations to work jointly together, first in environmental education and later in environmental conservation. The Ford Foundation, for example, has been a major partner for both the Chinese government and NGOs in numerous areas of environmental protection and sustainable development. The political barrier was broken and the administrative taboo removed under these collaborative activities which effectively bridged the gap between the state and civil society. Although environmental NGOs were still constrained by limited resources and capacity, they were able to gain increasing legitimacy by playing a part in the official effort to protect the environment through their diligent efforts in environmental education. This laid down the foundation for them to cultivate closer interactions with the government and channel their influence in the environmental policy regime.

In sum, the environmental NGOs subscribed to a non-confrontational approach to prevent any political conflicts with the government within a politically less tolerant setting throughout the 1990s, which allowed them the necessary time and space to grow. Their constructive efforts in environmental education under this apolitical strategy enabled them to dissipate political suspicion from the regime and to acquire a legitimate role to play in China's environmental governance. A decade's capacity building in environmental education and green awareness building has made them organizationally more prepared and competent to play an active role as institutional opportunities in China's environmental governance system have gradually emerged under the Hu-Wen administration's green development platform.[75]

Cultivating Environmental NGOs as Institutional Support under the Hu-Wen Administration

Although the Communist regime has been reluctant to accord environmental NGOs an institutional status in environmental protection, it has been increasingly evident that governments at all levels have difficulty getting environmental policies effectively implemented and pollution control regulations strictly enforced without active public support. Indeed, the political system of China has become increasingly fragmented under the market economic reform,[76] and in many situations it appears that the party-state has to work with civil society organizations for effective governance, particularly in the provision of social services and environmental protection.[77] After assuming the supreme leadership in 2003, Hu Jintao has steered his administration to adopt new strategies for development, such as the "Scientific Development Concept" and "Harmonious Society", with policy priorities set to ensure social stability and sustainable development. As social harmony and green development have emerged as a national strategic framework, this has provided stronger policy rationale for governments to cultivate and engage environmental NGOs as supporting forces to improve their administrative capacity for environmental protection. In return, this has created a more favourable institutional setting for environmental NGOs to develop their organizational strength, build trust with the government, and expand their policy influence.[78]

The influence of the green NGO sector has been growing since central government officials have gradually come to realize its contribution as a possible ally in the fight against rampant industrial pollution and ecological destruction at local levels. Environmental NGOs have indeed been actively performing the role of watch-dogs over corporate regulatory compliance and disclosing enterprises' unlawful polluting practices. In particular, leading environmental officials of the Hu Jintao administration have increasingly strategically considered that the capacity of the central government in exercising environmental stewardship could be strengthened from a closer collaboration and consultation with environmental NGOs in both policy formulation and regulatory enforcement. Most notably, Pan Yue, a Deputy Minister of the Ministry of Environmental Protection, has been a close friend of the leaders of many environmental NGOs in Beijing.[79]

Environmental NGOs have not been slow to capture these political opportunities to build constructive working relationships with governments. The encouraging signal here is that they had been able to influence environmental policy making through both formal and informal channels. Since the government has begun to develop institutions to incorporate social elites and source public preferences in environmental governance,[80] a few environmental NGOs have been given access to policy decisions within explicit or implicit political agendas. For example, NGO leaders have become members of the two traditional representative institutions in the Communist political system, namely, the Chinese People's Political Consultative Conference (CPPCC) and the National People's Congress (NPC), and thus they can now take part in environmental legislation and policy making.[81] For example, Liang Congjie, one of the founders of Friends of Nature, was a member of the CPPCC and proposed numerous bills for environmental protection. Many Chinese environmental NGOs also use informal channels, such as the mass media, the internet community, and research outreach, to mobilize resources and participate in environmental protection.[82] The most popular and effective way is to cultivate friendships and personal relationships with governmental officials through *guanxi* networks. As the founders of many environmental NGOs are members of social elites, their personal connections with government agencies have helped them communicate with senior officials and participate informally in environmental policy making and implementation.[83]

In the environmental legal regime, environmental NGOs have found a way to channel their input to improve existing environmental laws and regulations. After many years of advocating the importance of public participation in the environmental policy process, the Law of Environmental Impact Assessment, adopted by the National People's Congress in 2003, and the Regulation on Environmental Impact Assessment of Planning, promulgated by the State Council in 2009, have incorporated public consultation in different stages of the environmental planning and impact assessment process. As a result, some polluting projects proposing to locate their sites in conservation areas have been stopped by the central government in recent years as a result of the joint efforts of environmental NGOs and public protests. One of the most famous events is the collective efforts of environmental NGOs to stop the construction of hydropower stations on the Nu River in Yunnan Province. A few environmental NGOs, particularly those based in Beijing, have already developed their capacity in policy advocacy and organizing collective actions. They have also displayed their legal competence to relate their causes to relevant environmental rules and regulations when petitioning the government and appealing to the general public.[84]

Assessing China's Success
in Meeting Three Major Green Challenges

To what extent has China coped with the green challenges discussed above and achieved some positive results along the policy lines of developing a low-carbon economy under the broader framework of sustainable development? China's changing institutional context for building an affluent and environmentally-aware society has created a favourable setting for the government to drive polluting industries towards a green transformation through tougher regulatory control and stricter enforcement. In addition, China's emerging status as one of the world's two economic giants should, in theory, have put it in the advantageous position of assuming global environmental leadership in addressing climate change and moving the country toward a low-carbon trajectory. However, China's lack of a tradition of public participation has rendered it difficult to cultivate environmental NGOs as an institutional support for improving its overall capacity for environmental protection.

On the whole, there is room for optimism, particularly when one considers the various favourable institutional developments established to improve environmental governance in China in recent years. These include a stronger pro-environment orientation on the part of the central leadership stratum, the emergence of a properly-formulated national green development strategy, an increasing level of support for the enforcement duties of the environmental protection agencies of local governments, advancement in the technological levels in greener production, the provision of more avenues for public participation in the implementation of environmental policies, and a higher degree of societal support for environmental issues. All of these factors have apparently strengthened China's spiritual and material basis for its quest to attain a green socialist modernization.

In assessing a nation's prospects of achieving its stated environmental policy objectives, four policy aspects need to be considered.[85] The first is innovative capacity, which refers to the sum of all opportunities for the advancement of innovations and representation of new interests.[86] The second is strategic capacity, which refers to the government's ability to co-ordinate and, over an extended period of time, to implement long-term objectives.[87] The third is consensual capacity, which refers to the government's ability to achieve negotiated solutions within the framework of co-operative political styles.[88] The last aspect is economic capacity, which refers to the government's ability to achieve sound economic performance.[89]

In conducting this assessment exercise in relation to China's environmental policy performance, we may consider the regulatory control of polluting industries to be a local-level challenge, the cultivation of environmental NGOs as an institutional support to be a national-level challenge, and the taking-up of environmental leadership in addressing climate change in the international community as a global-level challenge. Table 2 summarizes our overall assessment of China's environmental policy performance in dealing with these three major green challenges. The conditions for tightening regulatory control over polluting industries have been building up under the central government's green instructions of "cleaner production" and "saving energy and reducing emissions". Enterprises have been encouraged to seek technological innovations to replace their polluting modes of production and produce environmentally friendly products in order to meet increasingly stringent emission standards and comply with stricter pollution control regulations. The days of weak enforcement and lax control are gone due to the strong national consensus that has been reached on the need to reduce the environmental costs of economic growth. In addition, the enlarged strategic capacity of the Hu-Wen administration in steering environmental stewardship is fully manifested in its ability to guide the nation's development pathway toward a low-carbon trajectory in the Twelfth Five-Year Plan. However, variations in local economic capacity will affect the degree to which the central government can ask local jurisdictions across the nation to introduce equally uniform and

Table 2:
An Assessment of China's Environmental Policy Performance in Tackling the Green Challenges of Strengthening the Regulation of Polluting Industries – Taking up Global Environmental Leadership, and Cultivating Environmental NGOs as an Institutional Support

	Innovative capacity: From low to high
Regulatory control of polluting industries: adopting cleaner production and building a circular economy	Medium 1. The central government has stressed the importance of technological innovation in "energy saving and emissions reduction" and developing a low-carbon economy. 2. Local governments encourage polluting industries and enterprises to seek a green transformation through production innovation. 3. Individual polluting industries and enterprises have acquired greater innovative capacity under stricter regulatory control and legal requirements. 4. Both national and local information systems have turned green to cater to environmental interests and provide support for environmental innovations.
Taking up environmental leadership in addressing climate change (international) and creating a low-carbon economy (domestic)	Low 1. The central government has continued to press rich industrialized countries to share their low-carbon technology with China. 2. Only a small number of low-carbon pilot projects have been initiated by the central government, but local governments have limited capacity in charting local-level policy frameworks to support low-carbon development.
Cultivating environmental NGOs as an institutional support for improving the capacity of environmental protection	Medium 1. The National People's Congress and the State Council have launched new laws and regulations to encourage public participation in environmental policy and planning. 2. Many local governments are still development oriented, and thus they are likely to resist the participation of NGOs in the policy process.

Strategic capacity: From low to high	Consensual capacity: From low to high	Economic capacity: From low to high
Medium to high 1. The central government's commitment to stricter regulatory control of pollution has grown increasingly strong in the quest to develop a low-carbon economy. 2. The political will for stricter enforcement varies among local governments in jurisdictions with divergent levels of economic development. 3. The political and administrative capacity for regulatory enforcement of both provincial and local governments has been growing with greater local public support. 4. The resource base for regulatory control has been strengthening under an improving material basis.	Medium to high 1. The central government has designated green values as the core values for the nation's economic development strategy. 2. Non-governmental stakeholder groups support stricter regulatory control. 3. Provincial and local governments increasingly see pollution control as a high priority issue. 4. Local people have increasingly shifted their attention from material well-being to improvement of the quality of the living environment.	Medium 1. China's national economic performance is among the best in the Third World, but the gap is still quite visible when compared with Western industrial economies. 2. The gap in economic capacity between local governments in coastal and inland regions has been widening. 3. The economic capacity of industrial enterprises for regulatory compliance has on the whole been improving.
Medium to high 1. The central government has assigned a high priority to climate protection measures to ensure the country's energy security position. 2. The central government and some local governments are committed to developing a new and globally competitive clean energy sector.	Low 1. The central government has assigned a high priority to tackling climate change but lower levels of governments accord a higher priority to energy conservation and economic development. 2. Local measures and actions do not conform to any nationwide, standardized criterion for measuring and evaluating low-carbon initiatives.	Low 1. China's ability to promote further economic growth through the pursuit of a low-carbon economy is quite uncertain. 2. China continues to rely on UN and international funding to help finance the cost of purchasing low-carbon technology.
Medium 1. The Ministry of Environmental Protection has established collaboration with the environmental NGO community and uses them as watchdogs to monitor local governments and firms. 2. For local environmental NGOs, the institutional channels of public participation are still under-developed, and in many situations they have to use informal channels to exert their influence on local governments and firms.	Medium 1. The Chinese government has shown that it is willing to engage NGOs in environmental protection, and a few Beijing-based NGOs have become more active in national policy advocacy. 2. Environmental NGOs have weak capacity in policy advocacy and research. Many of them still focus on education and conservation projects.	Medium 1. In recent years, there has been more funding from both government contracts and domestic donations to environmental NGOs. 2. Environmental NGOs are still constrained by limited financial resources, and most of them rely too much on international funding.

tough standards in regulatory enforcement without giving due consideration to local economic needs.

The conditions for China to assume global environmental leadership in addressing climate change issues are the least fulfilled. The innovative capacity of the Chinese government and its ability to provide proactive environmental stewardship have remained limited, as it continues to rely on the West for much of the world's latest low-carbon technologies. China would find it difficult to convince developed countries to help serve its strategic move to build a low-carbon economy. It is also far from certain that the Hu-Wen leadership has secured a national consensus on a proper blueprint for implementing this green transformation, given the disparities in levels of economic development between the inland and coastal regions. Despite the fact that China has become the world's second largest economy, its overall economic capacity has yet to reach parity with those of industrialized economies. This apparent limitation will continue to restrict China's ability to assume a leading role in global environmental governance.

Finally, the prospects of cultivating environmental NGOs as a supporting institution are mixed. Most frustrating of all, the existing instrumental approach to engaging environmental NGOs in the environmental policy process does not allow them to play an influential role. In addition, the strategic capacity of the central government, as well as those of local government, may not be strong enough to make environmental NGOs into proxies, following their policy moves in environmental governance. A national consensus on building a constructive working relationship with environmental NGOs at the local level has yet to emerge as local governments, in general, have remained suspicious of the motivations and operations of environmental NGOs. Local governments are resistant to the liberal idea of granting environmental NGOs more access to local policy processes. The central government and local governments are apparently worried about the growing influence of environmental NGOs, as the latter have acquired stronger economic capacity through both local and international networks. However, the non-confrontational approach adopted by most environmental NGOs, together with their proven records in environmental education and their emerging role as China's environmental ambassadors in the international arena, may help them win the trust of the central administration and local governments in the long run.

In short, it is highly likely that the Chinese government will be able to tighten its grip on polluting industries through more stringent environmental regulations and stricter regulatory enforcement, consequently driving them to pursue a green path of industrial growth. However, the prospect of China assuming global environmental leadership in addressing climate change issues is rather dim, as its green institutional strength remains underdeveloped. Finally, China is still struggling to cultivate environmental NGOs as its faithful supporters helping to implement its policy instructions. In conclusion, China has made some gains in its quest for a greener future, but the tasks ahead remain formidable challenges as it contemplates the next phase of economic and institutional reforms.

Acknowledgments

The research for this paper was partially funded by the project "Changes in the Enforcement of Environmental Regulations in China: A Longitudinal Study of Environmental Enforcement Officials in Three Cities" of the Research Grants Council of the Hong Kong Special Administrative Region (RGC No.: PolyU 5469/10H) and that of "Environmental Governance in China: A Cross-sectional Perspective" supported by the Departmental Research Fund for New Academic Staff (Project No.: 4-ZZ8A) of the Department of Management and Marketing, Hong Kong Polytechnic University. Research for a part of the paper was also funded by a Seed Funding for Basic Research Grant of the University of Hong Kong.

Notes and References

1. http://www.footprintnetwork.org/en/index.php/GFN/page/national_assessments/

2. WWF International, China Ecological Footprint Report 2010, p. 4. http://assets
   .wwfcn.panda.org/downloads/china_ecological_footprint_report_2010_en_low_res.pdf

3. See A. J. Hansen, *China as An Environmentally Responsible Global Citizen.* China Paper No. 5, Centre for International Relations, The University of British Columbia, 2010.

4. See Qu Geping, "The Role of Environmental Impact Assessment in Economic Development", in A. K. Biswas, ed., *Environmental Impact Assessment in Developing Countries*, London, The United Nations University, 1987, pp, 219–228.

5. See C. W. H. Lo and S. W. Leung, "Environmental Protection and Popular Environmental Consciousness in China". In J. Y. S. Cheung, ed., *China Review 1998*, Hong Kong, The Chinese University Press, 1998, pp. 501–541.

6. "Report on the Outline of the Ninth Five-Year Plan for National Economic and Social Development and the Long-Range Objectives to the Year 2010", *Beijing Review*, No. 15, 24–30 June 1996, p. xi.

7. Zhu Rongji, "Guanyu guomin jingji he shehui fazhan di shige wunian jihua gongyao de baogao" (The Outline of the 10th Five-Year Plan of National Economic and Social Development of the People's Republic of China), *Zhongguo zhengzhi*, Vol. 4, 2001, p. 27–28.

8. See Qu, "The Role of Environmental Impact Assessment in Economic Development".

9. See Lo and Leung, "Environmental Protection and Popular Environmental Consciousness in China", pp. 504–507.

10. C. W. H. Lo and S. S. Chung, "China's Green Challenges in the Twenty-First Century". In J. Y. S. Cheng, ed., *China's Challenges in the Twenty-first Century*, Hong Kong, City University Press, 2003, pp. 722–725.

11. See Lei Shan and Xiaojie Liu, "Empirical Modeling and Appraising of Saving Society: The Case of China", *Ecological Indicators*, Vol. 8, Issue 3, May, 2008, pp. 316–317.

12. See the 11th Five-Year Plan, http://www.gov.cn/english/special /115y_index.htm.; Wen Jia Bao, "Progress report on the Chinese government, 2008", 7 July 2009, from http://www.gov.cn/gongbao/content/2006 /content_268766.htm. In Chinese.

13. UNDP China, *China and a Sustainable Future: Towards a Low Carbon Economy and Society*, China Human Development Report 2009/2010. Beijing, China Publishing Group Corporation; China Translation & Publishing Corporation. http://www.undp.org.cn/pubs/nhdr/nhdr2010e.pdf

14. See the 12th Five-Year Plan, http://news.xinhuanet.com/politics/2011-03/16/c_121193916.htm. In Chinese.

15. Ministry of Environmental Protection, *China Environment Yearbook 2008*, Beijing, China Environment Yearbook Press, 2009. In Chinese.

16. *Ibid.*

17. *Ibid.*

18. National Bureau of Statistics and Ministry of Environmental Protection. *China Statistical Yearbook on Environment 2009*. Beijing: China Statistics Press, 2010. In Chinese.

19. State Environmental Protection Administration. "2008 Report on China's Environmental Status" retrieved 10 August 2010, from http://jcs.mep.gov.cn /hjzl/zkgb/2008zkgb/200906/t20090609_152536.htm. In Chinese.

20. Ministry of Environmental Protection, *China Environment Yearbook 2007*, Beijing, China Environment Yearbook Press, 2008. In Chinese.

21. Ministry of Environmental Protection, "2008 Report on China's Environmental Status".

22. *Ibid.*

23. National Bureau of Statistics and Ministry of Environmental Protection, *China Statistical Yearbook on Environment 2008*. In Chinese.

24. Ministry of Environmental Protection, "2008 Report on China's Environmental Status".

25. C. W. H. Lo, " Environmental Management by Law in China: The Guangzhou Experience" *The Journal of Contemporary China*, No. 6, Summer, 1994, pp. 39–58.

26. See M. Palmer, "Environmental Regulation in the People's Republic of China: The Face of Domestic Law", *The China Quarterly*, No. 156, 1998, pp, 788–808.

27. See C. W. H. Lo and Y. S. F. Lee. 2009. Environment. In J. Y. S. Cheng and K. Y. Lo, ed., *China's Thirty Years Reform: Change and Regularity*, Hong Kong, City University of Hong Kong Press, Chapter 14. In Chinese.

28. X. Y. Ma and L. Ortolano, *Environmental Regulation in China: Institutions, Enforcement, and Compliance*, New York, Rowman and Littlefield,2000; and C. W. H. Lo, G. E. Fryxell and W. H. H. Wong, "Effective Environmental Regulation with Little Effect: The Antecedent of the Perceptions of Environment Officials on Enforcement Effectiveness in China", *Environmental Management*, Vol. 38, No. 3, 2006, pp. 388–410.

29. *Ibid.*

30. "Communique on Environment", *Beijing Review*, Vol. 44, No. 25, June 21, (2001), p. 6.

31. E. Economy, The River Runs Black: The Environmental Challenge to China's Future, Ithaca, NY, Cornell University Press, 2004.

32. See C. W. H. Lo and G. E. Fryxell, "Governmental and Societal Support for Environmental Enforcement in China: An Empirical Study in Guangzhou", *The Journal of Development Studies*, Vol. 41, No. 4, May, 2005, pp. 558–589.

33. C. W. H. Lo and S. Y. Tang, "Institutional Reform, Economic Changes, and Local Environmental Management in China: The Case of Guangdong Province", *Environmental Politics*, Vol. 15, No. 2, April, 2006, 190–210.

34. Pearl River Environment News, Constructing Harmony, Pursuing Excellence: The First Special Issue on the Original Record of the Guangzhou Classic on Achieving a Model City, Guangzhou Environmental Education and Publicity Centre, Guangzhou, 2006. In Chinese.

35. State Environmental Protection Administration, *China Environment Statistical Report 2000–2006*, Zhongguo Huanjing Kexue Chubanshe, Beijing, 2000–2006. In Chinese.

36. C. W. H. Lo, G. E. Fryxell, and B. van Rooij, "Changes in Enforcement Styles among Environment Officials in China", *Environment and Planning A*, Vol. 41, Issue 11, 2009, pp. 2706–2723.

37. National Bureau of Statistics and Ministry of Environmental Protection, *China Statistical Yearbook on Environment 2008*.

38. News report on pollution in Huai river: http://www.zgcaifu.com /web/caifuzazhi/shehui/20100504/677.html. 2010.

39. China Environmental Awareness Program, *2007 China General Public Environmental Survey*. Chinese Academy of Social Sciences, 2008.

40. See, for example, K. E. Swanson, R. G. Kuhn and X. Wei, "Environmental Policy Implementation in Rural China: A Case Study of Yuhang, Zhejiang". *Environmental Management*, Vol. 27, 2001, pp. 481–491.

41. See Lo and Leung, "Environmental Protection and Popular Environmental Consciousness in China".

42. C. W. H. Lo, G. E. Fryxell, and Yundoing Liao, "Environmental Regulation in Guangdong Province: A Survey of Environmental Officials in County-Level Jurisdictions", in J.Y.S. Cheng, ed., *Guangdong: Challenges in Development and Crisis Management*, Hong Kong, City University Press, 2010, pp. 266–301.

43. S. Y. Tang, C. W. H. Lo and G. E. Fryxell, ,"Governance Reform, External Support, and Environmental Regulation Enforcement in Rural China: The Case of Guangdong Province", *Journal of Environmental Management*, Vol. 91, 2010, pp. 2008–2018.

44. Lo, Fryxell, and Yundoing Liao, "Environmental Regulation in Guangdong Province", pp. 291–293.

45. *Ibid.*, pp. 293–295.

46. PBL Netherlands Environmental Assessment Agency. "Chinese CO_2 emissions in perspective, 2007". Retrieved 22 October 2010, from http://www.pbl.nl/en/news/pressreleases/2007/20070622ChineseCO2emission sinperspective.html

47. A. Ang. "China Tops US in Carbon Emissions: Researchers Cite Industrial Growth", *The Boston Globe*, 21 June 2007.

48. A. Chang, "China: Rich Nations Wrong To Criticize Its CO_2 Emissions While Buying Its Products", *Insurance Journal*, 22 June 2007. Retrieved 22 October 2010, from http://www.insurancejounral.com/news/international /2007/06/22/81037.htm.

49. J. Watts, "China Ready for Post-Kyoto Deal on Climate Change." *Guardian*, 6 May 2009. Retrieved 22 October 2010, from http://www.guardian.co.uk /environment/2009/may/06/china-seeks-climate-change-deal.

50. "China Unveils Climate Change Plan", *BBC News*, 4 June 2007. Retrieved 22 October 2010, from http://news.bbc.co.uk/2/hi/6717671.stm.

51. Watts, "China Ready for Post-Kyoto Deal on Climate Change".

52. Chang, "China: Rich Nations Wrong To Criticize Its CO_2 Emissions While Buying Its Products",.

53. National Development and Reform Commission, "China's National Climate Change Programme", 2007. Retrieved 21 July 2010, from http://www.ccchina.gov.cn/WebSite/CCChina/UpFile/File189.pdf. In Chinese.

54. *Ibid.*, p. 28.

55. PBL Netherlands Environmental Assessment Agency, 2007.

56. Y. Qi, M. Li, H. B. Zhang and H.M. Li, "Translating a Global Issue into Local Priority: China's Local Government Responses to Climate Change", *Journal of Environment and Development*, Vol. 17, No. 4, 2008, pp. 379–400.

57. Caijing, "China commissioned 'Provincial Climate Change Programs' Project", 2008: http://www.ccchina.gov.cn/cn/NewsInfo.asp?NewsId=13044 (accessed on 21 July 2010). In Chinese.

58. The five provinces are Guangdong, Liaoning, Hubei, Shaanxi and Yunnan.

59. The eight cities are Tianjian, Chongqing, Shenzhen, Xiamen, Hangzhou, Nanchang, Guiyang and Baoding.

60. National Development and Reform Commission of the People's Republic of China, *Notice Regarding the Launch of Low-Carbon Provinces and Low-Carbon Cities Pilot Program*, 2010: http://qhs.ndrc.gov.cn/dtjj /t20100810_365271.htm (accessed on 6 September 2010). In Chinese.

61. W. Ni and G. Zeng, "Exploring City Development Path from Low-Carbon Economic Perspective", *Inquiry into Economic Issues*, Vol. 5, 2010, pp. 38–42. In Chinese. X. L. Zhang, ,"Building a Low-Carbon Market System in Hangzhou", *Hangzhou Science and Technology*, Vol. 2, 2010, pp. 43–46. In Chinese.

62. G. Y. Zhuang, "How Will China Move Towards Becoming a Low Carbon Economy?" *China and World Economy*, Vol. 16, No. 3, 2008, pp. 93–105.

63. W. L. Liu and C. Wang, "Low-Carbon City: Its Implementation and Development Patterns", *China Population, Resources and Environment*, Vol. 20, No. 4, 2010, pp. 17–22. In Chinese.

64. Qi et al., "Translating a Global Issue into Local Priority ».

65. X. Bai, "Integrating Global Environmental Concerns into Urban Management: The Scale and Readiness Arguments", *Journal of Industrial Ecology*, Vol. 11, No. 2, 2007, pp. 15–29; X. L. Yuan and Y. Y. Zhong, "Low-Carbon Cities in China: Practice and Framework Setup", *Urban Studies*, Vol. 17, No. 5, 2010, pp. 42–47. In Chinese.

66. See Economy, The River Runs Black.

67. Yiyi Lu, "Environmental Civil Society and Governance in China", *International Journal of Environmental Studies*, Vol. 64, No. 1, 2007, pp. 59–69.

68. P. Ho, "Greening Without Conflict? Environmentalism, NGOs and Civil Society in China", *Development and Change*, Vol. 32, 5, 2001, pp. 893–921.

69. X. Y. Zhan and S. Y. Tang, "Political Opportunities, Resource Constraints, and Policy Advocacy of Environmental NGOs in China", *Public Administration*, forthcoming.

70. Established in 1994, Friends of Nature is usually regarded as the first environmental NGO in China. See http://www.fon.org.cn/channal.php?cid=2. However, Liu Detian claimed that his Black-Beak Gull Protection Association, which was founded in 1991, was the first environmental NGO in China. See http://blog.sina.com.cn/s/blog_490d171b0100q2m0.html.

71. J. Schwartz, "Environmental NGOs in China: Roles and Limits", *Pacific Affairs*, Vol. 77, No. 1, 2004, pp. 28–49. See also Ho, "Greening Without Conflict?".

72. C. W. H. Lo and S. W. Leung, "Environmental Agency and Public Opinion in Guangzhou: The Limits of a Popular Approach to Environmental Governance", *The China Quarterly*, Vol. 163, 2000, pp. 677–704.

73. See Ho, "Greening Without Conflict? Environmentalism, NGOs and Civil Society in China".

74. Ma and Ortolano, *Environmental Regulation in China: Institutions, Enforcement, and Compliance*. See also Schwartz, "Environmental NGOs in China: Roles and Limits".

75. Zhan and Tang, "Political Opportunities, Resource Constraints, and Policy Advocacy of Environmental NGOs in China".

76. K. G. Lieberthal, "China's Governing System and Its Impact on Environmental Policy Implementation", *China Environmental Series*, Vol. 1, 1997, pp. 3–8 (Washington DC: The Woodrow Wilson Center). See also K. G. Lieberthal, "Introduction: The 'Fragmented Authoritarianism' Model and Its Limitations," in K. G. Lieberthal and D. M. Lampton (eds.), *Bureaucracy, Politics, and Decision Making in Post-Mao China*, Berkeley, CA: University of California Press, 1992, pp. 1–29.

77. T. Saich, "Negotiating the State: The Development of Social Organizations in China", *The China Quarterly*, No. 161, 2000, pp. 124–141.

78. P. Ho, "Embedded Activism and Political Change in a Semiauthoritarian Context", *China Information*, Vol. 21, No. 2, 2007, pp. 187–209. See also Zhan and Tang, "Political Opportunities, Resource Constraints, and Policy Advocacy of Environmental NGOs in China".

79. Tang and Zhan, "Political Opportunities, Resource Constraints, and Policy Advocacy of Environmental NGOs in China".

80. Andrew J. Nathan, "Authoritarian Resilience", *Journal of Democracy*, Vol. 14, No. 1, 2003, pp. 6–17.

81. S. Y. Tang and X. Y. Zhan, "Civic Environmental NGOs, Civil Society and Democratisation in China", *Journal of Development Studies*, Vol. 44, 3, 2008, pp. 425–48.

82. Guobin Yang, "Environmental NGOs and Institutional Dynamics in China", *The China Quarterly*, Vol. 181, 2005, pp. 46–66.

83. Tang and Zhan, "Political Opportunities, Resource Constraints, and Policy Advocacy of Environmental NGOs in China". See also Jiang Ru and L. Ortolano, "Development of Citizen-Organized Environmental NGOs in China", *Voluntas*, Vol. 20, No. 2, 2009, pp. 141–168.

84. Zhan and Tang, "Political Opportunities, Resource Constraints, and Policy Advocacy of Environmental NGOs in China".

85. M. Janicke, "Conditions for Environmental Policy Success: An International Comparison", *The Environmentalist*, Vol. 12, No. 1, 1992, pp. 53–57

86. *Ibid.*, p. 54.

87. *Ibid.*

88. *Ibid.*

89. *Ibid.*

15

Challenges and Prospects of Reforestation in Contemporary China: The Case of the Grain for Green Project

Jie GAO
Jia GUO

In 1999, the Chinese central government launched the "Grain for Green" project (*tuigeng huanlin*, hereafter referred to as the GFG project) in order to alleviate the country's severe land degradation and deforestation problems. [1] The GFG project is by far the most influential reforestation policy in the history of the People's Republic of China. It is designed to provide economic incentives for farmers to convert steep croplands into forests and reforest barren mountains. At the beginning of its implementation, the GFG project was enthusiastically welcomed by local governments and farmers. It has achieved noticeable progress in increasing China's forest coverage, reducing soil erosion and promoting farmers' incomes. [2] However, after just five years, in 2004 the central government dramatically reduced the scale of the GFG project because of the unexpected excessive expansion of the project in local regions. At the same time, the quality and survival rate of the trees newly planted under this project proved far from satisfactory. It is fair to say that the GFG project had encountered a huge setback. Since then, China's reforestation progress has been stagnant.

Prior research has mainly focused on examining the negative impacts of the GFG project, such as the poor quality and low sustainability of the project. [3] Studies on how the design of the GFG project gave rise to these problems are still rare. This chapter fills this gap. It will address the following questions: Why has the GFG project, an incentive-based policy well accepted at the local level, resulted in unexpected outcomes? What lessons could be learned from the problems in the implementation of the GFG project? Further, what can be done to promote the sustainability of the GFG project?

This chapter has two objectives. First, it examines why the GFG project has been excessively expanded in local areas and what problems are caused by the expansion. As we will show, the central leaders adopted a campaign-style approach to conducting the GFG project, which aimed to mobilize local officials and farmers to achieve reforestation targets rapidly, with less attention to the consequences and sustainability of the project. In particular, the compensation system of the GFG project provided strong incentives for local governments to expand the scope of converted croplands excessively. The funding provided by the GFG project for improving the quality of reforested lands was insufficient. Hence, farmers had weak incentives to improve the low survival rates of trees newly planted under the GFG project. Second, based on a case study of Wuqi County (under the administration of Yan'an City in Shaanxi Province), this chapter reports some useful experiences that may help to resolve the reforestation dilemma in local China. Our field research in Wuqi County shows that it is important to motivate local governments and farmers to take the initiative in participation in reforestation. In Wuqi this is achieved through educating local officials and farmers about the real purpose of the GFG project. Evidence suggests that the county has achieved impressive results in improving the sustainability of the GFG project. After the decline of central funding in 2003, the county government continued to make an effort to improve the quality of reforested lands and develop off-farm industries that support farmers to conduct further reforestation. The central government was impressed by Wuqi's successful practice in conducting the GFG project and encouraged other localities to learn from it.

The data for this study are drawn from national statistics, such as the central and local forestry yearbooks and government documents related to the GFG project. In addition, this study uses primary data collected in in-depth interviews with local officials in Shaanxi and Inner Mongolia in 2008. The interviewees comprised a total of nine officials in Shaanxi and six officials in Inner Mongolia. At the time of interview, these officials were working in the forestry bureaus at provincial, city and county levels. Shaanxi and Inner Mongolia were selected because these two provinces rank as the top two among all provincial-level governments for the total amount of croplands reforested under the GFG project. The relatively mature experience of these two provinces in conducting the GFG project is important to observe the problems in implementation and local officials' coping strategies. In addition, these two provinces have similar geographical features, for example, they both face water scarcity and soil erosion, and they receive the same level of compensation from the central government. In this regard, a comparison between the two provinces helps to illustrate why local officials adopted different strategies to cope with similar reforestation challenges.

Greening China:
The Grain for Green Project

A daunting challenge for the Hu-Wen administration and China's next generation of leadership is environment deterioration, an expensive price that the country has paid for its remarkable economic growth over the past three decades.[4] China nowadays suffers from major environmental problems such as land degradation, air pollution, water pollution and scarcity, deforestation and desertification. The seven major rivers in China, the Huai, Hai, Liao, Songhua, Yangtze, Pearl and Yellow, have been seriously polluted.[5] Two-thirds of the rural population suffers from diarrheal disease because of lack of access to adequate clean water.[6] Almost 750,000 people die from diseases caused by air pollution per year.[7] As Economy points out, China's environment has taken a "great leap backward" and the country urgently needs an "environmental revolution of a magnitude equal to the sweeping economic reform launched by Deng Xiaoping".[8]

Deforestation is one of the most prominent environmental problems in China. According to the Food and Agriculture Organization, China's forest cover rate was 22% in 2010, just 70% of the world average level and ranking the second lowest in East Asia.[9] The low forest cover triggers off other environmental crises such as soil erosion, desertification and flooding. At present, deforestation contributes to 31.8% of desertified lands, which leads to serious sandstorms in northern regions. The amount of eroded lands, 80% of which are located in western China, reaches 3.56 million square kilometres, which is nearly 37% of China's total territory.[10] Forest degradation also undermines its capacity for accumulating carbon and speeds up the emission of CO_2. The carbon stock in living forest biomass in China was 30 million tonnes per ha in 2010, ranking as the second lowest in East Asia.[11] According to data of the United Nations, in 2006 China replaced the United States as the foremost emitter of CO_2.[12] Furthermore, the loss of over 30% of forests is a major cause of flooding in the Yangtze and Yellow river areas.[13]

In 1998, the Yellow River suffered the most severe flood since 1949. About 4,000 people lost their lives in this disaster and the direct economic loss was RMB 200 billion. This event pushed the central leaders to take firm action to increase forest coverage in China. The GFG project was initiated in this context. In 1998, the State Council circulated "Several Opinions on Reconstruction after the Disaster" (*Guanyu zaihou chongjian de ruogan yijian*), which clearly required local governments to "convert arable lands to forests or grasslands" in order to prevent further soil erosion and flooding.[14] In 1999, former premier Zhu Rongji visited six provinces in north, south and southwest China. His tour started a pilot of the GFG project. In 2000, the GFG project was incorporated into the Western Development Campaign (*xibu dakaifa*), which was the benchmark of the regional policy of the Jiang Zemin-Zhu Rongji administration.

The main idea of the GFG project is to provide economic incentives for farmers to convert steep croplands with a slope over 25 degrees into forests and grasslands (reforestation) and to plant trees on barren mountains and lands (afforestation).[15] Farmers would receive compensation in the form of cash or grain from the central government. The compensation was to be transferred to farmers via local governments. The GFG project was first piloted in Gansu, Shaanxi and Sichuan provinces in 1999 to test its effectiveness. From 1999 to 2001, more provinces were involved in the GFG project when the central leaders saw local officials' soaring enthusiasm to participate. By 2002, the GFG project covered twenty provinces. In 2002, the State Council released "Several Opinions on Further Improving the Grain for Green Project" (*Guanyu jinyibu gaishan tuigeng huanlin zhengce cuoshi de ruogan yjian*), which further extended the scope of the GFG project to the rest of the country.

Another guiding document, the "Regulation on the Grain for Green Project" (*Tuigeng huanlin tiaoli*), was also enacted in late 2002 to regulate local reforestation work.

The central government's target of reforestation increased significantly, from 980,000 ha in 2001 to 4,830,000 ha in 2002. The ambitious goal set by the central government was to convert 14,670,000 ha of steep croplands into forests and to afforest an equal area of barren lands and mountains by 2010.[16] The original budget for achieving this goal was set at RMB 220 million. In order to ensure that local officials would make an effort to realize these targets, the central government added reforestation as a new criterion in the performance measurement of local governments. Local government at each level is assigned quantified cropland-to-forest targets. In many localities, such as Shaanxi and Inner Mongolia, these targets are mandatory. Senior officials of the forestry bureau at the corresponding level are held responsible for fulfilment of the assigned targets. If they fail to accomplish the targets, they will be "vetoed" in the year-end evaluation – that is, the forestry bureau will be banned from participating in the evaluation and therefore lose the opportunity to get any bonus, regardless of their successful accomplishment of other job duties. Meanwhile, responsible leadership officials might receive a warning and penalties such as bonus reduction.

By 2006, the GFG project covered 25 provinces, 2,279 county level governments, 32 million rural households and 124 million farmers.[17] In terms of the amount of central funding and coverage of population and areas, the GFG project is thought to be the largest conservation project in the developing world. The state budget on this project is about two and a half times that of the Three Gorges Dam and thirteen times that of the Qinghai–Tibet railway project.[18]

Excessive Expansion of the Project and Consequent Problems

The GFG project has achieved certain progress such as increasing forest cover in the target regions, accelerating structural changes of the agriculture sector, securing food production and increasing the incomes of farmers.[19] However, this massive cropland-to-forest campaign almost ceased in 2004 because of problems caused by excessive expansion of the project throughout the country. Figure 1 shows a significant increase in reforested cropland and afforested barren land from 1999 to 2003 in China. In 1999, the area of reforested land was 382,000 ha, yet the area peaked at 3.4 million ha in 2003, with an increase of 27% on the area in 2002 (2.6 million ha).

Figure 1: Total Amount of Reforested Croplands and Barren Lands

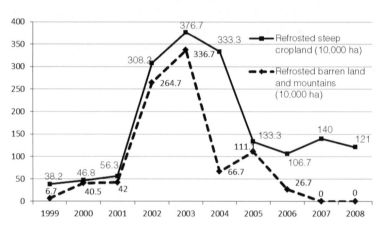

Source: Data in Figures 1–5 and Chart 1 all come form authors' calculation of the data in *Zhongguo Linye Tongji Nianjian* (*China's Forestry Yearbook*) (Beijing: Zhongguo Linye Chubanshe, 2000-2008) and internal documents that contain the amount of central subsidies allocated to the GFG project.

The three pilot provinces (Gansu, Shaanxi and Sichuan) quickly exceeded the original cropland-to-forest targets assigned by the central government within three to four months in 1999.[20] According to some scholars' calculations, in the three provinces, the actual number of counties carrying out the project was 312 in 2000 although the central government had approved just 174 of them.[21] Local officials in these counties had included extra towns and villages in the project partly in the hope that farmers in those localities could also gain benefits from it.[22] Figures 2 and 3 show the expansion in Shaanxi and Inner Mongolia. In 1999, Shaanxi Province converted a large area of cropland (210,000 ha) to forest because it was the pilot site of the GFG project. The amount decreased in the next year only because the national target was shared by more provinces that participated in the GFG project. The expansion started from 2001 and peaked in 2003. Within three years, the amount of reforested land in Shaanxi increased rapidly from 46,000 ha in 2001 to 280,000 ha in 2003. By 2007, a total of 922,000 ha of cropland was converted to forest and about one million ha of cropland was reforested in Shaanxi. Likewise, in Inner Mongolia, the amount of reforested land peaked at 350,000 ha in 2003 with an increase of 31% compared with 233,000 ha in 2002.

Figure 2: Reforested Cropland in Shaanxi (10,000 ha)

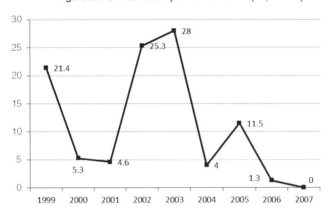

Figure 3. The Amount of Reforested Croplands in Inner Mongolia, 2000–2007 (10,000 ha)

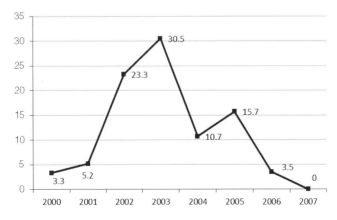

Note: The data for Inner Mongolia in 1999 is not included because Inner Mongolia started to implement the GFG project in 2000.

The expansion of the project forced the central government to spend more. In 2007, the central government expanded the original budget of the project (RMB 220 billion for 1999–2010) to RMB 430 billion from 1999 to 2018. Apart from the burden on the central budget, the subsidies were not used effectively. When local officials assigned the central reforestation quota to farmers, they tried to include as many farmers as possible into the subsidies scheme regardless of whether these farmers' lands qualified for reforestation or not. One local official described such an allocation method as "sprinkling peppers thinly" (*sa hujiaomian*).[23] The GFG project requires local government to convert steep arable land with an incline of over 25 degrees. However, many local governments were so keen on expanding the scope of the project that they even allowed farmers to convert normal cropland. Plot selection was not based on ecological concerns but on the convenience of accessing the cropland.[24] The study by Xu and Tao shows that almost 38% of reforested lands have an incline of less than 15 degrees.[25] In some localities, in order to gain more subsidies, local governments forced farmers to reforest lands but refused to provide financial assistance to farmers who had trouble in maintaining the survival rate of trees planted.[26] Some scholars have pointed out the problem that in some cases local governments retain central subsidies for their own use. As a result, the compensation that a farmer actually receives is far less than the amount he or she should receive from the central subsidy scheme. This triggers rising public anger at the local governments and jeopardizes the stability of local governance.[27]

The expansion of the GFG project also generated serious difficulties in maintaining the survival rate of newly planted trees. The northern part of China often suffers from water scarcity, which leads to a very low survival rate of trees. For example, in Inner Mongolia, only 56% of trees newly planted under the GFG project survived in 2007. This rate is far from achieving the central government's requirement, which is to maintain the survival rate at 80%. In the northern part of Shaanxi, the survival rate is even less, ranging from 20% to 40%.

The unintended consequences of the implementation of the GFG project forced both central and local governments to withdraw from it to some extent. The year 2003 marks a milestone change. Since then, the central government has greatly reduced the target for the amount of arable land that should be converted to forest. As Figure 4 shows, the area of steep arable land converted to forest decreased sharply from 3.36 million ha in 2003 to 0.67 million ha in 2004. After 2007, the central government no longer assigned quantified quotas for local governments. It also suspended the task of converting the remaining 1.06 million ha of sloping croplands, although at that time about 45% of steep land, with a slope over 25 degrees, had not been converted. Moreover, the central government now only provides half of the value of subsidies for farmers who continue to convert croplands into forests after the expiration of compensation.

Figure 4: Reduction of Converted Steep Croplands in China, 1999-2008

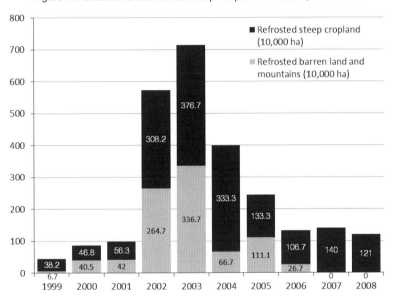

The decline of central subsidies significantly weakened the incentives of local officials and farmers to continue implementing the project. Since 2006, some farmers have begun to re-farm their croplands because they fear that they will not receive adequate subsidies by planting trees.[28] Local governments began to shirk their responsibilities of taking up the cost of monitoring the project and compensating for reforested lands.[29] Owing to the central policy adjustment in 2007, local governments are required to provide financial support for reforestation in the locality so as to improve the sustainability of the GFG project.[30] However, local governments, particularly those in the Yellow River region, are reluctant to use the local budget to pay for subsidies, encourage complementary planting (*buzhi buzhong*) or support the follow-up industries crucial for sustainable environmental improvement. [31] One county in Inner Mongolia made no efforts at all to provide financial support for farmers.[32] Instead, the county officials kept calling for more central government subsidies in order to ensure the continuation of the project.[33]

The Compensation System: What Went Wrong?

The GFG project highlights the shortcomings of using a campaign-style approach with short-term effects to resolve environmental problems that need long-term attention and inputs. The logic underlying the design of the GFG project is that large-scale reforestation can ameliorate China's deforestation problems, and mobilizing farmers to plant new forests is a fast and effective means to that end. According to one account, the central leaders' decision to launch the GFG project was actually too hasty. The design of the GFG project was worked out quickly without adequate discussion within the bureaucracy concerning the appropriateness of the incentive mechanism and the sustainability of the project. [34] The decision-making process somehow ignored the useful experiences and lessons of conducting other afforestation programs in China.[35] As a result, the design of the GFG project overemphasized the area of converted land and paid less attention to the quality and sustainability of the reforestation efforts.

The compensation system is the key factor that led to the excessive expansion of the project and the low sustainability of reforestation. Farmers were incentivized to convert a required area of cropland to forest each year. According to the central policy, farmers in the upper regions of the Yangtze River received 2,250 kg of grain per ha of forest and pasture redeveloped every year, and farmers in the upper and middle reaches of Yellow River received 1,500 kg of grain per ha of reforested land every year.[36] The grain subsidies were changed to cash subsidies at the value of RMB 1.4 per kg after 2004.[37]

In addition to grain subsidies, farmers received living subsidies of RMB 300 per ha of reforested land each year. The duration of payment of subsidies differs according to the type of planting. Food and living allowance subsidies were paid for five years for land converted to grassland in 1999–2001 (two years after 2002), five years for land converted to economic forest *(jingjilin)*, and eight years for land converted to ecological forest *(shengtailin)*.[38] Furthermore, if farmers planted trees or created grasslands on their own cropland, they could get another RMB 750 per ha each year as seed subsidies. Chart 1 shows the distribution of the major types of central subsidies by the end of 2007. By then, the central government had spent about RMB 157.5 billion (including grain subsidies to the value of RMB 123.4 billion) on the GFG project.[39] The majority of the subsidies (87%) is for food and living allowances. Seed subsidies of RMB 19.6 billion account for just 13% of the total expense.

Chart 1: Distribution of Central Subsidies by 2007

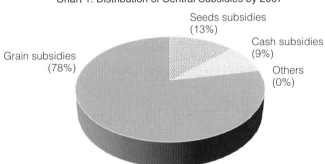

Seeds subsidies
(13%)

Cash subsidies
(9%)

Grain subsidies
(78%)

Others
(0%)

The economic compensation from the central government indeed played a crucial role in mobilizing local officials and farmers to participate in this project. Yet, since the majority of the compensation was in the form of grain and living subsidies, local officials and farmers treated the subsidies as the same as the subsidies they received from poverty alleviation programmes, and overlooked the purpose of reducing deforestation and soil erosion. For both local officials and farmers, the GFG project was more like a poverty reduction policy. Participating in the GFG project brought attractive funding and helped to improve farmers' incomes, which consequently enlarged the amount of local tax revenue. In some localities, farmers even complained to the forestry bureau officials because their croplands were not selected for reforestation, although this farm land did not meet the criteria of the GFG project.[40] Under such circumstances, local officials were spurred to expand the scope of reforested lands in order to obtain more subsidies from the central government.[41]

In some other cases, local governments played a more active role in expanding the scope of the GFG project. For example, some local governments decisively expanded the GFG project in order to fulfil the central reforestation targets as fast as possible.[42] For example, in 2003 Ningxia Province announced an ambitious goal to make a "great leap forward". The target assigned to the province by the central government was to convert a total area of 340,000 ha of cropland within eight years, yet the provincial leaders decided to expand the scope to 480,000 ha and to achieve this target within three years![43] In addition, journalists of Xinhua news agency visited Shaanxi, Gansu and Ningxia in 2004 and found that some local governments asked farmers to stop farming and prepare land for planting trees before they had received that year's reforestation quota from the central government.[44] Some farmers who conducted land preparation for tree planting in early 2004 subsequently did not qualify as participants of the GFG project and consequently encountered serious difficulties in making a living since the central plan reduced sharply in that year.[45]

As only a small portion of the central subsidies (13%) is used for seed subsidies, farmers actually lack sufficient incentives to conduct complementary planting, which is crucial to maintain the quality of reforestation. Besides, the actual expense of maintaining the survival of newly planted trees is much higher than was anticipated by the central planners, due to serious water scarcity, land degradation and loss of trees caused by animals.[46] The actual expense varies across localities. The cost of complementary planting in Inner Mongolia is RMB 1,500–2,250 per ha, whereas the annual seed subsidy of RMB 750 per ha that farmers receive is clearly insufficient.[47]

Moreover, developing ecologically and economically sustainable activities, such as off-farm and forestry related industries, is essential to bolster the sustainability of the GFG project and improve the well-being of farmers.[48] Normally farmers could earn more from working in the off-farm industries, yet building such industries is beyond the investment capacity of individual farmers. In this regard, part of the central subsidies should be used for this purpose. However, the compensation system of the GFG project does not cover the expense of these activities and provides little incentive for local officials to invest in such off-farm and forest industries.

Promoting Sustainable Reforestation:
A Case Study of Wuqi County

Since the mid-2000s, the GFG project has largely lost ground. Reforestation in China has encountered a bottleneck and needs to find a way out. Our field research shows that the experience a county in northwestern China may offer some useful lessons. Wuqi County is under the administration of Yan'an City in Shaanxi province. In 2008, it had a population of 129,000. It is a typical locality in the loess plateau region, where the land features hills and gullies of yellow soil. In this arid region, agriculture is largely rain-fed.[49] However, the region suffers from severe water shortages. In 2007, the annual rainfall in Wuqi County was 478.3 mm whereas the average rainfall of Shaanxi Province was 638.9 mm in that year.[50] In addition, extensive farming and open grazing has heavily degraded the ground vegetation. By the end of 1998, 3,696 km² of the total 3,791.5 km² of the county's territory suffered water and soil erosion, with 153,000 tons of topsoil per km² washed downstream.[51]

Figure 5: The Reforestation Target for Wuqi County to Accomplish
from 1999 to 2007

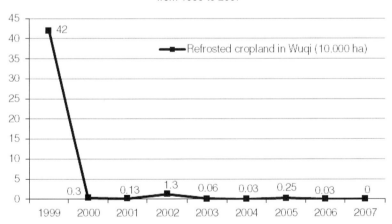

Wuqi County has implemented the GFG project since 1999. As Figure 5 indicates, in that year the county converted almost all the cropland with an incline of over 25 degrees (about 104,000 ha) even though the centrally imposed target for the county was only about 42,000 ha. By 2008, according to the central target, the county could receive compensation for a total of 63,000 ha of cropland converted to forest.[52] However, since Wuqi had *de facto* converted about 104,000 ha in 1999, it had 41,000 ha of converted cropland that did not earn any central subsidy. In addition, about 13,000 ha of cropland with an incline of over 25 degrees had not yet been converted.[53] Furthermore, the terrible water scarcity contributed to the low survival rate of trees in the county. In March 2008, farmers in Wuqi had to replant trees for the project over an area totalling 12,000 ha, which accounted for 10% of the county's total reforested area.[54] Obviously, the county government shouldered a heavy workload and financial burden to conduct complementary planting and pay for a large area of un-compensated converted cropland.

Measures to Promote Sustainable Reforestation

However, county officials did not shirk in the face of these difficulties. On the contrary, they have taken many measures to improve the sustainability of the GFG project in the locality. After 2003, when central funding decreased, unlike counties that sought continued central assistance, Wuqi County decided to use its local budget to invest in the GFG project. Notably, local funds are mainly used to consolidate previous outputs and maintain sustainability of the reforested areas. For example, lack of sufficient funding for administration has been a major obstacle for local governments to monitor and inspect the progress of the GFG project.[55] Because some villages are located in remote areas, it may take the monitoring officers a few months to complete the whole inspection process. Under the GFG project, the expense of monitoring is imposed on the local budget, which is one major reason for some local governments to shirk in conducting the GFG project.[56] However, Wuqi County issued an annual budget allocation earmarked to fund the administrative operation of the Forestry Bureau. From 2003 to 2008, the average budget for this purpose in Wuqi was about RMB 1 million per annum. Officials of the County Forestry Bureau indicated that this funding from local government was very important to sustain the GFG project.[57]

The county government also took action to improve the survival rate of trees newly planted under the GFG project. The most influential endeavour has been to adjust the forest structure, a policy decided in 2007. In the past, in order to achieve rapid increase of forest cover within a short period of time, Wuqi County farmers planted a large number of sea-buckthorn trees on cropland because this type of tree grows fast and costs less. In 2008, the area of Wuqi County planted with sea-buckthorn reached 35,000 ha, which accounts for 56% of the total area of converted cropland. However, such a forest structure, dominated by one single tree species, has a higher risks of damage from insect attacks. In many years, the sea-buckthorn plantations in Wuqi County have suffered from insect attacks. The county had to implement more complementary planting to deal with this problem.[58] In order to change the situation, since 2007 the county has provided an annual budget of RMB 20 million to adjust the forest structure and develop a mixed-type forestry.[59] Such efforts greatly increase the anti-drought capability of trees and reduce the risk of insect attack.[60]

To deal with unconverted steep cropland and converted land that was not compensated, the county invested RMB 120 million in creating the "national afforestation park" in 2008. [61] The establishment of the national park also aimed to consolidate the sustainability of the GFG project since farmers could benefit from local ecological tourism and were not tempted to remove trees from their cropland. Moreover, the county invested a lot in developing "green industry" such as products made from sea-buckthorn and other off-farm industries related to forests. A number of companies were established to produce a healthy drink from sea-buckthorn. These off-farm and forestry-related industries offered many job opportunities for local residents, including farmers. All these efforts helped to maintain the sustainability of the GFG project in the long term.

Explaining the Wuqi Model

Why would local officials of Wuqi County act differently from officials in other localities, though they faced similar challenges? The story dates back to the year 2001, when Wuqi County was selected to participate in an international forestry cooperation programme: the Sino-German Financial Cooperation on Afforestation.[62] Wuqi County stakeholders learned from the cooperation programme with regard to approaches and ideas of conducting sustainable reforestation. The programme was funded by Kreditanstalt für Wiederaufbau (hereafter referred to as the KFW), a German bank with a core mission of promoting sustainable development in developing countries. The KFW has had working relations with China since the 1980s.[63] It works closely with the forestry sector in China and is highly praised by Chinese officials.[64] As a number of scholars and government officials indicate, apart from providing financial support, the KFW plays an important role in introducing successful experiences of sustainable reforestation in different countries, training local officials and farmers, and establishing models for further development.[65]

The KFW provided a great deal of training to local officials and farmers in Wuqi County during the cooperation.[66] As Economy indicates, afforestation programmes in China lack appropriate incentives, proper technologies and capable staff.[67] Training is crucial to resolve these problems. In Wuqi, the trainers were forestry experts from Germany or from research institutes in Shaanxi Province.[68] The trainees included local forestry officials and farmers. Almost all the forestry officials in Wuqi were involved at least once in the training, including Wu Zongkai, who was in charge of the GFG project in the county. The major objective of training was to enhance the trainees' understanding of the necessity and importance of ecological conservation and sustainable reforestation. For farmers, the training focused on explaining the importance of complementary planting and maintaining the survival rate of planted trees, and enhancing their knowledge and skills to work in off-farm industries. Training for local officials mainly aimed to educate them about the importance of assisting farmers to conduct complementary planting, and developing forestry-related industries.[69]

The KFW's training changed the mindset of local officials and farmers to one where the quality of reforestation and its sustainability are more important than the size of reforested areas. As one local official of the Forestry Bureau said, "We now recognize that the local government should spend more money on helping farmers to conduct complementary planting if they fail to meet the required survival rate of trees and do things that may harm the sustainability of the project in the long run."[70]

The KWF's training also taught farmers, local officials and forestry experts how to work together in decision making on crucial reforestation issues. Farmers were encouraged to make their own decisions on planning, the selection of plots and the species of trees to be planted. They were also trained on how to negotiate with the Forestry Bureau officials about the amount of financial support.[71] Since 2002, Wuqi has been using such a participatory approach to conduct the GFG project. Wu Zongkai raised this issue openly when he talked about the difficulty in adjusting forest structure in the county. He said that he was impressed by the way the KFW carried out afforestation. The participatory approach respected local farmers' decisions and allowed farmers to plant trees that they thought were appropriate.[72] More importantly, the participation of farmers and experts in decision making helped to improve the trees' quality and capacity for preventing insect attacks.

Wuqi's effort in conducting the GFG project achieved impressive progress. After conducting the GFG project for ten years, the overall rate of forest cover in Wuqi County had increased significantly, from 19.2% in 1999 to 62.9% in 2009, which equals to twice the world average level and three times the average level for China. The erosion modulus, an indicator of the speed of water and soil erosion, declined from 15,300 t/km^2 in 1997 to 5400 t/km^2 in 2007.[73] The remarkable achievement both in ecological improvement and initiatives to consolidate the project in Wuqi drew the attention of central government. In recent years, the State Forestry Administration has sent senior officials to the county from time to time to observe and learn successful experiences. Other localities are also encouraged to adopt the so-called "Wuqi Model". In September 2009, Wuqi hosted the Tenth Year Anniversary of the GFG Project. At the meeting, local officials made a keynote speech to introduce Wuqi's experiences of conducting the GFG project. A number of state and local officials attended the meeting and visited the field of reforestation and the national park in the county.[74] With increasing attention given to the Wuqi Model, the small spark may start a prairie fire of China's "green revolution" in the near future.

Conclusion

This chapter examines how and why the GFG project, China's most influential and "expensive" reforestation policy over the past sixty years, has resulted in unexpected outcomes. It shows that in order to achieve rapid and efficient reforestation in local areas, the GFG project is designed to place a higher emphasis on the quantity rather than the quality of the reforested lands. Local officials and farmers are incentivized to focus on achieving the targets of reforestation with fewer concerns on issues such as ecological sustainability. As a result, the GFG project was excessively expanded in some areas, which imposed a huge burden on the state budget and led to low sustainability of the project.

To some extent, the challenges of implementing the GFG project illustrate the problems of using a campaign-style policy approach to resolve China's environmental problems. For decades Chinese reformers have used a campaign-style policy approach to deal with natural disasters and particular environmental crises.[75] Under this approach, the central leaders initiate a campaign and local officials are then given concrete policy goals to fulfil. Our study of the GFG project shows that a campaign-style policy approach may be effective in mobilizing local officials and the public to accomplish the state's environmental improvement plans with a fast effect in the short term. Yet such a policy approach may instil in them the mindset that targets should be met regardless of the negative consequences. In the long run, it is important for policy makers to place at least equal, if not more, emphasis on a policy instrument's usefulness in maintaining sustainable improvement of the environment.

This chapter also shows some useful experiences to deal with the problems of the GFG project by examining the successful practice in Wuqi County in Shaanxi Province. In a nutshell, the Wuqi Model highlights the importance of motivating local officials and farmers to take the initiative actively to promote sustainable reforestation. To achieve this end, one way is to educate local officials and farmers on the importance of, and knowledge and skills about, promoting sustainable reforestation. In addition, farmers' participation in decision making on crucial reforestation issues may enhance their sense of responsibility in protecting the environment. We acknowledge that Wuqi's success is based on some factors that are not replicable in other localities, such as the assistance from international cooperation, open-minded local officials who are willing to support experiments, and financial capacity that can actually afford investment needs. However, Wuqi's case still sheds light on strategies that can be used to deal with the difficulties of the GFG project, if conditions permit. It might become a benchmark for counties that are willing to find effective solutions and have the capacity to afford similar experiments. Chinese reformers have expressed that the reform in the next five years will pay more attention to striking a balance between economic growth and environmental improvement. The GFG project is still a crucial issue on the agenda of the top leaders. Recently it was reported that the central government has decided to invest a total of RMB 220 billion in the GFG project in the coming decade.[76] The money needs to be spent wisely. Reforestation in China, as in other developing countries, is an arduous task that needs continuous inputs and attention from the state leaders, local bureaucracy and the public. We hope that this study can offer some insights into the problems of the previous reforestation policy and possible directions for improvement.

Notes and References

1. Some studies use the term "Slope Land Conversion Programme".

2. Lijun Wu, Qing Liu, Yue Li, Xuan Zhao and Tiezhen Zhao, "Quanguo tuigeng huanlin gongcheng jinzhan chengxiao zongshu" ("Report on the development of the Grain for Green project"), *Forestry Economics* 9 (2009), pp. 21–37.

3. Michael Bennett, "China's sloping land conversion program: institutional innovation or business as usual?" *Ecological Economics* 65, No. 4 (2008), pp. 699–711; State Forestry Administration, *Guojia Linye Zhongdian Shengtai Gongcheng Shehui Jingji Xiaoyi Jiance Baogao 2004* (*The Report on Monitoring and Assessment of the Socio-Economic Impacts of China's Key Forestry Programs 2004*) (Beijing: Zhongguo Linye Chubanshe, 2005); Jintao Xu and Ran Tao, "Grain for Green or grain for gain: an empirical evaluation of the sloping land conversion program in China," in Dali Yang (ed.), *Discontented Miracle: Growth, Conflict, and Institutional Adaptations in China* (New Jersey: World Scientific, 2007); Emi Uchida, Jintao Xu and Scott Rozelle, "Grain for Green: cost-effectiveness and sustainability of China's conservation set-aside program," *Land Economics* 81:2 (2005), pp. 247–264. Chunmei Wang, "Evaluation of the economic and environmental impact of converting cropland to forest: a case study in Dunhua County," *China Journal of Environmental Management* 85:3 (2007), pp. 746–56; Jintao Xu and Yiying Cao, "The sustainability of converting the land for forestry and pasture," *International Economic Review* 3:4 (2002), pp. 56–60; Xiaoyan Zhang and Gaihe Yang (eds.), *Zhongguo Xibei Diqu Tuigeng Huanlin Huancao Yanjiu* (*The Study on the Grain for Green Project in Northwest China*) (Beijing: Kexue chubanshe, 2005); Emi Uchida, Scott Rozelle and Jintao. Xu, "Conservation payments, liquidity constraints and

off-farm labor: impact of the Grain for Green program on rural households in China," *American Journal of Agricultural Economics* 91:1 (2009), pp. 70–86.

4. Kristen Day (ed.), *China's Environment and the Challenge of Sustainable Development* (Armonk NY: M.E. Sharpe, 2005); Elizabeth C. Economy, *The River Runs Black: The Environmental Challenge to China's Future* (Ithaca NY: Cornell University Press, 2004); Elizabeth C. Economy, "The great leap backward?" *Foreign Affairs* (2007), http://www.foreignaffairs.com/articles /62827/elizabeth-c-economy/the-great-leap-backward (accessed 1 March 2011); Elizabeth C. Economy, "China's next revolution," *Current History* 107, No. 710 (2008), p. 293; Abigail R. Jahiel, "The contradictory impact of reform on environmental protection in China," *The China Quarterly*, 149 (1997), pp. 81–103; World Bank, China: *Air, Land and Water, Environmental Priorities for a New Millennium* (Washington DC: World Bank, 2001).

5. Day, *China's Environment and the Challenges of Sustainable Development*, p. 6.

6. World Bank, *Cost of Pollution in China: Economic Estimates of Physical Damage*, 2007, http://siteresources.worldbank.org/INTEAPREGTOPENVIRON MENT/Resources/China_Cost_of_Pollution.pdf (accessed 29 Feburary 2011).

7. Economy, "China's next revolution," p. 293.

8. *Ibid.*, p.294.

9. Food and Agriculture Organization, "Global forest resources assessment 2010", 2010, http://www.pefc.org/images/stories/documents/external /KeyFindings-en.pdf (accessed 27 Feburary 2011).

10. Ministry of Environmental Protection of the PRC, *Quanguo Shengtai Baohu Shiyiwu Guihua* (*The Eleventh Five-Year Plan on Ecological Protection in the People's Republic of China*), 2006, http://www.china.com.cn/policy/txt/2006-11/08/content_7333898.htm (accessed 28 Feburary 2011).

11. Food and Agriculture Organization, "Global forest resources assessment 2010."

12. Carbon Dioxide Information Analysis Center, *Carbon Dioxide Emissions* (*CO$_2$*) (United Nations, 2007).

13. Day, *China's Environment and the Challenges of Sustainable Development*, p. 237.

14. State Forestry Administration (ed.), *Tuigeng guanlin zhidao yu shijian* (*Practice Guidance for the Grain for Green project*) (Beijing: China Agricultural Science and Technology Press, 2003), p. 4.

15. Since 2005 the GFG project has also required local governments to enclose hills for natural afforestation (*fengshan yulin*), but only a small portion of the GFG project resources are used for this purpose.

16. Bennett, "China's sloping land conversion program," p. 699.

17. Wu et al., "Report on the development of the Grain for Green project."

18. Michael Bennett and Yucai Li, "Tuigeng huanlin gongcheng shi zhongguo

shengtai wenming jianshe de weida shijian" ("The Grain for Green project is the greatest practice in the history of ecological conservation in China"), *Forestry Construction* 5 (2009), pp. 3–13; World Wildlife Fund, "Reports suggest China's 'Grain-to-Green' plan is fundamental to management of water and soil erosion," 2003, http://www.wwfchina.org/english/loca.php ?loca=159 (accessed 21 February 2011).

19. State Forestry Administration, "Program progress and achievements," 2010, http://english.forestry.gov.cn/web/article.do?action=readnew&id=201001141 130506500 (accessed 27 February 2011).

20. Zhigang Xu, Michael T. Bennett, Rao Tao and Jintao Xu, "China's sloping land conversion program four years on: Current situation and pending issues", *FED Working Papers No. FE20050016*, 2004, http://www.fed.org. .cn/pub/workingpaper/200522421342888115.pdf (accessed 28 Feburary).

21. *Ibid.*

22. Interviews with local forestry bureau officials in November 2008 in four counties of Shaanxi and Inner Mongolia.

23. Interview with an official of the Provincial Forestry Bureau in Inner Mongolia on 18 November 2008.

24. Ting Zuo, Gubo Qi and Xiuli Xu, "Implementation gap of the policy: a case study of the role of county forestry bureau in the implementation of Grain to Green program," *Forestry Economics* 9 (2006), pp. 11–15.

25. Jintao Xu, "Grain for Green or grain for gain," pp. 249–250.

26. Muyi Kang, Shikui Dong and Hongyan Qin, Xibu Shengtai Jianshe Yu Shengtai Buchang (Ecological Construction and Ecological Compensation in West China) (Beijing: China Environmental Science Press, 2005), pp. 104–5.

27. Kefei Hong, "Hunan nongmin shangfang bei ding chongji zhengfu" ("A farmer was detained because he petitioned to complain of local officials taking away his compensation of the Grain for Green project"), *China Youth Daily*, 23 June 2010, http://news.163.com/10/0623/08/69RP6KBO00014AEE .html (accessed 28 Feburary 2011).

28. State Forestry Administration, *Guojia Linye Zhongdian Shengtai Gongcheng Shehui Jingji Xiaoyi Jiance Baogao 2007* (The Report on Monitoring and Assessment of the Socio-Economic Impacts of China's Key Forestry Programs 2007) (Beijing: Zhongguo Linye Chubanshe, 2008); Yong Wu, Haifeng Mao, Chunhui Zhao and Zhenxiang Lian, "Jingti, tuigeng huanlin de hongli zhengzai bei fugeng qinshi" ("Be careful! The achievement of the Grain for Green Project is being eroded by re-farming"), Ban Yue Tan (China Comment) (2010), pp. 53–55.

29. Kang et al., *Ecological Construction and Ecological Compensation in West China*, p.110; Zhang and Yang (eds.), *The Study on the Grain for Green Project in Northwest China*, p. 4.

30. State Council, "*Guowuyuan guanyu wanshan tuigeng huanlin zhengce de tongzhi*" ("*The notice on improving the Grain for Green Project*"), 2007, http://news.xinhuanet.com/video/2007-09/10/content_6699214.htm (accessed 25 February 2011).

31. Dong Huang and others, "A report for monitoring and assessment of the socio-economic impacts of conversion cropland to forest project," *Forestry Economics*, Vol. 9 (2009), pp. 65–73.

32. Interviews with officials of the forestry bureau in a county of Shaanxi Province on 9 November 2008. The name of the county is not reported here because local officials requested us not to release the information.

33. Interviews with local forestry bureau officials in Inner Mongolia on 19–20 November 2008.

34. Fengtao Li, "Wo xiang Zhu Rongji zongli jianyi xibu tuigeng" ("I recommend Premier Zhu Rongji to launch the Grain for Green project in Western China"), *China Economic Weekly*, 2009, http://www.china.com.cn /economic/txt/2009-09/29/content_18623901.htm (accessed 15 Feburary 2011).

35. The first attempt to convert arable land to forests through economic incentives was the "2605" project funded by the United Nations World Food Program in Xiji County (Ningxia Province) during 1982–1986. It offers a good lesson for the GFG project. After successful implementation of the project from 1983 to 1986, based on international grants and technologies, the entire policy outcome was reversed back to the status quo ante. Farmers returned to farming as soon as the subsidies expired.

36. State Council, "Several opinions on further improving the Grain for Green Project (Guanyu jinyibu wanshan Tuigeng Huanlin Zhengce cuoshi de ruogan yjian), 2002, http://www.mlr.gov.cn/zwgk/flfg/xgflfg/200507/ t20050721_639143.htm (accessed 27 Feburary 2011).

37. The change was made because food shortage may occur if grain subsidies are directly allocated as compensation on a consistent basis. State Forestry Administration, *Tuigeng Huanlin Tiaoli*, (*Regulation on the Grain for Green Project*), 2002, http://news.xinhuanet.com/zhengfu/2002-12/25/content _669840.htm (accessed 28 Feburary 2011).

38. The distinction between economic trees and ecological forests is vague and hard to define clearly. Four criteria are adopted based on the standards issued by the State Forestry Administration in 2001, namely; density of trees, type of trees, allocation of vegetation and operational measures. Generally speaking, since economic forests make less contribution to ecological conservation (only 30% that of ecological forests), the central government requires no less than 80% of converted land to be ecological forests on a county basis. However, the distinction is argued among forestry experts because local government can actually use loopholes. See Lizhen Yan and Qingwen Min, "Discussion on the concept and proportion of economic forest and ecological forest in returning cultivated land to forest," *Research of Soil and Water Conservation* 11:3 (2004), pp. 50–53.

39. Can Liu, Bin Wu and Yonghua Lu, "Zhongguo tuigeng huanlin gongcheng jiqi suo chansheng de yingxiang" ("China's conversion of cropland to forest project: progress and its impact"), *Forestry Economics*, No.10 (2009), pp. 41–46.

40. Interviews with forestry bureau officials in Shaanxi in November 2008.

41. Xu, and Tao, "Grain for Green or Grain for Gain," pp. 249–50.

42. *Ibid.*

43. Junxiao Du, "Ningxia tichu tuigeng huanlin banian renwu sannian wancheng" ("Ningxia proposed to take three years to finish the reforestation task designed to be done within eight years"), 2003, http://www.people.com.cn/GB/huanbao/55/20030402/960980.html (accessed 26 February 2011).

44. Xuecheng Jiang, Gang Chen and Guoliang Zhu, "Daxibei repan tuigeng huanlin ruanzhuolu" ("Northwest China prays for soft landing of the decline in central subsidies for the Grain for Green project"), 2004, http://news .xinhuanet.com/banyt/2004-08/05/content_1718462.htm (accessed 25 February 2011).The primary purposes of land preparation prior to planting are to create a soil structure favourable for tree growth, to incorporate residues and to control weeds and diseases. Planting delayed too long after land was prepared may cause low quality of trees or crop growth.

45. *Ibid.*

46. Interviews with forestry bureau officials in Inner Mongolia on 19–20 November 2008.

47. Kang et al., *Ecological Construction and Ecological Compensation in West China*, p.110.

48. Christine Jane Trac, Stevan Harrell, Thomas M. Hinckley and Amanda C. Henck, "Reforestation programs in Southwest China: reported success, observed failure, and the reasons why," *Journal of Mountain Science* 4:4 (2007), pp. 275–292; Emi Uchida, Jintao Xu, Zhigang Xu and Scott Rozelle, "Are the poor benefiting from China's land conservation program?," *Environment and Development Economics* 12:4 (2007), pp. 593–620; Qin Tu, Lei Zhang and Arthur Mol, "Payment for environmental services: the sloping land conversion program in Ningxia Autonomous Region of China," *China & World Economy* 16:2 (2008), pp. 66–81.

49. Shunbo Yao, Hua Li and Guangquan Liu, "Agricultural productivity changes induced by the sloping land conversion program: an analysis of County W in the loess plateau region," in Yin Runsheng (ed.), *An Integrated Assessment of China's Ecological Restoration Programs* (London: Springer, 2009), pp. 219–33.

50. County Government of Wuqi, "Wuqi xian tuigeng huanlin gongzuo huibao cailiao" ("Working report on the Grain for Green project in Wuqi County in 2007"), *Shanxi Tongji Nianjian 2008* (*Shaanxi Statistical Yearbook 2008*) (Beijing: Zhongguo tongji chubanshe, 2008).

51. Yao, Li and Liu, "Agricultral productivity changes induced by the sloping land conversion program."

52. Shannxi Provincial Forestry Department, "Shaanxi 1999–2008 jihua renwu yilan biao 1999–2008" ("Task plan in Shaanxi from 1999–2008"), internal document.

53. Interviews with forestry bureau officials in Wuqi County of Shaanxi Province on 6 November 2008.

54. *Ibid.*

55. *Ibid.*

56. Interviews with forestry bureau officials in Shaanxi and Inner Mongolia in November 2008.

57. Interviews with local forestry officials in Wuqi County of Shaanxi Province on 6 November 2008.

58. Yuan Lihua, "Linfen jiegou tiaozheng yige bude bushuo de huati" ("Forestry structure adjustment: an issue that cannot be ignored"), *Shannxi Daily*, 3 August 2009, http://bbs.cnwest.com/archiver/tid-104925.html (accessed 21 February 2011).

59. Jianhong Feng, Xuefeng Wang and Dongquan Liang, "Canyu shi fangfa zai zaolin xiangmu zhong de yunyong yu yiyi" ("The application and implication of the participatory approach in afforestation"), *Shaanxi Agricutural Science* 2 (2008), pp. 198–200; Lihua Yuan, "Forestry structure adjustment: an issue that cannot be ignored."

60. Liqiang Bai, Junbo Wang, Weibing Zhang and Yin Lu, "Zhongde caizheng hezuo zaolin xiangmu de jidian chuangxin zhichu" ("Innovation in Sino-German financial cooperation of afforestation"), *Shaanxi Forest Science and Technology* 1 (2005), pp. 41–43.

61. Interviews with forestry bureau officials in Wuqi County of Shaanxi Province on 6 November 2008.

62. Feng et al., "The application and implication of the participatory approach in afforestation", pp. 198–200.

63. Arne Gooss, "KFW's commitment to the forestry sector in China," paper presented at the International Forum on Investment and Finance in China's Forestry Sector held in Beijing in 2004.

64. Bai et al., "Innovation in Sino-German financial cooperation of afforestation," p. 41.

65. Zhen Wen, Yin Lv and Juan Wang, "Waizi siangmu de shishi cujin shaanxi linye fasheng jubian" ("International aid program enhances forestry development in Shaanxi"), *China Forestry*, No. 1A (2009), pp. 32–33; Tianming Pan, "Waiyuan xiangmu zaolin chengxiao tanjiu" ("The study on the effectiveness of international aid for afforestation"), *Forestry Economics*, 5 (2007), pp. 72–76; Janelle Plummer and John Taylor, *Community Participation in China: Issues and Processes for Capacity Building* (Earthscan/James & James, 2004); State Forestry Administration, "Deguo fuxing xindai yinhang pinggu zhongde caizheng hezuo zaolin xiangmu" ("KFW assesses China-German financial cooperation programme"), 2006, http://www.forestry.gov.cn/portal/main/s/112/content-302912.html (accessed 1 March 2011). Natural Resource Management Division Asia of KFW, "Financial cooperation with the P.R. China", 2008, internal document.

66. State Forestry Administration, "Linye wuchang waiyuan tongji" ("Internal reference on international grants on afforestation"), 2004, internal document.

67. Economy, *The River Runs Black*, pp. 108 and 23.

68. Interview with officials of KFW conducted in Beijing in July 2009.

69. County Government of Wuqi, "Wuqi xian tuigeng huanlin gongzuo huibao cailiao" ("Working report on the Grain for Green Project in County Wuqi"), 2007, internal document.

70. Interviews with forestry bureau officials in Wuqi County of Shaanxi Province on 6 November 2008.

71. *Ibid.*

72. Lihua, "Forestry structure adjustment: an issue that cannot be ignored."

73. County Government of Wuqi, "Working report on the Grain for Green Project in Wuqi County."

74. State Forestry Administration, "Linyeju zai Wuqixian zhaokai tuigeng huanlin gongcheng shizhounian zongjie dahui" ("The State Forestry Administration held the Tenth Year Anniversary of the Grain for Green project in Wuqi County"), 10 September 2009, http://www.gov.cn/gzdt /2009-09/10/content_1413917.htm (accessed 1 March 2011).

75. Lester Ross, "Obligatory tree planting: The role of campaigns in policy implementation in post-Mao China," in David M. Lampton (ed.), *Policy Implementation in Post-Mao China.* (Berkeley CA: University of California Press, 1987), pp. 230–231.

76. "Weilai shinian zhongyang chi liangqianyi tuigeng huanlin" ("The central government will spend RMB200 billion in the Grain for Green projct"), *Wenwei Po*, 19 August 2010, http://paper.wenweipo.com/2010/08/19 /CH1008190012.htm (accessed 27 February 2011).

16

Observations on Education Policy under Hu's Leadership and Wen's Administration: The Past and the Next Decade

Steven HOLM

Introduction

Since the founding of the People's Republic of China in 1949, and especially during the era of reform and opening up, China has witnessed historical changes and scored remarkable achievements in the field of education. According to the Common Programme of the Chinese People's Political Consultative Conference, which served as the *de facto* constitution at that time, education in the People's Republic of China should serve the nation, be scientific and universal, and education would be universalized step by step.[1] In 1954, the Constitution of the People's Republic of China further recognized the right to education.[2]

Since 1978, China's economy has started to transform from a planned economy to a market economy. The Communist Party of China (CPC), committed to serving the people, has attached great importance to education and put it at the top of the national development agenda. By prioritizing education and speeding up its modernization, China's educational reform and development has embodied the determination and effort of the entire nation.

Hu Jintao and Wen Jiabao have directed China to approach the leading role in the world. The attention and leadership of the CPC

Central Committee has focused on the development of education as well. Helping more people gain access to education and raising the educational level of the people has constituted the core of the CPC Central Committee's blueprint to rejuvenate the country. The education system was forged alongside the initiation of a brand new socialist system, whose take-off could be credited to the foresight of a Marxist ruling party.

Since the founding of the People's Republic of China, and the initiation of reform and the opening-up policy, China has followed a path of developing socialist education with Chinese characteristics and made tremendous progress. China has (1) established the largest education system in the whole world, (2) universalized nine-year, free "obligatory" education, close to the average level of medium-income countries, (3) sought to popularize higher education, marking a historical breakthrough in China's education history, and (4) risen to be a country rich in human resources, successfully turning itself into a country rich in human talent.

The universalization of nine-year obligatory education and the popularization of higher education symbolize a new level in Chinese civilization in a large country with a population of 1.3 billion. Much attention has to be paid in order to make a suitable judgement.

Background of the Education Reform and Development

To gain some understanding about education in China after the opening-up policy was introduced, we need to understand and analyse the important education policies, and how the opening-up policy influenced educational reform.

From the 1950s, the theories and practice of education in China were deeply influenced by those of the USSR. The Cultural Revolution downplayed the importance of education, emphasizing the function of education as serving proletarian politics. In the post-Mao period, China could not afford large investment in education. China's leaders modified the policy of concentrating education resources at the university level, either ideologically or financially, in the education of a few students. Although designed to facilitate modernization, it conflicted directly with the Party's principles. The policy that produced an educated elite also siphoned off resources that might have been used to accomplish the provision of nine-year education faster and to equalize educational opportunities. The policy of key schools has been modified over the years. Nevertheless, China's leaders believed that an educated elite was necessary to reach their modernization goals.

With the opening-up policy, China's education policy continued to evolve. Under Deng Xiaoping's pragmatic leadership, it was necessary to develop science, technology, and intellectual resources and to raise the education standard and level of the population to meet the goals of modernization. Demands for education in new technology, information science, and advanced management expertise were levied as a result of the reform of the economic structure and the emergence of new economic forms. China needed an educated labour force to feed and provision its population.

By 1980, achievement was once again accepted as the basis for admission and promotion in education. This fundamental change reflected the critical role of scientific and technical knowledge and professional skills in the "Four Modernizations". Political activism was no longer regarded as an important measure of individual performance. The development of commonly approved political attitudes and political background was made secondary to achievement. Education policy promoted expanding enrolments, with the long-term objective of achieving universal primary and secondary education. This policy contrasted with the previous one, which pursued increasing enrolments for egalitarian reasons. The commitment to modernization was reinforced by plans for nine-year obligatory education and for providing good quality higher education. However, the Constitution Law was amended in 1982 so that citizens have duties in addition to the right to education.[3] Education should serve the construction of social modernization and vice versa.

In January 1985, the Chinese government initiated a wholesale reform of education. Deng Xiaoping's far-ranging educational reform policy involved all levels of the education system. He aimed to narrow the gap between China and other developed countries. Modernizing education was critical to modernizing China. In May 1985, when China was restructuring its economy, a National Conference on Education Work was convened, the first of its kind since the reform and opening up started. Devolution of educational management from the central to the local level was the means chosen to improve the education system. Centralized authority was not abandoned, as evidenced by the creation of the State Education Commission. However, emphasis on the political function of education and the relationship between education and the superstructure was replaced by emphasis on the economic function of education and the relation between education and productivity.

According to the Resolution by the CPC Central Committee in its "Decision on the Reform of the Educational System", adopted at the 1985 Conference, the essential purpose of the educational reform was to improve the quality of the people, to produce more and better human resources. The reform had become an important agenda item for the Chinese government. Reform of the education system was necessary to guide the education activities in order to implement economic and political development. They were (1) to give the responsibility of managing basic education to local governments and to implement nine-year obligatory education step-by-step, (2) to adjust the structure of secondary education and to vigorously develop vocational and technical education, (3) to reform the enrolment planning and job assignment for graduates from tertiary institutions, and to increase the authority of tertiary institutions in running schools, and (4) to impose the regulation requiring principals to take responsibility for their education institutions gradually. Academically, the goals of reform were to enhance and universalize elementary, junior and middle school education, to increase the number of schools and qualified teachers, and to develop vocational and technical education. A uniform standard for curricula, textbooks, examinations, and teacher qualifications was established. However, considerable autonomy and variations in and among the autonomous regions, provinces, and special municipalities was allowed.

The National Conference on Education Work recognized five fundamental areas for reform to be discussed in connection with implementing the policy. The reforms were intended to produce more able people; to make the localities responsible for developing basic education and systematically implement a nine-year obligatory education programme; to improve middle-level education and develop vocational and technical education; to reform the graduate assignment system of higher institutions and to expand their management and decision-making power; and to give administrators the necessary encouragement and authority to ensure smooth progress in educational reform. Further, the system of enrolment and job assignment in higher education was changed, and excessive government control over colleges and universities was reduced.

The Resolution also put forward a series of recommendations including reform of the management system and structural adjustment in education. The document has since served as a guideline for the development of China's education system. At the 1985 Conference, Deng Xiaoping pointed out that the nation's strength and sustained economic development depended heavily on the educational level of the workforce and on the quantity and quality of intellectuals. Good education would produce a huge supply of human resources that would outnumber those of any other country. With quality education and a good socialist system, China would surely attain the goals.

A number of important instructions by Deng Xiaoping are set out below:

- "Education should be oriented towards modernization, the world and the future";
- "We should make every effort to develop education, even if it means slowing down our efforts in other sectors";
- "Leaders who neglect education are either short-sighted or immature, and they are therefore unable to lead the drive for modernization."

Through these brilliant expositions, Deng Xiaoping raised the overall requirements for the development of China's socialist educational endeavour, based on the historical destiny of the Chinese nation and the current trend of global expansion. They have served as strategic guidelines for the reform and development of contemporary Chinese education.

In 1986 the Obligatory Education Law[4] established requirements and deadlines for attaining universal education tailored to local conditions and guaranteed school-age children the right to receive education. The Obligatory Education Law divided China into three categories: (1) cities and economically developed areas in coastal provinces and a small number of developed areas in the hinterland; (2) towns and villages with medium development; and (3) economically backward areas. Universal basic education should be provided in each in turn. People's congresses at various local levels were, within certain guidelines and according to local conditions, to decide the steps, methods and deadlines for implementing nine-year basic education in accordance with the guidelines formulated by the central authorities.

In 1985 about 96% of primary-school-age children were enrolled in approximately 832,300 primary schools.[5] Under the Obligatory Education Law, nine years of basic education would be provided. Primary schools were to offer free tuition and be reasonably located for the convenience of children attending them;[6] students would attend primary schools in their neighbourhoods or villages. Parents would pay a small fee per term for books and other expenses such as transportation, food and heating.[7] Previously, fees were not considered a deterrent to attendance, although some parents felt even these minor costs were more than they could afford. Under the education reform, students from poor families received stipends, and state enterprises, institutions and other sectors of society were encouraged to establish their own schools. A major concern was that scarce resources were conserved without causing enrolment to fall and without weakening the better schools. In particular, local governments were warned not to pursue middle-school education blindly while primary school education was still developing, or to wrest money, teaching staff, and materials from primary schools. Chinese secondary schools are called middle schools and are divided into junior and senior levels. In 1985 more than 104,000 middle schools (both regular and vocational) enrolled about 51 million students. Junior middle schools offered a three-year course of study, which students began at twelve years of age. Senior middle schools offered a two- or three-year course, which students began at the age of fifteen.

The reform did not provide for compulsory education in China, just obligatory education, which indicated the educational stakeholders required to enhance the implementation of the popularization of basic education. The stakeholders might include central or local officials, educators and teachers, parents and citizens. They were responsible for providing education to the children but no one took the ultimate responsibility. As a further example of the government's commitment to nine-year basic education, in January 1986 the State Council drafted a bill that made it illegal for any organization or individual to employ youths before they had completed their nine years of schooling.[8] The bill also authorized free education and subsidies for students whose families had financial difficulties. According to analysts, inadequate funding causes high drop-out rates in poorer regions.[9]

When the Chinese government began to reform the education system, emphasis was placed on the reform of power and responsibility of the administrative organization, ignoring the reform of education in terms of the organization of education itself. Provincial-level authorities were to develop plans, enact decrees and rules, distribute funds to counties, and administer directly a few key middle schools. County authorities were to distribute funds to each township government, and these were to make up any deficiencies. County authorities were to supervise education and teaching and manage their own senior middle schools, teachers' schools, teachers' in-service training schools, agricultural vocational schools, and exemplary primary and junior middle schools. The remaining schools were to be managed separately by the county and township authorities.

The student enrolment and graduate assignment system was also changed to reflect more closely the personnel needs of modernization. By 1986 the state was responsible for drafting the enrolment plan, which took into account future personnel demands, the need to recruit students from outlying regions, and the needs of trades and professions with adverse working conditions. Moreover, a certain number of graduates to be trained for the People's Liberation Army were included in the state enrolment plan. In most cases, enrolment in higher education institutions at the employers' request was extended as a supplement to the state student enrolment plan.

In higher education, many of the problems continued, in 1987, that had hindered the development of this sector in the past. Funding remained a major problem because science, technology study, research and study abroad were expensive. Because education was competing with other modernization programmes, capital was critically short. Another concern was whether or not the Chinese economy was sufficiently advanced to make efficient use of the highly trained technical personnel it planned to educate.

The development of a free market for education accelerated with Deng Xiaoping's southern expedition in 1992 in which the paramount leader declared a policy of further opening of the Chinese economy to the outside world and urged the Chinese people to adopt market institutions to promote economic growth. This policy further encouraged the establishment of non-government financed educational institutions. Private funding in China included funds raised or spent by three types of schools: (1) private or non-government schools; (2) public schools which were leased for private operation, or parts of which were operated and financed independently, or financially independent colleges or schools that were set up by public universities or their affiliated units, and (3) tuition and fees charged by public schools.

From 12 to 18 October 1992, the Fourteenth CPC National Congress was convened in Beijing. Jiang Zemin called on the whole Party and the whole nation to make education a strategic priority and strive to upgrade the ethical and educational levels of the whole population, considering this an essential move towards China's modernization. In 1993, the "Outline of Reform and Development of Education in China" was enacted by the Central Committee of the Communist Party and the State Council. The principles of the reform of the education system insisted on the socialist orientation and fostered builders and successors of the socialist cause with all-round development morally, intellectually and physically. The principles were expected to motivate the enthusiasm of various levels of government, and the whole society with teachers and students. They were also expected to improve the quality of education, the level research and the efficiency of school management. These helped to promote education to serve socialist modernization.

To implement the reform, China planned (1) to reform the system for running schools, (2) to deepen the reform of the educational system for secondary education and continue to perfect the management system of running schools in separate levels and managing schools in separate levels, (3) to deepen the reform of the higher education system, (4) to change the enrolment regulations and the regulation of the assignment of graduates in tertiary institutions, (5) to perfect the regulation of graduates' training and academic degrees, (6) to reform the mechanism of funding in higher education institutions and to play a full macro-adjustment role in school funding, (7) to reform the enrolment and graduate placement in middle professional schools and technician schools in the light of tertiary institutions, (8) to push the reform of the intra-school management system focusing on the reform of personnel regulation and allocation regulation, (9) to deepen the reform of the regulation of personnel and labour in accordance with the reform of education system, and (10) to speed up the construction of educational legal regulation, to establish and perfect the system of law and supervision enforcement and to move gradually to the track of managing education by law. The reform mainly focused on macro-management and higher education. It also dealt with the relationship between the central government and local governments, among governments, schools and various dimensions of society.

On 14 June 1994 the second National Conference on Education Work was held in Beijing. Jiang pointed out in his speech at the opening ceremony that the development of education should always be given strategic priority throughout the whole process of socialist modernization and failure to recognize its importance would be a historical mistake and result in delayed development. The substantial national evaluation of universities in 1994 resulted in the massification of higher education as well as a renewed emphasis on elite institutions. By 1999, primary school education had become universal throughout the areas where 90% of China's population lived, and nine-year obligatory education was established throughout the areas with 85% of the nation's population.

On 15 June 1999, at the third National Conference on Education Work, Jiang emphasized again that the Party and people of all nationalities should continue to support the development of education for the purpose of making China strong and prosperous. Party committees and governments at all levels were called upon to regard education as a strategic priority and incorporate it into the overall plan of modernization. Reformers realized that the higher education system was not meeting modernization goals and that additional changes were needed. "Decisions on Deepening the Educational Reform and Improving Quality-Oriented Education in all Ways" was promulgated by the Central Committee.

In order to provide good conditions for quality oriented education, the contents of the 1999 education reform were (1) to basically make the nine-year obligatory education universal and gradually eliminate illiteracy in young and middle-aged people, (2) to adjust the structure of education, to enlarge the scale of senior secondary education and higher education so as to reduce the pressure of entering higher schools and to provide more educational opportunities for the qualified, (3) to formulate a new education system to match the needs of the socialist market economy system and the needs of the educational laws, to be communicated and connected with different kinds of education and to provide more study opportunities for graduates, (4) to give more power to the provinces in managing local education and to promote the integration of education and the local economy and social development, (5) to liberate thought, change ideas and enthusiastically encourage and support all walks of society to set up schools in different ways so as to match the increasing education needs of the people, and to formulate the new pattern in which schools are mainly run by government, and (6) to accelerate the reform of the regulation of enrolment and examination and the regulation of evaluation so as to change the situation that one's whole life should be decided by one examination.

The education policy played a crucial leading role in the course of educational development and economic reform. It was an integral part of the government's public policies. The document was issued, drawing up an overall plan for establishing a vigorous educational system with the Chinese socialist characteristics in the early twenty-first century. In the same year, the State Council approved the "Action Plan to Revitalize Education towards the Twenty-first Century" which was submitted by the Ministry of Education. This defined the important tasks of the educational sector in carrying out the strategy of revitalizing the nation by science and education at the turn of the new century.

Education Reform and Development
Meeting the Challenge
of the Last Decade under Hu's Leadership
and Wen's Administration

Under the leadership and administration of the CPC Central Committee and the State Council, the whole nation implemented the scientific concept for development, promoted the construction of the harmonious society of socialism and attained new achievements in economic reform and opening in the past decade.

A high technology revolution characterized by information technology was on the way. The globalization of the economy and information made an increasing serve competition of overall power among the countries of the world. The knowledge-based economy emerged and international patterns were adjusted. Faced with the information competitive capitalism, China took the implementation of the strategy of vitalizing the nation by science and education as a key to realize the great goal of modernization. Education in the construction of socialist materialism and spiritual civilization took on the significant historical mission of advancing the nation's quality and capacity of innovation and creativity.

As China went from being the eighth largest economy to the second in this decade, the GDP per capita reached over US$4,000 in 2010 and its comprehensive strength and international competitiveness have moved to a new stage. The state development should start to cater with the informational competitive capitalistic world. China's progress has been impressive but there are reports showing a slowdown in the expansion of average and widening regional disparities. In recent years, the public expenditure on education has been stagnant as a share of GDP and unevenly distributed. Public investment in primary education has been inadequate, especially in rural and poor regions where the possibility of private funding is limited.

The prestige associated with higher education caused a greater demand for it. But in the past many qualified youths were unable to attend colleges and universities because China could not finance enough university places for them. In China a senior-middle school graduate was considered an educated person, although middle schools were viewed as a training ground for colleges and universities. While middle-school students were offered the prospect of higher education, they were also confronted with the fact that university admission was limited. Middle schools were evaluated in terms of their success in sending graduates on for higher education, although efforts persisted to educate young people to take a place in society as valued and skilled members of the work force.

National examinations to select students for higher education are an important part of China's culture and entrance to a higher education institution is considered prestigious. Hence in 1998 the Chinese government proposed a plan intended to expand university enrolment to ensure a greater output of professional and specialized graduates (Table 1). An adjunct to the plan aimed to develop elite world-class universities. This rapid expansion of mass higher

Table 1: Number of New Entrants of Schools of All Types and Levels Providing Formal Programs (in thousands)

	1949	1965	1978	1980	1985	2000	2005	2006	2007	2008	2009
A. Higher Education											
1. Postgraduates	0.242	1.456	10.708	36.16	46.871	128.484	364.831	397.925	418.612	446.422	510.953
2. Undergraduates in Regular HEIs	30.6	164.2	401.5	281.2	619.2	2206.1	5044.6	5460.5	5659.2	6076.6	6394.9
3. Undergraduates in Adult HEIs					787.8	1561.5	1930.3	1844.4	1911.1	2025.6	2104.8
B. Secondary Education								35209.8	35485.9	35186.9	35087.1	34924.0
B1. Senior Secondary							15333.9	16190.3	16501.9	16491.2	17039.5
1. Senior Secondary Schools											
Regular Schools	71.1	458.9	6929.1	3834.0	2575.1	4726.9	8777.3	8712.1	8401.6	8370.1	8303.4
Adult Schools				500.5	1076.1	304.7					
2. Secondary Vocational Schools						3867.5	6556.6	7478.2	8100.2	8121.1	8736.1
Regular Specialized Sec. Schools	97.4	208.5	447.0	467.6	668.3	1325.9	2411.3	2788.9	2972.9	3037.8	3117.1
Adult SSSs				1522.2		533.9	479.5	461.6	520.0	558.3	868.9
Vocational High Schools		556.7		240.6	984.9	1503.9	2482.1	2880.2	3021.8	2906.6	3131.7
Skilled Workers Schools			257.0	331.3	355.4	503.8	1183.7	1347.6	1585.5	1618.4	1618.4
B2. Junior Secondary Education							19875.8	19295.6	18685.0	18596.0	17884.5
1. Regular Junior Secondary Schools	341.2	2998.9	20059.8	15509.1	13494.0	22633.0	19765.2	19236.2	18637.5	18561.7	17863.9
2. Vocational JSSs				66.6	176.1	322.7	110.6	59.4	47.5	34.3	20.6
3. Adult JSSs		2508.1		1948.1	2370.2	146.7	0.0	0.0	0.0	0.0	
C. Primary Education and Others											
Regular Primary Schools	6800.0	32960.2	33153.6	29423.4	22981.7	19464.7	16717.4	17293.6	17360.7	16957.2	16378.0
Pre-school Education Institutions						15311.1	13562.4	13912.5	14336.1	14827.1	15468.6
Correctional Work-Study Schools					3.2	4.4	3.5	4.0	4.4	4.8	3.9
Special Education Schools			5.9	5.9	9.2	52.9	49.3	49.8	63.4	62.4	64.0

education has resulted not only in a strain in teaching resources but also in higher unemployment rates among graduates.

The great development of general further and higher education in China has been made but there remain some issues and problems. Restructuring, through consolidations, mergers and shifts among the authorities who supervised institutions, was aimed at addressing the problems of small size and low efficiency. Higher vocational education was also restructured, and there was a general tendency there to emphasize elite institutions. Based on national data and field investigation, further reform and development was required.

In the spring of 2007 China conducted a national evaluation of its universities. The results of this evaluation would be used to support the next major planned policy initiative. Academics praised the *fin-de-siècle* reforms for budging China's higher education from a centralized, closed, monopolized and static system into one characterized by more diversification, decentralization, openness and dynamism. The reforms stimulated the involvement of local governments and other non-state sectors.

In 2008, over six million college graduates needed to obtain employment. The employment rate of graduates was recorded at just 70%. Graduates in different disciplines had varying levels of difficulty in seeking employment. Those from employment-oriented vocational colleges were more apt to find jobs. In October 2008, the Ministry of Education admitted that the expansion of enrolments in university that began in 1999 was a mistake. The result had been a lower quality of teaching due to the enormous increase in the number of students. At the same time it was noted that this decentralization and marketization had led to further inequality in educational opportunity. The study-aid policy, student loan policy, study-aid fund and scholarship system did not receive suitable attention, which led to a large number of students with financial difficulties.

For non-obligatory education, China adopted a shared-cost mechanism, charging tuition at a certain percentage of the cost. Meanwhile, to ensure that students from low-income families had access to higher education, the government initiated effective means of assistance, with policies and measures such as scholarships, work-study programmes, subsidies for students with special economic difficulties, reduction or exemption of tuition fees and state stipends. Abundant cases were found where students met with financial difficulties. The rectification of unauthorized fee collection[10] was one of the focal points. Since these were covert and unlawful activities, even government departments did not produce accurate figures for investigation. The Ministry of Education reported 170,000 investigation groups organized in 2002 and 145,000 primary schools and 41,000 junior secondary schools were checked. RMB420 million received from students was found to be unauthorized. Since the Sixteenth CPC National Congress in 2002, the Central Committee has recognized that human resources are the primary resources of a nation and play a crucial role in the overall progress in reform and opening up and socialist modernization. Thus it proposed the strategy of building up the strength of the country with talented people, and formulated the strategic plan to make education the first priority and to build China into a strong nation rich in human resources.

To recap the measures described above, in 1985 the CPC Central Committee "Decisions on Education Reform" was adopted by the first National Conference on Education Work. The Central Committee and the State Council later released the "Outline of China's Education Reform and Development" (1993), the "Decisions on Deepening Education Reform and Promoting Quality Education" (1999) and the "Decisions on Further Strengthening Education in Rural Areas" (2003). These documents were appropriate blueprints for promoting China's education reform.

In 2003, under the guiding principles of Deng Xiaping's theory of "Three Representatives" (introduced by Jiang Zeman), the new government was represented by the leadership of Hu Jintao and the administration of Wen Jiabao. The CPC Central Committee focused on the difficulties and keys of building a well-off society in an all-round way. The new government attached greater importance to the work of education in rural areas which showed the firm belief and practical behaviour of the Central Committee and the State Council to set up the party for the public and to govern for the people.

In March 2004, the State Council approved the "Action Plan for Invigorating Education 2003–2007" which was submitted by the Ministry of Education. The plan was imbued with scientific, prospective and operating features, which offered a better policy guarantee for establishing the well-being of society and promoting human development in an all-round way.

The traditional governance system and outdated policy-making process resulted in the mixing up of old and new and even of levels in the area of educational policies. Some of the policy-making actions revealed the trend of centralizing power and strengthening administrative control. Some policy-making processes were rather too hurried, without transparency and lack of democratic and open practice. Education in China confronted a historical turning point, from meeting fundamental needs to the pursuit of good and ideal education.

The focus on growth has led to uneven development and rising income inequality in the country – between the coastal, and the interior and western regions; across provinces, within provinces, and between rural and urban areas. Inequality in education reflects social inequality. Provincial-level authorities were to develop plans, enact decrees and rules, distribute funds to counties, and administer directly a few key secondary schools. They should distribute funds to each township government, which were to make up for any deficiencies. County authorities were to supervise education and teaching and manage their own senior middle schools, teachers' training colleges, teachers' in-service training, agricultural vocational schools, and exemplary primary and junior middle schools.

The purpose of the national education authority tried to safeguard children's rights to education. In terms of legislation, it reconstructed the protection of rights to education. From the administrative perspective, it should be impartial and establish an accountable system for the implementation of obligatory education. The nation and government should be responsible for abolishing disparity in education, reshaping educational aims, setting up the funding for the obligatory education system, regulating schools and avoiding school-age children dropping out of education.

The total funding for obligatory education gradually increased from 2000 to 2007, with efforts taken by the central and local governments (Tables 2 and 3). The budgetary funds grew rapidly with a higher proportion of the total financing, while investment in western China as well as in primary and secondary education went up promptly. The total budget was increasing and the budgetary ratio grew year by year. These resulted with the concerns of governments at all levels and the establishment of financial guarantee for the funding system.

Table 2: Education Expenditure Per Pupil at Primary Level[11]

	2000	2002	2004	2006	2007
Beijing	2907.14	4553.12	6411.28	7985.58	10684.09
Shanghai	3715.22	5559.40	9038.51	11632.49	13591.86
Zhejiang	1577.21	2372.95	3583.49	4347.87	5234.73
Guangdong	1331.28	1798.88	2115.06	2406.76	2850.92
Hunan	559.80	860.22	1299.61	2076.93	2680.71
Hubei	447.15	621.41	853.06	1170.74	1628.08
Guangxi	611.03	913.98	1117.31	1555.03	2034.71
Guizhou	418.23	643.04	819.24	1197.18	1628.08

Table 3: Education Expenditure Per Pupil at Junior Secondary Level[12]

	2000	2002	2004	2006	2007
Beijing	4362.04	5584.91	7763.04	12848.64	16945.83
Shanghai	4413.52	6106.60	9990.49	13623.59	15728.94
Zhejiang	2359.28	3168.61	4917.79	6097.74	7105.53
Guangdong	1889.53	2511.99	3081.76	3490.06	3978.73
Hunan	849.60	1078.26	1418.97	2216.05	2893.97
Hubei	1308.49	1655.96	1951.67	2840.45	3202.80
Guangxi	857.95	1234.47	1422.49	1868.76	2443.15
Guizhou	648.37	873.25	1040.07	1464.12	1961.97

As the resource base of local governments differed, the capacity to finance basic education also varied (Tables 2 and 3). Local governments were authorized to levy education surcharges and schools were authorized to charge fees, engage in income-generating activities, and accept donations from society in order to generate extra-budgetary resources to supplement the budgetary allocation.[13] The average expenditure figures significantly understated the disparity between rural and urban areas within these provinces. China should enact a better fiscal transfer system and put more investment towards helping alleviate the cause of underachieving rural education. The money allocated for rural education must be fully implemented and used for its specified purpose only.

Unfair distribution of resources in cities and the countryside as well as a shortage of teachers in rural areas has resulted in unequal education among school children. China should put more efforts into improving school conditions and raising teachers' incomes in rural areas, particularly in remote mountainous regions. There is a strong built-in incentive for teachers to avoid working in poor areas. Remote places, particularly in areas in the western region with ethnic minority populations, have difficulty recruiting and retaining qualified teachers. Substitute teachers who are less qualified had been recruited to do the job.

Education policy was moving from external to internal issues and from the construction of hardware to the renewal and upgrade of software. Once universal free obligatory education is achieved, it will be necessary to reach consensus on reform through emancipating the mind and public discussion on the issues of how to determine the goal of modern education in the next phase and what is good and ideal education.

Free obligatory education was developed further after the Obligatory Education Law (Amendment) came into effect in 2006.[14] The government launched an ambitious policy to abolish miscellaneous fees in obligatory education in the rural areas.[15] This reform increased fiscal transfers from the central government to regional governments to finance rural obligatory education. This new money was used to compensate rural schools for the abolition of miscellaneous fees for all students, to provide free text books to students, to subsidize boarding fees, to support essential non-personnel costs and school maintenance and reconstruction, and to contribute to the payment of teachers' salaries in poor counties. This massive investment in obligatory education aimed to support the goal of building a harmonious society and establishing the socialist new villages.

The 2006 amendment introduced a mechanism designed to allocate education funds between central and local governments. The Obligatory Education Law clearly stated that obligatory education was free and it secured government sponsored funding. It stipulated measures designed to promote the development of obligatory education and make it compulsory. Public primary and junior middle schools were forbidden from transforming into or sponsoring private schools. Schools were not permitted to require any tests for admission. They were barred from separating students by ability and were required to be non-discriminatory. Thus the goal of developing well-rounded students was stressed. A system of accountability was introduced to supervise illegal fee collecting activities and school security was emphasized.

According to the new funding policies, rural obligatory education, school expenditures, school maintenance and reconstruction and aid for needy students would be partly covered by the central government funding. Financing for schools has increased dramatically. In the western regions of China, the central government was responsible for 80% of miscellaneous fees and subsidies for public funds.

With free education available for rural students, making education more accessible for migrant children in urban areas became an urgent issue. The migrant population has increased with economic development and it includes a considerable proportion of school-age children. This floating population is large, highly mobile and difficult to control. Educating migrant children is becoming a prominent problem. Central government policy stipulated that urban governments were responsible for providing education for migrant children. Children were required to be allocated places in public schools, but this was difficult to accomplish in reality. The number of migrant workers in cities would continue to increase and the educational rights of migrant children would remain an important concern for a long time. Providing equal education to migrant children should be covered in the education planning of any regional areas, but the problem remained unresolved.

The number of migrant children kept increasing. With industrial and economic development, migrant workers initiated the serious problem of children left behind in rural areas. Children of migrant workers in urban areas and children left behind in rural areas accounted for about 50 million people. In the urban areas, there exhibited district features in family and became permanent residents. Facing this situation and the new policy generated by the central government, some local governments adopted measures for education for migrant children. The focus shifted from equal opportunity to equity in education, but the problems were continuous. In 2007, the government continued regulating the fees charged for educational purposes and balancing the allocation of education resources. It focused on regulating system reformed schools, improving the facilities of poorly equipped schools, encouraging reasonable faculty flow and reforming the high school entrance examination. The selection of schools was a serious problem in big cities where the principle of equality in education had been eroded. Schools could sell their educational opportunities for huge profit. Many local governments have begun to regulate reformed schools. Private schools, schools run by the private sector but subsidized by the government, and schools run by the government but subsidized by the private sector, were investigated, regulated and subsequently not permitted to separate students based on ability, or to request extra money. However, relevant education departments were still not clear how to prevent the selection of schools based on performance instead of quality of teaching and how to raise funds to support such schools.

The development of Chinese economy clearly affected the development of Chinese education as well. The central government and local governments continued to regard education as the first priority and did not aim at educational equity until 2007. Educational equality in terms of accessibility, if not quality, remained a mirage for many children of migrant workers in China. Beijing deserves praise for planning to remove one educational hurdle for these children. It considered opening some of its senior high schools, the vocational schools in particular, to qualified migrant children. The city governments, however, did not specify what qualifications these children should have.

Despite the unclear definitions, Beijing was moving in the right direction. The schooling of migrant workers' children was difficult as families move from the countryside to cities or from cities to cities. A different set of challenges emerged centring around the education of migrant children. Massive internal migration has occurred from rural to urban areas, within provinces and across provinces. Starting from 2003, opportunities for rural children to attend public school in urban areas were provided in accordance with children's residence status. Up to that point, public schools in the cities could still refuse to admit migrant children because of the residence system. Moreover, most rural children were denied entry to senior high schools in cities. These schools prepared the students with the final tuition for the national college entrance examinations. Without a permanent urban residence permit, the migrant students were not allowed to sit for the exams in cities and consequently the senior high schools in cities turned the migrant children away.

Table 4: Gross Pupil Intake Enrolment Rates[16] (%)

Year	Primary	Junior age 12–14	Pre-vocation	Senior	IHEs age 18–22
1991	109.5	69.7	23.9		3.5
1992	109.4	71.8	22.6	26.0	3.9
1993	107.3	73.1	24.1	28.4	5.0
1994	108.7	73.8	26.2	30.7	6.0
1995	106.6	78.4	28.8	33.6	7.2
1996	105.7	82.4	31.4	38.0	8.3
1997	104.9	87.1	33.8	40.6	9.1
1998	104.3	87.3	34.4	40.7	9.8
1999	104.3	88.6	35.8	41.0	10.5
2000	104.6	88.6	38.2	42.8	12.5
2001	104.5	88.7	38.6	42.8	13.3
2002	107.5	90.0	38.4	42.8	15.0
2003	107.2	92.7	42.1	43.8	17.0
2004	106.6	94.1	46.5	48.1	19.0
2005	106.4	95.0	50.9	52.7	21.0
2006	106.3	97.0	57.7	59.8	22.0
2007	106.2	98.0		66.0	23.0
2008	105.7	98.5		74.0	23.3
2009	104.8	99.0		79.2	24.2

Obligatory, but not exactly compulsory, education in China was carried out by local governments and followed a system of top-down administration; the distribution and scale of schools were based on the distribution of permanent residents in the locality. The large inflow of migrant children to cities exerted great pressure on local primary schools. The number of planned admissions was greatly exceeded, thus increasing the local financial burden. While frequent and large-scale mobility was allowed, children of migrant workers were either denied admission or asked to pay extra fees. The central government reform of the educational system was thus required. Permanent urban residence permits should not be a requirement for migrant children. To ensure equal and quality education for them, the government should work harder to reach out and connect with them. That was a challenge the government could not turn away from.

After enacting the Obligatory Education Law in 2006, the state tried to establish a new subsidy system for students with special economic difficulties. The target of free obligatory education was achieved in most rural areas after 2007. In 2008, China increased the amount of funds for obligatory education, becoming a part of the public financial security system and thus free obligatory education could be realized (Table 4).

The adjustment of education policy by increasing investment, improvement of educational resources allocation and preventing the problem of arbitrary fee-gathering was not on the schedule to address the question of improving governance of education. Exam-oriented education has caused most students to lose out and that was the largest problem of the system. Chinese students should receive good quality education, instead of being forced to do large amounts of homework just to get good scores in the examination. While many people travel, go shopping or just rest at home during the Golden Week holiday, many students continue their hard work. "To gain the highest score possible, most students are expected to do homework for several hours each day".[17] It is a pity that students, who have been made into "slaves of homework", cannot relax even during holidays. Young people are therefore often overloaded with homework and have no time to develop their own interests and potential talents. Education in essence is human resources training, which is crucial to the Chinese people's future. If children are forced to do too much homework or cite from ancient texts, they cannot give full play to their own creativity. The short-sighted, exam-oriented education system must be changed, or else it will eventually curb society's overall growth.

Higher education was experiencing the dilemma of improving quality or intensive developing. The stagnancy of reform in the governance structure in higher education, the problem of loans, severe bureaucracy and corruption in education and academic fields, continued to be under addressed although they were of intense interest to the public. Some observers believed that it would be more realistic to train a literate work force of low-level technicians instead of research scientists. Moreover, it was feared that relying on examinations to recruit the most able students might advance people who were merely good at taking examinations. Educational reforms also made some people uncomfortable by criticizing the traditional practice of rote memorization and promoting innovative teaching and study methods.

Hu Jintao has always reminded the country that China must promote reform and innovation in the education system and aim to establish a modern national education system; it must improve the patterns of educational management and funding, training models, educational contents and teaching methods so as to enhance educational quality and provide a powerful driving force for educational development in China.

China's education sector has made substantial progress and formed a relatively complete educational system nationwide. Higher, secondary and primary education as well as adult education took initial shape with full-time education, continued education and part-time education all developing together, producing a huge, well educated workforce for all regions in the country.

Education is seen by all the players in the "China Rises" story as both an ends and a means to economic success. The history of China demonstrates that education is the catalyst for expanding the capabilities of individuals to have the choice to do more, to live a long life, to escape avoidable illness, and to have access to the world's stock of knowledge. For the country as a whole, the level of adult literacy skills is an indicator of enhanced personal welfare and improved productivity. In a virtuous cycle, improved productivity increases wages which in turn leads to further possibility for expanded educational opportunities which will result in even higher per capita incomes. Expanded educational opportunities and higher per capita incomes are inversely correlated with infant mortality rates and fertility rates and positively correlated with rising life expectancy and gender equity. China evidently has long struggled with the issue of educational access and equity, ranging from dramatic political movements to the demographic realities of rural-urban change. Who gets educated will remain one of the central issues of education in China for the foreseeable future. Thus China must carefully reflect on the past as well as the future to examine how to make the present education system as democratic as possible.

With the support and leadership of the CPC Central Committee, China has made great headway in its reform of educational management, school administration, funding and related institutional development. Reform has been carried out in (1) the management of basic education, where free obligatory education has been universalized both in urban and rural areas, (2) the management of higher education, the training capacity of universities and colleges and research funding, (3) the management of vocational education to serve every member of society, (4) the educational management system, with more autonomy in decision making, (5) the school administration system with public-funded schools and private schools thriving at the same time, and (6) educational funding as the main resource supplemented by funding through other channels.

Efforts have been made to promote educational opening up. China has witnessed significant improvement in its international standing and influence, and has developed educational cooperation and exchange relations with 184 countries and regions and international organizations like UNESCO. China has improved its education-related laws and regulations so as to provide strong back up for education reform and development. A number of legal documents have been promulgated as well.

All these reform measures have demonstrated the determination and courage of the CPC Central Committee and the State Council in carrying out education reform. Investment in education has increased in recent years. The proportion of the overall budget allocated to education has increased gradually (Table 5).

According to a Ministry of Education programme, the government set up an educational finance system in line with the public finance system, strengthened the responsibility of governments at all levels in educational investment, and ensured that their financial allocation for educational expenditure grows faster than their regular revenue. The programme also set out the government's aim that educational investment should account for 4% of GDP in a relatively short period of time.

Table 5: Changes in State Financial Investment in Education from 1980[18]

Education expenditures in year	Total finance (billion Yuen)	State finance (billion Yuen)	Ratio of GDP %	Budget finance %
1980	–	13.489	2.99	–
1985	–	26.290	2.93	–
1990	–	56.398	3.04	–
1991	73.1	61.7	2.86	–
1992	86.7	72.8	2.74	14.4
1993	105.9	86.7	2.51	18.7
1994	144.8	117.4	2.51	15.3
1995	187.7	141.152	2.32	15.1
1996	226.2	167.1	2.35	15.3
1997	253.1	180.2	2.36	14.7
1998	294.9	203.2	2.41	18.8
1999	334.9	228.7	2.55	13.8
2000	384.9	256.261	2.58	13.13
2001	463.7	305.701	2.79	13.66
2002	548.0	349.140	2.90	14.12
2003	620.8	385.062	2.84	14.01
2004	724.3	446.586	2.79	14.14
2005	841.9	516.108	2.82	13.84
2006	981.5	634.836	3.01	14.4
2007	1214.8	828.021	3.22	16.26
2008	1585.6	1044.963	3.48	16.32

Education is directly related to social equality, and there is no sense talking about a fair society without fair education. The government offers free education for nine years and has achieved a lot in the education field in the past twenty-five years. It could not ignore the overall unfairness that existed in the field of education. Fairness throughout an education system is the hallmark of a fair society, but children in China's rural areas either could not attend school or dropped out from classes for various reasons. And though most of children could attend primary and middle schools, the education quality in some of them was hardly good enough to ensure that they could acquire proper knowledge to survive with dignity in today's world. The problem lay in the unfair distribution of educational funds and resources. Only by eliminating the existing unfairness in the education system could Chinese society ensure fair education for one and all.

With the support and attention of the CPC Central Committee and the State Council, breakthroughs have been made in key areas and registered preliminary progress regarding some key issues. (1) Enrolment and examination assessment patterns have undergone positive changes. In thirty-one provinces, autonomous regions and municipalities, breakthroughs have been made in reform of senior high school entrance examinations and college entrance examinations through a number of pilot reforms. (2) Progress has been made in the reform of educational structure. By vigorously developing vocational education and higher education, a more balanced structural composition has been created for education of various types and at various levels. (3) As an important component in quality education, curriculum reform in basic education has made significant progress, and (4) teachers' overall qualifications have been enhanced.

It is not fair to say that a profound reform in China's education sector is in full swing. Even Hu Jintao has also always paid attention to the children of migrant workers. Hu visited students' dormitories and asked about their life in school. He told the students that migrant workers constituted an important force in China's development endeavour and made enormous contributions to our economic and social development, and efforts were being made to provide education opportunities for the children so that they could grow up healthily and happily like other children in the cities. The unfair situation continued, however.

Promoting equity in education, free nine-year obligatory education has been made available to all children, urban or rural, throughout the country. The Chinese government has reformed and adjusted the mechanism for ensuring funding for rural obligatory education since 2006. Urban students undergoing obligatory education were exempted from tuition and other fees in 2008. Nine-year obligatory education was fully incorporated into the national financial security system. This did not mean that the problems had been solved completely and adequately, however.

The Chinese government is active in promoting balanced obligatory education. The government prioritized rural areas, outlying poor areas and regions inhabited by ethnic-minority groups in allocating public educational resources, and implemented programmes such as "National Obligatory Education in Poor Areas", "Building Boarding Schools in Western China's Rural Areas", "Modern Distance Education for Elementary and Middle Schools in Rural China", "Renovating Junior Middle Schools in Central and Western China" and the "Plan for Special Education in Central and Western China". These policies intended to narrow the gap between urban and rural areas and between different regions and guarantee that disadvantaged groups had access to education.

The financial aid system has also improved. The Chinese government adopted a national scholarship system, student subsidy system and national student loan system applicable to regular institutions of higher learning and vocational schools. It provided more financial aid to ensure that students from families with financial difficulties could continue their studies. By the end of 2009 some 90% of students from secondary vocational schools and 20% of university students had received financial aid on a total of 43.06 million occasions. Since 2009 students from poor rural families studying at secondary vocational schools and students studying agriculture-related subjects in such schools have been exempted from tuition fees. The government imposed a wage reform ensuring the payment of rural teachers should not be lower than that of local civil servants, on 1 January 2009.[19] The government has issued many preferential policies to encourage teachers, college graduates as well as normal schools' students to go to the countryside to teach.

China has paid great attention to the protection of rural migrant workers' rights and interests. Rural migrant workers are a special group of workers that has emerged in the process of China's reform and opening up, industrialization and urbanization. They have made great contributions to the economic and social development of the country. The State Council established the Joint Conference System to coordinate and guide the work on rural migrant workers across the country in 2006. China eliminated many unreasonable restrictions on rural migrant workers seeking jobs in cities, strengthened work safety and public health training, expanded social insurance to cover more migrant workers, established a retirement pension scheme, which ensured continuity of one's retirement insurance wherever he or she lived, and carried out supporting programmes. "China should enact a better fiscal transfer system and put more investment towards helping alleviate the cause of underachieving rural education. The money allocated for rural education must be fully implemented and used for its specified purpose only."[20] Almost 80% of the migrant workers' children were receiving free obligatory education at public schools in urban areas by the end of 2009, and the number of migrant workers covered by insurance for work-related injuries, medical insurance and basic retirement insurance for employees of enterprises in urban areas had increased.

Three decades of economic reform and market opening up ushered in the era of economic clout for China. Continuous ascent to power in the international arena cannot depend solely on the impetus generated by operating a global factory. China must participate in numerous bouts, contending with great powers worldwide for superiority in education and scientific technology. Wen Jiabao pointed out that the improvement of education was a prerequisite for nurturing talent and the foundation of building up a great country.

The Planning of the Next Leaders and Educational Policy and the Strategic Plan of the Next Decade

It is believed that education is of fundamental importance for China's long-term development and that human resources are the basis of long-term prosperity. China has ushered in a new era of reform and opening up. While striving to achieve economic and social development, the country also takes up an important mission to produce high-quality human resources to aid the reform and opening up and socialist modernization.

The CPC Central Committee has attached great importance to improving education quality in the process of educational reform, in the face of new requirements of modernization and new expectations of the people in recent years. The Chinese government pledges to improve the quality of education and to enable people to enjoy fairer education through more investment and reforms in the coming decade.

Whenever crucial points in China's social and economic development have occurred, the CPC Central Committee and the State Council have formulated important strategic documents to offer guidance to the education reform and development. The most significant issue recently was the formulation of the "Outline of China's National Plan for Medium- and Long-term Education Reform and Development (2010–2020)". Since the research and formulation of the Outline was launched in August 2008, Hu Jintao has given much attention to it, issued many important instructions and visited primary and secondary schools, universities and institutes for research.

Wen Jiabao acted as the Director of the Steering Committee of the Outline, published two significant articles and chaired many meetings for the Outline. He presided over a meeting of the National Science and Technology Education Leading Group to discuss the formulation of the Outline. He emphasized that this was the first education outline since China had entered the twenty-first century. During the policy formulation process, suggestions from various parties were welcomed. He assured that the principle of democracy should be upheld and the wisdom of the people collected. He conducted more than five meetings convened to discuss the Outline in early 2009. According to Wen, the government should strive to produce a high-quality outline which should be in line with people's interests, national conditions and future trends.

Wen reaffirmed education as a priority for the government in 2009. He stressed the importance of free and equal access to obligatory education in poorer areas, the development of the vocational education sector, and reform of the education system to nurture creative and practical generations of graduates. He pointed out that education was the cornerstone of national development and, since education reform had an important bearing on the future of the country and people, and was a big concern to every family and student, the Outline should reflect the will, the determination and strategic vision of China, give hope to people and promote their confidence in the education sector.

The fourth National Conference on Educational Work was held in 2009. The solicitation of public opinions for the Outline triggered enormous enthusiasm for the belated educational reform and public participation in this process. It was published after more than a year's consultation.

On 21 June 2010, the CPC Political Bureau meeting called for the prioritization of quality improvement as the core mission in educational reform and development. A scientific concept of educational quality was adopted and educational content was emphasized. The meeting pointed out that reform and innovation should be a strong driving force for educational development. Innovative methods should be introduced in human resource training, school administration, educational management, teaching content, teaching methods and tools. They would pursue the further opening up of the field of education. Hu presided over this meeting of the Political Bureau, which reviewed and approved the Outline. According to the meeting, education must be developed in order to build a strong nation. Human resources and education are crucial to the future development and rejuvenation of the Chinese nation.

The Outline identifies three main tasks; development, reform and guarantee, each of which contains six elements as well. First, the six development tasks are; in pre-school education, compulsory education, senior secondary education, vocational education, higher education, further education, and with special emphasis on education for ethnic minorities and special education. Second, the six reform tasks are; in the talent training system, the examination and enrolment system, the school system, the education provision system, the administration system and the further development of international cooperation and exchanges. The six guarantee tasks are; in strengthening the Party and government leadership over education, building up the teaching cohort, ensuring educational input, accelerating education informationization, promoting the management of education in accordance with laws and regulations, and implementing major programmes and reform pilots. The contents are structurally constructed in order to touch every area of the Chinese educational system.

The government has committed itself to markedly raising educational levels generally, as evidenced in a Ministry of Education programme. By 2020, of every 100,000 people, 13,500 will have had junior college education or above and some 31,000 will have had senior high school schooling. Rates of illiteracy and semi-literacy will fall below 3%, and average schooling duration across the population will increase from today's eight years to nearly eleven years. The major targets are set out in the following table (Table 6).

Table 6: The Major Targets of Educational Business Human
Resources Development by Years[21] (in ten thousands)

	2009	2015	2020
Pre-primary			
Kindergarten enrolment	2658	3400	4000
K1 net enrolment rate (%)	74.0	85.0	95.0
K2 net enrolment rate (%)	65.0	70.0	80.0
K3 net enrolment rate (%)	50.9	60.0	70.0
Nine-year obligatory education			
In schools	15772	16100	16500
Enforcement rate (%)	90.8	93.0	95.0
Senior stage education			
In schools	4624	4500	4700
Enforcement rate (%)	79.2	87.0	95.0
Vocational education			
Middle level in schools	2179	2250	2350
Higher level in schools	1280	1390	1480
Higher education			
In registration	2979	3350	3550
In schools	2826	3080	3300
Research students	140	170	200
Net enrolment rate (%)	24.2	36.0	40.0
Continuous education			
In service	16600	29000	35000
Number with higher education	9830	14500	19500
Labour force average education (years)	9.5	10.5	11.2
Rate with higher education (%)	9.9	15.0	20.0
New labour force education (years)	12.4	13.3	13.5
Rate with higher education (%)	67.0	87.0	90.0

All these unprecedented innovations are crystallizations of the consensus and efforts of the whole of Chinese society in promoting education development.

The Plan has proposed many innovative ideas, and education will serve as the driving force for the future development of the Chinese nation. Many policies in the Plan have touched upon "tough issues" in the reforms. The Plan proposes to "increase the proportion of fiscal education expenditure to total GDP to 4% by 2012". Education reform this time shall reflect the determination, will and strategic foresight of the Chinese nation to develop education and build up the people's confidence in China's education system.

The fundamental purpose of education reform is to improve the quality of the whole nation. In the twenty-first century, the central government has stressed repeatedly that education is an issue of public concern and will benefit future generations of Chinese. China must make sure that Chinese development relies on the people and promotes them in the process of educational development. The Party and the government are duty bound to ensure the people's access to education and believe that only by doing so are they promoting social justice and building a harmonious socialist society.

At the meeting in July 2010, Hu urged the government and the whole country to work hard to promote sound education development in the new era. Wen stressed the need for local governments to break away from old concepts and institutional limitations and explore new methods of educational development. After the formulation of the Plan, local governments would put forward their own roadmaps, timetables and agenda as soon as possible, based on local conditions, to promote all-round reform nationwide. However, a number of ideas proposed in the Plan are not new; they were already specified in the 1993 "Outline for China's Education Reform and Development" as well as in relevant legal documents promulgated in recent years. Actual implementation of these ideas therefore depends heavily on the genuine efforts of the government and authorities.

Discussion and Conclusion

Since the founding of New China in 1949, and especially since the reform and opening-up policies were introduced in the late 1970s, the Chinese government has actively implemented the principle of respecting labour, knowledge, talent and creativity, and has adopted a series of policies and measures to boost employment and develop education, science and technology, culture, public health and social security. Recently it has been striving to create a favourable environment and conditions for the people's all-round development.

Education has a direct bearing on the future of the country. It plays an important role in promoting the development of all economic and social undertakings. Today the world is undergoing considerable development, change and readjustment. Science and technology advance day by day, and competition for qualified human resources is intensifying. China is now standing at a new historical point. It relies on to maintain steady and rapid economic development and to achieve the goal of building a moderately prosperous society.

China can firmly implement the strategy of developing the country with technology and education and of building up the strength of the country with talented human resources. Thus it must prioritize educational development by putting it in a strategic position, and promote all-round, coordinated and sustainable development. They strive to turn China into a country with advanced development in human resources and guarantee talent and human resources to build a moderately prosperous society and realize the great rejuvenation of the Chinese nation.

China is a developing country with the largest population in the world. People are a vast reservoir of human resources. Actively developing human resources is a significant aim of the Chinese government, which it has been cherishing and unremittingly advancing as a major undertaking. On 14 March 2011 Wen said that education, science and technology are keys to a country's development.[22] China's rise should rely not only on its economic size, but on cultivating talent and the progress of science and technology. The Chinese government brings into full play the potential ability and value of each individual and promotes the people's all-round development. The aim is to provide powerful labour and intellectual support for China's modernization drive and to realize its transformation from a country rich in human resources to one with powerful human resources.

Although China is now the world's second largest economy, its education still lags behind. A Western proverb goes "Time and tide wait for no man." Facing a new global framework along with new challenges, China should seize the moment and grab the opportunity, accelerating the speed, to develop education so that its institutions rank among the world's top universities. While cheap labour has been a key factor in generating high growth over the past three decades, it has also contributed to profound income disparities, especially in recent years. And persistent, widening inequality might cause social crises that could interrupt growth. China must avoid such a scenario. If wages could increase in some meaningful way, it would indicate that the economy might finally reach the next stage of development, during which income disparities would be narrowed.

Many people are disgruntled at the state of public education in China, inequity being one of the chief reasons.[23] Disparities are obvious between key primary and junior schools and their non-key counterparts. Other problems are the short supply of kindergartens and the high cost of putting children into such schools. There are regional inequities in education. Large classes are still ubiquitous in inland areas. The quality of education in the western regions lags far behind other areas and the drain of talent from there has been severe. It is true that educational reforms are moving forwards faster in some regions than others. The problem is that the local level of education services cannot catch up with the expectations and requirements of the public. Parents blame current education methods for blocking attempts to ensure students are well-rounded when they graduate.

In accordance with the requirements of the socialist market economy system, and to promote sustainable development and social harmony, the Chinese government pays attention to the fundamental function of the market in deploying human resources, while vigorously promoting institutional reforms in the fields of economics, science, technology and education, constantly deepening the reform of the cadre-related system, and pursuing the strategy of rejuvenating the country through science and education and that of strengthening the nation with trained personnel and a proactive employment policy.

The sagacious word rings true. Yet it imposes hefty responsibility and long-term devotion to meet the goal. China does not possess one of the world's first-class universities at present, but it has established and improved the human resources development mechanism to train, attract, use and support talented people, and accelerated human resources legal construction, thereby opening up a human resources development path conforming to China's national conditions.

Along with its economic and social development, and improvement in people's living standards, China has made remarkable headway in its human resources development. But as a developing country, China is still faced with many problems such as great challenges in employment, structural imbalance in human resources development, and lack of high-level, innovative people. China faces unprecedented opportunities and challenges in the sphere of human resources development. This remarks caused ripples of public comment on the issue. Lack of openness to ideas and creativity has long been a headache for China's education system. Qian Xuesen, well known as the "Father of Chinese Rocketry", showed his concern when he was in his 90s, when he noted that China's universities have perennially failed to adopt scientific methods to cultivate creative talents. He cited the deep-seated feudalism of long history, and the tendency of students to be copy cats rather than innovators. He added that a good student should be able to innovate, rather than being rooted in rote memorization. The view to be a valuable and true reflection of the reality, the courage to acknowledge the deficiency makes customized solutions possible, hence the premise of progress.

In the new phase of the new century, the Chinese government should put people's interests first, concentrate its care on all-round human development, and encourage and support everyone to make contributions and become accomplished in one or more fields. It should build a complete lifelong education system with the focus on making education more equitable and improving educational quality as the core, so that all the people can enjoy their rights to education, make progress and apply what they have learned to practice.

At least, we should have a basic understanding about what is known as education reform in China. It has been heard about for a long time. The reformative discourse is not new, but an old tune. This was the education agenda of the advanced countries during the 1980s. If we read through the education policy documents comparing the Chinese government today with those of the western countries during the 1980s, we can understand the present situation in China. There is old wine flowing into a new bottle. We can read about what was called human capital investment in the 1970s. The education reform was brought about in the western countries under fiscal crisis. This legitimating crisis or rational crisis caused a series of educational reform movements in western countries. The processes are continuous, and are also causing effects in developing areas. China today asserts the importance of education. The social conflicts are still serious, inequality is extended as well, but the educational system is helpless. On the contrary, the inequality is extrapolated by education.

Notes and References

1. The common programme of the Chinese People's Political Consultative Conference, adopted by the First Plenary Session of the Chinese People's on 29 September 1949. Article 47: In order to meet the extensive requirements of revolutionary and national construction work, universal education shall be carried out, secondary and higher education shall be strengthened, technical education shall be stressed, the education of workers during their spare time and that of cadres at their posts shall be strengthened, and revolutionary political education shall be accorded to both young and old-type intellectuals. All this is to be done in a planned and systematic manner.

2. Article 94: Citizens of the People's Republic of China have the right to education. To ensure that citizens can enjoy this right, the state establishes and gradually expands schools of various types and other cultural and education institutions.

3. Article 46: Citizens of the People's Republic of China have the duty as well as the right to receive education.

4. 义务教育法: The CRP's official translation is the Compulsory Education Law. Article 2: The state shall institute a system of nine-year compulsory education.

5. By 1980 the percentage of students enrolled in primary schools was high, but the schools reported high drop-out rates and regional enrolment gaps (most enrollees were concentrated in the cities).

6. The law has failed to guarantee the funding of compulsory education, thus forcing many schools, particularly those in the impoverished rural regions, to either continue to collect the tuition fees or impose various "miscellaneous fees" on their students in the name of "voluntary donations", "fund-raising for school construction" or "after-school tutoring fees".

7. Article 10: The state shall not charge for the tuition of students receiving compulsory education. The state shall establish a system of grants-in-aid to support the school attendance of poor students.

8. Compulsory Education Law, Article 11: No organization or individual shall employ school-age children or adolescents who should receive compulsory education.

9. Xin Zhiming, http://english.caijing.com.cn/2004-10-10/100013860.html (accessed March 2011).

10. Unauthorized fee collection in education refers to the actions that set up fee collection items, expanded scopes for fee collection and increased fee collections, violating the relevant laws, regulations and rules of the state and provincial governments.

11. Xiaoli Du, "The Analysis of Investment and Expenditure on Compulsory Education in China, 2000–2007," in Guorui Fan (ed.) *Educational Policy Observatory Book 2* (Shanghai: East China Normal University Press, 2010), pp. 64–71.

12. Du, "The Analysis of Investment and Expenditure on Compulsory Education in China, 2000–2007."

13. Excessive charges by schools have become a major reason behind the increasing rate of rural drop-outs in recent years. The drop-out ratio for rural primary and junior middle schools in 2004 was 2.45% and 3.91% respectively, while the figure in the less developed central and western regions was much higher.

14. Adopted at the Fourth Session of the Sixth National People's Congress on 12 April 1986, and amended at the 22nd Session of the Standing Committee of the Tenth National People's Congress on 29 June 2006. Article 2: The State adopts a system of nine-year compulsory education.

15. Article 2: The State adopts a system of nine-year compulsory education. Compulsory education is education which is implemented uniformly by the State and shall be received by all school-age children and adolescents. It is a public welfare cause that shall be guaranteed by the State. No tuition or miscellaneous fee may be charged in the implementation of compulsory education. The State shall establish a guarantee mechanism for operating funds for compulsory education in order to ensure the implementation of the system of compulsory education.

16. Data from the website of the Ministry of Education http://www.moe.edu.cn (accessed March 2011) and Department of Development and Planning Ministry of Education, *Education Statistics Yearbook of China 2008* (Beijing: People's Education Press, 2008), p. 15.

17. "Lessons to learn on education reform," *China Daily*, 16 June 2003.

18. Data from the Statistical Department, Ministry of Education; http://www.moe.edu.cn (accessed March 2011); *The Chinese Statistics Year Book 2006 and 2008*; *The Chinese Education Finance Statistics Year Book*; Yang Dongping, *China's Education Blue Book 2003, 21st Century Education Development Research Institute* (Beijing: Higher Education Press, 2003), pp. 22 and 256; Department of Development and Planning and Ministry of Education, *Education Statistics Yearbook of China 2008* (Beijing: People's Education Press, 2008), p. 623; 黄河清和张敏(2009)〈免费义务教育政策分析〉于 范国睿(2009)编，《教育政策观察》(上海：华东师范大学出版社)，页 135；李贞《公平义务教育与中国财政体制改革研究》(北京：经济科学出版社，2009) 页 78.

19. *The China Daily*, http://www.chinadaily.com.cn/business/2009-09/12/content_8685276.htm (accessed March 2011).

20. "Equity Best Way to Solve National Education Problem," *People's Daily*, 3 March 2009.

21. Source: *The Outline of China's National Plan for Medium and Long-term Education Reform and Development (2010–2020)*.

22. "GCP-Obsessed Criteria Wrong," *Shanghai Daily News*, 15 March 2011.

23. Zhou Wenting, "Content with Schools Falling," *China Daily* (Hong Kong) 3 March 2011, at Nation/P05.

17

Strengthening Political Education in Chinese Universities in the Hu Jintao Era: A Critical Reading of the CPC's No. 16 Document (2004)

Qinghua WANG

Introduction

Close contextual reading suggests that the promulgating of "Views of the Communist Party of China Central Committee (CPCCC) and the State Council on further Strengthening and Improving University Students' Political Education" (called No. 16 Document, or *Zhongyang 16 hao wenjian* 中央 16 号文件, by the party-state) in August 2004[1] has been the most significant event in the politics of Chinese higher education since Hu Jintao became General Secretary of the Communist Party of China (CPC, or the Party) in 2002 at the 16th Party Congress. Over thirty documents have been issued subsequently to materialize the principles raised by No. 16 Document.[2] This document is aimed at strengthening political education among university students and hence ensuring the CPC's leadership, with the immediate objective being to improve the attractiveness and teaching effectiveness of political education courses.

Many new developments have occurred, among which this study will examine the following: replacing the 1998 scheme of political education courses for undergraduate students – i.e., the teaching scheme regarding the structure and contents of political education courses – with the 2005 scheme; intensifying the "disciplinary construction" (*xueke jianshe* 学科建设) of political education by setting

515

up the "first-order discipline" (*yiji xueke* 一级学科) of "Marxist Theory;" placing the production of political education textbooks (*jiaocai jianshe* 教材建设) under the sponsorship of the "Project on Research and Construction of Marxist Theory" (*makesi zhuyi lilun yanjiu he jianshe gongcheng* 马克思主义理论研究和建设工程); building up a competent corps (*duiwu* 队伍) of political education teachers; and professionalizing the training and upgrading the status of political advisors. From the point of view of the Hu regime, great progress has been made on these matters.

Maintaining that it is No. 16 Document that imprints the character of Hu Jintao's rule on China's higher education, this study will offer a critical reading of this important document. The purpose is to shed light on our understanding of the politics of Chinese higher education, and more generally, of the features of the Hu Jintao regime. As Hu's rule is expected to end in 2012 at the 18th Party Congress, China scholars will soon need to review the Hu regime, and this study is an attempt of this kind. More directly, because Party control over higher education in post-Mao China, a crucial aspect of the politics of Chinese higher education, has been inadequately studied in the extant literature, an examination of No. 16 Document and the accompanying measures is a timely and needed addition to the scholarship.

The literature on higher education in post-Mao China consists of scholarship from several disciplines, primarily education and, to a lesser extent, political science, economics, sociology and history. Despite the diversity of disciplinary approaches, the literature as a whole has not paid sufficient attention to the role of the CPC in higher education.[3] Students of Chinese politics have published some research on higher education politics in the 1980s, e.g., on the student movement in 1989.[4] For the post-1989 era, they have touched upon topics such as students' political attitudes,[5] Party recruitment of students,[6] and post-1989 leaders' patriotic education.[7] But, overall, the politics of Chinese higher education in the reform era has been outside the purview of mainstream China studies.

As for educational specialists, who are the primary contributors to the extant scholarship, they view depoliticization,[8] marketization (e.g., marketizing graduate placement, importing market mechanisms into talent cultivation, and encouraging universities to generate revenues outside of state funds), and de-Sovietization (i.e., replacing the previous Soviet-type model of talent cultivation and administration by that of the West) as three principal features of developments in Chinese higher education.[9] With a few exceptions,[10] they have tended to place stress on Chinese culture, history, markets, economic growth, and globalization. The variable of the CPC is not their primary focus.[11]

This chapter begins with a sketch of why No. 16 Document originated and how it was implemented. It then offers a critical reading of this document and ends with some concluding remarks.

The Making and Implementing of No. 16 Document

On 18 March 2004, it has been said, Hu Jintao became worried when he read an internal report entitled "Investigation on the Teaching Situation of Political Education Courses in Universities", a report that was based on covert investigations and interviews in many Beijing universities. Feeling that there was an urgent need to improve the attractiveness of political education courses, Hu ordered the Propaganda Department of the CPC Central Committee and the Ministry of Education (MOE hereafter)[12] to take action. The objective was to "improve the teaching situation of political education courses obviously within several years".[13] This event is called General Secretary Hu's "March-18 Order" (*san-yiaoba zhishi*, 3-18 指示) in the official and academic discourses. A chain reaction followed.

In August of the same year, No. 16 Document was promulgated. This is a significant event in that "it is the first time in the CPC and the PRC histories that a document focusing on how to strengthen and improve university students' political education is jointly issued by the CPC Central Committee and the State Council".[14] No. 16 document has been highly praised as a "framework-natured" (*gangling xing* 纲领性) document guiding political education work for the new century.[15] On 17 and 18 of January 2005, the CPC Central Committee held the National Conference on Strengthening and Improving University Students' Political Education ("the 2005 National Political Education Conference" hereafter), the only one of its sort in the Hu era. Hu Jintao and other top leaders attended the conference, and Hu delivered a speech to mobilize the whole country.[16] In July 2005, the General Offices of the Propaganda Department, MOE, and the Central

Committee of the Communist Youth League (CYL) began to check and supervise the work of sub-national governments and universities. This move is to ensure that the latter have materialized the spirit of No. 16 Document and "the 2005 National Political Education Conference", and have implemented measures stipulated by supplementary documents.[17]

Since 2009, China's propaganda machine has been mobilized to celebrate the fifth anniversary of the promulgation of No. 16 Document and to publicize successful experiences of its implementation. Relevant journal articles, edited books, and news reports can be easily found in China. For instance, beginning with issue 8 of 2009, the leading political education journal *Studies in Ideological Education* (*Sixiang jiaoyu yanjiu* 思想教育研究)[18] has included a special section named "An Overview of Achievements since the Promulgating of No. 16 Document". On 23 May 2010, Xinhua News Agency had a special report entitled "Summary of Achievements in the Work of Strengthening and Improving University Students' Political Education".[19] During 25–28 May 2010, *China Education Daily* published a series of news articles under the headline "An Overview of New Measures and New Developments of University Students' Political Education in the Past Five Years".[20] Many provinces and universities have also published edited books to publicize their achievements, e.g., the two well-regarded policy reports sponsored by the Shanghai municipal educational department, *Exploration and Development of Political Education in Shanghai Universities since the Party's 16th Congress*, and *Research Report on the Construction of the Corps of Political Education Teachers in Shanghai*.[21]

Since Hu's "March-18 Order", MOE has been playing a leading role in materializing the principles of No. 16 Document, with the Propaganda Department coming next. In October 2004, MOE held a special colloquium (*zuotanhui* 座谈会) to pass on Hu's will within the circle of educational officials, to mobilize universities nationwide, and to discuss how to take specific actions.[22] In April 2005, MOE issued "Outline on Publicizing the Study and Implementation of the Spirit of the Centre-Promulgated No. 16 Document (2004), and of the National Conference on Strengthening and Improving University Students' Political Education" ("Outline on Publicizing" hereafter).[23] This "Outline on Publicizing" was circulated throughout the country, and all universities were required to hold study sessions and make specific policies.

"Outline on Publicizing" has been by far the most comprehensive and developed document concerning political education in universities in the PRC's history. It specified that in the twenty-first century, efforts should be made to strengthen political education work in the following eight areas: the teaching of political education courses; the teaching of "current situations and policies"; the teaching of philosophy and social sciences courses; the political, professional, and moral qualities of teachers; social practice; campus culture; the CYL and CPC organizations among students, and other student associations; and the corps of political education workers in universities.

The supplementary documents that followed described specific measures in the eight arenas outlined above. "Political education courses in universities are the principal channel (*zhu qudao* 主渠道) of political education work towards university students".[24] In fact, the view that political education courses are regarded as the "principal channel" of political education work has been repeatedly emphasized in the post-1989 era.[25] By contrast, the other aforementioned areas are normally called "important channels" of political education work in the official discourse. The subtlety in using the two different expressions – "principal channel" and "important channels" – suggests that on the one hand political education teaching is a matter of prime importance, and strengthening political education work in other areas also serves political education teaching on the other.

Last but not least, the strengthening of political education is carried out as a key component of the "Project of Research and Construction on Marxist Theory". On 27/28 April 2009 when this project was launched, Li Changchun (李长春), standing member of the CPC Politburo who is in charge of ideological work, called it the Party's "life project" (*shengming gongcheng* 生命工程). In other words, this project is so important that the Party's continuous rule is directly involved.[26] This project has three tasks: strengthening research on classical works of Marx, Engels, and Lenin to achieve a more accurate understanding of Marxism; strengthening research on Sinicized (*zhongguohua* 中国化) Marxism; and writing textbooks for political education courses and social sciences, incorporating Sinicized Marxism of the reform era into the new textbooks, and nurturing a more competent corps of young and middle-aged political education teachers.[27] Sinicized Marxism is a product of applying basic principles of orthodox Marxism to the Chinese reality at different historical times, and at present it is comprised of Mao Zedong Thought, Deng Xiaoping Theory, the "Three Represents" Theory, and "Scientific Outlook on Development". Strengthening research in this regard is intended to build "philosophy and social sciences with Chinese characteristics" and to counterbalance influences from Western ideologies and socio-political theories brought about by China's deep integration into the world in the twenty-first century. The launching of the "Project of Research and Construction on Marxist Theory" is thus a new-round ideological campaign to safeguard China's ideological security and maintain Party rule. Our understanding of No. 16 Document should be placed against this large backdrop.

Strengthening Political Education: A Critical Reading of No. 16 Document

No. 16 Document consists of three parts, nine sections, and thirty articles. Part One consists of the first three sections, which analyse the current situation that political education work in universities is facing, and point out the guiding principles and main tasks of strengthening political education. Part Two includes the second three sections, stipulating the principal channel and main approaches of conducting political education. Part Three includes the final three sections, stressing the importance of providing organizational support, favourable larger environment, and strong leadership for political education work. In the following analysis, I will make reference to some of the main supplementary documents (e.g., "Outline on Publicizing") wherever necessary.

The Hu Regime's Views on Ideological Remoulding and Political Education

Above all, Article One stipulates that "Strengthening and improving university students' political education, enhancing their political-ideological qualities, and nurturing students into builders and successors of the cause of building socialism with Chinese characteristics" are of "great, far-reaching, and strategic importance". [28] "In particular, the status of students' political-ideological qualities has a direct impact on the prospects and fortunes of the Party and state."[29] At "the 2005 National Political Education Conference" Hu Jintao warned:

> The struggle between enemy forces and us for winning over our next-generation youth is still very intense and complicated. We absolutely cannot be not on alert. Under this context, when striving to enhance their scientific-cultural and physical qualities, we must also try our best to enhance university students' political-ideological qualities, to lead them to establish correct ideals and beliefs, to enhance their capabilities of making political judgments, and to effectively keep away and resist the ideological infiltration of enemy forces.[30]

What is at stake is that failing to perform well in political education work may incur the risk of turning students into "Party grave-diggers" (*juemu ren* 掘墓人), as shown by the 1989 student movement, a nightmare for the Party in which students wanted Western-style democracy and rejected Party leadership. Thus, "Universities should place political education as the first priority of their work"[31] and ensuring students have "qualified" political-ideological qualities is an indispensable part of university training. Students nurtured by universities should be "competent builders and reliable successors of the socialist cause".[32] The foremost criterion to evaluate whether university students are "qualified" or not is to see their political-ideological qualities.[33] The so-called qualified political-ideological qualities are that students are reliable successors of the socialist cause, measured by how well they uphold Party leadership and endorse Party-sanctioned views and policies. It is political education that assumes the Party-assigned task of ideologically remoulding students.

In short, the Hu Jintao regime views political education work as crucial for the persistence of Party leadership, and its endeavours of strengthening political education aim at ideologically remoulding students and ensuring they possess Party-desired political-ideological qualities.

Replacing the 1998 Scheme of Political Education Courses with the 2005 Scheme

Political education courses are also labelled "Two Sets of Courses" (*liangke*, 两课), i.e., courses on Marxist Theory, and courses on Communist Ideology and Morality (*sixiang pinde ke* 思想品德课). The first set of courses has existed since the founding of the PRC, and their main contents are orthodox and Sinicized Marxist theories. The second set appeared in the early 1980s, and strive to help students foster communist moral qualities and citizenship values. When Hu Jintao came to power, the scheme of political education courses for undergraduate students was the "98 scheme" (*98 fangan*, 98 方案), formed in June 1998, before which universities adopted the "85 scheme" (*85 fangan*, 85 方案), announced in August 1985 (see Table 1).

As political education courses are mandatory for all students and have long been valued as the "principal channel" of political education work, extraordinary efforts have been made to follow Hu's "March-18 Order". In late March 2004, the Propaganda Department and MOE formed a leading small group to investigate the teaching situation of political education courses in universities. The investigation went on for almost nine months, and was undertaken primarily in universities in Beijing, Shanghai, Guangdong and Shanxi. As a leading official from MOE's Division of Social Sciences commented, "Since the founding of the PRC, there has never been an investigation on this issue conducted at such a breadth and width".[34] In December 2004, based on the principles raised by No. 16 Document, the leading small group created a draft version of "The CPCCC Propaganda Department and MOE's Views on Further Strengthening and Improving Political Education Courses in Universities", which was discussed and approved by the Standing Committee of the CPC Politburo in January 2005.[35] This document was then officially issued one month later. It summarized that problems in political education teaching included:

> The foundation of disciplinary construction is relatively weak, teaching contents are repetitive, the qualities of textbooks are uneven, teaching methods are monotonous, and the teaching is not pertinent and is not sufficiently

Table 1: The Two Schemes of Political Education Courses
for Undergraduate Students

Versions of political education courses	Courses on Marxist Theory	Courses on Communist Ideology and Morality
Political education courses of the 1998-version (98 *fangan*) (unit: teaching hour)	1. Essential Theories of Marxist Philosophy (54 teaching hours); 2. Essential Theories of Marxist Political Economy (40 for students of Science and Engineering; 36 for students of Arts and Social Sciences); 3. Conspectus of Mao Zedong Thought (40 for students of Science and Engineering; 54 for students of Arts and Social Sciences); 4. Conspectus of Deng Xiaoping Theory (70); 5. Current Global Political Economy and International Relations (36; for students of Arts and Social Sciences).	6. Communist Ideology and Morality (51); 7. Foundations of the Law (34); 8. Current Political Affairs and Policies (1 teaching hour per week).
Political education courses of the 2005-version (05 *fangan*) (unit: credit)	1. Essential Theories of Marxism (3 credits); 2. Conspectus of Important Thoughts of Mao Zedong Thought, Deng Xiaoping Theory, and "Three Represents" (6);[36] 3. Outline of Modern and Contemporary Chinese History (2).	4. Foundations of Communist Ideology and Morality and the Law (3); 5. Current Political Affairs and Policies (2).

Sources: (1) The CPCCC Propaganda Department and MOE, "Guanyu putong gaodengxuexiao 'Liangke' kecheng shezhi de guiding ji qi shishi gongzuo de yijian" ("Opinions on establishing and implementing political education courses in universities") (June 1998); (2) The CPCCC Propaganda Department and MOE, "Zhonggongzhongyang xuanchuanbu jiaoyubu guanyu jinyibu jiaqiang he gaijin gaodengxuexiao sixiang zhengzhi lilunke de yijian shishi fangan" ("Scheme for Implementing The CPCCC Propaganda Department and MOE's Views on further strengthening and improving political education courses in universities") (March 2005). These two documents are in MOE, *Selected Important Documents*, pp. 252–256, and 422–425 respectively.

effective; the number of political education teachers is not enough and their comprehensive qualities need to be improved, outstanding young and middle-aged political education teachers who can be leading scholars in the political education field are lacking; many universities to varied extents have not attached sufficient significance . . . ["]37

To tackle these problems, the Hu regime has taken a range of measures. The following sections will discuss some of the major measures one by one.

In March 2005, a new teaching scheme, the 2005 scheme (*05 fangan*, 05 方案), was announced to replace the *98 fangan*. As Table 1 shows, the *98 fangan*'s "Communist Ideology and Morality" and "Foundations of the Law" were reorganized as the *05 fangan*'s "Foundations of Communist Ideology and Morality and the Law". The *98 fangan*'s "Essential Theories of Marxist Philosophy" and "Essential Theories of Marxist Political Economy", along with newly added contents on scientific socialism, were combined into the *05 fangan*'s "Essential Theories of Marxism". "Conspectus of Mao Zedong Thought" and "Conspectus of Deng Xiaoping Theory" of the older scheme, along with the then new "Three Represents" theory of Jiang Zemin, were restructured as "Conspectus of Important Thoughts of Mao Zedong Thought, Deng Xiaoping Theory, and 'Three Represents'". Also, the *05 fangan* added a new course, "Outline of Modern and Contemporary Chinese History". The number of teaching hours devoted to the new scheme count about 9.3% of the total student teaching hours, remaining roughly the same ratio in spite of the reduction of number of courses.

In addition to reducing some repetitive contents and merging relevant courses into new ones to make political education teaching more succinct, a more important objective is "to make the teaching content of each course closer to the current times, closer to China's actualities, closer to students' concerns, and more timely reflecting the development in practices and theoretical innovations of building socialism with Chinese characteristics".[38] To this end, the new teaching scheme focuses more on Sinicized Marxism in the reform era, i.e., Deng Xiaoping Theory, "Three Represents" Theory, and "Scientific Outlook on Development". While orthodox Marxism remains one important component, the *05 fangan* concentrates primarily on new developments of Sinicized Marxism and on how to explain current politico-socio-economic affairs more convincingly.

Adding "Marxist Theory" as a "First-order Discipline"

Another important development is to intensify the "disciplinary construction" of political education by upgrading political education from a "second-order discipline" (*erji xueke*, 二级学科) to a "first-order discipline" (*yiji xueke*, 一级学科), manifested as the adding of the "first-order discipline" of "Marxist Theory". To understand this, some background knowledge is in order.

According to the "List of Doctorate- and Master's Degree-Conferring Disciplines and Majors" at the postgraduate level, there are twelve "categories of discipline" (*xueke menlei*, 学科门类), encompassing Philosophy, Economics, Law, Education, Literature, History, Sciences, Engineering, Agriculture, Medicine, Military, and Management, as well as 88 "first-order disciplines" and 381 "second-order disciplines". In general, each category of discipline includes one or more "first-order disciplines". "Second-order discipline" is a sub-category of first-order discipline and each first-order discipline includes one or more of the former. For example, under the category of discipline of Law, there are four first-order disciplines, i.e., Law, Political Science, Sociology, and Ethnography, each of which has several second-order disciplines, to make 27 in all.[39]

In the PRC context, disciplinary construction refers to how a discipline matures. It encompasses disciplinary status, theories and methodologies, teachers and researchers, curriculum design and training schemes, and the impact on society, as well as the growth of bachelor's, master's, and doctoral programmes. Upgrading the status of a discipline brings crucial benefits. Because China's higher education is primarily state-run, there exists a state-designated disciplinary hierarchy, according to which a discipline receives corresponding treatments from the government. The upgrading is institutional in that it is often accompanied by government investment of resources, such as increasing the state-assigned quotas of teaching posts and student enrollment, and allowing more universities to establish more programmes of study.

The disciplinary construction of political education formally began in 1984 when political education was established as a bachelor's programme of study in twelve universities, and 360 students were enrolled.[40] Beginning from 1987, political education teachers and other full-time political education personnel in universities were officially granted the career status of teachers.[41] Ten universities began master's programmes in political education in 1988.[42] In 1996, political education was upgraded to a doctorate-conferring discipline, and Renmin, Tsinghua, and Wuhan universities became the first to admit doctoral students. In the 1997 "List of Doctorate- and Master's Degree-Conferring Disciplines and Majors", political education was renamed "Marxist Theory and Political Education" and was designated a second-order discipline.[43]

By 2004, when No. 16 Document was issued, the discipline of political education was known as "Marxist Theory and Political Education", was a second-order discipline and belonged to the first-order discipline of Political Science, which was in turn under the category of discipline of Law. The relevant disciplines of Marxist Philosophy, Political Economy, Scientific Socialism and the International Communist Movement, and History of the Chinese Communist Party, all of which were second-order disciplines, belonged to the first-order disciplines of Philosophy, Theoretical Economics, Political Science, and Political Science respectively, as well as under the categories of discipline of Philosophy, Economics, Law, and Law respectively.[44]

In December 2005, the Hu Jintao regime added "Marxist Theory" as a first-order discipline. The previous "Marxist Theory and Political Education" was renamed as "Political Education". Along with the above-mentioned political education-related disciplines, these were taken out from their previous superordinate first-order disciplines, and placed into "Marxist Theory" as its subordinate second-order disciplines. Specifically, "Marxist Theory" consists of six second-order disciplines; "Essential Theories of Marxism", "Research on Sinicized Marxism", "Research on Essential Issues in Modern and Contemporary Chinese History", "Political Education", "History of the Development of Marxism" and "Research on Marxism in Other Countries".[45] In July 2007, "Marxist Theory" was upgraded to a discipline that has post-doctoral research centres, and 25 post-doctoral programmes in "Marxist Theory" were established.[46]

According to the government, the discipline of political education and the discipline of "Marxist Theory" added in 2005 are defined as follows:

- "The discipline of 'Political Education' is a discipline that adopts Marxist theories and methods, that is specially devoted to researching into how people's political qualities come into being and develop and how to conduct political education, as well as aiming to help people foster correct outlooks on the world, life, and values."[47]
- "The discipline of 'Marxist Theory' is a discipline that researches the essential theories and scientific system of Marxism in its totality. This discipline researches essential theories of Marxism and the history of its formation and development, researches its circulation and development around the world, especially researches the theories and practices of Sinicized Marxism. This discipline also applies products of the research on Marxism to Marxist theory education, political education, and the work of political education."[48]

Although literally speaking the second definition is for the discipline of "Marxist Theory", it could be regarded as a broad definition of the discipline of political education. The rationale is that the task of political education work in Chinese universities is to ensure students possess the political-ideological qualities desired by the Party. All six second-order disciplines of Marxist Theory are instituted for this purpose. Seen in this light, the Hu regime's purpose in setting up Marxist Theory is a move of upgrading the discipline of political education from a second-order discipline to a first-order discipline.

As Jin Huiming (靳辉明), a renowned Party theorist at the Chinese Academy of Social Sciences, interpreted in an authoritative tone, the first-order discipline of Marxist Theory was assigned three tasks: nurturing specialized talent (i.e., master and doctoral students in Marxist Theory) for the healthy disciplinary development of Marxist theory; providing disciplinary backing for political education courses to enhance the teaching effectiveness; and securing China's ideological security through strengthening the guiding status of Marxism in the ideological arena.[49] Party theorists and political education teachers have written a great deal on the second task. For instance, on 19–21 July 2007 – under the sponsorship of "Research on the Disciplinary

Construction and Training Scheme of Marxist Theory", a research project commissioned by the State Council Academic Degree-Conferring Committee in June 2006 and led by Professor Gu Hailiang (顾海良)[50] – a "Symposium on relationships between the disciplinary construction of Marxist Theory and political education courses" was held at Xinan University (Sichuan Province). Consensus was reached on a number of issues, basically representing the views of the government.

Gu Hailiang wrote, "providing solid disciplinary backing (*xueke zhicheng*, 学科支撑) for the construction of political education courses (*kecheng jianshe*, 课程建设) is one important reason for setting up the discipline of 'Marxist Theory', and is one important task for the disciplinary development of 'Marxist Theory'".[51] Enhancing the effectiveness and persuasiveness of political education courses is one key indicator of measuring the success of disciplinary construction of "Marxist Theory".[52] The four second-order disciplines – (1) Essential Theories of Marxism, (2) Research on Sinicized Marxism, (3) Research on Essential Issues in Modern and Contemporary Chinese History, and (4) Political Education – correlate to and are expected to provide direct disciplinary backing for the four political education courses respectively: (1) Conspectus of Essential Theories of Marxism, (2) Conspectus of Important Thoughts of Mao Zedong Thought, Deng Xiaoping Theory, and "Three Represents", (3) Outline of Modern and Contemporary Chinese History, and (4) Foundations of Communist Ideology and Morality and the Law.[53]

With respect to the means for "Marxist Theory" to provide disciplinary backing, it was specified that graduate programmes in Marxist Theory should take into account the special features of the profession of political education teachers in matters of the setting-up of courses, graduate students' research areas, topics for students' master's or doctoral theses, students' social practices, and professional training. In so doing, the nurturing of new political education teachers could be improved. Existing political education teachers should conduct more research on key theoretical and practical issues that arise in their teaching. New research products should be transformed into supplementary materials for political education teaching. In-service training sessions or seminars should be held for existing political education teachers on a regular basis to enhance their comprehensive qualities.[54]

The Construction of Political Education Textbooks

In the pre-Hu era, there were many versions of political education textbooks of which the quality was uneven as most provinces had textbooks written by their own theorists. Holding that "High-quality textbooks are an important precondition for enhancing the teaching of political education courses",[55] the Hu Jintao regime decided to organize leading Chinese scholars in philosophy and social sciences to construct new textbooks. It ordered that "The teaching syllabi and textbooks of political education courses are placed into 'Project of Research and Construction on Marxist Theory'. The Propaganda Department and MOE are in charge of the work of writing teaching syllabi and textbooks."[56]

As Yang Guang (杨光), Chief of MOE's Division of Social Sciences, said in a 2009 interview, "The Centre (*zhongyang*, 中央) placed the four political education textbooks into the first-round key textbooks of the 'Project of Research and Construction on Marxist Theory', and has directly led the work of textbook construction. Top Chinese scholars have attended and indeed the whole nation has been mobilized for this work."[57] Specifically, the work of textbook-construction was officially launched in mid-March 2005. It began with issuing a call for bids, and several hundred scholars submitted their proposals on how to write the textbooks, out of which three were chosen for each political education course. After another round of review, one proposal was selected for each course. Four teams were formed for the four textbooks. Each team consisted of fifteen members and was led by a "chief scholar" (*shouxi zhuanjia*, 首席专家), who is a nationally renowned senior scholar. It was required that each team conduct careful investigations, and the strengths of other proposals were taken into consideration. The outlines for writing the four textbooks were submitted to the Centre and were approved in late September. By early March 2006, the first draft of each political education textbook was completed, and was then under careful review by scholars of the advisory committee of the "Project of Research and Construction on Marxist Theory", who are all top scholars in philosophy and social sciences in China. In one word, the extent of the significance attached to the construction of the political education textbooks is "unprecedented" in the PRC's history.[58]

Meanwhile, the regime repeatedly ordered that only textbooks produced by the Project of Research and Construction on Marxist Theory could be used. Other theorists and scholars, universities and provincial educational departments were prohibited from constructing political education textbooks in future. All the previous versions were also abolished.[59] Beginning from the autumn semester of 2006, for each political education course, it is required that all Chinese universities use one and the same textbook and teaching syllabus.

Jin Huiming summarized the Hu regime's requirements on construction of textbooks as "Three fully reflects" (*sange chongfen tixian*, 三个充分体现) and "One pertinently" (*yige you zhenduixing*, 一个有针对性). Namely, the writing of textbooks should "fully reflect the newest achievements in the Sinicization of Marxism, fully reflect the newest experiences in building socialism with Chinese characteristics, and fully reflect the newest developments in research on Marxist theories". Additionally, it should "pertinently address major problems that students are concerned with".[60] As a result, the new set of political education textbooks "have been commonly praised as the best, and also the most authoritative and scientific by teachers and students".[61]

Patronage-providing and Building up a Competent Corps of Political Education Teachers

Building up a competent corps of political education teachers has always been an important objective since the setting up of political education as an undergraduate major in 1984, especially since the early 1990s. But it has been a long-existing problem that the profession of political education teachers is not an attractive one. The image of political education work was severely damaged by the Cultural Revolution and the 1989 student movement. Recruiting new political education teachers and retaining existing ones was difficult in the 1980s and for several years following 1989.[62] To tackle this problem, post-Mao leaders have sought to provide preferential treatment for political education teachers, and the Hu Jintao regime is no exception. With a view that "political education teachers are an important part of university teachers, are propagators of the Party's theories, lines, and policies, as well as mentors and guides for students' healthy development",[63] the Hu regime has taken further steps to ensure the political-ideological qualities of political education teachers on the one hand, and to provide more patronage to them on the other.

The regime stipulated that "New political education teachers in principle must be Party members. . . . If political education teachers cannot stay in line with the Party Centre in regard to political principles, political stance, and political directions, they are not allowed to teach political education courses."[64] Accordingly, measures were implemented to screen incoming political education teachers' qualifications in terms of their political-ideological qualities, and also to ensure those of existing political education teachers through regular government-sponsored seminars and study sessions.[65]

Greater emphasis has been laid on political education teachers' professional and academic qualities. It is stipulated that new political education teachers must hold at least a master's degree in political education or a political education-related programme. New political education teachers are required to serve as part-time class directors or political advisors concurrently.[66] This measure aims to get new political education teachers steeped in the situations of students' political thinking, which in turn would make their teaching more pertinent to students' concerns. It has been a long-standing problem that students regard political education teaching as irrelevant to what they care about and hence feel little interest. Part of the reason is that political education teachers do not know much about students' actual concerns.[67]

The Hu regime announced that, starting in 2008, every year over 100 political education teachers would be admitted to a special in-service doctoral programme in "Marxist Theory", and they must stay in their current teaching positions for at least five more years after receiving the doctoral degree.[68] This measure amounts to a *de facto* giving away of doctoral degrees in political education in the name of specially-tailored programmes of study. In contrast, those who pursue doctoral degrees in other fields must pass strictly regulated admission tests, and, if admitted, must work hard for several years.

The 2005 decision to set up Marxist Theory as a first-order discipline is also a form of patronage. This decision was followed by the establishing of a large number of political education-related programmes, which resulted in more existing political education teachers being "upgraded" to become supervisors of master's students (*shuoshisheng daoshi*, 硕士生导师) and of doctoral students (*boshisheng daoshi*, 博士生导师). These two professional titles possess higher social status and would earn more respect.[69] Enhancing political education teachers' social status is intended to provide them some sense of pride or self-fulfilment in being a political education teacher.[70]

Professionalizing and Upgrading the Status of Political Advisors

The measures discussed so far all directly serve political education teaching. Among other measures that are not, upgrading the status of and professionalizing political advisors deserve our special attention. It is commonly held that "unprecedented" importance has been placed on the construction of the corps of university political advisors since Hu Jintao took office.[71] Consequently, political advisor has become a new type of position in universities and much of the attendant infrastructure for this profession has been instituted.

Before Hu, political advisors were called personnel of political work (*zhenggong renyuan*, 政工人员). In general they were university cadres doing other kinds of political work in universities and were not full-time political advisors. In contrast, the Hu Jintao regime upgraded the status of political advisors to the "backbone" (*gugan*, 骨干) of political education work with university students. Greater emphasis is laid on the political-ideological qualities of political advisors, which are regarded as the most important criterion in recruitment. As front-line Party workers, political advisors are required to stand firm with the Party Centre and work hard to maintain campus stability.[72] In April 2006, a National Conference on the Construction of the Corps of Political Advisors in Universities, the first one of its kind since the founding of the PRC in 1949, was held in Shanghai.[73]

Under the Hu regime, political advisors are expected to shoulder the following responsibilities: paying close attention to students' political thinking, recruiting students into the Party and developing grassroots Party cells among students; providing psychological counselling for students' mental health; providing advice and other help for students' job-hunting; managing other student affairs such as their study and financial assistance, etc. Political advisors should also actively join other university Party workers when emergent events on campus break out.[74] In addition to the outright ideologically-loaded political education work (e.g., recruiting students into the Party), student affairs such as study and campus life are also under the purview of political advisors. Taking care of these seemingly non-political student affairs is regarded as the work of everyday political education by the Hu regime. In so doing, political advisors are expected to instil Party-sanctioned values into students in a "stealthy" manner.[75]

In comparison with the pre-Hu era, the Hu regime's most innovative measure is to professionalize the training and career development of political advisors, making them professionals and experts. It was required that the main body of the corps of political advisors be full-time ones. For each 200 university students, there should be one full-time political advisor, and each grade of a school in each university must have a certain number of them. Furthermore, the Hu regime urged that political advisors should be treated as similar to teachers in regular disciplines of natural and social sciences in universities. The recruitment, training, and operations of political advisors are viewed as being as important as those of regular university teachers.[76]

Beginning from 2008, under the second-order discipline of "Political Education", MOE established a programme of study in "Political Advisor" (literally called "*fudaoyuan fangxiang*", 辅导员方向) aiming to admit students at the undergraduate, master's and doctoral levels on an experimental basis and to train professionals in political education work with university students.[77] These students are expected to join the profession of political advisors upon graduation. The rationale is that this profession is a science, and political advisors must possess certain knowledge and special training in order to perform their job well.[78] The newly established experimental programme of study in "Political Advisor" is precisely intended to provide disciplinary backing for the professional development of political advisors.

To make the profession of political advisors more attractive, more incentives and preferential policies have been provided following Hu's order. First of all, political advisors are given the double identity of teacher and cadre.[79] For the former, political advisors could choose to be promoted on the track of university teachers. Separate and specially-tailored criteria are instituted, and each university is required to establish a separate committee for the promotion of political advisors. In addition, political advisors are also given bureaucratic ranks, which in the PRC context means decent material and intangible benefits (e.g., higher social status, more income, and more rent-seeking opportunities). Many political advisors are promoted on the track of party-state cadres, e.g., section chief (*keji ganbu*, 科级干部) and division chief (*chuji ganbu*, 处级干部).[80]

Also, it was planned that between 2006 and 2010, 5,000 political advisors would be selected to study at master's level in political education and 500 for doctorates in political education.[81] These in-service training programmes are a *de facto* giving away of master's and doctoral degrees, like those that political education teachers have been offered, mentioned earlier.

Conclusion

From the official point of view, the efforts following Hu Jintao's "March-18 Order" have paid off. In a speech on 15 November 2009, Liu Guiqin (刘贵芹), Vice Chief of MOE's Division of Political Education Work, said that as a consequence of Hu's order, political education work in universities "has entered into the best development period since the founding of new China".[82] Liu Chuansheng (刘川生), President of the National Research Association of Universities on Political Education (*Quanguo gaoxiao sixiang zhengzhi jiaoyu yanjiuhui*, 全国高校思想政治教育研究会), was similarly positive. As he put it on 1 March 2010, "Since the implementing of No. 16 Document five years ago, university students' political education has made a breakthrough and has had evident achievements".[83]

Somewhat differently, based on MOE's own surveys, Yang Guang asserted that "Overall, the attractiveness and appeal of political education courses have been considerably increased, and the teaching effectiveness of political education courses has been obviously improved".[84] But Yang then cautioned that there were still many problems. "We hope that after five more years, political education courses can be really constructed as excellent courses and General Secretary Hu's objective of improving political education teaching obviously can be really realized".[85] In other words, the Hu regime's initial objective has been only partially met although the progress has been substantial.

Due to the lack of survey data that span at least the past five years, from scholars or from other non-governmental sources, it is difficult to judge if the actual achievements since 2004 could be hailed as "a breakthrough". Nevertheless, it appears a great deal has been done. The attendant infrastructure for political education work in universities has been instituted. Political education has become a formal and mature academic discipline in its own right. The contents of political education courses, which are primarily about the CPC's newly-raised theories and policies in the reform era, are becoming closer to what students actually care about and becoming less "*jia* (假, false), *da* (大, grandiose), and *kong* (空, hollow)". A more favourable institutional environment for the training and career development of political education teachers has been created, and political education teachers are acting more like teachers in regular disciplines. Political advisors are increasingly acknowledged as an independent and attractive profession, similar to teachers and administrators in universities.

Finally, by examining the context and objectives of the promulgation of No. 16 Document, as well as its main contents and accompanying measures, this study demonstrates that the Hu Jintao regime has been working very hard to strengthen political education and hence to ensure Party leadership in universities. As efforts devoted to matters such as investigating actual situations of political education teaching, constructing political education textbooks, and professionalizing the training of political advisors, have all been commonly praised as "unprecedented" in the PRC's history, as mentioned earlier, in comparison with its predecessors in the reform era, the Hu Jintao regime has been no less politically conservative. This study also suggests that in post-Mao China, the Party's laying great stress on higher education reforms and students' professional competence has been accompanied by concurrently devoting great efforts to strengthen the Party leadership in universities.

Notes and References

1. CPCCC and the State Council, Zhonggongzhongyang guowuyuan guanyu jinyibu jiaqiang he gaijin daxuesheng sixiang zhengzhi jiaoyu de yijian (Views of the CPC Central Committee and the State Council on further strengthening and improving university students' political education) (No. 16 Document hereafter) (August 2004), in Ministry of Education (ed.), Jiaqiang he gaijin daxuesheng sixiang zhengzhi jiaoyu zhongyao wenxian xuanbian (1978–2008) (Selected Important Documents on Strengthening and Improving University Students' Political Education (1978–2008)) (Beijing: Zhongguo renmin daxue chubanshe, 2008), pp. 376–384.

2. *Zhongguo jiaoyu bao* (China Education Daily), 28 May 2010.

3. Cf. Michael Agelasto, "Politics in charge: politically correct higher education in the People's Republic of China," *Education Journal*, Vol. 23, No. 2 (1995), pp. 51–52.

4. Stanley Rosen, "Political education and student response: some background factors behind the 1989 Beijing demonstrations," *Issues & Studies*, Vol. 25, No. 10 (1989), pp. 12–39; Shirin Rai, *Resistance and Reaction: University Politics in Post-Mao China* (New York: St. Martin's Press, 1991); Corinna-Barbara Francis, "The Institutional Roots of Student Political Culture: Official Student Politics at Beijing University," in Irving Epstein (ed.), *Chinese Education: Problems, Policies, and Prospects* (New York: Garland Publishing, 1991), pp. 394–415; Dingxin Zhao, "Decline of political control in Chinese universities and the rise of the 1989 Chinese student movement," *Sociology Perspectives*, Vol. 40, No. 2 (1997), pp. 159–182.

5. Stanley Rosen, "The effects of post-4 June re-education campaign on Chinese students," *The China Quarterly*, No. 134 (1993), pp. 310–334; Che-po Chan, "The political pragmatism of Chinese university students: 10 years after the 1989 movement," *Journal of Contemporary China*, Vol. 8, No. 22 (1999), pp. 381–403; Luo Xu, "Farewell to idealism: mapping China's university students of the 1990s," *Journal of Contemporary China*, Vol. 13, No. 41 (2004), pp. 779–799. For a more recent academic treatment of Chinese Youth's political attitudes, see Stanley Rosen, "Youth values and state-society relations," in Peter Hays Gries and Stanley Rosen (eds.), *Chinese Politics: State, Society and the Market* (London: Routledge, 2010), pp. 234–261.

6. Gang Guo, "Party recruitment of college students in China," *Journal of Contemporary China*, Vol. 14, No. 43 (2005), pp. 371–393.

7. Suisheng Zhao, "A state-led nationalism: the patriotic education campaign in post-Tiananmen China," *Communist and Post-Communist Studies*, Vol. 31, No. 3 (1998), pp. 287–302; Zheng Wang, "National humiliation, history education, and the politics of historical memory: patriotic education campaign in China," *International Studies Quarterly*, Vol. 52, No. 4 (2008), pp. 783–806; William A. Callahan, *China: The Pessoptimist Nation* (Oxford: Oxford University Press, 2010), chapter 2.

8. For example, King-lun Ngok and Julia Kwong wrote, "The concern that education should serve the new economic vision prompted depoliticization of Chinese education." See King-lun Ngok and Julia Kwong, "Globalization and educational restructuring in China," in Ka-Ho Mok and Anthony Welch (eds.), *Globalization and Educational Restructuring in the Asia Pacific Region* (New York: Palgrave, 2003), p. 164.

9. See, for example, Ruth Hayhoe, *China's Universities and the Open Door* (Armonk, New York: M. E. Sharpe, 1989); Ningsha Zhong, *University Autonomy in China* (Ph.D. diss. University of Toronto, 1997); Michael Agelasto and Bob Adamson (eds.), *Higher Education in Post-Mao China* (Hong Kong: Hong Kong University Press, 1998); Ka-Ho Mok, "Globalization and higher education restructuring in Hong Kong, Taiwan and Mainland China," *Higher Education Research & Development*, Vol. 22, No. 2 (2003), pp. 117–129; Ruth Hayhoe and Qiang Zha, "Becoming world-class: Chinese universities facing globalization and internationalization," *Harvard China Review*, Vol. 5, No. 1 (2004), pp. 87–92; Weifang Min, 'The legacy of the past and the context of the future,' in Philip G. Altbach and Toru Umakoshi (eds.), *Asian Universities: Historical Perspectives and Contemporary Challenges* (Baltimore MD: John Hopkins University Press, 2004), pp. 53–83; Ka-Ho Mok, "Riding over socialism and global capitalism: changing education governance and social policy paradigms in post-Mao China," *Comparative Education*, Vol. 41, No. 2 (2005), pp. 217–242; King-lun Ngok, "Globalization and higher education reform in China," in Nicholas Sun-keung Pang (ed.), *Globalization: Educational Research, Change and Reform* (Hong Kong: Chinese University Press), pp. 73–99.

10. In addition to Agelasto, "Politics in charge", two other notable exceptions are Wing-Wah Law, "The role of the state in higher education reform: Mainland China and Taiwan," *Comparative Education Review*, Vol. 39, No. 3 (1995), pp. 322–354; Su-Yun Pan, "Economic globalization, politico-cultural identity and university autonomy: the struggle of Tsinghua University in China," *Journal of Education Policy*, Vol. 21, No. 3 (2006), pp. 245–266.

11. For discussions on the methodological preferences of educational scholars, see John N. Hawkins, "Revolution and reform in education: prospects and problems," in John N. Hawkins (ed.), *Education and Social Change in the People's Republic of China* (New York: Praeger, 1983), p. 225; Glen Peterson and Ruth Hayhoe, "Introduction," in Glen Peterson, Ruth Hayhoe, and Yongling Lu (eds.), *Education, Culture, and Identity in Twentieth-Century China* (Ann Arbor MI: The Michigan University Press, 2004), p. 6.

12. In the PRC's history, the Ministry of Education has undergone several transformations and has had different names in different time periods. For the sake of this study, MOE will be used to refer to all of them.

13. "Interview with Yang Guang, Chief of MOE's Division of Social Sciences," *Sixiang jiaoyu yanjiu* (*Studies in Ideological Education*), No. 174 (2009), p. 9.

14. *Renmin ribao* (*People's Daily*), 16 October 2004.

15. *Ibid.*

16. http://info.jyb.cn/jyzck/200910/t20091029_319875.html (accessed on 18 July 2010).

17. http://www.moe.edu.cn/edoas/website18/info14078.htm (accessed on 22 August 2007).

18. *Studies in Ideological Education* is a monthly journal published by National Research Association of Universities on Political Education (NRAUPE) (*Quanguo gaoxiao sixiang zhengzhi jiaoyu yanjiuhui*) since 1985 and under the guidance of the Propaganda Department and MOE.

19. http://www.jyb.cn/high/gdjyxw/201005/t20100523_361863.html (18 July 2010).

20. *Zhongguo jiaoyu bao*, 25–28 May 2010.

21. Tiehui Wen (ed.), Lide shuren: dang de shiliuda yilai shanghai gaoxiao sixiang zhengzhi jiaoyu tansuo yu fazhan (Exploration and Development of Political Education in Shanghai Universities since the Party's 16th Congress), (Shanghai, Shanghai Renmin Chubanshe, 2009). Hu Hanji (ed.), Shanghai sixiang zhengzhi lilunke jiaoshi duiwu jianshe yanjiu baogao (Research Report on the Construction of the Corps of Political Education Teachers in Shanghai) (Shanghai: Fudan daxue chubanshe, 2009).

22. *Zhongguo jiaoyu bao*, 21 October 2004.

23. MOE, "Xuexi guanche luoshi zhongfa [2004] 16 hao wenjian he quanguo jiaqiang he gaijin daxuesheng sixiang zhengzhi jiaoyu gongzuo huiyi jingshen de xuanjiang tigang" ("Outline on publicizing the study and implementation of the spirit of the Centre-promulgated No. 16 Document (2004), and of the National Conference on Strengthening and Improving University Students' Political Education") (April 2005), in MOE, *Selected Important Documents*, pp. 437–450.

24. No. 16 Document, p. 376.

25. See, for example, MOE, "Several opinions of the MOE on strengthening and improving Marxist theory education in universities" ("Guojia jiaoyu weiyuanhui guanyu jiaqiang he gaijin gaodengxuexiao makesizhuyi lilun jiaoyu de ruogan yijian") (August 1991), in MOE, *Selected Important Documents*, p. 160.

26. Jin Huiming, "Guanyu makesizhuyi lilun yanjiu he jianshe gongcheng yu makesizhuyi lilun xueketixi he kechengtixi jianshe" ("'Project of Research and Construction on Marxist Theory,' and the construction of the discipline of 'Marxist Theory'"), *Sixiang lilun jiaoyu daokan* (*Journal of Ideological and Theoretical Education*), No. 107 (2007), p. 31.

27. CPCCC, "Zhonggongzhongyang guanyu jinyibu fanrong fazhan zhexue shehuikexue de yijian" ("Opinions of the CPCCC on further prospering and developing philosophy and social sciences") (January 2004), in MOE, *Selected Important Documents*, p. 367.

28. No. 16 Document, p. 376.

29. "Outline on publicizing," p. 439.

30. Quoted in MOE, Daxuesheng sixiang zhengzhi jiaoyu "shige ruhe" yanjiu (Research on the "Ten Hows" in University Students' Political Education) (Beijing: Higher Education Press, 2007), p. 245.

31. No. 16 Document, p. 383.

32. *Ibid.*, p. 377.

33. "Outline on Publicizing," p. 442.

34. *"Hu Jintao qinzi pishi gaoxiao zhengzhike tiaozheng"* ("Hu Jintao gives instructions on making adjustments in university political education courses"), http://news.people.com.cn/GB/4646134.html (accessed on 18 July 2010).

35. The CPCCC Propaganda Department and MOE, "Zhonggongzhongyang xuanchuanbu jiaoyubu guanyu jinyibu jiaqiang he gaijin gaodengxuexiao sixiang zhengzhi lilunke de yijian" ("The CPCCC Propaganda Department and MOE's views on further strengthening and improving political education courses in universities") (February 2005), in MOE, *Selected Important Documents*, pp. 416–421.

36. The name of this course was changed to "Conspectus on Mao Zedong Thought and Theories of Socialism with Chinese Characteristics" in August 2008.

37. The CPCCC Propaganda Department and MOE, "The CPCCC Propaganda Department and MOE's views on further strengthening and improving political education courses in universities," p. 417.

38. MOE, *Research on the "Ten Hows,"* p. 54; also see "Interview with Yang Guang," p. 9.

39. Source: State Council Academic Degree-Conferring Committee and MOE, "Shouyu boshi shuoshi xuewei he peiyang yanjiusheng de xueke zhuanye mulu" ("List of Doctorate- and Master's Degree-Conferring Disciplines and Majors") (June 1997), http://www.moe.edu.cn/edoas/website18/46/info12846 .htm (accessed on 22 August 2007).

40. MOE, "Jiaoyubu guanyu zai shier suo yuanxiao shezhi sixiang zhengzhi jiaoyu zhuanye de yijian" ("MOE's opinions on establishing the major of political education in twelve universities") (April 1984), in MOE, *Selected Important Documents*, pp. 33–35.

41. MOE, "Guanyu zai gaodengxuexiao xuesheng sixiang zhengzhi jiaoyu zhuanzhi renyuan zhong pinren jiaoshi zhiwu de shishi yijian" ("Opinions on granting the career status of teacher to full-time personnel on students' political education work in universities") (May 1987), in MOE, *Selected Important Documents*, pp. 95–97.

42. MOE, "Guanyu sixiang zhengzhi jiaoyu zhuanye peiyang shuoshi yanjiusheng de shishi yijian" ("Opinions on nurturing master's students in political education") (September 1987), in MOE, *Selected Important Documents*, pp. 120–121.

43. Cf., Bai Xianliang, "Gaige kaifang yilai sixiang zhengzhi jiaoyu xueke dingwei de huigu yu sikao" ("Reflections on our understanding of the nature

of political education discipline in the reform era"), *Sixiang lilun jiaoyu (Ideological and Theoretical Education)*, No. 5 (2009), p. 54.

44. MOE, *Research on the "Ten Hows,"* p. 55; State Council Academic Degree-Conferring Committee and MOE, "List of Doctorate- and Master's Degree-Conferring Disciplines and Majors."

45. State Council Academic Degree-Conferring Committee and MOE, "Guanyu tiaozheng makesizhuyi lilun yiji xueke ji suoshu erji xueke de tongzhi" ("Notice on adjusting the 'first-order discipline' of 'Marxist Theory' and its affiliated 'second-order disciplines'" (December 2005), in MOE, *Selected Important Documents*, pp. 469–478. "Research on Essential Issues in Modern and Contemporary Chinese History" was added as the sixth "second-order discipline" in April 2008.

46. Jin Huiming, "'Project of Research and Construction on Marxist Theory,' and the construction of the discipline of 'Marxist Theory,'" p. 32.

47. State Council Academic Degree-Conferring Committee and MOE, "Notice on adjusting the 'first-order discipline' of 'Marxist Theory' and its affiliated 'second-order disciplines,'" p. 477.

48. *Ibid.*, p. 470.

49. Jin Huiming, "'Project of Research and Construction on Marxist Theory,' and the construction of the discipline of 'Marxist theory,'" pp. 31–34.

50. Prof. Gu Hailiang, President of Wuhan University, used to be Chief of MOE's Division of Social Sciences Research and Political Education Work, and Party Secretary of Wuhan University. Professor Gu is a noted advocate for the importance of defending China's ideological security through political education work.

51. "Makesizhuyi lilun xueke jianshe yu sixiang zhengzhi lilunke guanxi bitan" ("Symposium on relationships between the disciplinary construction of 'Marxist Theory' and political education courses"), *Sixiang lilun jiaoyu daokan (Journal of Ideological and Theoretical Education)*, No. 105 (2007), p. 54.

52. *Ibid.*, pp. 53–71.

53. *Ibid.*; also see other theorists' views, e.g., Jin Huiming, "'Project of Research and Construction on Marxist Theory,' and the construction of the discipline of 'Marxist theory,'" p. 34; Fu Ruliang, Zhang Leisheng, and Tan Shun, "Makesizhuyi lilun xueke jiegou tezheng yu jianshe" ("Structure, features, and construction of the discipline of 'Marxist Theory'"), *Xueshujie (Academics in China)*, No. 134 (2009), pp. 75–77; Wang Shuyin, "Makesizhuyi lilun xueke fazhan de huigu yu sikao" ("Reflections on the development of the discipline of 'Marxist Theory'"), *Shoudu shifan daxue xuebao (shehui kexue ban) (Journal of Capital Normal University) (Social Sciences Edition)*, No. 161 (2008), p.13.

54. "Symposium on relationships between the disciplinary construction of 'Marxist Theory' and political education courses."

55. The CPCCC Propaganda Department and MOE, "The CPCCC Propaganda

Department and MOE's views on further strengthening and improving political education courses in universities," p. 419.

56. *Ibid.*

57. "Interview with Yang Guang," p. 10.

58. This descriptive account on how the work on the production of textbooks proceeded is based on a special news report dated 26 July 2006; see "Hu Jintao gives instructions on making adjustments in university political education courses."

59. See, for example, "Zhonggongzhongyang xuanchuanbu jiaoyubu xinwen chuban shu guanyu jiaqiang gaoxiao sixiang zhengzhi lilun ke jiaocai guanli de tongzhi" ("The CPCCC Propaganda Department, MOE, General Administration of Press and Publications") (January 2006), in MOE, *Selected Important Documents*, p. 479.

60. Jin Huiming, "'Project of Research and Construction on Marxist Theory,' and the construction of the discipline of 'Marxist theory,'" p. 32.

61. "Interview with Yang Guang," p. 10.

62. Cf. The CPCCC Organizational Department, *1989 nian zhuzhi gongzuo wenxuan* (*Selected Collection of Investigations on the Organizational Work in 1989*) (Beijing: The CPCCC Organizational Department, 1990), pp. 147–148.

63. The CPCCC Propaganda Department and MOE, "Zhonggongzhongyang xuanchuanbu jiaoyubu guanyu jinyibu jiaqiang gaodengxuexiao sixiang zhengzhi lilunke jiaoshi duiwu jianshe de yijian" ("Opinions of the CPCCC Propaganda Department and MOE on further strengthening the construction of the corps of university political education teachers") (September 2008), in MOE, *Selected Important Documents*, p. 532.

64. *Ibid.*, p. 533.

65. See relevant practices and experiences in Shanghai presented in a recent report, Hu Hanji, *Research Report on the Construction of the Corps of Political Education Teachers in Shanghai*, pp. 300–358.

66. The CPCCC Propaganda Department and MOE, "Opinions of the CPCCC Propaganda Department and MOE on further strengthening the construction of the corps of university political education teachers," p. 533.

67. Source: the author's observations and discussions with students.

68. MOE, "Guanyu zuohao 2008 nian 'gaoxiao sixiangzhengzhi lilun ke jiaoshi zaizhi gongdu makesizhuyililun boshixuewei' zhuanxiang jihua zhaosheng gongzuo de tongzhi" ("Notice on implementing the 2008 special plan of 'admitting political education teachers of universities to the in-service doctoral program in Marxist Theory'") (March 2008), in MOE (ed.), *Putong gaoxiao sixiangzhengzhi lilunke wenxian xuanbian (1949–2008)* (*Selected Documents on Political Education Courses in Regular Universities*), (Beijing: Zhongguo renmin daxue chubanshe, 2008), pp. 243–247; "Interview with Yang Guang," p. 11.

69. "Symposium on relationships between the disciplinary construction of 'Marxist Theory' and political education courses."

70. See interviews with Shanghai political education teachers, Hu Hanjin, *Research Report on the Construction of the Corps of Political Education Teachers in Shanghai*, pp. 150–151, 254. Also see "Interview with Yang Guang."

71. See, for example, Tiehui Wen, Exploration and Development of Political Education in Shanghai Universities since the Party's 16th Congress, p. 77.

72. MOE, "Putong gaodengxuexiao fudaoyuan duiwu jianshe guiding" ("Stipulations on the construction of the corps of political advisors in regular universities") (July 2006), in MOE, *Selected Important Documents*, pp. 492–493.

73. http://www.moe.edu.cn/edoas/website18/01/info26101.htm (accessed on 17 May 2010); Tiehui Wen, Exploration and Development of Political Education in Shanghai Universities since the Party's 16th Congress, p. 76.

74. MOE, "Stipulations on the construction of the corps of political advisors in regular universities," pp. 492–495.

75. The author's discussions with several full-time political advisors, Shanghai, 16 May 2010.

76. *Ibid.*; MOE, "Stipulations on the construction of the corps of political advisors in regular universities," pp. 492–495.

77. Tiehui Wen, Exploration and Development of Political Education in Shanghai Universities since the Party's 16th Congress, pp. 118–121.

78. *Ibid.*, p. 102; MOE, *Research on the "Ten Hows,"* p. 241.

79. MOE, "Stipulations on the construction of the corps of political advisors in regular universities," pp. 494–495.

80. The author's discussions with several full-time political advisors, Shanghai, 16 May 2010.

81. MOE, "2006–2010 nian putong gaodeng xuexiao fudaoyuan peixun jihua" ("Plan of training political advisor in universities: 2006–2010"), in MOE, *Selected Important Documents*, p. 498.

82. Source: Speech at a conference held by National Research Association of Universities on Political Education, 15 November 2009, *Sixiang jiaoyu yanjiu (Studies in Ideological Education)*, No. 175 (2009), p. 3.

83. Liu Chuansheng, "Zai quanguo gaoxiao sixiang zhengzhi jiaoyu yanjiuhui mishuzhang huiyi shang de jianghua" ("Speech at working conference of provincial secretaries of the National Research Association of Universities on Political Education"), *Sixiang jiaoyu yanjiu (Studies in Ideological Education)*, No. 178 (2010), p. 7.

84. "Interview with Yang Guang," p. 10.

85. *Ibid.*, p. 12.

18

Mending the Chinese Welfare Net: Tool for Social Harmony or Regime Stability?

Linda WONG

Abstract

After three decades of stunning economic growth Chinese society has become increasingly unequal and conflict ridden. Surveys and reports regularly chronicle public frustration and anger over such problems as unfair income distribution, corruption, unemployment, urban-rural disparity, environmental damage and social discrimination. Aggrieved groups like farmers, laid-off SOE workers, migrants, property owners, pensioners, and householders displaced by land resumption and urban development are becoming more vocal in rights talk and resistance action. It is plain that at the turn of the twenty-first century, the country is now gripped by waves of social discontent and popular protests and its social welfare system, an instrument to manage the social risks and failures of the market system, badly needs an overhaul. Since the late 1990s, the state has stepped up efforts to mend the Chinese welfare net. This chapter discusses what these measures are and what drives the state to improve on welfare engineering. It begins by contextualizing welfare reform against the policy agenda of enhancing social harmony. It then discusses policy innovation in five areas: introduction of social assistance; extension of social security; improving welfare provision for migrants; promoting, controlling, and assisting NGOs; and reforming health care to make it accessible for all. In reviewing the drivers for welfare reform, the author argues that recent welfare reforms are mainly motivated by concerns for social stability and regime preservation in an attempt to shore up the resilience of the authoritarian regime.

Introduction

China at the turn of the twenty-first century is gripped by waves of social discontent and popular protests. Surveys and reports regularly chronicle public frustration and anger over such problems as unfair income distribution, corruption, unemployment, urban rural disparity, environmental damage and social discrimination. Aggrieved groups like farmers, laid-off SOE workers, migrants, property owners, pensioners, and householders displaced by land resumption and urban development are becoming more vocal in rights talk and resistance action.[1] Their tactics, both legal and non-legal, range from petitioning, protests, legal contest, and even collective rebellion.[2] It is plain that after three decades of stunning economic growth, Chinese society has become increasingly unequal and conflict ridden. Its social welfare system, an instrument to manage the social risks and failures of the market system, badly needs an overhaul. Among the key shortcomings are the lack of a safety net, a patchy social insurance system, exclusion from welfare of migrant workers, underdevelopment of non-state welfare, and unaffordable health care for the rural masses and the poor. These failures are acknowledged by the state. Since the late 1990s, the state has stepped up efforts to mend the Chinese welfare net. This paper discusses what these measures are and what drives the state to improve on welfare engineering. It begins by contextualizing welfare reform against the state agenda of enhancing social harmony. It then discusses policy innovation in five areas: introduction of social assistance; extension of social security; improving welfare provision for migrants; promoting, controlling, and assisting NGOs; and reforming health care to make it accessible for all. In reviewing the drivers for welfare reform, the author argues that state welfare policies are mainly driven by concerns for social stability and regime preservation in an attempt to shore up the resilience of the authoritarian regime.

Social Contradictions
and the Agenda for Social Harmony

The new millennium marks a quarter century of China's experiments with a market system. Up until this time, the whole ethos of the reform has been to speed up economic development at all costs. As we all know, the growth that occurred has been stunning, an average of 9.8% per year.[3] As a result, living standards have improved tremendously. Social problems have mushroomed as well, exposing deep contradictions that gnaw at society. In 2002, three prominent Chinese intellectuals published an article entitled "The Most Severe Warning: Social Instability Behind Economic Prosperity" in *Strategy and Management*, an influential public policy journal in China. The paper warns that China has entered a new phase of social instability due to massive unemployment and redundancy, vast rural and urban disparity and regional inequality, a fast rising Gini coefficient, severe corruption, and large-scale environmental damage. Social discontent and grievances simmer among marginalized groups that have yet to share the fruits of growth. These include unemployed workers, migrant labourers, farmers, landless peasants, evicted urban households, poor people, and masses who suffer from official malfeasance and corruption.[4] If the ills of unemployment and unequal growth (or growth without redistribution) continue to be ignored, China may plunge into turmoil. Likewise, poll after poll conducted by the China Academy of Social Sciences has identified widening income disparity, soaring prices of health, unaffordable housing and education, rising unemployment, and gaps in the social security system as the most serious social problems.[5] There is wide consensus that the magnitude and seriousness of these social issues are threatening social and political stability.

The new administration headed by President Hu Jintao and Premier Wan Jiabao heeded these warnings. In October 2004, at the Fourth Plenary Session of the Sixteenth Central Committee of the CPC, Hu introduced the concept of harmonious socialist society (*shehui zhuyi hexie shehui*). In a seminar for senior cadres at the Central Party School in February 2005, he elaborated that "a harmonious society features democracy, the rule of law, equity, justice, sincerity, amity, vitality, peace with order, and the harmony between human beings and nature". Such a society is basically "people-centred" (*yi ren wei ben*). Its developmental path reflects a "Scientific Outlook on Development" (*kexue fazhan guan*), which stresses a comprehensive, coordinated and sustainable development approach.[6] Subsequently, the ethos of building social harmony set the keynote of social and economic development of the Eleventh Five Year

Plan (2006–2010). In Wen's work report to the third session of the Tenth NPC (March 2005), its importance is further elaborated: "a harmonious society gives full scope to people's talent and creativity, enables all the people to share the social wealth brought by reform and development, and forges an ever-closer relationship between the people and government".[7]

With the stern backing of the top leadership, the propaganda on social harmony attained the ideological height of an official campaign and social movement. At first, state and society applied the harmony discourse with all manner of reverence and hope. When the slogan was first mooted, policy pundits and intellectuals hailed it as a major policy shift from single-minded pursuit of economic growth and efficiency to concern for social development, social stability and social justice. More significantly it underlines the top leadership's concern to reduce social conflicts and balance the interests between different social groups in society. Nearly all people would agree that it is the absence of social harmony that lies behind the drive for social harmony. Social commentators liken the new emphasis on social issues to a sea change. Wang Shaoguang, for example, calls this "a great transformation" and "a historic shift of Chinese public policy".[8] In recent years, however, an increasingly cynical public have started to use the term in jest and sarcasm. Voices or acts that have been "harmonized" (*bei hexie*) actually means that such have been suppressed or obliterated, instead of denoting tolerance and acceptance of diversity. Such a turn may be unexpected.[9] It does belie the fact that Chinese society has seen an escalation of discontent or failure to enhance harmony.

The government has indeed hugely increased its social expenditures. In the wake of the 2008 financial tsunami, increase in social spending is designed as a part of the stimulus package to promote domestic consumption.[10] It is well agreed that without a sound social protection system, people will feel compelled to save up for health care, children's schooling, and retirement. This explains why in 2008, China's saving rate came to a staggering 51.3% while the spending rate was only 35.3% (versus 12% and 70% in the United States).[11] State commitment to safeguard the livelihood of the people has been translated into concrete plans for a livelihood enhancement project (*minsheng gongcheng*). One can glimpse the outline of this project by piecing together official announcements pertaining to improvements in social security, health care, education, employment and housing. For 2009 alone, state social spending was in the order of 700 billion *yuan*.

Mending the Welfare Net

Improving the coverage and effectiveness of the welfare system is now a strategic goal of the government. In the following sections, this chapter shall examine relevant developments over five areas, namely building up a social assistance system, expanding social insurance, reforming healthcare, encouraging and regulating NGOs, and developing the social work profession. The first two have a common objective to plug the loopholes of the current social security system and make it a better weapon against poverty and economic insecurity. Health care reform answers the acute need to provide healthcare for all and remove the major complaints against the current system. The NGO initiative aims at spearheading the growth of the third sector in welfare to meet unmet social needs. Developing social work education and deployment provides skill and human resources to help distressed individuals adapt to social change. The desired outcome of these measures is to enhance social harmony and stability in Chinese society.

Building up Safety Nets

Before 1978, the urban employing units and rural collectives provided the framework of social and economic security for the masses. State relief only went to people who have no families, no work ability, and no means of livelihood. Aid that was given was meagre, discretionary and full of social stigma.[12] The restructuring of urban industry created high unemployment as well as erosion of occupational welfare. Likewise, the disappearance of rural communes and the poor financial ability of village and township governments seriously weakened welfare support for the indigent.[13] The recreation of a safety net is absolutely crucial in relieving urban and rural poverty.

Shanghai was the first city to introduce social assistance for needy urban residents in the form of a Minimum Living Security System (MLSS, or *dibao*) in 1993. Its success prompted the state to replicate

Table 1:
Major Contents of China's Livelihood Enhancement Project

Social Security	Emphases	Improve urban retirement, healthcare and unemployment insurance.
		Pilot rural retirement insurance in 10% of counties.
	Investments	Expenditure for 2009: 293 billion *yuan*, of which 3 billion *yuan* goes to rural retirement insurance.
Health Care	Emphases	Deepen reforms in health care and drug administration.
		Improve rural cooperative health care system.
		Popularize basic health insurance for urban residents.
	Investments	Expenditure for 2009: 118 billion *yuan*, total expenditure of 850 billion *yuan* in the next three years.
Education	Emphases	Implement compulsory education in rural areas
		Enhance safety of primary and secondary school buildings in villages.
		Solve the schooling problem of migrant children residing in cities and towns with their parents.
	Investments	Expenditure for 2009: 198 billion *yuan*, of which 57.8 billion *yuan* goes to compulsory rural education.
Employment	Emphases	Aid to university graduates seeking employment in urban and rural grassroots areas and middle and western regions.
		Provide vocational training to unemployed persons and migrant workers.
		Support small and medium enterprises in creating employment.
	Investments	Expenditure for 2009: 42 billion *yuan*.
Housing	Emphases	Build low cost rental housing.
		Rebuild dwellings in slum areas.
		Rebuild dangerous dwellings in rural areas on pilot basis.
	Investments	Expenditure for 2009: 49.3 billion *yuan*, of which 33 billion *yuan* goes to low cost rental housing.

Source: *Hong Kong Economic Times*, 31 August 2009, p.A6 (compiled from various Chinese government websites).

it across the country. In 1997, in the wake of firm bankruptcies and massive lay-offs, the central government released the Circular on Building a Minimum Living Security System for All Urban Residents. In 1999, the State Council announced the Regulation on the Minimum Living Security System for Urban Residents, which institutionalizes the system of social assistance with regard to eligible targets, assistance standards, funding source, and application procedures. [14] The momentum to expand the scheme picked up after 2001 when the central state demanded local governments to "cover as many people as possible who qualify". By the end of 2002, recipient numbers had jumped to 20 million. In subsequent years, the number of beneficiaries stabilized at around 22 million; reaching 23.3 million at the end of 2008. The scope of the scheme can be seen in Table 2.

Table 2: Number of Social Assistance Recipients in Urban Areas

Year	Persons (million)	Growth Rate (%)
1999	2.66	
2000	4.03	
2001	11.71	190.8
2002	20.65	76.4
2003	22.47	8.8
2004	22.05	−1.9
2005	22.34	1.3
2006	22.40	0.3
2007	22.72	1.4
2008	23.34	2.8

Source: *Report on Civil Affairs Work of the Ministry of Civil Affairs in 2008*, at http://cws.mca.gov.cn/article/tjbg/200906/20090600031762.shtml, accessed on 14 April 2009.

A few caveats are needed. First, assistance rates are set by each locality, taking into account the number of poor people and the fiscal ability of the local state which funds the scheme. This gives rise to wide variations across cities. In 2008, Shanghai and Tianjin's MLSS standards were set at 400 *yuan* per month. In contrast, western provinces like Qinghai and Xinjiang could only manage 193 *yuan* and 156 *yuan* respectively.[15] It is not uncommon for poor areas to tighten up the eligibility to reduce their burden. Second, the actual aid received is lower than the aid standard given that MLSS is a supplement to make good the gap between actual income and the defined minimum. In 2008, the assistance standard averaged 205 *yuan* per month while the average monthly subsidy was 143.7 *yuan*.[16] These paltry grants are hardly enough to keep body and soul together. Three, MLSS is not administered by professional or government cadres; rather investigations and recommendations are handled by assistants employed by neighbourhoods (community residents' committees). It is generally agreed that these assistants lack the authority and competence to process the applications in matters of verifying incomes, unemployment status and family circumstances.

The introduction of social assistance in the countryside fell greatly behind urban developments. In the last decade, more affluent areas piloted programmes to improve social relief. Following rural taxation reform, which simplifies the tax structure and exempts peasants from agricultural tax, the government amended the rural relief regulation in 2006. The most significant shift was to change the source of funding from local levies to government allocations. In July 2007, the State Council released the "Circular on Building a Minimum Living Security System in All Rural Areas". The safety net vacuum in the hinterland was finally plugged. By the end of 2008, 43 million peasants received rural social assistance. The growth trend is shown in Table 3. For the under-developed areas in the middle and western regions, the lion's share of the financing comes from the central government.

A number of comments are apposite. First, both the assistance standard and actual grant are extremely low. In 2008, the average standard was 82.3 *yuan* per month while the actual payment averaged 50 *yuan*. Second, the variations in assistance standards are even more extreme than in the cities. In 2008, the most generous rates were found in Shanghai, Beijing and Tianjin (3,202 *yuan*, 2,546 *yuan* and 2,516 *yuan* per annum) where provinces like Gansu, Guangxi and Jilin set the poverty line at 680 *yuan*, 683 *yuan* and 693 *yuan* respectively.[17] Third, different groups get different treatment. The standard for childless elderly people without the ability to work or the means of livelihood ("five guarantee households") was 2,176 *yuan* per year if they were in residential care and 1,624 *yuan* if they lived in their own home. The actual subsidy per head averaged 2,056 *yuan* and 1,121 *yuan* respectively, depending on whether they were in residential care or living at home. Some people receive only temporary relief (8.31 million person/times in 2008). In addition, medical relief (42 million person/times) totalling 3.8 billion *yuan* was handed out.

Table 3: Number of Social Assistance Recipients in Rural Areas

Year	Persons (million)	Growth Rate (%)
2001	3.05	
2002	4.08	33.9
2003	3.67	−10.0
2004	4.88	32.9
2005	8.25	69.1
2006	15.93	93.1
2007	35.66	123.9
2008	43.06	20.7

Source: Report on Civil Affairs Work of the Ministry of Civil Affairs in 2008, http://cws.mca.gov.cn/article/tjbg/200906/20090600031762.shtml, accessed 14 April 2009.

Expanding Social Insurance

China's social security system is exceedingly complex. Since the early 1950s, social security for urban workers, previously known as labour insurance, covered compensation for old age, sickness, work injury and maternity. Up until the late 1960s, labour insurance was administered by trade unions. The attack on trade unions and labour agencies during the Cultural Revolution (1966–1976) destroyed the administrative framework. Subsequently the onus to fund and dispense social security was transferred to individual work units, changing its nature from social pooling to company-based benefit. The burden on state-owned enterprises (SOEs) became unbearable when they had to compete with non-state firms. To relieve the burden of SOEs, the state began experiments with social security. In the 1990s, social security reform became institutionalized. The former system of labour insurance gave way to a system of social insurance. Five components schemes are included to deal with the contingencies arising from retirement, medical treatment, unemployment, work injury, and maternity. Employees in SOEs benefitted first, followed by workers in collective owned enterprises, and later employees in the private and informal sectors. Policy and administration came under the ambit of the Ministry of Labour and Social Security (recently renamed Ministry of Human Resources and Social Security). At the city level (some at provincial level), social insurance bureaus were set up to handle the collection, distribution, and management of insurance funds. Another departure from old practice was a requirement for a joint contribution from employers and employees to replace sole funding by enterprises. Now, companies contribute an average of 20% of the wage bill to pensions, 6% to healthcare, 2% to unemployment compensation, and about 1% to work injury and maternity insurance. At the same time, employees pay an average of 8% of their wages for pension, 2% for health insurance, and 1% for unemployment benefit.

The population of China is aging rapidly, having attained the status of an aging society (where 10% of the population is 60 and above) in 1999. At the end of 2008, Chinese seniors (60 and above) amounted to 160 million, or 12% of the population.[18] By 2050, a quarter of the population will be elderly. Until recently, pension was only enjoyed by urban retirees. Two most important milestones marked the development of urban pensions. The first one was the State Council's "Decisions on Reforming the System of Retirement Insurance for Enterprise Employees" in 1991 which laid the foundation of modern pensions on the principles of joint contribution by employers and employees and creation of social pooling and individual accounts. The other marker was the "Decisions on Establishing a Unified Basic Retirement Insurance for Enterprise Employees" in 1997. Building on the basis of the 1991 document, the new decree unifies the former disparate pension schemes and extends coverage to all employees in urban enterprises. Significantly, employees in non-state firms and self-employed persons come under protection. From then on, the key task was to expand the coverage. From 1989 to 2008, enrolment in the basic retirement insurance scheme expanded very quickly, from 48.2 million persons to 218.9

million. The latter figure includes 165.9 million serving employees, 53.4 million retirees and 24.2 million migrant workers. Some observations are pertinent here. First, practically all working personnel in the formal sector and nearly 90% of retired workers have been covered. [19] Second, the participation of migrant workers is low, considering the estimated size of 140 million. Third, few employees in informal employment have enrolled. Basic pensions at best cover half of the eligible population.

Creating retirement protection for rural peasants is a bigger challenge. At present, 65% of Chinese elderly people live in the countryside but very few qualify for a pension. Experiments with rural pensions started in the 1980s and made encouraging progress under the tutelage of the Ministry of Civil Affairs. At the end of 1997, 82 million peasants had enrolled. In the 1998 state restructuring reform, the onus for rural social security passed to the Ministry of Labour and Social Security. Subsequently, pension experiments faltered. One factor behind the stagnation was lack of interest from the labour ministry, which has no experience with rural social security. More importantly, state leaders at the time had doubts about the feasibility of rural pensions. From 2002 onwards, membership of rural pension schemes stabilized at around 54 million. In 2007, the State Council gave approval for explorations into different types of retirement protection, reviving local interest in such schemes. [20] At the end of 2008, membership had increased to 55.95 million, with 5.12 million rural elders receiving pensions. [21] Up to the present, support for the elderly still falls primarily on their own labour and support from the family.

Reforms on health insurance have been more difficult than other types of insurance reform because of its complexity and multiple stakeholders. For much of the 1980s and 1990s, the guiding spirit in healthcare system reforms has been to reduce the financial burden of enterprises and the state. Many experiments were conducted but few succeeded. In 1999, the government finally introduced a Basic Health Insurance System for Urban Employees. Built on the principles of broad coverage at low standards, employer and employee contribution, and co-payment above stipulated ceilings, the scheme expanded quickly. In 1999, enrolment was 18 million. By 2008, this has risen to 318.2 million, comprising 149.9 million serving employees, 50.1 million retirees and 42.7 million migrant workers. A number of caveats must be added. First, the expansion in coverage has been remarkable. Most working employees and retirees in the formal sector are now covered. Second, migrant workers are still under-represented in the membership. Third, the basic scheme only covers urban employees and excludes non-working personnel like school children and housewives. This is a big loophole. Since 2007, many cities have explored ways to plug the gap, for example, creating health insurance schemes for school children and adolescents and allowing non-employees to join the basic scheme.

The introduction of the Temporary Regulations on Unemployment Insurance for State Owned Enterprise Employees in 1986 was a measure to complement the passing of the Trial Bankruptcy Law. At first, eligibility was restricted to a few categories of unemployed workers; in 1993, coverage was widened. Massive redundancy drives since the mid-1990s created the need to institutionalize a broader system of unemployment insurance. In 1999, the State Council released the Unemployment Insurance Regulations, which extends protection from SOEs to collective owned enterprises, foreign firms, joint ventures, and all types of employing units. From 1998 to 2000, there was a big rise in enrolment from 79.3 million to 104.1 million. After 2000, the scheme lost momentum. At the end of 2008, enrolment stood at 124 million,[22] much lower than for basic pension and health insurance. The reasons were attributed to the low income replacement ratio (20–30% of average wages in the local area), short duration of benefits (24 months maximum), and popularization of social assistance. There were likewise doubts about the efficacy of unemployment insurance, leading to uncertainties about its future. The ambiguous attitude belied state passivity in promoting the scheme.

Experiments with work injury insurance started in the mid-1990s as provided by the Labour Law (1995). Based on a no-fault principle, employees in all workplaces who suffer work related injuries have the right to claim compensation. Enrolment increased rather slowly until 2004 when the State Council promulgated the Regulation on Work Injury Insurance. As a result, participants jumped from 45.8 million in 2003 to 137.9 million in 2008, including 49.4 million migrant workers. As a matter of priority, the government plans to enroll all employees working in dangerous occupations like coal mines and construction in three years.

Maternity insurance protects women workers from loss of employment and income during pregnancy and childbirth, against a backdrop of gender discrimination and employer concerns about maternity costs. Experiments on maternity insurance started in Nantong and Qufu in 1998. In 1994, Pilot Measures in Implementing Maternity Insurance was released. Enforcement proved difficult. By 2001, only 34.55 million women workers were covered.[23] Even at the end of 2008, the coverage stood at 92.5 million, the lowest among all the five schemes. Only women in the formal sector are covered, leaving out women in the informal economy (where most women work) and in rural areas.[24] Official information and research reports are scarce.

Table 4: Scope of Social Insurance in 2008

	Participants (million persons)		Revenue (billion *yuan*)	Expenditure (billion *yuan*)	Accumulated balance (billion *yuan*)
Retirement Insurance	218.91 participants of which:		974.0	739.0	993.1
	Employees	165.87	Subscription: 801.6		
	Retirees	53.04	Financial		
	Migrant workers	24.16	Subsidy: 143.7		
	Rural participants	55.95			
Health Insurance	318.22 participants of which:		304.0	208.4	343.2
	employees	199.96			
	residents	118.26			
	retirees	50.08			
	migrant workers	42.86			
Unemployment Insurance	124.0 participants of which:		58.5	25.4	131.0
	migrant workers	15.49			
	recipients	2.61			
Work Injury Insurance	137.87 participants of which:		21.7	12.7	33.5
	migrant workers	49.42			
	recipients	1.18			
Maternity Insurance	92.54 participants recipients	1.4	11.4	7.1	16.8

Source: Statistical Communique on Labour and Social Security Development in 2008

Table 4 summarizes the scope of China's social insurance scheme at the end of 2008. Comparing the five schemes, a number of observations can be made. First, health and retirement insurance have the highest coverage; work injury and unemployment insurance schemes stand at the second tier while maternity insurance remains a limited scheme. Second, there are major exclusions, primarily rural peasants, migrant workers, and employees in the informal sector. For the peasantry, apart from limited forays into rural pensions, they are barred from organizational resources to meet life contingencies. This makes Chinese peasants and migrant workers second-class citizens in the state distribution regime. Third, the number of recipients in some schemes appears to be unjustifiably small, for example, unemployment and work injury benefits. This is difficult to explain against the backdrop of much publicized needs. Are the criteria of receipt too restrictive? Are there administrative problems in processing claims? Until one knows the answers, one has to be cautious in taking the official figures at face value.

In recent years, the 140 million migrant labourers working in Chinese cities have attracted attention from both government and society. Without urban status, migrant workers are treated as outsiders and suffer from discrimination. They are barred from state social services like social insurance, health care, and education for their children. Their lot has improved somewhat in the current decade since the government has gradually removed the official barriers to social security (and education). Now, a portion of migrant workers enroll in local social insurance schemes or join pension and healthcare insurance plans designed for migrants. However, many institutional hurdles bar the majority from participation. These include bureaucratic discrimination against outsiders, employers' reluctance to pay premiums, high thresholds of local schemes, distrust of migrants, and lack of portability of the benefits. It is the last problem that reduces migrants' incentive to enroll in local schemes, causing low participation and high withdrawal rates when they leave the city.[25]

Reforming Health Care

Difficulty in accessing affordable healthcare is a top social problem in China. "Hard to see a doctor, treatment is expensive" (*kanbing nan, kanbing gui*) is a common complaint of most citizens. Rural residents and uninsured persons regard sickness as a curse. A major illness can sink a family into poverty. Untreated sickness mars health and productivity, and yet only a quarter of the population have insurance coverage. For the rest, out of pocket payment is the only mode to access healthcare. The commodification of healthcare gives rise to widespread discontent. Other problems are equally daunting. Hospitals rely too heavily on the selling of drugs to finance their operation costs in light of serious underfunding by the government. Between 2002 and 2006, government funding accounted for only 10% of hospital revenue.[26] As doctors' pay is linked to the income they earn for the hospital, distorted incentives give rise to indiscriminate use of costly prescriptions and unnecessary treatment. For the country as a whole, healthcare costs have outstripped the increase in people's incomes. Between 1990 and 2006, outpatient costs jumped by twelve times and hospitalization costs by ten times, whereas people's incomes in urban and rural areas rose by just five and seven times.[27] Inefficiency in the use of healthcare resources and inequity of access pose obstacles in delivery of healthcare for all. According to the World Health Report 2000, China ranked 188th among 191 countries for fairness in healthcare finance and 144th for overall health system performance. So, domestically and internationally, the related problems are well recognized.[28]

To fill the vacuum of subsidized healthcare for rural residents, the Chinese government introduced a New Cooperative Medical Scheme (NCMS, or *xinnonghe*) in the countryside in 2003. This is a voluntary scheme subsidized by the central and local governments (20 *yuan* each for each participant, later increased to 40 *yuan*) with contribution from each peasant who enrolls (10 *yuan*) to help defray partial costs of hospital treatment. Adverse selection, poor governance, and low reimbursement level (from 10–30%) slowed its expansion in the beginning years. At the end of 2005, only 24% of peasants had joined up. Participation has since improved as the scheme becomes better known and government subsidies increase. In mid-2007, 720 million peasants, or 82.8% of the rural population, had become members.[29] At the end of 2008, the enrolment rate had risen to 91.5%.[30] The NCMS has two major flaws. First, outpatient costs are not covered. Second, reimbursement rates are very low. Patients still have to pay the lion's share of the treatment costs. Typically, one hospital admission accounts for 1.5 years' income of a rural resident.

The pressure to reform the healthcare system has come from public opinion, experts, and government ministries. In 2005, a think tank under the State Council concluded that the medical reforms of the last twenty years have failed, mainly due to the commercialization of public hospitals. In 2006, the central government set up the National Healthcare Reform Coordinating Group headed by the Ministry of Health and the National Development and Reform Commission to oversee the new round of medical reform. The taskforce was asked to draft a new healthcare reform proposal. In early 2007, the Coordinating Group invited seven organizations (Peking University, Fudan University, Beijing Normal University, Development Research Center of the States Council, World Bank, World Health Organization, and McKinsey) to submit proposals for healthcare reforms.[31] A consultation document was released in October 2008 after two years of intense debates and bargaining. The goal was to ensure equal access to basic health services by 2020. Medical care services are to be delivered mainly by non-profit hospitals. Both urban and rural dwellers are to be covered by medical insurance.[32]

In April 2009, the Central Committee of the CPC and the State Council jointly endorsed and issued a 13,000-word document titled "Guidelines on Deepening the Reform of the Healthcare System". The government will launch an initial three-year plan to invest 850 billion *yuan* (US$124 billion) to improve the healthcare system. The plan underscores the responsibility of the state to ensure accessible and affordable public services to all: "The government's responsibility in the basic health care system will be strengthened and the government should step up its responsibility in planning, financing, serving and supervising to guarantee the non-profit nature of public health care and promote equality". The short-term goal is to provide basic insurance coverage to 90% of residents, provide affordable medicines, and establish a network of urban and rural clinics at the community level by 2011. It envisages the building of 2,000 county hospitals and 29,000 township clinics as well as the upgrading of 5,000 township clinics within that time. The goal by 2020 is a comprehensive system offering basic healthcare, drugs and medical insurance. On the treatment of unprotected groups, all retired employees of bankrupt state enterprises and university students will be included in the basic medical insurance scheme for urban residents. Rural migrants working in cities will be allowed to join the urban scheme too. In terms of cutting costs, the government has decided on a formulary of basic drugs. The manufacturers will be appointed by the government through public bidding. The central government will set the price range for basic drugs and provincial governments will set the prices within the ranges. The prices of basic medical services provided by hospitals will also be decided by the government. The government also promised to strengthen its supervisory role in insurance and hospital operations.[33]

The initial comments have been favourable. The objectives to achieve equality of access, ensure healthcare for the poor, universalize insurance cover, control drug dispensation and costs, strengthen the supervisory role of the state, deliver primary services through a system of community-based clinics are all useful in meeting the goal of healthcare for all. At the same time and in the light of lack of details of the plan, many concerns remain unanswered. The more important ambiguities include financial resources, feasibility of building up grassroots clinics, manpower and skill shortages, hospital management issues, and policing of drug costs and supplies. In China, the challenge of public policy lies in enforcement. Effectiveness cannot be gauged until the blueprint becomes reality. Until now, policy distortion and implementation deficits have been chronic problems. To deliver this exceedingly ambitious and complex plan demands an inordinate amount of political will, financial and organizational resources, cooperation of stakeholders, and ability to work out detailed solutions to problems.

Promoting and Regulating Non-state Welfare

The liberalization of China's command system in the last two decades spawned an explosion of social organizations. Among different types of non-government organizations (NGOs), agencies that deliver social welfare services using non-state funds have grown rapidly. These normally register as non-state nonprofit enterprises or nonprofit organizations (NPOs). At the end of 2007, China had 173,915 NPOs, making up 45% of total registered NGOs.[34] NPOs enjoy tax exemption and preferential charges for the public utilities.

In China, non-state welfare organizations can be divided into five types; social welfare homes, children's homes, social welfare hospitals, urban welfare homes for the elderly, and rural welfare homes for destitute households. Non-state welfare homes have expanded very quickly, in particular residential care for seniors. Unable to meet the demand, the state promulgated the Provisional Regulations on the Registration and Management of Civilian-run Non-Enterprise Units in 1998 to provide incentives for NGOs. The decree specifies strict rules on the formation, operation, administration and dissolution of programmes. Before they can register with the Ministry of Civil Affairs, agencies must secure an official or professional sponsor willing to oversee their daily management. The dual supervision regime by professional sponsor and registration authority is very strict. Agencies unable to meet these conditions are forced to operate without registration or operate as a business enterprise. Each year, NGOs must pass an annual inspection by the civil affairs authorities before they can renew their licence.[35]

Among various types of non-state welfare organizations, the development of residential care facilities for urban elders is particularly noteworthy. As pioneer in non-state care, these agencies are products of the welfare socialization reform since 1998 with the aim of encouraging non-state actors to provide, fund and manage welfare programmes to meet societal needs. In the last decade, non-state old age homes expanded quickly. At the end of 2007, their numbers came to 41,000, operating a total capacity of some 2 million beds, exceeding the supply in state welfare homes.[36] In Shanghai, with seniors making up 21.6% of the population, NPO-run beds accounted for 52% of total supply, up from 1,851 beds in 1997 to 42,186 beds in 2008, a twelve-fold increase over the period.[37]

The rapid growth of non-state welfare can be attributed to favourable policies in the last decade to grant tax exemption, offer policy guidance and improve institution building. Taking Shanghai as an example, the last measure includes provision of a start-up subsidy (adding 10,000 beds each year during 2006–2010, at 5,000 *yuan* for each new bed), formation of a trade association, and introduction of an accident insurance scheme. However, formal codes and systems are one part of reality. In China, where legal norms are not well enforced, officials' attitudes and behaviour are influential. Researchers have found considerable vacillation of official attitudes towards non-state agencies. On the one hand, the state is anxious to unload the heavy burden of social welfare onto non-state actors. On the other hand, the state still keeps a watchful eye on civil society organizations for fear of insubordination, intransigence or loss of state authority. The result is wavering, inconsistent, and conflicting attitudes which impinge on policy and undermine support for NGOs. Currently, NPOs stand in need of financial support (both capital and on-going expenditure) from the government, help with land and buildings, staff training and recruitment, and delivering on the promised preferential policies. The strong regulatory framework, state distrust and limited support still constrain the growth and autonomy of the third sector in social welfare.[38]

Creating a Social Work Profession

In modern welfare systems, social work is a core profession that supplies the human resources and skills for personal intervention, community development, social planning, programme development, and citizen participation. In China, social work is often equated with voluntary work (or "good work") performed by party members, trade unions, women's federations, youth league cadres, and socially involved individuals. Until the 1990s, welfare services were either delivered in the workplace or run by civil affairs departments at different levels. Civil affairs cadres perform welfare administration functions while personal care for seniors, disabled, children and orphans is done by care workers and assistants. In city neighbourhoods, local cadres handle civil mediation while volunteers help to deliver care to needy people without family support.[39] Until the beginning of the 2000s, social work profession, social work posts, and social work services did not exist in China.[40]

The underdevelopment of social work is also attributed to the lack of social work education. From the 1950s to the late 1970s, social work and other social sciences disciplines were discontinued. In the 1980s, a small number of universities re-established social work courses. The formation of the China Social Work Association (1991) and the China Association for Social Work Education (1994) tried to promote the professionalization of social work. Expansion remained limited – by 2001, there were only 36 programmes – thereafter momentum picked up. By 2003, the number rose to 172. Now there are over 200 social work programmes producing 10,000 graduates each year. [41] Notwithstanding the proliferation of academic programmes, a number of problems are still prominent. First, most of the teachers lack proper social work education. Second, there is a shortage of supervised practicum and supervisors with practical social work experience. Third, curriculum, text books, theories and methodology are primarily adopted from Hong Kong and the USA, with little attempt at indigenization.[42] Fourth, there is difficulty in attracting good students because of poor pay, low social status, and lack of job openings in social work.

The professionalization, or at least the occupationalization, of social work moved forward in the middle of the decade. In 2004, the government passed the Regulations on the Occupationalization of Social Workers and in 2006, the Regulations on the Social Workers Occupational Standard System. These regulations define social work practice, scope and objectives. They also classify social work grades based on qualification and experience. Further, the Regulations on the Assessment of Professional Levels of Social Work divide social workers into three levels (assistant social worker, social worker, and senior social worker). The first national examination to qualify candidates for the assistant and social worker grades was held in 2008. Out of the 111,720 persons who took part, 18% successfully passed the examination.[43]

In theory, social work has attained the status of a profession alongside an expansion in tertiary education, with a standardized curriculum, common examination, and grade determination. Paradoxically, qualification to practice is not matched by posts in social work. Inside the government, there are no formal social work positions in welfare centres or in state bureaus. Some social workers find work in neighbourhood agencies. Most of the newly created social work posts are now found in NGOs. In Shanghai, Guangzhou, Shenzhen and Dongguan, NGOs are contracted by the government to provide social work services in hospitals, old age homes, rehabilitation centres, enterprises, schools, youth centres, neighbourhood agencies, legal clinics and the like. Most of the work is geared to personal intervention and helping agencies to handle grievances. The proliferation of social work NGOs in these cities warrants close watch. If these experiments spread to other cities, this has the potential for greater NGO activism and social work professionalization.[44] My interviews in Guangzhou in November 2009 and May 2010 suggest that such agencies face many constraints. A major drawback is the duration of service contracts, which are negotiated year by year, severely limiting continuity of service to clients. As a corollary, agencies encounter high staff turnover, which is a result of job uncertainty and lack of career prospects. More fundamentally, agency functions are mostly set by the government, including user targets and type of programmes. At the present time, social work NGOs function more like handmaidens of the local state than autonomous agencies and advocates for the disadvantaged.

What Drives Welfare Reform in Recent Years?

The above review of state efforts to improve the coverage and functionality of its welfare net identify considerable achievements. The agenda for social harmony has helped to increase political incentive and resources in the social sectors. Does this imply that economic growth has been replaced as the key imperative of the state? The answer is no. More attention to social issues is an attempt to address the lag in social development and strike a better balance between economic and social development. This is a step in the right direction. The improvements outlined above are certainly crucial in ameliorating the injustice and social ills that accompany three decades of break neck growth. This does not mean an abandonment of the goal for development.

"Everything we do we do to ensure that people live a happier life with more dignity and make our society fairer and harmonious", said Wen Jiabao when he addressed the NPC in March 2010. The audience broke into applause. This was the third time the premier had iterated the theme of greater dignity for the people within the space of one month.[45] Establishment intellectuals saw this as a sign of the government putting people first. Some hoped this could herald an expansion of the scope of legal and civil rights. On 23 March 2010, Zhang Ping, director of the National Development and Reform Commission, said at the China Development Forum that China should further expand domestic demand, spurring people's consumption in particular, to sustain the country's economic development:

To stimulate consumption is a long-term strategy, and represents a strong point of China's development . . . We will accelerate the adjustment of China's income distribution system and enhance help for low-income households through improving the social safety net, which will clear people's concerns when they consume.[46]

Zhang's remarks reveal a core motive in welfare improvement: to stimulate social consumption, especially among low-income groups. Improving safety nets and speeding up income distribution reform are both seen as tools to release the consumption power of the poor. What can one make of these utterances? To what extent do these concerns become drivers for welfare reform?

To unravel the mystery, one must review the position of welfare and work in the history of the PRC. Undoubtedly the two have an inseparable relationship. Deriving from this, the objectives of welfare reforms vary according to the requirements of economic and political transition in particular stages. In the socialist period, welfare was part of the socialist structure.[47] This saw welfare wedded to the work unit and collective systems while another, residual, aid system catered to people without work and families. The onset of economic reform, especially the reform of state-owned enterprises and the collapse of rural collectives, destroyed the bases of welfare provision. From the 1980s onwards, to enable enterprise to shed its social burdens, welfare reform was designed as a complement of economic reform.[48] With this in mind, social security responsibility was transferred to state social insurance bureaus while welfare services were also turned over to government, NGOs and community agencies.[49] In the countryside, social security and welfare programmes fell into disarray altogether. Further inroads of marketization and global competition hastened the demise of SOEs and gave rise to the problem of urban poverty. Loss of stable employment and social support created the need to introduce social assistance and institutionalize social insurance. Thus the late 1990s saw the extension of social protection to plug the loopholes of the existing welfare system to address the problems of rising unemployment, poverty and market failures in primary distribution.[50] In both periods (1980s and 1990s), the key theme is economic development. Deng Xiaoping's agenda to achieve a comfortable society (*xiaokang shehui*) put the stress on eliminating poverty (*jieque wenbao wenti*) and enhancing living standards. During Jiang Zemin's tenure, the success in attaining relative affluence in a general sense (*zongti xiaokang*) prompted a higher goal to achieve affluence in a comprehensive way (*quanmian xiaokang*).

The dawn of the twenty-first century saw China entering another critical stage. When Hu and Wen took over the reins as Party Secretary and Premier in 2003, the signs of social conflict were too prominent to be denied. Hu referred to some of the contradictions in his Report at the Seventeenth Party Congress:

> In light of the basic reality that China is in the primary stage of socialism, the Scientific Outlook on Development has been formulated to meet new requirements of development . . . At this new stage in the new century, China's development shows a series of new features which are mainly as follows: The economic strength has increased markedly, but the overall productivity remains low . . . The socialist market economy is basically in place, but there remain structural problems and institutional obstacles slowing down development, and further reform in difficult areas is confronted with deep-seated problems. A relatively comfortable standard of living has been achieved for the people as a whole, but the trend of a growing gap in income distribution has not been thoroughly reversed, there are still a considerable number of impoverished and low-income people in both urban and rural areas, and it has become more difficult to accommodate the interests of all sides. Efforts to balance development have yielded remarkable results but the foundation of agriculture remains weak, the rural areas still lag behind in development, and we face an arduous task to narrow the urban-rural and interregional gaps in development and promote balanced economic and social development . . .[51]

In the current period, it is clear that the presence of social contradictions has been the driving force for a programme to enhance social harmony. In other words, the lack of social harmony is the key factor in setting the agenda for a harmonious society. The state realizes that if systemic problems are not addressed further development is not possible. Seen in this light, the ultimate aim of social intervention is to eliminate contradictions that obstruct development. Social investment is a means to promote development;

increasing welfare is a desirable goal but its main justification to its contribution to social stability.

What about the relationship between the scientific outlook on development and social harmony? On this subject, Hu explains the dialectic as follows:

> To thoroughly apply the Scientific Outlook on Development, we must work energetically to build a harmonious socialist society. Social harmony is an essential attribute of socialism with Chinese characteristics. Scientific development and social harmony are integral to each other and neither is possible without the other. Building a harmonious society is a historical mission throughout the cause of socialism with Chinese characteristics, as well as a historical process and the social outcome of correctly handling various social problems on the basis of development. It is through development that we will increase the material wealth of society and constantly improve people's lives, and it is again through development that we will guarantee social equity and justice and constantly promote social harmony . . . we will spare no effort to solve the most specific problems of the utmost and immediate concern to the people and strive to create a situation in which all people do their best, find their proper places in society and live together in harmony, so as to provide a favourable social environment for development.[52]

In Hu's view, development and harmony cannot be separated. To have development, one needs harmony. To build a harmonious society, there must be development. The relationship between the two is like the chicken and egg puzzle. Either attribute can be treated as an end in itself or a means towards the end. Which is the more important? To Deng Xiaoping and Jiang Zemin, development is definitely paramount. Hu no doubt agrees but sees the impossibility of attaining development without harmony. Identifying his scientific development and social harmony agenda closely to the revolutionary ideals of Mao, Deng and Jiang ("building a harmonious society is a historical mission throughout the cause of socialism with Chinese characteristics"), he sees himself as heir to the communist dream to bring modernization and development to China.[53] Given such a legacy, development cannot but remain a paramount goal for the country.

The need to contain social conflicts has become even more urgent in the last two years. Journalist Qian Gang, for example, pointed out a sobering reality: that *hexie* (harmony) seemingly gets less media attention when compared with *wei wen*, short for *weichi shehui wending* (maintaining social stability). Hu's predecessor Jiang Zemin has emphasized "stability overrides everything" (*wending yadao yiqie*); the term *wei wen* came into currency after Hu assumed office. Qian observed that since 2008, the authorities have gone into overdrive to ensure order as it coped with a succession of major events which included the Tibetan riots, the Sichuan earthquake, the Beijing Olympics, the Xinjiang rebellion, the PRC's 60th anniversary, and the Shanghai Expo.[54] In acting to restore order, the regime has shown extreme nervousness and become more sternly repressive. Paradoxically, the outcome is the opposite; the more the attempts at maintaining stability, the more the instability (*yue wei wen yue bu wen*).[55] A vicious cycle seemingly takes this form: the stronger the urge to maintain stability, the stronger the repression on interest articulation by the masses, the greater the social injustice suffered by the voiceless, the more violent the public remonstrations, which in turn heightens the determination for *wei wen* and so on.

Chinese society and the world were stunned by a spate of five attacks on elementary schools and kindergartens that have occurred since March 2010. The tragedies resulted in seventeen deaths and eighty wounded. That fifteen of the fatalities were young children, the most innocent and treasured members of their communities, and that they were killed by knives, cleavers and tools compounded the horror. The public was even more shocked by the profiles and motives of the attackers, involving middle-aged men who seemed to be emotionally unhinged, doing poorly in life (unemployed, or jilted in love), and bearing a big grudge against society.[56] Wen saw these attacks as symptoms of "social tensions", commenting that long standing social concerns are partially to blame.[57] As well as boosting the security presence in schools, China needed to "handle social problems, resolve disputes and strengthen mediation at the grassroots level".[58]

No less shocking was a string of worker suicides. Within the space of five months from the end of 2009, twelve workers tried to end their lives by jumping (resulting in ten deaths) at the Shenzhen plant of

Foxconn. One of China's biggest electronics manufacturers owned by Taiwan's Hon Hai Precision Industry Company, Foxconn made the iPhone and electronic and computer parts for multinational companies that include Hewlett Packard, Sony, Microsoft, Nokia, and Apple. Like the school attacks, the victims are all migrant workers, they were born after 1980 and had been working at the plant for a year or less at the time of death. Coming shortly one after another, the tragedies rocked the world.[59] While the exact causes of their desperation remain unknown, the furious debates that followed highlighted many disturbing issues. These include low pay, harsh working conditions, the regimental and inhumane management regime of some companies, discrimination against migrant workers, their loneliness and lack of social support, the behaviour and psychology of the post-1980 migrant cohort, lack of autonomous trade unions to represent worker interests, negligence of the local state in protecting labour rights and so on. A group of academics openly blamed the company's management style and appealed for the abolition of the household registration system which made migrants second-class citizens in their own country. Even the New China News Agency raised the question whether it is time to end China's development model that relies heavily on foreign investment and exploitation of cheap migrant labour to make low value-added products, which also pollute the environment.[60] While the furor and soul searching continues, everyone holds their breath about even more suicides to come.

As the central and provincial (Guangdong) authorities pursue their investigations, the government at all levels is stepping up relevant measures. On 26 May 2010, Politburo Member Wang Lequan commanded public security departments at all levels to resolve problems and provide psychiatric services for "special groups" to prevent extreme incidents. At a forum on the comprehensive management of public security, referring to migrants, mental patients, drug users, and released prisoners among others, Wang said, "Problems for special groups concerning their livelihoods should be resolved with great efforts, and psychiatric consultations should also be provided for them".[61] So far, two of the attackers have been executed. The authorities has vowed to deal severely with anyone attacking schools, making clear that the police stand ready to shoot to kill.[62]

Such a statement is revealing. In handling cases like the school attacks and Foxconn suicides, a two-prong attack is considered necessary. One is severe punishment; the other is provision of treatment and social care. Such an attitude highlights the Janus-faced nature of welfare. Welfare provides help to individuals. At the same time, it stabilizes society. While the first attribute makes the supply of welfare desirable, the second makes its provision strategic. To Chinese leaders it is this second dimension that allows them and the rest of society to sleep in peace and let the growth engine run its course. In the West, welfare pundits call this function social control, social integration, shock absorbing, or control of deviance.[63] In China, the task is known euphemistically as enhancing social harmony or more baldly as maintaining social stability. Ultimately, keeping society under control is vital in preserving the political regime.

Political scientists suggest that authoritarian regimes are inherently fragile due to the absence of checks and balances, weak rule of law, over-reliance on coercion, over -concentration of power, and weak legitimacy.[64] The resilience of the political regime in China seems to challenge this assertion. Andrew Nathan attributes Chinese authoritarian resilience to a number of institutions that allow citizens to believe they have some influence over policy decisions and personnel, including local elections, letters and complaints systems, rights of action in administrative Law, more vocal people's congresses and market-driven mass media.[65] An analysis of the welfare initiatives undertaken in the last two decades indicates that institution building is not confined to the political arena. Welfare reforms are also part of the institutionalization process. Beginning in the 1980s, social security reforms became a complementary project to facilitate enterprise reform. In the 1990s, welfare state improvement extended social protection to ward off market risks and vulnerabilities. As the contradiction of rapid growth without fair distribution and social development becomes more acute, social investments acquire a strategic character variously to promote social consumption, facilitate development, and maintain social stability. Susan Shirk suggests that paranoia is the occupational disease of all authoritarian leaders and the Chinese suffer from a particularly acute form.[66] For the Hu-Wen administration, the state has definitely tried harder to repair the welfare net with the objective of making development more balanced and society more harmonious. To what extent welfare reforms can fulfil these goals remains an open question. Even though popular discontent and social tensions rise, there is no sign that the regime has lost the will or ability to contain political and social threats. Still, if political, legal, and social structural reforms are not in place before too long, dishing out more money to help the weak and uttering more sweet talk to comfort the victims may not be sufficient to ensure social harmony.

Note

An early version of this paper was presented at the Conference on Authoritarianism in East Asia, 29 June–1 July 2010, City University of Hong Kong, Hong Kong.

Notes and References

1. X. Ru, X. Y. Lu, and P. L. Li (eds.), *Blue Book of Chinese Society: An Analysis and Forecast of the Chinese Social Situation* (Beijing: Shehui kexue wenxian chubanshe, 2008, 2009, 2010).

2. D. Zweig, "To the Courts or to the Barricades: Can New Political Institutions Manage Rural Conflict?" in E. Perry and M. Selden (eds.), *Chinese Society: Change, Conflict and Resistance*, 2nd edition (London: Routledge, 2003); W. Hurst and K. J. O'Brien, "China's Contentious Pensioners", *China Quarterly*, No.170 (2002), pp. 345–360; K. J. O'Brien, and L. J. Li, *Rightful Resistance in Rural China* (New York: Cambridge University Press, 2006); M. Goldman, *From Comrade to Citizen: The Struggle for Political Rights in China* (Cambridge MA: Harvard University Press, 2005); C. K. Lee, *Against the Law: Labor Protests in China's Rustbelt and Sunbelt* (Berkeley CA: University of California Press, 2007); F. Chen, "Individual Rights and Collective Rights: Labor's Predicament in China", *Communist and Post-Communist Studies*, Vol.40, No.1 (2007), pp.59–79; F. Chen, "Worker Leaders and Framing Factory-based Resistance", in K. J. O'Brien (ed.), *Popular Protest in China* (Cambridge MA: Harvard University Press, 2008), pp. 88–108.

3. "Widen social security net to cover all, say experts", *China Daily*, 27 February 2009, http://www.chinadaily.com.cn/cndy/2009-02/27/content _7518032.htm (accessed 3 March 2009).

4. T. Saich, "Social Policy", in T. Saich, *Governance and Politics of China*, 2nd edition (Basingstoke UK: Palgrave Macmillan, 2004), pp. 268–304; G. C. Zheng, "China Enters the Post-Reform Era", in G. C. Zheng, *Structure the Harmonious Society. The Speech Recordings of Prof. Zheng Gongcheng* (Beijing: Renmin Chubanshe, 2005).

5. P. L. Li, G. J. Cheng, and W. Li, "Report on the State of Social Harmony and Stability in Chinese Society 2006", in X. Ru, X. Y. Lu, and P. L. Li (eds.),

Society of China Analysis and Forecast 2007 (Beijing: Social Sciences Academic Press, 2006); Z. Q. Xie, and J. Pan, "The Views of Party and Government Cadres on China's Social Situation in 2007–2008", in Ru, Lu and Li (eds.), *Blue Book of Chinese Society*, 2008.

6. J. T. Hu, "Construct a Socialist Harmonious Society", *Renmin Ribao*, 6 February 2005.

7. "Wen: China to build a harmonious society", *China Daily*, 2 February 2005.

8. S. G. Wang, "From Economic Policy to Social Policy: The Historic Shift of Chinese Public Policy Pattern", in K. L. Ngok and W. Q. Kuo (eds.), *Chinese Public Policy Review*, Vol.1 (Shanghai: Shiji Chubanshe and Shanghai Renmin Chubanshe, 2007).

9. G. Qian, "More Instability with More Stability Maintenance – A Contradiction in the Mainland", *Hong Kong Economic Times*, 21 May 2010, http://www.hket.com (accessed 24 May 2010).

10. "China to boost spending on welfare, medicare despite int'l financial turmoil", *China View*, 3 March 2009.

11. *Hong Kong Economic Times*, 31 August 2009, p. A6.

12. L. Wong, *Marginalization and Social Welfare in China* (London and New York: Routledge and LSE, 1998).

13. S. B. Yang, "The review and future prospects of China's sixty years' building up a system of social assistance", paper presented at the *First National Conference on Social Assistance in China*, 23–24 July 2009, Renmin University of China, Beijing; S. G. Wang, "The Great Transformation: Two-Way Movement in China since the 1980s", *Zhongguo Shehui Kexue*, No.1 (2008), pp. 129–148.

14. Yang, "The review and future prospects of China's sixty years' building up a system of social assistance"; Wang, "The Great Transformation".

15. L. X. Yang, "The impact of price fluctuations, income growth and local development on the definition of poverty line", paper presented at the *First National Conference on Social Assistance in China*, 23–24 July 2009, Renmin University of China, Beijing.

16. Ministry of Civil Affairs, *Report on Civil Affairs Work of the Ministry of Civil Affairs in 2008*, http://cws.mca.gov.cn/article/tjbg/200906 /20090600031762.shtml (accessed 14 April 2009); X. T. Liu, "Prominent problems in urban social assistance and policy suggestions", paper presented at the *First National Conference on Social Assistance in China*, Renmin University of China, 23–24 July 2009, Beijing.

17. Yang, "The impact of price fluctuations, income growth and local development on the definition of poverty line".

18. "China pledges to improve social welfare for senior citizens", *Chinaview.cn*, 6 February 2009, http://news.xinhuanet.com/english/2009-02/06/content _10775549.htm (accessed 9 February 2009).

19. Wang, "The Great Transformation"; National Bureau of Statistics of China,

Statistical Communique of the PRC on the 2008 National Economic and Social Development, 2009, http://www.stats.gov.cn/tjgb/ndtjgb/qgndtjgb /t20090226_402540710.htm (accessed 27 February 2009).

20. Wang, "The Great Transformation".

21. National Bureau of Statistics of China, Statistical Communique of the PRC on the 2008 National Economic and Social Development.

22. *Ibid.*

23. Huang 2002; Pan 2004; Hu, "Construct a Socialist Harmonious Society".

24. National Bureau of Statistics of China, Statistical Communique of the PRC on the 2008 National Economic and Social Development.

25. Wong 2009.

26. Ministry of Health of the PRC, *China Health Statistical Yearbook* (Beijing: Peking Union Medical College Press,various years).

27. National Bureau of Statistics of China, *China Statistical Yearbook 2007* (Beijing: China Statistics Press, 2008).

28. E. Gu, "Towards Universal Coverage: China's New Healthcare Insurance Reforms", in D. L. Yang and L. T. Zhao (eds.), *China's Reforms at 30 – Challenges and Prospects* (New Jersey and London: World Scientific, 2009).

29. Wang, "The Great Transformation".

30. National Bureau of Statistics of China, Statistical Communique of the PRC on the 2008 National Economic and Social Development.

31. Gu, "Towards Universal Coverage: China's New Healthcare Insurance Reforms".

32. "Much-anticipated health-care plan out for public consultation: medical reform scheme unveiled", *South China Morning Post*, 15 October 2008, p. A7.

33. "Health care reforms laid out for next 3 years: Analysts raise doubts about national medical scheme", *South China Morning Post*, 8 April 2009, p.A4.

34. Ministry of Civil Affairs, *China Civil Affairs' Statistical Yearbook 2008* (Beijing: China Statistics Press, 2009).

35. Saich, "Social Policy", pp. 38–62; L. Wong, "The Emergence of Non-state Welfare in China: Performance and Prospects for Civilian-run Care Homes for Elders", in J. Cheng (ed.), *Challenges and Policy Programmes of China's New Leadership* (Hong Kong: City University of Hong Kong Press, 2008); L. Wong, "The Third Sector and Residential Care for the Elderly in China's Transitional Welfare Economy", *The Australian Journal of Public Administration*, Vol.67, No.1 (2008), pp. 89–96.

36. Ministry of Civil Affairs, China Civil Affairs' Statistical Yearbook 2008.

37. Shanghai Civil Affairs Bureau, *Shanghai Social Welfare Annual Report 2008* (Shanghai: Shanghai Civil Affairs Bureau, 2009).

38. L. Wong, and N. Li, "Explosion, evolution and challenge: an initial follow up

study of NPOs specializing in elder care in Shanghai", paper presented in the *Fifth Cross-Strait Conference on Public Administration*, 20–21 August 2009, City University of Hong Kong, Hong Kong.

39. Wong, *Marginalization and Social Welfare in China*.

40. J. C. B. Leung. "The development of social assistance in urban China: the residualisation of social welfare", paper presented at *Provincial China Workshop 2008*, 27–30 October 2008, Nankai University, Tianjin.

41. *Ibid*.

42. M. C. Yan, and K. W. Cheung, "The Politics of Indigenization: Development of Social Work in China", *Journal of Sociology and Social Welfare*, No.33 (2006): 63–83; M. C. Yan, and M. S. Tsui, "The Quest for Western Social Work Knowledge and Literature in the USA and Practice in China", *International Social Work*, Vol.50, No.5 (2007), pp. 641–653; Y. G. Xiong, and S. B. Wang, "Development of Social Work Education in China in the Context of New Policy Initiatives: Issues and Challenges", *Social Work Education*, Vol.26, No.6 (2007), pp. 560–572.

43. Leung. "The development of social assistance in urban China: the residualisation of social welfare".

44. Ibid; W. J. Zhuang, and Q. Yu, "Innovation and practice in local government service purchase: analysis of two cases in social work service purchase", and R. H. Liu, "Shenzhen social work studies", papers presented at the *Guangdong-Hong Kong Conferences on Social Services*, 20–21 August 2009, Dongguan.

45. "China must reduce rich-poor gap", *China Daily*, 8 March 2010.

46. "Better social safety net key to domestic demand", *Shanghaidaily.com*, 24 March 2010.

47. J. Dixon, *The Chinese Welfare System 1949–1979* (New York: Praeger, 1981); N. W. S. Chow, *The Administration and Financing of Social Security in China* (Hong Kong: Centre of Asian Studies, University of Hong Kong, 1988); Wong, *Marginalization and Social Welfare in China*.

48. S. Y. Chen, *Social Policy of the Economic State and Community Care in Chinese Culture* (Aldershot UK: Avebury, 1996); J. L. Wu, *Understanding and Interpreting Chinese Economic Reform* (Mason OH: Thomson South-Western, 2007), Chapter 9 "Establishment of a New Social Security System"; A. Walker and C. K. Wong, "The Relationship between Social Policy and Economic Policy: Constructing the Public Burden of Welfare in China and the West", *Development and Society*, Vol.38, No.1 (2009), pp. 1–26.

49. L. Wong, "Welfare Policy Reform", in L. Wong, and N. Flynn, (eds.), *The Market in Chinese Social Policy* (Basingstoke: Macmillan, 2001), pp. 38–62; J. C. B. Leung, and R. C. Nann, *Authority and Benevolence – Social Welfare in China* (Hong Kong: Chinese University Press, 1995); C. K. Chan, K. L. Ngok, and D. Phillips, *Social Policy in China – Development and Well-being* (Bristol: Policy Press, 2008), Chapter 3 "Social policy in the context of economic reforms".

50. S. Cook, "After the Iron Rice Bowl: Extending the Safety Net in China", *Sussex: IDS Discussion Paper* Vol.377 (2000); F. L. Wu, "Debates and Developments: The State and Marginality: Reflections on Urban Outcasts from China's Urban Transition", *International Journal of Urban and Regional Research*, Vol.33, No.3 (2009), pp. 841–847; D. J. Solinger, "Social Assistance under Capitalist, Authoritarian Rule: Two Management Models in Chinese Municipalities", paper presented at *Conference on Authoritarianism in East Asia*, 29 June–1 July 2010, City University of Hong Kong, Hong Kong.

51. Hu, J. T., *Report at the 17th Party Congress*, 15 October 2007, http://www.gov.cn/english/2007-10/24/content_785505.htm (accessed 26 November 2007).

52. Ibid.

53. J. G. Mahoney, "On the Way to Harmony: Marxism, Confucianism and Hu Jintao's Hexie Concept", in S. J. Guo, and B. G. Guo (eds.), *China in Search of Harmonious Society* (Lanham MD: Lexington Books, 2008), pp. 99–128.

54. "Successive jumps tragedy: manifestation of the severe pain of societal transition, Foxconn worker slits wrists: the thirteenth suicide unsuccessful", *Hong Kong Economic Times*, 28 May 2010, p. A20.

55. Tsinghua University Social Development Research Project Group, "Report: to Achieve Long Term Peace through the Institutionalization of Interest Articulation", http://www.chinaelections.org/newsinfo.asp?newsid=176760 (accessed 11 May 2010); "To achieve long term peace through the institutionalization of interest articulation, say experts", *Zhongguo Qingnian Bao*, 19 April 2010, http://zqb.cyol.com/content/2010-04/19/content _3188971.htm (accessed 19 April 2010).

56. "'Social tensions' behind China school attacks", *BBC News*, 14 May 2010, http://news.bbc.co.uk/2/hi/asia-pacific/8681873.stm (accessed 15 May 2010); "China's Premier discusses school attacks", *NYTimes.com*, 14 May 2010, http://www.nytimes.com/2010/05/15/world/asia/15beijing.html?_r=1&scp=3 &sq=may+15+2010+china&st=nyt (accessed 15 May 2010).

57. "Man executed for east China kindergarten stabbing", *English.news.cn*, 30 May 2010, http://news.xinhuanet.com/english2010/china/2010-05/30/c _13323289.htm (accessed 30 May 2010).

58. BBC, "'Social tensions' behind China school attacks".

59. "Successive jumps tragedy", *Hong Kong Economic Times*; "Regimented lifestyle out of touch with new generation of workers, say expert, 200,000 workers to get pay rise", *South China Morning Post*, 29 May 2010, p.A4; "Twelve jumps in five months: another form of blood and sweat factory at Foxconn", *Ming Pao Weekly*, 29 May 2010, pp. 72–73.

60. "Successive jumps tragedy", *Hong Kong Economic Times*.

61. "China vows to take care of 'special groups'", *English.news.cn*, 26 May 2010, http://big5.xinhuanet.com/gate/big5/news.xinhuanet.com/english2010 /china/2010-05/26/c_13317404.htm (accessed 26 May 2010).

62. "Man executed for east China kindergarten stabbing", English.news.cn

63. P. A. Baran, and P. M. Sweezy, *Monopoly Capital: An Essay on the American Economic and Social Order* (Harmondsworth: Penguin, 1968); F. F. Piven, and R. A. Cloward, *Regulating the Poor: The Functions of Public Welfare* (New York: Vintage Books, 1972); C. Offe, "Advanced Capitalism and the Welfare State", *Politics and Society*, No.2 (Summer, 1972), pp. 479–488.

64. R. Dahl, *On Democracy* (New Haven CT: Yale University Press, 1998); B. Gilley, "The Limits of Authoritarian Resilience", *Journal of Democracy*, Vol.14, No.1 (2003), pp. 18–26.

65. A. Nathan, "Authoritarian Resilience", *Journal of Democracy*, Vol.14, No.1 (2003), pp. 6–17.

66. S. Shirk, *China – Fragile Superpower* (Oxford: Oxford University Press, 2007), pp. 52–53.

19

Sino-Vatican Relations in China's Rise: From Clash of Authority to Accommodation

Beatrice LEUNG

Introduction

The rise of China as a strong power is a popular topic for political discussion. China has attracted the attention of the international community with its continuous growth of 8% in GDP in the last two decades as well as its growth in military power. Japan's economic output totalled $1.288 trillion in the second quarter of 2010, a little less than China's $1.3337 trillion[1] Eventually China is getting to surpass Japan as the world's second-largest economy, an unprecedented position for a developing country. This success has brought threats as well as triumphs to China's foreign relations.[2]

The rise of China's economy was applauded by one economist: "the impressive thing in China is how well they have gone through what has been a really difficult time for most countries (financial crisis 2008) and kept growing at a strong pace".[3] On the other hand, China's national wealth is translating into political power, making it a target of criticism. China has become the world's second-largest economy but it is far from being a leader, as remarked by some political critics.[4] Some Western economists and politicians also see China's policy of export-led growth as the main cause of the global trade imbalance. China's economic strength may give it power and influence, but it does not always win friends and China is criticized for failing to translate economic power into "soft power".[5]

The sinking of the South Korean patrol boat *Cheonan* is a case to illustrate this issue. The international investigation confirmed that it was attacked by North Korea. China delayed for a month before offering South Korea, China's major trading partner, condolences on the deaths of its 46 sailors. Neither did China act on South Korea's invitation to review the evidence of the investigation. South Korea is very disappointed with China on this issue, having hoped that strong economic ties with China would turn into better diplomatic and military relations.

China's recent handling of long-simmering tensions over competing claims to islands and waters in the South China Sea has rung alarm bells in South East Asian countries that have China as their central trade partner. [6] This emerging geopolitical drama was underlined by a fascinating statement made in Hanoi at the end of July 2010 by Hilary Clinton, the U.S. Secretary of State. She told a regional meeting that the U.S. was willing to act as a mediator in talks over the islands in the South China Sea disputed by, among others, China. Many of the islands in question might be little more than rocks, but given that they are close to the sea lanes for a significant portion of world trade, they have huge strategic importance. As such, Hilary Clinton's speech is one of the most striking symbols of the diplomatic battle that will define Asia for the next few decades – a struggle between the U.S. and China to be the dominant voice. [7]

The Clinton statement had two goals. One was to emphasize that in Asian diplomacy, the U.S. is coming back. During the presidency of George W. Bush, some Asian governments felt that the U.S. had lost interest in the region. Whether this impression was justified or not, Clinton was telling Asia's leaders that the U.S. is not packing its bags any time soon. [8] The broad outlines of this strategy are not new – since the end of the cold war, Washington has approached China through a mixture of engagement on economic issues and diplomatic containment. The nuclear deal with India was partly motivated by such considerations. [9]

Over the last decade or so, China has stolen a march on the U.S. in Asia. The wars in Afghanistan and Iraq proved to be a strategic gift for Beijing. While the U.S. was chasing al-Qaeda, China settled border disputes with a string of once suspicious neighbours – from Russia in the north to Vietnam in the south (although not India). As a decade of double-digit growth in China helped shift the gravity of the Asian economy, Beijing drove pipelines into central Asia, invested in natural resources projects in Burma, Indonesia and the Philippines, and financed new ports in the Indian Ocean.

However, Hilary Clinton has laid a trap for Beijing in the South China Sea. If China stands up to U.S. interference in its backyard and presents itself as the regional power, it risks pushing China's threatening neighbours into the U.S. camp. Even Singapore's President Lee Kuan Yew, who has spent much of the past decade praising Beijing, in 2010 called on the U.S. to remain the Pacific's "superior power".[10] Indeed, this is the broader diplomatic test that China faces in Asia over the coming decades. The more dependent Asian countries become on China's economy, the more uneasy they will be about its power. Amid rising tensions, China has reportedly told other Asian countries not to discuss the issue among themselves. According to U.S. officials, Beijing also now says it considers the area a "core interest", alongside Taiwan and Tibet, and refuses to internationalize the South China Sea issue.[11]

The Pentagon's report on China again revealed U.S. rivalry attitude towards China. "The balance of cross-Strait military forces continues to shift in the mainland's favour," the report said, adding that China's moves pose a "new challenge to Taiwan's security". The report warned that the United States is maintaining the capacity "to defend against Beijing's use of force or coercion against Taiwan". The Pentagon report also noted, "Many uncertainties remain regarding how China will use its expanding military capabilities . . . The limited transparency in China's military and security affairs enhances uncertainty and increases the potential for misunderstanding and miscalculation."[12]

In other developments concerning China's naval forces, construction of a new PLA Navy base on Hainan Island in the South China Sea is "essentially complete", the report said. The base "will provide China with direct access to vital international sea lanes" and offer "the potential for stealthy development of submarines into the South China Sea".[13]

The Purpose of This Study

Indeed China is marching from being a strong power towards the status of a great power. Its dealings with religion in general and with institutionalized religion in particular thus becomes a test for China's "capacity in tolerating heterodoxy". The greater its success in this test, the more soft power China will have acquired and the better it can rise to the status of a great power. This chapter studies the changing Sino-Catholic relationship in the context of China's rise as a case study to illustrate how far Beijing is prepared to tolerate heterodoxy in its dealing with religious matters, which by nature generate an ideological conflict between atheist dialectic Marxist-Leninism and religious idealism.

My hypothesis is that for pragmatic purposes, as it is encountering international criticism, rivalry, suspicion and even adversity towards its rise, China would adopt an approach with the greatest toleration and accommodation the Chinese Communist Party has ever before exercised to acquire a Concordat with the Vatican, which is an icon of morality in world politics. For the sake of obtaining this Concordat between Beijing and Rome to improve China's international image, the clash of authority between Beijing and Vatican would gradually be reduced to accommodation in religious affairs. The present tight controls on religion, including Catholicism, at the grassroots is expected to be relaxed to conform with the accommodation.

Relations between Church and state have historically ranged from the relatively mild tensions in modern Western democracies[14] to the fundamental conflicts over authority found in authoritarian and Communist states. [15] Ideological incompatibilities and cultural differences have led to repeated clashes of authority in Communist China between advocates of atheist Communism and those who hold religious beliefs.[16] The problems involving the Catholic Church are more complex because its hierarchical structure poses extra challenges to the omniscience of the ruling Chinese Communist Party. [17] Catholicism, an institutionalized religion with a strong hierarchical structure, is a soft power which requires China to adopt a new approach in dealing with it at this stage, when the political landscape both internationally and internally has been shifting its balance with China's status as a rising power.

Sino-Vatican Relations in the Twenty-First Century

Sino-Vatican diplomatic relations were established in 1942 under the Nationalist government, and the relationship was broken in 1951 with

Mao Zedong's emphasis on class struggle and his intolerance towards heterodox ideology. Only after Deng Xiaoping initiated the modernization policy in 1978 was there a possibility for dialogue, with the view of establishing a Sino-Vatican Concordat. In November 1987 Zhao Ziyang, the then Secretary General of the Communist Party of China (CPC), met Cardinal Sin of Manila in Beijing and they agreed to let their aides-de-camp thresh out more details to initiate formal Sino-Vatican negotiations.[18] However, in the course of twenty-three years (1987–2010) it seems both sides have been unwilling to give too much in the way of concessions. Recently, however, when China wishes to improve its international image, and the Vatican sees that the Church in China is in no danger of falling prey to schism yet and it needs a warmer political landscape to allow the local Church to grow, the tide has turned. New hope for a Sino-Vatican reconciliation is seen at the far horizon.

The Sino-Vatican Negotiation: Issues and Progress

The Vatican's principal aim in negotiating for the normalization of its diplomatic relations with China is to obtain warmer relations with the People's Republic of China (PRC) for the normal development of the Chinese Catholic Church. For Beijing originally the only aim in the normalization of its relations with the Vatican was to isolate Taiwan further in the international community. By demanding the cutting off of Taiwan-Vatican diplomatic relations it could inflict a heavy blow to this island state, aimed at drawing Taiwan to the negotiating table for talks on unification. However, at this stage, the aim of Beijing in the negotiation has shifted to that of improving its international image, through establishing diplomatic relations with the Holy See, the role model of morality in international politics.

During the years of informal and formal talks between Beijing and the Vatican, the issues that were brought up for negotiation can be summarized into the following categories:

1. the arrangement to share power between the Vatican and the PRC in appointing Chinese bishops;
2. the method of unifying the official and non-official sectors of the Chinese Catholic Church;
3. the ways and means whereby the papal representative in Beijing relates to local bishops in the future; and

4. the ways for moving the Chinese papal nunciature from Taipei to Beijing with minimal disturbance and embarrassment to Taiwan.

Before a solution could be thought of to resolve the thorny issues stemming from these four categories with tolerance and accommodation, two new requests sprang out from Beijing in August1999 adding extra complexity to the unresolved problems. Beijing's two requests which touched the Vatican's nerves were: (a) the transfer of the ecclesial administrative power of local bishops to the civil authority, and (b) in the joint appointment of Chinese bishops, Beijing proposed to retain the current practice of selecting episcopal candidates by itself with the Vatican continuing to validate the government appointment. In the first place, the Vatican could not accept this suggestion, simply because the papal authority would be undermined in the Chinese Catholic Church contrary to Articles 333, 377.1 and 377.5 of the *Codex Iuris Canonici*.[19] In other words, this arrangement is not a Sino-Vatican joint appointment in a spirit of concord, but Beijing appointing the candidate and the Vatican validating the appointment.

In 2006, the Vatican sent a secret delegation to Beijing with a clear message that the Sino-Vatican negotiation had to be conducted amidst mutual trust. This meant that the Sino-Vatican negotiation was in deadlock at that time. In 2010, in contrast, negotiations between the Vatican and Beijing were going on rather smoothly. In February and June 2010 there were two sessions of formal talks, in Rome and Beijing respectively. In July 2010 two Vatican special envoys visited Beijing quietly for a discussion on some issues. The change that took place between 2006 and 2010 will be described in the next section.

An Advancement of Vatican's China Policy: A Shift of Paradigm

Vatican's China Policy: The Paradigm Shift versus Cardinal Zen

In 2006 Cardinal Zen Ze Kiun, the bishop of Hong Kong and an "old hand" of the Vatican's China policy, was at the pinnacle of the

Vatican hierarchy. His presence swung the pendulum in the Vatican administration from the soft-line to the hard-line approach. This is because Zen's Shanghai background and ten years of experience teaching in seminaries across China before becoming the prelate of Hong Kong gave him a good understanding of how the Bolshevik model of Communism has been operating in China. He is especially concerned with the matter of the clash of teaching authority in ideological matters, including the clash between the atheist dialectical of Marxist-Leninism and Mao Zidong Thought, and religious idealism.

Being the only Chinese person who had personal experience of Chinese communism in the Vatican's cabinet, Cardinal Zen's opinion on China policy gained weight in the Roman Curia. He persuaded the Vatican to put more emphasis on the well-being of Catholics in the unofficial sector (the underground sector), as well as caring more about the persecution and oppression of the Chinese Catholic Church. He also called upon the official sector (the open sector) of Chinese bishops to be courageous and stand firm to protect the Church's interest – so much so that Beijing regards Zen as an arch-enemy.[20] Above all, Zen did not hold the view that the Vatican should make too many concessions to Beijing.[21]

The departure of Cardinal Zen from the Hong Kong see at Christmas 2008 was a watershed in the Vatican's shift of paradigm in its approach to China.[22] Since then, the gradual shift of Vatican policy towards China has been swinging back to a soft-line approach. Due to the concessions of the Vatican, China responded by agreeing to consultation with the Vatican on episcopal candidates before Beijing's announcement of the appointment.[23] Therefore, these bishops are to be recognized both by the PRC government and the Vatican. This was eulogized by Church observers as a concession on China's side, amid hopes that a possible reconciliation would not be too far away.[24] However, Cardinal Zen held the opposite view and did not believe that Beijing really wants bishops to be appointed by the pope. He advocated that the Vatican's compromise should have a bottom line and in his opinion the Vatican should not compromise too much.[25]

In 2006, Cardinal Zen advised the Roman Curia to do two things which had long-lasting effects on the Sino-Vatican interaction. Firstly he advised the Vatican to open more channels to understand the real situation in China. Therefore, the China Affairs Commission was created in the Vatican administration in 2007. Secondly, he suggested a papal letter should be issued to Chinese Catholics giving them guidelines on pastoral questions.

From 2008, the Vatican's policy on China began a paradigm shift when the political landscape changed with the strong economic growth of China. Beijing had also been thinking of changing its strategy in the international arena to promote its image. China's Vatican policy thus underwent a review. The sending of a Chinese orchestra to the Vatican to play in the presence of the Holy Father was a tactic for Hu Jintao to boost his international image.[26] Therefore Zen's stepping down as bishop of Hong Kong was an important opportunity for the Vatican to swing back a little from the hard-line to a soft-line strategy. Without these shifts of policy, the Sino-Vatican negotiations would not have resumed.[27]

The China Affairs Commission of the Vatican

The Vatican, with the purpose of gaining a deeper understanding of China, considered setting up a committee on Chinese matters when its administration (the Roman Curia) acknowledged its inadequate knowledge of China. This commission, which advises the Vatican on up-to-date developments in Church-state relations in China, meets regularly to discuss special topics concerning the Chinese church.[28] The Commission met for the first time in January 2007.[29]

This is the second time in the modern history of the Roman Curia that it has set up a commission to deal with national affairs with articulation. The first one was created to advise the pope and the Vatican administration on the complicated issues of Catholic-Soviet relations. The China Affairs Commission comprises more than thirty appointed members, including five bishops from Hong Kong, Macau, and Taiwan, China experts and heads of Church agencies, and religious congregations which are aiding and studying China, as well as officials from the Vatican administration. The term of membership lasts for three years. The General Assembly holds its annual meeting for three days. The Standing Committee, which comprises officials in the Secretariat of the States and Propaganda Fides as well as the five bishops from Hong Kong, Macau and Taiwan, meets three times a year to oversee the recent developments in the Catholic Church in

China. A special subcommittee was established to deal with the question of the "formation of Church personnel in China".[30] This subcommittee is drafting some guidelines for all the Chinese women's religious orders to follow. This is to ensure that all of the Chinese religious sisters are functioning in the orbit prescribed by the canon law on religious life. These guidelines are very timely indeed since many of these female orders on the diocesan level, which were established in the 1980s, need administrative assistance in their ecclesial administration.[31] It is a response to the Vatican's China policy that the training of Church personnel and Catholic laity is a top priority. Although the Commission is mainly consultative in nature, its discussion agenda affects the priority of the Vatican's actions in China policy.

For the last three years, discussions in the China Affairs Commission have only focused on the uncontroversial question of formation, without stepping into the uncharted water of the sensitive issues in the Church of China, such as how to handle the relationship between the open church bishops and the underground bishops. Whether the lenient or militant approach should be adopted in dealing with Beijing has not been thoroughly discussed.[32] However, at the last meeting, in March 2010, it discussed the sensitive issue of the bishops' participation in the controversy of the Eighth Assembly of Chinese Catholic Representatives meeting which has been institutionalized in Beijing's bureaucracy. The meeting should have been held in 2008 but was postponed due to the opposition of the Vatican.

The Papal Letter to China 2007

At Zen's suggestion and through the request of the members of the China Affairs Commission, on 30 June 2007, Pope Benedict XVI issued a letter exclusively to Chinese Catholics. The letter gave them clear religious guidance on practising their Catholic faith.[33] Its title is *Letter of the Holy Father Benedict XVI to the bishops, priests, consecrated men and women and lay faithful of the Catholic Church in the People's Republic of China*.[34] The pope set out the purpose of this letter in the introductory part. Then he pointed out some important aspects of ecclesial life in China giving cause for concern, such as communion of the particular church and the universal church. He suggested pardon and reconciliation to resolve the problems of tension and division within the Chinese Church.[35] The pope did not recognize the present College of Catholic Bishops of China as the episcopal conference, because the "clandestine" bishops who are loyal to the pope are not part of it.[36] He also gave a guideline on the relationship between ecclesial communities and state agencies. In this context, the pope reiterates that "the principles of independence and autonomy, self-management and democratic administration of the Church . . . is incompatible with Catholic doctrine".[37] Here the pope alluded to the Chinese Catholic Patriotic Association as unacceptable. Then he addressed some of these matters and offered guidelines concerning the life of the Church and the task of evangelization for Chinese Catholics.[38] In the concluding part, the pope "revoked all the faculties previously granted in order to address particular pastoral necessities that emerged in truly difficult times".[39] On 24 May 2009 the pope issued an official explanation called the "compendium" on the papal letter, guiding Chinese clergy and laity to interpret the letter properly, especially on some sensitive issues on "unity" and others.[40] These new suggestions, originating from Cardinal Zen, led to a paradigm shift in the Vatican's considerations on China.[41]

Previously Beijing reacted very strongly to any unilateral action from the Vatican on the Chinese Church. For example, in 1981 the appointment of Bishop Dominic Tang as the archbishop of Guangzhou,[42] and the canonization of 102 saints in China in 1990, prompted the Chinese government to mobilize its propaganda machines at all levels to launch serious attacks on the Vatican on these two occasions.[43] The papal letter to China is the first papal instruction exclusively on the Catholic pastoral life within the territory of the PRC. On the provincial level religious cadres requested the Catholics not to read the letter by blocking the website which uploaded the text. However, when printed copies were issued, there was no way to keep the Chinese Catholics in ignorance of the pope's. On the national level, both the Party and the state organs did not say anything openly against the papal letter to China. This can be interpreted as demonstrating a change of Beijing's attitude, with leniency and toleration towards the Catholic Church. Although Beijing did not take the papal letter as an "interference [in the] internal affairs of China", yet local bishops were neither allowed to gather together nor to gather the priests of their own dioceses to discuss the implementation of the papal letter.

The Thorny Question of the Eighth General Assembly of Catholic Representatives

This meeting was a government-initiated assembly of the Chinese Catholic Patriotic Association (CCPA) and the Chinese Catholic Bishops College (CCBC). The highest authority ruling Catholics in China is no longer the CCPA nor the CCBC, but the meeting of the General Assembly of Catholic Representatives 全国天主教代表大会 (the Assembly), held every five years. The convening of the meeting, the number and selection of the delegates as well as any major issues, are studied and decided jointly by the two standing committees of the CCPA and CCBC. The Assembly receives reports from the CCPA and CCBC and elects the office bearers of both organizations. It also has the power to modify their constitutions and even to dissolve the CCBC.[44] In July 2004 the Seventh General Assembly of Catholic Representatives meeting was convened, in which Michael Fu 傅铁山, the controversial bishop of Beijing, was elected as the head of the CCPA and vice-president of the CCBC, and the bishop of Nanjing, Liu Yuanran 刘元仁 was elected president of the CCBC and vice-president of the CCPA. After Bishop Liu died in April 2005, Michael Fu became the acting president of the CCBC. When Michael Fu in turn passed away on 20 April 2008, Bishop Ma Yinglin 马英林, whose appointment had not been ratified by the Vatican, was entrusted to take care of its routine administrative work in the capacity of the Secretary of the CCBC, while he is also the vice-president of the CCPA. The last General Assembly of Catholic Representatives held its meeting in 1994. The Eighth Assembly of Catholic Representatives should have called its meeting in 2009, but due to the Vatican's opposition, it has been postponed, and the date of the next meeting has not yet been announced.

The Vatican was concerned about the participation of Vatican-approved bishops in this event. The meeting of the China Affairs Commission in March 2010 at the Vatican included a lengthy discussion on this issue and concluded that the Assembly contradicts what the pope wrote in his letter to Catholics in China.[45]

In the meetings of the General Assembly of Catholic Representatives, the participants elect the president of the bishops' college (CCBC), and the Assembly receives the CCBC's report and may revise the constitution of the CCBC. This means the CCBC and

CCPA are subject to the Assembly. This is equivalent to surrendering the ecclesial power of Chinese bishops to the civil authority. It is contradictory to Article 381-1 of the Canon Law which stipulates that the local bishop has the highest authority in his diocese in Church affairs, and he is accountable to the pope alone but not to the civil authority.[46]

However, after the China Affairs Commission meeting in March 2010, the Vatican made a compromise by expressing that the Assembly could be acceptable, but only if it were convened by the CCBC, whose president was to be selected freely by the bishops themselves without interference from external pressure.[47] This suggestion singles out the authority of bishops and the CCBC which, according to the Vatican, should be superior to the CCPA, and the CCBC should not be accountable to the civil authority, including the General Assembly of Catholic Representatives.

The General Assembly of Catholic Representatives is one of the whirlpools in which the clash of authority between Beijing and the Vatican took place. Previously, hardliners like Cardinal Zen requested the non-participation of all Chinese bishops because of the nature of the meeting, which allows the civil authority to usurp the Church authority. Now the softening of the Vatican's tone with an effort to compromise reveals that the Vatican administration is happy to establish a warmer relationship with China. At this stage of developments there have been several sessions of Sino-Vatican negotiations to discuss some sensitive but practical issues. Both parties understand that without concession, compromise and good will no result will come from the negotiations.

The Vatican Administration's Understanding of Communism in China: Bolshevik versus Menshevik

Until the appearance of Cardinal Zen, there was no ethnic Chinese in the Vatican to participate in decision making in its policy towards Communist China. The Vatican's understanding of Communism in China had been along European lines.

There are two schools of International Communism. Firstly, the hard-line approach, the Bolshevik model, which was adopted by the former Soviet Union and Eastern European States in the Cold War period, and is still employed by the PRC with the help of military force aiming at one-party dictatorship. Secondly, there is the soft-line approach – the Menshevik model – which does not aim at one-party dictatorship or the mobilization of military power to monopolize political power. Most Communist and Socialist parties in Western Europe have undergone a metamorphosis from the Menshevik model of Communism.

This problem in the Vatican's understanding of Communism is illustrated by the case of the Vatican representative sent to the Macau Special Administrative Region of China in 2008 to investigate the issue of the School of Christian Studies of the Catholic St Joseph's University of Macau, a subsidiary of the Portuguese Catholic University. First of all this European representative believed that Communism in China had faded away already, since China is now employing free market capitalism aiming at vigorous economic growth. Any visitors to China would get the impression that there is no difference between a big Chinese city which is loaded with commercialism and consumerism and any city in the capitalist West.[48] This investigator did not see any problem in the sensitive question of hiring a member of the CCP to be the Pro-Rector of the Catholic St Joseph's University. He failed to see the seriousness for a Catholic university of Communist infiltration, which is a major weapon of the Bolshevik model of Communism.[49] On the contrary, he found that it would be acceptable to have all the teaching staff of the School of Christian Studies who are mostly priests and religious, and naturally they are not Communists. He also considered it natural to have a Communist leading a university within the boundary of a Communist regime. In fact, it was the Catholic St Joseph's University that had initially invited a Communist member to take the leadership post, in exchange for reduced rent and other financial and academic benefits when the university initiated its new campus in a PRC-owned building and planned to set up a Beijing office for future student recruitment and other forms of cooperation with Mainland China.[50]

Apparently the Portuguese rector of St Joseph's University as well as the European Vatican representative are laden with the understanding of Menshevik Communism. They did not see how the Bolshevik model of Communism and its weapon of infiltration was practised in China, including in its Special Administrative Regions of Hong Kong and Macau.[51] However, at present the vice-rector of

Communist affiliation has not been removed. This can be interpreted as a sign of the Vatican's tolerance towards Communism?

The Internet Management and Pastoral Service Meeting in Macau

China is notorious for its vigorous control of internet communication, so much so that it is prepared to install in each new PC sold in China surveillance software called "Green-Dam Youth Escort". [52] This reflects that China has a policy of controlling internet communication by all means. The Vatican's Radio Veritas Asia, Chinese Section, planned to convene a meeting in May 2010 in Wenzhou (Zhejiang) 浙江温州 for the internet management of Church institutes. The purpose of the meeting was to improve skills in internet communication in the context of pastoral and evangelization services. It included updating techniques of internet communication and skills in news writing. The proposed meeting in Wenzhou vanished into thin air after a warning from the Chinese authorities two days before it was due to commence. However, the same meeting was convened in the Macau Special Administrative Region from 31 August to 3 September 2010. Beijing allowed all the participants coming from China to attend. Finally, forty internet managers from church institutes of various parts of China, from Inner Mongolia to Guangdong, attended. All the participants were young priests, sisters and lay men and women who are managers of their own religious websites, belonging to the open and the underground sectors of the Chinese Catholic Church.

The 100 percent attendance of Mainland participants speaks loudly enough of the tolerance of the PRC. In a social context with harsh surveillance of internet communication, China could easily interfere with the meeting or prevent it from ever going ahead by refusing visas to the Chinese participants or by various other means. In fact, the meeting was a four-day training course for information technology amateurs from the Mainland who are the managers of substandard websites. Hong Kong experts in mass media, and website and multi-media professionals from the Jesuit-owned Kuangchi Centre in Taiwan, shared their experience in the selection of information for the website, the characteristics of Catholic media, basic skills of news writing, and so on.

The Kaleidoscopic Development of the Chinese Catholic Church

A general overview

The actual extent of the revival and development of the Chinese Church is reflected in some basic statistics. In 1983 there were 300 Catholic churches in China, by 2008 there were 6,000. The number of Catholics is estimated to have risen from 3.3 million in 1986 to over 12 million in 2008 (including 5 million belonging to the official and 7 million to the underground sectors). In 1997, there were 1,500 Catholic priests. In 2004, there were 2,200 priests, three-quarters of whom had been ordained in the past twelve years. In 2008, there were 3,000 priests.[53]

In 1998, it was recorded that in the official sector there was one national seminary, six regional seminaries, seven provincial seminaries, and ten diocesan seminaries with 1,000 major seminarians and 600 minor seminarians in training. There were ten training centres for the underground sector with 800 seminarians (major and minor) in training. There were forty novitiates for religious sisters with 1,500 sisters under training in the official sector and twenty in the underground sector for the training of 1,000 sisters.[54] There were 6,000 churches with 100 bishops and 3,000 priests. There were 1,000 seminarians in twenty-two seminaries and preparatory schools plus 400 underground seminarians in ten underground seminaries, as well as 5,000 sisters with fifty convents in the open and underground sectors of the Chinese Church (most of them are under the age of 35).[55]

These transformations of the Chinese Church life took place under the Bridging Church programme initiated in 1982 at the suggestion of the late Pope John Paul II, who requested the overseas Catholics to assist in building a bridge between the Chinese Church and the universal Church.[56] Foreign Catholic missionary institutes supported this revival of the Chinese Church. Overseas relations and Chinese friends cooperated with local Catholics who could find their way to even remote villages and deserted areas. From 1987 onwards it was not too difficult to the Mainland from Hong Kong, Macau and Taiwan. Thus, priests, sisters, laity and foreign missionaries whose missionary institutes were originally in the Mainland were able to contact their home dioceses again, and bring them substantial help both materially and spiritually.

More concrete exchanges were developed during the 1990s. A few theology students from the Mainland were sent to train in Hong Kong, and professors from Hong Kong could give some courses in Mainland seminaries. Hong Kong priests, sisters and laity played a great role in the liturgical renewal and in the promotion of biblical study. The liturgical reform was officially approved for the whole country in 1992. The new liturgical celebrations in China, with the full participation of the faithful, are performed with a great solemnity which has largely disappeared in the West, according to the observation of Fr. Jean Charbonnier, a Church analyst.[57]

The Jesuits' Kuangchi Society has published books on a wide range of subjects concerning Christian life and thought, providing useful tools for learning more about their faith. Kuangchi radio and television produces radio programmes which are regularly fed into the Vatican-run Radio Veritas in Manila and thence to China. A full course of theology on the air was later channelled to Shanghai, and a print out in hardcopy distributed throughout China.[58] During 1980s and 1990s, 20,000 volumes of library books which had been acquired from Jesuit colleges and universities in the USA were shipped to the Shanghai seminary.[59]

Theological Formation in Europe, the USA and the Philippines

Bishop Aloysius Jin Luxian of Shanghai was the first bishop in the Mainland to send seminarians and priests to study abroad, preparing them to teach in local seminaries in days to come. From 1993 onwards students were sent to the USA, France, Germany, Belgium, Ireland and Italy to study. Missionary institutes which had previously worked in China before 1949, e.g., the Jesuits, the Maryknoll Fathers, Columbans, Claretians, Franciscans, Trappists, and Divine Word priests as well as may religious sisters, were happy to respond to the call from Chinese bishops who sought to send seminarians and priests abroad for further studies. The sending of church personnel abroad is a kind of exchange between Mainland China and the outside world and represented a real breakthrough for the Chinese Church after four or five decades of separation. From within this cohort new bishops were appointed recently, one of them holding a doctoral degree from abroad, and others master's degrees.[60]

The Philippines is second to Europe and the USA as a favourite place for Chinese sisters and priests to be sent to further their studies. The Institute for Consecrated Life in Asia is mainly filled with a cohort of nearly one hundred Chinese priests and sisters in language training and a two-year course in Theology. As usual the result of the intensification of priestly formation has no uniform result. However, many overseas student priests and sisters have now gone back to China, the staff of seminaries is largely composed of these young professors who have returned with an open mind.[61]

Kaleidoscopic Services Rendered to China

Apart from education, which is untouchable by any religious denomination according to Article 36 of the Constitution of the PRC, overseas Chinese and foreign Catholics discreetly offer the Church in China their services in every possible way, including giving short formation courses in doctrine and the Bible in city parishes, and assisting the religious orders in spirituality and ecclesial administration. These are experienced religious who have just stepped down from their administrative posts in Taiwan, Hong Kong and Macau as important religious superiors. They also give retreats and courses on human development to priests and sisters who could not find the same resources within China. Consequently, after attaining the charisma of the hosted religious missionaries, some local religious, with the consent of local bishops and either individually or as a group, were allowed to change into foreign missionary institutes. Physically these Chinese religious are in China, but institutionally and judicially they are members of international missionary institutes backed up by foreign missionaries.

For many missionary institutes, when religious vocation in the West has declined drastically, China is the reservoir of vocations providing manpower to church service. Take a certain religious order of women in Taiwan for example; it has 50 members in Taiwan, but has more than 100 members in China. It is a classical case of this issue. All of these overseas religious men and women are waiting to establish their work base in China with the expected relaxation of religious control after the Sino-Vatican reconciliation occurs.

Service to the Poorest of the Poor

The remote villages for lepers, handicapped people and abandoned children are the targets for the service of missionaries either from Hong Kong, Macau and Taiwan or abroad. This is part of the endeavour of bridge building. Usually the overseas visitors have allied with local religious to upgrade the provision of the institutes or the level of professional staff. Social services to the weak and poor as well as those in the margins of society have started to gain momentum and seen positive effects. These services are lubrication for the social friction when the gap between the rich and poor is getting bigger and bigger.[62] These services to the weak and abandoned as well as alleviating their poverty are acknowledged by the new head of the Religious Affairs Bureau of the PRC, Wang Zuoan 王作安, as an important force to stabilize the social community and to set up a harmonious society.[63] This is the first time that the Chinese civil authority has adopted a more positive attitude towards religion by openly acknowledging the contribution of religious groups to society.

The Appointment of Chinese Bishops

The appointment of Chinese bishops has been a very thorny question, manifesting a real clash of authority between Beijing and the Vatican. In August 1999 Beijing added extra complexity to the unresolved problems in the Sino-Vatican negotiations by proposing to retain the current practice of selecting episcopal candidates by itself and the Vatican continuing to validate the government appointment. Beijing's requests touched the Vatican's nerves, simply because papal authority would be undermined in the Chinese Catholic Church, according to Articles 333, 377.1 and 377.5 of the Canon Law.[64] In other words, this suggestion is not a Sino-Vatican joint appointment in the spirit of concord, but Beijing appointing the episcopal candidates and the Vatican only passively accepting the government's choice.

There has been no unilateral ordination since December 2007, when the ordination of Bishop Gan Junquo 甘俊邱 of Guangzhou (Guangdong) was done by unilateral government appointment, although the candidate secretly sought papal approval. Starting from 2010, through some informal channels Beijing solicited the opinion of the Vatican administration on the candidates before proceeding with the appointment of Bishop Tu Guang 杜江 of Bameng and Bishop Meng Qinglu 孟清禄 of Hohort (both in Inner Mongolia), Bishop Shen Pin 沈斌 of Haimen (Jiangsu), Bishop Cai Pingrui 蔡炳瑞 of Xiamen (Fujian), Bishop Yang Xiaoting 杨晓亭 of Yenan (Shaanxi), and Bishop Xujiwei 徐吉伟 of Taizhou (Jiangsu).[65]

This is a very positive sign of progress towards the joint appointment of bishops. At this stage the Vatican's consent is given under two conditions; the acceptable morality and the ecclesial loyalty of the candidate. Then there is an agreement that the Chinese Foreign Affairs Office will seek the consent and approval of the Vatican on the particular candidate. When the Vatican's opinion is solicited formally before the ordination, then we have reason to believe that the joint appointment with Beijing and Rome in the spirit of concord is not far away.[66] In China, according to Beijing's calculation, all together there are 97 dioceses (according to the Vatican administration, there are 138 dioceses). Among the 97 "official" dioceses, there are currently 37 or 38 vacant sees waiting for new bishops.[67]

An Unclear Picture

Beijing's Treatment of Chinese Catholics: Conflicting or Accommodating

In Beijing's encounter with the Chinese Catholic Church and the Vatican, it appears that China has been adopting a "schizophrenic" approach. This is a typical behaviour of the CCP since the Mao era. In addition to the positive signs of tolerance and concessions in the issue of the appointment of bishops, and in the General Assembly of Catholic Representatives, in reality, Beijing seems to be offering olive branches to the Vatican in its recent contacts by releasing the symbol of opposition, the underground bishop Julius Jia Zhiguo 贾治国 of Zhengding 正定 (Hebei) in July 2010.[68] On the other hand, however, two Chinese Catholic priests of 宣化 in the same province were detained in the same month.[69] After the release of Bishop Julius Jia Zhiguo from prison, Baoding of, Hebei Bishop James Su Zhimin 河北保定苏志民主教, who had been "disappeared" for thirteen years, Bishop Shi Anchang of Yixian (Hebei) 河北易县施安祥主教 as well as some underground priests and Catholic lay people were still under detention.[70]

The government keeps a tight watch to prevent the bishops of the open sector from engaging in a dialogue with the government or communicating among themselves. They have only to listen and obey. They are ordered to leave for destinations they do not know. They are summoned to meetings without knowing the agenda. They are given speeches to read which they have not written and which they were not even given the chance to read beforehand. Those of the official community are treated as slaves or, even worse, as dogs led with a chain, as criticized by Cardinal Zen.[71] Also the treatment of the official sector (the open sector) as well as the unofficial sector (the underground church) of Chinese Catholics has been more strict than before. The religious policy on the grassroots level has been considerably screwed down, much tighter than in the early period of Deng's Modernization Era. Moreover there is an intensification of militant control of religious affairs under Hu Jintao, especially after the 2008 Tibet riots. There is an upgrading of surveillance of religious organizations by moving the control from the public security level to the national security level.[72] In the government's religious policy there is no sign of the concessions and relaxation of control which are the prerequisites for successful Sino-Vatican negotiations.

We have reason to believe that the change of Catholic policy in Beijing would meet obstacles when the realization of the Sino-Vatican Concordat eliminated the interest of the Chinese Catholic Patriotic Association (CCPA), which might vanish into thin air eventually. This is because the CCPA is unacceptable to the Vatican as alluded to in the papal letter of 2007.[73] The hard-line Cardinal Zen more than once pointed out that the CCPA is a major obstacle to Sino-Vatican reconciliation.[74] Local religious cadres and officials allied with CCPA for their own vested interest would like to keep the status quo without normalization of the Sino-Vatican relationship. Therefore they might not follow properly the order of Beijing in dealing with religious affairs. On the other hand, in the climate of modernization since 1978, the central government has increased problems in directing local governments to function according to the will of Beijing and to implement the national policy correctly when local interest is more attractive than orders from Zhongnanhai.

China's Policy Towards Religion: A Paradigm Shift

In Deng's reign, Yeh Xiaowen 叶小文, the then head of the Religious Affairs Bureau, told the cadres that the current policy on religious freedom was to eliminate the influence of religion in the current socialist regime.[75] Of course at that time it seems that China was more lenient towards religions compared with the iron hand of the Mao era. However, in Yeh's time control of religions including Catholicism has been reported. Yeh's successor, Wang Zuoan 王作安, has not made a clear statement on changing China's religious policy, however in Wang's most recent speech on 18 August 2010 we can see the subtle change of the party-state's policy towards Catholicism. Wang spoke to the youth representatives of religious personnel who participated in a seminar organized by the government to train religious leaders. Unprecedentedly, the theme of his speech is the desire to intensify the formation and education of religious personnel. In this speech he reported that: "the General Secretary, Hu Jintao, has an earnest hope and expectation for religious leaders. He raised a norm for religious personnel as follows: 'on politics, they are reliable, on academic attainment they are accomplished, and on conduct and behaviour they are exemplified'. We must work according to this standard to establish a group of qualified religious personnel." Wang also mentioned some inappropriate conduct of religious personnel, such as being "thin in religious faith, relaxed in observing religious regulations, negligent in spiritual training and crazy for worldly comforts and so on [which] prevails with various degrees of seriousness". Wang held the opinion that all these deficiencies erode the substance of religious life and should be taken care of.[76] Here is, for the first time, an indication that China's policy towards religion in general has changed so much that a CCP official should be concerned for the spiritual well-being of church personnel.

Putting aside the Party's political considerations, the CCP and the Vatican's leaders share more or less the same concern for the conduct and behaviour of religious personnel as well as their spiritual attainment. Beijing and the Vatican now have a common concern about the religious quality of the Chinese Catholic Church. However, in the project of campaigning for better morality, the central government has invited not religion but Confucianism to engage in this project where religion is the reservoir of moral power. Was this because the CCP still harbours suspicion that religion can usurp the teaching authority of the Party?

Considerations on the Sino-Vatican Rapprochement

China's View of the Vatican

Catholicism as a reservoir of moral power

Sending the Chinese Orchestra to the Vatican to play for the pope was a public relations tactic to boost the image of Hu Jintao. This action indirectly symbolized that, for China, the Vatican with the Holy See is an icon of morality imbued with soft power and is influential in the international community. The funeral of Pope John Paul II in April 2006 attracted 200 heads of state and 8 million participants from all parts of the world. On the occasion of the funeral of its head, the Vatican demonstrated its attractiveness in moral power in the Western world. Since China would like to integrate itself into the international community, diplomatic relations with the Vatican would be a great help to upgrade its political status in the Western world.

Religious freedom versus international reputation

The long entanglement between Beijing and the Vatican in negotiations lasting twenty-three years without result presents a negative image of China. In terms of territory, China is so huge and the Vatican is so tiny (less than one square mile), and the Vatican only asks for religious freedom which for the democratic West is as natural as breathing air. Public opinion would not be on Beijing's side when the Vatican has been wooing China for normalization but Beijing turns its back against it. Moreover, on many occasions, Chinese delegations cannot avoid meeting the representatives of the Vatican in many gatherings of international institutions where the Vatican is an observer. Now China wishes to put itself on the bench of great powers, friendship with the Vatican would be a help if China is willing to exchange religious freedom for its international reputation.

The Taiwan Factor

For Beijing originally the sole aim in the normalization of its relations with the Vatican was to isolate Taiwan further in the international community by demanding the cutting off of Taiwan-Vatican diplomatic relations. As mentioned above, the aim was to inflict a heavy blow to the island state and thus draw Taiwan to the table for negotiations on unification. In Ma Ying Jeou's administration, Taiwan experienced good economic gains from the Mainland, but Beijing has received no political gain from Taiwan in return in terms of unification. The formulation of a Sino-Vatican Concordat is equivalent to the severing of Taiwan-Vatican diplomatic relations. The Vatican is the only European state with which Taiwan has diplomatic relations. The resumption of the Sino-Vatican negotiation in 2010 can be interpreted as a gesture to Taiwan, requiring the latter to give more political concessions to Beijing which can monitor the speed and contents of the Sino-Vatican negotiation.

The Hong Kong Catholic Church as an Example

The relationship between the Catholic Church and the state in Hong Kong under British colonial rule can be seen as a case study with positive elements for Beijing to consider. Since London did not infringe on the religious freedom of its colonies, the fundamental elements of Catholicism in Hong Kong could be upheld. The Hong Kong Catholic Church operated with and for the colonial government in many ways, helping to stabilize society by offering educational, social and medical services to the poor and needy. For many years, from after the Second World War until 1997, the government could monitor the Church by channelling its resources, making the Church work as its "contractor", following policies from London to provide services for the government.[77] Even in the riots of 1967 the Church did not join the protest. It did not enhance the social movement by playing a framing role.[78] However, when the Catholic Church in Hong Kong detected a threat to religious freedom post-1997, even though in a remote way, it acted quite differently compared with its behaviour in the colonial period. [79] This illustrates that allowing the Catholic Church to function without too much interference and channelling its energy to serve the poor and needy is the best strategy. The British did it successfully in Hong Kong for the last 150 years of the colonial period. Could it be a good example for Beijing to think about?

The Vatican's View of China

The troubled European Church

The situation of the Catholic Church in Europe is reflected in the complaint by a reputed Church writer, George Weigel, that "seemingly endless stories of clerical sexual abuse, and the mismanagement of these sins and crimes by Catholic bishops, are not the only story to be told about the church at the end of the first decade of the 21st century". [80] Pope Benedict XVI's vision of Christianity in the West today is as a "creative minority" (a term he borrows from British historian Arnold Toynbee). By "minority", Pope Benedict means a church that is no longer a culture-shaping majority but rather a subculture, which of course is no more than a concession to sociological reality. By "creative", he means a subculture clear about its own identity, and passionate about infusing that energy and vision into society. [81] The Church does not crown itself with triumphalism as before when Europe was the home base of the Catholic Church. Now Europe accepts Christians in general and Catholics particular as a "creative minority" and Christendom in Europe is shrinking. After the Reformation in the sixteenth century, Catholic missionaries were sent to the New World to expand Christendom to compensate for the shrinking of Catholic influence in Europe. With rapid growth in the Chinese Catholic population, is China becoming the new world for the expansion of Christendom?

The Catholic Church in China is as normal as any local church

For the time being, the Chinese Catholic Church, which is beginning to be eroded by economic materialism, is as normal as any local church outside China.[82] The Vatican has little worry that schism would prevail in China even though there are two sectors (open and underground) of the Chinese Catholic Church. Based on the papal letter of 2007, the ecclesiastical administration can be carried on along the right track assisted by fundamental guidelines working for reconciliation.

The normalization of Sino-Vatican diplomatic relations offers a chance to relax government pressure and provides a warmer political climate for the Chinese church to grow, and to intensify the spiritual formation of the Church personnel and the laity. Therefore the Vatican administration is rather firm on doctrinal issues in bargaining with Beijing and is not prepared to concede more in the negotiations. The Vatican's bottom line can be found in the papal letter of 2007, in which the Vatican does not ask much from Beijing, but it only that the Catholic Church in China should function as normally as any local church in every part of the world.

Conclusion

While China's rise attracts a mixture of admiration, suspicion and rivalry from the international political arena, for pragmatic reasons, China has attempted to enhance its capacity by taking up the challenge of tolerating and accommodating heterodoxy in dealing with institutional religion, i.e., Catholicism. The more its success in this test, the more soft power China can acquire and the better it can rise to the status of a great power.

Both in Beijing and Rome one has witnessed the shift of paradigms. The Vatican's China policy has swung back and forth between hard line and soft line, depending whether the hard-line Cardinal Zen was in or out of the Vatican hierarchy. However, the establishment of the Vatican's China Affairs Commission and the Papal Letter to China of 2007 reveal that the Vatican had never before paid close attention to the ecclesial issues of the Chinese Church.

Since 2010, the Sino-Vatican negotiation has been in full swing, and concessions from both the Vatican and China have been detected on some sensitive issues, such as the thorny question of the Eighth General Assembly of Catholic Representatives and the appointments of bishops. The kaleidoscopic development of the Chinese Catholic

Church leads one to believe that the ice is beginning to break. However, such optimism is clouded by some harassment coming from the local government level causing doubt as to whether Beijing is adopting a conflicting or accommodating policy towards the Vatican, and whether a "schizophrenic" approach is still practised by religious cadres at all levels.

Nevertheless, new political and ecclesiastical developments both in China and the Catholic Church have provided a new impetus to both parties. For example, the troubled European Church and Catholics becoming a minority in the West offered new impetus for the Vatican to consider Catholic expansion in China. The exchange of religious freedom for an enhanced international reputation can resolve the problem of gaining friends for China in the international community. Is it a good incentive to formulate a Sino-Vatican Concordat? Is the Catholic Church under the British in Hong Kong a good case for Beijing to ponder on how to utilize the Church to deal with the problem of poverty?

Notes and References

1. Keiko Ujikane, "Japan Economy Is Overtaken by China as Growth Weakens". *Bloomberg Businessweek*. 17 August 2010.

2. Andrew Batson et al., "China Is Set To Take No. 2 Economy Spot". *The Wall Street Journal Europe*. Brussels. 16 August 2010.

3. Ibid.

4. "China Becomes World's Second-Largest Economy But It's Far from Being a Leader". *The Christian Science Monitor*. Boston MA. 16 August 2010.

5. Batson et al., "China Is Set To Take No. 2 Economy Spot".

6. Geoff Dyer, "Power Play in the South China Sea", *Financial Times*, London 10 August 2010, p. 9.

7. Batson et al., "China Is Set To Take No. 2 Economy Spot".

8. Dyer, "Power Play in the South China Sea".

9. *Ibid.*

10. "Singapore PM says US presence in Japan benefits Asia, boosts stability". BBC Monitoring Asia Pacific, London, 21 May 2010.

11. Batson et al., "China Is Set To Take No. 2 Economy Spot".

12. BBC Monitoring Asia Pacific, London, 17 August 2010.

13. *Ibid.*

14. Michele Dillon, *Catholic Identity: Balancing Reason, Faith and Power.* Cambridge: Cambridge University Press 1999. Robins and Robertson, *Church-State Relations: Tension and Transition.* Oxford and New Brunswick NJ: Transaction Books 1987. G. Moyer (ed.), *Politics and Religion in the Modern World.* London: Routledge 1990. Eric Hanson, *Catholic Church and World Politics* New Jersey: Princeton University Press 1987.

15. Eric Hanson, *Catholic Politics in China and Korea.* New York: Orbis Books 1980. H. H . Stehle, *Eastern Politics of the Vatican, 1917–1979* trans. by S. Smith. Ohio: Ohio State University Press 1987. Beatrice Leung, *Sino-Vatican Relations Problems of Conflicting Authority, 1976–1986.* Cambridge: Cambridge University Press 1992. George Weigel, *The Final Revolution: The Resistance Church and Collapse of Communism.* New York: Oxford University Press 1992. Leo Goodstadt, "Politics and Economic Modernization in 21st-Century Asia: Potential Conflicts and their Management" in Beatrice Leung (ed.), *Church and State Relations in 21st Century Asia.* Hong Kong: Centre of Asian Studies, University of Hong Kong 1996.

16. Pedro Ramet and Sabrina Ramet (eds.), *Religious Policy in the Soviet Union.* Cambridge: Cambridge University Press 1993. Donald Treadgold, *The West in Russia and China: Religious and Secular Thought in Modern Times.* Cambridge: Cambridge University Press 1973.

17. Pedro Ramet and Sabrina Ramet, *Catholicism and Politics in Communist Societies.* Durham NC: Duke University Press. 1990. Adam Michnik (ed.), *The Church and the Left.* trans. by David Ost. Chicago: Chicago University Press 1993. Szajkowski Bogdan, *Next to God: Poland, Politics and Religion in Contemporary Poland.* New York: St Martin's Press 1983.

18. Revealed by Fr. Jose Calle SJ, who accompanied Cardinal Sin in the latter's meeting with Zhao Ziyang in November 1987.

19. Can. 333: Romanus Pontifex, vi sui muneris, non modo in universam Ecclesiam potestate gaudet, sed et super omnes Ecclesias particulares earumque coetus ordinariae potestatis obtinet principatum... Can 377.1: Episcopos libere summus Pontifex nominat, aut legitime electos confirmat. Can. 377.5:Nulla in posterum iura et privilegia electionis, nominationis, praesentationis vel designationis Episcoporum civilibus auctoritatibus conceduntur. *Codex Iuris Canonici.* Typis Polyglottis Vaticanis. 1983.

20. It was acknowledged by Zen that he was classified as an arch-enemy, when he was interviewed in September 2007.

21. Dorian Malovic, *Mgr. Zen, un homme en colère. Entretiens avec le cardinal de Hong Kong* 陈日君照亮公义的枢机 Trans. 吴颖思 et al. Hong Kong: Next Media Group 2007, pp. 81–114.

22. The news of Zen's retirement was announced at Christmas 2008, but he officially retired in a ceremony on 15 April 2009. *Kung Kao Po (Catholic Chinese Weekly*, Hong Kong), vol. 3400, 19 April 2009, has a special issue to commemorate Cardinal Zen's retirement as bishop of Hong Kong.

23. Beijing had solicited the opinion of the Vatican on episcopal candidates through informal channels since 2009.

24. "Zen Refutes Articles on Beijing-Vatican Deal". *UCAN*. 29 July 2010. http://www.ucanews.com/2010/07/29/zen-refutes-article-on-beijing-vatican-deal/ (retrieved on 12 August 2010).

25. Cardinal Zen. "Does Beijing Really Want Bishops Appointed by the Pope?". *UCAN*. 29 July 2010. http://www.ucanews.com/2010/07/29/does-beijing-really-want-bishops-appointed-by-the-pope/ (retrieved on 22 August 2010). "Compromise has a Bottom Line, Cardinal Zen said". *UCAN*. 7 April 2010. http://www.ucanews.com/2010/04/07/compromise-has-a-bottom-line-cardinal-zen-says/ (retrieved on 22 August 2010). "China-Holy See Relations Expected To Develop Slowly in 2010". *UCAN*. 8 January 2010. http://archives.ucanews.com/2010/01/08/china-china-holy-see-relations-expected-to-develop-slowly-in-2010 (retrieved on 22 August 2010).

26. Elisabetta Povoledo. "China Orchestra Plays for Pope for First Time, Hinting at Thaw", *The New York Times,* 8 May 2008. http://www.nytimes.com /2008/05/08/world/europe/08vatican.html?_r=1 (retrieved on 8 September 2010).

27. The latest two sessions of the Sino-Vatican negotiations took place in February 2010 and June 2010 to be held in Rome and Beijing respectively.

28. Malovic, Mgr. Zen, un homme en colère.

29. *Ibid.*

30. An anonymous member of the China Affairs Commission was interviewed, and this person passed this information to the author in 12 August 2010.

31. Some young Chinese ladies mostly from rural families were collected by local bishops for a religious life without following a rule and orders as stipulated in canon law. Art. 608–704, *Codex Iuris Canonici*

32. This was the opinion of the same anonymous member of the China Affairs Commission.

33. This was revealed by Zen when he was interviewed by this author on 28 April 2009. For the papal letter see: http://www.vatican.va/holy_father /benedict_xvi/letters/2007/documents/hf_ben-vi_let_20070527_china_en.html (accessed on 1 May 2009).

34. The Papal Letter to China. See the Vatican website: http://www.vatican.va /holy_father/benedict_xvi/letters/2007/documents/hf_ben-vi_let_20070527_china _en.html (retrieved on 12 August 2010)

35. Section 6, The Papal Letter to China.

36. Section 8, The Papal Letter to China.

37. Section 7, The Papal Letter to China.

38. Section 7, The Papal Letter to China.

39. Section 18, The Papal Letter to China.

40. For the compendium, see the Vatican's website: http://www.vatican.va

/chinese/pdf/2Compendium_zh-t_en.pdf (retrieved on 26 May 2009).

41. *South China Morning Post*, *Ming Pao* and *Hong Kong Economic Review*, 25 May 2009.

42. Dominic Tang SJ, *How Inscrutable His Way! Memoirs 1951–1981*. 2nd edition. Hong Kong: n/p 1991, pp. 136–139.

43. In fact, numerous articles from the provincial level issued criticism of this issue as well as attacking the Vatican after this leading article was launched: 国家宗教局发言人发表关于梵蒂冈"封圣"问题的谈话 http://www.sina.com.cn 2000 年 10 月 01 日 20:42 新华网 http://www.cathlinks.org/saint-cn.htm (retrieved on 12 August 2010).

44. Jean Charbonnier, *Guide to the Catholic Church in China 2008*. Singapore: China Catholic Communication 2008.

45. This was revealed by two Commission members when they were interviewed in August 2010.

46. Can. 381-1. Episcopo diocesano in diocesi ipsi commissa omnis competit potestas ordinaria, propria et immediate, quae ad exercitium eius muneris pastorallis requiritur, exceptis casusis quaeiure aut Summi Pontificis decreto supremae aut alii auctoritati ecclesiasticae reserventur. *Codex Iuris Canonici*..

47. This was revealed by one Commission members when he was interviewed in August 2010.

48. This was the remark of the Vatican representative, whom the author interviewed in Macau in September 2008.

49. Philip Selznick, The Organizational Weapon: A Study of Bolshevik Strategy and Tactics. Illinois: Free Press 1960.

50. The author met the investigator sent from a Portuguese Catholic University [?] and had a long talk with him. The views cited here are those of the investigator whose report went to the Catholic University in Portugal as well as the Vatican.

51. The author has a meeting with the Vatican representative when he was sent to investigate the question of having a Communist as the pro-rector of the St Joseph's University in September 2008.

52. http://hk.search.yahoo.com/search?p=%E4%B8%AD%E5%9C%8B%E7%B6%B2%E7%AB%99%E7%AE%A1%E5%88%B6green+dam&fr2=sb-top&fr=FP -tab-web-t&rd=r1 (retrieved on 22 August 2010).

53. "A Chronology of the Catholic Church in China in the Context of Selected Dates in World and Chinese History". *Tripod*. Vol. XIII no.76 (July-August 1993): 19-76. China Catholic Communication, *Guide to the Catholic Church in China 1993*. Singapore: 1993, pp. 10–18. China Catholic Communication, *Guide to the Catholic Church in China 1997*. Singapore 1997, pp. 10–18. China Catholic Communication, *Guide to the Catholic Church in China 2000*. Singapore 2000, pp. 8–14, 18–20. China Catholic Communication, *Guide to the Catholic Church in China 2004*. Singapore 2004, pp. 18–20. Jean Charbonnier, *Guide to the Catholic Church in China 2008*. Singapore: China Catholic Communication 2008, p. 24.

54. *Ibid.*

55. Charbonnier, *Guide to the Catholic Church in China 2008.* p. 24. "A Chronology of the Catholic Church in China 2007-2008", 57–58.

56. Beatrice Leung, "The Catholic Bridging Effort with China". *Religion, State and Society* 28 (June 2000): 185–195.

57. Jean Charbonnier, "How Chinese Catholics Renewed the Church in China". *Tripod* no.155 (Winter 2009): 55–69.

58. Unfortunately the broadcast of Radio Veritas has been blocked by the Chinese government since 2007.

59. Charbonnier. "How Chinese Catholics Renewed the Church in China".

60. In the ordination of 2010 alone, Yang Xiaoting 杨晓亭 bishop of Yenan 延安 diocese holds a doctoral degree in Theology from Rome, and Li Cheng 李晶 bishop of Yinchuan 银川 diocese in Ningsha 宁夏 province holds a master's degree from Germany. More are coming on this way. Usually all candidates study abroad and return to China with a master's degree, but with a few exception, after negotiation with the local bishops and the hosting institute. It is the policy that the resources should be spread more widely to more candidates than concentrating on a few gaining a doctoral degree.

61. Charbonnier, "How Chinese Catholics Renewed the Church in China".

62. According to a report by the Guangdong Consultative Conference, in Guangdong province there are 3 million people living below the poverty line. Guangdong is the richest province in China, where the GDP of the richest (RMB$176,271 in Shengzhen 深圳) is 30 times that of the poorest (RMB $5,472 in Meizhou Wuhua). Source: "全国最富省广东穷人 300 万" *Ming Pao.* 3 September 2010, A19.

63. This was acknowledged by the head of the Religious Affairs Bureau. Wang Zuo an "jia qiang zhong jiao jiao zhi ren yuan de pei xun he jiao yu" — zai di er jie zhong qing nian ai guo zhong jiao jie dai biao ren shi yan tao hui shang de jiang hua .[Intensifying the Formation and Education of Religious Personnel] – a talk in the Second Conference for the Young and Middle-Aged Representatives of Patriotic Religious Sectors] 王作安 "加强宗教教职人员的培训和教育" — 在第二届中青年爱国宗教界代表人士研讨会上的讲话 (18 August 2010).

64. Can. 333: Romanus Pontifex, vi sui muneris, non modo in universam Ecclesiam potestate gaudet, sed et super omnes Ecclesias particulares earumque coetus ordinariae potestatis obtinet principatum.....Can 377.1: Episcopos libere summus Pontifex nominat, aut legitime electos confirmat. Can. 377.5:Nulla in posterum iura et privilegia electionis, nominationis, praesentationis vel designationis Episcoporum civilibus auctoritatibus conceduntur. *Codex Iuris Canonici.* Typis Polyglottis Vaticanis. 1983.

65. This was revealed by an anonymous person who is close to the Religious Affair Bureau on 2 September 2010.

66. The author got this information from those who are near the Foreign Affairs Department in Beijing in October 2010.

67. The figures are given by Beijing.

68. *Kung Kao Po*. 18 July 2010, p. 20.

69. *Kung Kao Po*. 13 June 2010.

70. *Kung Kao Po*. 3 October 2010, p. 16.

71. Zen, "Dialogue? Confrontation?"

72. This was revealed by a religious cadre working in a location in central China in a private interview with the author in Macau on 13 May 2009.

73. Section 7, the Papal Letter to China 2007.

74. 「获委任枢机后陈日君主教响应刘柏年讲话」在平安抵岸全靠祂 — 陈日君枢机公教报文集（1996-2009）香港：公教报，2009. pp. 295–296

75. Ye Xiaowen, "Danqian woguode Zhongjiao wenti-guanyu Zhongjaio Wuxin de jaidantao" [The contemporary religious questions of the motherland: re-investigation on the five characters of religion] in *Zhonggong Zhongyang danxiao baogao xuan [Selected Reports of the Party Central School]* vol.101, no.5 (1996): 9–23 (internally circulated document)

76. Wang Zuo an "jia qiang zhong jiao jiao zhi ren yuan de pei xun he jiao yu" ′ zai di er jie zhong qing nian ai guo zhong jiao jie dai biao ren shi yan tao hui shang de jiang hua .[Intensifying the Formation and Education of religious Personnel] – a talk in the Second Conference for the Young and Middle-Aged Representatives of Patriotic Religious Sectors].

77. Beatrice Leung and Chan Shun Hing, *Changing Church and State Relations in Hong Kong, 1950–2000*. Hong Kong: Hong Kong University Press 2003. chapter 3, pp. 23–46.

78. Beatrice Leung, "Hong Kong Catholic Church: A Framing Role in Social Movement" in Khun Eng Kuah Pearce and Giles Giuheux eds. *Social Movements in China and Hong Kong: The Expansion of Protest Space*. University of Amsterdam Press. pp. 245–258.

79. Leung and Hing. Changing Church and State Relations in Hong Kong. chapter 6, pp. 107–124.

80. http://ncronline.org/blogs/all-things-catholic/four-questions-about-popes-trip-uk.

81. http://ncronline.org/blogs/all-things-catholic/four-questions-about-popes-trip-uk

82. The bishop of Shanghai, Jin Luxian, more than once either openly or private expressed this concern both in writing and in speeches. This author interviewed him in 2001 when we met at Germany, he held the same opinion.

Epilogue

Joseph Y. S. CHENG

By mid-2011, when the leadership succession process was in full swing, the strengths and weaknesses of the Hu-Wen administration had become more conspicuous. China's economy grew at an annual average of 9.9% during the period 1979–2009, and 10.7% during 2001–2009. Economic growth dropped sharply to 6.1% in the first quarter of 2009 due to the global financial tsunami, but the Chinese economy rebounded with a growth rate of 9.2% in 2009 and 10.3% in 2010. By the end of the latter year, China's GDP surpassed that of Japan, and it became the second largest economy in the world. In 2009, China's exports fell 34% because of the slump in global demand for China's goods; but in the following year, China's foreign trade achieved an increase of 34.7%, amounting to US$2,973 billion.[1]

In 2011, the Chinese authorities considered an economic growth rate of 8% per annum as healthy and desirable, and their major worry was inflation, especially the overheated real estate market. In 2010, China's exports rose 31.3% and imports 38.7%. As imports grew faster than exports, China's trade surplus shrank by 6.4% to US$183.1 billion. In the first quarter of 2011, China even reported a trade deficit of US$1.02 billion.[2] There was an obvious consensus among Chinese leaders and economists even before the global financial tsunami that China's economic growth should rely less on exports and investment in infrastructure and instead should depend more on domestic consumption. Hence the brief trade deficit needed not be a bad sign; it might help to reduce the international pressure on the Chinese authorities to appreciate the *renminbi*. But pressure was not reduced, as China's foreign exchange reserves broke the US$3 trillion mark at the same time. Other economic statistics for the quarter continued to paint a bright picture. GDP grew at a rate of

9.7%, compared with 9.8% in the previous quarter; exports and imports increased 26.5% and 32.6% respectively, amounting to US$399.64 billion and US$400.66 billion.

In November 2010, inflation reached a 28-month high of 5.1% year-on-year, compared with the government's targeted ceiling of 3% for 2010. The November consumer price index hike was mainly caused by the 74% increase in food prices (food having a 34% weight in the index) and a 14% rise in housing prices. The Chinese leadership was very concerned about the potential impact of inflation on social stability. The statement released after the Central Economic Work Conference held at the end of the year revealed the Chinese authorities' determination to curb inflation: "The priority (for 2011) is to actively and properly handle the relation between maintaining steady and relatively fast economic growth, economic restructuring and managing inflation expectations."[3]

Inflation in China is highly sensitive to increases in the price of basic livelihood commodities, and thus disproportionately affects low-income groups. In the context of high income inequalities, rising inflation naturally generates social grievances and even instability. The Chinese authorities do not only rely on the usual macro-economic tools of raising interest rates and the reserve requirement ratio for banks to fight inflation. The National Development and Reform Commission even condemned the multinational corporation Unilever for "illegally disseminating news of price hikes" which sparked panic buying of shampoo and detergents in March 2011. Subsequently Unilever was fined two million *yuan*.[4] The episode illustrated the tremendous concern for social stability on the part of the Chinese authorities, especially in the wake of the "jasmine revolution".

On the eve of the Tiananmen Incident in 1989, there was similar panic buying when the inflation rate exceeded 20%; the Chinese leadership certainly had this in mind. Rising real estate prices presented another challenge. Accommodation ownership is a symbol of improvement in living standards at this stage of China's development; when the dream of possessing one's own accommodation is crushed, people become much more acutely aware of the social inequalities and the gap between the haves and the have-nots. This is exactly why, while the Hu-Wen leadership has attempted to build a basic social security net covering the entire population in recent years, it has also committed itself to build 36 million units of social security housing (*shehui baozhang fang*) in the Twelfth Five-Year Programme period (2011–2015), with ten million units to be completed in 2011. This demonstrates that the Hu-Wen leadership considers a basic social security net the principal policy programme to contain social grievances and maintain social stability, and now affordable housing in the urban sector has become a part of the social security net to be established. Meanwhile, in the 2011 budget, it was observed that the expenditure on the maintenance of stability (public security) amounted to 624.4 billion *yuan*, exceeding military expenditure which amounted to 601.1 billion *yuan*.[5]

The global financial tsunami has reinforced the importance of upgrading China's industrial structure, spending more on research and development, stimulating domestic consumption where the building of the social security net will make a contribution, reducing China's dependence on exports, stepping up the urbanization process, etc. Improvement in the quality of life, urbanization, and the better supply of social services in turn would contribute to the expansion of the tertiary sector, and this is in line with the Chinese leadership's plan to secure a more balanced economic structure.

The demand to stimulate domestic consumption and the concern for the maintenance of social stability have facilitated the Chinese leadership's pledge to promote social justice and improve income distribution. Hence protection of labour rights and raising wages have become legitimate demands; the Chinese authorities adopted a tolerant attitude towards the labour strikes in the early summer of 2010. In the Twelfth Five-Year Programme, the Chinese authorities promise that the growth of people's incomes should be in line with economic development, and improvement in labour remuneration should be in line with that in labour productivity. Further, efforts should be made gradually to raise the share of people's incomes in national income distribution and the share of labour remuneration in the initial income distribution. Finally, it is planned that the per capita disposable income of urban residents and the per capita net income of rural residents should grow more than 7% per annum in real terms in the programme period.[6]

Sustainable growth is becoming a more significant goal after more than three decades of rapid growth, and environmental protection, climate change, energy intensity, etc., have become serious concerns. International pressures have also grown because of China's increasing weight in the international economy; but Chinese leaders and Chinese people are aware that these policy objectives are in China's own interests. This awareness, however, still appears weak when challenged by greed, corruption and vested interests.

The maintenance of impressive economic growth and social stability means that the leadership succession process will not be challenged, and that the broad policy programmes of the Hu Jintao era would be closely followed by Xi Jinping with adjustments naturally but not significant reversals. Hu Jintao will have a decisive say in selecting the new members of the Political Bureau in the Eighteenth Party Congress in 2012, and the youngest members are expected to become the top leaders in 2022.

Its rapid economic recovery since the global financial tsunami has strengthened the argument that China needs a strong government to concentrate on economic and social development; and the advantages of a strong government were well demonstrated by the prompt response to the global crisis including the four-trillion *yuan* economic stimulus package, the launch of major infrastructural projects, and various measures to reduce unemployment. The rise of China's international status contributes to the legitimacy of the regime too, as the Chinese people desire an improvement in China's international influence, and national pride has been fully exploited by the Chinese leadership. The latter has been cautious not to accept the notion of a "G2" though.

Chinese leaders today probably feel well justified postponing the issue of political reforms which has been neglected for a decade or so. Wu Bangguo's statement at the recent annual session of the National People's Congress (NPC) in March 2011 was representative of this attitude. Wu, Chairman of the NPC Standing Committee, rejected the ideas of a multi-party system, pluralism in the guiding ideology, separation of powers and a bicameral legislature, a federalist system and full implementation of a system of private ownership. The leadership succession process emphasizes stability and continuity, and serious debates on policy lines tend to be avoided. Even if Xi Jinping is a Mikhail Gorbachev-type of reformer (he does not appear so), he still needs some years to make his own key appointments to consolidate his power base before he will be in a position to introduce bold reforms. As Hu Jintao will likely follow Jiang Zemin's precedent and continue to serve as chairman of the Party Central Military

Commission for two more years after his retirement as Party General Secretary, Xi will not be able to make important military appointments on his own until late 2014 or early 2015. Hence significant political reforms will be unlikely in the coming years. In late 2010 and early 2011, Premier Wen Jiabao made a number of open appeals for political reforms, but his seemed to be the lone voice among Chinese leaders. There are no indications of serious political reforms being scheduled.

The increasing integration of the Chinese economy with the world economy implies that China will be more affected by global business cycles; and the global financial tsunami had a significant impact on the unemployment of migrant workers at the end of 2008 and the first half of 2009. The successors of Hu-Wen will definitely continue to complete the establishment of the basic social security net to maintain social stability which certainly has become even more challenging in the context of rapid economic growth. Issues like inflation and real estate prices have already become closely related to the leadership's serious concern about social instability.

Real estate prices deserve attention because this issue is a microcosm of the policy challenges facing Chinese leaders at this stage of development. In the first place, satisfaction of the urban population's demand for housing has increasingly become a part of building of the social security net and a significant factor in reducing social grievances and improving people's satisfaction with government performance at all levels. In fact, if real estate prices were allowed to rise continuously, the central government would be perceived as powerless in tackling the vested interests including local governments, major property firms and speculators. Yet the bubble should not be allowed to burst suddenly because many people including the growing middle-class will be hurt if real estate prices sharply decline. More significant still, local governments heavily depend on land sales to generate revenue in support of the expanding social services. Since the tax reforms in 1994, more and more revenues go to the central government, while local governments have to shoulder the burden of an expanding supply of social services. The central government is reluctant to increase fiscal revenues for local governments at its expense, it much prefers to use its power of granting transfer payments to maintain its control of local governments. Recently, the latters' debts have attracted considerable attention.

According to a study by Goldman Sachs, at the end of 2009 the total debts of various levels of government in China amounted to 15.7 trillion *yuan*, about 48% of China's GDP in the year. The debts of the central government amounted to 20% of the annual GDP, those of the local governments 23%, and the rest were non-performing loans absorbed by the state-owned asset-management companies from the restructuring of the state-owned commercial banks in 2000–2001.[7] The central government with its healthy revenues and impressive foreign exchange reserves would not consider the debts an unbearable burden, not so for many local governments.

A study by the Ministry of Finance in 2005 already indicated that many provincial governments had accumulated debts exceeding their respective annual fiscal revenues, and that their debt-service ratios surpassed 10%. The situation in the wake of the global financial tsunami was certainly worse because local governments had to come up with matching funds to attract investment from the central government's fiscal stimulus package. More serious still, the debt problems of many local governments were well hidden, and a significant proportion of their debts were not yet their direct debts, i.e., they did not have to repay them immediately. But when their corporations went bankrupt, they would have to assume the responsibility of loan repayment. Chinese leaders were aware of the problem and in June 2010 the State Council issued a notice demanding local governments to tighten the management of their corporations regarding the finance of local projects.[8]

When Chinese leaders became concerned about the impact of inflation and real estate prices on social stability, they naturally tightened the suppression of dissidents. The arrest of Ai Wei Wei in April 2011 was a conspicuous case in point. At the same time, many dissidents, human rights lawyers and critics were also arrested, placed under house arrest, forbidden to travel abroad etc. There were also stricter controls on the "underground churches".[9] These phenomena continued to reflect the sense of insecurity on the part of the Chinese authorities, and that to protect the Party regime's monopoly of political power, they were willing to pay the price of tarnishing China's international image and weakening its "soft power".[10]

In the leadership succession process, Bo Xilai's political gestures in Chongqing perhaps revealed some important political indicators. In contrast to Xi Jinping, Li Keqiang, Li Yuanchao and others who are assured of positions in the Political Bureau Standing Committee of the Communist Party of China (CPC) in the coming Party Congress and therefore have been keeping a low profile, Bo instead had to attract attention in order to secure a satisfactory portfolio in the Political Bureau Standing Committee after 2012. His strong position on law and order probably had an appeal to the people who were in general worried about the law and order situation; though as an issue of concern as reflected in public opinion surveys, its relative priority had declined in comparison with inflation, employment and the gap between the rich and poor. What was more significant was his controversial attempt to revive the revolutionary traditions. This attempt demonstrates that in Chinese politics today, political showmanship is increasingly an asset. Premier Wen Jiabao is another conspicuous example. Moreover, while the revival of revolutionary traditions appeals to the conservative Party leadership, implicitly it represents a critique of the market economy today. Apparently Bo Xilai wanted to exploit the dissatisfaction of the under-privileged groups in Chinese society who feel nostalgic for the socialist era.

In the foreign policy sector, China's recent perceived assertiveness was not well received, especially in Asia. The fishing boat incident in the vicinity of the Diaoyutai (Senkaku) Islands in September 2010, China's refusal to condemn the Kim Jong Il regime over the sinking of the *Cheonan* in March 2010 and the shelling of Yeonpyeong in the following November, and the confrontational military exercises in the Yellow Sea and South China Sea in the same year, all cost China dearly in its relations with its neighbours including Japan, South Korea and ASEAN. These incidents have strengthened their hedging strategies involving more spending on the military and enhancing their security ties with the United States. These trends in turn have facilitated the Obama administration's high-profile "return to Asia" and at the same time its endeavour to limit China's regional influence.

Chinese leaders are under domestic nationalist pressure not to be seen to be weak in dealing with the United States and Japan; they are also aware that China's rising international status has become an important source of the Party regime's legitimacy. Hence there is a trade-off between domestic gains and diplomatic costs in terms of assertiveness in foreign-policy positions. When the Chinese Vice-President, Xi Jinping, visited Singapore in November 2010, he declared that China "sees all countries, big and small, as equals. It endeavours to address problems and differences through peaceful dialogues and uphold regional peace and stability by working with all parties."[11]

At the same time, China successfully resisted the United States' pressure to appreciate its currency in various recent international forums ranging from the G-20 summit to the APEC informal leaders' meeting. China still needs a peaceful international environment to concentrate on its modernization, and it will continue to avoid confrontation with its neighbours and other major powers. [12] Improvement of its military capabilities, including the building of a blue-water navy, would certainly make reassuring its neighbours about its peaceful rise a much more challenging task.

In sum, on the eve of the Eighteenth Party Congress scheduled in 2012, China's leadership succession arrangements appear to be smooth and predictable. The economic success also helps to maintain the continuity of the existing policy programmes under the new leadership. The challenges of potential social instability and the accumulation of social grievances would prompt the leadership to step up the building of a basic social security net covering the entire population, while the scope of the net would continue to expand. The central government has the financial resources, but many local governments are already in heavy debt. The Chinese authorities are confident that respectable economic growth rates can be maintained in the near future, and they will accord higher priority to the issues of quality and sustainability of growth as well as social justice. Resistance from vested interests is expected. The tendency to avoid serious political reforms will continue.

As China's economy is well integrated with the global economy, it will be more affected by the world business cycles. Chinese leaders will have a larger say in international economic forums reflecting China's increasing influence, but they will be expected to assume greater responsibilities. China's diplomatic assertiveness will strengthen the hedging strategies of its neighbours too, reducing China's appeal as an engine for regional economic growth. The great success so far will make the tasks ahead more challenging.

Notes and References

1. For the statistics on China's economy in 2010, see http://www.china.com.cn/economic/txt/2011-01/20/content_21779966.htm. See also John Wong, "China's Economy 2010: Continuing Strong Growth, with Possible Soft Landing for 2011," *East Asian Policy*, Vol. 3, No. 1 (2011), pp. 13–26.

2. For the statistics on China's economy in the first quarter of 2011, see http://www.etnet.com.hk/www/tc/news/categorized_news_detail.php

3. "More policies to curb inflation," *China Daily*, 12 December 2010. The conference was chaired by President Hu Jintao.

4. "China's unilever fine a warning to others: experts," *AFP*, dispatch from Beijing, 11 May 2011.

5. *Ming Pao* (a Chinese newspaper in Hong Kong), 6 March 2011.

6. Zhou Heng, "Dingceng sheji' liuda gouziang" ("Six major ideas in the 'top design')", *The Mirror* (a pro-Beijing monthly in Hong Kong), No. 406 (May 2011), pp. 11–14.

7. Qiao Hong and Song Yu, "Qianzai fangchan tiaozheng he zhengfu guodu jiedai de fengxian pinggu" ("Risk assessment of potential real estate adjustments and excessive debts of governments)", *Research Report of the Goldman Sachs Group*, 10 May 2010.

8. Huang Yanfen and Wu La, "Difang zhaiwu fengxian: Xianghuang, chengyin ji dui shehui de yingxiang" ("The debt risks of China's local governments: status, causes and impact on society"), in Ru Xin, Lu Xueyi and Li Peilin (eds.), *Shehui Lanpishu: 2011 Nian Zhongguo Shehui Xingshi Fenxi yu Yuce (Bluebook of China's Society: Society of China Analysis and Forecast (2011))* (Beijing: Social Sciences Academic Press (China), 2011), pp. 229–243.

9. Chen Pokong, "Zhonggong zhengce zouxiang jiduanhua" ("Chinese Communist Party policies go to extremes"), *Open Magazine* (Hong Kong), No. 293 (May 201), pp. 19–21.

10. See Joseph S. Nye, Jr., *Soft Power: The Means to Success in World Politics* (New York: Public Affairs, 2004).

11. Zheng Yongnian, Lye Liang Fook and Chen Gang, "China's foreign policy in an eventful 2010: facing multiple challenges in a deteriorating external environment," *East Asian Policy*, Vol. 3, No. 1 (2011), p. 33.

12. Li Mingjiang, "Non-confrontational assertiveness: China's new security posture," *RSIS Commentaries* (S. Rajaratnam School of International Studies, Nanyang Technological University, Singapore), No. 80/ 2011 (16 May 2011), pp. 1–3.

Authors

Chris King-Chi CHAN has been an Assistant Professor in the Department of Applied Social Studies at the City University of Hong Kong since 2009. He graduated from the University of Hong Kong. After working a number of years as a labour organizer, he came to the University of Warwick in the UK where he studied an MA in Comparative Labour Studies from 2004 to 2005 and was awarded a PhD in sociology in 2008. He is the author of the book *The Challenge of Labour in China: Strikes and the Changing Labour Regimes in Global Factories*, New York: Routledge (2010). He also published a number of articles in international journals, including *The China Quarterly*, *Journal of Contemporary Asia* and *Industrial Relations Journal*.

Joseph Y. S. CHENG is Chair Professor of Political Science and Coordinator of the Contemporary China Research Project, City University of Hong Kong. He is the founding editor of the *Hong Kong Journal of Social Sciences* and *The Journal of Comparative Asian Development*. He has published widely on the political development in China and Hong Kong, Chinese foreign policy and local government in southern China. He has recently edited volumes on *Whither China's Democracy? – Democratization in China since the Tiananmen Incident*; and *Guangdong – Challenges in Development and Crisis Management*. He was chairman of the Hong Kong Observers, 1980–82; and convener of Power for Democracy, 2002–04. He has been a Justice of Peace since 1992; and was the founding president of the Asian Studies Association of Hong Kong during 2005–07. In 2006–08, he served as the secretary-general of the Civic Party. He is now involved in the launch of the New School of Democracy.

Jie GAO is Assistant Professor at the Department of Public and Social Administration, City University of Hong Kong. Her teaching and research interests are in performance management and public administration reforms in the mainland China. Her current research focuses on the design and implementation of the Chinese target-based performance measurement system in local governments at the county and township levels. Her publications appear in SSCI journals in the fields of public administration and China studies, such as *Administration & Society*, *Australian Journal of Public Administration*, *Public Administration and Development* and *The China Quarterly*.

Mobo GAO is the Chair of Chinese Studies at the Centre for Asian Studies and Director of the Confucius Institute at the University of Adelaide. Professor Gao's publications include four monographs and numerous journal articles and book chapters. He is the author of the critically acclaimed book *Gao Village* and of *Introduction to Mandarin Chinese*, which are widely used at tertiary institutions. Professor Gao's most recent publication is *The Battle for China's Past: Mao and the Cultural Revolution*.

Jia GUO is currently working as an Assistant Professor in the School of Management at Beijing Normal University. She obtained B.A. and M.A. from Peking University, and her Ph.D. in political science from the University of Hong Kong in 2010. Her research focuses on environmental policy and the policy process in China, in particular, policy learning during environmental policy implementation.

Steven HOLM is an experienced educator in Hong Kong. Staring from his Diploma in Education at The Chinese University of Hong Kong, education policy and moral values have surrounded his working content. He graduated from the Chinese Academy of Social Science, and got a Master's degree in Jurisprudence (Sociology). He also obtained a Master's in Cultural Studies from Lingnan University. For attainment of Doctor of Philosophy, he has researched into the policy of financing education in Hong Kong; the moral, cultural and political perspective of the thesis was certified. These various perspectives of studies have given him great benefits on promoting education and policy analysis. He had presented many education policy research papers in different academic conferences, where he had the opportunity to meet with related research experts discussing experiences and sharing different views. Concerning the development of education in Greater China and the new rising network society, he focuses on policy implementation of the relationship between content and development, with the comparison of different regional policies. ˈ

Chin-fu HUNG is Associate Professor at the Department of Political Science and Graduate Institute of Political Economy, National Cheng Kung University (NCKU), Taiwan. He holds a PhD in Politics and International Studies from the University of Warwick, UK. Dr Hung's main research interests include the political and economic transition of China, the impact of the information and communication technologies upon political development and democratization, and the socio-political development in East and Southeast Asia. He has written various articles on topics of cyber participation and the Internet politics of democratic and (semi-)authoritarian states in Asia.

Ronald C. KEITH received his Ph.D. in Politics at the School of Oriental and African Studies, University of London, 1977. He is currently Professor of China Studies, Griffith Business School, Griffith University, Brisbane. Since 1989 when he published the Macmillan book, *Diplomacy of Zhou Enlai*, he has maintained a special interest in Chinese foreign policy particularly as it relates to the leadership of Zhou Enlai. His recent books on China's international relations include the Routledge 2005 volume, *China as a Rising World Power and Its Response to Globalization* and the Pluto 2009 volume, *China from the Inside Out: Fitting the People's Republic into the World*. For relevant background to the current chapter see his article, "Zhou Enlai heping gongchu waijiaode dangdan yiyi: Xianzhizhuyi yu lixiangzhuyide wanmei jiehe", ("The contemporary relevance of Zhou Enlai's five principles of peaceful coexistence: a consummate synthesis of realism and idealism"), in Xu Xing, (ed.), *Ershiyi Zhou Enlaide xinshiye* (*New 21st Century Perspectives on the Study of Zhou Enlai*), Vol. 2 (Beijing: Zhongyang wenxian chubanshe, 2009), pp. 991–1004.)

Willy Wo-Lap LAM is a Professor of China Studies at Akita International University, Japan; and an Adjunct Professor of History and Global Economy at The Chinese University of Hong Kong. A journalist, author and researcher with 35 years of experience, Dr. Lam has published extensively on areas including the Chinese Communist Party, economic and political reform, and Chinese foreign policy. Dr. Lam is the author of six books on China, including *Chinese Politics in the Hu Jintao Era* (M E Sharpe, 2006); *The Era of Jiang Zemin* (Prentice Hall, 1999); and *China after Deng Xiaoping* (John Wiley & Sons, 1995).

Yok-shiu F. LEE is an Associate Professor in the Department of Geography at the University of Hong Kong. He earned his PhD degree in Urban Planning from the Massachusetts Institute of Technology. His current research projects include a study of the problem of conserving urban cultural heritage assets in China's transitional economy, examining this issue through in-depth case studies of Shanghai and Guangzhou. He has published research papers in international journals such as *The China Quarterly*, the *Journal of Contemporary China*, *World Development, Environmental Politics*, the *Third World Planning Review*, and the *International Development Planning Review*.

Beatrice Leung received her Ph.D. in 1988 from the London School of Economics and Political Science, the University of London majoring in International Relations. She is the Honorary Fellow at the Centre for Greater China Studies, the Hong Kong Institute of Education. She is the author and editor of seven books and has published more than forty scholarly articles in academic journals and in books. The latest one is *Casino Development and Its Impact on China's Macau SAR* (co-edited with Sonny Lo) and published by City University of Hong Kong Press, 2010.

Jun LI has more than 20-year experience in China political science research and is the author of over 30 publications and conference papers. She obtained her bachelor's degree in political science from Central China Normal University in 1991, and a master's degree in the same subject from and Wuhan University in 1998. She served as an official in Organization Department of CPC and a lecturer in Peking University of Technology respectively until 2004 when she furthered her studies at the City University of Hong Kong and received his PhD degree in public and social administration in 2008. Dr. Li, as the member of Association of Chinese Political Studies, has rich experience in academic exchange. In 2011 her paper was recommended for inclusion into the China Goes Global conference held by Harvard University. Currently, Dr. Li is an associate professor in charge of research on public and social policy, public administration at the Research Center of Social Work in the Ministry of Civil Affairs, PRC.

Yang LI graduated from City University of Hong Kong with a major of Economics and Finance and obtained a master's degree. He was a research associate for Dr. Baozhi Qu at the Department of Economics and Finance, City University of Hong Kong, during the time when the book chapter was written. He also provided support for the teaching of the Gateway Education course "China in the global economy" at the same university. He is currently a consultant at a major international consulting firm.

Feng LIN is an Associate Professor of Law at the School of Law of City University of Hong Kong and Director of the Centre for Chinese and Comparative Law. He is also a practicing Barrister in Hong Kong. He was a visiting scholar at Harvard Law School in Fall semester 2010. He obtained his LLB from Fudan University, Shanghai, LLM from Victoria University of Wellington, and Ph.D. from Peking University. His primary research interests are constitutional law, administrative law, and environmental law. He is widely published and his most recent edited book is 《百年宪政与中国宪政的未来》（2011）.

Carlos Wing-Hung LO is a Professor in the Department of Management and Marketing at the Hong Kong Polytechnic University. His main research interests are in the areas of law and government, environmental governance, cultural heritage management, corporate environmental management, and corporate social responsibility, within the context of China and Hong Kong. Currently he is researching environmental regulatory control and corporate environmental management in the Pearl River Delta Region. He has had major publications in *Law and Policy (2010),*the *Journal of Public Administration Research and Theory* (2009), *Environment and Planning A* (2009 & 2003), the *Journal of Cross Cultural Psychology* (2008), the *American Journal of Comparative Law* (2005), the *Journal of Public Policy* (2003), *World Development* (2001), and *The China Quarterly* (2000 & 1997).

Stefania PALADINI is an economist specialized in international trade, strategic commodities and geopolitics. She is at present Senior Lecturer at Coventry University. Before relocating to UK, she has spent several years in Hong Kong and China appointed as Italian trade commissioner and advising companies about trade and investment in Asia. Her current research interests are Chinese politics, Asian presence in Latin America and government policies regarding strategic materials. Among her last publications: "Shopping abroad the Korean way: a study in resource acquisition" in *Korea 2011*, BRILL.

Baozhi QU is currently Assistant Professor at the Department of Economics and Finance, City University of Hong Kong. He received his B.A. and M.A. from the Renmin University of China and Ph.D. in Economics from University of Pittsburgh, USA. His research interests are in the areas of financial economics and economic development with focus on the following fields: institutions, finance and trade; corporate finance and governance; banking; and Chinese economy. He has published a number of papers on various academic journals in the fields of economics and finance both in English and Chinese.

Alvin Y. SO is Chair Professor in the Division of Social Science at Hong Kong University of Science and Technology. His research interests include social class and development and comparative and historical sociology. He is the author of *Social Change and Development* (Sage 1990), *East Asia and World Economy* (co-author with Stephen Chiu, Sage 1995), *Hong Kong's Embattled Democracy* (Johns Hopkins University Press, 1998). His co-edited volume *Handbook of Contemporary China* is forthcoming from World Scientific in 2011.

Qinghua WANG is an Assistant Professor of Political Science in the School of Public Economics and Administration and the Center for Public Governance, Shanghai University of Finance and Economics, China. He received his Ph.D. in political science from the University of Oregon in 2007. He works primarily on the politics of China's higher education. His current research interests also include modern state-building in contemporary China, and official ideology and Chinese intellectual discourse. He has published (or will publish) in *Asian Perspective* and *Journal of Contemporary China*. "

Linda WONG is a Professor at the Department of Public and Social Administration, City University of Hong Kong. Her research interests span the fields of social welfare, comparative social policy and China studies. Among her works are *Marginalization and Social Welfare in China, Social Change and Social Policy in Contemporary China, The Market in Chinese Social Policy, Social Policy Reform in Hong Kong and Shanghai,* and *Rural-Urban Migrant Workers in China: Issue and Social Protection.* Her articles have appeared in *Journal of Social Policy, Social Policy and Administration, Public Administration Review, International Migration Review, Journal of Contemporary China, Pacific Affairs, Asian Survey,* and *Australian Journal of Public Administration.*

Xueyong ZHAN is an Assistant Professor in the Department of Management and Marketing at the Hong Kong Polytechnic University. He obtained his Ph.D. in public administration from the University of Southern California. His current research focuses on environmental governance, public and nonprofit management. His recent research articles have been published in *Public Administration* (forthcoming), the *Journal of Policy Analysis and Management* (2009), and the *Journal of Development Studies* (2008).

Index

P

State Organization Chart of China

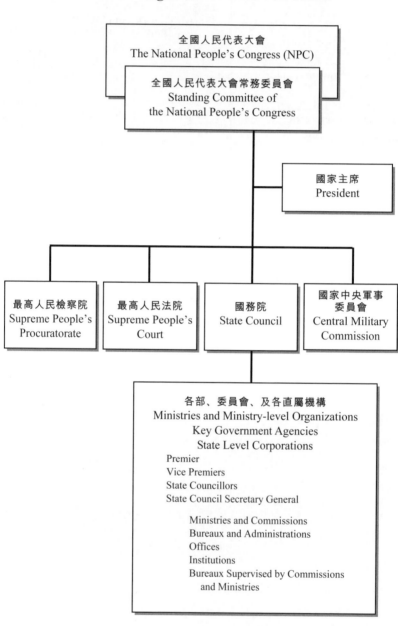

全國人民代表大會
The National People's Congress (NPC)

全國人民代表大會常務委員會
Standing Committee of
the National People's Congress

國家主席
President

最高人民檢察院
Supreme People's
Procuratorate

最高人民法院
Supreme People's
Court

國務院
State Council

國家中央軍事
委員會
Central Military
Commission

各部、委員會、及各直屬機構
Ministries and Ministry-level Organizations
Key Government Agencies
State Level Corporations
Premier
Vice Premiers
State Councillors
State Council Secretary General

Ministries and Commissions
Bureaux and Administrations
Offices
Institutions
Bureaux Supervised by Commissions
and Ministries

Map of China